D1135096

615.7827 J717
Jones, Helen C.
Marijuana question   an answer
NBCA   720292000590635

615.7827
J717

Link Library
Concordia College
Seward, Nebraska

DEMCO

THE
MARIJUANA
QUESTION

Cannabis sativa

615.7827
J717

☘ THE ☘
MARIJUANA
☘ QUESTION ☘

AND SCIENCE'S SEARCH
FOR AN ANSWER

HELEN C. JONES

AND

PAUL W. LOVINGER

WITH A FOREWORD BY

C. EVERETT KOOP, M.D. Sc.D.
Surgeon General

Link Library
Concordia Teachers College
Seward, Nebraska

DODD, MEAD & COMPANY

NEW YORK

Copyright © 1985 by Helen C. Jones and
Paul W. Lovinger
All rights reserved
No part of this book may be reproduced in any form
without permission in writing from the publisher.
Published by Dodd, Mead & Company, Inc.
79 Madison Avenue, New York, N.Y. 10016
Distributed in Canada by
McClelland and Stewart Limited, Toronto
Manufactured in the United States of America
Designed by Kingsley Parker
3 4 5 6 7 8 9 10

Library of Congress Cataloging in Publication Data

Jones, Helen C.
   The marijuana question.

   Includes bibliographical references and index.
   1. Marihuana—Physiological effect.   2. Marihuana—
Social aspects.   3. Drug abuse.   I. Lovinger, Paul W.
II. Title.
QP801.C27J66   1985   615'.7827   84-10277
ISBN 0-396-08398-4

CONTENTS

PART II

CANNABIS AND THE PSYCHE

PART III

CANNABIS AND SOCIETY

FOREWORD

According to the most recent National Survey on Drug Abuse (1982), 50–60 million Americans have tried marijuana and approximately 20 million are current users. Marijuana is, by far, the most widely abused illicit drug. The gravity of the problem became more evident as its usage by children and teenagers increased during the seventies. Usage by high school seniors reached a peak in 1978 when 37.1 percent of the graduating class reported current use and 10.7 percent reported current daily use. The lifetime prevalence of daily use by high school graduates from the classes of 1976–1982 was 24 percent; i.e., about one-fourth of high school graduates had used marijuana daily for at least one month. This is an astonishingly large percentage of our youth who have placed themselves seriously at risk for the adverse biological, developmental, psychological, and social consequences of heavy marijuana use. Though we do not yet know the full extent of the nature of the risks to which these youngsters have exposed themselves, to quote the summary of the 1982 Institute of Medicine study of marijuana and health:

> Our major conclusion is that what little we know for certain about the effects of marijuana on human health—and all that we have reason to suspect—justifies serious national concern.

We in public health are not only concerned about the adverse effects of marijuana on the user; there also are undoubtedly major effects, unrecognized as yet, on nonusers as well. We know that marijuana impairs performance and judgment. To what extent marijuana has contributed to vehicular accidents is unknown, but there is reason to believe it is significant. Nor do we know to what extent marijuana has contributed to society's burden of crime and the erosion of a respect for the law.

Marijuana poses many social issues, as well as the scientific and medical issues. The authors help us to understand the many aspects of the social phenomenon in which we are immersed—the extraordinary growth in the past 20 years of the abuse of illicit drugs. And though they clearly have reached the conclusion, as have most experts, that marijuana is a serious health risk, they allow the reader to make up his own mind from the data. There is no confusion of opinion and fact. Here is the lay reader's opportunity to understand what we know and what we don't about marijuana.

C. Everett Koop, M.D. Sc.D
Surgeon General,
U.S. Public Health Service

ILLUSTRATIONS

✳   ✳

Photos and Drawings

Figures

❋ THE ❋
MARIJUANA
❋ QUESTION ❋

OVERVIEW

"*The very first time I smoked it, I didn't get high. . . . I did the second. . . . I was with a group of people in my room in college and we had records, some baroque oboe concerto or something, and as soon as the thing finally connected and hit in my brain, all of a sudden the music seemed more beautiful. Everything just seemed so happy and mellow. It was very comforting. Colors seemed more vibrant. It seemed, in a sense, as if maybe it was free from the sort of grimness and painfulness of normal life.*

"*I remember falling down and rolling on the floor, as did a couple of other people who were with me, in sort of giggles of laughter. I mean everything seemed so happy and merry. I suppose it was like fairyland or where the elves live or something. I mean it was just a different, different world. All more vivid and glowing and whatnot. . . .*

"*In many ways, life today is so unpleasant and so full of hassles, so full of many negative things—lots of pressures and stresses—and so ugly in so many ways, that it's hard to blame somebody if they all of a sudden think that they have found something that is much more beautiful and gives them this kind of pleasure that is so different from anything they've ever seen before, where everything seems so nice and harmonious. Gosh— it's pretty tempting!*" —Nathan (a former user of marijuana)

Some spell it "marijuana." Others spell it "marihuana." People can't even agree on how to spell it, much less what to do about it.

Not only is the word spelled in different ways; it is used to mean various things. So let us define a few terms and present some basic facts. After that, we will outline the book's philosophy and format.

In this volume "cannabis" serves as a general term referring to the plant *Cannabis sativa* or its crude drug products. The two main drug products are marijuana and hashish. "Marijuana" consists of any part of the plant that has been crudely prepared for smoking, primarily by drying. "Hashish" essentially is resin from the plant.

1

Substances found only in cannabis (as well as chemical derivatives of these substances) are "cannabinoids." The main cannabinoid is delta-9-tetrahydrocannabinol, the principal "psychoactive"—mind-affecting—ingredient of marijuana. It is often abbreviated "Δ^9-THC" or simply "THC" (although technically there are ten other THC compounds).

"Indian hemp" used to be a common term for marijuana. The United Nations lists 265 other terms for it (including marijuana preparations but excluding resin). The choice of plant parts and the way they are prepared vary from place to place. Definitions differ confusingly. For instance, Merriam-Webster narrowly defines "cannabis" as "the dried flowering spikes of the pistillate plants of the hemp." At the other extreme, U.S. laws have included under "marihuana" all parts of the cannabis plant, its resin, its seeds, or anything produced from them (excluding certain nondrug products).

* * *

Cannabis (accent on the first syllable) has been cultivated since antiquity, until lately, grown less for mind-altering use than for industrial, medicinal, and other purposes. Possessing scores of varieties, it is produced and used in widely varying climes and cultures throughout the world. Modern-day marijuana seekers have looked to the tropics for "good pot," but the scene is changing. Any cannabis seeds can flourish almost anywhere.

The Swedish botanist Linnaeus is credited with establishment of the plant's scientific Latin name in his *Species Plantarum* of 1753, although earlier writers referred to *Cannabis sativa*, meaning planted hemp. (We saw the phrase identifying a line drawing of the cannabis plant in the 1542 book *De Historia Stirpium* by German botanist Leonhard Fuchs.) Most botanists consider the genus *Cannabis* to possess just a single species. Some have disagreed, recognizing separate Indian and European species, for instance.

Categorizing by THC content yields two main types of plant (with variations in between): the drug type, chief source of marijuana; and the fiber type, used to make hemp ropes and other products. That dichotomy can be credited to scientists of the Marihuana Project at the University of Mississippi, where the only legally grown marijuana in the United States has been produced under federal contract since 1968. In North Carolina its leaves, small stems, and flowering tops are aged, chopped, and rolled in the manner of tobacco cigarettes to provide standard marijuana cigarettes for research; the strongest ones contain just flowering tops. This research marijuana is of Mexican lineage, and so is the drug's name *(mariguana* or *marihuana).*

Cannabis users usually smoke it, either in a marijuana cigarette—a "joint" or "reefer"—or in a pipe. In some countries smokers mix their marijuana or hashish with tobacco. Some marijuana consumers eat or drink it prepared in food or beverage. Fanciers of "hashish oil" or "hash oil" (a highly concentrated chemical extract of marijuana) may add it to tobacco cigarettes or heat it and inhale its vapor.

Cannabis is no simple drug but a mixture of at least 426 compounds, including at least 62 cannabinoids. The proportions of these compounds vary from one variety of plant to another, even from batch to batch of one variety. While it is mainly THC that intoxicates or "stones" users, making them euphoric or "high," some of the other cannabinoids too have psychoactive properties and even nonpsychoactive ones may be biologically active. Few cannabinoids have been studied in depth for their bodily actions, let alone interactions. From the cannabinoids in the plant material, the body evidently produces hundreds more. Burning yields thousands of additional chemicals. (See the supplement.)

For centuries writers have described the psychological effects of cannabis. Early research workers had to rely on the natural plant and its crude extracts. The complexity of its chemistry and biological actions limited the scientific study of cannabis until the mid-1960s, when the isolation and synthesis of THC in Israel—coinciding with an explosion in marijuana use among American college students—paved the way for a vast increase in research. More than 7,000 scientific papers on the subject have come out since then.

The U.S. government launched its first intensive research program on cannabis in 1967 through the National Institute of Mental Health. A dozen or more federal agencies have supported research, principally the National Institute on Drug Abuse. From the start, a major federal concern has been to furnish scientists with marijuana and cannabinoids. Confiscated material was used before the government could provide the scientists with specially grown cannabis, beginning in 1969. Along with research reefers, mostly of about 1, 2, or 3 percent THC, experimenters get "placebos"—marijuana cigarettes with the cannabinoids extracted—for comparison or "control." Those experimenting just with THC get a synthetic version of the compound (either in capsules, in solid form, or in alcoholic solution, all made lately in southern California).

Comparing studies can be like comparing pineapples and kumquats. An experiment using THC, the compound, is not the same as an experiment with marijuana, the crude bits of plant. Observing the immediate effects of a cigarette or capsule does not indicate what the long-term effects will be. Smoking and ingestion may produce different results. Inhalation delivers more THC to the bloodstream and delivers it quicker than the oral route.

The pieces of information from a microscopic tissue study, an objective mental test, and the quizzing of a subject ("How high are you, on a scale of zero to ten?") do not directly compare, though all may, or may not, fit into the cannabis jigsaw puzzle.

Canine data is not feline data. Even two varieties of mouse may react differently.

One study may compare drug users with nonusers, in some test of their ability or fitness. Another study may test only drug users, comparing their performance before and after they take the drug.

The time chosen for collection of data can make a difference. So can the background and perhaps bias of the person collecting or interpreting the data.

Two scientists studying the chronic effects of a substance on human beings may arrive at two vastly different outlooks if one chooses to examine healthy users and the other starts with ailing patients who have used the substance.

Results of human experiments can hinge on a variety of factors, in addition to health, that usually can be better controlled in animals. Among the factors are age, sex, and social status; use of other drugs; whether subjects have used the drug under investigation; and, if so, how recently, how heavily, and for how long.

Animal results may or may not apply to human beings. They and we may differ in sensitivity to a drug or even respond in contrary ways (for example, in heart action when dosed with THC). On the other hand, animals are particularly useful for testing toxicity, examining tissues and organs, and observing reproduction and offspring. Rodents—short-lived, rapidly generating, and cheap—are most commonly used.

Inasmuch as effects often vary drastically with the size of the dose, the matter of dosage is essential. If a dose is too large, toxicity of the dose as such can distort the results, if not kill the animal (though large doses may be valid for some purposes). Yet laboratories figure dosage in divergent ways. For example, many scientists relate one species to another simply according to amount of drug per unit of body weight (milligrams per kilogram, or mg/kg). Some others believe that different species rate different relative doses (based on metabolic rate, for example).

Calculations of dosage in humans are not always precise, least so in studies of long-time use. Terms like "heavy" and "light" use can have many interpretations. Even specifying the number of joints per period of time may not be enough. Different smokers roll them and smoke them differently. Moreover, they may have access to cannabis of unequal potency. The THC content of street marijuana, according to government analyses, has ranged from a mere trace to more than 13 percent.

The strength of cannabis is subject to change. Fresh, green cannabis plant is not very potent. THC in its native state occurs mainly as part of THC acid, which is inactive. Aging begins to free the active THC from the acid group; heat, particularly the heat of combustion, advances the reaction rapidly. Unused, marijuana will reach a peak strength and ultimately deteriorate.

Cannabis is classified as an intoxicant, a stimulant, a depressant, and a hallucinogen. You cannot be sure whether a dose of marijuana will act in one or another—or more than one—of these capacities. At different times, someone's reactions can vary both in nature and intensity (from high to low) in response to similar doses (whether large or small).

Smokers sharing a joint can respond in different ways. For example, Dan, an occasional user, may react to a few puffs with an intense "high" while Frank, a chronic user, becomes scarcely high at all. What is strong marijuana to one is weak to the other, who has gained tolerance, decreased sensitivity to the drug. At another time, either smoker may react otherwise, perhaps in a surprising way, depending on his mental state, the setting, the marijuana's potency, and his use of another drug or alcohol.

THC, which is highly soluble in fat and nearly insoluble in water, remains in fatty tissues of the body for a relatively long time. One dose can take weeks, maybe months, to eliminate completely. Thus a regular smoker may never be free of cannabinoid.

* * *

In going through the voluminous drug literature issued since the marijuana boom began, we see problems both of style and substance.

The popular publishing world, largely ignoring the hazards of the most widely abused of the illegal drugs, has turned out a multitude of works glorifying the drug and encouraging the drug habit. These publications have been profitable. They have given marijuana devotees what they want: support more than science.

In general, while the readable works are unscientific, the scientific works are unreadable. You can find some of the world's worst writing between the covers of scholarly tomes. In this book we try to avoid the dilemma. We aim for a book that is clear and enjoyable enough for the general reader while factual and detailed enough for the serious student of the subject.

The scientific literature contains more than 9,000 studies on cannabis, cannabinoids, and cannabic effects. We selected more than 300 of them and describe them in this book. They are not necessarily the best studies from the standpoint of scientific method, but they are the ones that we consider most notable or quotable.

We also interviewed scores of cannabis users and ex-users (respondents to classified ads and other sources developed by us over the years), and we faithfully quote their replies to our questions, though we have changed the names.

Of course cannabis research goes on. We paint the picture the way we see it in 1984. It is admittedly an incomplete picture, perhaps even a confusing one, for some research studies contradict one another. We cannot explain all of the contradictions, but we can explain our viewpoint.

When it comes to drugs, the phrase "innocent until proven guilty" cannot hold. For the safety of the public, a drug must be presumed guilty until proven innocent—that is, harmful until found safe. This essentially has been the law in the United States since 1962. Any manufacturer wishing to introduce a new drug to the market has the burden of demonstrating to the Food and Drug Administration by controlled research that the drug is safe as well as effective.

While the use of marijuana is ancient, its scientific study is relatively new. Plainly it is no lethal poison. Neither is it a charmed herb that can do no wrong. It is a highly complex substance whose long-range effects have not been exhaustively tested.

The scientific knowledge of cannabis held by the marijuana-smoking population generally is sparse and obsolete. Those favoring the drug often point to a handful of studies showing scant differences between small groups of smokers and nonsmokers, or in smokers before and after smoking, in some aspect of body or mind. Such research, they say, proves there is nothing wrong with "pot," "grass," "dope," "weed," "herb," "tea," or "Mary Jane."

Those studies (which can be interpreted in different ways) give only a partial picture. To ignore other, more ominous signals coming out of the world's laboratories is foolhardy.

*   *   *

In separate experiments in different laboratories, a doctor periodically places mice in smoke-filled chambers; scientists inject or paint rodents with tar and resin extracted from similar smoke; a pathologist saturates human embryonic lung tissue with such extracts and transplants it to guinea pigs. No tumors or hardly any develop.

This is not cannabis research. The smoke, tar, and resin came from tobacco cigarettes. A prosmoking writer gathered several such studies in a 1957 book to try to disprove the "cigarette-cancer theory."

Among the more than 40,000 studies on the subject of tobacco and health, one can dig out some showing no detrimental effects. But the evidence to the contrary now is overwhelming. The smoking gun has been found. The role of that common habit in deadly disease has been proven beyond a reasonable doubt to the satisfaction of the world's medical and scientific communities. Millions have abandoned the cigarette habit to avoid joining the millions it has sent to their graves.

Now a new type of smoking sweeps the Western world.

Nobody can yet say definitively whether cannabis smoking is as injurious as tobacco smoking. Scientists continue to investigate the matter in laboratories, while a vast number of young people in effect serve as guinea pigs in a decades-long experiment. The ultimate answer to the marijuana question awaits the future.

* * *

Our format is out of the ordinary. Sandwiched between these preliminary pages and a commentary near the end are three main parts, dealing with the impact of cannabis on (I) several vital systems of the body, (II) the brain and mind, and (III) various aspects of society.

The parts are divided into sections, each devoted to a particular human system or societal concern. The majority of sections lead off with personal accounts of the effects of cannabis smoking. The sections, totaling sixteen, are subdivided as shown in the table of contents.

Taking the place of footnotes, various passages in small type appear here and there to elaborate on the main text, furnish technical detail, or add related information. Read them or skip them as you wish.

In the back we identify sources for our material. There are some 750 citations. The source notes are keyed to reference numbers in the text, which follow accounts of studies, reports, and so on. The research works bearing on a specific topic often are presented approximately in order of date of publication.

Unless otherwise indicated, a mention of a difference (or lack of difference) between a drug group and a nondrug group or between presmoking and postsmoking figures implies that the data passed (or failed) some standard test of statistical significance. Figures may be rounded.

You can read the parts and sections of this book in any order you choose.

* * *

Many thanks to all who cooperated in our quest for the facts.

We have strived for accuracy. If any errors have crept in, we offer our apologies.

PART I

 CANNABIS
AND THE BODY

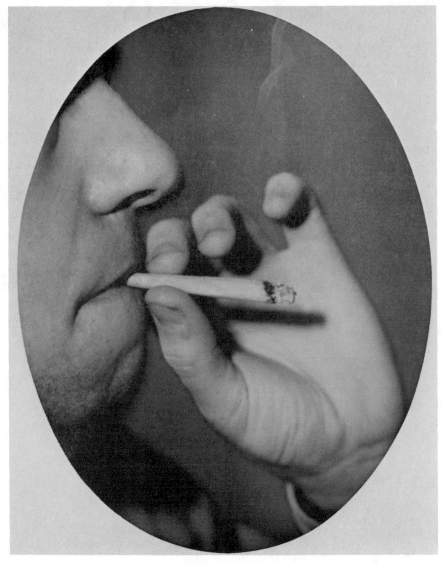

Smoking a joint.

THE
LUNGS
AND
RESPIRATORY SYSTEM

• *"I've smoked marijuana heavily for ten years. Practically every day for ten years I've been stoned. I'm worried that there may be damage to my lung."* —Betty (long-time user, trying to quit)

• *"Cigarettes make me cough but marijuana cleanses the lungs. . . . I have a little sister who has had chronic asthma. . . . In light doses the smoke soothed and relaxed the respiratory system. . . . In heavy doses any type of smoke is harmful to the lung."* —Pete (chronic user and marijuana advocate)

• *"I cough a lot, especially when I get up in the morning. It's hard to say whether it's from marijuana or cigarettes. A friend of mine, who just smokes marijuana, says he has kind of asthma when he smokes a joint."* —Charlie (chronic user)

• *"There are a lot of hot things going into your lungs and it's going to cause a little cough and stuff in your throat. I used to sing a little. I always knew if I didn't smoke grass I'd be able to sing better."* —Rhoda (long-time user, trying to quit)

• *"If I smoke too much of it, it just affects my lung. The better the pot, the worse the effects. It will just make me cough. It will make phlegm in the morning."* —Alice (chronic user)

11

• *"I have bronchitis and my doctor told me I shouldn't smoke pot. He said any kind of smoke is going to irritate your bronchioles. I've had it for a long time."* —Millie (chronic user)

• *"I do definitely feel that it does have a negative effect on your respiratory system. . . . I get a stuffed nose when I smoke a lot."* —Bert (chronic user)

• *"After 2½ years of smoking cigarettes and marijuana, I felt my lungs couldn't handle both. I felt if I gave up one or the other, I could survive. I chose to give up pot. The combination of cigarettes and marijuana made me feel like I was going to suffocate. I became aware of how I was cutting off the circulation to all the little passages of my lungs and it frightened me."* —Rosemary (ex-user)

• *"Sometimes I would feel very bad. I would hyperventilate sometimes because of overuse of hashish . . . being overdosed, so to speak. . . . Interestingly, I wasn't a smoker—you know, a cigarette smoker."* —Hiram (ex-user)

• *"[Marijuana caused] irritations—very pronounced in my throat and nasal passages. . . . Hash was a little stronger. It burned my throat even more."* —Quentin (ex-user)

• *"It was hard on my respiratory system and I had congestion in my lungs. . . . I had a definite sore throat."* —Oscar (former user except for "a puff once in a while")

• *"Occasionally I would observe a certain shallowness of breath, which I still experience from time to time. . . . It seems to me that any intake of smoke into the lungs is not a wise idea, and as far as I know it tends to constrict the vessels in the lungs."* —Pierre (ex-user)

• *"I smoked heavily one night, came home, and kept passing out. I kept feeling I couldn't get my breath."* —Wendy (ex-user)

• *"Inhaling it really hurt [my chest] sometimes . . . especially first thing in the morning. It feels like I had pulled something. . . . I think it [the smoke] physically stretches the lung muscles. . . . It was a sharp pain like if you dived into a cold pool and held your breath for a long time and then came up."* —Donna (ex-user)

• *"My son started smoking marijuana when he was eleven years old. He used pot for five years. . . . In the eighth grade he developed chronic sore throats, bronchitis, and chest pain. I took him to the doctor and the doctor said the pain was because of the inflammation of the lining of the lungs due to his bronchitis. . . .*

"After he had been off marijuana for six to nine months, his sore throat, bronchitis, and chest pain went away." —Viola (Georgia mother)

1

In a Nutshell

It's obvious. At least it seems obvious to us. The lungs and the treelike tubes of the respiratory system are not designed for the breathing of smoke—any kind of smoke, whether from wood, paper, tobacco, or marijuana. Lungs do the job of exchanging good and bad air, taking in oxygen and getting out carbon dioxide, while fending against invading particles and disease. They can't do much of a job when overwhelmed by pollutants.

> Put in more formal language by scientists Rosenkrantz and Fleischman: "The architecture of lungs has evolved to achieve an efficient exchange of gases coincidentally with defense mechanisms adequate to remove reasonable quantities of particulates. The design of the microanatomy of the pulmonary tree was probably not intended to cope with the continuous onslaught of smoke ingredients."[1]

Medical observations of smokers as well as laboratory experiments on animals and human beings have provided a fund of information about the effects of cannabis smoke on the breathing system. A lot more facts are needed before the world's knowledge of cannabis matches that of tobacco, but evidence already available suggests that frequent marijuana smoking can produce certain respiratory problems at least as serious as those caused by tobacco.

Marijuana-breathing lungs may take double punishment. They are battered by many of the same harsh gases and particles that occur in tobacco smoke, and they may also be attacked by THC and other cannabinoids.

Evidence that heavy, habitual cannabis smoking can deteriorate the lungs—more so on top of tobacco smoking—comes from patients seeking medical help for respiratory troubles who have reported histories of chronic use of marijuana or hashish, and from medical researchers studying animals or humans who have observed differences between the lung tissues of users and nonusers.

Repeated, heavy cannabis use by humans has produced (1) cell changes like those that herald the approach of major lung disease, (2) measurements showing the air passages narrowing and the lungs handling less air than normal, (3) more of certain respiratory symptoms compared with

14

those of nonsmokers, and (4) signs of possible deficiencies in the lungs' defenses.

In animal projects by three separate teams of investigators, malignancies have developed in hamster lung samples exposed to fresh marijuana smoke, in lungs of live rats injected with marijuana smoke condensate, and in lungs of live mice injected with THC.

> "One cannot help but consider the analogy to tobacco smoking, where much clinical and scientific evidence has incriminated tobacco smoke as either a causative or accessory factor in the development of irritative, inflammatory, and neoplastic [tumorous] bronchopulmonary disease," said Bernstein et al. of Harvard Medical School.
>
> Among the reasons to suspect a potentially injurious effect of cannabis use on the lungs, they pointed out, is "the almost ubiquitous occurrence of throat discomfort and irritation associated with marihuana smoking."[2]

Marijuana likes the lungs, though the sentiment is not necessarily reciprocated. The lungs are the first vital organs the smoke hits, and the drug gets further cracks at them through the blood. The lungs receive all that the heart pumps before the blood goes to the rest of the body. Having the highest blood flow of any bodily tissues, they have the most opportunity to pick up THC.[3] Thus marijuana reaches the lungs even when taken in other ways than smoking.

After giving animals THC by injection or force-feeding (1965–1972), several European and American researchers could detect the drug in lung tissues.

> First, C. J. Miras of the University of Athens, Greece, injected radioactive THC—extracted by chromatography from cannabis plants grown in an atmosphere of C-14-carbon dioxide—into the abdomens of male rats. (Dose: 6 mg/kg—milligrams per kilogram of body weight.) After an hour and a half, they were killed and various organs were counted with a scintillation spectrometer.
>
> He recovered rather low amounts of radioactivity, mostly from the liver (4.86 percent of the injected dose), but also from the testes, kidneys, lungs, thymus, heart, brain, muscles, spleen, and spinal cord, in that order (0.58 percent to 0.02 percent).[4]

* * *

> Agurell et al. in Sweden made the "striking observation" of a "high amount of radioactivity in the lungs" after injecting rabbits and rats intravenously with THC labeled with H-3 (0.1 to 0.6 mg/kg in rabbits).[5]

* * *

> Klausner and Dingell in Tennessee found far more drug in the lung than in eight other tissues when they injected rats intravenously with C-14-THC (4 mg/kg).[6]

* * *

Kennedy and Waddell at the University of North Carolina used autoradi-
ographs—images on photographic film produced by a radioactive emulsion in the
test substance—to study lengthwise sections of female mice treated with C-14-
THC (about 20 mg/kg).

Injections in veins brought relatively high concentration of radioactivity to the
lungs (and liver) within twenty minutes. After twenty-four hours, much of it had
migrated to fatty and connective tissues, but spots of high radioactivity remained
in the lungs. Three hours after injection under the skin, some radioactivity had
entered the lung, although much less than other tissues.[7]

Again in North Carolina, at the Research Triangle Institute, Freudenthal, Martin,
and Wall used the same method to study mice and observe its distribution in
fifteen organs.

Mice given 0.65 mg of THC intravenously had after two hours "very high ra-
diolabel" in the lungs as well as adrenal gland, brown fat, corpora lutea, liver,
and spleen. Two hours after THC was forced into mice's stomachs, it was less
concentrated and more evenly dispersed in the lungs (and spleen) than in the above
organs (and intestine) but more concentrated than in the remaining tissues.[8]

2

The *Ganja* Experience

Observations of marijuana smokers in various countries have long linked
the habit to respiratory ailments. Although some of the old investigations were not scientifically controlled and the element of tobacco smoking
was not always taken into account, they are of some interest.

The report of the Indian Hemp Drugs Commission, 1893–94, represented an early attempt to investigate the effects of cannabis smoking
on health and society. The inquiry was more like an opinion poll than
a scientific study.

Some seven decades later the report was used in the United States to
justify the smoking of marijuana, although the report offered many un-
favorable observations about the weed. For example, one of the conclusions was that the habitual smoking of strong hemp (cannabis) drugs caused
chronic bronchitis. Some witnesses connected it to asthma as well.

Cannabis users in India have consumed it in three main forms, which are in
ascending order of potency: *bhang*, the leaves and other parts of the wild or cultivated cannabis plant, commonly taken by mouth as a beverage or confection;
ganja, the dried flowering tops of the cultivated female cannabis plant with coat-
ings of resin that oozes from the plant; and *charas*, the pure resin (equivalent to

hashish). The latter two are mostly smoked, usually combined with tobacco, although sometimes they are eaten.[9] The THC content was estimated (in 1973) to be about 1, 3, and 5 percent by weight, respectively.[10]

The hemp drugs commissioners reported that doctors in India often prescribed the inhaling of *ganja* smoke for asthma and bronchitis patients. On the other hand, they cited evidence that tended to indicate that both afflictions might be induced by habitual *ganja* smoking. While doubtful as to the asthma, they found the evidence more convincing that the drugs might cause bronchitis or bronchial catarrh.

"The inhalation of ganja smoke may very possibly first act as a pulmonary sedative, diminishing the secretion of mucus, and after long continuance as an irritation increasing mucus secretion, and giving rise to a chronic bronchitis. . . ."

The cannabis was commonly smoked together with tobacco in a pipe. It was the pyridine produced that acted as a pulmonary sedative, the commissioners wrote. Hemp drugs aside, they added—in a statement that today's tobacco companies might quote in the manner of the pro-pot partisans—"the tobacco smoke may be thus of value in both bronchitis and asthma."

However, they went on to to say: "But long-continued smoking, whether of ganja or of any other substance, doubtless results in the deposition of finely divided carbonaceous matter in the lung tissues, and the presence of other irritating substances in the smoke ultimately causes local irritation of the bronchial mucous membrane, leading to increased secretion, and resulting in the condition which is described as chronic bronchitis in ganja smokers."

Under direction of the British secretary of state, the colonial government of India had appointed the commissioners—four Britons and three Indians. They were to study the cultivation of the hemp plant, drug preparation and trade, social and moral effects on the Indian people, and whether to ban the drug. The governor-general, in his instructions, strongly hinted that stringent resrictions were not a good idea.

During a six-month tour to thirty cities throughout the provinces, the commission took written or oral testimony from 1,140 "witnesses," based on a questionnaire with seventy questions. The witnesses were mainly officials, practitioners of western and native medicine, landholders, traders, professionals, missionaries, and spokesmen for associations.

Only two of them said the excessive use of hemp produced no "noxious effects," while 847 (74 percent) said it did produce such effects. Just 243 (21 percent) saw no ill effects from the moderate use of hemp, while 643 (55 percent) did see harm in it. (Some declined to give an opinion.)

The commission acknowledged that it was impossible to get reliable data, many of the drug users being illiterate peasants who combined their hemp consumption with other vices. But despite the muddy data, the commission reached a definite conclusion: Excessive use of hemp drugs is harmful; moderate use is not. It neglected, however, to explain the difference.

As to respiratory diseases, many witnesses attributed them to the hemp drugs while others did not. Examples follow:

"Assistant Surgeon Soorjee Narsain Singh . . . stated that habitual moderate consumers of bhang, ganja or charas do not apparently suffer from any injurious effects . . . Durg Dass Lahiri . . . a private medical practitioner, said, 'I have ..ot seen any evil results mentioned when taken moderately, but it is very difficult to keep to moderation.' . . . Pyari Sankar Dass Gupta . . . a private medical practitioner . . . and a member of a temperance association . . . submitted three papers. . . . In one paper the witness states: 'The smokers of ganja often suffer from hoarseness of voice produced by the continual inhalation of its fumes, giving rise to sore throat, bronchitis, and carbonaceous phthisis [wasting away].' . . . Assistant Surgeon Upendra Nath Sen . . . states that bronchitis and asthma are common complaints of ganja smokers. Madhab Krishna Dass . . . a private practitioner . . . considers that smoking may cause dysentery, bronchitis or asthma. . . . Rakhal Das Ghoash . . . has apparently seen no ill effects caused by the drug. The remaining witnesses in this class clearly failed to discriminate between the moderate and excessive use, and their evidence has not been considered. . . .

"Fifteen native practitioners were examined. Bijoya Ratana Sen . . . considers that the habitual moderate use of ganja or charas . . . may in some cases cause bronchitis, dysentery, or asthma. Witness No. 126 . . . and witness No. 153 . . . both consider the moderate use harmless. Piyari Mohan . . . states, 'I know it causes dysentery, and I believe owing to its heating power it can cause bronchitis and asthma.' . . . Kedareswar Acharjya . . . remarks . . . 'As to asthma, I have not seen any typical case originating from ganja smoking. I know that a chronic catarrhal condition of the air passages with a certain amount of spasm is the misfortune of many old ganja smokers. I know a friend who suffered from chronic bronchitis, and in whom asthmatic fits were induced by attempts to smoke ganja.' "

And so on and so forth.

Another observation in this nineteenth century report from India could describe today's use of marijuana in the United States. The smoke is "inhaled into the lungs in a similar manner as sometimes in cigarette smoking. In ganja smoking, however, the inspiratory act is far greater and more prolonged, a larger volume of smoke entering the lungs than in cigarette smoking."

The report concluded that cannabis should remain legal but be restricted and taxed. It received the approval of five commissioners (W. Mackworth Young, president; H. T. Ommanney; A. H. L. Fraser; C. J. H. Warden; and Kanwar Harnam Singh) while two commissioners dissented (Soshi Sikhareswar Roy and Lala Nihal Chand).[11]

Let us linger awhile more in India, where a family of doctors, the Chopras, have been writing on drug habits since 1928. A survey of "1,238 hemp-drug addicts," reported in 1939 (by R. N. and G. S. Chopra) included physical examinations, and nearly two out of five turned out to have respiratory disorders. Thirty-four years later, a clinical study (by G. S. Chopra) of 124 more users found that close to half suffered from respiratory ailments.

R. N. Chopra and G. S. Chopra reported in 1939 on the 1,238, who comprised 772 users of *bhang* and 466 users of *ganja* and/or *charas*. They were examined "in the field" in different parts of India, the process taking eight years. All but six were men; few women indulged in the habit.

The system of the body that hemp drugs appeared to affect most severely, next to the central nervous system, was the respiratory. Altogether 39.4 percent of their cases involved some disorder of the respiratory tract, the Chopras wrote.

"Chronic sore throat and pharyngitis are common among the habitués. Even when these drugs are taken in the form of a drink, they give rise to a feeling of constriction and hoarseness in the throat which in some cases may lead to a certain amount of difficulty in speaking. When smoked along with tobacco and other ingredients, there is always some irritation and congestion of the buccal and pharyngeal mucous membrane.

"The throat was examined as a routine in all our cases and it was found that 485 or 39.18 per cent of individuals suffered from tonsillitis and pharyngitis." The incidence of chronic bronchitis and emphysema were very high, 22.1 percent and 4.5 percent, respectively, mostly among *ganja* and *charas* smokers. The emphysema was "no doubt brought on by the constant and repeated fits of violent coughing to which ganja and charas smokers are subject."

Inhalation of *ganja* and *charas* with tobacco, unlike the process of smoking tobacco alone, was done with "considerable force . . . and a large volume of smoke is inhaled as deeply into the lungs as possible."

The frequency of tuberculosis was high, particularly among *ganja* and *charas* smokers, but the reason could be economic, according to the writers, for the majority were poor and ill-nourished and lived in bad hygienic conditions in overcrowded places. Cannabis usually was smoked in company through a common pipe, and this may have added to the chances of contracting the disease.

Among *bhang* users, 6.5 percent had chronic bronchitis, 5.8 percent asthma, 2.3 percent emphysema, and 3.2 percent tuberculosis. Among users of *ganja* and *charas*, 47.9 percent suffered chronic bronchitis, 13.7 percent asthma, 8.2 percent emphysema, and 5.4 percent tuberculosis.

Unfortunately, the drug users were not compared with nonusers.[12]

* * *

Dr. Gurbakhsh S. Chopra, director of the Calcutta Drug Addiction Clinic and the Research Field Centre (Nabha, Punjab), reported on the 124 in 1973. The subjects, all regular users, volunteered information and allowed themselves to be examined after taking their doses. The author discussed physiological effects only briefly and made it clear he considered them relatively minor compared with those of other psychotoxic drugs, including alcohol. But the subjects had such ailments as dryness of throat, irritating cough, laryngitis, pharyngitis, bronchitis, asthma, and dyspnea (difficult breathing). There were 61, or 48.3 percent, who suffered respiratory ailments.

The patients were grouped into four categories, based on average daily THC consumption, ranging from 40 to 350 mg of THC. The lightest users averaged nineteen years of age and a year and a half of use; the heaviest averaged forty-two years of age and eighteen years of use.

In the light-use group, there were twenty-nine respiratory sufferers; paradoxically the heavy-use group had eight.

Other adverse physical effects recorded (aside from the mind and nervous system): conjunctival (eye mucous membrane) congestion, forty-four users; tachycardia (rapid heart action) or throbbing in the head, thirty; malnutrition, wasting, or anemia, nineteen; dyspepsia and minor liver damage, four. Youths suffered most from adverse effects.

This study had no control group either.[13]

The smoking of *ganja* (marijuana) has been a widespread practice among laboring men in Jamaica, despite the illegality of the substance.

It appears to be associated with an "emphysema-bronchitis syndrome," according to Dr. John A. S. Hall, chairman of the Department of Medicine at the Kingston (Jamaica) Hospital.

> Testifying at a Senate committee hearing in 1974, Dr. Hall said that over the years he had routinely asked all patients at the initial interviews whether they used *ganja*. His team saw about 5,000 a year. Only about 3 percent would acknowledge using the drug, but they enabled him to study its effects, immediate and long-term. He enumerated long-term effects in four categories: respiratory complications, gastrointestinal tract involvement, metabolic effects, and personality changes. We will quote him only on the first:
> "An emphysema-bronchitis syndrome, common among Indian laborers of a past generation, who were well known for their ganja smoking habits, is now a well recognized present-day finding among black male laborers. Indeed, one of our cases died from the acute pulmonary embolism and at autopsy demonstrated spontaneous thrombosis of the pulmonary artery. In the autopsy room in general, the barrel-shaped emphysematous chest is a common finding in Rastafarian cultists. This raises questions of their smoking habits and the possible action of toxic metabolites from acting on the pulmonary parenchyma [tissue]. . . ."
> He did not compare them with nonsmokers or cite any statistics.
> Men in the Rastafarian religious cult in Jamaica smoke marijuana heavily.
> The Jamaican physician also reported gross declines from normal blood sugar levels in three of eight cases an hour after heavy *ganja* pipe smoking. He observed a constant craving for sweets in many habitual smokers, often keen appetitite generally, yet an absence of obesity that hinted of "some interference with the metabolic pathways for depositing body fat."[14]
> Dr. Hall wrote us that he was finding "a relationship between ganja and bleeding stomach ulcers on a seasonal basis." Further observations were pending.

A prominent study of Jamaicans compared thirty chronic *ganja* smokers and thirty "nonsmokers," all laboring-class men. The comparison produced differences in blood chemistry, and test results seemed to indicate also an association between smoking and the functioning of the lungs.

Reports on the study judged chronic, heavy smokers to be at greater risk of "functional hypoxia," that is, deficiency of oxygen in bodily tissues. Moreover, smokers tended to score lower on tests of respiratory function, though not significantly so. The investigators suggested that smoking per se might be responsible for the differences. Normally the smokers consumed their *ganja* with tobacco in home-rolled cigarettes.

Note that eighteen of the so-called nonsmokers had smoked marijuana in the past, seven or eight still occasionally smoked it, and the majority of each group currently smoked tobacco cigarettes.[15] So a clear-cut comparison between cannabis smokers and nonsmokers was not made (let alone a determination of whether cannabis-related respiratory ills could have killed or laid up any less fit smokers).

The book *Ganja in Jamaica* by Vera Rubin and Lambros Comitas (1975), emphasizing psychological and anthropological findings, was widely publicized. Typically, news stories reported how a Jamaican study of marijuana had given it a clean bill of health, and they omitted a statement in the final summary that "it appears that the [respiratory] risk of chronic cannabis smoking may parallel the risks of chronic tobacco smoking."

About twice as many *ganja* smokers as controls fell into the lowest third of scores for each of three tests of lung function: forced vital capacity (the maximum volume of gas that can be expelled after a deep breath), forced expiratory volume in one second (the volume of air expelled in the first second), and peak flow rate (expiration in volume per minute).

While the differences lacked a 0.05 statistical significance, authors Rubin and Comitas felt the results indicated some association between smoking and respiratory function. Furthermore, "Correlations of number of years of *ganja* smoking" with the latter two measurements "are significant at the .05 level."

Arterial blood gas percentages were determined, and at rest smokers tended to have less oxygen than controls, "indicating poorer oxygenation of blood for smokers." After exercise, oxygen values leveled and smokers' blood had significantly less bicarbonate (alkali). Each time, smokers' carbon dioxide tended to be lower.

To a significant extent, *ganja* users had elevated blood hemoglobin and packed red blood cell volume, "suggesting lowered oxygen-engaging capacity of hemoglobin due to hypoxia induced by smoking." About twice as many smokers as controls had a low count of monocytes and of eosinophils, types of white blood cells.

Only two "significant physical abnormalities" appeared, chronic bronchial asthma and a form of neuropathy. They both occurred in smokers, but the authors saw no evidence to relate the conditions to cannabis.

Twenty-seven *ganja* smokers also smoked tobacco cigarettes. Nineteen controls smoked tobacco. The *ganja* smokers had engaged in the habit for a mean of seventeen and a half years, range of seven to thirty-seven; they currently smoked daily a mean of seven *spliffs* (*ganja*-tobacco cigarettes), range of one to twenty-four; and potency averaged 2.8 percent THC, ranging from 0.7 to 10.3 percent.

Professor Eric K. Cruickshank, then head of the Department of Medicine of the University of the West Indies, conducted the medical portions of the Jamaican cannabis project. The Research Institute for the Study of Man, in New York City, performed the study for the National Institute of Mental Health. Joint principal investigators were Vera Rubin and Lambros Comitas.[16]

* * *

"A federally contracted study of marijuana smoking in Jamaica, where the consumption by heavy users is said to be 10 to 25 times that of their American counterparts, has failed to confirm any serious adverse effects," began a forty-paragraph story in *The New York Times* (1975) when the book was published.

3

Is It Carcinogenic?

Lung cancer used to be a rare disease before cigarette smoking caused the graphs to soar. It is well known that the burning of a Camel or Kent or Lucky Strike produces carcinogens, cancer-producing substances. Carcinogens exist in nature or emerge as the product of burning or other chemical activity.

Burning destroys some of the 426 compounds in cannabis and creates thousands of others. The smoke introduces many known toxic chemicals, such as carbon monoxide, hydrogen cyanide, and nitrosamines. These and many other poisonous substances occur in the gas phase of the smoke from a marijuana joint and from a tobacco cigarette in similar concentrations. Among the particles in marijuana smoke, chemists find considerably more of the carcinogenic hydrocarbons than in tobacco smoke's particulate phase.

Various scientists view cannabis smoke as a potential source of cancer. The additional possibility that THC and some of the other sixty-one cannabinoids themselves are carcinogenic has been raised.

*   *   *

" . . . It is extremely difficult to produce a lung cancer in an experimental animal with tobacco smoke. Instead, when an extract of tobacco tars is painted on the skin of mice, tumors and cancer can be induced." (Dr. Sidney Cohen, 1979.)[17]

In the early 1970s at least three teams of American researchers independently performed experiments of the latter type to find out whether marijuana smoke, like tobacco smoke, had cancer-causing properties. Each collected an extract from marijuana smoke and smeared it on the shaved skin of live mice. (The marijuana extracts were dissolved in acetone. As a check, other mice were painted with acetone alone.) One team also analyzed the marijuana smoke for toxic and tumor-producing ingredients.

Examining the affected tissues after periods of time, all three teams found that abnormal changes had taken place in the cells of marijuana-treated mice. Two of the three (Magus and Harris, and Cottrell, Sohn, and Vogel) found the results to be characteristic of approaching cancer. The third (Hoffmann et al.) expressed doubt but—finding marijuana smoke to contain 50 percent more of the cancer-causing hydrocarbons than tobacco smoke—considered marijuana's possible carcinogenicity a "reasonable question" to study further.

The late R. D. Magus and L. S. Harris (University of North Carolina School of Medicine) applied the tar yields from marijuana cigarettes to mice three times at two-day intervals and did the same with tobacco cigarette tar.

Specimens taken on the eighth day revealed "dose-related sebaceous gland destruction, dermal lymphocytic infiltration, epidermal hyperplasia with acanthosis" in all marijuana and tobacco groups but not in the control mice. "These effects are typical of those produced in the mouse skin test by known carcinogenic compounds such as polycyclic hydrocarbons."[18]

*   *   *

Cottrell, Sohn, and Vogel (Jefferson Medical College, Thomas Jefferson University, Philadelphia) painted some mice with marijuana smoke condensate and others with benzopyrene (a carcinogenic compound in tobacco cigarette smoke) daily for five days. Two days later each group showed "complete metaplasia [abnormal transformation of cells] of all sebaceous glands in mouse skin." Control mice remained normal.

Since the effect of the marijuana smoke condensate correlated well with the carcinogenic tendency of tobacco smoke condensates, "we anticipate that cannabis will prove to be carcinogenic."[19]

*   *   *

Analyzing concentrates, Hoffmann, Brunnemann, Wynder (American Health Foundation, New York City) and Gori (National Cancer Institute, Bethesda, Maryland) found that a number of toxic chemicals were present in tobacco smoke and marijuana smoke in approximately the same amounts: ammonia, hydrogen cyanide, acrolein, acetonitrile, benzene, toluene, and nitrosamines.

They discovered polynuclear aromatic hydrocarbons (which are formed during incomplete combustion of organic matter) in the smoke of both marijuana and tobacco, but in much higher amounts in marijuana. Their reason: marijuana does not burn as well as tobacco. They listed the strong carcinogen benzopyrene, benzanthracene, and the naphthalenes.

After receiving tar treatment three times weekly for up to seventy-four weeks, 6 of 100 "marijuana mice" had developed skin tumors, all benign, while 14 of 100 "tobacco mice" had developed skin tumors, malignant in two cases. The experimenters "rarely" had observed skin tumors in similar mice after treatment with acetone solvent alone. Respectively 1, 2, and no mice suffered lymphomas (malignant tumors) in marijuana, tobacco, and control groups; and 25, 22, and 31 mice acquired lung adenomas (benign tumors). "Tar" was defined as particulate matter in smoke.

The experimenters hesitated to relate the study directly to human beings in the absence of pertinent epidemiological data, but they deemed the carcinogenicity question worthy of more investigation, particularly because of marijuana smoke's relatively high content of polynuclear aromatic hydrocarbons.[20]

Our Supplement, E, contains a chemical comparison of marijuana and tobacco smokes, based on analyses by Hoffmann, Brunnemann et al.

In 1970 the Leuchtenbergers, a husband-and-wife cancer research team
in Switzerland, began pioneer experiments on the biological effects of
fresh marijuana smoke on the lungs. Having experimented earlier with
tobacco cigarettes, they became interested in the respiratory and genetic
effects of marijuana cigarettes and in seeing how the two kinds compare.
The couple cultured more than 5,000 samples of lung tissues, from
human beings as well as from mice and hamsters.

They found abnormal changes in cells of mouse and human lung
samples exposed for a short time either to tobacco or marijuana smoke
or a combination of the two. Both types of smoke brought similar results, although marijuana produced more marked changes and so did
marijuana mixed with tobacco. Some of the changes appeared "precancerous."

Malignant cells developed in hamster lung samples exposed for months
to marijuana-only cigarette smoke. When the cells were injected into
live mice, malignant tumors appeared at the places of injection.

The Leuchtenbergers concluded that the smoke from marijuana cigarettes had a harmful effect on human and animal lung tissues and cells,
and that long-term marijuana smoking might lead to lung cancer.

Working in the cytochemistry department of the Swiss Institute for Experimental Cancer Research, at Lausanne, were Professor Cecile Leuchtenberger, Ph.D.,
head of the department, a biologist educated in the United States and Europe;
and Professor Rudolf Leuchtenberger, M.D., an experimental pathologist. They
did their marijuana work until 1980, supported by the World Health Organization.

They performed three main types of experimental lung studies:

A. They exposed cultured samples from lungs of mice to fresh smoke from
standard tobacco cigarettes without marijuana. Then they exposed the same lung
cultures to smoke from cigarettes made from both tobacco and marijuana. Doses
were low (two puffs of 8 milliliters a day for five days). As a control, similar cultures were left untouched by smoke.

Lung samples exposed to smoke from regular cigarettes did not look much different from the control samples.

But adding marijuana to tobacco cigarettes produced a smoke that was (in the
words of Cecile Leuchtenberger) "much more harmful to these mouse lung cultures than was the smoke from tobacco cigarettes without marijuana." Smoke from
the marijuana-tobacco mixture brought "morphological and cytochemical alterations in cells" of the lung samples. These alterations were of "a significantly higher
degree" than those caused by tobacco-only cigarettes.

In the samples exposed to the tobacco-marijuana smoke, "there was a marked
increase in size of nuclei and nucleoli, accompanied by abnormal shapes of cells,
lagging of chromosomes, and crisscross formations. . . . This indication of ab-

normal proliferation was accompanied by a significant increase of mitotic index and by stimulation of DNA synthesis." (DNA is short for deoxyribonucleic acid, the genetic material.)

For example, when lung samples were exposed to tobacco-marijuana smoke, the number of one type of abnormal cell alteration (epithelioid cells with four DNA) was at least three times greater and as much as seventeen times greater than samples exposed to smoke of tobacco-only cigarettes, depending on whether the THC content of the marijuana was 0.4 percent or 4 percent, Madame Leuchtenberger said.

B. Here they used human lung cultures, both from adults and fetuses. They compared the effects of the smoke from tobacco-only cigarettes with those from marijuana-only cigarettes. Volumes of smoke (25 milliliters) and periods of exposure (up to two months) were larger than those in the mouse study in order to resemble more closely the volume of smoke inhaled by human smokers. (That volume was estimated at 35 ml a puff.)

The changes in human lung cultures were very similar after exposure to marijuana smoke and after exposure to tobacco smoke. Each type of smoke stimulated abnormalities in DNA synthesis and in cell division; irregular, abnormal growth of the cultures; and variability in number and DNA content of chromosomes.

However, these disturbances were more severe after exposure to marijuana smoke than after exposure to tobacco smoke.

C. Questions to be answered were these: Does continued exposure from tobacco or marijuana cigarettes bring a sequence of changes progressing to malignancy? Are such changes produced only by the whole smoke or only by the gas vapor (smoke without particles, tar, or nicotine)?

Both hamsters and mice were used. For varying periods of time, the Leuchtenbergers exposed cultures from hamster lungs to the different types of smoke (four to six puffs of 25 ml each on three consecutive days a week). In addition, some cultures were left untouched as a control. Three stages were observed in all smoke-exposed cultures:

I. A toxic effect on a number of cells (damage or destruction), after a week of exposure or less.

II. Abnormal proliferation of the remaining cells, after three to ten weeks of exposure.

III. Malignant transformation of cells, after three to six months of exposure.

In stage I marijuana showed less cytotoxicity than tobacco (fewer cells destroyed). But in stage II the "proliferative alterations . . . were especially striking" after exposure to marijuana smoke. "Proliferation was particularly noticeable after exposure to the gas vapor phase of marijuana, nucleoli, nuclei, and cytoplasm increasing enormously." Furthermore, abnormalities in cell division were more marked from marijuana (any phase) than from tobacco.

In stage III, malignancies occurred, whether in the marijuana or the tobacco cultures. When cells of such cultures "were injected into nude mice, fibrosarcomas were observed at the place of injection within 10 to 20 days. . . ." After one to two years a considerable number of the control cultures, untouched by smoke, displayed malignant changes and caused the same reactions when injected into mice.

"It appears, therefore, that smoke from marijuana cigarettes accelerates malignant transformation of culture lung cells as does smoke from tobacco cigarettes.

. . . Mainly gas-vapor-phase constituents were responsible for enhancing malignant transformation," inasmuch as smoke with the particles (and THC) filtered out caused such result.[21]

Chemists burned about 2,000 marijuana cigarettes plus 2,000 tobacco cigarettes and analyzed the smoke. They discovered more than 150 chemicals in marijuana smoke that could be suspected of causing cancer. Marijuana smoke possessed "a considerably higher content of potential carcinogens" than tobacco smoke, according to Professor Milos Novotny in Indiana and associates.

Novotny and Lee, both of Indiana University, and Bartle of the University of Leeds, England, had set out to analyze marijuana smoke for "the potent carcinogens, polynuclear aromatic hydrocarbons." Using a smoking machine, they burned about 2,000 cigarettes of Mexican marijuana (2.8 percent THC) and an equal number of standard tobacco cigarettes.

Their detailed studies resulted in "identification of over 150 polynuclear aromatic hydrocarbons in marijuana smoke condensate." There was "a larger proportion of heavier polynuclears encountered in marijuana smoke compared to tobacco." Reporting in 1975 on their findings, they listed the chemicals and amounts found in both marijuana and tobacco.

"It should be noted that the well-known carcinogen benzo(alpha)pyrene is enhanced in marijuana smoke by 70% over that present in tobacco smoke," they wrote. Among other marijuana constituents found by the chemists were indenopyrene, which they noted was a known carcinogen, and dibenzopyrene, which had been reported to produce respiratory cancer in hamsters. They were not sure how carcinogenic many of the other chemicals were because "most of them had never been synthesized or isolated in a pure state for biological experiments."[22]

The late surgeon Alton Ochsner of New Orleans was said to have performed 20,000 operations. Best known for his long battle against tobacco, he claimed to have seen and treated more lung cancer patients than any other doctor. It was in the 1930s, on witnessing an unexpected upsurge in lung cancer among smokers, that he suggested cigarette smoking as a cause of the disease.

We asked Dr. Ochsner whether marijuana smoking could cause cancer. "I do not think we know enough about the effects of marijuana to say that it is cancer-producing," he replied (in 1980). But he added, "The changes it causes in the larynx, which can be seen very readily in marijuana smokers, are much worse than the changes caused by tobacco."

Noting the years it takes for the production of a cancer to become evident, he predicted that in time marijuana would prove "just as carcinogenic as tobacco—and, of course, it is detrimental in other ways as well." He cited harm to the brain.

Dr. Ochsner published his theory in 1939, with Dr. Michael De Bakey. A piece on lung cancer in the *Journal of Surgery, Gynecology, and Obstetrics* announced: "In our opinion the increase in smoking with the universal custom of inhaling is probably a responsible factor, as the inhaled smoke, constantly repeated over a long period of time, undoubtedly is a source of chronic irritation to the bronchial mucosa."[23]

In a letter to us, Dr. Ochsner wrote: "My conviction that there was a relationship between cigarette smoking and cancer of the lung was a serendipitous one.

"When I was a medical student at Washington University [St. Louis] in 1919, there was a case of cancer of the lung admitted to the Barnes Hospital, which was our teaching hospital, and, as usual, the patient died. Our professor of medicine, Dr. George Dock, who was an eminent pathologist, as well as an eminent internist, had the two senior classes witness the autopsy because, as he said, the case was so rare we would never again see another case as long as we lived. . . .

"I did not see another case until 1936. I had come to Tulane as professor of surgery in 1927. In 1936, at the Charity Hospital in New Orleans, I saw nine cases of cancer of the lung in six months, a condition that seventeen years previously I was not supposed to see for the rest of my life. . . .

"This was an epidemic and there had to be a cause. They were all men, they all had smoked cigarettes heavily, and they all began smoking in World War I. I looked up and found that there were very few cigarettes consumed until the First World War, so I had temerity at that time to say that I thought the cause of this new epidemic was cigarette smoking.

"The evidence was pretty nebulous then, but now we have the proof. Cancer of the lung is increasing more than any other cancer in the body. It is by far the most frequent cause of cancer death in men, and it is predicted in another two years it will be the most frequent cause of death in women. All other cancers in the United States are remaining about the same or decreasing. . . . It is the one cancer that we know is preventable, because all but about 4% of lung cancers are caused by smoking.

"Of greater hazard, of course, is the effect of tobacco on the heart and blood vessels. Heart and blood vessel disease are the principal causes of death in the United States, and tobacco is the principal cause of these conditions. I am convinced that if people will stop smoking, cancer of the lung will revert back to the same rarity it was when I was a medical student."

In 1980, when an asbestos company sued cigarette companies in response to suits by asbestos workers, Dr. Ochsner lent his support. He said, "The tobacco industry is the principal cause of death in the United States. I have seen or operated on more cancer cases than any other living person. No patients I have operated on had lung cancer from asbestos." He said smoking caused that disease, plus heart trouble, strokes, aneurysms, and emphysema. "There's not one damn thing good about tobacco except that it kills bugs."[24]

Dr. Ochsner died in 1981 at the age of eighty-five, following heart surgery at Ochsner Medical Foundation Hospital, which he had founded. He was the author of four books on smoking and health and taught more than 3,000 medical students.

In two sets of rodent experiments, some rats injected with marijuana tar by Cottrell and Vogel in Pennsylvania developed lung cancer and other cancers; and many cases of lung cancer occurred in mice injected with THC by Szepsenwol and associates in Florida. (Details on both projects will follow in "The Cells and Chromosomes," 3.)

Biopsies by the U.S. Army in Germany and by Tashkin *et al.* in Los Angeles turned up possibly precancerous cell changes in airways of heavy, habitual cannabis smokers. (More in 4, this section.)

4

Some Studies of Smoking and Sickness

Early in the seventies, army medical officers studied American soldiers stationed in Europe who had smoked hashish for at least a few months. Surprisingly for men so young, their smoking was often associated with sore throat, bronchitis, sinusitis, and other ailments.

Examinations of bronchial tissues revealed abnormalities of the kind associated with heavy cigarette smoking and lung cancer. The abnormalities were much more common in those who smoked both hashish and (tobacco) cigarettes than in smokers of one or the other, although they also occurred in hashish-only smokers. Months of hashish smoking, particularly by the tobacco smokers, appeared to be making more impact on the lungs than years of tobacco smoking alone.

In a 1971 survey of a thousand U.S. soldiers in Germany, close to half smoked hashish and the majority of the smokers blamed ailments on the hashish. Leading the list, sore throat had afflicted nearly one in every four.

> The survey was run by Forest S. Tennant, Jr., then a medical corps officer with the Third Infantry Division, U.S. Army in Europe. He helped start some of the first drug and alcohol rehabilitation efforts in the armed forces and later he helped develop such programs for U.S. Army units throughout Europe. On leaving the army, he became a consultant, researcher, and drug-treatment director in the Los Angeles area.
>
> Testifying before a 1974 Senate committee hearing, Dr. Tennant said that when he went to Europe in 1968, he thought of cannabis as "a rather harmless drug." He learned that "a major difference between hashish and marijuana from the medical point of view is the irritating effect of hashish on the respiratory tract."
>
> Hashish was cheap in West Germany, costing only $1 to $1.50 a gram, or about $28 to $43 per ounce. The resinous material, smoked in pipes, was many times stronger than the marijuana in the U.S.A. at that time.

"In early 1971 we surveyed 1,018 U.S. Army soldiers by anonymous question-naires: 492, 48 percent, had used hashish in West Germany," Tennant told the senators.

By the hashish smokers' own accounts, the drug had caused sore throat in 122 smokers (25 percent); headache, 70 (14 percent); running nose, 43 (9 percent); emotional problems, 42 (9 percent); bronchitis, 30 (6 percent); diarrhea, 23 (5 percent); and no bad effects, 205 (42 percent). About 14 percent of the hashish smokers indicated that they had visited an army physician for an ailment caused by hashish. (Some suffered more than one.)

Among the medical cases that came to the attention of Tennant and other army doctors in 1969 and 1970, he said, were "respiratory problems that were related to hashish consumption. . . . We found that sinusitis, pharyngitis, and bronchi-tis were extremely common among these heavy hashish smokers. And this is rather surprising, because, even though you can get bronchitis and emphysema and these sort of problems from cigarette smoking, one usually must smoke cigarettes for 10–20 years to get these complications. We became alarmed about this because we began seeing these complications in 18-, 19- or 20-year old men."

Over a three-year period, he and colleagues studied 720 hashish smokers who sought medical care at the Würzburg, West Germany, U.S. Army Hospital. "Over one-half—392—smoked small quantities of hashish and came to us for minor re-spiratory complaints—sore throat, sinusitis—or for information about the adverse effects of hashish. The other subjects exhibited findings of significant psychiatric disease."

One of the major concerns was "whether hashish may also lead to cancer as does cigarette smoking." So in 1971 Tennant and two other army physicians (Major Roderick Guerry, a pathologist, and Lieutenant Colonel Robert Henderson, an ear-nose-throat specialist) began a study that involved bronchial biopsies of thirty-six soldiers, seventeen to thirty-six (mean age: twenty-one).

Thirty were hashish smokers, who had smoked between 25 and 150 grams for three months to two years. All thirty were found to suffer chronic bronchitis. The biopsies revealed abnormal cells in twenty-four of them. Of the six who did not use hashish, only one (a tobacco cigarette smoker, aged thirty-two) showed such abnormalities.

"The abnormalities found in the bronchial biopsies were the same that are as-sociated with heavy cigarette smoking and cancer of the lung," the doctor testi-fied. According to research into cigarette smoking, "it takes between five and twenty years to develop precancerous lesions in the lungs from cigarette smoking alone."

The presiding senator, Strom Thurmond, said, "You are talking here about chronic cigarette smokers, who smoke a pack a day or more?"

"Yes, sir."

"And with the chronic hashish smokers, as much change took place in three months as you would normally find in chronic [tobacco] smokers who have been smoking a pack or more a day for many years?"

"That is right."

"Those are very impressive figures."

"Now, the interesting thing about this is that we had seven of these 30 smokers that did not smoke cigarettes; they only smoked hashish and two of them had these precancerous lesions. You might say that two out of seven is not very many. But you have got to realize that you do not normally find this particular lesion unless you have smoked [tobacco] for a long time.

"Now, the other thing about this study: we had 23 people who smoked both hashish and cigarettes. . . . And all of these people had abnormal lesions in the biopsies. And therefore, our conclusion, at least based on our evidence, is that it would appear that people who smoke both hashish and cigarettes develop these precancerous lesions at an amazingly early age, and that smoking hashish alone may cause this also."[25]

Microscopic examination of the tissues sampled in the biopsies revealed these abnormalities (per Tennant, 1980):

"Atypical cells" in 23 of 23 cigarette-hashish smokers, 2 of 7 hashish (only) smokers, 1 of 3 cigarette (only) smokers, and 0 of 3 nonsmokers.

"Squamous metaplasia" in 21 cigarette-hashish smokers, 1 hashish smoker, 1 cigarette smoker, and 0 nonsmokers.

"Basal cell hyperplasia" in 14 cigarette-hashish smokers, 1 hashish smoker, 0 cigarette smokers, and 0 nonsmokers.

All hashish or combination smokers complained of respiratory symptoms, nearly all reporting chronic cough and the majority shortness of breath. Most showed rales or wheezes. One cigarette-only smoker complained of chronic cough. The cigarette-only smokers and nonsmokers had no other complaint and exhibited no symptom on examination.

The data are not sufficient to determine if hashish-only smoking is more detrimental to the pulmonary system than cigarette-only smoking, Tennant wrote. They indicate, however, that "hashish plus cigarette smoking is more deleterious than smoking either one alone. . . . It is unknown if these abnormalities may possibly lead to emphysema or carcinoma of the lung, although this is a reasonable assumption" because the tissue abnormalities—particularly squamous metaplasia (scaly transformation)—have been associated with those diseases. It is also "reasonable to assume" that marijuana too (though not a part of the study) may produce similar abnormalities if smoked chronically with cigarettes.[26]

*　*　*

At the Senate committee hearing, a description of the marijuana vogue as "a new experiment in cancer epidemiology" and a warning that society might be raising a crop of young "respiratory cripples" came from Professor (later Sir) W. D. M. Paton of the pharmacology department at the University of Oxford, a medical doctor and coauthor of the textbook *Pharmacological Principles and Practice*. He testified:

"Like the tar from cigarettes, reefer tar is carcinogenic when painted on mouse skin. Cannabis smoke produces changes in cultures of lung disease. . . . THC in low concentration resembles the carcinogen methyl-chlolanthrene in generating malignancy in rat embryo cells incubated with a marine leukemia virus, but is slower in action. The irritant effect of the smoke on the respiratory tract is well known to users and is associated with bronchial pathology.

"These effects are becoming very important. Originally, one was uncertain about their significance, and about what the balance would be between the facts that more cigarettes than reefers will normally be smoked in any one day, whereas inhalation and retention of the smoke is much deeper and more efficient with the reefer. . . .

"But now lung damage, in the form of emphysema, is being repeatedly recorded. . . . Emphysema is normally a disease of much later life; but now the quite unexpected—to me, at least—prospect of a new crop of respiratory cripples early in life, is opening up.

"Originally, I thought the cancer risk was the main problem; cannabis has never been used extensively in a society with an expectation of life long enough to show a carcinogenic effect in man, until recent years. In effect, a new experiment in cancer epidemiology started five to ten years ago.

"To this I would now add respiratory pathology generally; and because it shows itself early, just as with cigarette smoking, bronchitis is an early warning of that pathology. . . ."[27]

* * *

Robert G. Heath, chairman of the Tulane University (New Orleans) psychiatry and neurology department, telling the senators of his monkey-brain experiments, mentioned that two monkeys had died after 3½ and 5½ months of heavy marijuana smoking and was asked if he blamed the smoke.

"Yes," he replied. "I think I will have to speculate, but there is an awful lot of junk in marijuana that is bound to be extremely harsh and irritating. Marijuana is much more harsh and irritating than tobacco and produces considerable irritation in the respiratory tract of these animals. We feel this was the reason the two animals developed pneumonia and subsequently died."[28]

"Smoke for Science and Dollars," read an ad soliciting marijuana-smoking collegians in Boston. Thereupon seventeen of them inhaled smoke from a special machine, and Dr. Louis Vachon and associated physicians at Boston University School of Medicine (1973) learned that a single marijuana dose had "a striking bronchodilator effect." That is, it expanded the airways, unlike tobacco smoke which constricted them.

At the University of California at Los Angeles, medical Professor Donald P. Tashkin and colleagues (1973) determined that marijuana-cigarette smoking and oral THC both dilated the airways, in asthmatic as well as normal subjects, and that the effect lasted for hours.

The Boston and Los Angeles studies led to premature talk of marijuana's therapeutic benefits to the lungs. Longer-range studies in the same cities would tell another story.

For each subject in the Vachon experiment (fifteen men and two women), airway resistance decreased and specific airway conductance and expiratory flow at one-fourth of vital capacity increased within twenty minutes after igniting of 3.2 mg of marijuana. High doses (2.6 percent THC), given to nine subjects, induced quicker and greater changes—for instance, a 45 percent mean increase in the flow rate—than low doses (1 percent THC), to eight.[29]

In thirty-two healthy, young, male marijuana smokers observed by Tashkin, Shapiro, and Frank, specific airway conductance reached a peak in fifteen to thirty minutes of marijuana smoking (cigarette of 1 or 2 percent THC) or three hours after THC ingestion (10 to 20 mg) and remained elevated for the hour and six hours of the respective tests.[30] In ten asthmatic subjects, specific airway conductance increased 33 to 48 percent after their smoking (2 percent THC) and 14 to 19 percent after THC ingestion (15 mg) but not after placebos.[31] Following induction of bronchospasm by Tashkin et al. (1975) in eight asthmatic subjects through exercise or methacholine inhalation, marijuana and sprayed isoproterenol both corrected it immediately.[32]

Of forty-eight young, male marijuana smokers examined in a sweeping pair of Harvard Medical School studies (1974 and 1976), two-thirds displayed abnormalities of lung function. Tobacco was not the cause: many never had smoked it and previous studies of tobacco smokers in similar groups had not shown such abnormalities.

Bernstein and associated scientists commented (1976): "In the absence of other risk factors and in the presence of a very positive history of marijuana use in these subjects, it seems reasonable to assume these changes to be related to marijuana and on this basis to sound a note of caution regarding the possible long-term deleterious effects of this substance on the lungs."

> The first study tested twenty volunteers in Boston City Hospital. During five nonsmoking days before a three-week smoking period, impaired vital capacity (VC) was found in twelve subjects, of whom four also showed impairment in one-second forced expired volume (FEV). Two others failed the latter test only. Of the fourteen subjects with abnormalities, only six had a history of tobacco use. The twenty volunteers were equally divided into "casual" and "heavy" users, and so were the fourteen. Smoking of 2 percent-THC marijuana cigarettes brought some deterioration in eight within an hour, including significant FEV impairment in two heavy users earlier rated abnormal in VC.[33]
>
> In the second study, using twenty-eight subjects in McLean Hospital, Belmont, Massachusetts, the medical researchers observed no respiratory tract symptoms but did note "clinically significant" pulmonary function results in the presmoking period. These included VC reductions in six subjects, three of whom never had smoked tobacco. Also eighteen subjects, including the six, had one-second FEV/VC ratios of 90 percent or greater. "This type of abnormality is strongly suggestive of the presence of restrictive disease of the lung such as interstitial fibrosis or other types of pulmonary disease that may be produced by chronic inhalation of irritating substances."[34]
>
> Jerrold G. Bernstein, M.D., psychiatrist and clinical pharmacologist, has been assistant clinical professor of psychiatry at Harvard Medical School.

In Los Angeles, Dr. Tashkin and colleagues continued their research (1976), testing the lung functioning of twenty-eight healthy, young, male marijuana smokers before seven or eight weeks of free smoking in a hospital. Presmoking results mostly fell within normal limits. Heavy smoking during the experiment brought "mild" but definite narrowing of the airways, both large, medium, and small. Examination of a few subjects in a week and a month showed the condition reversing. Smokers were not compared with nonsmokers in that study.

In a later study (1980), Tashkin and group gave a battery of lung-function tests (in a hospital) to the 28 plus 46 similar subjects, likewise examining 115 controls (in a mobile laboratory). Marijuana smokers scored poorer than controls in two tests. The impairment was "mild but significant."

Marijuana users who smoked no tobacco (fifty) compared just as unfavorably whether matched with tobacco-smoking controls or nontobacco-smoking controls; the two control groups measured alike. Thus "habitual marijuana use causes abnormalities in the large airways of young individuals that are not produced, at least to a detectable degree by the chronic smoking of more than 16 tobacco cigarettes a day." Statistically the readings stayed in the normal range and the marijuana smokers did not feel breathless even during exertion, yet it remained an open question whether disease might develop after more years or decades of smoking.

Subjects in the 1976 study had habitually smoked cannabis between four times a week and several times a day (for unspecified terms). Recruited by newspaper ads, they were segregated in a special ward for ninety-four days and examined in many ways by different investigators at UCLA's Neuropsychiatric Institute. Dr. Tashkin, a chest physician and head of the Lung Function Laboratory, headed the respiratory investigations.

No smoking was allowed for the first eleven days. Measurements were made on the eighth no-smoking day and after at least nine hours of no smoking following forty-seven to fifty-nine days of smoking. Daily the young men smoked between one and twenty marijuana cigarettes (2 percent THC), an average of five, more than their regular consumption.

There were decreases in forced expired volume in one second (3 percent), diffusing capacity (8 percent), maximal midexpiratory flow (11 percent), and specific airway conductance (16 percent). The severity of the latter two conditions depended on the amount of marijuana smoked. Tashkin et al. thought the air flow obstruction stemmed from marijuana's repeated irritation of the respiratory epithelium (membrane lining the tubes) and the resulting inflammation. Yet they volunteered the opinion (for readers of the prestigious *New England Journal of Medicine*) that "customary social use of marihuana may not result in detectable functional respiratory impairment in healthy young men. . . ."[35]

The seventy-four in the 1980 study had smoked marijuana for at least two years, in most cases more than five years, from three times a week to several times a day. Testing came between twelve hours and one week after their last smokes.

Airway resistance tested one-fourth higher and specific airway conductance one-fourth lower than controls (the majority of whom were not questioned as to marijuana habits). Marijuana smokers displayed no abnormalities in three tests (maximal midexpiratory rate, closing volume, and single-breath nitrogen washout) believed to be sensitive indicators of obstruction in smaller airways in the early stage of chronic obstructive pulmonary disease.

Tashkin et al. wrote that chronic exposure to marijuana smoke mainly affected the larger airways, narrowing them, mainly through inflammation. Whether major pulmonary disease would develop had to be left to large-scale epidemiological studies. By this time they had no encouragement for "social" smoking.[36]

In 1980 testimony, Tashkin concluded that while the risks of chronic marijuana smoking could not be stated with certainty, a "fair body of information" suggested that marijuana "does have the potential to damage the lungs of man" and that "chronic respiratory irritation from long-term use" might harm the already damaged airways of asthmatics or chronic bronchitis sufferers. Hence the smoking of marijuana should be discouraged to prevent damage to the lungs.

He advised asthmatic sufferers not to smoke marijuana for relief—thus to disregard his earlier findings of acute airway dilation—because the smoke contains compounds that irritate the respiratory tract. Even THC alone has an irritating effect, and the higher the THC concentration in smoke, the greater that effect probably is. When five asthmatic subjects received THC in an aerosol, two suffered asthma attacks and all suffered coughing and throat irritation.[37]

Checkups of selected groups of users versus controls in Costa Rica and Greece (both 1976) failed to convince examiners of any cannabic role in pulmonary disease. All of those tested also smoked tobacco.

Forty Costa Ricans who had used marijuana for an average of ten years scored substantially the same in lung function tests as a matched non-marijuana group with comparable tobacco history.[38] In Greece, thirteen hashish smokers (30 percent) had bronchitis, against six controls (16 percent). The difference was pronounced insignificant and maybe due to a greater number of tobacco cigarettes smoked by the hashish users. Two users and one control showed signs of emphysema. Coughing and irritation of the pharynx "were common among the users," who had smoked hashish for an average of twenty-three years.[39]

Tashkin and Cohen (1981) speculated on the reasons for the contrasting American and Greek hashish findings: The GIs were patients seeking treatment while the Greek study excluded those with incapacitating illness. Also the two nationalities smoked differently, and "the rapid, deep, and prolonged inhalation technique favored by Americans might lead to greater deposition of irritating particulates in the larger airways and greater exposure of the peripheral airways to the more deeply penetrating and longer-retained gaseous irritants in the smoke."[40]

The effects of tobacco smoke and marijuana smoke were compared in canine experiments in Quebec. Daily for 900 days beagles each received smoke from four cigarettes, one type or the other, directly through tubes into the windpipe. Pathologists reported the most serious result to be bronchiolitis (that is, inflammation of the bronchioles, subdivisions of the bronchial tree), which was particularly marked in the marijuana-smoking dogs.

P. E. Roy and three others of Laval Hospital and Laval University, Quebec, used thirty-four female beagles in four groups: marijuana (3 grams daily, 1.5 percent THC), tobacco (3.2 grams daily, standard, nonfilter), controls with tracheostomy tubes, and absolute controls.

The researchers reported (1976) bronchiolitis with macrophage infiltration to be the most important pathologic change. Such a condition "can produce a lung emphysema." The operation itself also produced bronchiolitis, tobacco brought a little more, and to a significant extent "marijuana provoked a higher degree of bronchiolitis than tobacco." The tobacco group tended to have the smallest alveolar surface. The marijuana group had more squamous metaplasia in the trachea.[41]

Dr. Roy, M.D., has been a professor in the Department of Pathology, Laval University.

Scientists in Massachusetts discovered numerous abnormal changes in the lungs of rats made to inhale marijuana smoke for extended periods. The project involved the development of an automatic smoking machine and of a method of relating rodents' doses to humans', for the rats were supposed to represent habitual marijuana smokers. Experiments went on between 1973 and 1978, using close to 600 rats.

For different lengths of time, as long as a year, the animals periodically received varying numbers of puffs in the smoking machine. After about three months of smoke inhalation, changes occurred in their lungs. Their alveoli (air sacs) became inflamed, filling with cellular debris. The debris came from the disintegration of lung cells and from an accumulation of macrophages (cells that battle foreign bodies or engulf cellular debris), which had mobilized extensively.

As months of smoking went by, things got worse for the rats. Their lungs became more severely inflamed. An array of new lesions developed by six months, becoming worse after a year. More debris clogged the alveoli, and their walls thickened. There appeared enlarged lung cells with accumulated cholesterol—usually a sign of serious change in lung tissue and possibly an early warning of the coming of cancer in some cases (Dr. Harris Rosenkrantz told us).

The investigators allowed some rats a month to recover but the damage showed no signs of reversing, even when the duration of smoke exposure had been only three months.

The severity of the lung trouble was related to the length of time rats had smoked and the dose (number of puffs): light, medium, or heavy.

As a check, the researchers tested some rats with the smoke of placebo marijuana cigarettes (made of marijuana with cannabinoids removed). Changes developed among those rats too—particles and gases in the smoke causing inflammations—but the changes were less severe. In other rats, placed in the machine without smoke or just left alone, few if any adverse changes occurred.

Some rats periodically inhaled the smoke of research tobacco cigarettes for three months while others inhaled marijuana cigarette smoke.

The tobacco rats suffered lung changes like those of the placebo rats—that is, similar to the damage in the marijuana rats but less intense (though persisting after a thirty-day recovery period). From the abnormalities, outside observers could distinguish the marijuana lungs from the tobacco or placebo lungs.

Hence, while noncannabinoid particles and gases in the marijuana smoke play a role in lung irritation, "cannabinoids themselves may have a direct undesirable effect on pulmonary function" (Rosenkrantz and Fleischman).

> The (four) lung studies as well as studies of cannabis and reproduction took place under federal contract at the private EG&G Mason Research Institute, Worcester, Massachusetts, with Rosenkrantz as director of biochemical pharmacology.
>
> Several rats at a time entered the smoking machine, once daily in most cases, five to seven days a week, each time receiving four to sixteen puffs of 0.9 percent-THC marijuana usually, to vary the dose from 0.4 to 5 mg/kg. The doses produced blood levels of THC similar to those in human consumers of cannabis.
>
> The investigators observed no deterioration in lungs of rats exposed to smoke for 14 to 57 days. The main microscopic changes occurred in the alveoli and appeared after 87 days of exposure. Structural changes increased in severity after 180 and 360 days, and neither a 20-day nor a 30-day recovery period was enough to reverse the conditions.
>
> "A time and dose-related focal alveolitis or pneumonitis occurred. Pulmonary irritation progressed from extensive mobilization of alveolar macrophages and foreign body cell inflammation to more pronounced focal proliferative aberrations. After chronic exposure, the most striking morphological lesions were focal granulomatous inflammation and cholesterol clefts" (1979).
>
> Both the marijuana cigarettes and the inert placebo cigarettes proved fatally toxic to some rats. In fact, the latter killed more, probably by carbon monoxide poisoning.[42]
>
> Rosenkrantz wrote to us that for years he had alerted the National Institute on Drug Abuse to the fact that its so-called placebo cigarette was more toxic than its marijuana cigarette. "During the extensive solvent extraction of cannabinoids, many other type lipids are removed. The cannabinoid-free marijuana cuttings were inadvertently transformed so that remaining constituents were more easily pyrolized to carbon monoxide. In other words, puff for puff, more carbon monoxide is generated from 'placebo' cigarettes than marijuana (or tobacco) cigarettes, resulting in greater carbon monoxide poisoning (and lethality)."
>
> In various toxicological studies, therefore, he had to reduce some high "placebo" doses to avoid excessive carbon monoxide deaths.

Preliminary results of a new investigation by Tashkin and six teamworkers (1984) featured a striking discovery: "extensive, microscopic abnormalities" in marijuana smokers' airways—including changes that "have been correlated [elsewhere] with the development of chronic bronchitis, emphysema, and lung cancer." The investigators had sampled tissue from 20 subjects chosen at random from 201 mostly "heavy, habitual" marijuana smokers (a fourth of them women). Whether or not they smoked tobacco also (about half did smoke it), the 201 complained of more coughing, phlegm, and acute bronchitis than a control group of 52 that smoked nothing.

What of occasional, "social" marijuana smoking? Dr. Tashkin surmises that the degree of marijuana's impact on the respiratory system depends on the amount smoked. He hesitates to guess at what point a smoker begins to incur any risk.

Dr. Tashkin in mid-1984 gave to the American Lung Association in Miami Beach and to us preliminary highlights of his latest study at the UCLA Center for the Health Sciences, still in progress after a year and a half, under the auspices of the National Institutes of Health. His team had performed twenty biopsies of the carinae of the trachea, main bronchi, and labor bronchi and found some abnormality in each of the subjects. There were no control biopsies.

These were the respective findings for thirteen marijuana-tobacco smokers and seven smokers of just marijuana: (a) squamous metaplasia in 8 and 5, (b) basal cell hyperplasia in 11 and 3, (c) atypical changes in 6 and 3, (d) epithelial inflammation in 9 and 7, and (e) basement membrane thickening in 8 and 3. The changes qualitatively were similar in marijuana-tobacco smokers and marijuana-only smokers. Tashkin referred to other studies associating each of the first three changes with increased risk of cancer and each of the five with increased risk of emphysema and chronic bronchitis.

They are "changes one sees in much heavier and older smokers of tobacco" and then not usually in the same areas, the upper and central airways. Tobacco generally hits the peripheral airways, the bronchioles. Tashkin feared the "real possibility" of an eventual "epidemic of lung cancer at this fairly unusual site." The far end of each larger airway, where damage was observed, forms a bottleneck; when marijuana smoke narrows it by inflammation, more smoke may favor that spot, aggravate the inflammation, and "possibly even induce cancer because of much heavier and concentrated deposition of carcinogens at this site." The lesser surface area of the central portion of the tracheobronchial tree versus the smaller airways may be further reason for such concentration, which could make marijuana more of a cancer risk than tobacco, Tashkin theorized in an interview.

In pulmonary-function testing of all subjects and controls, a relatively high portion of marijuana smokers registered abnormal in specific airway conductance: 16 percent of those smoking tobacco too and 13 percent of those smoking just marijuana, against 4 percent of controls. The test measures resistance to air flow in the large airways and indicates a narrowing of the large air passages. This is not usually seen in tobacco smokers, even in the majority of those suffering lung disease.

These are the percentages of 98 marijuana-tobacco smokers, 103 marijuana-only smokers, and 52 nonsmokers, respectively, to complain of symptoms: (a) acute episodes of bronchitis, 15%, 13%, and 0% (b) chronic cough, 24%, 17%, and 0%; and (c) phlegm problem, 32%, 29%, and 13%. Smoking experience for most hovered around fifty "joint years"—joints per day times years—although the entry minimum was two joints a day for more than five years. The mean age was thirty-four. Pulmonary functions and symptoms were scored blindly; the scorer of tissue studies did not know which marijuana smokers also smoked tobacco. Tashkin and co-investigator Anne H. Coulson, research epidemiologist, contemplated future biopsies of nonsmokers and tobacco-only smokers.

Another major avenue of research bearing on cannabis and respiration involves the immune system, the body's defense program against disease. Studies indicate that cannabis may tend to hamstring the system in the lungs (and elsewhere). Details will follow in "Immunity and Resistance," 1 and 4.

5

Contamination

Marijuana smokers open themselves to additional sources of respiratory disease: one is fungus, notably aspergillus.

Cultured for aspergillus organisms at the Medical College of Wisconsin, in Milwaukee, twelve of thirteen samples of marijuana from smokers proved to contain the organisms. And in related tests, eleven of twenty-one marijuana smokers (52 percent) possessed antibodies against aspergillus, indicating past exposure to it, compared with one of ten nonsmokers so tested.

Dr. Steven L. Kagen urged (1981) that all illegally obtained marijuana be assumed to contain inhalable fungi capable of causing allergic lung disease, asthma, and other disorders. From the lungs, the fungus may spread throughout the organs of the body even though the patient may feel nothing.[43]

"I now have five patients with asthma which I believe to have been induced at least in part by the inhalation of fungi via marijuana smoking," he wrote to us. He said that aspergillus could cause death, particularly in patients with weakened resistance—for example, from anticancer drugs.

> Following are two case histories associating aspergillus with respiratory illness in marijuana smokers.
> 1. A seventeen-year-old boy was hospitalized at the National Institutes of Health (Bethesda, Maryland) with pneumonitis caused by aspergillus infection following heavy smoking of marijuana that had been buried in the ground for "aging." (Users say this practice increases the potency of the marijuana. Physicians say it increases the chances of exposure to fungus.) Culture of his marijuana and pipe yielded aspergillus.

Further, "of 10 samples of confiscated marijuana that we obtained through the Department of Justice Drug Enforcement Agency . . . two grew Aspergillus fumigatus and all showed heavy growth of a variety of saprophytic fungi," reported Dr. Michael J. Chusid and others (1975). They called marijuana "a potential hazard to individuals predisposed to Aspergillus infection."[44]

2. A habitual marijuana user, aged twenty-seven, was hospitalized for fever, wheezing, and cough—"allergic bronchopulmonary aspergillosis," was the diagnosis. Samples of his marijuana grew large colonies of three species of aspergillus. Dr. Roberto Llamas et al. at the Miami Heart Institute (Miami Beach, Florida) commented that "The use of marihuana may be particularly hazardous for the atopic [allergic] asthmatic subject, as this case report suggests" (1978).[45]

In 1968 an extract from a 700-pound batch of confiscated marijuana went to scientists and figured in experiments before the marijuana was discovered to have been contaminated with pig fat.

If experts can so err, smokers cannot have any greater assurance that their marijuana is pure. Said chronic smoker Dan, "I once had pot that was sprayed with hair spray. A friend gave it to me. After smoking it, I was coughing my head off."

Oxford University professor and scientist, W. D. M. Paton said at a U.S. Senate hearing that "near Oxford, people have bought horse manure and smoked it as cannabis. There are other similar examples that are known by people familiar with the field." Senator Gurney of Florida responded, "That's a pretty dirty trick." (Laughter.)[46]

Salmonellosis traced to marijuana, which may have been contaminated with animal feces, afflicted scores of people in Ohio and Michigan (1981).

> Marijuana samples obtained from several patients' households turned out to be infected with *Salmonella muenchen*, the same type of bacteria that was isolated from sixty-two patients. Most were teenagers and young adults with personal or household links to marijuana. They suffered diarrhea, fever, and abdominal pain, which were commonly bad enough to call for hospitalization. Marijuana smokers "may have been at additional risk because this drug has been shown to lower gastric acidity."[47]

Ungerleider et al. in Los Angeles (1982) discovered that marijuana cigarettes supplied them by the federal government were contaminated with substantial numbers of five types of disease-producing bacteria.[48]

Five people whom we interviewed told of smoking marijuana laced with PCP ("angel dust")—in all cases with unpleasant results, in four cases unexpectedly. Others said they had discovered bonuses of opium, cocaine, sugar, or oregano in their marijuana. One felt sure that his had been sprayed with the herbicide paraquat and that it hurt his lungs.

"When our group at the University of Mississippi reported that marijuana contaminated with paraquat was available on the streets in the U.S., the 'Great Paraquat Scare' erupted," wrote Carlton E. Turner, presidential drug adviser and formerly director of the Research Institute of Pharmaceutical Sciences (1981).

"Pro-drug groups and certain elements in the media agitated for a halt to the spraying program and implied that paraquat was causing lung damage to many marijuana smokers. Sadly, extensive research findings concerning marijuana's effects on the lungs were given little or no publicity. . . .

"To date, despite press reports to the contrary, *no single case of lung damage attributable to the presence of paraquat in marijuana cigarettes has been confirmed* [Turner's emphasis]. Lung problems, however, are known to occur with marijuana!"[49]

In August, 1983, five years after the spraying in Mexico had stirred up the fuss, something of a new paraquat scare came about when U.S. drug agents began spraying domestic cannabis fields, in Georgia.

A medical-scientific committee of the Institute of Medicine, in a report on cannabis and health (1982), raised the possibility that long-range exposure to marijuana sprayed with paraquat could result in serious and ultimately fatal lung damage ("diffuse interstitial fibrosis").

While more than 500 people had died from swallowing water solutions of paraquat, the committee considered the evidence on the effects of sprayed or smoked paraquat "too meager for conclusions." However, a chemical study (measuring up to a milligram of paraquat in smoke from a typical contaminated joint) and a hamster experiment (finding damage to the distal airways) "suggest that an individual who continued to smoke paraquat-contaminated cigarettes would be a candidate for serious lung injury. The prospect probably would be greatly heightened by the toxic effects of the combusted marijuana."[50]

A U.S. Public Health Service study (1983) estimated that nationally between 150 and 300 marijuana smokers inhaled hazardous amounts of paraquat each year.

> The 150 to 300 smokers, 100 to 200 of them in the Southwest, theoretically inhaled per year at least 500 micrograms of paraquat, a dose judged to represent a health hazard. In a year throughout the country 31.4 percent of marijuana smokers would be exposed to some paraquat, according to the projection.
>
> It was based not on any clinical cases but on (a) a survey in which 3.6 percent of 910 marijuana seizures between 1975 and 1979—or .63 percent of about 185 tons seized—contained detectable paraquat, most of it obtained in the Southwest; (b) an estimate that one-fifth of one percent of sprayed paraquat passes unchanged into marijuana smoke; and (c) various assumptions, for example that the country has ten million regular smokers, one million in the Southwest, who make monthly purchases of marijuana.

Supported indirectly by the United States, Mexico began spraying cannabis fields with paraquat in 1975. In 1978 Congress asked the secretary of health, education, and welfare to determine possible health hazards of paraquat to marijuana consumers. Consideration of any beneficial effects of the marijuana-destruction program was not part of the inquiry. (A companion program for eradicating opium poppies in Mexico was associated with a sharp decline in heroin deaths in the United States.)

However, Dr. Philip J. Landrigan of the National Institute of Environmental Health Sciences and three associated researchers in the Centers for Disease Control pointed out that "marijuana smoke has itself been shown to be a pulmonary toxin." They said the above agencies and the others in the U.S. Public Health Service maintain that "marijuana smoking is a hazard to health and ought to be discouraged."[51]

Paraquat is used in agriculture for such purposes as weed control in orchards and truck farms and defoliation to aid the harvest of soybeans.

6

Tobacco Versus Marijuana

Let us make a few comparative observations about the two favorite forms of smoking. First, bear in mind that many cannabis smokers smoke tobacco too, thus compounding the hazards.

In the Tashkin studies, subjects smoked as many as 20 marijuana cigarettes a day. In two experiments by Hembree and others (dealing with sperm), the subjects smoked up to 20 a day in one and up to 31 in another. The heaviest of a group of users surveyed in Costa Rica averaged 40 joints a day, sometimes reaching 100.[52]

In tobacco terms, twenty cigarettes is a full pack. It has often been said that marijuana, while it may be stronger than tobacco, is of less concern because, for one thing, "the daily exposure to marijuana smoke, even in extreme cases, is below the dose level of most tobacco cigarette smokers. . . ."[53] We see, however, that doses among some confirmed marijuana smokers reach or exceed the pack-a-day stage.

Of course, most users don't smoke that much, but the way they smoke makes a big difference. Addicts of Marlboro, Salem, Winston, etc., often inhale the tobacco smoke, of course. But few of them inhale it as frequently, quickly, and deeply and hold it in the lungs as long as regular marijuana smokers do in the United States.

"On a weight-to-weight basis," Dr. Tashkin said (in a 1984 interview) "marijuana is definitely more irritating than tobacco and conceivably could be more carcinogenic." He ascribed the extra harshness both to smoking technique and to physical and chemical characteristics of the smoke.

Nor do any cigarette smokers that we know use anything like a "roach clip" to hold the butt, or "roach," and then smoke it almost down to the last ember, the way the grass burners often do. Any roach left is likely to be a tiny one. "This difference in butt length suggests that at least a portion of the smoke delivered toward the end of a marijuana cigarette is hotter and subjected to less filtering than smoke which might be inhaled from a tobacco cigarette" (Harvard scientists said). [54]

Moreover, many "tokers" use "double-wide" papers to roll their joints more easily and burn them slower. The extra paper, of course, adds to the pollutants inhaled.

Furthermore, unlike the practice with cigarettes (except among the vagabond community), joints very often are passed from mouth to mouth. Many a smoker who would not think of putting a fellow diner's fork to his own lips, loses his qualms about microbes when the joint or pot pipe is passed around.

Then too, whereas the pipes found in a tobacco shop are all essentially similar, the "head shop" stocks a wide variety of smoking devices—including "bongs," "carburetors," "power hitters," and so forth—to gather all the smoke from the burning marijuana and blast it into the smoker's lungs.

As milder cigarettes make their appearance on the tobacco counter, marijuana's potency climbs. Filter-tipped joints are not common, nor is kindness to lungs a selling point for pushers. No peddler of illegal drugs talks of "mildness" and "low tar content." The customer wants the strongest he can afford for the maximum effect. Smoking as such is not the object. He wants to get high or stoned. He doesn't think of his lungs.

SEX,
REPRODUCTION,
AND
OFFSPRING

- *"The first time that I got high on a joint, it was in a college dorm. I was seventeen. It was also the night I lost my virginity. I believe that they were related. I think because of the euphoria that resulted from my use of the drug, my inhibitions were lowered and I gave in to something I'd been hesitant about."* —Rosemary (ex-user)

- *"[Marijuana] made me more hornier. . . . We always wanted to have women up there at our parties simply to get them stoned . . . for sexual purposes."* —Quentin (ex-user)

- *"Marijuana can lead to a breakdown of morals. It can in the sense that it tunes you more into your sensual self, because all of a sudden your body awareness is heightened and you feel all buzzy and it's easier for you to be seduced. Ha, ha! I know—I've done it myself. You get a chick high and it's easier to seduce her. The same if somebody is bisexual and they're trying to turn somebody on to the bisexual world.*
  "You get high and you're all kicked back and the world is all so nice and you feel so good and why not try this and why not try that—what does it matter? It's like you lose your reason, and before you know it, you're doing something that you didn't believe before you could do." —Ira (ex-user and former pusher)

- *"When I was fifteen was the first time I ever got involved with someone that way. And actually I think what was part of it was there had been*

43

some smoking . . . that whole intensification of sensual feelings, hearing, taste, smell—I think that sexual feelings really go along with it. . . .

"I think that higher parts of myself were shut off. . . . I was just totally into a sensual experience. . . . Some sort of moral perception just went out the window. It's just living for the moment of that pleasure." —Carol (ex-user)

- *"Being high, it was easier to see the darker side of morality, especially in terms of relationships, primarily with women, sex. It was easier to excuse thoughts, opinions that I might somewhere in my heart consider immoral or improper or reprehensible. It was easier to relate to opinions that society may not approve of. It was easier for me to approve of bisexuality or homosexuality in others and perhaps in myself when high. The same thing occurs when I consume alcohol. . . .*

"I had a tendency when I first started toward premature ejaculation when I was stoned. I have no problem with it when I'm not stoned, and that to me was definitely a negative factor." —Pierre (ex-user)

- *"In the few times that I smoked and had sex, I'd say that about thirty percent of them were intensified. The other seventy percent it even caused some disturbance in me, that is, in the ability to function . . . mainly to erect."* —Hiram (ex-user)

- *"I started when I was nineteen years old, eleven years ago. . . . I enjoyed the high. It was very pleasant, very mellow. It made me feel relaxed. It's very good for making love also, very sensual. . . . It makes me horny. . . .*

"I've had some hormonal changes and I haven't had a period in five years. I've been told by my doctors it's not an alarming thing but there's a very good chance that the marijuana has caused that. . . . I'm divorced. I have no children." —Betty (long-time user, trying to quit)

- *"I'm definitely less sexual when I'm high. I don't like having sex when I'm high. Generally I get groggy and sleepy and not able to direct my energy the right way. I can think of a couple times I had sex [after marijuana] and it did affect my performance."* —Bert (chronic user)

- *"It makes you hornier. It kind of keeps your mind on sex. It kind of works you up a bit, which isn't always so good."* —Charlie (chronic user)

- *"For me marijuana was a real sexual turn-on. I was totally absorbed in sex but at a primitive level. I wanted to gorge in sex the same way I want to gorge on foods I liked. My capacity to relate to my partners in other ways was blunted and relationships never seemed to develop very far."* —Imogene (ex-user)

• *"I was fourteen when I started smoking pot. . . . It exaggerated any sort of fear all out of proportion, so it had the effect that I wouldn't want to face them, overcome any of them. I just wanted to hide from them. I didn't really grow at all personality-wise. . . . I was just coming into that [puberty] and I was afraid of girls. As a result I didn't really develop that part of me very fully."* —Steve (ex-user)

• *"In the beginning a few times I had a lot of strong erotic feelings and I made love a few times when I was stoned and that was very pleasurable. . . . I think I had more of an erection. I had the sense like my entire consciousness was in my penis. . . .*

"I don't feel marijuana is an aphrodisiac. It just enhanced sex in the beginning of use. After a while it didn't increase sexual feelings. It's possible it decreased them." —Gregory (occasional user, former chronic user)

• *"The night I first felt the effects . . . I felt sexually aroused. . . .*

"I found marijuana heightened my sexual activity. . . . It tends to release a certain tension in my solar plexus. When I'm high, I'm more relaxed. I'm more open to pleasure. I also tire out more easily. . . .

"Alcohol with marijuana would wipe out my memory and cause blackouts. . . . I spent a night with my boyfriend after we'd been smoking pot and drinking. In the morning I said to him, 'I'm sorry I didn't do anything last night. I just blacked out.' He said, 'Are you kidding? We screwed for an hour.' . . .

"When I was pregnant, being high decreased my feelings of nausea. I smoked alone, every day or every other day. In the third month I had an abortion. When I do have a child, I intend to not smoke or have any alcohol, coffee, tobacco, or marijuana three months before I conceive. It might have an effect on my child. If you're getting high, the baby's getting high, and that's not fair. I don't think it's something a child under thirteen should get involved with, willingly or unwillingly." —Kathy (light user, former heavy user)

1

The Sexes

In 1970 a professor at the State University of New York at Stony Brook surprised 564 male and female undergraduate students attending his lecture course in the sociology of deviance and delinquency by passing out a questionnaire asking about their sex lives and their use of illicit drugs.

Their responses indicated that sexual behavior and use of drugs, particularly marijuana, were very closely related, at least on that college campus. Marijuana smokers were considerably more likely to engage in premarital intercourse than nonsmokers. The more frequent the smoking, the more likely a student was to have had sexual relations in the past six months, and the greater the likelihood that multiple partners were involved. And the first sexual experience generally took place earlier in life for the more frequent smoker than for the less frequent smoker.[1]

Of course, to say that marijuana correlates with sexual activity is not to say that marijuana causes it, or vice versa. An attitude favorable to drugs and a permissive attitude toward sex may both be part of the same subculture.

Cannabis's reputation as an aphrodisiac dates to ancient times. Young users have long claimed that the weed stimulates desire, enhances enjoyment, and—up to a point—may even improve performance. An experiment with mice suggests that this phenomenon is more than just "mental," at least among males: it may have to do with a drug-induced rise in sex hormone.

Nearly any substance will arouse aphrodisia if the consumer believes it will. Marijuana increases the power of suggestion. It can also release inhibitions and relax the partners. In some cases the relaxation turns to drowsiness and sleep may replace sex.

For many users, marijuana does heighten the pleasurable sensations of touch, at least in the early stages of use. Also, it often extends the sense of time, so that the pleasure seems to go on and on. Some contemporary authors have dwelled on such phenomena in rapturous detail. Observers in nations with centuries of experience with the cannabis plant, however, view it somewhat differently. They point to the stifling effects of heavy use.

"The subjective impression of slowing of time might, indeed, confer on the performer a very unusual gratification in an orgasmic experience, if it is extended from 30 secs to 30 min," wrote Chopra and Jandu, reporting to the New York Academy of Sciences on marijuana's effects on 275 chronic users in India (1976). "These effects are more common with a low dosage. When taken in moderate doses, the effects are somewhat similar to those of alcohol: the drug induces the desire but makes performance impossible. The chronic use of the drug leads to a sad condition, where the lack of desire may also be coupled with inability to perform."[2]

We know of no scientific experiment to show what marijuana does to actual sexual performance in humans. A two-year experiment testing the drug's effect on male sexual arousal, to be financed by $121,000 in federal funds, had been scheduled at Southern Illinois University until, in 1976, Congress cut off the funds for the project. The design of this "sexpot" experiment was too much for congressmen. It would have exposed male marijuana smokers to pornographic films and measured responses by means of instruments attached to their sexual organs![3]

The effects of cannabis on reproduction has been the subject of hundreds of scientific reports in medical and scientific journals. Most of them describe experiments performed in the 1970s, largely on animals. A few studies involve humans. The rat is the most common test animal, the mouse next. Rabbits, monkeys, dogs, guinea pigs, hamsters, sheep, bovines, chimpanzees, chicks, and fish have been tested on occasion. Most experiments have used THC or crude extracts of cannabis, administered by mouth, stomach tube, or injection. Some experiments have involved marijuana smoking by people or animals.

In humans, the male's reproductive system has been studied far more often than the female's. Under guidelines set by the Food and Drug Administration, experimenters have not been allowed to give cannabis to women able to have children or to people under age eighteen of either sex.

We will summarize a few of the hundreds of findings before discussing selected studies.

The male system: Cannabinoids decreased the function of the male sex gland, the testis, in all species studied. They decreased its metabolic activity, usually lowered transiently the level of sex hormone, and shrank or disabled the seminal vesicles, prostate, and epididymis. Prolonged intake of cannabinoids inhibited the development of sperm. But the effects of cannabis were reversible. Reproductive functions ultimately recovered after the drugging was discontinued.

The female system: Most of the experiments have been performed on rodents. In nonpregnant rats prolonged intake of marijuana extract or

THC alone usually (though not always) resulted in impaired uterine functions. Heat cycles became irregular or disappeared entirely; sometimes the uterus atrophied; levels of pituitary luteinizing hormone dropped temporarily, disrupting ovulation.

In pregnant rats high doses of THC (though not always lesser doses) held down weight gain and reduced prolactin (milk-producing hormone), considerably decreasing milk secretion. When marijuana preparations were administered to rats and mice, particularly in substantial amounts during the first half of gestation, litter size was reduced, often fetal growth was stunted, and sometimes the frequency of deformed offspring increased.[4]

The primates have been tested. One experiment showed no apparent reproductive or sexual effect on chimpanzees from long-term drugging of one sex or both up to six weeks before impregnation. But later experiments found THC disrupting the reproductive system of female rhesus monkeys: it produced effects ranging from infertility—which lasted for months after the drug was discontinued—to high-risk pregnancies. THC transferred to suckling young in several species.

According to one study, women's use of marijuana before and during pregnancy apparently produced nervous disorders in their offspring. Similar human studies suggested that marijuana influenced birth and offspring in other ways.

Male-female relations: Cannabis had an inhibiting effect on mounting, insertion, and ejaculation by male rats and mice.

In humans—according to subjective accounts of sexual experiences rather than experiments—marijuana in the short run often stimulated and prolonged sexual feelings and behavior. But in the long run, the drug, particularly in large doses, often tended to inhibit sex activity.

*   *   *

During five years of interviews, the Masters and Johnson Institute in St. Louis, Missouri, obtained information on the effects of marijuana on sex in 800 men and 500 women, ages eighteen to thirty. Most of the men (83 percent) and women (81 percent) indicated that marijuana enhanced their enjoyment of sex. Specific questions and answers, however, showed the reasons to be nonsexual.

The marijuana did not affect desire, performance, or orgasm. Both men and women cited such factors as increased sense of touch, more relaxation, and being more in tune with the partner. Most said that if the partner was not "high," the effect was unpleasant.

Of men who used marijuana daily, nearly one in five was impotent—twice the frequency of "potency disorders" among nonusers and relatively light users. Among women, no relationship was found between intensive use of marijuana and impaired sexual functioning.

Dr. Robert C. Kolodny and coauthors Masters and Johnson reported in a 1979 sexual medicine textbook: "It was found that while fewer than 10 percent of a control group of men who had never used marihuana and a group who used marihuana once or twice a week experienced potency disorders, almost one fifth of the men using marihuana on a daily basis were impotent."[5]

2

Males

In approximately A.D. 77, the Greek physician and pharmacologist Dioscorides wrote in his classic text on medicinal plants that the eating of cannabis could "quench geniture," that is, inhibit procreation. He did not explain.

The text of this passage in De Materia Medica, as translated and annotated in 1655 by John Goodyer, English botanist, goes as follows (some punctuation added): "KANNABIS EMEROS. Cannabis sativa. Hemp. Cannabis [some call it Cannabium, some Schoenostrophon, some Asterion, ye Romans Cannabis] is a plant of much use in this life for ye twistings of very strong ropes; it bears leaves like to the Ash, of a bad scent; long stalks, empty; a round seed, which being eaten of much doth quench geniture, but being juiced when it is green is good for the pains of the ears."[6]

About nineteen centuries went by before actual scientific work began on the effects of cannabis and its preparations on sex and reproduction. But other early scholars bequeathed their observations.

Galen, the second century Greek physician, writer, and adviser to Roman emperors, maintained that hemp cut off the semen.

A similar statement, that the eating of hemp "dries up the semen" and generates "effeminacy," is attributed to al-Razi, Moslem philosopher (865–925).

Numerous medieval Arabic writers are quoted as relating the use of hashish (then meaning any form of cannabis) to homosexuality. Some of them were openly homosexual themselves. Hashish was said to make normal young men effeminate, weaken the will to resist advances, and help procure boys.

From the sixteenth century al-Antaki: "Addicts may think that it strengthens sexual intercourse. This may perhaps be so in the beginning, but then it loosens the sinews because of its cold temper."[7]

The Indian hemp drug commissioners, in their 1890s investigation, asked this question: "Does the use of hemp tend to produce impotence?" Among medical witnesses, 53 percent (174) of 329 answered the question in the affirmative.

> Of "private practitioners," 57 percent (69) of 122 replied as did Nimar Charan Das, physician of Bengal: "Hemp, if taken for a long time, produces impotency." Of "superiors," 40 percent (43) of 107 agreed, as did 62 percent (62) of 100 "subordinates."
>
> The impotency question was preceded by these: Is the moderate use of any of these drugs practiced as an aphrodisiac? Is it so used by prostitutes? Is the use for this purpose more injurious than its use as an ordinary narcotic, and, if so, how?
>
> One Russick Lall Dutt, surgeon-lieutenant-colonel of Bengal answered this way: "These drugs are feeble aphrodisiacs, and are often used by immoral men and women as well as the upper classes of Muhammedans and Hindus who from abuse lose their sexual powers. Medicinally it is not injurious, and as such it is generally used. Excessive habitual use causes impotence. I have seen [it] in more than a dozen instances."[8]

The 1939 Indian study of 1,238 cannabis users—all but six of them males—discovered varying effects on sex, even opposite effects. Only one out of every six reported unqualified stimulating results from any hemp drug. Furthermore, the rate of sterility among those interviewed came to nearly double the rate in the general population of India.

> The survey, by Chopra and Chopra, showed these effects, according to 772 habitual *bhang* users and 466 habitual users of *ganja* and *charas*: 15.6 percent felt some aphrodisia after taking the drugs; 20.0 percent had felt sexual stimulation in the early stages but after habitual use of the drugs for a number of years they felt sexual depression instead; 39.6 percent felt the sexual faculties depressed from the beginning. More *ganja* and *charas* users felt stimulation (40.3 percent) than *bhang* users (2.2 percent). But more people felt stimulation from smaller and moderate doses than those who took large doses (more than twenty grains).
>
> Fertility was studied. Married or formerly married users numbered 686; they had been taking the drugs for about fifteen years on the average. The incidence of sterile marriages was 2 percent (5.7 percent among *ganja-charas* users and 0.4 percent among *bhang* users), nearly double that of the normal but less than an eighth that of opium addicts. The fact that *ganja-charas* users had higher rates of stimulation but lower rates of fertility than *bhang* users, according to the Chopras, might have to do with the former's low societal status and morals.
>
> They wrote: "Hemp drugs have been commonly used for their aphrodisiac effects in this country. Some even believe that they restore sexual power in cases of impotence and for this reason they have found their way to and are used in houses of ill fame somewhat like alcohol in western countries. On the other hand, saintly

people who wish to renounce worldly pleasure use hemp drugs for suppressing sexual desires. . . .

"Like alcohol it depresses the higher cerebral centres. . . . The stimulant or depressant sexual effects would thus appear to be purely a psychical phenomena in both the cases."[9]

Gynecomastia is a simple ailment to diagnose. A man suffering it possesses enlarged breasts. In 1972 and 1974 surgeons Harmon and Aliapoulios of Cambridge Hospital in Massachusetts reported seeing fourteen patients with gynecomastia, and in all of them the condition appeared after heavy cannabis use. All had undergone normal puberty and none had taken any female hormone.

Three of the men stopped smoking and reported the condition reversing.

The physicians followed up those observations with experiments in which THC stimulated the development of breast tissue in male rats.

In a letter to a medical journal, Doctors Harmon and Aliapoulios told of examining the first three gynecomastia patients, all in their twenties.

"Marihuana use by the patients was remarkably intensive. Marihuana smoking was clearly the main life activity of two of these patients and had been for six years in one case and two years in another."

The doctors speculated on the chemical similarity between THC and the female sex hormone estradiol. "Both are polycyclic hydrocarbons with phenol rings."

Their letter concluded: "With the increasing use and possible legalization of marihuana, previously unrecognized clinical phenomena associated with its prolonged and heavy use should be looked for by practicing physicians."[10]

They reported later in another medical journal that three of the fourteen patients chose to have the breasts removed by surgery. An examination of the tissues showed a proliferation of female-type ducts.

The doctors gave male rats five-times-weekly injections of THC (1 mg/kg) or other substances beneath the skin and later graded the mammary tissues according to degrees of development.

In one experiment, twenty rats received thirteen injections, half with THC solution and half with solvent alone. In another experiment, forty rats received either THC, DES (diethylstilbestrol, a synthetic female hormone), THC plus DES, or saline solution.

Rather significant statistical differences signified that only the THC—alone—served to "stimulate the development of rat breast tissue."[11]

The development did not approach the magnitude of breast formation in female rats, especially those lactating, Dr. Aliapoulios told us in a letter (1981). ". . . Not enough time was allowed for any differences to be seen on the external surface of the bodies of these animals. These changes are quite subtle, microscopic but definite in nature. . . ."

Later two other physicians, Cates and Pope, described a study of eleven patients who underwent surgery for gynecomastia at the U.S. Army

Hospital in Nuremberg, Germany, 1971–74. Although five of them admitted using cannabis, this fact did not seem very significant inasmuch as nearly half of the GIs in the area smoked it.

> They had questioned each patient one to six months after his operation and matched each (in age, race, rank, unit, and duration in Europe) with a control. Five patients admitted using cannabis (one other, amphetamines) in the six months before surgery. Six of the controls said they had used it in the previous six months.
>
> The doctors therefore concluded that their evidence failed to show an association between gynecomastia and use of cannabis, contrary to the other report. But they acknowledged that lack of hormonal data, the small number of patients, and the possibility that some subjects withheld or forgot facts attenuated their conclusion.[12]

In addition to the cases recorded in the medical journal, Dr. Aliapoulios personally tended to thirty more cannabis smokers with gynecomastia up to autumn of 1983. He had written us earlier (1981) that through "discussions with practicing endocrinologists and physicians in all parts of the country" he learned that "this phenomenon now is widely accepted as fact." In the patients he had seen as a hospital chief of surgery in Worcester, Massachusetts, there was "a diminution in breast size following the cessation of marijuana in most but not all cases."

Meanwhile, as an army surgeon in Washington, D.C., Dr. Harmon also saw additional patients with gynecomastia that he thought to be related to marijuana smoking, although the relation could not be verified because of the reluctance of soldiers to admit their use of illicit drugs. We asked how marijuana caused gynecomastia. "Probably it affects the hypothalamic-pituitary control of the release of FSH and LH which are two hormones produced in the brain which control sexual function. There is evidence to support this mechanism, but it is not firmly proven," he said in a letter (1983).

Dr. Donald Cooper, health services director and team physician at Oklahoma State University, told us, "I see stoned kids and I can almost pick them out. . . . I've even had some gynecomastia in a couple of kids . . . in the last year, and one of them was one of my football players. . . . His breast was enlarging and the breast plate of the shoulder pad was rubbing it. And he said . . . 'It's tender. . . . It's swelling on me. I must have an infection.' And I said, 'I don't think you have an infection. I think you're using too much marijuana.' It startled him. . . . He went off the marijuana and his breast went back down in about three weeks."

*   *   *

In interviews with more than 2,000 marijuana users, the majority of them male, the late Professor Hardin B. Jones, of the University of California at Berkeley, was often told that marijuana relaxed them socially, made it easier to find sex partners, and increased the pleasure of sexual relations.

However, many other interviewees reported to him that marijuana caused a wane in their sexual satisfaction, drive, or dreams; some men reported inability to perform and even physical pain. Frequently in those cases, marijuana had been conducive to sex at first but increasingly produced the opposite effect as use continued and doses increased.

Cannabis weakens will power, enhances the power of suggestion, and sometimes leads to activity that the user normally would avoid, he pointed out. "For instance, approximately one out of every five students who comes to me for advice is troubled by a homosexual encounter in which he participated while high on marijuana. The student is troubled by the episode and seems to feel that the encounter has caused subsequent difficulty in relationships with the opposite sex."[13]

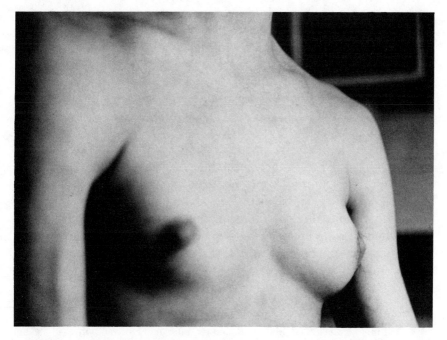

A young man who has smoked marijuana heavily for several years. According to Doctors Harmon and Aliapoulios, his drug history was the cause of his gynecomastia, that is, enlarged breasts. (Courtesy of Medical World News.)

At the time of his death in 1978, Professor Jones was planning to undertake a study of the relation, if any, between cannabis use and homosexuality.

> He had hypothesized in 1970 that marijuana users possessed "less than usual male hormone because they appeared less virile and had less sexual activity." An application for a Federal grant to test this idea was turned down.
> He told a Senate committee in 1974 that about half of male users showed diminished masculinity, most marked in those least physically active.[14]

There are other hints of a feminizing trend in male users (and, to some extent, a defeminizing effect on female users, as we will see later).

The initial observations regarding gynecomastia led to various investigations of the effect of cannabis on the principal male sex hormone, testosterone.

In 1974 Dr. Robert Kolodny and colleagues of the Reproductive Biology Research Foundation (later called the Masters and Johnson Institute) in St. Louis reported having examined twenty frequent marijuana smokers and found the levels of their testosterone to average 44 percent less than in a comparative group of men who never had used marijuana. How low his testosterone level had fallen seemed related to how much a man smoked. Heavy smokers also had low sperm counts.

Citing other research linking testosterone to ambition, Dr. Kolodny raised the possibility that the sluggishness and lack of motivation often found in regular marijuana smokers might be related to their decreased testosterone levels.

Human and animal experiments in his field (Kolodny told Senate investigators) pointed to further possibilities that might have serious consequences: "disruption of sperm production . . . birth defects . . . impairment of hormone balance . . . either inhibition of puberty or disruption of normal sexual differentiation during fetal development."

Testosterone is necessary for the development and maintenance of male sexual organs and secondary male sexual characteristics as well as for the functioning of the organs.

> The subjects, twenty heterosexual men, aged eighteen to twenty-eight, said they had smoked marijuana at least four days a week for at least six months and during that time had taken no other drugs and no more than fourteen ounces of alcohol a week. They had smoked between five and eighteen joints weekly (mean of 9.4) for between 1½ and 8 years (mean of 3½).
> The researchers found another twenty men who had used no drugs at all in the past six months and who matched the others in age, cigarette-smoking history, and other criteria. All forty received medical examinations and two blood tests each on mornings a month apart.

Testosterone in the blood plasma averaged 416 (ng/100 ml) in the marijuana users and 742 in the nonmarijuana group. The count appeared related to dosage. With three exceptions, those who had averaged ten or more joints a week (eleven men) showed significantly lower testosterone levels than those who used less than ten (nine men): the readings were 309 and 503. (The figures refer to nanograms per 100 milliliters of blood plasma. A nanogram is a U.S. billionth of a gram.)

Three of the men discontinued marijuana and in each case the testosterone increased markedly—between 57 percent and 141 percent after a week, more after two weeks. This suggested that the marijuana's testosterone-lowering effect may have been just temporary.

Six smokers (of seventeen so tested) had sperm deficiencies. Whether abstention from marijuana would raise sperm counts was not tested. The group mean for men smoking ten or more joints a week was 27 million per milliter versus 68 million for lighter smokers, a significant difference. The heavier smokers differed significantly from the lighter also in having a lower level of follicle-stimulating hormone (which stimulates formation of sperm in the testes).

Two of the twenty smokers indicated that their sexual functioning was impaired. One who had been suffering impotency on and off for a year was advised to stop using marijuana; he did so and had no further problems of that sort (at least as of ten months later). The other, who reported having been impotent for half a year, refused to stop smoking.

A standard test measuring the testes' capacity to produce testosterone (stimulation with human chorionic gonadotropin) was run on four smokers. All four responded normally, suggesting that marijuana's effect "is not directly on the male sex organs, but is at a higher regulatory center," said Dr. Kolodny, physician and medical school teacher.

He told of two male patients (not part of this study) who had used a lot of marijuana for a long time and who each had impotency and lowered testosterone. In both cases the patients discontinued marijuana and their sexual functioning returned to normal.[15]

Seven months after the Kolodny study appeared, the same medical journal published a seemingly contradictory finding by Dr. Jack H. Mendelson and colleagues of the Harvard Medical School and McLean Hospital.

In a special hospital ward they had studied twenty-seven men, measuring testosterone daily every morning before, during, and after a twenty-one-day period of marijuana smoking. They found no statistically significant changes in levels (except that five subjects showed correlations between rising doses and diminishing testosterone), nor did the "casual" users differ significantly from the "heavy" users. Therefore they concluded that the Kolodny study was not corroborated.

The subjects ranged in age from twenty-one to twenty-six. Twelve of them, who had smoked for 3 to 8 years (mean of 5.3 years) and averaged 11½ times a month, were designated as "casual" users. The other fifteen, who had smoked for 3 to 9 years (mean of 5.6) and who averaged forty-two marijuana cigarettes a month were called "heavy." No nonsmoking group was used.

After thorough physical examination, there was a five-day period of abstinence, followed by a twenty-one-day period in which subjects could buy and smoke as many joints as they wanted. Each contained about a gram of roughly 2 percent THC. Most smoking took place between 8 A.M. and midnight. Blood tests were taken each morning, 8:30 to 9:00, for thirty-one days (in addition to other biological and psychological tests).

The mean average plasma testosterone levels during the base period were 988 for the "casual" users and 1,115 for the "heavy" users, not significantly different from one another. During the three week smoking period, the groups smoked 54.3 and 119.5 joints (mean average) respectively. The researchers found "no statistically significant differences in testosterone levels" in either group at different times or between the two groups, and no relation between the amount smoked and testosterone level.

The Mendelson team made twenty-one pairs of observations for each subject to correlate the number of marijuana cigarettes smoked and the level of testosterone. One of the "casual" users and four of the "heavy" users displayed significant relationships.[16]

Kolodny followed up (1976), giving marijuana to thirteen men hospitalized at the University of California at Los Angeles. Tested three hours after they had smoked, their testosterone had dropped an average of a third.

The thirteen subjects, aged twenty-one to twenty-seven, all had used marijuana regularly in the past. They spent ninety-four days in the ward. For the first week and a half they did not smoke. On the tenth day blood samples were taken six times within three hours, and the concentration of testosterone remained relatively steady (dropping 5 percent after one hour).

Two days later each subject got a blood test and his first dose of marijuana (a single cigarette with 900 mg at a strength of about 2.2 percent THC). Now the testosterone soon dropped substantially and kept going down. Three hours after the day's first test, in which the testosterone levels averaged 779, the average level had sunk 39.9 percent to 505. A substantial decrease was found in every man, as much as 48 percent.

The subjects proceeded to smoke marijuana daily for nine weeks and then abstain from marijuana for one week. A blood test was taken, testosterone averaging 639. Each thereupon smoked three marijuana cigarettes in succession. Then five more blood tests were given in three hours and testosterone sank progressively, reaching a low of 432, a drop of 32.4 percent.

Both times, the marijuana smoking brought significant decreases in luteinizing hormone. In the male this hormone stimulates the development of interstitial tissue in the testes and their secretion of testosterone.

What is the significance of a person using marijuana daily and having a persistently low testosterone level? Kolodny was asked this question at a panel discussion (during a federally sponsored cannabis research conference in Savannah, Georgia, in 1974).

"The metabolic effects of testosterone, such as its nitrogen retention properties, its stimulation of erythropoiesis [production of red blood cells] and its assistance in the maintenance of skeletal mass, would certainly seem to be important ones."

Just how, say, a 40 percent reduction in testosterone might alter them was not known, he said.

"We can only speculate as to what the potential effects would be on sexual function. But I think there is at least a possibility that in men with marginal—either procreative or sexual—functions that a lowering of their testosterone level might result in difficulty in conception or in partial or complete impotence. I have certainly seen a number of cases of this over the past year."[17]

Elsewhere (in Senate testimony, 1974) Kolodny referred to these two theoretical possibilities related to his findings:

"Since at least some of the active constituents of marijuana have been shown to cross the placenta, there may be a significant risk of depressed testosterone levels within the developing fetus when this drug is used by a pregnant woman. Since normal sexual differentiation of the male depends on adequate testosterone stimulation during critical stages of development, occurring approximately at the third and fourth months of pregnancy, it is possible that such development might be disrupted.

"Theoretically, there is also the possibility that marijuana use by the prepubertal male may delay the onset or completion of puberty or may interfere with bone growth, if a suppression of pituitary or hypothalamic function occurs."[18]

Meanwhile, tests on seventy-six Costa Ricans (1976) found the levels of testosterone to be "no different in users than in their matched controls" and turned up "no relationship between levels of marijuana use and testosterone levels."

However, in San Francisco trials, testosterone declined in men consuming sizable oral doses of THC but rose when they discontinued the drug.

As part of a many-sided Costa Rican–American investigation, blood samples for each of thirty-eight marijuana smokers and thirty-eight nonsmokers were collected on two mornings, three to seven days apart. The mean testosterone levels were 564 for the user group and 549 for the controls.

Those users who smoked an average of ten or more marijuana cigarettes (thirteen men) had a mean level of 522—5 percent below the level of their matched controls: 550. The difference was not significant.

Smokers and controls each had fathered a mean of 2.6 children.

Dr. W. J. Coggins with eight others declared it difficult to reconcile the findings with the (first) Kolodny study. "Our subjects have smoked marijuana for longer periods of time, in larger quantities than those reported in the St. Louis study. The lack of correlation between higher levels of marijuana use and lower testosterone levels within our subject group further mitigates against a cause and effect relationship between marijuana use and testosterone levels. It is possible that a tolerance to marijuana develops that overcomes some inhibitory action of marijuana on the hypothalamic-pituitary axis or on the end organ, the testis."

The report concluded that chronic marijuana users had "minimal differences in health status from nonusers of the same sociocultural class and age" (up to fifty)—although single blind examinations found the marijuana users to have more positive serologic tests for syphilis, less globulin, less hematocrit (concentration of red blood cells), more eye congestion, and less bilirubin (bile pigment). Questioning disclosed that "users more frequently experienced indigestion, nausea, and abdominal pain than non-users." Users indicated more frequent use of other drugs and vapors. ("Inhalation of gasoline or paint thinner to obtain a high was reported by nineteen of the users and two of the controls")[19]

Dr. Coggins was then professor in the Department of Community Health and Family Medicine, University of Florida College of Medicine. Later he became dean of the College of Community Health Sciences, University of Alabama School of Medicine.

✻   ✻   ✻

Coggins et al. referred to an unpublished, closed-ward experiment by Dr. Reese T. Jones that produced "transient decrements in testosterone levels that returned to baseline levels when drug administration was discontinued." Dr. Jones confirmed this when queried at the Langley Porter Neuropsychiatric Institute in San Francisco (1981).

The decrease was significant statistically but not necessarily biologically. Part of a thirty-day study in 1975 (mentioned in "The Heart and Circulatory System"), the testosterone tests remained uncompleted because funds ran out.

The story of a series of experiments conducted over the years at the University of Texas Health Science Center (San Antonio) could be titled "Of Mice and Men." Reports that heavy, chronic use of marijuana was having a sexual effect on young men inspired Susan Dalterio and Andrzej Bartke to feed drugs to hundreds of mice and see if anything happened to male functions.

• First they observed that the taking of either THC or CBN (cannabinol, a nonpsychoactive component of cannabis) by both immature and adult male mice decreased their testosterone and pituitary hormone. Suppression of copulatory behavior followed within four hours after THC and three weeks after CBN (1980).

• However, studies of this sort, showing cannabinoids suppressing hormones and sexual activity, ran counter to the "abundant, although mostly anecdotal evidence that marijuana can act as an 'aphrodisiac.'" Subsequent, one-hour experiments seemed to resolve the apparent contradiction. Dose and time made the difference.

In the first ten minutes, testosterone increased in response to all doses of THC given. But only the smallest dose kept it elevated for as long as an hour. The larger doses dropped the hormone below normal level within twenty minutes. Male mice given THC usually could engage in normal copulation only if the female was introduced immediately (1981).

(In human studies too, diverse doses and varying intervals between

THC exposure and blood sampling may help explain the divergent effects of THC on testosterone.)

• Later (1982) the Dalterio team discovered some reduction in fertility plus hints of genetic impairment (chromosomal abnormalities) in male mice repeatedly fed cannabinoids. Those effects carried over to some of the treated mice's offspring. The repeated drugging of male mice was associated also with an increase in fetal loss.

The team also drugged female mice to observe the sexual effects on male offspring. (See 4, this section.)

"In our laboratory studies in mice, we have observed reductions in testosterone and pituitary hormone . . . in both immature and adult male mice after a single oral feeding of THC," testified Dr. Dalterio, research assistant professor of pharmacology and obstetrics and gynecology, at Senate committee hearings (1980). The pituitary hormones normally activate the testis.

"It is also possible that THC may directly affect the testis, since other investigators have reported that THC can suppress protein synthesis and enzymatic activity, and we have observed a THC-induced decrease in the production of testosterone in testes removed from laboratory animals and exposed to cannabinoids. . . ."

In an article (1981) she and colleagues speculated that "the anecdotal reports on the aphrodisiac effects of marijuana and the evidence for suppression of testicular activity after heavy use of this substance are not contradictory, but represent effects of different doses or different phases in the temporal sequence of physiological changes induced by marijuana."

In the earlier experiments the mice received 50 mg/kg of drug in sesame oil or the oil alone. The later experiments gave either 0.5, 5, or 50 mg/kg of drug in oil or the oil alone.

A graph indicated that at 0.5 mg/kg the levels of testosterone during the hour experiment (seven measurements) doubled the control levels. At either 5 or 50 mg/kg the levels of testosterone more than doubled the control level in the first ten minutes but thereafter sank almost to a tenth of control.

THC acted even in mice lacking the pituitary. (The gland, in the base of the brain, produces gonadotropins, hormones that stimulate the sex organs.) When the experimenters gave both THC and human chorionic gonadotropin to normal mice and to those with no pituitaries, higher testosterone levels resulted than when they gave gonadotropin alone (by injection).[20]

*   *   *

In the latest set of experiments, male mice repeatedly fed CBD (cannabidiol, a nonpsychoactive cannabis component) impregnated fewer females than control mice. Neither THC nor CBN changed the impregnation rate.

Male mice repeatedly given cannabinoids or crude marijuana extract showed more chromosomal abnormalities (translocations, aneuploidy, and polyploidy) than control mice.

Such exposure of male mice to THC, CBN, or CBD increased the rate of fetal loss. The CBD exposure also increased postnatal deaths.

Moreover, among surviving offspring of the sires treated with THC or CBN, a larger proportion were infertile or failed to produce normal litters. CBD did not have that effect.

Chromosomes in testes from eight offspring with birth defects were examined and rearrangements observed in two of the testes. This finding indicated to the researchers that "cannabinoids are capable of inducing chromosomal aberrations in germ cells and of producing genetic mutations."

Dr. Dalterio and associates treated 112 mice with drugs or oil. The drugs were given three times a week for five weeks. The research team (including a zoologist from Kuwait) intentionally set the dose per body weight (50 mg/kg) at a dozen times that which a human might take, observing that the behavioral effects in the mice lasted about five hours, comparable to the duration in humans.[21]

Case reports suggest that use of marijuana by boys entering adolescence may interfere with their sexual development.

• Professor Hardin B. Jones studied three young men, ages eighteen to twenty, who had used marijuana through adolescence and whose sexual development had been thereby disturbed. He wrote that they attained sexual maturity within a few months after giving up marijuana.[22]

• The University of North Carolina's pediatrics department described a "pubertal arrest" in a boy who had smoked at least five joints a day since he was eleven. Not only had his mother condoned it—she had supplied him with the marijuana! Seen at sixteen and at seventeen, he still had not attained puberty and his bone growth was delayed.

The North Carolina pediatricians last examined their patient at seventeen after he had abstained from marijuana for three months. They noted some development: growth accelerated, sex organ enlarged, testosterone count increased from 82 to 394, and luteinizing hormone was up.

Having excluded most other potential causes, Kenneth C. Copeland, M.D., and two other physicians postulated (1980) that "this patient's unusually heavy marihuana usage inhibited luteinizing hormone secretion, resulting in diminished testosterone production. His pubertal arrest also may have been aggravated by a direct inhibitory effect of marihuana on the testes."[23]

• A Georgia mother told us (1981) her son had smoked marijuana for five years, since he was eleven. At sixteen, smoking several times daily, "he was underweight, had poor color, and didn't grow. There was no sexual maturity. . . .

"After he had been off marijuana for six to nine months, he started to gain weight and to grow taller. He matured sexually, could grow a beard. His facial and body hair started to grow, and he developed broad shoulders and muscle mass. He is now in his third year of recovery. He is six feet, two inches tall and weighs one hundred eighty pounds."

* * *

Modern evidence supporting the warning of the ancient Greek physicians that *kannabis* could inhibit semen and begetting emerged from the following four sets of studies (reported between 1974 and 1980) as well as the first Kolodny study. There was some indication that sperm could recover, however, once the drug was given up.

● In Jaipur, India, V. P. Dixit and two others determined that daily injections of mice with cannabis extract held down the development and number of sperm, ultimately halting sperm production entirely, and caused degeneration in immature sperm and accessory sex tissues. But all of those changes reversed in time after treatment was discontinued.

> After twenty-five days of abdominal injections at 2 mg, Dixit et al. of the University of Rajasthan found: a decrease in the number of developing sperm; regression in Leydig cells (interstitial cells in the testicle, which secrete sex hormone), their cytoplasm scanty and nuclei shrunken; degenerating cells, immature sperm, and fibrous material from the testis appearing in the seminal duct; and a 37 percent decrease in the amount of RNA (ribonucleic acid) in the testis.
> The same daily treatment for forty-five days completely arrested the production of sperm. There were significant decreases in testicular weights, suggesting damage to the organ; drastic decreases in weights of seminal vesicles; and involution of the thymus gland.
> But ten treated mice (of forty used) allowed to recover for sixty-three days completely recovered; all of their functions proved normal (1974).[24]
> Zoology Professor Dixit wrote us (1981) that in a recent experiment of his in presbytis monkeys, chronic oral administration of cannabis extract (14 mg/kg) for ninety days "caused testicular lesions, resulting in mass atrophy of the spermatogenic elements."

● Cecile and Rudolf Leuchtenberger and associates in Switzerland compared the effects of short-term exposure to smoke of marijuana cigarettes and tobacco cigarettes on spermatids (formative spermatozoa) in mouse testis cultures.

The spermatids in the tobacco-treated cultures did not differ from those of controls (untreated cultures) in structure or in content of DNA, that genetically essential acid. But many of the spermatids in the marijuana-treated cultures had smaller nuclei and were low in DNA.

Similar results ensued when living mice were used. Male mice inhaling smoke from marijuana cigarettes developed a disturbance in their production of spermatozoa and an increased frequency of spermatids with low DNA content.

Serious genetic consequences can result if a sperm from a low-DNA spermatid fertilizes an egg, the Leuchtenbergers pointed out.

> After exposure of the testis cultures to the marijuana smoke, "a considerable number of spermatids had smaller nuclei and showed less staining with basic dyes" compared to those of control and tobacco cultures; furthermore, "there was a statistically significant increased frequency of spermatids carrying a DNA complement lower than 1 DNA" (the normal amount of deoxyribonucleic acid). Marijuana had that effect in eleven out of twelve trials.
>
> Overall about half of the marijuana spermatids had the low DNA content, compared with about one-fifth of the tobacco spermatids and about one-fifth of the control spermatids. The couple examined 1,750 spermatids in 500 cultures. These were exposed daily for two to six days to as many puffs of marijuana smoke or two to four puffs of tobacco cigarettes. The lower number of tobacco puffs had to do with "the relatively high cytotoxic effects of this type of smoke on the cultures."
>
> The cultures also were exposed to just the gas vapor phase of marijuana smoke, with cannabinoids filtered out. It did not have the above effects.[25]

• Experiments in which marijuana apparently lowered sperm production in young men—counts dropped 30 to 70 percent after a month of heavy smoking—were reported by Dr. Wylie C. Hembree and others at Columbia University College of Physicians and Surgeons in New York City.

> Five male volunteers, aged twenty to twenty-seven, were admitted to New York State Psychiatric Institute for the first experiment. All were regular marijuana smokers, consuming no less than three to five joints a week. Medical examinations found them normal.
>
> They underwent a drug-free period of two or three weeks. Starting with one joint (2 percent THC), they added another every two days until reaching eight a day. After that they were asked to smoke at least ten a day. Four kept this up. One smoked as many as thirty-one in a day. After four weeks of smoking, they had a two week "washout" period.
>
> Sperm counts began decreasing during the smoking period, becoming particularly depressed after the smoking period. Decreases ranged from 30 to 70 percent. Drops in concentration were not so drastic, especially for two subjects, but still statistically significant.[26]
>
> In a similar experiment, conducted at the same place, sperm samples were received from sixteen regular marijuana smokers, aged eighteen to twenty-nine. Following at least three weeks of no smoking, they smoked between eight and twenty joints (2 percent THC) daily for four weeks.
>
> There was a significant reduction in sperm concentration. The reduction occurred in twelve of the sixteen subjects, three to five weeks after the start of smoking, persisting at least two weeks. Concentration remained low until the end of

the study, sixty days after the start of smoking, although a trend toward base levels was observed.[27]

An internist and reproductive endocrinologist, Dr. Hembree has been associate professor of medicine and of obstetrics and gynecology.

• In Greece, Stefanis and Issidorides tested sperm of four chronic hashish users, finding cell nuclei low in the essential amino acid arginine. The latter also discovered abnormalities in structure of the sperm cells. (Details in "The Cells and Chromosomes," 2.)

3

Females

Old scientific literature (since 1851) records the utilization of cannabis by doctors to stimulate uterine contractions, alleviate labor distress, or treat menstrual ills, and such folk use as the smoking of cannabis by South African tribal women to stupefy themselves during childbirth. Pharmacologists experimenting in India (1963) observed a solution of cannabis resin restraining induced contractions of an isolated rat uterus.[28]

In 1965 C. J. Miras at the medical school of the University of Athens, Greece, reported on a series of experiments with rats and cats that explored diverse aspects of the action of hashish. Large doses of cannabis resin given with food to 100 rats for half a year generally "reduced the reproductive activity of the treated animals" and caused "a rather high incidence of death in the mothers . . . on the second or third day after delivery" even though treatment had ended for most. "The newborn rats developed normally" nevertheless.

The experiments included a pilot study of the distribution of radioactive cannabinoid in rats. Later, other investigators used radioactivity to trace the passage of drug from mother to fetus in other rodents.

Among other findings, cannabis resin (250 mg/kg) when dissolved in olive oil and injected into the peritoneal cavity reduced body temperatures, prolonged the effect of barbiturate, and induced depression in rats. It lowered the pulse in cats.[29]

* * *

Later Dr. Idänpään-Heikkilä, medical scientist from Helsinki, Finland, and others at the Texas Research Institute of Mental Sciences, Houston, synthesized radioactive THC to learn when and to what extent the drug crossed the placenta. They drugged twenty-four pregnant hamsters (2 mg/kg) on either the sixth or fifteenth day of gestation, destroying them at intervals (15, 30, or 120 minutes, or 24 hours).

After injection through the peritoneum, radioactivity crossed within fifteen minutes, reaching peak concentration in the fetus within thirty minutes, as assayed by a scintillator. Fetuses of hamsters so injected during early pregnancy contained nearly three times as much radioactivity as fetuses of hamsters treated in late pregnancy. This difference was "even more noticeable" after injection under the skin. Either way, the placenta took up much more radioactivity than the fetus, which contained much more than the maternal plasma or brain. Radioactivity persisted in all fetuses after twenty-four hours.

Chromatography proved that unchanged THC crossed the placenta; this compound accounted for 55 percent of the radioactivity in the placenta and 25 percent of the fetus's radioactivity.[30]

* * *

Two research teams in North Carolina made analyses of pregnant mice injected with radioactively labeled THC.

Kennedy and Waddell observed radioactivity in fetal tissues at all time intervals studied (twenty minutes to twenty-four hours) after injection (by two methods) into the mothers at twelve days of gestation. Fetal concentrations of radioactivity, generally low, registered the heaviest in the central nervous system.[31]

Freudenthal, Martin, and Wall observed some radioactivity in fifteen-day fetuses, high concentrations in mammary glands and yolk sac placentas, and very high concentrations in corpora lutea, two hours after injection (by two methods).[32]

Late in the sixties, four letters to the editor of *The Lancet*, the British medical journal, raised the specific question of whether cannabis was teratogenic, that is, caused abnormal development of fetuses.

• First, Persaud and Ellington in Jamaica reported that single injections of cannabis resin in pregnant mice caused considerable stunting, though no apparent malformations. Such injections (16 mg/kg into the abdomen) on days one through six of gestation killed the fetuses.[33]

• The same researchers later wrote that when they gave thirteen pregnant rats similar injections at smaller doses (4 mg/kg) on days one through six of gestation, they found (on day twenty) a high incidence of malformation, fetal death, and retardation. Of ninety-three fetuses, fifty-three were malformed.[34]

• Hecht, an Oregon pediatric geneticist, and others then told of a baby whose parents had taken LSD and cannabis before and during pregnancy and who was born with a missing hand and forearm. (The mother's chromosomes were normal. The father's were unknown; he had committed suicide.)[35]

• Carakushansky et al. in Syracuse, New York, thereupon described the misshapen hands and feet of a baby whose mother was believed to have taken LSD and cannabis in pregnancy. (The defects were webbing, stunting, lack of nails, and a clubfoot.)[36]

Within a decade, Rosenkrantz of Massachusetts could list thirty-three investigations into the same question by far-flung scientists testing seven animal species. Eight of the studies seemed to show a teratogenic effect from cannabis or THC but twenty-five did not show such effect. The contradiction is not easily explained. Species and dose did not make a difference.

An extensive project using mice, rats, and rabbits turned up few abnormal fetuses but did produce hundreds of fetal deaths in Dr. Harris Rosenkrantz's laboratory. In experiments through the 1970s, Rosenkrantz and coworkers examined about 1,000 pregnant animals before and after treatment with marijuana smoke or THC and observed more than 10,000 embryos or fetuses, he told us.

At least twice as many fetal deaths occurred in pregnant animals exposed to marijuana smoke as in control (unexposed) animals, regardless of species.

Pure THC, given to other pregnant rats and mice by stomach tube, did similar damage or worse—large doses sometimes wiped out entire litters. Yet neither the THC nor the marijuana smoke induced physical defects in survivors.

Rosenkrantz said he had undertaken the experiments because of the controversial findings of deformities and the shortage of information about how marijuana inhalation affected the fetus. He aimed to simulate human smoking. This simulation was achieved by developing a smoking machine to deliver the animal equivalent of human doses and by blood analyses to verify that the levels of THC circulating in the animals resembled those in human marijuana smokers, he reported. "We have mimicked the smoking conditions somewhere between the naive and experienced marijuana consumer."

The set of experiments demonstrated "the unequivocal embryocidal effect" of marijuana and THC. Unlike the sporadic and controversial reports of teratogenicity (abnormal development), the increased incidence of death in the uterus was a common observation by his research group and others, Rosenkrantz noted.

What is the message to young women? (Senator Mathias of Maryland asked the question in a 1980 hearing.) Rosenkrantz sees "a potential hazard" in the use of marijuana by pregnant women, particularly in the early days of pregnancy. His studies suggest, not that a baby would be

born deformed or necessarily smaller, but "you may lose a baby . . .
because you have been using marijuana."

With the machine controlling the volume and duration of each puff, 4 to 16
puffs from three simultaneously burning marijuana cigarettes provided a THC range
of 0.8 to 3.8 mg/kg, or a plasma level of 70 to 300 ng/ml in mice and rats and
20 to 50 ng/ml in rabbits. The range of THC levels in plasma of human male
marijuana smokers had been reported at 40 to 500 ng/ml (nanograms per milliliter).

Mice and rats got this treatment daily between days six and fifteen of gestation
and rabbits between days six and eighteen, the critical days for the animals' organ
formation. Six to twelve animals were exposed at one time. Control groups either
received cannabinoid-free smoke ("placebo" treatment) or entered the machine
without smoke ("sham" treatment).

Through surgery early in pregnancy, a scientist would determine the number
of infants due each dam. Then drugs were given. Later another scientist dissected
the mother and delivered the babies. The difference between the number of embryos counted and the number of infants born represented developing offspring
that died in the uterus and were resorbed (or partially resorbed) into the system of
the pregnant animal.

Following is the average percentage of fetuses lost to each species when exposed
to marijuana smoke at the above doses and when "sham-treated" (without smoke):
Rabbits—marijuana 4%, controls 1%.
Rats—marijuana 3.1%, controls 1.6%.
Mice, CD-1 strain—marijuana 1.9%, controls 0.7%.
Mouse dams of the Swiss-Webster strain lost 120 of 1,015 fetuses (12.7 per-
cent) after exposure to marijuana smoke but lost only 17 of 284 fetuses (6.0 per-
cent) when "sham-treated."

When exposed to "placebo" smoke, fetal resorptions averaged 2 percent in rabbits, 2.2 percent in rats, 0.7 percent in CD-1 mice (same as the "sham" controls),
and 7.9 percent in Swiss-Webster mice. All represented significant differences from
the respective marijuana figures except the rats. An additional, abbreviated inhalation study of twenty-four rats at a larger dose, 5 mg/kg, showed 4.2 percent
of fetuses resorbed in the marijuana group, compared with 1.6 percent in the
"sham" group and 2.1 percent in the "placebo" group.

The total number of embryos/fetuses examined in the inhalation studies was
about 4,000, including 800 rabbits, 1,800 rats, and 1,400 mice (both strains).
These studies used about 410 dams.

Results for each species did not depend on the amount of marijuana smoke
given. In the stomach-tube feedings, however, results did vary with dose.

At the seventh to ninth days of gestation, two to five stomach treatments with
larger doses of THC (12.5 to 600 mg/kg, usually 50 mg/kg) sufficed to kill some
embryos in rats and mice.

"Some of them were excessive doses to deliberately see what was the worst situation that could occur in terms of teratogenicity. Then we reduced the oral doses
so they were comparable to what human oral doses would be," said Rosenkrantz
at the E G & G Mason Research Institute.

Why were the infants taken prematurely by cesarean delivery instead of allowed
a natural birth? "That's a protocol that was established by the regulatory agencies," he explained. The main reasoning appeared to be "to avoid potential deaths

during delivery through the birth canal so we wouldn't know if it was an *in utero* death or a death due to parturition." (A few spontaneously were born prematurely—alive.)

In one study (conducted by Dr. Robert W. Fleischman, the institute's pathologist and teratologist, 1980) mothers were opened up at different intervals to find out whether embryos died in the early days or in the late days of gestation (which takes about nineteen days in a mouse). Consequently, "we're more secure in saying that cannabis is embryotoxic and not necessarily fetotoxic, but others have shown that *in utero* deaths occur at a later time in gestation too. . . ."

During "the preliminary experiments that our client, the National Institute on Drug Abuse asked us to carry out by the standard protocol . . . we noticed these *in utero* deaths and we recommended that we try to look at how early this occurs, so that we know that if a woman is smoking in the first trimester, she may have already caused damage to her fetus. . . ."[37]

Dr. Akira Morishima of Columbia University observed many abnormalities in fertilized egg cells of female mice that had been repeatedly injected with THC when sexually immature. The experiment was designed to simulate the effects of prolonged exposure to the drug on girls' oöcytes (immature egg cells). Whereas a male's sperms regenerate, a female's stock of egg cells is limited at birth and no new ones are created. "Therefore," said Dr. Morishima in 1980 testimony, "any genetic damage inflicted on these cells should be permanent." (More in "The Cells and Chromosomes," 2.)

☆   ☆   ☆

Marijuana extract or synthetic THC given by mouth to one parent or both over a four-year period had no apparent effect on sexual activity, reproduction, or offspring of seven chimpanzee couples in New Mexico. At the time of impregnation, between a month and a half and a year and a half had elapsed since the last dose.

"All of the animals readily copulated with their mates," David M. Grilly and two coworkers reported (1974). They concluded that "normal, healthy infants can be reproduced in instances where one or both parents had previously experienced long-term exposure to marihuana."

Six of the fathers and three of the mothers took a drug between 50 and 254 times, THC dosage averaging 1.0 to 2.1 mg/kg. There was one fetal death. Seven offspring were born, all apparently normal. This percentage of normal births, 87.5, compares with about 77 percent of 77 births to marijuana-free parents during eight years in the chimpanzee colony at Holloman Air Force Base, Alamogordo, New Mexico.[38]

The rhesus monkey, a pale brown primate from India, common in zoos and favored in medical research, is a first-rate animal to use in studying the feminine reproductive system. Its female has a menstrual cycle that closely resembles the menstrual cycle in women. Also, its response to marijuana is similar to the human's response at roughly equal doses, scientists say.

In the latter 1970s two overlapping sets of experiments on THC's effects on the reproductive system of the female rhesus monkey were conducted independently in Texas and California. Neither scientific team knew the other was doing similar work.

At 1980 Senate committee hearings, two women scientists in charge of the teams, both associate professors at medical schools—Carol Grace Smith from Maryland (heading the Texas experiments) and Ethel Sassenrath from California—summarized the results.

"It now appears evident," Dr. Smith said, summing up five years of work, "that marijuana, or THC, can produce disruptive effects on the reproductive system."

Apparently the disruption takes place indirectly. The drug appears to disrupt nerve pathways in the brain, above the pituitary, inhibiting that gland from secreting sex hormone to the ovaries.

In this way, marijuana or THC "can produce infertility in the female monkey that can last for several months, even after discontinuation of drug use. But in healthy, adult monkeys, the hormonal effects appear to be completely reversible with time, after the discontinuation of drug use."

The first experiments were designed to find out whether THC affected female reproductive hormones. It did. THC injections caused temporary decreases in both luteinizing hormones (LH) and follicle-stimulating hormone (FSH).

These two hormones are among those controlling sexual development, fertility, and sexual function in human beings and animals. In the female, LH brings about ovulation, release of the ovum (egg) from the ovary. FSH, as the name implies, stimulates the development of the follicle (egg sac).

Later the monkey project was carried further to see whether hormonal changes caused by THC would in turn cause infertility, and this appeared to be the case. No monkey ovulated while receiving THC treatment or for months afterward. Still later (1983) the group observed that monkeys subjected to long-term treatment acquired tolerance to THC. Normal cycles with ovulation ultimately resumed despite drugging.

This was a joint project of specialists in pharmacology, neuropathology, obstetrics-gynecology, and reproductive physiology from four medical schools, headed by Dr. Smith, of the pharmacology department at Uniformed Services University of the Health Sciences, Bethesda, Maryland.

In the first phase of the experiments, five female monkeys were given injections of THC solution. All but the smallest dose caused substantial drops in the levels of LH and FSH within one to three hours. On the average, individual levels of LH dropped a maximum of 69 percent; FSH, a maximum of 56 percent. The doses were said to be comparable to those of marijuana smokers (between 0.6 and 5.4 mg/kg). The magnitude of the drop did not depend on the amount of the dose. However, the bigger the dose, the longer the depression in each hormone lasted—between twelve and twenty-four hours. This effect reversed in twenty-four to forty-eight hours, regardless of dose. Injections of solvent alone caused no decreases.

THC also inhibited the secretion of the pituitary hormone prolactin, which could be important in milk production in nursing mothers. Prolactin dropped promptly and significantly for all the female monkeys—an average of 84 percent for the group.

The effects of crude extracts of marijuana and pure THC were about the same.

Next Smith et al. examined three rhesus monkeys for normal menstrual cycles, about 28 days long. Daily THC (2.5 mg/kg) for 18 days disrupted the normal pattern. None of the monkeys ovulated before next menstruation, which took up to 141 days. Ovaries were observed through a laparoscope.[39]

When the group (1983) similarly dosed three rhesus monkeys thrice weekly for up to 230 days, it took an average of 116 days for regular menstruation to resume, after which hormones and ovulation returned to normal.[40]

* * *

THC or cannabis derivatives have lowered the secretion of gonadotropins (LH and FSH) in animals whose ovaries were removed. Pertinent experiments began with rats (B. H. Marks, 1973) and included rhesus monkeys (N. F. Besch et al., 1977).

Exactly how the THC works in holding back those hormones is not known, but "the involvement of hypothalamic neuro-endocrine processes seem very likely," Dr. Smith and associates theorized.

In both sexes, the disruptive effects of cannabis "appear to be mediated primarily through an inhibition of gonadotropin secretion, although direct effects on the gonad and other reproductive tissues may occur with the chronic use of the drug."[41]

Dr. Sassenrath, following Dr. Smith in testimony, generally confirmed her findings. She added some observations of her own, based on five years of work by her group at the California Primate Research Center, University of California at Davis, home of about 2,000 simians.

A behavioral biologist, she too (with associates) had experimented on rhesus monkeys, which she called "a close counterpart" to humans both in reproductive hormone function and in the interrelations between mother and fetus during pregnancy. Monkeys consumed THC on cookies or fruit, foods they liked. The THC, in doses approximating those of chronic marijuana smokers, produced an array of effects on female reproductive functions.

"These effects range from interference with conception in the newly drug-exposed female to high-risk pregnancies in the long-term drugged female," she said. Drugged mothers lost four times as many babies as undrugged mothers.

Behavioral changes in offspring appeared also, and Dr. Sassenrath called attention to the possibility of functional problems in children born to marijuana smokers.

She noted that the risk to reproduction from the use of marijuana "has not been already recognized in clinical practice" and "would be difficult to recognize in the human population. However, it should be remembered that the role of alcohol in reproductive risk was not recognized until a decade ago, although it had long been suspected and is now acknowledged as a syndrome which is not rare."

Dr. Sassenrath's work on reproduction in rhesus monkeys followed three years of work on THC and behavior in the same species. In the later study her group observed over fifty pregnancies, involving eleven undrugged monkeys and eight drugged ones. The eight, five females and three males, received THC daily for three to five years. An alcoholic THC mixture was dropped on the monkeys' foods. The dose (2.4 mg/kg) was meant to approximate the amount of THC taken by the daily smoker of one or two joints.

Some of the results are listed below.

Conception: The rate was over 90 percent for both drugged and undrugged females. In the newly drugged females, however, conception was delayed for three to five menstrual cycles. In comparison, there was no delay for the chronic THC-taking monkeys or the undrugged monkeys.

The differences are explained by "the level of tolerance to the drug." Tolerance develops in the brain centers that control reproductive hormones.

Pregnancy: The drugged mothers gained significantly less weight during the 5½ months of pregnancy than the undrugged mothers, and they lost 40 percent of their babies (abortions, fetal deaths, stillbirths, and early infant deaths), contrasted with a 10 percent loss for undrugged mothers.

Offspring: Newborn male offspring of THC-treated mothers weighed a little less (but significantly so) than those of undrugged mothers. Offspring of THC mothers appeared normal on the surface. But examination of the tissues of the dead offspring showed "developmental abnormalities." Most of these involved retarded growth or development.

The survivors showed no physical abnormalities. But differences in their behavior were turning up. In playing with other monkeys they were hyperactive, they overresponded, and they lacked normal caution, testified Dr. Sassenrath, of the university's psychiatry department.[42]

In observations of the same monkey offspring, conducted by Mari S. Golub (1981), the young of THC-treated mothers generally proved comparable to peers in "regulation of activity level, environmental responsiveness, problem solving, and social interaction," but there were some group differences, notably "the occurrence of prolonged periods of visual attention in the THC offspring." In a standardized test, the experimental and control offspring, aged one to two years, viewed projected slides through two peepholes and the frequency and length of visits to the peepholes were measured. The THC monkey (not exposed to any drug since weaning at 3½ months) tended to fix its attention on a novel stimulus.[43]

"The normal monkey, when he is put into a new environment, will look over the whole environment and check everything and then go back to what's interesting. The THC monkey will hit something that's novel and stay with it," said Dr. Sassenrath in an interview. "This is not a very adaptive thing to do. If they're out in the wild and they're in a new place and they don't keep their eyes out for what's going on all around, they just aren't going to be there very long."

In a two-year study at the Masters and Johnson Institute in St. Louis, women who used marijuana had shorter menstrual cycles and a greater number of defective menstrual cycles than women of the same ages who did not use marijuana. Furthermore, the level of prolactin (a hormone associated with milk production) was lower in the marijuana group. But

These are two monkey mothers and their babies at the University of California at Davis. The mother at the left (shown nursing its baby) has never taken a drug. The mother at the right has been treated with THC in food for an extended period. She is pictured the day after her latest treatment. "The mothers did not behave in exactly the same way toward their infants," said Dr. Ethel Sassenrath of the psychiatry department. Undrugged mothers exhibited "more affectionate and protective behavior." As the right-hand photo illustrates, drugged mothers were "not as protective and tended to reject their infants more often." They were more likely to be irritable and detached.

the marijuana users had higher testosterone levels—the opposite of the trend in male marijuana users.

While acknowledging that use of alcohol and smallness of sample— twenty-six marijuana users—left the study inconclusive, the scientific team indicated that the findings were of concern both to women trying to conceive and those trying *not* to conceive, to nursing mothers, and to girls wanting to become normal women.

At a 1979 conference and in 1980 testimony, Joan Bauman described the study of the effects of chronic marijuana smoking on woman's hormonal system.

The researchers had selected twenty-six women, aged eighteen to thirty, who appeared healthy and indicated that they had used marijuana at least three times a week for the preceding six months while avoiding other drugs. They were com-pared with a control group of seventeen women who said they never used mari-juana. At least thirteen blood samples were extracted from each woman through-out her menstrual cycle. (Most were studied for two cycles.)

The marijuana smokers used it between ten and twenty-eight days (mean of 17.6 days) per cycle. Those in the control group used none. Of course the mar-ijuana belonged to the users and its strength could not be determined.

Following are some results, comparing the marijuana group with the control group. Serum prolactin: consistently lower in the marijuana group. Testosterone: mean levels higher in the marijuana group; this reaction was the opposite from that in young men. Gonadotropins—LH and FSH: levels similar in the two groups. Estrogen and progesterone: levels similar in the two groups but the normal rise after ovulation was slower in the marijuana group (ten days versus five). Length of the menstrual cycle: shorter in the marijuana group (26.8 days versus 28.8 days). Cycles with inadequate luteal phase (less than eleven days): more in the mari-juana group (31.0 percent versus 9.7 percent). Failure of ovulation: more in the marijuana group (10.6 percent compared to 3.1 percent), the difference not sta-tistically significant.

Though pointing out the study's limitations—the marijuana group drank twice as much alcohol as the control group, the marijuana belonged to the subjects and its potency and purity was not known, and the frequency of use was reported by the subjects—Dr. Bauman told the Senate committee what this and related stud-ies might mean in practical terms:

"The incidence of chronic marijuana use has increased dramatically in recent years, primarily among the young: those of pre-pubertal, pubertal and reproduc-tive age. Animal research over the last few years has clearly indicated that THC is capable of affecting the female endocrine system, while our preliminary re-search indicates similar effects may occur in young women using the drug. These potential effects must be confirmed and studied more closely.

"Blockage of ovulation and defects of the luteal phase of the menstrual cycle are of obvious concern to those trying to conceive, while changes in menstrual cycle length and the timing of ovulation are of equal concern to those attempting conception or certain types of contraception.

"Decreased prolactin levels might interfere with lactation or with reproductive function in other ways: the role of prolactin in the normal menstrual cycle is as yet imperfectly known.

"Suppression of gonadotropic levels, particularly at puberty when the sensitive feedback mechanisms of the menstrual cycles are maturing, could cause delay of puberty with deleterious psychological effects or speculatively could lead to long-term fertility problems.

"Change in androgen production or metabolism might result in acne, hirsutism or voice-deepening.

"Prolonged effects on ovulation such as found in rhesus females during the cycle after treatment with THC might have serious implications for marijuana users who rationalize that reproductive consequences of drug use can be circumvented by abstinence from marijuana at the time when they may wish to become pregnant."[44]

* * *

That marijuana works through the brain in suppressing LH and FSH is demonstrated by research on nonreproductive women reported in the Kolodny textbook:

"Studies of acute marihuana use by women who were either post-menopausal or who had previously had their ovaries removed surgically demonstrated that marihuana lowers pituitary gonadotropin levels by approximately 35 percent. . . ." This indicates that "the effect of marihuana is centrally mediated."[45]

4

The Newborn

Once an infant is born, can its mother then proceed to take marijuana without fear for her child? If she is nursing it, no. This answer follows from several studies of lactating (milk-secreting) rodents, sheep, monkeys, and humans and their respective progeny.

The first two were performed by Alexander Jakubovic, Patrick McGeer, and associates, of the psychiatry department at the University of British Columbia (1973, 1974).

They injected radioactively labeled THC into two lactating mother rats. The drug and its metabolites (products) appeared in various organs of twenty suckling infants. The experimenters had dissected the infant rats at different intervals, from four to seventy-two hours, examining the brain, heart, liver, lung, spleen, and stomach. Cannabinoid was present in all organs at all times. Amounts were substantial.

In addition, they found that the drug, given to lactating rat mothers, was "capable of bringing about structural and biochemical changes in the suckling rat brain cells."

Later, giving three lactating ewes injections of the radioactive THC, they observed radioactivity in the sheep milk at all time intervals studied, from four hours to four days after treatment. The drug also showed up in the waste matter of a lamb suckling from one of the ewes. ". . . The excretion of notable amounts of radioactivity by a lamb suckled by a ewe which had been given a single low dose of THC indicates that at least some of the drug and its metabolites can be transferred to a growing infant at a critical period of development," they wrote.

> Radioactivity appeared in all organs of the rat pups studied, at four intervals after single injections under the skin with THC labeled with carbon-14 (53 mg/kg). After seventy-two hours the stomach contained the highest radioactivity, indicating that infants received a constant supply of drug via the mother's milk.
>
> With colleague Hattori using the electron microscope, the scientific team found "a highly significant decrease of ribosomes attached to the nuclear membrane of brain cells in the suckling rats." (The ribosome, a particle consisting of ribonucleic acid and protein, is the site of protein synthesis in the cell.) Among controls, 40 percent of the nuclear membrane surface contained ribosomes. The figures for cells of pups four and twenty-four hours after THC administration to their mothers were 21 percent and 25 percent, respectively.[46]
>
> "Considerable radioactivity" appeared in the sheep milk at four hours after intravenous injection (with either 0.02 or 1 mg/kg). THC and various unidentified metabolites persisted in milk of the three ewes for ninety-six hours. The ewes discharged a seventh of the radioactivity in the first forty-eight hours, far less in milk than in excreta. The lamb too excreted radioactivity all that time. (Its mother had received the 0.02 mg/kg dose.)[47]

Monkey mothers' milk and marshmallows figured in a similar experiment reported in 1976 by Fu-Chuan Chao, of the University of San Francisco, and five others. The subjects were eleven lactating squirrel monkeys and their babies. When the mothers were fed marshmallows injected with radioactive THC, some of it appeared in their milk—relatively more than in the ewes' milk—and some turned up in the infants' waste matter.

> At the time of the observations the infants ranged in age from three to six months. The mothers had been receiving THC orally for months. One day they received their dose (2 mg/kg) with a radioactive tracer.
>
> During a twenty-four-hour observation period, about 0.2 percent of the labeled THC appeared in the milk and 43 percent in the excreta of the mother monkeys. Infants suckling within six hours after their mothers got the labeled dose excreted an average of 0.13 percent of the labeled THC within eighteen hours after suckling.[48]

A sensational tabloid might have made something of this 1975 study of drugging and baby swapping in Canada's capital, except that the subjects were rats.

Psychology professor Peter A. Fried reported housing each of ten virgin females with "two naive male rats." The male rats apparently lost their naiveté, for nine females became pregnant.

Daily through most of their three-week pregnancy, the mothers entered a special smoke box. Five inhaled marijuana fumes and four—"controls"—got pot without active ingredients.

Two of the five marijuana-inhaling mothers failed to produce live offspring, except for one pup—which the mother ate the first day. Inside her was evidence of nine fetal fatalities.

At birth the marijuana pups weighed, on average, 7 percent less than the control pups. Then Fried switched half of the pups to mothers in the opposite group, with these results:

• Control-born pups nursed by marijuana mothers lost in relative weight (compared with control pups staying with their own mothers) but caught up after weaning, at three weeks of age.

• Marijuana-born pups nursed by control mothers gradually reached the weights of controls.

• Marijuana-born pups remaining with their own mothers sank even lower. Their weight measured 9 percent less than controls at weaning and 7 percent less after three months, when all the other groups were even.

• All pups born to marijuana mothers moved around much less than the others at one week of age (though differences disappeared a week later) and were late getting incisors and (particularly the marijuana-born-and-bred pups) opening their eyes.

So cannabis taken by mothers during pregnancy continued to hit their young during suckling. Either way, it stunted the babies. Those drugged only in the womb or through the milk could recover. But those doubly dosed suffered long-term handicaps.

From one to nineteen days after impregnation, rats received a maximum of about 3.3 mg of THC from marijuana cigarette smoke (1.1 percent THC), according to Fried of the psychology department at Carleton University, Ottawa.

Control mothers gave birth to fifty pups, marijuana mothers to thirty-nine pups, all live. At birth, marijuana males weighed nearly 8 percent less than control males while marijuana females weighed nearly 6 percent less than control females. Weights of pups born and nursed by marijuana mothers amounted to 13 percent less than controls at 1½ weeks of age.

An electromagnetic "activity sensor" showed less than a tenth as much motion by week-old pups born to marijuana mothers, compared with the others. Five tests of reflexes and physical features registered about normal.[49]

The plot thickens, as Fried traces certain effects of the smoke through the two succeeding generations of rats.

When the four groups of rat pups in the above experiment attained the adult age of six months, each of sixteen of the males and sixteen of the females acquired a lover (or two).

Fried's next observations indicated that "rats exposed to marihuana smoke during embryological development may be less fertile" than those not so exposed. Animals in the former category had some smaller reproductive organs than the others, achieved fewer impregnations and pregnancies, and took somewhat longer to mate and gestate.

The grandchildren of the smoking females weighed less than normally born rats—the differences persisting beyond weaning—and were slower to open eyes and get incisors. In all of these respects, they resembled their parents during the latter's puphood. Fried suggested that the retardation of the grandpups was a genetic effect of cannabis smoke administered two generations earlier.

> Ovaries weighed close to a third less in the (two groups of) marijuana-born rats than in the (two groups of) normally born rats. Prostate, seminal vesicles, and to some extent adrenal glands also weighed less in the former. Testicular weight did not differ.
>
> Among the former, one of eight males and two of eight females proved fertile; among the latter, six of eight males and three of eight females were fertile.
>
> Compared with their control counterparts, the pups of the second filial generation descended from marijuana smokers weighed 9 percent less when a day old and 12 percent less when thirty days old. There were no malformations or differences in litter size.[50]

Weekly injections of mice with THC at moderate doses beginning a few days after birth did not interfere with their normal development and reproduction. But the treatment did cause "a high mortality rate" among their offspring. So reported Szepsenwol (in Florida) and associates (1979).

Apparently THC did the damage by cutting off milk secretion in the mammary gland and causing starvation. Baby mice that had no milk in their stomachs the day after birth survived and developed normally when transferred to lactating female mice for nursing. THC stemmed the milk flow apparently by decreasing luteinizing hormone and prolactin, according to the experimenters.

"Another finding, which greatly surprised us, is the development of malignant tumors by the THC-treated mice," they wrote. Rates of lung cancer and sarcoma (cancer of connective tissue) were high in those mice, although THC seemed to inhibit the development of mammary cancer. (Details in "The Cells and Chromosomes," 3.)

> The original aim of the experiment, said the researchers (of Florida International University, Miami, and the University of Puerto Rico), was to find out if THC had the effects of an estrogen (female hormone), being similar in chemical structure. It did not.
>
> Hundreds of mice were injected, under the skin, with either delestrogen in sesame oil, which limited weight of mice; sesame oil alone, which did not retard growth or reproduction; or THC (20 micrograms) in sesame oil (0.05 ml), which did not hold back growth or reproductive capacity but caused "high mortality" in newborn pups.[51]
>
> In the C57 Black/6 strain of mouse, only one litter in ten survived. In the BALB/c strain, which made up most of the mice, eight out of ten litters survived, Dr. Szepsenwol informed us (1982).

Another phase of the University of Texas mouse series saw male offspring's sexual functioning suffering after their mothers took cannabinoids, even a nonpsychoactive one. More specifically:

• Female mice in midpregnancy that consumed either THC or CBN (cannabinol) had male fetuses with much less testosterone than a normal group of mice.

Dr. Dalterio explained (at a 1980 Senate hearing) that the critical period for development as a human male or female occurs in the first third of pregnancy, earlier than in the mouse. Changes in testosterone levels at such critical times, whether for humans or animals, can result in males or females with physical features of the opposite sex and possible sterility later in life.

• When female mice took either drug just before and after they gave birth, long-range sexual alterations resulted in their male offspring.

"They have been exposed only through the placenta and through milk. And yet, after they went through puberty, we see changes in sexual behavior, changes in hormone levels that apparently are due to the early exposure to marijuana," summarized colleague Dr. Bartke (at the thirteenth annual convention of the Society for the Study of Reproduction, Ann Arbor, Michigan, 1980).

In terms of the human child's development and behavior, he called any use of marijuana by pregnant women "potentially unsafe."

> Some details on the latter study: Fertile female mice were "housed with a sexually experienced male" and checked daily for signs of copulation. About a day before they gave birth, sesame oil was applied to the females' tongues. The oil

was either plain or mixed with THC or CBN (50 mg/kg). In addition, each mother received a dose on the day of birth and daily doses for six more days.

At birth each litter was culled to six males, which were weaned at twenty-one days of age. At maturity (sixty to eighty days) males were tested for copulatory activity. Then they were given blood tests and killed for a study of various organ weights.

Copulatory behavior was tested for one hour and found to be suppressed in the mice from mothers treated with cannabinoids. Mice in both the THC and CBN groups took more time to mount than did untreated mice. Only four of nine THC mice mounted, whereas all of fourteen normal mice mounted. There were fewer mounts in the CBN group than in the latter group.

Other significant differences: The THC group (seventeen mice) showed increased body weights, reduced testes weights, and more LH than the untreated animals (twenty-eight mice). The CBN group (twenty mice) displayed a moderate decrease in FSH.[52]

We now return to Fried (1980), who studied humans as well as rats. With the cooperation of two hospitals, sixteen obstetricians, and 291 expectant women, he assembled what might be the first body of data on the effects of marijuana use by mothers-to-be on their offspring (except for case histories).

In interviews one-fifth of the women reported using marijuana in the year before and/or during pregnancy.

Eighty-nine babies received standard behavioral tests when they were two or three days old. Compared with babies of nonusers or infrequent users, those born to women who smoked marijuana regularly before and during pregnancy—nine—had "a significant increase in symptoms associated with nervous system abnormalities." The latter infants displayed marked tremors and startles. Moreover, notably more of the latter failed to respond normally to lights shined at them.

Marijuana apparently made no difference in normality of births and physical condition of offspring.

Once the study was well under way, came the discovery that three babies born to regular marijuana users had a "shrill, high-pitched, catlike cry" not heard among the offspring of those abstaining from marijuana. Such a cry has been reported among infants newly born to heroin and methadone addicts and is considered "a symptom of drug withdrawal."

While acknowledging that "many desirable control procedures were not possible in this study" and that the small number of subjects limited the statistical techniques, Fried concluded that "even with this relatively small sample there is clear evidence that in the newborn there are measurable correlates of regular marijuana usage by mothers-to-be at quantities as low as five joints per week."

Fried indicated (1982, 1983) that at thirty days, the abnormalities were fading, and at one year, marijuana babies appeared normal in development and behavior. He was continuing to gather data.

In the 1980 study, two trained raters, unaware of the mothers' drug histories, tested the infants according to the Brazelton behavioral scale. Tobacco and alcohol use correlated with marijuana smoking before and during pregnancy.[53]

Fried informed us (1984) that when twenty women who smoked over five joints a week through pregnancy were matched for use of alcohol, nicotine, and caffeine with twenty controls, the newborn infants of the marijuana smokers differed from the other babies in tremors, startles, response to light, and cries. At thirty days, most marijuana babies were crying normally, and fewer of them than before—but still more than controls—differed in the other respects, Fried said. He speculated that the symptoms might signify marijuana withdrawal or delayed nervous development.

Two nursing mothers who smoked marijuana daily in pipes took samples of their milk to a North Carolina laboratory to be analyzed for THC. The milk did contain THC, more of it in the heavier smoking woman. Later she provided a sample of her infant's feces, which was found to contain THC plus a relative abundance of THC metabolite. She agreed also to have her milk and blood sampled simultaneously about an hour after a smoke. The milk had eight times as much THC as the blood plasma.

"These findings indicate that THC is concentrated and secreted in human milk and is absorbed by the nursing baby," Mario Perez-Reyes, M.D., and Monroe E. Wall wrote (1982). "Because the effects on the infant of chronic exposure to THC and its metabolites are unknown, nursing mothers should abstain from the use of marijuana."

Analysis of the fecal sample (by gas-liquid chromatography and mass spectrometry) suggested "that the THC present in the mother's milk was absorbed and metabolized by the infant, because the proportion of 11-OH-THC and 9-carboxy-THC to the parent compound was much higher in the feces [two to one] than in the mother's milk [one to twenty-two]."

Samples of the infants' urine brought in initially by the mothers tested negatively. They were advised not to smoke and nurse but one continued to do so. She had smoked marijuana seven times a day for eight months while nursing. The other had smoked it once a day during seven months of nursing. Both were in their late twenties. Their infants were reported developing normally.

So reported Perez-Reyes of the University of North Carolina School of Medicine and Wall of Research Triangle Institute in a letter to the New England Journal of Medicine.[54]

Further studies of the newborn and their mothers in the eastern and western United States (1982), found that smoking marijuana during pregnancy made a difference.

Ralph Hingson of the Boston University School of Medicine and associates examined 1,690 newborn babies and interviewed their mothers, 181 of whom avowed having smoked marijuana during pregnancy. At birth, the infants of the smokers weighed on average 105 grams less than the infants of the nonsmokers. Furthermore, women who smoked marijuana during pregnancy were six times as likely as nonusers to deliver infants with "fetal alcohol syndrome." Such infants had either (a) two or more physical deformities or (b) small openings between eyelids, plus either (c) small head size or (d) small weight or length.

Sander Greenland of the School of Public Health at the University of California at Los Angeles reported to us two pertinent studies he conducted. One examined 313 babies delivered at home, 41 of them born to marijuana users. Another examined 35 babies of marijuana users, compared with 36 nonusers (matched for age and number of children). In each Greenland study, the mothers who smoked marijuana when pregnant had more labor problems (prolonged, protracted, or arrested labor) and their infants had more meconium staining (expulsion of intestinal waste matter into the fluid that surrounds the fetus—often due to fetal distress during birth).

> Hingson et al. reported that women who smoked marijuana less than three times weekly while pregnant delivered babies (at Boston City Hospital) averaging 95 grams less than those who never smoked marijuana, while those who used marijuana three or more times a week had babies that were 139 grams lighter than those of nonusers.
>
> In contrast, women who smoked a pack of tobacco cigarettes or more daily during pregnancy delivered babies 83 grams lighter than those who did not smoke tobacco.
>
> Use of alcohol showed no effect on either infant growth or fetal alcohol syndrome, but since few mothers reported chronic heavy drinking, no conclusion could be reached on adverse effects of this factor. The research had aimed to "assess the impact of maternal alcohol consumption on fetal development when confounding variables were controlled." The report played down the effect of any one variable and stressed the danger of "a life-style that combines smoking, drinking, marijuana use, etc. . . . ."
>
> Deformities observed in determining fetal alcohol syndrome included ear anomalies, heart murmurs, limited joint movements, small nails, large hemangiomas (benign tumors of blood vessels), epicanthic folds (skin over the eyes), long philtrum (groove amid the upper lip), odd creases on palms, and broad, low nasal bridge.[55]

* * *

> Dr. Virchel Wood, hand surgeon of Loma Linda, California, told us (1984) he had seen misshapen hands with fingers missing or barely formed in babies of drug users. "In the last ten years I have had nine cases that I feel could be drug-related." In all of them the mother had taken marijuana and alcohol during pregnancy. In seven of them she also took other drugs, such as LSD and heroin. The

father too used drugs in at least some cases. Dr. Wood said that multiple drug use made it hard to assess the cause and that "maybe it is just coincidental that these mothers who smoked marijuana had deformed children. But I feel it is a strong possibility [that marijuana was a factor] and is something we should be watching for."

* * *

"Based on the minimal data available, there is no known increased risk to pregnancy from marijuana consumption. . . . Drawing conclusions is premature," said Christine Kelley, coordinator of the California Teratogenic Registry, a program by the University of California, San Diego, pediatrics department to educate and counsel on substances that may cause birth defects. As for the studies of monkeys and women, "We do not consider the results of animal experiments applicable to humans. In the human studies there were so many confounding variables and the number of babies studied was small. I would not want to base warnings on them." Responding to our inquiry (1984), Mrs. Kelley expressed the personal view that "until more is known about marijuana, pregnant women should avoid it." She explained, though, that the registry "gives facts but does not make recommendations about drug use."

THE
HEART
AND
CIRCULATORY SYSTEM

※   ※

- *"I stopped smoking marijuana for two reasons. Marijuana speeded up my heart so greatly, I had heavy palpitations and felt like it was jumping out of my chest. The next morning after smoking, when I was no longer stoned, I was depressed and paranoid."* —Prudence (ex-user)

- *"I definitely had less lasting strength, less stamina. It was tied in with shortness of breath. . . . My heart would beat faster when I was high."* —Steve (ex-user)

- *"In the beginning I had faster heartbeats that were scary. You could hear it."* —Gregory (occasional user, former chronic user)

- *"My breathing was more rapid and I was more conscious of it. I used to think I could hear my heart beating. . . . It seemed to me as if it was beating louder and probably faster. It was more noticeable when you actually took a puff or a drag than it was two or three hours later."* — Anna (ex-user)

- *"It seemed to increase my heart rate. . . . It would pound if I was high and I would exert myself. I could definitely feel my heart more if I was under the influence. . . . When one is sober and gets up suddenly, there is a feeling of blacking out. If I was very stoned, it would be more intense."* —Pierre (ex-user)

• *"I would feel cold when on marijuana. I would feel like my temperature had dropped."* —Oscar (former chronic user)

• *"Sometimes I get real cold, like my circulation is cut out—which makes sense: smoking affects your oxygen in your blood."* —Alice (chronic user)

1

A Sad Study and a Short Summary

Articles in medical journals usually are written in a dry fashion, devoid of soul. But in recording the observations of two physicians in Morocco, the pages of a 1960 issue of the French periodical *Archives of Diseases of the Heart and Blood Vessels* reflect frustration and melancholy.

Doctors Sterne and Ducastaing treated twenty-nine impoverished young men who were being increasingly crippled by arteritis, inflammation of the arteries. Toes would be amputated, the disease would subside, but then it would recur. Feet or whole legs would be lost; again, a reprieve, but nothing helped for long. The physicians could not save their patients.

Belatedly they found out that all twenty-nine patients were heavy smokers of *kif*, cannabis. When smoking reached a peak, so did the disease. After surgery, back the men went to their pipes.

The symptoms were those of a "senile arteritis," not an ailment one would expect among youthful people. Such inflammations of the arteries were very frequent in the regions where *kif* intoxication prevailed, the authors reported.

The twenty-nine men, ages twenty-five to thirty-five, belonged to "poor classes and led hard lives." Observations were made in Meknes and Casablanca, both in private practice and at the Maurice-Gaud Hospital of Casablanca, where 2 percent of all wintertime patients suffered the disease: obliterative arteritis of the lower limbs.

This was the only circulatory disorder claiming the attention of doctors in North Africa. The authors contrasted these cases with the relative immunity of the Arabs to atherosclerosis, hypertensive disease, coronaries, and so on.

Trouble would start in the cold months. Hobbling would progress to immobility in days or weeks, the feet painful, pussy, and pulseless; possibly ulcerous and gangrenous. At that advanced stage, the patients would go to the hospital. When queried, they would state that their problems began very recently.

"The patient is released from the hospital missing a few toes or a foot. He will return after a few weeks or at latest the following winter with a recurrence on the other side or on his stump. His general condition will worsen. His weight will fall and death is the almost inevitable end of those arteritis cases within two or three years." (No fatality figure was given. The authors left Morocco, perhaps before following each case to its conclusion.)

". . . We believe that we can state that those arteritis cases are connected with the consumption of cannabis indica. That stupefying plant is used a good deal in Morocco. The dried leaves and the flowery tips are . . . smoked either mixed with tobacco or pure in small, special pipes. . . .

"The consumption of Indian hemp is of course forbidden and punished, but in reality an active, illegal traffic takes place. It is easy to obtain it for a reasonable price and very poor individuals who lead difficult lives easily find refuge in that artificial paradise."

Cannabis's role in causing the arteritis "was revealed to us by a patient who, after we gained his confidence, indicated to us that the three upsurges of the disease had each time followed a particularly distressful period of his life during which he started smoking an abundance of the Indian hemp. . . .

"Systematic inquiry was rendered difficult by the fact that the patients naturally were trying to conceal a habit sought out by the police. However, we received admissions of addiction in twenty out of twenty-nine cases." Only 6 percent of nonarteritic patients surveyed indicated that they used cannabis.

"For the most part they were heavy smokers, having reached a high degree of tolerance, who absorbed an average of fifteen pipefuls per day. In several cases of intermittent addiction, an upsurge due to resumption of the addiction was observed."

The only effective treatment that the authors found was surgical suprarenal removal. Pain would soon disappear and ulceration would scar. "But the results do not last. The patient leaves and resumes his addiction, and the arteritis continues its progress."[1] (The above is translated from the French.)

Those were by far the most serious cardiovascular complications in human beings described in any scientific report on cannabis that we have read. Most of the pertinent studies have tested acute effects, the immediate response to a joint or a dose of THC; a few have examined volunteers after some weeks of drug taking. Such studies have not put the finger on marijuana as a source of mortal disease. But all of them have evoked noticeable, often spectacular effects. In fact, what is probably the most common physiological effect of cannabis and its leading ingredient, THC—though an effect that users often ignore—involves the heart. It is tachycardia, an abnormally rapid heart action.

Again and again, experiments have shown the human heart responding to marijuana by picking up speed. Both smoking and ingestion have accelerated the pulse rate, smoking having the quicker and greater effect. In a typical case, Joe's pulse quickens promptly with a few puffs, doubles within half an hour, and continues on the rapid side for an hour and a half.

Blood pressure has reacted variably. It may rise somewhat in one experiment, stay put in a second, and drop in a third. The subjects may have been lying, sitting, and standing, respectively. Pressure (lying) also has diminished in response to frequent and heavy drugging. After such dosing, the pulse has been known to fall instead of rise. In some people, loss of pressure (standing) can occur at low doses. Some individual reactions deviate drastically. Theories to explain the phenomena diverge too.

On occasion, unexpected abnormalities have appeared in electrocardiograms upon the consumption of THC or marijuana, particularly in chronic users. Abnormal circulatory responses have been observed also.

Marijuana smoking has hastened angina pectoris attacks in cardiac patients. Doctors feel that such patients should not use cannabis. Usually the subjects chosen for experimentation have been young and apparently healthy. Medical scientists are not yet agreed on whether the changes in heart and blood vessels produced by cannabis will harm the health of such people.

Pending a definitive answer, one should bear in mind the lessons of tobacco. It took many years—and lives—before the link between tobacco smoking and heart disease became plain, as medical Doctors William Pollin and Reese T. Jones have pointed out (respectively testifying and writing for the National Institute on Drug Abuse). Two other points that they raise heighten the significance of that analogy:

• Tobacco claims more lives by afflicting the heart than by causing cancer.

• Cannabis seems to have more of an effect on the heart than does tobacco.

> "It is clear that marijuana changes heart function . . . increases heart rates . . . changes the distribution of blood . . . does cause significant increase in angina in individuals who do have preexisting heart disease," Dr. Pollin testified before a Senate subcommittee (1980) as director of the national institute.
>
> Of what consequence these effects will turn out to be is not yet known, he said. But he noted:
>
> "It took at least fifteen years, between the time of the first and the second Surgeon General's report on the health consequences of smoking, before it became apparent that though there are perhaps some 80,000 to 100,000 deaths due to lung cancer based on smoking each year, that deaths due to coronary effects of smoking are at a substantially greater number than those due to carcinoma effects of smoking."[2]

✻   ✻   ✻

> "The lessons learned from chronic tobacco use are worth considering. It was only after many years of use by millions of people that cardiovascular disease associated with tobacco use was recognized. Even now the exact mechanisms are scientifically debatable." So wrote Reese Jones, San Francisco scientist (1980).
>
> "Assuming that smoking cannabis has some similarity to smoking tobacco . . . one may assume that long term chronic effects will be different from the more commonly reported and easily studied acute ones."

Supporting the first assumption is the fact that "THC seems to have far more profound effects on the cardiovascular system than does nicotine."[3]

2

Experimental Chronicle

The experimental history of cannabis and the cardiovascular system embraces many broad studies testing an array of mental and physical effects. In some old cases, observers simply described their experiences after consuming hemp extract; in others, doctors recorded the symptoms of medicinal or experimental takers. Controlled studies focusing on the human heart have been relatively scant. We will not dwell on the lower creatures, which in this area make dubious stand-ins for human beings: Single doses of THC lower pulse rate and blood pressure in experimental animals.

The French psychiatrist Moreau ate hashish and indicated imprecisely that one dose stimulated as did coffee or tea; increased dosage slightly quickened the pulse; and a large dose made the heart beat no stronger or faster than usual despite a feeling of unusual intensity and resonance (1845).[4] Another doctor, H. C. Wood, Jr., of Philadelphia, recorded that he ingested roughly 25 grains of an extract of male hemp grown for fiber and 3½ hours later, having become grossly intoxicated while calling on a patient, "I counted my pulse and found it 120, quite full and strong" (1869).

In objective European accounts of cannabis extract ingestion, Lichtenfels and Froehlich reported pulse increases in ordinary trials but a drop to 16 beats in one exceptional case (1852) and Windscheid saw a healthy young man who reacted to three grams with a weak pulse of 172 the first day and 120 the second (1893). Dontas and Zis measured increases of 10 to 50 pulsations a minute and usually diminution of blood pressure in medical students smoking hashish experimentally in Greece (1929). And Skliar and Iwanow noted marked palpitation and accelerated pulse in fifty-two cannabis smokers in Russia (1932).[5]

The Indian Hemp Drugs Commission reported (1894) that a rhesus monkey that inhaled *ganja* smoke 181 times in eight months developed "an excessive accumulation of fat" in the pericardium and a tendency to such accumulation in the heart muscle and abdominal organs. (More in "The Brain," 3.)

Let us dip again into the 1939 Indian memoir of Chopra and Chopra. In describing the effects of hemp drugs on the human heart and blood vessels, they were rather vague: 85 individuals, nearly 7 percent of the

1,238 hemp takers examined, displayed "involvement of the cardiovascular system"—and so on.

The Chopras recorded blood pressure before and after smoking by 100 smokers of *ganja* and *charas* (hashish). Rising pressure was common. In experienced "addicts," blood pressure rose slowly. In new users, a few pulls on a pipe produced "a sharp rise of blood pressure followed by a rapid fall with the onset of symptoms of intoxication" and possibly collapse, the blood pressure remaining low for a considerable time. "The heart rate was considerably increased." The drinking of liquid hemp extract, however, did not necessarily accelerate the heart.

In 893 cases, some 72 percent of the sample, they observed eye congestion and reddening. Yellow discoloration of the eyes also was common among those who had indulged for many years. General health often showed deterioration.

> Of the eighty-five individuals showing "involvement" of the cardiovascular system, "10 complained of palpitation, cardiac distress and breathlessness." Four people suffered "congestive heart failure and fullness of the veins in the neck." There was "arrhythmia," an alteration in rhythm, in two cases. Extra beating was found in "a number of cases," clearing up after the smoking habit was abandoned.
>
> The eye congestion, though more marked right after smoking, would persist long after intoxication, Chopra and Chopra wrote. The deposit of a yellow pigment "is a very important sign by which addiction to hemp drugs, particularly ganja and charas smoking, can be diagnosed. The congestion of the transverse ciliary vessels may persist for many years after the drug has been completely withheld. We observed this sign in almost all the mental cases in Indian Mental Hospital at Ranchi who gave a history of prolonged indulgence in hemp drugs even after five to ten years' stay in the hospital where they had no chances of indulging in these drugs."
>
> The Chopras gave liquid extracts of Indian hemp to ten people, including nontakers of drugs, in addition to the 100 regular smokers. "In man the effect on the heart varied according to whether the fumes of the ignited drug were inhaled or the drug was taken by the mouth." Inhalation in moderate doses always accelerated the heart—"four to five whiffs of ganja pipe were sufficient to increase the pulse rate to 100 per minute or even more; the effects disappeared within half to one hour." Administered by mouth in "medicinal doses," any quickening, if it occurred at all, was insignificant; larger doses that produced "narcotic effects" caused a marked slowing of the heart.
>
> In a study to determine minimum fatal doses, 2 to 10 grams of drug killed cats in four to seventy-two hours, depending on the strength of the preparation (*charas* being the strongest and *bhang* the mildest). Usual autopsy result: "cardiac failure."[6]

The report of Mayor LaGuardia's Committee on Marihuana (1944) climaxed a rather comprehensive experiment on the immediate effects of cannabis. Volunteers in New York City, mostly prisoners, swallowed marijuana extract and were examined in many ways. Measured quantities of drug were administered, but its strength was unknown. The "most consistent" bodily effect was a faster pulse. As subjects grew intoxicated, their hearts usually began speeding up. Pulses increased between thirty and sixty beats per minute. The heart rate seemed to change with the mental state. Nine of the subjects, including seven users and two nonusers, showed abnormal electrocardiograms before and after taking marijuana. For two others, both users, normal tracings turned abnormal following the taking of marijuana. Blood pressure varied but generally rose with the pulse.

Subjects numbered seventy-seven, all but five of them prisoners. Forty-eight had smoked marijuana.

Dr. Samuel Allentuck reported that the pulse reached its peak rate in 1½ to 3½ hours. "The maximum increase was from 30 to 40 beats per minute in most instances but in some it was from 50 to 60 beats." From the peak, the rate declined sometimes sharply, at other times gradually. It was "greater in states of euphoria with talkativeness, laughter, and body movements." As these symptoms subsided, the pulse rate fell accordingly.

Blood pressure was less consistent. "Thus, in one instance, with an increase of 30 beats per minute in pulse rate, the blood pressure rose 20 mm. Hg. [millimeters of mercury]; in another, with a rise in pulse rate of 50 beats per minute, the blood pressure remained unchanged. The diastolic pressure in general followed the systolic."

In four subjects the pattern of electrocardiographic abnormalities resembled that in patients with rheumatic heart disease, as interpreted by Dr. Robert C. Batterman.

Among other results were increases in blood sugar, in the urge to urinate, and in appetite, particularly for sweets, and some nausea and vomiting. Intensity of these and the pulse and pressure changes did not vary with dose. No circulatory, pulmonary, gastric, or kidney changes were observed.

"All the effects described are known to be expressions of forms of cerebral excitation, the impulses from this being transmitted through the autonomic system. The alterations in the functions of the organs studied come from the effects of the drug on the central nervous system. . . . A direct effect on the organs themselves was not seen," Dr. Allentuck wrote.[7]

Ten medical interns, including the experimenter, consumed cannabis pills in a South African hospital and took notes on their experiences while observers and nurses recorded clinical changes and behavior.

Heartbeats in all subjects accelerated—"in one case the pulse rate, initially 56, rose to 80, but in all the other cases the rate rose to between 120 and 140," Frances Ames reported (1958). The rapid action "persisted for several hours before the pulse gradually returned to its original level."

Several subjects complained of "intense . . . discomfort" in the chest,

over the heart. "A most interesting and striking feature" in all was reddening of the eyes, sometimes with swelling of the eyelid. All developed
"moderate coldness of the extremities and in some cases fingers and toes
looked pallid." Blood pressure rose moderately in some.

> After taking four pills, at Groote Schuur Hospital in Cape Town, Dr. Ames
> experienced "some paraesthesiae [tingling] of hands and feet, was conscious of
> coldness and had a bad headache. My pulse rate remained more or less normal
> unless I exerted myself, when it immediately rose from 80 to 120. I developed
> slight conjunctival suffusion [reddened eyes] and had a diuresis [increased urina-
> tion]. The effects of the drug lasted for 11 hours."
>
> When the experiment was repeated on three subjects several months later, the
> accelerations were much reduced and the main abnormality noted in heart rate
> was greater instability than usual. It accelerated rapidly on exertion.
>
> Five subjects complained of tingling over the nose and around the mouth. Five
> complained of headache. Nausea was common. "An invariable complaint was
> marked dryness of mouth." Urine volumes, compared before and after the drug-
> taking, increased in six of seven cases. "Fasting blood-sugar estimations," made
> at half-hour intervals for 2½ hours, showed little change from normal.
>
> One likened his physical symptoms to a violent adrenaline (epinephrine) re-
> lease—"it was like having the visceral effects of panic and a mental sense of panic
> without cause and without alarming thoughts in my head."
>
> The ten volunteers, eight men and two women, were in the twenty to thirty
> age group. All but one took (without water) four to seven pills, "according to body
> weight and temperament." Each pill contained one grain (65 mg) of resinous
> cannabis extract, with licorice and tragacanth added.
>
> One subject took forty-eight pills (3.1 grams or a ninth of an ounce of canna-
> bis) and suffered, among other ailments, severe abdominal cramps that persisted
> for two days. The author blamed the pains in part on the licorice but did not
> explain how the subject came to take so many pills, except to say he was "inad-
> vertently given an overdose."[8]
>
> Dr. Ames has been head of the Department of Neurobiology at the same hos-
> pital and senior lecturer in neurobiology and associate professor at the University
> of Cape Town. Incidentally, none of the ten subjects acquired a drug habit, she
> informed us.

Delta-9-THC was isolated by 1964, and researchers made the most of
it. Among the pacesetters, Isbell and group reported (1967) what happened when subjects received THC cocktails to drink and THC-spiked
cigarettes to smoke in Lexington, Kentucky. Those studied were some
forty prisoners serving time for narcotics violations.

Based on changes in pulse, the experimenters found THC much more
potent when smoked than when swallowed. While THC caused no significant changes in blood pressure, "pulse rates at rest were consistently
elevated."

Conducting the experiment at the U.S. Public Health Service Hospital, Dr. Harris Isbell and five others called it "the first demonstration of hashish-like activity of a tetrahydrocannabinol of *known* chemical structure in man."

Tested weekly, subjects got drinks of THC (0.12 and 0.48 mg/kg) in ethanol and cherry syrup; also tobacco cigarettes injected with THC (0.05 and 0.20 mg/kg); and also placebos with no THC. ". . . Potency of delta-9-THC after smoking calculated from changes in the peak pulse rate was 2.6 times that after oral ingestion. . . ."

No matter how they took the THC, all the subjects recognized its effects as similar to those of marijuana. They all reported changes in mood, usually euphoric. Observing marked distortions in reality at higher doses, the authors concluded that "delta-9-THC is a psychotomimetic [psychosis-imitating] drug and its psychotomimetic effects are dependent on dose."[9]

An experiment on eight prisoners by Isbell and Jasinski (1969) compared the effects of THC (smoked) with LSD (injected). The medical effects clearly differed, though not the psychological effects. LSD increased blood pressures, temperatures, and size of pupils, and lowered the threshold for the knee-jerk reaction. THC had none of those effects but caused a much greater increase in pulse rate. Unlike LSD, THC produced minor eye problems: "injection of the conjunctivae and pseudoptosis" (reddened eyes and flabby lids).[10]

Warning signs emerged from a Michigan project specifically designed to test the effects of marijuana smoking on the heart, at least in young men of normal health. Doctors Johnson and Domino gave low doses to ten subjects (1969) and high doses to fifteen others (1971).

Again marijuana smoking upped heart rate. The degree of increase was related to the dose nearly two-thirds of the time. The fast heartbeats usually reached a peak in half an hour and persisted at least an hour and a half. Blood pressure rose at higher doses, apparently related to dosage. Two high-dose recipients also responded with "premature ventricular contraction" (PVC).

The doctors cautioned that the three symptoms indicated that "marihuana should be used with caution by people with heart disease. Like nicotine and caffeine, marihuana may be a cause of PVCs in susceptible individuals."

The speeding heartbeat was not restricted to inexperienced marijuana smokers. One who smoked marijuana daily could tolerate a large dose "with little change in his outward behavior or conversation. . . . However, his heart rate increased from 55 to 120 after a 30 mg. [THC] dose."

In the low-dose study, subjects smoked between two and five marijuana cigarettes. Experts could not agree on whether each contained 0.2 or 0.5 percent THC. In the high-dose study, subjects were told to smoke "until they were as high as they had ever been on marihuana and felt they could not smoke any more. This required from one to 4 cigarettes," 2.9 percent THC each. Subjects were twenty-

one to thirty-three years old. The experimenters were with the University of
Michigan (Ann Arbor) and Lafayette Clinic (Detroit).[11]

An ingeniously mechanized experiment was conducted on ten male
volunteers by Renault and other members of the psychiatry department
at the University of Chicago (1971). Using spirometer, crucible, tubes,
lights, mask on subject's face and electrodes on his chest, the experimenters seemed primarily interested in inventing a method of administering measured doses of smoke. Nevertheless, they did measure some
effects on the heart.

Heart rate generally increased in a subject in proportion to the dose
of marijuana. At different sessions an individual usually responded to a
given dose in essentially the same way, but subjects varied greatly from
one another in their response to each dose; rates did not hinge on smoking experience. Large doses caused heart rates to increase to 140 to 160
beats per minute within ten to twenty minutes after the start of smoking.
A consistent effect of marijuana on cardiac rhythm was observed.

> Renault and associates "developed a system to deliver a measured quantity of
> smoke to a subject. . . . Linear dose-effect curves and the replicability of dose
> effects in the same subject from one session to another" attested to its reliability.
> Their device delivered the entire smoke output of a fixed amount of marijuana
> (in this case, 62.5, 125, 250, or 435 mg, 1.5 percent THC) to be inhaled through
> a mask connected to a spirometer. Four lights told the subject when to get "ready,"
> to "inhale" for five seconds, to "hold" the smoke in his lungs for fifteen seconds,
> and to "exhale." Electrocardiograms and tracings of heart rate and respiration were
> made at the same time. The subjects, aged twenty-four to forty-five, were six ex-
> perienced marijuana smokers (taking it at least weekly) and four who were inex-
> perienced (three never had tried it), all found in good health. All used tobacco.
> In addition to the drug, the subjects were tested with placebo marijuana. It
> produced no increase in heart rate.
> Regarding the effect of regular marijuana on heart rhythm: "The most direct
> effect is the suppression of the normal sinus arrhythmia" (variation in heart rhythm,
> the rhythm slightly accelerating on inhalation and slowing on exhalation). Inas-
> much as the vagus (cranial nerve) mediates this arrhythmia, "marihuana may have
> its effects on heart rate by altering normal autonomic tone." In a follow-up test,
> "marihuana suppressed the cardiac slowing during the Valsalva maneuver" (an
> effort to exhale against the closed glottis).[12]

In Washington, D.C., Galanter and colleagues (1972) had a dozen
chronic marijuana users do some smoking and rate their subjective feelings. Generally the higher a pulse increased, the "higher" a subject felt.

Three of the twelve were studied further. After they smoked (inactive
marijuana cigarettes injected with THC), concentration of THC in the
blood soon reached a peak and sharply declined, correlated with their

changes in pulse. Subjective symptoms peaked later and dissipated more gradually.

> For the three, whose THC was labeled with radioactive carbon, both plasma concentration of THC and pulse increment were at their peaks when tested fifteen minutes after the start of smoking and they diminished abruptly. The subjective experience, though, was at its summit in one hour and took hours more to fade away.
>
> "This suggests that the delta-9-THC concentration is more closely related to changes in pulse than to changes in subjective ratings," reported Marc Galanter and others of the National Institute of Mental Health's clinical pharmacology laboratory.
>
> The twelve, men in their twenties, after smoking 10-mg-THC cigarettes rated their "highs" on a scale of zero to ten and also checked a list of sixty-two subjective symptoms. Their individual symptom scores correlated with their "high" scores and with their respective pulse increments.
>
> When subjects smoked placebos, some of the symptoms of intoxication appeared and heartbeats quickened slightly.
>
> In the three labeled subjects, plasma concentration and subjective reactions were tested nine times in twenty-four hours after smoking started.
>
> "Both the plasma concentration of delta-9-THC and the pulse increment peaked at 15 minutes and then rapidly declined. . . . The subjective experience, however, reached a peak at 1 hour and declined more slowly."
>
> Plasma concentrations were highly correlated with pulse increases, "but neither of these correlated significantly with the subjective measures. This suggests that the delta-9-THC concentration is more closely related to changes in pulse than to changes in subjective ratings."
>
> Results from THC and placebo (inert marijuana) were, respectively: Heart rate increase—44 and 7. Subjective "high"—5 and 2. Symptom checklist—32 and 18.[13]

With a rise in pulse rate, marijuana caused an increase in blood flow to the limbs of doctors smoking it for the first time. An English medical team headed by Beaconsfield so reported in the *New England Journal of Medicine* (1972), describing a study in Asia.

Some smoked tobacco for comparison. The pulse rate increased but not so much, and it did not remain high so long. Blood flow decreased in most cases, contrary to marijuana's effect.

After studying the effects of marijuana together with various medicinal drugs, the authors urged caution by physicians in administering medication affecting the heart and blood vessels in patients who might recently have smoked marijuana. Such treatment could "dangerously" enhance and prolong the rapid heartbeat caused by marijuana. How would doctors determine who those patients are?

"The age group most frequently involved in road traffic accidents is also the one that most commonly smokes marihuana." If a young traffic victim has a persistently rapid pulse that cannot be otherwise explained, it "might be related to cannabis smoked before the accident."

At the authors' London hospital, there were "circulatory disturbances in a number of accident cases that, at the time, we could not explain. On subsequent questioning, some of these patients admitted to smoking marihuana shortly before the accident."

> Peter Beaconsfield, M.D., and two others from the Royal Free Hospital Medical School in London, conducted the study. The subjects volunteering, nine men and a woman, were all doctors on the staff of "the University hospital where the study was undertaken"—the authors did not say where.
>
> Six subjects each smoked a marijuana cigarette (10 mg THC). The volume of blood flowing to forearm and calf increased (56 percent and 92 percent, respectively) and remained elevated at least half an hour while the flow to the hand rose modestly (29 percent) and soon fell to normal. Heart rate shot up from a mean of sixty-six beats per minute in the control period to eighty-nine "immediately after smoking" and ninety-two at half an hour. Changes seen in electrocardiogram tracings and lack of significant change in blood pressure suggested the "possibility that circulatory adjustments occur in other vascular beds." Skin temperatures in toes increased.
>
> Tobacco tests were made on three subjects. The pulse rate rose an average of fifteen beats per minute during smoking but fell to control values within half an hour. Systolic and diastolic pressures rose (10 and 5 mm of mercury, respectively), remaining elevated for up to half an hour. Skin temperature fell and blood flow decreased, except for forearm-calf increases in one subject.
>
> Effects of marijuana on top of other drugs: Propranolol prevented the tachycardia and increase in forearm flow. Atropine increased pulse rate but not forearm flow or blood pressure. Epinephrine (adrenaline) induced greater heartbeat, to about 100 a minute.
>
> The increases in pulse rate and limb blood flow induced by cannabis seemed to involve "beta-adrenergic vascular mechanisms" for there were no such responses after marijuana-smoking by subjects pretreated with propranolol, a "beta-adrenergic blocker." On top of marijuana, treatment with atropine or anesthetics containing epinephrine could enhance and prolong a patient's tachycardia for "a dangerously long period."[14]

"Marihuana may affect the heart, and its repeated use may have cumulative effect." And if that is the case, long-term use "could prove to be detrimental to health." Wisconsin pharmacologists Kochar and Hosko came to that conclusion (1973) after taking electrocardiograms of seven young men given THC.

Before consuming the drug, by ingestion, the subjects all had normal electrocardiograms. After they took substantial doses of THC, changes appeared in tracings of six out of seven men, abnormal changes in three. Only two never had smoked marijuana and they showed no changes aside from pulse increases. The heaviest smoker developed "PVCs, a potentially serious change." The first two subjects tested, weekly users, generated tracings that resembled the pattern seen in cases of inflammation or injury to the heart membrane. So startling were the changes in the first subject that the two investigators cut the dose of THC by one-fourth in the remaining six subjects.[15]

JAMA, the American Medical Association's journal, editorialized in an issue that featured the Kochar-Hosko report: "Though the primary target of addictive psychoactive substances is the brain, the heart does not always remain unmolested. It may become involved directly, as in alcohol cardiomyopathy, or indirectly, as in bacterial endocarditis of heroin addicts. Evidence is accumulating that even marihuana, which causes no apparent cardiac distress, does not spare the heart. . . .

"Is the effect of the drug cumulative? If it is, then cardiovascular involvement in habitual, heavy, marihuana smokers may become a cause for concern." For the time being, however, the editorial cautioned against overreading the electrocardiograms in cannabis users and misdiagnosing heart ailments where none existed.[16]

Each subject received THC in flavored corn oil twice and just the oil five times, not knowing which was which. Small and large THC doses were given (0.2 and 0.3 mg/kg, except one 0.4) at least four days apart, the small dose said to be roughly equivalent to the amount of THC delivered by the smoking of a marijuana cigarette.

Following consumption of large doses, pulse rates increased in all subjects except one, a once-a-week smoker, who showed no changes at all. Two others who used marijuana weekly showed S-T-segment and T-wave changes, which "simulate pericarditis or an epicardial injury pattern and may be due to a direct effect of THC on the myocardium."

After taking a large dose, a subject who had smoked marijuana about three times a week developed the PVCs, five per minute; and one who had smoked it only three times in the past three years showed only an increase in heart rate. All abstained for two weeks before the study.

The above effects appeared in electrocardiograms taken 2½ hours after consumption of THC. Twelve hours after, the increased heart rate had persisted in five subjects; the other changes had reversed. Nobody felt any cardiac symptoms.

The study was conducted in 1971 at Wood Veterans Administration Medical Center, Milwaukee, where Dr. Kochar was then a research fellow (and later associate chief of staff for education and an internal medicine specialist). Dr. Hosko (Ph.D.) was with the Medical College of Wisconsin, Milwaukee.[17]

The smoking of marijuana by angina pectoris patients before exercising substantially hastened attacks. California physicians Aronow and Cassidy reported this finding in *The New England Journal of Medicine* (1974). In earlier studies, Dr. Aronow had found tobacco cigarettes producing such effects.

Testing ten middle-aged patients, they told each to smoke one marijuana cigarette and then "bicycle." On the average, the marijuana cut nearly in half the subjects' usual exercise time before the onset of angina pectoris. Substituting a placebo cigarette (inactive marijuana) also decreased the time, but only by a twelfth.

The doctors theorized that each type of cigarette caused carbon monoxide in the smoker to rise, interfering with delivery of oxygen to the heart muscle. In addition the active marijuana raised blood pressure and heart rate, probably increasing the demand for oxygen. The demand exceeded the supply of oxygen, bringing the chest pains earlier after less exertion.

Smoking one marijuana cigarette caused a 48 percent decrease in exercise time until the onset of angina pectoris; the placebo brought a 9 percent decrease. There were increases in resting heart rate, systolic and diastolic blood pressures (sitting), and venous carboxyhemoglobin after marijuana smoking. The placebo too increased the carboxyhemoglobin.

The subjects, mean age of forty-seven, each had been smoking a pack of tobacco cigarettes daily and none had ever smoked marijuana before. All suffered stable angina pectoris with evidence of severe coronary-artery disease. They gave consent after being informed of the risks. Each inhaled ten puffs of smoke from a marijuana cigarette (about 20 mg of THC) and, at another time (in double-blind manner), ten puffs from a placebo.[18]

Dr. Aronow was chief of cardiovascular research and professor of medicine at the University of California, Irvine, and chief of the Cardiovascular Section at the Long Beach Veterans Administration Medical Center. Dr. Cassidy was respectively assistant professor of medicine and a staff cardiologist at those institutions.

Bernstein and fellow scientists at the Harvard Medical School, in a broad pair of studies (1974 and 1976), came up with an array of pertinent observations of forty-seven marijuana smokers who could smoke as much as they wanted during three weeks of voluntary hospitalization.

Posture and tolerance both modified the effects of marijuana smoking. Generally marijuana diminished the blood pressure somewhat, especially lowering the systolic pressure with subjects standing. While they stood, the tachycardia or accelerated pulse usually caused by marijuana was especially pronounced. With the buildup of drug, came a lessening of the tachycardic effects.

Relatively fast pulse and somewhat low blood pressure tended to persist throughout the three-week smoking period (based on comparison with five-day nonsmoking periods that preceded and followed it). Occasionally some subjects reacted to marijuana with higher pressure and lower pulse.

In the first study, electrocardiograms recorded some irregular heart rhythms in all subjects and some premature beats in two subjects. In that study "we found the physical performance level of our subjects to be generally below what one would expect normally for healthy young men."

These were among the findings in blood pressure, electrocardiograms, and tolerance in the first study, using ten "heavy users" and ten "casual users" in Boston City Hospital:

Blood pressure: Lowest pressures were measured within an hour after smoking, when systolic pressures of six heavy users and two casual users in the standing position fell at least 20 millimeters. This was "probably due to the vasodilator [blood vessel-expanding] action of the drug, not adequately compensated for by increased heart rate." Three casual users had some occasional increases in systolic pressure following smoking. In such cases, the theory was that the tachycardia, increasing the cardiac output, overrode the effect of vasodilation.

Electrocardiograms: Smoking triggered "minimal" effects. One subject had premature atrial contractions and another had premature ventricular contractions. Many "prominent sinus arrhythmias" were observed.

Tolerance: When successive marijuana cigarettes were smoked in a short time, each succeeding cigarette raised the pulse a lesser degree. Moreover, tachycardic responses often were less pronounced in the latter part of the three-week smoking period than in the beginning part.[19]

Among comparable findings in the second study, using fifteen "heavy users" and twelve "casual users" in McLean Hospital, Belmont, Massachusetts, were these:

Blood pressure: During the smoking weeks, measurements were quite variable, tending to be a little low, particularly systolic pressure and in the standing position. During actual smoking, the general trend was to somewhat lower systolic pressure and slightly elevated diastolic pressure, although occasionally the former climbed too.

Electrocardiograms: No abnormalities were observed, but in view of the findings in the previous study and those of other researchers, "a history of marijuana use may be helpful in understanding an otherwise puzzling cardiac rhythm disturbance in a healthy young individual with no other signs of heart disease."

Tolerance: Sometimes the pulse hardly increased following smoking, or it even dropped, especially when a subject had been smoking multiple marijuana cigarettes within a relatively short time. In such a subject, the pulse-rate increase with each successive cigarette tended to diminish.[20]

In contrast to the speeding heart and increased or unchanged resting blood pressure seen after single doses, prolonged, frequent THC ingestion in large doses resulted in slowing of the heart rate and lowering of the blood pressure in hospitalized volunteers in San Francisco.

Medical doctors Benowitz and Jones (1975) dispensed THC capsules to a dozen healthy young men every four hours, night and day, for eighteen to twenty days. The doctors discovered that the drugging had resulted in the development of tolerance, not only to more THC ingestion but to marijuana smoking too. Also, they drew abnormal circulatory reactions to various maneuvers, which suggested disturbance in the functioning of the sympathetic nervous system.

> Before getting THC, each subject smoked a marijuana cigarette, whereupon each one's heart rate increased (mean increase: forty-five beats). After several days of ingestion of up to 210 mg of THC a day, modest but significant decreases in systolic and diastolic blood pressure and heart rate occurred with subjects supine.
>
> Standing brought clearly low blood pressures. The pressures sank to the point where the subjects grew dizzy and two of them fainted. But after some days of continued THC consumption, the low pressures on standing disappeared, while plasma volumes increased markedly. Body weights increased during the drug period, plunging afterward. Heart rates dropped from an average of about sixty-eight beats per minute before THC ingestion to about sixty-one a couple of weeks into the THC period. After drug treatment stopped, blood pressures were back to normal within one day, pulses within one week.
>
> "A striking observation is the development of marked tolerance to the tachycardia produced by smoked marijuana as a result of prolonged ingestion of oral THC," Neal L. Benowitz and Reese T. Jones reported. Cross-tolerance between smoked and oral cannabis was tested by periodic dispensing of marijuana cigarettes.
>
> "Impaired circulatory responses to standing, exercise, Valsalva maneuver, and cold pressor testing" (the hand placed in ice water) suggested to the physicians an inability of the sympathetic nervous system to function properly.
>
> In explaining the opposite reactions seen in different experiments, they offered a hypothesis that THC has two effects on man's sympathetic nervous system, "producing excitation with single doses and inhibition with prolonged administration."
>
> The subjects, all experienced marijuana smokers (aged twenty to twenty-seven), spent thirty days in a research ward of San Francisco's Langley Porter Neuropsychiatric Institute. Pre-THC observations of each subject served as his control.
>
> Cardiovascular examination was made about two hours after each 8 A.M. dose. The dose (likened to the average in the previous, Boston experiment) was acknowledged to be high for Americans but "not beyond what is smoked or ingested in India, Afghanistan, or Jamaica."[21]

A combination of "social (moderate) doses of alcohol and marijuana" brought severe distress to experimental subjects in Boston. The results led Doctors Sulkowski and Vachon to caution (1977) that "it could be dangerous for some individuals under certain conditions, e.g., in the presence of cardiac or central nervous system disorders." They knew of no treatment for the reactions, which included nausea, instability of the autonomic nervous system, impaired behavior, and psychological pain.

Four of seven subjects, each taking a screwdriver cocktail followed in an hour by a marijuana cigarette, developed the nausea within a few minutes and threw up. Others could barely move for hours. Heart rates of six increased between 35 and 60 beats per minute. However, one man's heart rate dropped from 150 to 36 beats as he lay supine; it rose when he sat up.

"The same variable pattern was noted for blood pressure, but with more moderate increases. Intense reddening of the conjunctivae, marked skin pallor, and profuse cold sweating were also observed. The subjective distress and physiological signs dissipated slowly in 3 to 4 hours," reported the physicians, psychiatry teachers at Boston University School of Medicine.

The subjects were men, aged twenty to twenty-nine, screened for health. They were all "experienced social users" of both marijuana and alcohol who combined them often to increase the "high" despite nauseating results. The drink contained 1 g/kg of ethanol in orange juice; the cigarette, 18 mg of THC. Subjects got three combined treatments (in random order), but in one treatment they smoked just placebo marijuana and in another the drink contained only a smell of alcohol.[22]

* * *

Manno et al. in Indianapolis had reported (1971) that pulse rates and eye congestion of twelve male volunteers increased as doses of smoked marijuana increased, and that adding alcohol further enhanced both the magnitude and duration of each effect.[23]

Thirty men, regular pot users, smoked 11,170 marijuana cigarettes in sixty-four days for the benefit of research. Among results: the development of tolerance to both the objective and subjective effects of marijuana, as seen in the lessening of the tachycardia and the subject's "high." The tolerance developed within two or three weeks of daily smoking. Marijuana induced milder and shorter lived effects on heart rate and subjective state in the heaviest smokers than in the lighter smokers, reported Nowlan and Cohen (1977).[24]

This research was part of a comprehensive, ninety-four-day cannabis study at the University of California at Los Angeles. Within that framework, Shapiro and Tashkin performed a variety of tests suggesting that marijuana smoking (at least by healthy, regular smokers) increases the amount of blood discharged by the heart each minute, accomplishing this by causing the heart to beat faster, rather than pump harder. In addition, marijuana usually lessened the amount of exercise that a man could do before wearying.

Shapiro and Tashkin measured cardiac output and left-ventricular function in seventeen men at various times during the ninety-four-day study by simultaneous echocardiograms, phonocardiograms, electrocardiograms, and pulse records. A "slight tolerance" developed to the effect of marijuana on heart rate.

On the average the cardiac output and pulse increased 28 percent and 30 percent, respectively, immediately after smoking. Fifteen minutes after, the stroke volume (amount of blood ejected by the left ventricle at each beat) dropped while other indices of left-ventricular performance did not change. In six men, cardiac output was measured also by the injection of green dye into one arm and sampling of blood from the other. Right after they smoked, output increased by a fourth, pulse rate rose by half, and pressure hardly changed. "Therefore the increase in cardiac output after marijuana smoking seems to be related solely to an increase in heart rate."

In eleven experienced marijuana smokers, injections of propranolol (a beta blocker) failed to prevent tachycardia. So the researchers disagreed with those (like Beaconsfield et al.) who attributed the tachycardia to "beta-adrenergic" stimulation.

Ten men did increasingly difficult exercises on a bicycle ergometer. Pulse rate rose accordingly to as high as about 180 beats a minute. Heart rate always was greater after marijuana than after placebo at given work loads. Eight of the ten became exhausted and quit sooner with marijuana. The other two exercised longer with marijuana. "Possibly, premature achievement of a maximum heart rate during exercise after marijuana smoking diminishes peak exercise performance."[25]

The smoking of one marijuana cigarette brought immediate increases in left-ventricular performance as well as heart rate, followed soon by a large discharge of norepinephrine. The experiment was performed on healthy young men. But such excessive hormonal discharge "could adversely affect patients with heart disease," according to Gash of San Diego and three other medical doctors (1978).

> The subjects, who were not heavy cannabis users, each smoked placebo (inert marijuana) on one occasion and regular marijuana (6 mg of THC) on another. After the latter was smoked, both heart rate and left ventricular performance (tested by ultrasound measures of internal diameter shortening) increased at once and remained high for at least an hour in fourteen men examined.
>
> Within half an hour after the marijuana smoking, the levels of norepinephrine in the blood plasma also rose, remaining high for at least two hours; four of the fourteen plus four others were so tested.
>
> "These marihuana-induced increases in plasma norepinephrine and the tachycardia are similar to alterations that occur after smoking nicotine-containing cigarettes and could be harmful to patients with cardiovascular disease," wrote Dr. Arnold Gash, cardiologist of the Department of Medicine, University of California at San Diego, and the others.[26]

The elevated heart rate induced by marijuana rose much higher after exercise, and marijuana "severely retarded the return of the heart rate to resting levels." Because of the drug, it appears that the heart must work harder while less oxygen is delivered to it. Thus those who exercise after smoking marijuana may have to pay "a physiologic price," not yet known.

This view was expressed by Avakian and coworkers (1979) at the University of California at Santa Barbara (Institute of Environmental Stress and Department of Ergonomics). They had six young men smoke marijuana and pedal a bicycle machine. When under the influence of marijuana, all subjects felt the exercise to be most strenuous.

> Regular users of marijuana but not tobacco, the subjects (aged twenty-one to twenty-seven) abstained for twenty-four hours before the experiment. Every subject at different times (1) smoked marijuana, (2) smoked placebo, and (3) did not smoke. In each case there was a rest period, treatment or control, a fifteen-minute exercise period, and a fifteen-minute recovery period.
>
> During rest, the average marijuana pulse rate stood at 34 percent (twenty-six beats) above control. Five minutes after exercise, the difference had widened to as much as 51 percent. At the end of the recovery period, the marijuana heart rate remained 37 percent above the control heart rate.
>
> Under control conditions, the pulse rate returned to normal by the end of the recovery period.
>
> Marijuana showed no effect on pulmonary ventilation, oxygen consumption, or blood pressure, Edward V. Avakian, research physiologist, and the others reported.[27]

Dr. Adam Sulkowski, psychiatrist and teacher at Boston University, has studied more than 100 users of marijuana between the ages of eighteen and thirty. He told us that they would suffer heart problems unless they quit the habit.

Every user displays some reliable signs of indulgence, Dr. Sulkowski said, citing increase in heart rate and reddening of the eyes. The first is a dose-related symptom, which can be used to figure roughly how much marijuana one has smoked, though users do not seem to pay attention to it. (This is something we too have observed. While all that furious cardiac activity goes on, the typical smoker paradoxically feels lulled into a sense of security.)

Reacting to a dose of 10 to 20 milligrams of THC, "in many cases the heart rate goes to 130 to 150 beats per minute, the normal being 60 to 70 beats per minute. It is unusual, but it can go as high as 170 to 180 beats per minute. When marijuana is smoked, the heart rate increases within five to ten minutes. In oral doses it takes twenty-five to thirty minutes. . . .

"The chest pain commonly felt by chronic marijuana users may be due to the overstimulation of the heart muscle. As marijuana smokers age, they will have heart problems unless they stop smoking."

3

Lethality

The question asked by *JAMA*—"Is the effect of the drug cumulative?"—
was, in effect, answered affirmatively by Professor W. D. M. Paton of
Oxford University, a prominent British pharmacologist and physician,
in U.S. congressional testimony (1974).

He stressed the fact that THC and other cannabinoids are highly soluble in fat, dissolving only slightly in water. Such solubility gives a substance like THC an affinity for the fatty material in cell membranes, he
added. According to the professor, several results follow from that physical property: passage of the cannabinoid into body, brain, and every cell;
its tendency to persist in the body, because it sits in the fatty areas that
the body's watery system cannot wash out; and its accumulation in those
areas.

"Fat affinity and cumulation in the body in themselves are not necessarily harmful. . . . The fundamental test is a biological one, whether
toxicity is cumulative.

"This has been found to be the case for a mouse; it requires one-tenth
as much cannabis to kill if given in repeated daily doses as if given in a
single dose. Similar cumulative toxicity has been found for THC and
in other animals and by more delicate methods than lethality. Infer-
ences must not be drawn, therefore from responses to single exposures
to the likely effect of repeated doses."

Turning from mouse to man, Professor Paton cautioned that cannabis could prove fatal by its changes in the heart of a chronic user and
by its action in dilating blood vessels. Under some circumstances, he
said, these in turn could lead to heart failure or a drain of blood from
the brain, respectively.

". . . One wishes that all cannabis users were aware of these possibilities."

> Paton pointed to three ways in which cannabis could "cause or facilitate death
> although proof in a particular case would be difficult.
> "A. It produces a considerable tachycardia, and this may be associated with
> electrocardiographic changes and ventricular extrasystoles. It is not at all impos-
> sible that this, in unfavorable circumstances in a chronic user, could progress to
> ventricular fibrillation and death.

"B. It causes a dilation of peripheral blood vessels, corresponding to the hypotensive action in animals. This probably underlies the 'fainting attacks' reported in the literature as well as by my own contacts. This involves 'postural hypotension,' in which the capacity of the body to correct for the upright position fails, and the blood drains from the brain. As with other hypotensive drugs, if the subject could not become horizontal either deliberately or by falling—for example, because he was in a chair—blood supply to the brain might fail.

"C. Cannabis, chiefly because of its cannabidiol content, can potentiate and prolong the action of barbiturates—as well as other drugs used in medical treatment. This could mean that a nonlethal dose of barbiturate became lethal."[28]

Tachycardia is an acceleration of the heart rate. *Ventricular extrasystoles* are extra heartbeats, originating in the ventricles. *Ventricular fibrillation* is a condition where the ventricular contraction becomes uncoordinated and cardiac output fails. *Hypotension* is abnormally low blood pressure.

✻ ✻ ✻

According to scientist Harris Rosenkrantz (1982), death of experimental animals given acute lethal doses usually results from cardiac arrest or respiratory failure. The former appears to be the major cause of death, inasmuch as artificial respiration only delays death from such doses. In acute lethality tests, the lower the animal species, the greater the potency of THC; for most other effects, potency is directly related to body size of the species, rodents being much more resistant than monkeys.

In chronic animal studies, many times lethality is delayed. Animals may survive initial doses but then die suddenly weeks later—possibly from accumulation of THC or metabolites in the body.[29]

Paton's warning may sound odd. Many others—particularly those wishing to illustrate how mild and inoffensive the drug is—have declared that taking cannabis cannot be fatal or that nobody has ever died from it.

"It is impossible, in my opinion, for a person to take a lethal overdose of cannabis," said Dr. Lester Grinspoon of Harvard Medical School (1980), in describing the "slight" physiological effects of the drug. "In the long period over which this drug has been used, there has not been a reliably documented instance of death from marijuana overdose, and this is because the amount needed for intoxication (the effective dose) is so much less than the amount needed to produce death (the lethal dose)."[30]

While marijuana smoke and oral THC often have proven fatal to test animals, truly enough, cannabis does not rank high on the list of human poisons. But reports of human cannabis fatalities are not unknown, though they are rare. Their reliability is a matter of opinion. Paton found the following Belgian case study to be "rather convincing."

A report, by members of the Department of Toxicology of the State University of Ghent, of "a fatal intoxication . . . due to cannabis smoking" appeared in a Belgian journal in 1969. A twenty-three-year-old man was found dead one morning, presumably in his room, along with large amounts of cannabis herb and resin plus a water pipe. The autopsy showed no evidence of either a natural or a violent death, so they performed a classical toxicological analysis.

Tests of bodily fluids and tissues proved negative for alcohol, barbiturates, narcotics, and a host of other drugs and poisons. Only one chemical turned up (by the process of thin-layer chromatography): cannabinol, an ingredient of cannabis. Having examined the samples five days after death, the toxicologists said, they recognized that other cannabis compounds apparently had oxydized and disappeared.[31]

Another 1969 report, from Istanbul University, concerned an American boy of sixteen found dead in a dormitory in Turkey. No explanation could be found for his death, outside of a toxicological analysis showing the presence of compounds of *asrar*—cannabis—in internal organs and urine.[32]

Physician Gurbakhsh S. Chopra, of Calcutta, India, contended that an enormous dose of *charas*, pure cannabis resin or hashish, could cause death. As an example (in a United Nations periodical, 1971) he recalled two prisoners in the central jail in Lahore in 1928 who had been addicted to the substance but were forced to forgo it upon being locked up.

"They suddenly obtained a large amount of the drug and consumed larger doses than they had been accustomed to taking. The effect was a rapid onset of coma, vomiting, strenuous breathing, marked congestion of conjunctiva, and coldness, followed by collapse," wrote Dr. Chopra. The postmortem examination showed only marked congestion of the internal organs, he added (without specifying his role).[33]

Older literature describes three other fatal cases in India in which large cannabis overdoses were blamed (1880, 1904).[34]

A few witnesses before the Indian Hemp Drugs Commission (1893–94) referred to cases of "sudden death" after a deep draw on a pipe of the drug. The commission tried to probe some cases and did not consider the causes of death satisfactorily explained. However, in its report, it theorized that "a very prolonged pull at a *chillum* [pipe] might possibly cause spasm of the glottis, producing asphyxia, or the products of the destructive distillation of the resin might cause paralysis of the respiratory centre or of the heart."[35]

Dr. Gabriel G. Nahas, New York physician and scientist, mentioned several cases of accidental deaths of children who had smoked hashish from water pipes in Egypt, his native land (but he gave no details, 1973).[36]

A French soldier in Paris was found in a coma with no apparent cause, according to a French medical publication (1971). When he awoke four days later, he admitted having smoked nine or ten pipefuls of a hashish-tobacco mixture. He said that his intention was to commit suicide and that this method of taking one's life had been used by others in the drug culture of western Europe.[37]

Walton T. Roth, M.D., of Stanford University, California, and fellow investigators (1973) reported this incident among several cases of fainting by experimental subjects given cannabis. A man of thirty-five smoked a marijuana cigarette, something he had done often without ill effects. Five minutes later "he complained of difficult breathing and an inability to see, and then suddenly fell from the chair to the floor." For a time he was "unresponsive" and neither pulse nor blood pressure could be detected. "The subject spontaneously revived after several minutes." (He remained intoxicated for two hours, with pulse and blood pressure somewhat elevated.)[38]

IMMUNITY
AND
RESISTANCE

☀   ☀

- *"I think it's a tonic. I'm much healthier than I would be if I didn't smoke it."* —Pete (chronic user and marijuana advocate)

- *"Brian is a very handsome young man, about six-three, weight a hundred eighty. Really likes his bod. He doesn't like to be sick. His mother and I kept reading about the loss of immune response when you smoke marijuana. We kept talking to him about that because he kept having infections. Every time he'd get a scratch, it would get infected and fester.*
    "He went through a year when he had bronchial infections, nasal infections, ear infections, three abscessed teeth—and we said, 'That's what's doing it' and he kept saying, 'Aah, you people don't know what you're talking about.'
    "But he really was upset about being sick all the time and was finally ready to try anything. So we said, 'Look, what have you go to lose? Why don't you quit smoking marijuana for three months? What's the big deal?'
    "He quit smoking marijuana for three months and he got well—no more infections. I don't know if that's what did it; he doesn't know but he believes that's what did it. It worked." —Bob, father of Brian (then sixteen, who had smoked marijuana for about fifteen months)

- *"I think I was much weaker healthwise. I got colds a lot more frequently."* —Steven (ex-user)

- *"Rick began smoking pot when his alcoholic father left home about a year and a half ago. He got into it heavily fast. For most of a year, Rick was smoking ten joints a day. He got into all kinds of trouble with his family and the law, and his mother asked that he be admitted to our live-in center.*

"*He got sick a lot. In one year's time of heavy pot use, he had colds, coughs, bad lung infections, chronic bronchitis, and severe chest pain with even mild exertion.*

"*After cutting way down on his pot use, he was sick less and generally felt better and his grades went up, but he was still so short-winded, he couldn't run a block. After three months of no pot use, he was able to enter a foot race and run six miles with no chest pain.*

"*His relationships with people improved. We noted that rather than instigating trouble at the center, he was more trustworthy and able to take responsibility.*" —Jenny, drug-rehabilitation counselor for Rick (then sixteen)

• "*If I was getting sick and I smoked marijuana, it seemed like it would bring my resistance down. I think smoking pot uses up vitamin C.*" —Joe (ex-user)

• "*I smoked pot off and on for the past three years. I couldn't see it did anything harmful to my health.*" —Horace (ex-user)

• "*My health has always been good.*" —Anna (ex-user)

1

Health And The Macrophage

Can cannabis lead to illness by weakening the immune system, the body's natural defenses against disease? Several laboratory findings raise the suspicion that it can. But some other studies fail to confirm those findings. Immunity, as much as any other facet of the cannabis story, has been marked by contradictory observations and scientific disagreement.

Experiments testing cannabis's effects on cells that battle intruders flourished in the early and mid-1970s. The first experiment of this sort (as far as we know) was reported in 1971 and dealt with the lung macrophage.

The macrophage is a type of cell in various bodily tissues that actively defends the body. It counterattacks invading organisms or particles and devours them. It consumes tumor cells and cellular debris too. In the lung, the macrophage stands in the front line of defense. Its main job is to stop anything breathed in that could cause disease, engulfing and absorbing it.

Scientists began in the sixties to study the effects of tobacco smoke on the defenses of the lungs. A 1969 New Mexico experiment used a technique called "lavage" (which rhymes with "mirage") to wash out material from the airways in order to examine the cells. More of the smokers' cells than the nonsmokers' cells were macrophages (93 percent compared to 63 percent). The theory was that more lung macrophages might be produced in smokers than in nonsmokers "because of the need to remove the inhaled products of cigarette smoke."[1]

In San Francisco Philip E. G. Mann, M.D., extended the study to marijuana. The same lavage technique was used to extract the material from the lungs. Working for over a year, Dr. Mann laboriously counted between 4,000 and 12,000 cells from each of ten subjects, measured cells, examined their structures, and tested their effectiveness.

He discovered "a significantly greater percentage of macrophages" among the cells washed from nonsmokers than those from smokers—the reverse of the findings in the tobacco study. Of four nonsmokers tested, 84 percent of their cells were macrophages; of six smokers studied, macrophages came to 63 percent (exactly the percentage for nonsmokers in the tobacco study).

The reduction in macrophages "may affect the capacity or character" of the marijuana smoker's defenses against inhaled organisms and particles, Dr. Mann wrote.

Even more difficult than tallying tens of thousands of cells (with the aid of an ordinary microscope) was studying the internal structures of different cells (by means of an electron microscope). Comparison of marijuana smokers' and nonsmokers' macrophages revealed differences in inclusions, objects taken in by cells. Most inclusions in the marijuana macrophages resembled those reported in tobacco smokers' macrophages.

Tests of macrophage effectiveness involved samples from tobacco smokers as well as marijuana smokers and nonsmokers. There was no difference in the ability of any of the three groups of macrophages to consume dead *Candida albicans*, an infectious, yeastlike fungus.

Comparison of macrophages from marijuana smokers and nonsmokers showed no significant differences in cell size, volume of cellular and other material, or the number of multinuclear macrophages recovered. The sediment of marijuana smokers included a greater percentage of other cell types besides macrophages (red and white blood cells and epithelium).

Inclusions in macrophages from the marijuana smokers contained distinctive, "highly electron-dense zones" and other features not found in nonsmokers' macrophages but reported seen in tobacco smokers' macrophages: many "dense angular zones," large "pale areas," and "curving, fiber-shaped clear areas." Needle-shaped structures and small pale areas appeared often in the marijuana smokers' macrophages but seldom in those from the nonsmokers.

Macrophages from marijuana and tobacco smokers showed no difference in ability to adhere to glass, although each group of macrophages showed greater glass adhesion than those of nonsmokers.

The lavage procedure involved anesthetizing the trachea, inserting a catheter, directing it into a segment of the bronchus with the aid of a fluoroscope, washing the segment with saline solution, recovering the fluid, and gathering the sediment by means of a centrifuge.

For the structural study macrophages were obtained in this way from eight marijuana smokers and four nonsmokers, each group half men and half women, all in their twenties. The macrophage count used two fewer marijuana smokers. The functional study used macrophages from seven marijuana smokers, eleven nonsmokers, and nine tobacco smokers. Mean age of the latter two groups was fifty-four. Macrophages from fifteen of them were lavaged from lungs removed in surgery.

Dr. Mann, an anesthesiologist, conducted the work at San Francisco's Mt. Zion Hospital, assisted by colleague Dr. Theodore Finley, who developed the lavage procedure, and Dr. Allen B. Cohen of the University of California Medical Center.[2] (A decade later, Mann was working in anesthesia at Kaiser-Permanente Medical Center in San Rafael, California.)

2

Kif in the Rif

Kif is the Moroccan term for cannabis. People in Morocco's Rif, a coastal mountain region south of Gibraltar, smoke it heavily in pipes.

In 1971 and 1972 Doctors Gabriel Nahas and Phillip Zeidenberg, of Columbia University, and Claude Lefebure, French ethnologist, traveled to that region to survey cannabis smoking. A Moroccan health official informed Dr. Zeidenberg that heavy users were more susceptible to tuberculosis, a major public health problem there. The official even quoted a well-known expression, *"Kif* makes a bed for tuberculosis." Of course, poor living conditions may have contributed to the susceptibility. But the people appeared to be in a state of "general physical deterioration" seemingly related to chronic cannabis smoking, in Dr. Nahas's view.

This observation, he recalled later, led him to look into the effects of the drug on the immune system. Egyptian-born Nahas was research professor of anesthesiology at Columbia University's College of Physicians and Surgeons. A physiologist and pharmacologist, he had spent decades studying in laboratories the effects of different drugs on bodily functions.

Back from Morocco, Nahas got together with a French anatomy professor visiting the United States, Daniel Zagury from Reims, who specialized in studying lymphocytes, white blood cells that fight disease. The latter would use mice in his laboratory to see what effect, if any, marijuana had on those cells and their process of division.

Zagury and coworkers injected mice with THC and collected and incubated their lymphocytes. Additional THC stimulated the lymphocytes to grow and divide. In contrast, THC had no effect when added to cultured lymphocytes from five undrugged mice.

"Our conclusion was that THC acted as a stimulant to lymphocyte activity," Nahas wrote.

> The mice got three small injections in three weeks. Lymphocytes were collected from the spleens of five rodents. When extra THC was added, it appeared as though the lymphocytes had taken up defense against the THC.

The experiment had been designed to test a hypothesis involving tolerance. It was known that animals became more tolerant to THC as drugging proceeded. Could the immune system have something to do with it? The experiment seemed to give a positive answer, but later experiments contradicted this one.[3]

The next step was to find out the effects of THC on human lymphocytes. Nahas collaborated with immunologists Nicole Suciu-Foca and Jean-Pierre Armand as well as cell geneticist Akira Morishima.

Armand took blood from several Columbia University staff members who smoked marijuana several times a week. The lymphocytes from the marijuana smokers displayed a lower growth activity than that of the nonsmokers' lymphocytes.

"This was a surprise!" Nahas recalled. They had expected greater activity from lymphocytes of marijuana smokers, based on Zagury's experiment. But exactly the reverse turned up. The experiments differed in several ways: subject, exposure, drug, method. The first exposed mice briefly to THC. The second involved humans who had smoked marijuana for an average of four years.

Nahas and colleagues obtained 132 more volunteers, through ads, and repeated the experiment. The volunteers, all male, included 51 chronic marijuana smokers, aged sixteen to thirty-five; the rest were nonsmokers of marijuana, twenty to seventy-two.

The lymphocytes' activity was gauged by a standard test of immunity: blast (formative cell) transformation. It entailed taking blood samples, isolating the lymphocytes, incubating them with substances that normally stimulate cell growth, adding radioactive thymidine, and finally measuring the amount of thymidine incorporated into the lymphocytes. The chemical thymidine serves as a cellular building block.

In comparison to nonsmokers of marijuana, the smokers as a group had a two-fifths lower thymidine count, and therefore a substantially diminished lymphocyte response. About three-fourths of the marijuana smokers showed what appeared to be decreases in "cell-mediated immunity" when their lymphocytes were contrasted with those of nonsmokers.

Dr. Suciu-Foca compared the response to that found in cancer patients and organ transplant patients. The results were rather similar. Surgeons have given transplant patients drugs to inhibit their immune defenses so that their bodies do not reject the organs.

The scientists studied the T-lymphocyte, one of the two kinds of active lymphocyte. Also called T-cell (carrying out "cell-mediated" immunity), it seeks to consume or kill cancer cells, viruses, poisons, or foreign bodies—perhaps including, alas, organ transplants. The other kind is the B-lymphocyte, or B-cell, which works by making an antibody, a pugnacious protein that recognizes a specific enemy, such as a species of bacteria. (This is "antibody-mediated" or "humoral" immunity.)

Much as an invaded country needs to mobilize, the body has to increase its army of white blood cells rapidly when attacked by germs or other alien substances. The cell reproduces by dividing in two, after reaching its limit of growth by absorbing essential chemicals from outside. It was the amount of radioactively marked chemical absorbed by the lymphocyte cells that was gauged in this and several other experiments in order to test the fitness of those lymphocytes.

Dr. Suciu-Foca and Dr. Morishima worked for Columbia University's College of Physicians and Surgeons. The former was chief of the Laboratory of Clinical Immunology. She had perfected experimental methods used in the cannabis studies. The latter was a pediatrics professor. Armand worked with the Cancer Institute of the University of Toulouse, France (Nahas's medical alma mater).

The researchers secured their subjects from advertisements in The Village Voice. The marijuana smokers, median age twenty-two, had smoked at least weekly (an average of four times a week) for at least a year (an average of four years) and taken no other drugs, apart from tobacco and alcohol by some. The control group of eighty-one "healthy volunteers" had a median age of forty-four.

Samples of venous blood were collected and placed in a centrifuge to spin the lymphocytes from the red blood cells.

Together with a nutrient plus three mitogens, the lymphocytes went on a transparent plate and into an oven to be incubated for three days. The mitogens, substances that stimulate cell growth and division, were pokeweed (a weed), PHA (phytohemagglutinin), and MLC (mixed lymphocyte culture, made from lymphocytes of normal subjects, treated with an antibiotic to kill cells but not their property as antigens).

In the last hours of incubation, the workers added thymidine containing tritium, a radioactive isotope of hydrogen. The compound thymidine is incorporated into DNA (deoxyribonucleic acid, essential to cell division); the radioactivity serves to trace the thymidine's movement.

Then they "harvested" the cultures and washed away everything but the cells. A MASH (multiple automatic sample harvester) sucked the lymphocytes into test tubes, preparing them for a scintillation counter, a device giving a printed record of radioactivity. By measuring the radioactivity, they could compare the amount of thymidine taken up by the different groups of lymphocytes.

Following are the measurements of radioactivity for each group of lymphocytes when treated with MLC, in counts per minute (rounded):

Marijuana smokers—16,000.
Nonmarijuana controls—26,000.
Cancer patients (primary tumors)—15,000.
Transplant patients—12,000.
Uremic poisoning patients—12,000.[4]

In one of several variations, rats and humans shared the spotlight. Lymphocytes from each species were treated as in the other experiments except that THC went into the cultures, not into the creatures. Cell growth in each (as measured by thymidine incorporation) was restrained partially or totally, depending on the THC concentration, Armand, Hsu, and Nahas reported.[5]

The effect of other cannabinoids besides THC on lymphocytes from human nonusers figured in an experiment by Nahas, Morishima, Dr. Bernard Desoize, and Joy Hsu. They cultured the lymphocytes with several substances isolated from marijuana, adding two chemicals to stimulate the lymphocytes.

They found the ability of the lymphocytes to grow and divide inhibited, partially or almost completely; the extent of the inhibition depended on dose. But even more important: THC was not the only cannabinoid to suppress the growth of those cells, which are necessary for immunity. Four psycho-inactive substances in marijuana produced similar effects. In fact, they seemed even stronger than THC in their suppression.

". . . THC is 'psychoactive,' impairs psychomotor performance, and is considered the major biologically active substance of marihuana. In this experiment it is made clear that not only is THC immuno-suppressive but that also the two nonactive substances in marihuana CBN and CBD have a similar effect," Nahas testified in 1974.

The casual user of marijuana would not have the amount of cannabinoid in his system corresponding to the dose that produced those test-tube changes. But the concentration of cannabinoid in the blood plasma and tissues of the long-term, chronic marijuana user could reach that level, allowing for cannabis's cumulative effects, according to the experimenters.

They tested aspirin, caffeine, and alcohol by the same method. It took between twenty and fifty times more aspirin or caffeine than cannabinoid to inhibit the growth and division of the lymphocytes. Alcohol was not even in the same ball park: 10,000 times more alcohol than cannabinoid had no inhibiting effect at all. A concentration of that sort in a human would be fatal.

Besides delta-9- and delta-8-THC, the experiments used natural cannabidiol, cannabinol, cannabichromene, and cannabicyclol. They were mixed with blood serum, in different concentrations. At different times, PHA and MLC were used to stimulate growth and division of the lymphocytes; both gave similar results.

The researchers employed the blast transformation test, with variations. THC inhibited thymidine incorporation by the lymphocytes; or, put another way, it appeared to thwart DNA formation. The degree of inhibition (varying from a tenth to nearly total) depended on the concentration of blood serum in the culture medium (0.5 to 10 percent). Inhibition was nearly complete in fifteen minutes.

The same concentrations of THC restrained incorporation of uridine and leucine (apparently into RNA and protein) as well as thymidine. Complete figures were not reported, but a graph indicated that concentrations of cannabidiol and cannabinol somewhat lower than the concentration of THC would stop thymidine incorporation induced by PHA after three days of culture. A much higher concentration of aspirin or caffeine was needed to achieve that result; the two had about equal potency. The chart was not large enough to accommodate alcohol.[6]

When a scientist has something to say, he is expected to say it abstrusely in a scientific journal that few read except other scientists. Nahas displayed unorthodox conduct for a scientist. Vocal in his opposition to marijuana, he wrote a book warning of the "deceptive weed" and used the news media to try to make the public aware of his findings. Critics consequently shot down his scientific work as "biased."

A 1974 press release of his declared that "habitual marijuana smoking weakens the body's immunology defenses and inhibits the division of the cells that specialize in the defenses." He called the results of the 132-subject study "the first evidence that marijuana usage induces cellular damage in man."

The promarijuana lobby followed up with its own release, primarily attacking Nahas himself, his "prejudiced" book and his "self-righteous fanaticism." It also gathered a few medical and scientific supporters for some more specific criticisms, such as the "lack of clinical evidence" that marijuana smokers were falling ill more often. Nahas did not deny this.

Later, at the Senate Judiciary Committee hearing on May 16, 1974, the counsel asked Nahas if he concluded from his experiments that marijuana suppressed immunity.

"Well, in the test tube, yes," he replied. As yet no facts linked marijuana smoking to, say, increased virus disease or cancer. It was just that the lymphocytes of marijuana smokers did not respond the way the lymphocytes of others did to the usual laboratory test of immunity.

Senator Gurney, the chairman, wanted clarification. Was Nahas saying there was no experimental proof that marijuana prevented resistance to disease? The latter replied, "There have not been enough actual observations. But if I were to bet personally, I would certainly bet that the incidence of disease in chronic marijuana smokers would be much greater than in those who do not smoke marijuana."[7]

✻   ✻   ✻

Nahas's five-page news release, issued on January 25, 1974, a week before the date of scientific publication of the large study, had secured press and broadcast attention and such headlines as "Marijuana Found to Weaken Defenses Against Sickness."[8]

A few weeks later contrary headlines appeared, such as "Experts dispute claim that pot leads to illness."[9] They arose from a ten-page news release issued from Washington, D.C., on March 8 by the National Organization for the Reform of

Marijuana Laws (NORML), a procannabis lobby. The first three and a half pages attacked Nahas himself. The first four "experts" quoted were all members of the NORML Advisory Board: Doctors Lester Grinspoon (Harvard psychiatrist and author of *Marijuana Reconsidered*), Norman Zinberg (chief of psychiatry at the Washingtonian Center for Addictions, Boston), Andrew Weil (author of *The Natural Mind*), and David E. Smith (director of the Haight-Ashbury Free Clinic, San Francisco).

Dr. Grinspoon, the medical community's foremost defender of cannabis, was quoted attacking Nahas's book *Marihuana: Deceptive Weed* as "psychopharmacologic McCarthyism."

While affirming that "Dr. Nahas's work deserves careful consideration," Dr. Zinberg made clear that he was not the one to give it. Describing Nahas's "long-held conviction" of marijuana's danger, a conviction that "has gone beyond simple prejudice," he said that if the laboratory findings conformed to reality, clinicians would have seen a deluge of infections among millions of young people passing joints around, surely in the colleges, where marijuana use included "over 50% of the population."

Dr. Weil, unconvinced that the impairment was caused by chronic marijuana smoking, called it "retrospective reasoning" to draw that conclusion by studying chronic marijuana smokers. "The only legitimate way to test a hypothesis is by prospective experiment," he said. Examine subjects, give some of them marijuana, then observe changes in the immune system. (He did not address the ethical problem of making drug users out of nonusers.)

Among others quoted were Dr. Thomas G. Wegmann, Harvard biologist, who criticized the lack of statistical analysis and low standard error, and Dr. R. Bjornsen of the University of Minnesota, who found the age difference of smokers and controls "inappropriate." (The Nahas scientific article did point out, however, that "an inverse correlation exists between cellular immunity," as reflected in laboratory tests, "and aging.") Maintaining that "some, and perhaps all" subjects had used other drugs (without saying how he knew), Dr. Bjornsen referred to a 1971 German study of leukocyte inhibition by aspirin and accused Nahas of "a willfully misleading thing" by failing to mention such studies (but cited no evidence for the accusation).[10]

* * *

Shortly Nahas did investigate other drugs. He wrote (in *Keep Off the Grass*) that while "all drugs added in large enough amounts will also produce cell damage," the effects of other drugs tested "nowhere matched the cellular damage done by THC." He and associates tried aspirin first, finding that it took ten to twelve tablets to depress lymphocyte replication.

Next, caffeine: "Since caffeine is rapidly inactivated by the body, it never reaches sufficient concentrations in tissues to produce a change in lymphocyte function. When we added alcohol in concentrations rarely reached in the bloodstream of man, the division of lymphocytes was not impaired. We even tried LSD and found that it too never reaches a high enough level in the tissues to cause cell damage *in vitro* [in the test tube]".

In a medical journal, a scientific pair from Rutgers University (New Jersey), Segelman and Segelman, suggested that the smoking of tobacco could have led to the same results (per a 1969 study by Vos-Brat and Rümke) and that the results could have been distorted if THC united with PHA, a mitogen.

The answer of Nahas et al. (in the same issue): the percentage of tobacco smokers was the same, 30 percent, in the marijuana group and in the control group.

"In addition, the greatest depression in lymphocyte transformation was observed in a 16-year-old high school student who had smoked marihuana, but not tobacco, daily for 2 years." But after he had abstained for a couple of months, his "blastogenic response" had risen to the level of the control group.

As to the question of the THC reacting with PHA: they had experimented by incubating the two for five hours and adding them to normal lymphocyte cultures. The "blastogenic response" was similar to that seen when THC and PHA were added without previous incubation. [11]

3

Dispute Over Lymphocytes

From other regions came scientific reports contradicting the human immunity studies. Similar experiments, using the same kind of test, yielded different observations.

"Our findings," reported White and colleagues in Washington, D.C. (1975), "differ completely from those of Nahas and his coworkers." Comparing a dozen marijuana smokers with an equal number of control subjects, they found essentially no difference in "blastogenic responses" between the groups.

Their results indicated, they said, "that long-term marihuana smoking had no significant effect on the functional status of T and B lymphocytes." In other words, chronic marijuana smoking did not seem to impair immunity. The reasons for the discrepancies are not clear.

White et al., at Washington's Veterans Administration Hospital, picked eleven men and a woman, aged nineteen to thirty-two, who had smoked marijuana at least once a week for a year, an average of 3.4 times weekly for 4.8 years. Twelve "matched control subjects," who said they never had smoked marijuana and who denied other forms of drug abuse, also were selected. All twenty-four were questioned and examined for health.

Cell transformation was tested, using PHA and pokeweed to stimulate T- and B-lymphocytes, respectively. The experimenters noted no significant difference between the smokers and controls. (T-lymphocytes from nine of twelve smokers showed greater counts than the controls. B-lymphocytes from seven of twelve smokers showed lower counts than the controls.)

They offered two possible explanations for the different results: The earlier investigators "did not describe the health status of their subjects." (Nahas et al. had described their fifty-one subjects only as "healthy volunteers.") Another possible variable was the time elapsed between smoking and blood sampling. "It is possible that impaired lymphocyte responses may be detectable only within a relatively short period after smoking," and the earlier subjects might have smoked more during that period. (In addition, the average frequency of marijuana use in the earlier study, "four times a week," was about 18 percent higher.)[12]

Likewise, in an experiment by Lau of Michigan and associates (1975), lymphocytes from eight chronic marijuana smokers taking capsules of crude marijuana extract responded normally to the same test. And when the lymphocytes were cultured without the usual chemical stimulant, they did even better than lymphocytes from controls.

> After taking placebos for six days, eight hospitalized young men consumed increasing doses of marijuana extract for four days and 210 mg of THC a day for two weeks. When PHA was used fully as a mitogen, no substantial difference could be found in the thymidine count between the same subjects at different times or between the subjects and controls (not described in the report but presumably nonsmokers).
>
> Without PHA, however, for some reason the marijuana cultures incorporated 1.4 to 1.8 times the amount of thymidine as control cultures (same subjects or others).
>
> R. Jane Lau of the University of Michigan and others concluded that "THC in doses of 210 mg/day orally does not inhibit lymphocyte responses to PHA."[13]
>
> Professor Hardin B. Jones criticized the study for its small number of smokers and controls and its use of unrefrigerated blood samples after time lags up to twenty-four hours, unlike Nahas's 1974 study, which it purportedly rebutted.[14]

Skin testing is a common index of immunity. A foreign substance is applied to a patient's skin and applied again at a later date. If the skin does not react, it indicates a possible failure of the immune system.

At the University of California at Los Angeles, the antigen DNCB was applied to upper arms of twenty-two young marijuana smokers. All twenty-two developed the normal sensitivity to it, for when the DNCB was reapplied, after two weeks, they all reacted with redness, hardening, or blistering of the skin.

For comparison, Silverstein and Lessin reviewed the skin-test records of sixty cancer patients in the same age range. One-fifth of them had failed to react to DNCB.

The pair wrote that skin testing "may be a better gauge of overall immunocompetence" than any currently used (1974) test-tube measure of lymphocyte function because "skin testing closely correlates to clinical prognosis in cancer patients. . . .

"Since responses were normal in the chronic marijuana users we tested, it would appear that chronic marijuana smoking does not produce a gross cellular immune defect that can be detected by skin testing."

> This experiment used no controls, but in addition to their review of the sixty skin-test records (at UCLA's Division of Oncology, Center for the Health Sciences) the researchers referred to pertinent published reports. These showed that 96 percent or 267 of 279 normal individuals and 70 percent or 384 of 548 cancer patients of all ages developed sensitivity to DNCB (2,4-dinitrochlorobenzene).
>
> Other antigens used were monilia, mumps, purified protein derivative, and Varidase. Seventeen subjects reacted to two or more, three subjects reacted to only one, and two subjects reacted to none.
>
> The ages of the subjects ranged from twenty-one to thirty. A "chronic marijuana user" regularly smoked it at least three times a week for a minimum of six months. He could use tobacco and alcohol but not other drugs.[15]
>
> Some scientific writers have downgraded the value of skin testing in cannabis research, Hardin B. Jones for one: The immune responses of skin cells "may not be affected by marijuana. Skin cells are exposed to much less THC than are blood cells."[16]
>
> Nahas wrote, in response to Dr. Silverstein's study, that "our findings indicated a *depressed*, not a suppressed immune response. And such a depressed response might not show up with a DNCB skin test."[17]

Thirteen young men who indulged regularly in cannabis and eight who abstained from it "did not appear to be clinically distinguishable." But clear differences emerged when a research team probed their immune systems with a variety of tests at an Indianapolis clinic.

"The most striking differences" between marijuana smokers and nonsmokers involved the ability of their PMN (polymorphonuclear leukocytes, white blood cells of a certain type) to consume dead yeast, reported Petersen, Lemberger, and others (1975). An average of only 58 percent of the smokers' PMN demonstrated such ability, compared with 90 percent from the nonsmoking group.

Furthermore, when those cells from smokers did display any appetite, "they were prone to engulf only one or two yeast cells, in contrast to cells from nonsmokers which would engulf numerous [yeast] cells until their shape was distorted." (Such gluttony is a healthy sign in PMN and other phagocytes, cells which also make meals of germs and miscellaneous debris.)

Several blood measurements evinced no difference between the two groups and blast transformation did not prove conclusive, but with another method (the rosette) T-lymphocyte levels of smokers clearly dropped.

The researchers judged that marijuana smoking "does appear to affect immune mechanisms" although they could not explain the "clinical significance" of their findings. The two groups had received medical examinations and appeared in equivalent states of health.

In the rosette method, sheep's red blood cells will rim lymphocytes when properly processed. "The mean percentage of T-lymphocytes found in the lymphocyte population of marihuana smokers was less than that found in nonsmokers." Individual smokers showed depressions as much as two-fifths below the norm. Meanwhile, the mean percentage of smokers' B-lymphocytes increased slightly.

"Lymphocytes obtained from marihuana smokers did not appear to be as responsive to mitogenic (PHA) stimulation as were the lymphocytes from nonsmokers." Comparison of the mean percentages revealed no statistical difference between the two groups, but large variance among individual smokers "suggests that some of the subjects did have an inhibition in the responsiveness of their [T] lymphocytes to mitogenic stimulation."

Immunoglobulin and complement levels, blood chemistries, and hematologic values from marijuana smokers did not seem to differ significantly from those of the control group.

The smokers, aged twenty-two to twenty-six, had used marijuana at least weekly for a minimum of one year. None had habitually used other drugs. Six of the controls never had smoked marijuana; none had used it in six months. Each group had some tobacco smokers. The twenty-one volunteers were studied as outpatients at the Lilly Clinic in Indianapolis.[18]

The seesaw continued up and down. We return briefly to the sweeping, ninety-four-day study at the University of California at Los Angeles. Among those voluntarily smoking marijuana daily for sixty-four consecutive days were a dozen healthy young subjects having their immune systems examined. The research team calculated B- and T-cell populations, lymphocyte responses to stimulation, and immunoglobulin levels. Immunoglobulins are protein molecules that act as antibodies, providing immunity against specific pathogens (microorganisms or substances that can cause disease).

T- and B-cells behaved similarly: the overall number of each sank at first but became normal by the end of the smoking period. However, two subjects ended with B-cell depressions. From start to finish, both serum immunoglobulins and test-tube responses of lymphocytes generally were normal. The number of marijuana cigarettes smoked daily did not affect the results.

The way the data started out led a spokesman prematurely to announce preliminary agreement with Nahas on T-lymphocytes.[19] But by the end, Dr. Gary S. Rachelefsky and coresearchers had to report (1976), "Our findings appear to dispute other reports describing an association between chronic marijuana smoking and decreased . . . immunity."

Why the contradictions, and why did the initial findings show depressed lymphocytes? As an explanation, they suggested "impurities or other chemicals incorporated into 'street' marijuana. None of the previous authors could be sure that their test subjects were not using any other medications or illicit drugs. Even the ingestion of aspirin can inhibit the in vitro [test tube] reactivity of lymphocytes."

"A recent viral infection could also influence lymphocyte function," added the authors (from UCLA's departments of pediatrics, surgery, biomathematics, and psychiatry). "None of our patients were ill. . . ."

In the preceding six months, the hospitalized subjects had smoked marijuana three to six times a week (six men) or at least daily (six men), used other drugs no more than three times, drunk no more than five ounces of hard liquor and twenty-one glasses of wine or beer a week, and smoked no more than ten tobacco cigarettes a day. They and twelve nonhospitalized controls, matched for age, were twenty-one to twenty-eight.

Blood samples were tested for T-cells (rosette and blast response to PHA and mixed leukocytes), B-cells (rosettes and the presence of surface membrane immunoglobulins), and serum levels of immunoglobulins G, M, and A (radial diffusion).[20]

In New York, Nahas, Davies, and Osserman (1979) performed a further immunoglobulin experiment with a remarkably different outcome from that in Los Angeles. Weekly for two months they took blood samples and measured concentrations of four immunoglobulins from fifteen confined, "clinically healthy," chronic marijuana smokers and from nineteen "control subjects."

The concentration of immunoglobulin-G (the principal immunoglobulin in human blood) was consistently lower in the marijuana group than in the control group, about 15 percent lower overall. A month of smoking (sandwiched between two fortnights of abstinence) did not make much difference.

Concentration of immunoglobulin-D (a rare one of uncertain function) ran three and a half times as high in the marijuana group as in the control. The groups did not differ significantly in immunoglobulins M and A. Scoring was done in blind fashion (the scorer not knowing which sample was which).[21]

4

Animal Contributions

Note that the scientific differences and the contradictory results involved the studies of human marijuana smokers. When it came to animal experiments, the findings were fairly consistent (an exception being the Zagury-Nahas project).

The experimentation favored rodents. Monkeys figured in one study (a by-product of an investigation into cannabis and the brain). The researchers probed T-cells, B-cells, and macrophages.

The goal of one group differed from the rest. In approaching a novel mouse experiment, investigators at the Medical College of Virginia in Richmond (1974) took the position that suppression of immunity could sometimes be desirable. Pioneer work in organ transplants had been performed at the college, and they wondered if THC would alter the role of T-lymphocytes in rejecting transplants.

Levy, Munson, and colleagues grafted skin from black mice onto white mice. They gave some of the white mice THC daily, through a stomach tube. Others received no THC. All skin grafts were rejected, but the grafts on the drugged mice lasted longer than those on the undrugged mice. The THC prolonged graft survival between one-fifth and two-fifths, depending on dosage. At the maximum dose, it mimicked a traditional immunosuppressive drug, which was used in this experiment for comparison. So THC had diminished the animals' immune responses—and the researchers were pleased.

> The Virginians administered THC daily to the recipient mice for seven days before grafting the skin onto the rodents' backs and continued the drugging until rejection took place. Making daily observations, they pronounced a graft rejected when they could no longer support the mouse by lifting it by the graft.
>
> Grafts of the control group of mice lasted about sixteen days. THC extended the graft survival to close to twenty, twenty-one, twenty, and twenty-three days on the average at doses of 25, 50, 100, and 200 mg/kg respectively. An established immunosuppressive agent (6-mercaptopurine, 25 mg/kg administered daily for eleven days, starting the day before grafting) extended the survival to 23½ days.
>
> The study embraced various tests besides the grafting, all involving comparison of THC-treated mice and undrugged mice. The investigators assessed the effectiveness of lymphocytes by the blastogenic test and by the capacity to produce antibodies.
>
> The drug "produced depressions of both cell-mediated and humoral immunity. . . . Both T- and B-cell reactivity were depressed upon single and multiple treatments with delta-9-THC." All doses but the smallest (25 mg/kg) lowered the blastogenic response in both types of lymphocyte. The highest dose (200 mg/kg) significantly suppressed the formation of antibodies.
>
> They also examined the overall reticuloendothelial system (cells that ingest particles) by an established test of the mice's ability to clear colloidal carbon from the blood vessels. Oddly, only doses of 25 and 100 mg/kg seemed to depress the system. And they observed diminished sizes and numbers of spleen cells from drugged mice.[22]

The monkey study, in New Orleans, while giving credence to the impaired-lymphocyte position, suggested that the impairment could be temporary.

Five rhesus monkeys smoked marijuana two, five, or fifteen times a week for six months by means of a special smoking machine. They were probed, before and after, for two different signs of immunity: their lymphocyte responses and their levels of immunoglobulin.

At the end of the six-month smoking period, tests showed lymphocyte responses down in all five smoking monkeys; and immunoglobulin levels down in the (two) heavier smoking monkeys.

Three months into the smoking period, the lymphocyte responses had shown no change. Tested between one and two months after the smoking ended, the lymphocyte responses were back to normal, Daul and Heath reported (1975).

> Dr. Carolyn B. Daul conducted the study at Tulane University's School of Medicine in the laboratory of Dr. Robert G. Heath (whose work is described in "The Brain," 3).
>
> Concanavalin A, PHA (two concentrations), and pokeweed (testing B-cells) were the mitogens. Lymphocyte blastogenic responsiveness to the first of these in culture was reduced in all monkeys smoking marijuana: "high" dose, 59 percent; "medium," 66 percent; and average for "low," 47 percent. The "high" and "medium" monkeys showed impairment in response to PHA (higher concentration) and pokeweed also, 58 percent and 57 percent, respectively. (The smokers had sixteen other reductions and two increases, none statistically significant.) Between one and two months after smoking, all responses had returned to about the pre-smoking levels.
>
> After "high" or "medium" dosing, reductions were registered in immunoglobulin-G, 20 percent, average; and immunoglobulin-M, 26 percent average. Neither immunoglobulin sank significantly after "low" dosing. These changes (measured by "radial immunodiffusion analysis") seemed to indicate less effective humoral immunity, but the pokeweed test did not diminish the B-cell response in the "medium" monkey. Immunoglobulin was not checked again later.
>
> "Our data indicates that the observed changes in cellular reactivity are transient; they occur only during the period of 'chronic' marihuana usage and return to initial responsivity within 1–2 months after the drug usage is discontinued," said the report. No changes were observed three months after smoking began, so cannabis had its effect sometime between three and six months. The exact way in which it worked posed a puzzle. And what all of this meant in terms of the animals' actual defenses against illness remained unclear.[23]

The immune system of the rat has shown considerable sensitivity to cannabis and components, more so than that of the mouse.

Dr. Gary L. Huber, of Harvard Medical School, and associates in Boston incubated flasks of rat macrophages with *Staphylococcus albus* bacteria and marijuana smoke. The smoke impaired the ability of macrophages to consume the bacteria. Smoke-treated macrophages destroyed markedly fewer bacteria than untreated macrophages. The higher the dose, the fewer bacteria were destroyed.

Whatever it was that harmed the macrophages occupied the gas phase of the smoke. Filtering out of particles made it evident that the THC was not the culprit. Besides, THC-free, placebo marijuana smoke had the same effect on the macrophages, and, furthermore, pure THC had no effect on them at all.

Tobacco smoke depressed the macrophages in much the same way as marijuana smoke did. Tobacco smoke possesses at least 2,000 components and while the total for marijuana is not known, its burning can be assumed to generate a large number of substances, Huber's report said (1975).

Summing up: The notion "that marihuana is harmless has enjoyed considerable acceptability without concrete support. Our data demonstrate that fresh whole marihuana smoke is cytotoxic to the alveolar macrophage, the key defense cell of the lung."

> After three hours of incubation, control (untreated) macrophages had destroyed about 79 percent of the bacteria. Macrophages exposed to doses of marijuana smoke (about 2 percent THC) ranging from 8 to 2 ml (milliliters) destroyed between about 11 percent and 67 percent of the bacteria, respectively. Macrophages exposed to those doses of tobacco smoke knocked out about 18 percent to 50 percent of the bacteria, respectively. (Tests of smoke without macrophages found it somewhat toxic to bacteria—8 ml of marijuana reduced bacteria by 11 percent—so figures are corrected to eliminate this factor.)
>
> Filtering marijuana smoke through glass fiber showed that the gas phase contained the macrophage toxin. Running the gas through water washed away the offending substance, which appeared unstable inasmuch as stale smoke lost most of it. Tobacco smoke acted similarly in all respects.
>
> The researchers believed that the marijuana "cytotoxin" somehow impaired the macrophage's function of phagocytosis (a cell's engulfment of foreign matter) without actually killing the macrophage.[24]

A later study by Dr. Huber and coworkers compared the effects of tobacco and marijuana on the lung defenses of rats forced to breathe smoke (1979). The rats were showered with an aerosol of *Staphylococcus aureus* bacteria. By means of a smoking machine, many of them then sniffed smoke from cigarettes—tobacco for some, marijuana for others. Other rats received no smoke at all. Afterward isolated lungs were examined and the amount of surviving bacteria determined.

Both types of cigarette impaired the lungs' bacteria-killing activity but marijuana appeared to impair it notably more than tobacco.

With marijuana, the extent of impairment in lung defenses varied with dose. The same could be said of tobacco above a certain dose, but at low doses tobacco did not impair defenses and even seemed to stimulate them.

At comparable doses marijuana appeared "significantly more toxic to the alveolar bactericidal activity of the lung than tobacco smoke," Huber et al. reported.

Compared with the nonsmoking rats' performance, tobacco added one-fifth to the time required to "inactivate" bacteria while marijuana more than doubled the time, based on the smoke from fifteen cigarettes. "Inactivation" involved (1) mostly the killing of bacteria in the lung, mainly by macrophages; but also (2) physical clearance from the lung by cilia and mucus.

An aerosol apparatus had showered dozens of rats with bacteria labeled with radioactive phosphorus. Half of the rats served as controls. The others received ten minutes of exposure per hour for five hours to smoke from tobacco or 2-percent-THC marijuana (a total of three to thirty cigarettes). Then at intervals the research workers destroyed rats, removing the lungs and homogenizing them in nutrient broth.

By counting the radiation remaining, they could figure out how much bacteria a rat had physically cleared from its lungs. By incubating diluted samples of the lung mixture for forty-eight hours and counting the bacteria colonies that formed, they could determine the quantity of living bacteria still in each rat, and hence the quantity killed.

The research marijuana cigarette burned more rapidly than the research tobacco cigarette and delivered about half of the latter's total particulate matter and half of its carbon monoxide. But the blood concentrations of carboxyhemoglobin (a compound formed by carbon monoxide and the blood's hemoglobin in carbon monoxide poisoning) were similar in marijuana-exposed and tobacco-exposed rats. Marijuana of course contained no nicotine.[25]

At the University of Guelph, Ontario, Canada, researchers found that THC given to live rats appeared to interfere with macrophages in a chemical way. It seemed to depress the level of MIF (migration-inhibition factor, a substance released by sensitized T-lymphocytes), which normally stimulates the defense activity of macrophages. The decrease "may be related to the impaired cellular immunity observed in regular users of cannabis," said Gaul and Mellors (1975).

They gave immunized rats abdominal injections of THC solution. Hours later they examined abdominal ooze from the rodents. The effect of MIF (in getting migrating macrophages to stand and fight) was reduced in drugged rats—to as low as one-tenth that of undrugged rats. The degree of depression depended on dose (the more drug, the more depression) and time elapsed between drugging and testing (at fifteen hours, MIF hit bottom).[26]

Then in Ness-Ziona, Israel, Aviva Chari-Bitron of the official Israel Institute for Biological Research used motion picture microphotography to observe the movement of macrophages taken from rats' lungs. THC paralyzed them.

Whereas alcohol had no effect on the movement of the macrophages, a large concentration of THC caused "a spectacular inhibition of cell motility leading to actual paralysis without noticeably changing the macrophages shape."

In another experiment, THC in a lesser amount released some of the macrophages' lysosomal enzymes, proteins responsible for breaking down foreign particles. The more THC, the more enzymes emerged.

Finally, whereas immersing the macrophages in a salt solution did not damage them, adding a large amount of THC did. The cells disintegrated.

Lung macrophages, again, are considered "the first line of pulmonary defense and are exposed to the inhaled hashish before it enters the bloodstream or is metabolized," the biological researcher pointed out (1976).

The paralysis of rat alveolar macrophages followed an exposure to THC in 30 micromolar solution. The presence of 10 micromolar THC induced the release of the lysosomal enzymes.

The macrophages were "relatively resistant to osmotic shock, with little loss of viability," in 0.2 percent sodium chloride solution. Adding 35 micromolar THC "causes complete cytolysis of the cells, accompanied by extrusion of lysosomal hydrolytic enzymes."[27]

We note that even the smallest concentration of THC used in Chari-Bitron's experiments exceeded by far the concentration that other researchers have found in the blood of smokers. Of course, the accumulation of THC in tissues is a factor to be considered.

Another set of Massachusetts experiments on that little-loved species investigated B-cells and the "humoral immune response." Dr. Harris Rosenkrantz and colleagues dosed rats daily for five days. The doses were designed to equal those of human users. Some rats received THC by forced feeding and others breathed in the smoke of marijuana cigarettes by means of a smoking machine. Still others received no drug.

Each rat got an injection of sheep's red blood cells to stimulate its body to make antibodies. After five days the rats were destroyed and their blood exposed to the sheep blood to see how much specific immunity had built up. Two indexes of immunity showed substantial depressions for THC- and smoke-treated rats compared with untreated rats: counts of antibody-forming cells in the spleen and measurements of hemagglutination (the clumping together of red blood cells). THC and smoke also caused some decline in weight of the spleen (an organ in which lymphocytes and other defense cells form).

"It seems reasonable to conclude that pure delta-9-THC at reasonable doses is immunosuppressive in rodents and that cannabinoids in marihuana smoke have a similar effect since placebo [inactive] marihuana smoke did not elicit an equivalent inhibition," Dr. Rosenkrantz wrote

(1976). So it was evidently cannabinoid chemical and not the smoke as such that caused the suppression of the B-cell responses.

> The mean decreases in the number of antibody-forming cells in spleens of marijuana-smoking rats compared with placebo smokers were about 52, 59, and 77 percent at THC doses of 0.7, 2, and 4 mg/kg, respectively. The decline for rats fed THC, in sesame oil, also hit 77 percent at the top dose, 10 mg/kg. At top doses, hemagglutination declined 41 percent for marijuana smokers and 66 percent for THC-fed rats while spleen weights declined 18 and 15 percent, respectively.
>
> Values for placebo-treated rats (given inactive smoke or fed sesame oil only) were similar to those that were untreated or "sham-treated" (put in the smoking machine but not given smoke).
>
> The study also observed inhibition in the central nervous system and decreases in exploratory activity, temperature, respiration, and growth, particularly at high doses. The changes were greater, occurred much sooner, and tended to reverse quicker after inhalation than after gastric intake.
>
> Antibody-forming cells were counted by the "localized hemolysis in gel (LHG) plaque formation" test, developed in the 1960s.
>
> Rosenkrantz conducted the study as a Clark University (Worcester, Massachusetts) biochemistry professor.[28]

Another investigation into the humoral immune reaction was undertaken "because of the conflicting reports concerning the effects of marihuana on the immune system in humans, presumably due to difficulties of experimental design" (1980). So reported Dr. Arthur M. Zimmerman, zoology professor at the University of Toronto, cell biologist and pharmacologist, who collaborated in this study with his wife, Dr. Selma Zimmerman, natural sciences professor at York University. The experimental design was a rather complicated one.

THC brought depression in B-cell immunity when injected in immature mice also injected with sheep's red blood cells. The inhibition varied with dose. It was reflected in results of four different tests. There were several control groups for each test. "Our studies clearly show that antigen-challenged mice display a reduced immune response when treated with THC." CBD and CBN, two nonpsychoactive ingredients of cannabis, caused no such effect.

> THC's suppression of the antigenic response was manifested in reductions in weight of spleen, number of splenic antibody-forming cells, hemagglutination titer, and percentage of splenic white pulp to total spleen volume.
>
> Mice of similar weights had been evenly distributed in the different groups (antigen plus drug, antigen plus vehicle, antigen alone, drug alone, vehicle alone, and untreated controls). On each of four straight days, drug-treated animals received injections (within the peritoneal cavity) of 1, 5, or 10 mg/kg of THC, or 25 mg/kg of cannabidiol or cannabinol. The antigen groups received, besides drug or vehicle, a single injection of sheep red blood cells on the first day.[29]

A Pennsylvania rat experiment rates a mention here (and in "The Cells and Chromosomes," 3, in further detail). Doctors Cottrell and Vogel injected a solution of marijuana tar in the animals and later discovered some to have lymphoma, that is, cancer of the lymph nodes, and other types of tumor. Rats injected only with solvent did not become sick in any way.

(Found in many parts of the body, the lymph nodes are small, rounded bodies that furnish lymphocytes to the blood. Also acting as filters for the lymph, the fluid that bathes the tissues, they prevent bacteria and other foreign particles from entering the bloodstream.)

Eight of twenty-five rats died of cancer, including three lymphomas; and six more died from other illness, including four cases of pneumonia—leading to speculation by Dr. Cottrell that "maybe the cannabinoids messed up the immune system."

✻   ✻   ✻

In 1983 staff members of the Medical College of Virginia performed experiments on guinea pigs to determine whether THC would modify herpes simplex virus infection, inasmuch as the drug "has been shown to have immunosuppressive effects" and "herpes genital infections are reaching epidemic proportions in the United States," to quote Guy A. Cabral, the principal investigator.

They chose guinea pigs because these animals mimic humans in their herpes reactions. Given the virus intravaginally, the female guinea pigs usually go through the spectrum of the disease, with swelling, lesions, and possible recurrence.

Ninety-nine guinea pigs were so treated with virus. Fifty-nine of them first had been injected with THC and continued to receive THC for three weeks (a total of twelve injections per animal). The drugged animals had a worse time than the undrugged ones: the disease was more severe, lasted longer, and (at some dose levels) took more lives. All of the dead animals were found to have virus in the brain.

The lesson, Cabral says, appears to be that use of cannabis either immediately before or at the same time as exposure to herpes "may either lead to exacerbation of a previous herpes infection or enhance your chances of getting infected with herpes and cause a more serious disease."

THC was injected intraperitoneally beginning one day before infection and continuing for three weeks, four consecutive daily treatments a week, at 0.2, 1, 2, 4, 10, or 25 mg/kg. Controls were injected with vehicle or untreated. The 4 and 10 mg/kg courses evoked the most pronounced results; four days of these treatments were intended to translate roughly to the smoking of ten to thirty joints by a human over a four-day period.

While 35 percent of controls died, deaths amounted to 50, 63, and 64 percent in the 2, 4, and 10 mg/kg THC groups, respectively. While half of the controls suffered lesions, between 75 and 86 percent of the THC groups had lesions, excluding the 25 mg/kg group (67 percent, not significant).

The virus (HSV2) was "very strongly neurotropic" (had a strong affinity for neural tissue) "and the treatment with delta-9 enhanced the spread of this virus to the central nervous system," said Dr. Cabral (Ph.D.), associate professor of microbiology and immunology, in a telephone interview. The guinea pigs' specific or nonspecific resistance appeared to have broken down. The investigators were checking further to see whether THC enhanced the replication of virus. Doctors Albert E. Munson, F. Marciano-Cabral, P. Coleman, Louis S. Harris, S. G. Bradley, and Eric Mishkin also worked on the project.

5

Do Users Suffer More Illness?

Do marijuana smokers suffer more illness than nonsmokers? No scientific study that we know of has addressed the question specifically. Small groups of smokers and nonsmokers often have been compared without showing any glaring health differences. Of course, investigators have not usually chosen ill people as subjects.

While valuing the laboratory research, we see a need for statistical studies specifically comparing the incidence of various types of disease among cannabis smokers and nonsmokers—or the incidence of cannabis smoking among different types of patients. Such studies might consider the possibility of contagion through the sharing of joints and the consequences of other unhealthy ways of drug life, including the devouring of junk food to satisfy the "munchies" often accompanying pot smoking.

Some observers, like the following, have professed to find infections more profuse among the smokers.

"Because there has still been no centralized pooling of information from parents, physicians, and marijuana users themselves, the practical implications of the lab findings are still not established," Marsha Manatt has written for the National Institute on Drug Abuse. "However, the author's extensive interviews with pediatricians, parents, and young users indicate increasing bronchitis, sinusitis, flus, and viral infections; data from these interviews have not been systematically analyzed."[30]

Dr. Frederick Lundell, senior psychiatrist and director of the adolescent clinic at The Montreal General Hospital, wrote that in the late sixties, when he directed the mental assessment and guidance clinic at The Montreal Children's Hospital, "marijuana casualties began turning up with distressing frequency." Making a follow-up study of 100 cases, he found marijuana users sharing certain characteristics. These included paranoia and deterioration in concentration, comprehension, and short-term memory. "They also had a high incidence of respiratory and other infections."[31]

Dr. Ingrid L. Lantner, Cleveland, Ohio, pediatrician, having treated or counseled more than fifty marijuana smokers and spoken with a thousand more after giving talks in person or on the air, noticed that adolescents often complained of ailments related to the use of marijuana. These included tiredness, sleep disorder, depression, lack of motivation, chest pain, hacking cough, lung irritation, and, among the girls, irregular menstrual cycles. "We physicians used to see teenagers mainly in connection with sports or for routine physical examinations," Dr. Lantner told us. "But now they have throat infections, bronchitis, and lung problems that hang on."

Munson and Fehr (1983), reviewing 106 studies on cannabis and the immune function (including mouse experiments by Dr. Munson at the Medical College of Virginia), accepted it as a fact that marijuana reduced resistance to infection. They expected the degree of this lowered resistance to range in different individuals from slight to fatal, usually being minor.

"It is likely that we would now be aware of profound changes in the resistance of human cannabis smokers if these occurred frequently," Munson and Fehr wrote. On the other hand, to establish that marijuana causes common infections to break out a little more often or become a bit worse would take epidemiological data on large numbers of users, which are lacking, they pointed out. "This type of effect could ultimately be a significant public health issue," particularly among those with immune disorders or whose immunity has been otherwise suppressed, such as cancer and transplant patients.[32]

6

The Liver

The liver, largest gland of the body, has more than 100 functions, including the detoxifying of poisons and the formation of antibodies. Among vital duties, it produces bile, blood-clotting agents, and plasma proteins, and it breaks down unwanted substances, regulates sugar, and metabolizes fats. As for cannabis and cannabinoids, it is the main organ for their metabolism.

A few studies exist on the reaction of smokers' livers to cannabis, leaving the matter still in doubt. We cite five:

• The New York Mayor's Committee on Marihuana reported (1944) no clinical evidence of liver damage in any subjects before or after ingestion of marijuana concentrate. An unspecified number received—and all passed—a standard test of the liver's efficiency in cleansing the blood of injected blue dye (bromsulfalein).[33]

• Kew and colleagues in Johannesburg, South Africa (1969), performed liver-function tests on a dozen chronic marijuana smokers, finding evidence of at least "mild liver dysfunction" in eight. Of the eight, liver biopsies on three (who had shown abnormal biochemistry) uncovered striking cell degeneration plus pronounced arteriole disease in one of the three. Reportedly the smokers, young males, never had taken drugs intravenously; only three drank, moderately; and all were well fed. They had used marijuana for two to eight years.

The idea for the study derived from a discovery of cirrhosis in a young man who had smoked marijuana heavily for over three years. He had drunk alcohol but apparently too lightly to cause cirrhosis.[34]

• Tennant and fellow army doctors (1971) detected no liver enlargement, jaundice, or laboratory evidence of liver disease in any of thirty-one hashish-smoking American soldiers tested in Germany. The patients had smoked very heavily for six to fifteen months.[35]

• Giving fifty marijuana smokers liver tests, Hochman and Brill in Los Angeles (1971) perceived disturbances in ten. But detailed questioning of the ten unexpectedly revealed a history of long-term alcohol use and current heavy drinking. Before the examinations began, all had denied ever being alcoholic.

They were asked to stop drinking for a month. At the end of a month, nine of the ten tested normal.

Indicting the alcohol as the culprit, Hochman and Brill nevertheless conjectured that "Possibly the combination of heavy use of alcohol and marihuana presents an additional risk beyond the risk of either alone, since the liver is the principal organ of metabolism of both substances."[36]

• A finding of more enlarged livers among hashish smokers than non-smokers was the only long-term medical difference discerned in a many-faceted Grecian study, aside from cellular and personality distinctions. Eight (18 percent) of the former group had enlarged livers, compared with one (3 percent) of the latter. Five investigators blamed the condition on alcoholic drinking (Boulougouris et al., 1976).[37] To a sixth, "The significance of this finding remains obscure" (Fink, 1977).[38]

THE
CELLS
AND
CHROMOSOMES

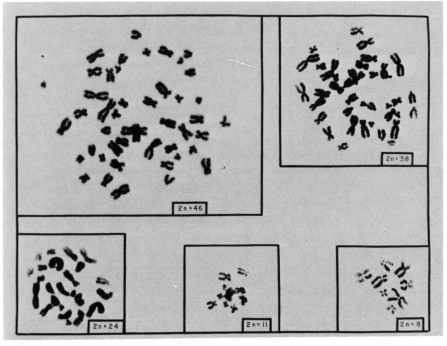

2n=46

2n=38

2n=24

2n=11

2n=8

Doctor Morishima's exhibit.

1

Genetic Question

The U.S. Senate does not customarily study chromosomes as part of its official business, yet here were members of its judiciary committee busy examining photographs of the microscopic things, magnified a thousand times. The chromosomes came from five lymphocyte cells about to divide. One had the normal forty-six chromosomes. The others contained thirty-eight, twenty-four, eleven, and eight chromosomes.

"What is the significance of a cell with twenty-four or eleven or eight chromosomes?" asked J. G. Sourwine, the chief counsel.

"These are abnormal cells, which are seen only in a very small percentage among the normal controls," replied Dr. Akira Morishima.

"Will they take part in reproduction?"

"They probably will, at least for one or two generations, but after that I have no evidence to support whether or not they can or cannot."

The chromosome shortages appeared in cells of chronic marijuana smokers, conjuring up for Dr. Morishima visions of immunity breakdowns, development of cancer, genetic mutation, and birth defects. This was supposition, and a long distance on the road of knowledge remained to be traveled. But the witness cautioned, in his 1974 testimony:

"It was only two years ago that diethylstilbestrol, once a commonly prescribed female hormone, was implicated in vaginal cancer of female offspring of mothers who were treated with this agent some fifteen to twenty years before.

". . . The effect was not seen in the mother at all. She never expressed adverse effect, and it was only when the female offspring reached beyond the pubertal age, cancer of the vagina was discovered. . . .

"So I believe that similar kinds of situations can occur in the marijuana usage."[1]

* * *

Chromosomes are the blueprints of the body, carrying genetic information in the form of genes. Composed of DNA (deoxyribonucleic acid) and proteins, the chromosomes are elongated structures in the nucleus of each cell. They hold a hereditary pattern, either for new cells of one's own body, or—in the case of one's sex cells—for offspring. The usual human cell contains forty-six chromosomes, except for a sex cell (that is, sperm or egg) which has twenty-three. Along each chromosome are 1,000 or more genes, the basic genetic units.

Damage to chromosomes in sperm or egg cells can harm the development of offspring. In other cells, damaged chromosomes can pose danger to health. Normally there are very few of them.

THC added to normal human blood in test tubes has not increased the number of chromosomal abnormalities. Tests of actual cannabis smokers, however, have been contradictory. Some have shown increased defects in chromosomes and others have not.

Research reports that began issuing in 1967 showed the illicit hallucinogenic drug LSD apparently causing breaks and rearrangements of human chromosomes. In a pacemaking study, cultured white blood cells presented a marked increase in chromosomal damage when treated in the laboratory with LSD (M. M. Cohen et al., Buffalo, New York).[2]

". . . To determine if delta-8-THC would cause similar aberrations when added to human blood cultures," Neu and colleagues experimented late in the decade at the Upstate Medical Center in Syracuse, New York. For three days they incubated whole blood from five normal individuals, adding the drug at four different concentrations after the second day.

Delta-8-THC drastically curbed cell division in white blood cells, more so as concentrations increased. But the drug did not cause the number of chromosome breaks or gaps to increase over the control cultures (untreated samples). That is, no more than 5 percent of cells had those abnormalities. No other structural changes were found.

> Delta-8-tetrahydrocannabinol is an ingredient of cannabis that seems to produce the same biological effects as delta-9-THC. The former is less plentiful and more stable. They are isomers, having the same chemical formula but some different properties because of different ways in which their atoms are linked.
>
> Delta-8-THC caused "a drastic decrease in the mitotic index," that is, the percentage of cells undergoing mitosis, the process of cell division. The index decreased from about 8 percent to zero at high concentration (50 or more micrograms per milliliter of medium). To a much lesser extent ethyl alcohol, the solvent for the drug, lowered the index when used alone in control cultures. "Less than thirty metaphases were available for analysis in cultures with the higher delta-8-THC concentrations. . . ."[3]

LSD research proliferated. The last three years of the sixties yielded about three dozen papers on the genetic impact or lack of impact of that drug. Dorrance and two fellow physicians in southern California came up with another (1970), including an additional illicit hallucinogen in their study. They ascribed their interest in the question of hallucinogens and chromosomes to "the obvious public health problem and the conflicting nature of published reports."

Besides fourteen users of LSD and other drugs and ten "normal controls," they studied nine young people who had used marijuana and no other "psychedelic drug." The marijuana group included "both light and relatively heavy users." The LSD group included thirteen who had used marijuana. (Presumably the control subjects never had used mind-altering drugs.)

The researchers cultured blood samples and analyzed lymphocytes, counting abnormalities in chromosomes among the three groups. The frequency of broken chromosomes in the marijuana, LSD, and normal groups turned out to be about the same statistically.

> Marijuana usage had varied from four cigarettes, spread over a year, to two or three per week for a year and a half. The time of the last smoking ranged from one month to twelve hours before sampling.
> "The only abnormalities noted in any group were chromatid breaks and fragments." The mean rate of breakage for each group:
> Marijuana—0.86%, 7 of 816 cells. (The seven came from five users, including three of four women subjects.)
> LSD (lysergic acid diethylamide)—0.76%, 8 of 1,284 cells.
> Control—0.79%, 8 of 1,018 cells.[4]

Also prompted by the LSD research, Gilmour and others (1971) examined some 4,000 white blood cells from subjects in New York City: fifty-six psychoactive-drug users, divided into five groups; sixteen nonusers of drugs; and seven with a history of considerable irradiation.

The irradiated subjects showed by far the most aberrations in chromosomes, followed by multidrug users, heroin addicts, psychiatric patients treated with phenothiazine, amphetamine users, those who smoked marijuana lightly and the nonusers of drugs, in that order.

The multidrug group comprised eleven subjects, all of whom used marijuana heavily as well as other drugs, and seven of whom used LSD. The figures for all eleven were combined, thus muddying the data. In any event, noting that the drug results "were largely accounted for by a few subjects with more than one aberration each," the researchers played down the effects of drugs on chromosomes. They speculated that other factors, such as viral infections, might be responsible.

> For each group, this was the percentage of cells with one or more chromosomal aberrations, either breaks or rearrangements: irradiated, 6.0 percent; heavy marijuana, LSD, etc., 2.2 percent; heroin, 2.2 percent; phenothiazine, 2.0 percent; amphetamines, 1.6 percent; light marijuana, 0.8 percent; and controls, 0.5 percent.
> The drug users were twenty-seven men and twenty-nine women; the controls, seven men and nine women. All told, they had 4,121 of their cells examined under a microscope. Of five researchers, three were from New York University School of Medicine, the rest from University of Michigan Medical School.

Most of the "light marijuana" group, thirteen subjects, used it no more than once a month; a few used it about twice a month.[5]

Nine inquiries into possible damage to human chromosomes from cannabis alone, made public between 1972 and 1978, are outlined below.

Four of the studies found chromosomal defects. The other five found no such defects. In the four studies finding defects, regular users were compared with others. The five finding no defects included one study comparing regular users with others, one THC test-tube experiment, and three experiments testing subjects before and after taking cannabis. But four of the latter five studies (all but the test-tube one) had serious flaws.

Note that the chromosome studies are not completely comparable. At best, differences exist, not only in experimental design, but in ways of processing samples, scoring defects, and handling data. The marijuana and its usage vary from study to study, typical of cannabis work generally. The scientists have not even agreed on precisely what, if anything, constitutes harm to chromosomes besides outright breakage.

There are some common procedures, however. The researcher questions volunteers to rule out damage to chromosomes from other factors, such as radiation or illness. From specimens, he (or she) isolates certain cells (white blood cells are preferred for technical convenience), immerses them in a nutrient broth, adds a stimulant, and incubates them until they reach the metaphase, a brief stage of cell division when chromosomes are clearly visible. Then he fixes and stains the cells, spreads them on slides, and examines the chromosomes under a microscope.

• In Lucknow, India, medical teachers Kumar and Kunwar studied chromosomes from bone marrow of seven men, aged forty to fifty-seven, who had been smoking or drinking cannabis preparations for fifteen to twenty years. The pair found an increased frequency of abnormality in the cannabis group, compared with a group of twenty-five nonusers. (The abnormalities: "gaps, breaks, hyperdiploid cells [too many chromosomes] and . . . a ring 'X' chromosome.")

Whether the long use of cannabis made the chromosomes abnormal or "whether these chromosomal abnormalities make a person addicted to cannabis" was a question on the minds of Kumar and Kunwar.[6]

• One well-publicized chromosome study dealt with thirty-three Jamaicans, eighteen of whom had smoked *ganja* for at least ten years, three *spliffs* (cigarettes of marijuana mixed with tobacco) per day.

Examining cultured blood samples, researchers at the University of the West Indies counted breaks and gaps in 9 of 381 (2.4 percent) of the smokers' cells and 10 of 341 (2.9 percent) of the "control" cells.

From their examination of an average of twenty-two cells per subject, they concluded, "It appears that chronic Cannabis usage has no significant effect on the mitotic chromosomes of human peripheral blood lymphocytes in the Jamaican man."[7]

Abundant publicity on the experiment, when the broader study of cannabis in Jamaica came out in book form, failed to point out that at least eighteen of thirty "controls" had smoked cannabis and others consumed it in other forms. "Ganja is taken by both smokers and controls in tea and tonics for medicinal purposes and occasionally in food," avowed Dr. Erik K. Cruickshank, codirector of the Jamaica project's clinical studies.[8]

> Cultured cells from thirty men in each of the two groups were to be analyzed, however, as a report to the sponsoring U.S. agency acknowledged, "cultures from 12 users and 15 controls failed to produce adequate results for analysis. . . . Part of this high failure rate was due to a bad batch of calf serum used in our culture medium."[9]
>
> Dr. Marigold J. Thorburn, M.D., a lecturer in pathology who directed the chromosome study in Kingston, Jamaica, 1970–71, wrote us from the child health department at the University of the West Indies that "the high failure rate of the original cultures . . . were due to matters entirely beyond our control . . . associated with the many constraints of doing scientific research in a developing country where communications, transportation and funding are limited. Due to the above constraints we were unable to repeat the investigations although we had proposed to do so at the time."
>
> She noted that "the selection of controls for the study was not undertaken by us. . . . According to the information that we were given, the 'controls' that were subsequently discovered to have been using cannabis were withdrawn from the study and not included in the results that we published."
>
> The reports that we saw by other participants in the Jamaica project said nothing of any change in controls.

• An experiment by Stenchever and Allen in Salt Lake City resembled the Neu research and reached the same conclusion.

They exposed 2,737 white blood cells from four healthy donors to delta-9-THC, culturing for seventy-two hours. As in the Neu project, they found "no increase in the incidence of chromosome breaks or gaps in any of the study cultures when compared to controls," 903 untreated cells. (In the two groups, respectively, 2.2 percent and 2.7 percent of cells had breaks.) Heavy THC concentrations stopped cell growth.

The study of cannabis by Dr. Stenchever—obstetrician, cell geneticist, and university professor—was an outgrowth of a study he had made of reproductive failure in couples. ". . . It became apparent that almost without exception when we found chromosome breakage in these people we could elicit a history of marijuana use . . . and we were finding no damage in pure LSD users. . . ." Consequently, he did not accept the results of his THC experiment as conclusive.[10]

In contrast to the test-tube study, Stenchever and associates later compared lymphocytes from the blood of forty-nine marijuana users with those of twenty nonusers and found more chromosomal breaks among the marijuana group (students at the University of Utah). A hundred cells from each individual went under the microscope and 3.4 cells per user had breaks, contrasted with 1.2 cells per nonuser. (Scoring was "blind," the scorer not knowing which cells were which.)

There were no statistical differences in breakage rate between (A) twenty-seven subjects who used two joints a week and twenty-two lighter users, (B) twenty-two subjects who also used other drugs and twenty-seven marijuana-only users, and (C) twenty-nine male users and twenty female users.

Thus the data seemed to implicate marijuana in chromosome damage. How often the users had smoked it, whether they also took other drugs (twenty-two also took amphetamines, barbiturates, heroin, LSD, mescaline, and tranquilizers), or whether they were male or female had nothing to do with the extent of the damage. (Caffeine did not seem to influence the extent of chromosome damage either, although the control sample here was too small to draw a conclusion: only six of the forty-nine did not drink coffee, tea, or cola.)

It remained unclear which chemical in cannabis was doing the damage—THC apparently was not the vandal—or "whether or not this chromosome-breaking agent is capable of causing abnormalities of unborn children, an increased mutation [genetic change] rate, or an increased incidence of cancer. . . . All of these possibilities are potentially there," said Stenchever.[11]

• Nichols and coworkers analyzed white blood cells from thirty volunteers given oral doses of marijuana extract, hashish extract, or synthetic THC over periods of five or twelve days. Comparing chromosome breakage in cells sampled before and after treatment, they detected no increase that could be attributed to those substances.

The wide-spreading project (with blood drawn in California and processed in a New Jersey laboratory, assistance of a geneticist from Sweden, and publication in a Dutch scientific journal) established that the taking of cannabis or THC by mouth in up to a dozen daily doses did not necessarily cause a measurable breakage of chromosomes. It shed no light on the genetic effects of long-term cannabis smoking. The subjects, healthy young males, all "had some experience with marihuana" (although no exposure to drugs in the week preceding the experiment). The study did not compare them with nonusers.

> Dr. Warren W. Nichols, M.D., head of the cytogenetics department at the Institute for Medical Research in Camden, New Jersey, noted in a letter to us "that each individual served as his own control" by providing a blood specimen before receiving any of the substances under test and "that the levels obtained then and after the various dosage combinations were well within outside control levels, [in studies] performed many times in this laboratory and outside laboratories" (no details given).
>
> Over the course of the five or twelve days, a subject received either two doses or daily doses, each comprising 20 mg of THC (vehicle unspecified). Blood was drawn before and 2½ hours after the first and last dose. Scoring was blind.[12]

• The use of hashish was widespread in West Germany in the early 1970s when Herha and Obe of the Free University of Berlin made chromosomal analyses of white blood cells from twenty chronic users (including four women) and twenty nonusers.

Compared to nonusers, hashish smokers showed statistically more major aberrations ("exchange type aberrations [chromatid interchanges, dicentric chromosomes]"). The pair advised caution in linking usage to genetic damage "because one cannot be sure that the effects . . . are caused by hashish alone." Seven subjects were opiate addicts and twelve had taken LSD. Nine subjects had histories of hepatitis, and the aberration rate was somewhat heavier in this group.

All things considered, however, Herha and Obe deemed their results and past research "a strong indication of a possible genetic risk of chronic Cannabis usage."[13]

• Matsuyama and coworkers in southern California performed two experiments that they said failed to show any effect of marijuana on chromosomes, at least among experienced users. But they acknowledged both studies to be inadequate.

First, twenty-one male volunteers smoked marijuana containing either 1 percent, 2 percent, or 0 percent THC, a cigarette a day, for twenty-eight days in a Los Angeles hospital research ward. Then lymphocytes were analyzed. The frequency of breaks, compared before and after smoking, doubled in the 1 percent group, changed little in the 2 percent group, and remained the same in the 0 percent group.[14]

Later they analyzed lymphocytes of thirteen male volunteers smoking marijuana in the same hospital ward. The smoking of four to ten (2 percent) joints daily for seventy-two days, following a twelve-day nondrug period, did not increase the overall frequency of breaks. (Breaks increased in six men and decreased in five.)

Matsuyama himself criticized the two experiments: Neither included a group of nonusers of drugs for comparison. All subjects had experience with marijuana. In the first study, two laboratories analyzed the same blood samples and cultures but came up with grossly different figures.[15]

• Fifteen men who had smoked pure hashish almost every day for ten to thirty years and an equal number of "normal" men yielded blood samples to Miras and colleagues of the medical school at the University of Athens, Greece, for chromosomal analysis of white cells.

The analysts found smokers' rates of breakage and numerical aberration (too many or too few chromosomes) "far exceeding" those for nonsmokers. The abnormalities "could be reasonably associated with hashish as they do not seem attributable to any of the usual causes such as the effects of irradiation, viruses or chemicals. We believe that hashish gives rise to irregular mitoses [cell divisions] similar to what has been demonstrated with certain chemical agents, as well as with X-rays."

In a United Nations report, they wrote that breakage caused by hashish might or might not mend; either way, the damage could doom the cell and, they suspected, encourage tumors and deformed offspring.

They did not report the nonusers' test results or the result of any statistical test. In the hashish smokers the percentage of cells with breaks averaged 13 percent; with numerical aberrations, 24 percent.

> All of the fifteen hashish smokers showed some kind of chromosomal irregularity. A table listed "breaks" in chromosomes of eleven smokers, "hypoploidy" (chromosome shortage) in fourteen, "hyperploidy" (chromosome surplus) in nine, "asymmetrical chromosomes" in thirteen, and "dicentric chromosomes" in three. The individual percentage of cells with such irregularities ranged from twenty-five to sixty-nine—and that, coincidentally, was the range in age.[16]

2

Cellular Activity

The cell is the smallest unit of structure of living things that is capable of functioning independently. Among its functions is reproduction, which it achieves by dividing. In the process it needs to manufacture protein and the nucleic acids DNA and RNA. (The first is deoxyribonucleic acid, a basic genetic material. Found in the nucleus of each cell, it is considered to be the self-reproducing component of chromosomes and the carrier of hereditary information. The second is ribonucleic acid, another essential constituent of the cell, found in both the nucleus and the cytoplasm, and understood to control protein production.)

Various scientists studying chromosomes (Neu, for instance) as well as scientists studying immunity have observed a tendency of cannabis to curb the process of cell division, at least in white blood cells.

Those performing the Jamaican chromosome study reported that "the administration of cannabis resin to both human and rat cultures resulted in a lowering of the mitotic rate," that is, the percentage of cells undergoing mitosis, the cell-division process. "A dose-response relation was observed; at higher concentrations of the drug the mitotic depression was greater." And at a certain point, cell division halted completely.

> The point was a concentration of 200 micrograms of resin per milliliter of medium.
>
> In other experiments, the Jamaican investigators did not find mitotic inhibition in cell cultures from cannabis smokers or rats injected with cannabis resin (compared with controls). But they did not estimate the quantities of THC in blood of subjects at the times of sampling.
>
> They speculated, in *Teratology* (a journal specializing in the study of fetal abnormalities): "Although toxic effects seen in vitro [in glass] are not necessarily the same in vivo [in life], it is possible that high concentrations of the drug achieved even temporarily by heavy users might have an inhibitory effect on the proliferative capacities of embryonic or germ cells."[17]

A number of scientists have noted that cannabinoids appeared to thwart the cell's synthesis of nucleic acids and proteins. Early in the seventies, at least two teams in the United States and Canada—separately studying rats' brains at about the same time—indicated the possibility of such a phenomenon. Each used great amounts of drug.

• Luthra, Rosenkrantz, and others in Massachusetts gave live rats THC or crude marijuana extract for twenty-eight or ninety-one days, respectively, via stomach tube. When analyzed, brains of treated animals had considerably less protein and RNA than controls (the amounts related to dosage in the THC group). The scientists thought THC broke down the molecules or prevented their buildup or both.[18]

• Jakubovic and McGeer in Vancouver, Canada, incubated slices of brains of rats, both adults and pups, with cannabinoids and radioactive leucine and uridine. THC and cannabidiol similarly inhibited the incorporation of the leucine into protein and the uridine into nucleic acid—

the younger the animal, the more the inhibition.

With associate Hattori, they also injected cannabinoids into infant rats and examined brain cells under the electron microscope. Delta-9-THC and two other psychoactive cannabinoids (delta-8-THC and 11-OH-delta-9-THC, but not three other cannabinoids) each brought about a reduction in the number of ribosomes (particles involved in cellular synthesis of protein) attached to membranes inside the brain cells. The reductions varied with dose and time and were reversible. Similar results ensued in brain cells of suckling rats after THC-injections in their mothers.[19]

Later, Jacubovic and McGeer used rat testes to study the synthesis of protein and nucleic acid in the presence of a variety of cannabinoids. They incubated the tissue with the cannabinoids and measured the extent to which the cells incorporated various essential chemicals.

All of the cannabinoids that they tested, whether psychoactive or not, tended generally to deter the synthesis of nucleic acid and protein, and often lipids (fats and fatlike substances) as well. In general, the more psychoactive cannabinoids had the greater influence.

> The chemicals used were uridine, orotic acid, thymidine, adenine, and glucose, all radioactive for purpose of measurement. Psychoactive cannabinoids tested were delta-8-THC, delta-9-THC and its derivative SP-111A, and 11-OH-delta-9-THC. Less psychoactive or psycho-inactive cannabinoids tested were cannabidiol, cannabinol, cannabigerol, and 8-beta-OH-delta-9-THC.
>
> The pair had chosen the testis to study primarily because nucleic acids and proteins were known to be synthesized rapidly during sperm production. Further, they thought that an interference with that process of synthesis might explain the decline in sex-gland function observed among cannabis users.[20]

Zoology Professor Arthur M. Zimmerman of the University of Toronto has been studying the effects of cannabinoids on cells and their functions since 1970 with his wife, Selma, natural sciences professor at York University, among collaborators. These are some results:

A. In a series of experiments on the one-celled animal *Tetrahymena pyriformis*, chosen as a model cellular system, THC introduced to cultures depressed its reproduction and metabolism. At "modest" doses, the drug delayed the division of cells and held down increases in cell population, the effects varying with dosage; and the drug lessened the synthesis of DNA, RNA, and proteins, as gauged by the decreased incorporation of (radioactive) precursors, chemical building blocks.

B. Are cannabinoids mutagens, substances able to cause mutations, changes in genes or chromosomes? Several standard test-tube assays (using bacteria and cultured human cells) apparently answered the question negatively.

C. Later, though, cannabinoids injected in mice "at dosages relative to human use" stimulated "positive mutagenic response." Compared with undrugged mice, treated mice displayed more abnormal changes in appearance of sperm—although their sperm ultimately returned to normal—and more chromosomal abnormalities in red blood cells, bone marrow cells, and developing sperm cells.

Zimmerman summarized (1980): "The studies reported show that THC suppresses cell growth, cellular metabolism, and the immune response in laboratory studies." The *in vitro* (test tube) studies displayed little or no mutagenic effect, but those *in vivo* (live) showed "a potentially harmful effect, which may be attributed to cannabinoid treatment. One could conclude from these studies that delta-9-tetrahydrocannabinol (THC) is a weak mutagen."[21]

Zimmerman found the tetrahymena to be an excellent model for studying the effects of drugs on cells because the cells could easily be induced to divide simultaneously and because much was known about that protozoan. Intermittent heat treatment would induce the cells to divide together. THC at 9.6 micromolar concentration, for example, delayed division for fifteen minutes; depressed the colony growth rate 11 percent; and reduced the incorporation of uridine into RNA by 70 percent, thymidine into DNA by 30 percent, and phenylalanine into protein by 35 percent.[22]

Zimmerman initially concluded that the cannabinoids were not mutagens when THC failed to alter salmonella bacteria or induce chromosomal abnormalities in cultured human fibroblasts and neither THC nor three other cannabinoids encouraged precancerous DNA synthesis in those fibroblasts.[23]

One index for assessing whether chemical compounds are mutagens is "sperm head morphology. . . . An agent displays a positive mutagenic response when sperm abnormalities exceed the 3 percent level." Male mice treated with THC or CBN (cannabinol), but not mice treated with CBD (cannabidiol), exceeded that level when scored thirty-five days after the last of five intraperitoneal treatments. Normal sperm has a smooth, kidney-shaped head with a prominent hook; abnormal sperm heads are either folded, hookless, banana shaped, or amorphous.[24]

In chromosomal analyses, excessive abnormalities appeared in red blood cells of mice treated with THC, CBN, or CBD; abnormalities in mouse spermatocytes (developing sperm cells) tripled after THC treatment but reversed after seventy-two days; and bone marrow cells of cannabinoid-treated mice showed three to seven times as many abnormalities as normal.[25]

Akira Morishima's interest in cannabis stemmed from a study he made for the City of New York of genetic changes in cells of heroin addicts. "The vast majority of heroin addicts we were able to study smoked marijuana, at least on occasions, and therefore it became important to examine separately the effects of marijuana," he said. Dr. Morishima, a cell geneticist and pediatrician on the Columbia University medical faculty, who was born and educated in Japan, studied marijuana's effects at length. He came up with these findings:

A. In each of three microscopic studies of cultured lymphocytes, samples from young, male, habitual marijuana smokers contained a significant number of cells with too few chromosomes. From tens of thousands of cells examined, habitual smokers had two to four times as many cells with chromosome shortages as nonusers.

B. When cultured with THC, lymphocytes from nonusers showed more than the normal number of "segregational errors of chromosomes," the chromosomes dividing improperly during cell division. The incidence of such errors in users was normal before and after smoking but elevated during a smoking period.

C. In an experiment "to imitate the effects of prolonged use of THC upon egg cells of sexually immature girls," fertilized eggs from young female mice injected with THC had more than triple the nuclear abnormalities of controls.

The data suggested to Morishima that "marijuana results in severe disruption of normal processes by which chromosomes are transmitted to succeeding generations of cells in a precise and orderly fashion," and that THC, acting as a poison and a mutagen, disturbs the chromosomes during cell division and may hurt early embryonic development.[26]

Morishima counted the number of cells with thirty or less chromosomes. (Cells with thirty-one or more chromosomes were classified as normal to allow a margin for error.) The percentages of these "hypoploid metaphases" came to:

• About 31 percent of cells from three smokers who smoked marijuana at least weekly—compared with about 7 percent from three nonusers. "This incidence was so high that I have not encountered a comparable phenomenon in any other clinical situations in fifteen years of experience in cytogenics," Morishima testified. (Further, 60,173 cells of the marijuana smokers showed a lower "mitotic index" than 59,000 control cells: 2.4 percent versus 5.9 percent in the process of cell division.)[27]

• About one-quarter of cells from five who smoked marijuana more than three times a week—compared with about one-tenth among ten nonusers. (Results for five lighter smokers barely differed from control figures but technical problems marred the study.)[28]

• About 36 percent of cells from five smokers (at least ten joints a week) sampled during a heavy-smoking period in a hospital. This was double the count for seven nonusers and nearly triple the smokers' score during an earlier, three-week, drugless period. But counts returned close to normal ten days after the users stopped smoking. They had been "encouraged to smoke as many marijuana cigarettes as possible" for four weeks, and they averaged fourteen a day. (The presmoking count did not include one subject who refused to cooperate until he got his marijuana.)[29]

Segregational errors, scored in blind fashion, came to 3.5 percent of eight non-users' treated cells (cultured for three days at a 3.2 micromolar concentration). Incidence of spontaneous errors in twenty-five healthy men who never had used cannabis (including the eight above) was 1.3 percent of 3,304 dividing cells.

Of 1,383 cells from users, the rates before, during, and after smoking were 1.2, 2.0, and 1.3 percent, respectively.

Morishima classified six categories of these errors. An example is "bridge formation," in which an elongated chromosome lies across the space created by two split nuclei. Another is "unequal segregation," a difference in size, therefore in the amount of chromosome material, between the two separating nuclei of a dividing cell.[30]

In the egg cell experiments, female mice received daily THC injections from the age of twenty-six days until they reached sexual maturity two weeks later. Untreated males mated with them. Two days later the fertilized eggs were recovered. Abnormalities had occurred in 37.5 percent of cells recovered from THC mice, compared with 10 percent in cells obtained from controls. The abnormalities included "degenerating nucleus . . . premature hatching . . . and unequal nuclear sizes."[31]

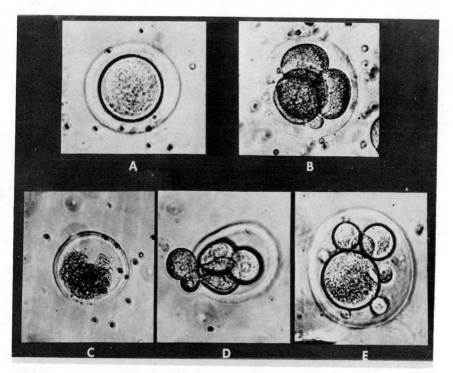

The Morishima mouse-egg experiment. A and B are normal ova in the one-cell and four-cell stages, respectively. The other ova, from THC-treated mice, display "degenerating nucleus" (C), "premature hatching of nuclei" (D), and "unequal nuclear sizes" (E).

Various other investigators in different countries have found cannabis or cannabinoids to interfere with cellular activity. Elsewhere we cite most of the following findings by four groups of scientists.

• Neu and colleagues, primarily studying the effect of delta-8-THC on lymphocyte chromosomes, observed no damage but did notice that the drug drastically reduced cell division.

• The Leuchtenbergers in Switzerland, testing cultured cells from the human lung, found that both marijuana smoke and tobacco smoke—but more so marijuana—stimulated abnormalities in DNA synthesis, cell division, growth of cultures, and the number and DNA content of chromosomes. In hamster lung samples, either marijuana smoke or tobacco smoke caused cells and DNA to proliferate to the point of malignancy. When they introduced marijuana smoke to mouse testis cultures, it increased the frequency of spermatids with low DNA content—while tobacco smoke caused no such effect—and similar results ensued when live mice inhaled marijuana smoke.

"One of the most striking observations on human cell cultures," Professor Cecile Leuchtenberger wrote us later, "is the difference of response to vitamin C between human breast cancer cultures exposed to marijuana smoke and human breast cancer cultures exposed to tobacco smoke." Among the tobacco-exposed cells, vitamin C prompted a reduction in abnormal growth. Meanwhile, among the marijuana-exposed cells, vitamin C had no such effect; in fact, abnormal growth accelerated. The data suggest that marijuana smoke not only stimulates "abnormalities of cell growth" but also interferes with "cell metabolism relating to vitamin C."

• Dixit and colleagues in India recorded that mice injected daily with cannabis extract suffered degenerating cells and a substantial decrease in RNA in the testis, deterioration in both nucleus and cytoplasm of Leydig cells (testicle tissue that secretes sex hormone), arrested development of sperm cells, and ultimately total sperm stoppage.

• Nahas and coworkers, culturing lymphocytes to learn cannabis's effect on immunity, discovered that marijuana smokers' cells absorbed considerably less thymidine (a building block of DNA) than nonusers. Later he and his group noted that THC and several other cannabinoids deterred the synthesis of DNA, RNA, and protein in normal, cultured lymphocytes in the laboratory.

*   *   *

Meanwhile, Blevins and Regan in Tennessee (1976) looked into the effect of THC on cultured human and mouse cells. It restrained the incorporation of thymidine, uridine, and leucine (all radioactive) into DNA, RNA, and protein, respectively.

At low concentration, THC reduced the synthesis of the nucleic acids 11 to 17 percent but had no effect on protein synthesis. At high concentration, it reduced nucleic acid synthesis 37 to 58 percent and protein synthesis 30 to 40 percent.

> The pair (with the health sciences department of East Tennessee and the biology division of the Oak Ridge National Laboratory, respectively) cultured, according to standard procedures, normal human fibroblasts, human neuroblastoma (cancerous) cells, and mouse neuroblastoma cells.
>
> Low and high concentrations were 101 and 3,145 nanograms of THC per milliliter of cell medium. The high concentration was at least a dozen times above the blood level of marijuana smokers, however. "Because of the manner in which successive dosages of delta-9-THC lead to accumulation, consideration of the effects of delta-9-THC concentrated in body tissues (and thus its effects on macromolecular synthesis and physiological action) is necessary."[32]

Costas N. Stefanis and Marietta R. Issidorides, both of the University of Athens, Greece, studied cells of fifty-two men, including thirty-four long-term hashish smokers and eighteen nonusers of cannabis who smoked tobacco regularly. From blood samples, they examined white cells microscopically and also tested them with chemical stains to identify certain substances by color. Sperm cells of four users and four controls were similarly tested.

In white blood cells of the hashish users, they frequently observed structural changes and consistently found chemical changes. Twenty-one of the users' cell nuclei had appendages called drumsticks, "characteristic of the female sex" but not of normal men. One of the chemical findings was decreased (compared with controls) arginine content in lymphocyte nuclei. Nuclei of smokers' sperm had the same shortage. (Arginine, an amino acid, is part of the protein in chromosomes.)

"Our results clearly demonstrate," they reported (1976), "that in man chronic cannabis use leads to alteration of the cellular metabolism, which is particularly evident in the nuclear area." Observations in blood cells and sperm indicated that "the state of the chromatin is altered under the effect of cannabis." (Chromatin is the substance that makes up the chromosomes. It consists of DNA and protein.)

The two Greek researchers said the sperm apparently was normal in reproductive capacity because it displayed normal shape.[33] Later, however, scrutinizing the samples through an electron microscope, Professor Issidorides detected structural abnormalities and revised her opinion. The three main abnormalities, in order of frequency, were undeveloped or missing acrosome (a caplike covering on the front end of the sperm cell); spotty chromatin; and forms of nucleus characteristic of immature sperm, suggesting the arrest of maturation in chronic users. Details of sperm structure are normally controlled by heredity, so the fact that cannabis interferes with these details supports the idea (propounded by Zimmerman et al.) that the cannabis interacts with the chromosomes, she said (1979).[34]

Among other changes in users were these, found in neutrophils (white blood cells that stain easily with neutral dyes): a loss of phospholipids from the membrane and outer cytoplasm; mostly deformed, irregular cell surfaces; uniform increase in arginine-rich histones; and in varying degree an increase in glycolipids in the cytoplasm.

The subjects, paid volunteers, on the average began smoking hashish at age sixteen, continued for twenty-five years, and at the time of examination used it twice a day, three grams daily. Nothing was reported about any children they had fathered.[35]

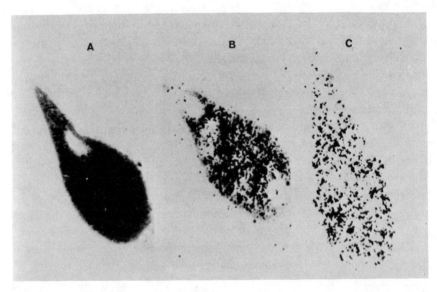

These are spermatozoa from Greek men, as the electron microscope pictures it. Tested for the amino acid arginine (by the ammoniacal silver reaction), they showed distinct differences between hashish smokers and nonsmokers, per Stefanis and Issidorides. A dense black reaction in a sperm cell of a nonsmoking man (A) indicated arginine-rich protein, as expected from normal sperm. In contrast, sperm cells from chronic smokers of hashish (B and C) gave a spotty reaction for arginine. (Courtesy of Listen *magazine.)*

This sobering theoretical account of microscopic events set in motion by the introduction of cannabinoid to the body came from unpublished notes (1978) by the late Professor Hardin B. Jones of Berkeley, California.

"THC has a high affinity for absorption by fat," he wrote. "Fat in tissues is mostly combined with proteins and these are called lipoproteins. Lipoproteins of the blood carry the THC absorbed from marijuana smoking. Lipoproteins that are a part of cell structures become increasingly burdened by THC as it is retained and accumulates with repeated intake.

"Paton and his colleagues at Oxford have led the way to understanding these properties of THC and the accumulation of it on the lipoproteins of the cell membranes; concentrations on the outer and inner cell membranes may be several hundred times greater than the concentration in blood plasma.[36]

"As THC accumulates in the body, the burden on cell membranes increases. These membranes have important functions in cell metabolism—in providing the cell with oxygen and food, in the elimination of waste products, and in providing surfaces where some of the crucial chemical events of cell life take place.

"Alteration of the cell membranes probably has a lot to do with the fact that functions of cells are somewhat altered by THC. Cell division is slowed; separation of chromosomes on the completion of cell division is erratic so that one daughter cell gets more and the other equally less than the usual number of chromosomes. Chromosomes may be formed improperly during DNA synthesis so that some are broken and others may have irregularities.

"The nature of these changes suggests that the THC has not affected the central mechanisms in cell division directly, for that would lead to lethal effects, and THC isn't an immediate threat to life, even at usual high doses. What happens is interference by THC with the usually precise events in proper synthesis of new constituents of cells (DNA, RNA, and proteins).

"Thus, with heavy, regular marijuana use, the process of cell division is slowed and handicapped and there are more chromosome errors than usual. This is of potential consequence because the accumulation of cellular genetic errors is believed to contribute to aging, malformation of embryos, genetic impairment of offspring, and cancer."

3

Cancer in Rodents

Cancer developed in rats injected with marijuana tar (that is, the condensate from the smoke) for fifty-eight weeks in Reading, Pennsylvania. Medical Doctors John C. Cottrell, pathologist, and Wolfgang H. Vogel, clinical pharmacologist, injected acetone solutions of marijuana tar into thigh muscles of twenty-five rats three times a week. An equal number received similar injections of the acetone alone.

None of the latter group became ill at all. "The only thing they did was get fat and grow," Dr. Cottrell remarked. Fourteen of the marijuana rats died—eight of them from cancer.

Sarcoma (cancer of connective tissue) showed up first. "Then rats began to die from what we thought initially was pneumonia—until we examined the lungs microscopically and found out it was carcinoma" (cancer of tissue lining); two rats had it. Three rats each had sarcoma and lymphoma (cancer of lymph nodes).

The doctors had imitated a tobacco experiment of the early sixties. "We followed the design exactly, except that we used marijuana instead of tobacco." Analysis of the marijuana tar isolated "a surprising amount of benzopyrene," a well-known cancer-causing substance, more than in tobacco.

In the tobacco experiment (by Druckrey, cited in the 1964 surgeon general's report, *Smoking and Health*), a fifth of the rats developed cancer, sarcoma at the site of injection. In the marijuana experiment, more rats—nearly a third—got cancer, of more types.

Doses were large. The heaviness of the dosage may have accelerated cancer development; nevertheless the experiment has relevance to human marijuana consumers if the theory holds true that carcinogens in any amount are dangerous because of a cumulative effect, the pathologist explained.

Injections began at St. Joseph Hospital in Reading in October, 1975, building up to 60 mg of tar after several weeks. They ended in December, 1976, when the first cancer appeared, a fibrosarcoma in a foot of one rat. Three rats (including that one) had fibrosarcomas at points of injection. The six noncancer deaths in-

cluded four from pneumococcal pneumonia and two from hemorrhagic pancrea-
titis. All rats were of the DUB (SD) strain.

Concentration of benzo(alpha)pyrene was 1.5 mg/ml of crude tar.

The study ended in July, 1977, but had not been published in a journal by the
time of our long distance interview (1982).

*   *   *

A writer on food additives (Michael F. Jacobson, 1976), observed that "just
because extremely high dosages of a chemical are harmful does not mean that
high levels or normal dietary levels will be harmful. . . .

"Cancer, however, does *not* appear to be one of the effects that occurs at high
dosages, but not at low dosages. If tumors are caused by feeding an animal large
amounts of a chemical, we must assume that small amounts will also cause tumors, although less frequently. The 1958 food additive law recognizes the importance of eliminating carcinogens from our food supply by banning any additive that 'is found to induce cancer when ingested by man or animal.' "[37]

The discovery of cancer in mice injected with THC—a discovery that
surprised the researchers, who had been studying reproductive effects of
the drug—was made in Florida under the direction of Dr. Josel Szepsenwol, M.D., research professor at Florida International University in
Miami.

They gave weekly injections of THC in sesame oil to 216 mice of one
strain (BALB/c) for an average of seventeen months, and 118 of them—
55 percent—developed cancer. There were seventy-three lung tumors,
twenty-one sarcomas (cancer of connective tissue), and twenty-four
mammary tumors.

The rates of lung cancer and sarcoma in mice treated with sesame oil
alone were far below those for the mice treated with THC in sesame oil;
completely untreated mice had lower rates yet. But when it came to
mammary cancer, the sesame oil–only group had by far the highest rate;
the THC group came next. (See table 1.)

"We are obtaining now the same results with mice of another strain,
the C57 Black/6, which is considered cancer-resistant," Dr. Szepsenwol
informed us. The mice were acquiring the same kind of tumors—from
injections of cannabinol as well as THC. By autumn of 1983 over a
hundred mice of the latter strain had been tested.

"I feel that THC and also CBN, or cannabinol, both are carcinogenic," Dr. Szepsenwol said. But he added the qualification that "THC
may inhibit mammary cancer to some extent."

Why did his group find tumors when so many other investigators
studying rodents and cannabinoids did not? The others do not study the
carcinogenic effects and do not perform such long-term experiments, he
said. He usually keeps the mice until they become sick and start losing

weight. In most cases they have reached an advanced age. Then he dispatches them and cuts them open for examination.

Injections began at the age of three to five days. If the life expectancy of a mouse is "two to three years," an average animal received THC treatments for half to three-fourths of a normal lifetime.

The amount of THC injected weekly under the skin of each mouse approximately equaled the amount of THC received per week by a typical marijuana smoker (adjusting for difference in body weight), Dr. Szepsenwol said.

> The dose to each mouse was 20 micrograms.
>
> All of the sarcomas and close to a fifth of the mammary cancers in the THC group originated at the points of injection. The location of injection had no relation to the lung cancers.
>
> Most of the mice died or were killed at ages between 500 and 700 days, a few in each group at younger ages.
>
> In a related project, synovial sarcomas, rhabdomyosarcomas, and fibrosarcomas developed at points of injection with cannabinol, cannabidiol, and THC in eight mice of both strains. (1983).[38]
>
> Dr. Szepsenwol was born in Poland and, before joining the biological sciences department at Florida International, was associated with the Universities of Geneva and Buenos Aires, Yale and Emory (Atlanta) Universities, and the Universities of North Carolina and Puerto Rico (in that order). While possessing a medical degree, he never practiced medicine but was primarily an anatomy professor. His research interests have centered on experimental embryology, tissue culture, and cancer. We were in touch by mail and telephone (1981–83).
>
> Earlier experiments by Virginia medical researchers in which THC temporarily retarded cancer growth are described in "Medicine," 4.

TABLE 1

CANCER IN MICE

Results of Dr. Szepsenwol's Experiment on 438 Mice of the
BALB/c Strain (Figures are rounded. Mammary cancer percentages
pertain only to females.)

| | NUMBER OF MICE | | AVERAGE AGE IN DAYS | NUMBER OF MICE WITH CANCER | LUNG CANCER | MAMMARY CANCER | SARCOMA |
	Males	Females					
UNTREATED MICE	73	78	668	13 (8%)	3 (2%)	9 (12%)	1 (1%)
SESAME OIL MICE	36	35	558	27 (38%)	5 (7%)	21 (60%)	1 (1%)
THC MICE	86	130	524	118 (55%)	73 (34%)	24 (18%)	21 (10%)

PART II

CANNABIS AND THE PSYCHE

THE
BRAIN

- *"I'm afraid of brain damage—that's the big thing, loss of memory. . . . I believe that brain damage can occur if pot is used excessively. I also feel to a certain extent pot dulls your senses a little bit. However I also feel it's a worthwhile exchange for some of the benefits."* —Bert (chronic user)

- *"It definitely made me a mush-brain. . . . I couldn't read a book or do my homework. Once I managed to go to French class. I was lighting a joint and ignited my own curls. I remember my embarrassment. A couple curls went."* —Rosemary (ex-user)

- *"It enhances my hearing and my sensitivity and gives me more intellectual activity."* —Pete (chronic smoker and marijuana advocate)

- *"I started realizing that I felt really stupid when I smoked pot. . . . I started thinking it would make me permanently stupid. . . .*
"I took an IQ test when I was heavy into pot at sixteen. I just freaked out. I couldn't do anything. I'm usually good at those puzzles. I scored ninety. The last IQ test that I took before I started taking pot was one-fifty-four in the fourth grade. I was about eleven. . . .
"I really think pot makes you stupid. . . . I refuse to talk to anyone who is smoking it. People aren't coherent. . . .
"I think my thoughts were a lot sharper before and I was a lot more imaginative." —Janet (ex-user)

- *"I'm hoping you could answer some questions for me. First of all I started smoking pot when I was in high school about five years ago. I smoked regularly for about six to seven months. I started feeling more & more depersonalized & spaced even if I hadn't smoked pot. I quit smoking, hoping that I would start feeling good again but I kept getting worse. I feel like I no longer have any person within me. Since it's been several years since I've smoked and I haven't noticed any improvement, would I be correct assuming brain damage? . . .*

"If I'm one of the persons that it caused brain atrophy, is there any hope in ever getting well? Every doctor I've talked to, said pot couldn't cause me to feel this way, but I didn't feel this way before I used pot. Do you know of any medication that might be of help to me? Do you think Bio Feedback would help? I'm so desperate for any suggestions!" —Art of Oklahoma (in a letter)

"Since I wrote you, I had several tests taking at a local clinic. They took X-Rays of my head and several blood tests and they didn't find anything wrong.

"I did write Dr. ———. . . . He suggested I might go to a psychologist . . . I did go to one for awhile, but he didn't do anything for me.

"A friend referred me to a doctor in a nearby town which did a test and it did show there was something wrong in the brain stem. He prescribed some tablets. . . . I still feel worse more & more. I'm really getting scared now." —Art of Oklahoma (in another letter, a year later)

• *"There was general confusion, in the last couple years especially. When I wasn't high, my vision was muddled. The air wasn't completely clear, something like if you look under a microscope and see vibrating cells. . . .*

"If I was asked a question, the answer wouldn't come right away. Things didn't seem to flow out as easily. Just like there was a big pile of junk to wade through before talk would come out. . . .

"I was feeling the effects two or three months after I quit. There's still some tinge [a year after], sometimes shyness." —Steve (ex-user)

• *"Some synapses were affected by the THC. . . . Childhood memories would come to me in vivid color. . . . But I get into a conversation and forget the subject of conversation. . . . It's like senility."* —Kathy (light user, former heavy user)

• *"I was intensely involved with marijuana for only a year. . . . After my drug experience I continued to be hazy in my mind. I'm normally not a very organized person, but I've felt that I just became so much more disorganized and I remained so much more disorganized as a result of the bombardment that I put on my brain . . . much more loose, much more able to forget facts, forget faces. . . . It lasted. . . . I stopped when*

I was fourteen or fifteen, and I'm twenty-nine, so that's fourteen years."
—Lewis (ex-user)

• *"I had PCP once. Somebody passed around a joint that tasted real weird. I got stoned in a real weird way. You can hear brain cells sizzling on the grill. I knew I was losing some parts of my brain. I knew it would. I got real mad. We knew who did it. It was this friend of ours' brother. He just wanted to get us real high. I told him it was real uncool."* — Alice (chronic user)

1

In General

What's the difference between the brain and the mind? Are they one or are they separate? If the mind is separate, where is it? These questions and the like have engaged philosophers for millennia. For the sake of clarity, not of argument, we are separating the two. So we need to define our terms.

We regard "brain" as an organ, "mind" as a general term referring to the brain's actions, past and present. You cannot see a mind. You can see a brain, or an electronic image of one.

But seeing the wrinkled, three-pound collection of billions of cells tells nothing about the consciousness it represents—all the thinking, perceiving, remembering, willing, feeling, and imagining it has done. Is it the brain of a scholar, simpleton, scoundrel, or saint? All the world's psychobiologists with the most advanced equipment couldn't tell. No one yet knows what changes take place in the brain when it does what it does, when it learns new things, when it makes up its mind.

Medical science has shown that life can go on with a substitute heart, real or fabricated. But the brain is king on life's chessboard; once this piece is checkmated, the game is over. Notwithstanding such supreme importance, the brain remains the least understood organ of the body. The hows and whys of the brain's inner space rival outer space when it comes to mysteries beckoning to science.

The reason for the puzzlement lies partly in the incredible complexity of the brain's composition. It isn't easy to grasp the working of perhaps 15 billion neurons (nerve cells)—each neuron connecting, through the aid of chemicals, with thousands or tens of thousands of others—nearly an infinity of possible hookups—maybe billions of electrochemical impulses fired instantaneously to and from glands, muscles, and sense-receptors for a single fleeting thought or action!

But can part of the problem be that the brain resists the unraveling of its secrets?

One can readily see smoke-scarred lungs and compare them with healthy lungs. But one sees the two respective brains and they look alike.

Seeing may be believing, but to assume the converse—that not seeing calls for disbelieving—is faulty thinking. Some experimenters have an-

159

nounced discovery of structural or chemical brain changes in animals and, in some cases, in humans, caused by cannabis. Others have reported finding nothing. Some find persistent changes in functioning of the human or animal brain; others, none. Scientific critics have faulted and defended studies on both sides.

Brain research today remains an infant science, and—in the cannabis field particularly—enormous gaps remain. Yet while far from conclusive, the evidence is nonetheless grimly suggestive. For drug users to accept the negative findings but brush off the positive ones may be risky.

Dr. William Pollin, director of the National Institute on Drug Abuse, made these pertinent comments to congressional committees:

"Overall, of the studies [of cannabis and the brain] reviewed, the majority have suggested enduring impairment occurs. The quality of studies in this area, in particular, is highly variable, leaving the issue in significant doubt" (1979).

"It is entirely possible to have impairment of brain function from toxic or other causes that is not apparent on gross or microscopic examination of the brain" (1980).

"Additional research is needed, particularly with regard to any subtle changes in brain functioning that may occur as a result of marijuana use" (1981).[1]

Reese T. Jones, M.D., of San Francisco, has pointed out: "In science, particularly when dealing with drug effects, it is impossible to prove the absence of something or to prove that something will not happen."

Studies turning up no neurological differences between users and nonusers usually have selected relatively moderate smokers; possibly lasting impairment comes from higher doses or from marijuana's interaction with some other factor. One has to consider the total weight of evidence and the way studies were conducted, according to Dr. Jones, himself a noted cannabis researcher.

"If one considers neuro-chemical data from test tubes, animal data, clinical case reports, survey data, controlled laboratory data, and semi-controlled field studies, the weight of the evidence so far is that lasting neuro-psychological impairments are possibly but not inevitably associated with some undetermined level of heavy, prolonged cannabis use," he wrote (1980).[2]

The brain-mind separation used here is somewhat arbitrary, and the two sometimes will overlap, but for the most part it goes this way:

Here in "The Brain" we describe direct observations of brains, or impulses or images of the brain, after consumption of cannabis by people or animals. We look at experiments studying the course of cannabinoids in the body and brain, and we review studies investigating possible brain

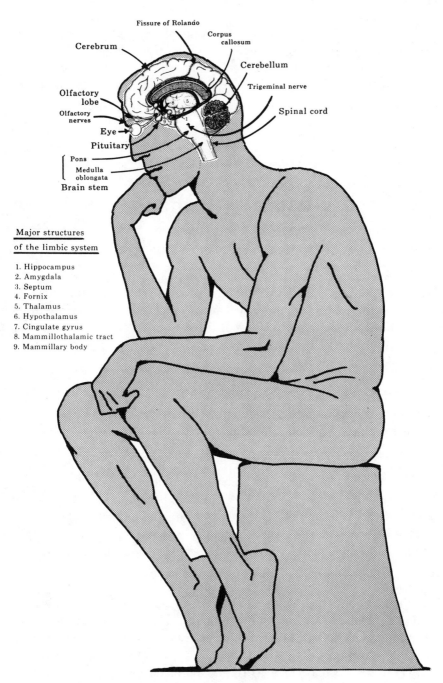

Fissure of Rolando
Corpus callosum
Cerebrum
Cerebellum
Olfactory lobe
Trigeminal nerve
Olfactory nerves
Spinal cord
Eye
Pituitary
Pons
Medulla oblongata
Brain stem

Major structures
of the limbic system

1. Hippocampus
2. Amygdala
3. Septum
4. Fornix
5. Thalamus
6. Hypothalamus
7. Cingulate gyrus
8. Mammillothalamic tract
9. Mammillary body

*The Brain in Use.
(With apology to Rodin.)*

injury from cannabis. Generally, human studies come first and animal studies follow.

In "The Mind" we will summarize some of the multitude of cannabis studies showing people using their brains—or misusing them, as the case may be. We have selected twenty-five such studies or groups of studies. They are arranged historically in each of three categories: (1) intoxication, (2) long-term use, and (3) psychic illness.

2

Mainly Humans

Julius Axelrod won the 1970 Nobel Prize for physiology, with two others, for studies in the chemistry of the nervous system and the effects of drugs on the brain. He and associates investigated mind-altering drugs for years at the National Institute of Mental Health of the U.S. Public Health Service (Bethesda, Maryland), where he has been chief of the clinical science laboratory.

The increasing use of marijuana, despite ignorance as to what happened to it in the body, generated their interest in the drug. In 1964 the isolation of the principal active ingredient in marijuana, THC, had permitted rapid progress in knowledge of the drug and its fate in human bodies.

"We developed sensitive methods to measure THC in the blood and urine of man," Axelrod told a Senate committee.

The scientific team, including Louis Lemberger and others, injected radioactively labeled THC into veins of human volunteers—two young women and two young men, none of whom ever had taken marijuana—and drew blood samples periodically, measuring the THC content.

The amount of the compound in plasma diminished rapidly at first. Within an hour, the decline slowed greatly; most of the drug was gone from the blood—but not from the body. "THC and its biochemically transformed products continued to be excreted in the urine for more than a week," Axelrod said.

The quick decrease of the drug in the blood represented "a redistribution of marijuana active principles from the blood into tissues including the brain. . . ." It also represented "chemical transformation. The metabolic alteration of THC takes place mainly in the liver. In man the psychological effects of marijuana are greatest in fifteen minutes after injection, begin to diminish after one hour, and are largely dissipated by three hours. This is consistent with the initial fast disappearance of the drug from the blood."

The slower disappearance of THC from the body presumably meant that some tissues retained it, releasing it slowly. "The observation that THC and its transformation-products persist in humans for long periods of time indicated to us that the drug and its metabolites [products of metabolism] would accumulate in some tissues when taken repeatedly."

This led to an experiment to find out which tissues THC settled in and to verify that repeated doses built up its concentration in those tissues. They injected radioactive THC into rats. Far more drug found its way into the fat than into any other tissue examined, and it accumulated steadily with repeated administration.

After a single injection of THC there appeared "barely detectable concentrations of THC in the brain, but after repeated administration there was a gradual accumulation of the drug in the brain."

In people, most of delta-9-THC is chemically transformed. An important product of this transformation was identified as 11-hydroxy-THC. Axelrod's and other laboratories found this chemical to have essentially the psychic effects associated with marijuana, the euphoria and anxiety.

Axelrod confirmed (in replies to questions at the Senate hearing, 1974) that:

• THC unquestionably is a toxic substance.

• When taken repeatedly and heavily, so that it accumulates in the brain, it probably leads to brain damage. At least this is "a good assumption," yet to be proved.

> Those investigating the course of THC in the human bloodstream and organs postulate that it disappears from the blood in two overlapping phases. The first is rapid: part of the THC is distributed to the tissues while part is metabolized into other cannabinoids. The second is slow: THC released from the tissues back into the blood is metabolized and excreted.
>
> Lemberger et al. (1970–72), measuring plasma levels of C-14-THC, placed the former phase at "a few hours," and half of the latter phase at fifty-seven hours for the marijuana nonusers tested (twenty-eight hours in tests of four regular marijuana users). Ten minutes after injection, the metabolites were present at concentrations higher than those of the parent compound. They too disappeared in fast and slow phases. And in a week, close to 70 percent of the total administered drug, now nearly all in metabolite form, was found in subjects' feces and urine.[3]

✻   ✻   ✻

Hunt and Jones in San Francisco (1980), using slightly different techniques, calculated that half of the terminal phase of elimination from the plasma took about twenty hours when they injected C-14-THC in six marijuana smokers. They figured too that initially the tissues absorbed about 70 percent of the plasma's THC, the rest being converted to metabolites, and that the majority of the radioactivity was recovered in excreta on the first day. Extensive protein binding of metabolites delayed clearance by the kidneys. THC, with its high lipid solubility, may survive longer in fat people than in thin ones.[4]

Of greater importance for health than THC's longevity in the body is the persistance of the dozens of THC metabolites, which have terminal half-lives of fifty hours or more in the blood, Reese T. Jones commented (1983). He noted that after one dose, up to a fifth of the metabolite produced can remain in the body a week later and complete elimination can take a month or more. Clinical investigators reporting subtle cumulative effects of cannabinoids even in infrequent users may be seeing the consequences of accumulation of THC and metabolites, Dr. Jones added.[5]

"There seemed to be a striking difference between the bright lively youngster of 14 who was interested in fishing and shooting and was able to strip down and maintain a motorcycle, and the retarded, slothful, emotionally labile, and intolerant man of 22." This is a quotation from one of the most frequently cited and controversial scientific reports in the drug field, issued by British neurologist Archibald M. G. Campbell and three colleagues in 1971.

In the pages of *The Lancet* they described a "pattern of cerebral atrophy in a series of young men who smoked cannabis." Cerebral atrophy, they explained, "indicates irreversible brain damage." Test results suggested that "regular use of cannabis" could produce such atrophy, which was otherwise rare in young people, Dr. Campbell and the others told readers of the English medical weekly.

Campbell used a diagnostic procedure that is usually termed pneumoencephalography, which he called air-encephalography. Exacting and hazardous, causing the patient days of headaches and nausea, it has generally been replaced by other techniques. Even then it was becoming rare. Essentially it entails X-ray photographing of cavities in the brain, called the ventricles, after cerebrospinal fluid (which flows through them) is removed and replaced with air to provide visual contrast.

The report compared the sizes of the ventricles in ten young, habitual cannabis smokers with those in thirteen patients of similar age (presumably with no cannabis habit) who had undergone air-encephalography but been found normal. Campbell found increases in size of the ventricles in each of the ten. More empty space meant less brain substance; some of it had wasted away.

A coworker, psychiatrist Myrddin Evans, reviewing the study in 1974, after Campbell's death, saw significance in nine out of ten cases. The results still were "positive and disturbing," however he tempered his conclusion. That regular, heavy smoking of cannabis resin—he specified resin—might produce cerebral atrophy was a "possibility" calling for urgent investigation.

Detailing each ventricle expansion, the Campbell paper likened the changes to "parkinsonism" and "the atrophy of old age and arteriosclerosis." While measurements found in the smokers might be normal in people aged sixty to eighty, "they are abnormal for this age group." The ages of the ten ranged from eighteen to twenty-eight, averaging twenty-two. Cannabis-smoking histories varied from three to eleven years (including temporary abstinence), an average of six.

The first four of the ten patients had been referred to Campbell, at Bristol Royal United Hospitals, for neurological investigation of headaches, memory loss, behavior change, mental impairment, or, in one case, epilepsy. All four "had been to some extent poly-drug takers." However, "a common factor in all four histories was prolonged heavy cannabis smoking."

The next five patients, all with histories of prolonged and intensive cannabis smoking, had been referred from an addiction center headed by Evans at Whitchurch Hospital, Cardiff, Wales.

The tenth was an emergency patient hospitalized for a drug overdose. He had been taking large amounts of cannabis and amphetamine and some LSD.

Dr. Evans understood all of the patients to smoke "one half or one ounce weekly of concentrated material," that is, cannabis resin, also called hashish. "It was common practice to mix the resin with shreds of ordinary tobacco, and all patients had taken other drugs of dependence. . . ."

All ten patients had taken LSD, at least a couple of times; eight had taken amphetamines; three had taken other drugs, including barbiturates, sedatives, and opiates; and two had drunk a good deal of alcohol. Further, three had suffered head injuries. Campbell did not consider the consumption of the other drugs or alcohol as significant and described the head injuries as minor. Critics, however, have made much of those points.

Campbell and his associates recognized that "Cerebral atrophy is known to occur in alcoholism," but said, "Only two of our cases . . . had taken much alcohol, and alcoholism is unusual in heavy cannabis smokers." A common pattern was to start on amphetamines and soon smoke cannabis regularly. "L.S.D. had also been taken, but cannabis became the predominant drug in all cases. . . . Morphine, heroin, or cocaine had not been taken in any significant quantities. . . . Although amphetamines and L.S.D. may have an added effect, they are rapidly metabolised and excreted and would not seem likely to have the cumulative effect on nervous tissue of the fat-soluble components of cannabis."

Campbell and group acknowledged that cerebral atrophy could stem from severe head injuries. ("For many years the production of cerebral atrophy in professional boxers was not realized.") Three of the patients had been struck on the head but "we do not consider that their head injuries played a part in the enlargement of the ventricular system." They were "minor" injuries. A variety of diseases, congenital or acquired, likewise can cause such atrophy, but "We found no such causes for cerebral atrophy in this series of ten drug addicts."

Critics have suggested that the patients were abnormal before they began smoking cannabis. Anticipating this criticism, Campbell and group said that "in at least three cases where we know the history intimately these individuals were entirely normal before they started drug-taking."

An admitted difficulty was in the choice of so-called controls. To estimate the normal size of the ventricles, "we reviewed the X-ray films and notes of all cases investigated by air encephalography in our neuroradiological unit in which the findings had been reported at the time as normal." Those with abnormal physical signs were excluded. This left as controls thirteen patients, aged fifteen to twenty-five, seven females and six males, who had been referred because of symptoms such as headaches and fainting spells.

The work concluded by calling for further studies of long-term effects of cannabis smoking on the nervous system, including additional X-ray tests. (No cannabis researcher repeated the encephalographic technique used by Campbell, although at least two X-ray brain studies of marijuana smokers, using a safer method, did follow.)

The Lancet commented editorially, in the issue that presented the Campbell study, that the authors had demonstrated significant atrophy. "What is not certain is whether these changes are caused by the use of cannabis. Comparison with normal controls is not enough to prove this point. The controls might more appropriately have been individuals with personality disorders without exposure to cannabis. . . ."

Ten letters, divided equally between support and censure, appeared in The Lancet in the two months after publication of the provocative piece (in addition to a letter by the Campbell team).

"The article by Dr. Campbell and his colleagues . . . was front-page news before the journal reached me here," began a letter from a New York academic, Mervyn Susser, to the London-based periodical. Declaring it grossly misleading to call the group of thirteen "controls," he deemed the study biased. Instead of picking the thirteen from the same population as the subjects and then comparing results, Campbell's group first had found them to be normal and then designated them "controls" because they were normal. He added that they failed to show that the so-called controls were not exposed to the factor that supposedly caused the abnormality—that is, cannabis smoking.

In their own letter, Campbell and coworkers partially accepted the first criticism. The word "controls" was incorrect in the context of animal experimentation. They should have called the thirteen "comparative cases of a similar age group." The nature of air-encephalography had limited the doctors (ethically) to patients who had already taken the test. But they still considered their comparisons important. Their "control" measurements agreed closely with comparable measurements of twenty-five normal patients (average age thirty-two) who had undergone air-encephalography, in an American study (1969).[6] Additionally, after completing their paper, Campbell and his associates studied air-pictures of an amphetamine addict of fifteen years' duration. The pictures showed no atrophy.

They never said whether the "controls" had used cannabis. Evans, in his 1974 article, said only, "None were drug dependent." Nor was the fate of the patients made known.

The *Lancet* piece summarized the case histories of all ten cannabis smokers. Here is the preceding portion of the history quoted in part above.

"A 22-year-old unemployed man complained of difficulty in recalling recent events, and also of periods of amnesia with occasional headaches. He described permanent alteration of vision after some years of drug abuse, with alteration of bright lights into colours: 'On a sunny day I have a lot of extra colour without drugs—that's very nice.' There was no history of birth injury, trauma to the head, or significant past illness.

"He had a 7-year history of drug abuse, starting with cannabis and amphetamine at age 15. Cannabis remained the chief drug, although he had also taken a large amount of L.S.D. and occasional barbiturates. He left school aged 15 and then had 4 months at sea with the Merchant Navy. Since then he had been unable to hold any job for long, and has not worked for the past 4 years. Over the previous 18 months his mental state had rapidly deteriorated, with intermittent confusional states and paranoid psychosis."

He had no abnormal neurological signs, but the X-ray films found parts of his lateral ventricles "increased" (from the norm).

Linear or areal measurements of the lateral ventricles and the third ventricle (three of the four brain ventricles) showed significant differences in all of them between the "controls" and drug-abuse groups, though some parts remained "normal."

An example of a significant difference: for "controls" the mean area of the left lateral ventricle (measured by a planimeter) was 2.6 square centimeters (range 1.2 to 3.7) while for "cases" it was 3.9 (range 2.2 to 5.8).

Campbell used "the standard air-encephalography technique." With the patient seated, sedated, and locally anesthetized, some cerebrospinal fluid was removed and air (about 25 ml) was injected into the lower back (the lumbar subarachnoid space). X rays of the head were taken with the patient seated, supine, and prone.

Campbell and the others cited as ailments that could cause cerebral atrophy in young people: head injury at birth, severe childhood infections involving encephalitis, congenital syphilis, toxoplasmosis, vascular lesions, hereditary disease such as Huntington's chorea, and demyelination.

They drew a parallel between the syndrome of sleeping sickness (encephalitis lethargica) and the picture presented by "chronic abuse of cannabis and L.S.D.," citing "a reversal of sleep rhythms, hallucinations, and mental changes" in "some" of their patients.

The cannabis smoking had spanned six years in three patients; seven years in three patients; and three, four, five, and eleven years in one patient each. The extent of other drug use was described as follows:

Amphetamines—"not much," ten times, one year, four years, six years, seven years (twice), and twelve years.

LSD—two times (twice), "occasional" (twice), at least five doses, twenty times (twice), thirty times, and "large amounts" (twice).

Other drugs—"occasional" barbiturates (twice), mescaline and tranquilizer-antihistamine "occasionally," heroin four times, and barbiturates for four years with "occasional" morphine. (The use of cocaine, not in a "significant" quantity, was not detailed. Campbell's report ignored tobacco, which according to Evans was used "consistently and repeatedly.")

Among the four participants in the project were J. L. G. Thomson of the radiology department at Frenchay Hospital in Bristol and M. J. Williams of the department of medicine at Bristol Royal Infirmary.[7]

In its editorial, The Lancet said that the study "deserves careful scrutiny. . . . The atrophy is significant, and the difference from the normal air-encephalogram entirely justifies the authors' description and diagnosis. . . .

". . . Although the moderate summary of Dr. Campbell and his colleagues is entirely reasonable, it would be wise to avoid the conclusion implicit in their findings considered in isolation. It should not be assumed that cannabis was the sole cause of the changes demonstrated until other possibilities have been assessed in a wider context."[8]

Professor Susser, of Columbia University's public health school, wrote that he could accept the work "as a series of ten uncontrolled case studies." A control group is supposed to represent, as nearly as possible, the same population from which experimental subjects are drawn. It shows what to expect in that population when it comes to the condition under study. But the article never told what the encephalograms of such a comparison group would show. Assuredly it would have a greater risk of abnormalities than these investigators' "controls," because they started by choosing a group with normal findings. What they achieved this way was "to establish a set of criteria for their subjective judgments of the normality of the encephalogram."

He added that the Campbell group "neglected an equally important canon of research design. They provide no evidence for the assumption that the so-called controls in the study were not exposed to the factor—i.e., cannabis smoking—that supposedly caused the abnormalities in the cases."[9]

Dr. Robert C. Kolodny, endocrine researcher of St. Louis, commented on the Campbell study in 1974 at a Senate committee hearing, lumping it with many studies that are "severely limited by indiscriminately including multiple drug users, thus frequently raising more questions than providing useful information."

Because all ten men had taken LSD, some had taken other drugs, one had suffered convulsions, and "four had significant head injuries" (a questionable statement), Kolodny called the report's "speculative connection between cannabis use and brain damage . . . highly suspect."[10]

Responding to Kolodny's criticism, Professor W. D. M. Paton of the pharmacology department at Oxford University defended the Campbell work (having seen it developing and known the author) in a letter to Senator Edward J. Gurney, chairman of the hearing at which Kolodny, and also Paton, had testified. Major points:

1. Because multiple drug use is so common and pneumoencephalography is a major procedure that ethically requires valid medical reasons, "the authors did well to find 10 subjects with such a clear dominant pattern of cannabis use (several hundreds of doses)" and "much lower use of other drugs. They also did well . . . in identifying a group of the same age who were not drug users, apparently free of neurological disease, to provide an estimate of ventricular size in this young age range."

2. "Of all the drugs used by the subjects, there is little or no evidence that any of them are cumulative apart from cannabis."

3. Evidence already had appeared that cannabis could interfere with cell division and brain biochemistry, "making it perfectly possible that by either, or both mechanisms, loss of brain substance could occur."

4. Evidence had appeared suggesting that cannabis's action was "in the deeper parts of the brain, in regions near the ventricles" where atrophy might be occurring.

5. A similar study (but with no control group) had recently indicated that heavy alcohol drinking could produce brain atrophy (Brewer and Perrett, 1971), but the average age of patients was fifty, range thirty-nine to sixty-two. The results were compatible, "the high fat-solubility of cannabis compared to that of alcohol producing a similar but much earlier adverse action."[11]

*   *   *

In 1970 Von Zerssen, Fliege, and Wolf at the Max Planck Psychiatric Institute in Munich, writing to *The Lancet*, reported an investigation of "the hypothesis that addiction to drugs (hypnotics, tranquilisers, analgesics) can lead to irreversible brain damage." They did not specify the hypnotics, etc.

They used echoencephalography (also called ultrasound midline detection, a method of imaging certain brain structures through the echoes of ultrasonic pulses) to measure the third ventricle in thirty-four "drug addicts (male and female, aged 25-60) most of whom had no history of alcoholism, cerebral trauma, epilepsy, diabetes, or hypertension." They compared those subjects with an equal number of "neurotic and psychopathic patients with the same sex and age composition." The differences were "highly significant."

The lateral diameter for the addicts averaged 9.2 millimeters, beyond the "upper limit of normal, 7 mm." Four subjects registered below that limit, thirty above; while for the control group, the score was exactly reversed. "These results emphasize the need for care in prescribing drugs with specific actions on cerebral structures, and for early recognition and treatment of addiction," the authors concluded, without identifying any drug.[12]

Many brain examinations of cannabis users have used electroencephalographs, machines to record so-called brain waves, minute electric impulses that represent different activities in the brain. A technician operating such a machine places electrodes on various parts of the scalp. Electric signals from the brain are enhanced about a million times and converted to a graphic tracing called an electroencephalogram, EEG for short. The result is a set of wavy or jagged lines, each standing for fluctuations in voltage occurring in part of the brain.

The technique has been useful in diagnosing some diseases, including tumors and epilepsy. But it has flaws. It does not directly detect brain damage. Sometimes patients with brain disease have normal EEGs and patients with no other signs of such disease have abnormal EEGs. "Normal" or "abnormal" is a matter of opinion, though an opinion based on experience.

The following three studies all aimed to test immediate or short-term effects of cannabis on brain-wave recordings, not the debatable question of long-term changes. Even so, they did not come to any consensus.

• The New York Mayor's Committee (1944) made EEGs of fifteen subjects given oral doses of marijuana extract and "There appeared to be a relationship between the typical euphoric reaction produced by marijuana and an associated increase in the alpha activity seen in the electroencephalogram." But two subjects who took no drug showed a similar increase in alpha activity. The findings suggested that marijuana "is conducive to mental relaxation in some individuals."

• Contrarily, to Williams et al. in Kentucky (1946) results of a similar test suggested increased cerebral activity. The smoking of one to four marijuana cigarettes by eighteen subjects tended to lower the amount of alpha rhythm and increase recorded muscle activities—changes "seen in normal subjects during mental efforts such as concentration, calculation, or attention."

However, free smoking of marijuana by six subjects for thirty-nine days brought no such trends. EEG changes "thus appeared to parallel the observed changes in overt behavior, namely, initial stimulation followed by subsequent diminution of activity."

• The South African study by Frances Ames (1958) of ten medically trained subjects, including herself, included EEGs made before and three hours after consumption of resinous cannabis pills. "Six out of ten showed changes but they remained within the limits of normal": additional fast activity in four of the six, some slow activity in the other two. The tracings "gave no indication of the site of action of cannabis and at most merely indicated a general cerebral disturbance."

Several years after the marijuana fad burst forth, sundry research workers resumed the testing of brain wave reactions to the drug, and they too recorded minimal changes, with no signs of brain dysfunction. "On the whole," one group said of its sixteen recordings, "the tracings were consistent with the drowsy, sleepy state of the subjects, both without and with the drug, but showed little in the way of specific drug effects. . . ."[13] Some questioned their own studies. Had the marijuana become too weak?[14] Did they wait too long before recording?[15]

In the year that the Campbell study came out in Britain, another Campbell article describing young cannabis-using patients and comparing them with others had appeared in a Canadian medical journal. The author was psychiatrist D. R. Campbell of the University of Alberta (Edmonton), and unlike the British study, which created a stir internationally, his went little noticed.

He told of eleven patients of his, aged sixteen to twenty-two, "who developed psychotic reactions to cannabis and required psychiatric help." None had taken any other drug. EEGs of ten of the eleven (91 percent) were "abnormal." Dr. Campbell compared their EEG tracings with three other groups, each in the same age range:

• Eleven others using cannabis without apparent psychiatric problems—eight had abnormal EEGs (73 percent).

• Ten who had needed consultations for neurological problems ranging from headaches to convulsions—four abnormal (40 percent).

• Twenty-nine patients hospitalized for schizophrenia—eleven abnormal (38 percent).

The heavier incidence of EEG abnormality in cannabis users suggested that "the drug may be a factor in creating the EEG abnormalities as well as contributing to the psychotic reactions observed." But the sampling was small, the author acknowledged, and he urged further research.

The first group of eleven comprised patients of Campbell's in the past two years. The time between the taking of "marijuana or hashish" and the EEG recording ranged from two months to two days. The lightest user was a woman, twenty-two, who indulged three times two months earlier. At the other extreme: "one nineteen-year-old male who had taken marijuana continuously for three weeks and presented himself to Emergency in comatose state."

Only two (females) had a previous history of EEG abnormality (one migraine, the other epilepsy) before taking cannabis; both developed the psychoses after taking cannabis. (The doctor did not say how many others ever had EEGs.)

In the comparison group of eleven, five had used cannabis only, five had also used LSD, one had used both plus amphetamines. Of the cannabis-only five, "four had electroencephalograms compatible with epileptic disorders (all females)."

The twenty-nine had been hospitalized over the past three years and been given EEGs (presumably in that connection). Their degree of EEG abnormality was "comparable to studies reported in the literature." Campbell did not state whether they or the group of ten used cannabis.

The majority in all four groups were female.

A graph (but no figure or explanation) placed at about 15 percent the abnormal EEGs in the "normal population."

Campbell assigned the first interpretation of the EEGs to "a neurologist who knew only that they were done at the request of the psychiatrist." Later "a different interpreter, who had no knowledge of the groupings," read them again to check the degree of abnormality.

Each abnormality included "recurrent excess of sharp and theta wave activity . . . excessive theta wave activity . . . moderately severe slow dysrhythmia . . ." or "abnormalities compatible with convulsive disorder. . . ."

No statistical analysis was made.[16]

The study of sixty Jamaicans included electroencephalograms of all of them. Among smokers and controls, respectively five and three were ranked "abnormal," three and eight "equivocal," fourteen and nine "low voltage normal," and eight and ten "normal."

The authors of *Ganja in Jamaica* (1975) saw no significant differences. ". . . Most of the findings considered definitely abnormal or equivocal were focal in nature. It is very unlikely that these were caused by any medication or drug effect."[17]

*   *   *

From nightly EEGs and eye-movement tests on sleeping young men given either marijuana or alfalfa "joints" to smoke, Barratt and team in Galveston, Texas (1972, 1974), generalized that infrequent marijuana smoking increases slow-wave sleep (the more restful phase of sleep) but chronic use decreases it below normal. This effect, they thought, may account for the lethargic life style associated with heavy marijuana use.[18] Feinberg et al. in San Francisco (1975, 1976) reported "powerful effects on brain activity during sleep" but would not venture any interpretation of their own experiments in which relatively high doses of either THC or marijuana extract reduced rapid eye movement sleep at first but grossly increased it after drug withdrawal.[19]

Karacan et al. (1976) compared thirty-two long-term users and as many matched nonusers, each man paying about eight successive nightly visits to an EEG laboratory in Costa Rica. Given no drug but encouraged to smoke as usual by day, the users generated no evidence of major disturbances in sleep patterns.[20]

* * *

Subjecting brain-wave data to computer analysis, Hanley et al. (1976) discovered that "the inhalation of cannabis decreases the energy of the EEG signal." This suggested possible "anticonvulsant properties" because "sudden increases in the energy of the EEG signal" went with seizures.

> They could differentiate eighteen cannabis smokers from a matched group of nonsmokers by feeding impulses directly into a computer. (For example, analyses of phase shifts would segregate the two groups in at least 85 percent of cases.) Heavy smokers generally could be distinguished from moderate smokers, though with more difficulty. Used in an attempt to contrast brain waves before and after test smoking, the method ranked little better than pure chance.[21]
>
> It was part of the ninety-four-day study at the University of California at Los Angeles, in which other researchers suggested that intoxication might alter the relative roles of the right and left cerebral hemispheres ("The Mind," 1).

The methods of electroencephalography and echoencephalography figured in a study of forty-seven long-time hashish smokers and forty nonsmokers of hashish, all men, in Athens, Greece. (Both terms come from the Greek: *elektron*, meaning amber; *ekho*, echo; *enkephalos*, brain; *graphein*. to write.)

Only fourteen of the hashish users and twenty-one of the nonusers consented to echoencephalography, despite its being far safer and less distressful than pneumoencephalography (also derived from the Greek: *pneuma*, meaning wind). Through the reflection of ultra-high-pitched sound, the echoencephalography produced an image of one brain ventricle. The width of the ventricle "was found to be well within the normal limits" for the users and control group, and "the mean values were not significantly different."

Similarly, with electroencephalograms (given to all but one reluctant hashish smoker), "abnormal and borderline EEGs were found to be evenly distributed between the two groups and no characteristic EEG patterns could be identified" (Stefanis, Boulougouris, and Liakos, 1976).

Other participants in the investigation qualified the statement. "EEG records of chronic hashish users tended to have a higher amplitude than the records of control subjects" (Panayiotopoulos and others, 1977). "Hashish, marijuana, and THC-delta-9 each affected the EEG and performance on psychological tests in a characteristic pattern after inhalation. The effects were transient. . . .

"For these men, smoking large amounts of cannabis for extended periods did not result in clinical evidence of brain damage, but the number of users examined was small and the men were selected from among functioning and working members in the community" (Fink, 1977).

> In the EEG tests, the chronic hashish users had six borderline records (13 percent) and four abnormal records (9 percent) while controls had six (15 percent) in each category, based on blind interpretations by at least two electroencephalographers.
> According to the echo tests, none of the users exceeded the norm of a seven-millimeter width of the third ventricle. The mean measurement, 6.6, surpassed that of the controls, 6.3, by 5 percent, "no statistical difference."[22]

A "computerized axial tomography" or CAT scan is a modern X-ray method for examining soft tissues of the body. Inflicting little risk or discomfort on patients (unlike pneumoencephalography), the technique has become widely accepted in brain diagnosis.

Reports on two CAT studies of young marijuana smokers, twelve in the Midwest and nineteen in New England, appeared together in a 1977 issue of JAMA, The Journal of the American Medical Association. Two medical research teams, led respectively by Doctors Co and Kuehnle, had independently used that then new technique to check the sensational Campbell findings in England. Each measured smokers' brain ventricles and each found them to be within normal limits. Neither found evidence of structural change. They could not duplicate Campbell's findings of cerebral atrophy in young cannabis smokers.

Of course, the studies differed in choice of subjects (the Americans were healthier than the Britons) and in the amount of active drug taken (the Americans' cannabis probably was weaker) as well as in method. In each of the three projects, however, most of the subjects had used other drugs. Use of other drugs became a major ground for criticism of the British study.

> In computerized axial tomography X-rays scan the head in a series of contiguous "slices" and are measured from many directions. A computer collects and processes the resulting information. This provides printed density data and a reconstructed photographic image of each "slice."
> Both studies used male volunteers in their twenties. One study was conducted

in St. Louis by Doctors Ben T. Co and Donald W. Goodwin of the psychiatry departments of Washington University School of Medicine and the University of Kansas School of Medicine and others. Doctors John Kuehnle and Jack H. Mendelson at the Alcohol and Drug Abuse Research Center of Harvard Medical School and McLean Hospital, Belmont, Massachusetts, and others conducted the other study.

Dr. Co and colleagues measured the areas of the lateral ventricles, and reported, "Unlike Campbell et al., we did not find evidence of cerebral atrophy in young cannabis users." But they pointed out differences between the studies: first, in the methods, and second, in the fact that "most of Campbell's subjects had neurological or intellectual impairment, whereas our subjects did not. Finally, the potency of the cannabis used by the two groups may have been different."

Co et al. had screened subjects to rule out any physical or mental condition that could cause ventricular change. All but two had taken LSD; half had taken other drugs as well. Their cannabis histories averaged seven years (range: six to ten years). They averaged eleven joints daily (range: six to twenty joints). The potency of the marijuana was not known but it "may have been of low to moderate potency."

Those selected as controls were thirty-four males, aged twenty to thirty, who denied abusing drugs and who had undergone CAT scans for suspected nerve disorders but turned out to be normal.

An abbreviated table showed users tending to have larger ventricles than nonusers, but data in the article was too sketchy to imply any conclusions.[23]

In the Harvard study, Dr. Kuehnle and the others reported that "Independent and comparative analysis of all nineteen cases showed no evidence of abnormality. The ventricular system and subarachnoid spaces were normal in size and showed no indication of atrophic change." They presented no measurements at all and did not specify which ventricles they had measured. The only table dealt with subjects' drug use.

Subjects had finished participating in a thirty-one-day experiment in behavioral and biological results of marijuana use, conducted in a research ward of the same Harvard center. The subjects, "healthy men," were those who smoked the most. Their past history and observed behavior were described as showing "very heavy marijuana use," but this amounted to one or two joints a day at home and an average of more than five joints in the ward (about 100 mg of THC). Campbell et al. could not determine the doses used by patients, although an associate indicated that they had smoked cannabis resin, hashish.

Kuehnle et al. compared subjects with "a normal control series (persons with no neurological signs or symptoms from another series of volunteers given in a different study)."

Their findings of "lack of structural damage" to the central nervous system "do not, of course, rule out the possibility that marijuana may produce alterations of brain function that cannot be adequately measured with this technique."[24]

* * *

A posthumous article in the *Australian Medical Association Gazette* by Professor Hardin B. Jones made it known that "when I applied appropriate statistical tests to figures that Co supplied to me but that were not included in the report, I found the difference in the ventricle sizes of the users and the controls to be significant. The ventricles of the cannabis users were 25 per cent larger. The degree of exposures to cannabis and the sizes of the ventricles were about the same in the Campbell and the Co studies."

As for the Kuehnle study, Professor Jones had been working on an analysis of it when he died in 1978.[25]

"In 1976 an eighteen-year-old twelfth grader whom I had known since his fourth-grade year, attending the excellent and demanding private school in which I have consulted weekly for eleven years, came to see me in my private practice," said Dr. Robert C. Gilkeson, a Cleveland, Ohio, psychiatrist and professor at Case Western Reserve University School of Medicine (1980).

The boy, Steve, said his whole existence had "become a drag." He found he had even lost interests in "chicks."

". . . His entire life seemed to be going down the tube since the last trimester of his junior year. . . . His grades had fallen steadily off— failures, incompletes, and barely passables." Although his trouble used to be that he was too active and too involved, now "he was increasingly disinterested in everything and found himself constantly sitting by himself, or a similarly immobile group of peers, listening to high-volume rock music. He had become increasingly annoyed with anyone, including his peers, his parents, and his teachers, who demanded even the most reasonable of expectations from him." He saw life as a growing "hassle."

Steve had given up ideas of going to college to pursue a social-work career or joining the family business and had recently decided to become a keyboard player in a rock group. The fact that his only piano experience was some elementary lessons in the third grade would not matter, he felt, if he could just get himself to practice.

"Knowing himself to have been a more-than-adequate student, he felt his major problem lay in the fact that he could not initiate or sustain sufficient study efforts rather than that he could not understand the material itself. He admitted to having more trouble memorizing. . . .

"During the second interview with me he had brought along a long-overdue senior paper. I was surprised to note the markedly immature and disorganized penmanship, the numerous and obvious misspellings left unnoticed and uncorrected, the inadequate complexity of concepts, and the general superficiality and poor organization of the entire paper. Even more important to me was three reversals of the letters 'b' and 'd,' a classic finding in the learning-disabled youngster."

Since 1969 Dr. Gilkeson had observed teenagers who had trouble learning, and he had developed a method of testing their brain waves. He would take, not one, but two records—during two mental states.

First "we did a normal, standard EEG. . . . We had people come in, sit down, relax in a stimulus-free room with their eyes closed, lying back, not concentrating, not focusing, not supposed to have any tension, and certainly in a state that no educator, no parent, no employer wants them. We put the person in the most unnatural condition to do the 'normal' EEG." The purpose of the customary relaxation has been to avoid muscle movements, which influence the recording.

Wanting to examine his young patients in "an alert, aroused, conscious, focusing state," the psychiatrist added a wrinkle to EEG testing. He would ask a youngster to do a mental task, such as making a calculation or spelling a word backward. Normally this would speed up the brain waves. But youngsters with "learning disabilities" or "cognitive deficits" (shortcomings in the act or process of knowing) could not produce the normal fast-wave activity.

The report on Steve's tests, from a neurologist who had not seen him, described an "abnormal EEG" characteristic of a "diffuse encephalopathic process" (process of general brain impairment). For his age, the graphs appeared "markedly immature."

Gilkeson had a clue. The youth's problems began at about the time that he started smoking marijuana. He admitted doing it nearly every day.

The doctor showed him the report. It shook the boy. Gilkeson advised him to stop smoking for two months. He agreed.

On repetition, the EEGs remained abnormal but showed improvement. So had Steve's grades, memory, mood, and even speech, as documented on a tape recorder. He felt less depressed and irritable. Steve agreed to go without marijuana for another two months. After that time, the neurologist's report found him "within normal limits for age."

"Steve became our initial diagnostic EEG study of an adolescent youngster with chronic pot ingestion."

By 1980 Gilkeson had compiled electroencephalographic studies of fifty-three chronic marijuana users, aged thirteen to twenty. Fifty of them produced "abnormal" records. (The records of two heavy users could not be read because involuntary "twitching and moving of the eyelids, jaw, tongue, and lips" interfered with the brain waves.)

Those studying the brain generally agree, said Gilkeson, that the slower the frequency of its waves, the less complex intellectual functioning is taking place. Normally from the time of birth, the EEG "matures." Frequencies generally become progressively faster until about the age of eighteen to twenty, when the human brain reaches its intellectual peak. They stay level until about sixty-five or seventy, when they slow down. The most common finding in moderate to severe brain injuries, infections, and traumas is an abundance of slow-wave frequencies.

"In these kids [on marijuana] we see EEGs that are about the maturity level of eight-year-olds—although they are seniors in high school—in terms of the slow wave activity, the disorganization, the preponderance of a rhythm called theta . . . abnormal in the teenage population, and paroxysmal theta discharge, associated with a lot of dementias and various diseases with dopamine deficiencies."

Does the condition always reverse? "I have had kids whose EEGs have not improved in six months. I have had kids who have been on what seemed to me to be surprisingly high doses whose EEGs have cleared within twenty-three days." Then there were those whose records cleared but became abnormal again when they resumed marijuana.

If it should turn out that long-term invasion and disfigurement by cannabis ultimately destroys neurons (nerve cells), said Gilkeson, the victim has no second chance. They are the tissues in the body that are the most sensitive to injury, and unlike most other cells, they do not regenerate. ". . . Damage to these systems ends up with no growing back and no repair. Once gone, it's gone."

Dr. Gilkeson, as the final witness before the Senate subcommittee hearing testimony in 1980 on the health consequences of marijuana, spoke of accumulated evidence that cannabis and its active molecules mimic other drugs that hold back the production of catecholamines, chemicals thought to act as neurotransmitters (substances that transmit nerve impulses across gaps).

He thought it tied in with syndromes of fifty boys and girls he had studied, with the aid of neurologist Dr. John Gardner and technician Tom Widener. The teenagers had gotten "high" on marijuana at least twice a week for four months (abstaining for two to fifteen days before an EEG test). Their slow waves—like those of the poor learners—corresponded to a poverty of cognitive brain functions:

"With increasing slowing there is a universally accepted lowering of alertness and arousal . . . a lessened awareness and conscious experience of the sensing of time . . . less awareness of the specific sequence or order of events upon recall . . . a wandering of attention, and a decreasing richness, or complexity, and tightly related association of things, events, and concepts . . . much greater difficulty in sustaining continuous, sequential thought, without distractions and the occurrence of unrelated associations . . . a marked impairment of detailed, specific, and time-related memory of the thoughts and concepts experienced.

". . . The slower the activity, and the lower the arousal, the less the involvement of frontal activity, the more progressive the fall-off in alertness and high-order intellectual function."

Gilkeson called the frontal lobe "the final analyzer," taking sensory information relayed from the back of the head and—in the manner of a TV control director—mapping out action, or a stoppage of action.

The neurotransmitters it produces are dopamine, norepinephrine, serotonin, and gamma amino butyric acid. ". . . Depressant drugs such as alcohol, Thorazine, Haldol, lithium, and marijuana are the deactivators or decreasers of these neurotransmitters and . . . lower the arousal, alerting responses, while they impair highest-order learning functions and memory and slow the frequencies of the electroencephalogram."

Increasing evidence from neurophysiologists and their electron microscopes indicates, he said, that fat-loving cannabis invades and disfigures the neurons' membranes, which are fatty, and interferes with the cells' ability to carry out normal metabolic functions and to synthesize and respond to neurotransmitters.

"Loss of these most sensitive and last-to-develop cells leads eventually, not to death, but to the progressive loss of highest intellectual functions and what is known as normal behavior, and rather than kill the user directly, reduces him to mediocrity."

Gilkeson described marijuana as "a known neurotoxic agent, altering consciousness and lowering arousal, awareness, and cognitive functions. . . . With greater frequency than every 30 days, it must slowly accumulate in the brain and fatty tissues of the body until eventual saturation takes place. . . ." At that time the drug can be constantly found not only in cell tissues, but circulating in the blood stream and body fluids."[26]

* * *

"Current evidence has shown marijuana causes some chemical changes in the brain," said an Institute of Medicine study committee in *Marijuana and Health* (1982). The committee cited (a) studies in man and animals concluding that THC acts to inhibit acetylcholine nerve cell networks and (b) reports of marijuana's high-dose effects on nucleoprotein synthesis in animals. It could draw no conclusion as to any long-range changes in brain function or structure.

3

Monkeys And Others

What would happen if a monkey smoked marijuana? Rhesus monkeys have been falling victim to human curiosity on that score since the 1890s when one in Calcutta gave his life for the Indian Hemp Drugs Commission. Two scientists there tried such an experiment again in the thirties, and a brain researcher in New Orleans did it his own way in the seventies. (We will describe his work later.)

One Doctor Cunningham reported to the commission how he made a rhesus inhale *ganja* in a special chamber 181 times in eight months, 1893–94. Resisting the treatment in the earlier part of the experiment and trying to plug the tube carrying in smoke, the monkey evidently became addicted later on; he did not want to leave the chamber without his full dose and became uneasy on smokeless days. Symptoms commonly included unsteadiness, drowsiness, and "loss of will-power ac-

companied by optical delusions" that persisted long beyond other signs
of intoxication. Sometimes violent convulsions seized him and he lost
consciousness. In a postmortem, the "cerebro-spinal nervous centres"
appeared healthy.

Chopra and Chopra later subjected two monkeys to "frequent inha-
lations of ganja smoke" (half a gram to two grams of marijuana) for three
months to test addiction. At first their monkeys too had an aversion to
the contamination and it was hard to get them to inhale the fumes. They
became restless and often tried to close the hole through which the smoke
entered their chamber.

After three weeks of daily smoke, the animals began to show some
liking for it. After four weeks the monkeys became quiet and often reacted to the smoke by falling asleep or moving and sitting with difficulty, their eyes congested. Relatively small doses brought a reeling gait,
restlessness, and watery eyes. "The animals looked confused and this
condition continued for a considerable time after all other signs of active
intoxication had disappeared." (Within six months they died of dysentery.)

Brigade-Surgeon-Lieutenant-Colonel D. D. Cunningham, a professor of physiology at the Medical College, Calcutta, undertook his experimentation at the

A *young male rhesus monkey under the influence of THC at the University of California at Davis.*

request of the Hemp Drugs Commission. He did not specify the dosage.

At first the monkey "violently resisted introduction into the inhalation-chamber, was restless when the smoke began to enter it, and not unfrequently attempted to prevent its entrance by plugging the orifice of the supply-tube." Ultimately he "readily entered the chamber, resisted any attempts to remove him from it before he had a full dose, was restless and uneasy on days on which the treatment was omitted, and on two occasions on which he managed to make his escape from his cage, showed an evident desire to enter the chamber on his own account."

When removed from the chamber, if not asleep, the monkey was very unsteady on his legs and often could not even sit up without grasping the bars of his cage. He gazed about attentively at "nothing which seemed likely to excite his curiosity" and searched the floor for nonexistent objects until late in the day, long after other signs of intoxication from the morning treatment had disappeared. Sometimes when treated he was "suddenly seized with violent general convulsions and immediately became profoundly unconscious."

His general health was "excellent" except for appetite loss and some dysentery. After he was chloroformed, a postmortem examination showed an "excessive accumulation of fat in the tissues of the omentum, peritoneum, and pericardium, and the tendency to the establishment of a similar accumulation in the cardiac muscle, the liver, the pancreas and the spleen."

In another experiment, Cunningham gave two other monkeys *charas* (hashish) in milk. They took it for about two months and then suddenly they simultaneously refused any more. Outside of that, he found the experiment uneventful. In a third experiment, "serious morbid changes in the cerebral nervous centres" followed six weeks' inhalation of *dhatura* (jimsonweed) smoke by another monkey. No study used a control.

Dr. Cunningham made his inspections with the naked eye. While the commission had "no evidence of any brain lesions being directly caused by hemp drugs, as they have been found to be caused by alcohol and dhatura," it noted that "it is not improbable, though it has not been established by evidence, that prolonged abuse of the drugs may give rise in some cases to definite brain lesions resulting in a progressive weakening of all the faculties leading to dementia."[27]

* * *

The Chopras reached no general conclusions about addiction. The monkeys developed some tolerance and liking for the drug after repeated doses. "The desire for repeating a dose and the abstinence symptoms produced were not so intense as is the case with animals to whom opium is repeatedly administered."

They gave cannabis in different ways to cats, dogs, frogs, guinea pigs, mice, and rats, as well as monkeys and human beings, and described a variety of short- and long-range effects and (in animals) fatalities.

For instance, within an hour cats fed extracts "lost all sense of fear and repulsion when placed together with dogs who on the other hand became more docile and affectionate and did not attack or even show their usual antipathy to cats."

Frogs injected with extract became uncoordinated in half an hour or even (with large doses) paralyzed, but effects passed in a day or two.

The experiments proved "that the physiological effects produced by hemp drugs differ in different species of animals and in different individuals of the same species."

They divided cannabis's (mainly short-range) effects on the central nervous system into stages of (1) "primary stimulation and excitement," (2) "general depression and anaesthesia," and (3) "secondary stimulation or excitement, observed only in the case of toxic doses or in animals showing marked idiosyncrasy toward the drug."

They found it unreliable as a hypnotic, for it tended to give rise to listlessness, lack of concentration, and sometimes amnesia.[28]

"In studying animals intoxicated with hashish, it is possible to distinguish between a stage of excitement and a stage of paralysis," wrote Joachimoglu and Miras of Greece (1963) about their rodents. "Slight degrees of paralysis of the central nervous system can be determined by various tests. If the animals are placed on a stick and the latter is rotated with the fingers, the control animals do not lose their balance, whereas animals which have been given hashish fall off. The control animals can swim in water. After being injected with hashish, the animals cannot keep themselves above water. As soon as they sink and swallow water, they try with ataxic [uncoordinated] movements to reach the surface."[29]

Professor Miras reported (1965) experiments in which he injected radioactive THC in rats and recovered modest but measurable amounts of it in various organs, including the brain.[30]

Experiments by others on the rat and other animals showed THC persisting in the brain over periods of time. Ho and colleagues (1970) at the Texas Research Institute of Mental Science forced rats to inhale THC labeled with a radioactive tracer. They tested the distribution in different organs at intervals from twenty minutes to seven days. The amount in the brain was notable at the start and fell less than one-fourth in a week.[31]

At the same institute, in Houston, McIsaac and others (1971) injected eight squirrel monkeys with similarly radioactive THC and measured its distribution in seventeen brain areas at intervals. Both the monkeys and the brain concentration of drug were "high" at fifteen minutes and an hour. They descended at four hours, more so at twenty-four hours.

McIsaac and colleagues claimed to be able readily to relate the concentrations in specific regions to THC's behavioral, physiological, and mental effects. For instance, at fifteen minutes, the geniculate nuclei, "known to have connexions with the visual pathway," gave off a high level of radioactivity, particularly so "when visual perception was most distracted and when the behavior suggested the animals were hallucinating." Another example (which wouldn't require the reading of animals' minds) might be that the monkeys showed "pronounced motor incoordination," that is, they moved very clumsily, particularly one hour after injection (in veins with 30 mg/kg of THC). At that time, according to a table, the cerebellum—responsible for making movements smooth and coordinated—registered its greatest concentration of THC and this concentration topped that of any other brain part tested.[32]

* * *

Subjects led a rat-eat-rat existence in a series of Massachusetts studies testing the toxic effects of daily cannabinoid treatment over periods of time. Staffers of the Mason Research Institute gave them huge doses of THC or crude marijuana extract at first, via stomach tube; later gave THC in similar experiments but at smaller doses to approach human drug taking more closely; and still later administered pot smoke, in more modest doses yet. All told, more than 1,000 rats took the treatments in the three projects (1971–76).

• In the first study the experimenters reported the doses to be 30 to 300 times the usual human doses, "chosen specifically to induce toxicity in rats" (Thompson et al.). The first 1½ to 3 days of treatment brought generalized depression, abnormally slow breathing, and low temperatures. Within 3 days, death came to most of the higher-dosed rats. More females succumbed than males, some after only one dose.

Then tolerance developed. Many of the rats developed hyperactivity along with "increased irritability and fighting that resulted in severe wounds." Paradoxically these effects developed earlier and more intensely in the lowest-dosed rats, beginning after a week. After three or four weeks, the rats would devour each other's tails and paws. Tremors and convulsions developed in relation to dose.

Another phase of that study examined the brains of some rats after a month or three months on THC or crude marijuana extract, respectively. The drugs apparently lowered the brain's synthesis of protein and RNA (ribonucleic acid), and in some cases reduced the brain enzyme acetylcholinesterase as well, compared with undrugged rats. The amounts of the reductions varied directly with the dose in the THC group.

The main results issued from the 162nd annual meeting of the American Chemical Society, 1971, in Washington, D.C. The press quoted Rosenkrantz and Luthra as reporting "the first evidence" of damage (Associated Press) or basic chemical change (*Time*) in brains of animals exposed to marijuana over long periods of time—the periods equaled years in a human life—and advising doctors to watch for hyperactivity or convulsions in chronic marijuana smokers.

• In a later study, rats got the treatment for a month, three months, or six months in one of three doses. THC solution, forced into their stomachs daily, corresponded either to a human marijuana cigarette, a hashish cigarette, or a dose five times as strong as the hashish, according to the Mason scientists.

Rosenkrantz reported in summary that the study "implicated reasonable doses of delta-9-THC in undesirable behavioral changes highlighted by fighting aggression, convulsive activity, and lethal cumulative toxicity." And Luthra concluded that "chronic treatment with reasonable doses" of THC "introduces neurochemical and neurotoxicological manifestations" (causes chemical changes in nerves and poisons them), although most behavioral and neurotoxic changes appeared reversible. He added that they had correlated "behavioral aberrations" with neurochemical changes in four brain areas. But both men indicated that the lowest dose generally brought few if any changes.

Among the aberrations were depression or lack of coordination, followed by fighting in many higher-dosed animals and—months later—fighting in some low-dosed animals. There were also convulsions and "hypnotic trances" in many medium-dosed rats. As dosing continued in that group and in high-dosed rats, RNA concentrations went down and up in certain brain areas, varying for males and females; and brain enzymes rose for males and dropped for females. Brain weights generally rose.

After seizures, a number of higher-dosed rats showed such abnormal behavior as the "popcorn reaction"—involuntary vertical jumping—as well as running in circles and gnawing on cages.

• Finally rats received marijuana smoke through a smoking machine in three doses described as "relevant to man," the medium corresponding to the low of the previous study. Treatment lasted twelve, eighteen, twenty-seven, fifty-seven, or eighty-seven days. Behavioral and neurochemical changes resembled those observed in the other experiments but they came earlier and were less intense after prolonged treatment (Luthra reported). In a switch from the other two studies, more females than males showed fighting aggression.

> Doses in the three projects went as follows: Rats in the first two received drugs in sesame oil solutions; control rats got the oil only.
> First—50, 250, 400, or 500 mg/kg of THC; and 150, 750, 1,200, or 1,500 mg/kg of marijuana extract.
> Second—2, 10, or 50 mg/kg of THC.
> Third—0.7, 2, or 4 mg/kg of THC via inhalation. Controls received smoke of placebo (cannabinoid-free) marijuana.
> The first project produced three journal reports, two by Luthra and Rosenkrantz on brain. They had selected the "massive" doses to have "a greater proba-

bility of evoking adverse effects. If neurochemical lesions could be induced," they would "perform similar studies at lower doses approximating delta-9-THC concentrations used by man."

The second allowed a seven-fold increase in mg/kg dose to rats over humans (attributing this principle to Freireich et al., 1966). Many physiological and clinical tests were performed. Rosenkrantz reported that "absence of harmful changes in blood and tissue despite growth and organ changes indicated a functional impairment that did not threaten the animal's life because of unknown protective mechanisms."

Various organ weights increased, including brain weight 3 to 25 percent (dose-related) after 90 days and 16 percent (at higher doses) after 180 days. (Professor Hardin B. Jones suggested that edema, fluid retention, accounted for the increase in organ weights.)[33]

Behavioral highlights of the second Massachusetts study (in sequence) were: depression, decreased activity, or lack of coordination in many higher dosed rats; irritability, hypersensitivity, hyperactivity, or aggressiveness among many of them; fighting by medium-dosed rats; trance or convulsions among them; trance in low-dosed rats; deaths, mostly at high dose; tolerance among once-depressed rats; convulsions in the majority of top-dosed rats; fighting by the low-dosed rats; and normal behavior in rats allowed to recover for a month after the half-year of treatment.

Neurochemical highlights of that study: After 180 days, RNA declined in males at higher doses (11 to 21 percent) and in females at all doses (13 to 16 percent), while acetylcholinesterase increased in males (19 to 70 percent) but sank in females (8 to 45 percent). After 180 days plus 30 days' recovery, RNA values were normal, but the enzyme rose in males (11 to 43 percent) and females (14 to 17 percent).

In the third study, neurochemical changes again differed by sex. After 57 days, the females' cerebral enzyme dropped and the males' cerebellar enzyme rose some. After 87 days at the two higher doses, cerebral enzyme and cerebellar RNA rose some in females. And after 87 days plus a 20-day recovery period, cerebral enzyme dropped at the two higher doses for females and two lower doses for males (no high-dosed males having survived).

Dr. Rosenkrantz headed biochemical pharmacology at the Mason Research Institute, Worcester, Massachusetts. Luthra (whose 1974 journal article was part of his master of arts dissertation in biology at Clark University, Worcester) worked on the experiments as a graduate student and later as Rosenkrantz's toxicology assistant.[34]

The work of Jacubovic, McGeer, and Hattori in Vancouver, Canada, on brain cortex of rats can be mentioned again. THC and cannabidiol added to cultured brains of normal rats markedly inhibited the cells' manufacture of protein and nucleic acid, as measured by incorporation of radioactively labeled chemicals. Cells of the youngest rats, three days old, were affected the most.

When they injected THC and two other psychoactive cannabinoids into live rat pups, an electron microscope revealed a decrease in the number of ribosomes (particles where protein synthesis takes place) attached to membranes within brain cells. The declines were reversible and related to dose and time. Injections of THC in mothers caused such results in brain cells of suckling rats.

* * *

Some fussy rats occupied the cages in the pharmacology laboratory at the University of Toronto, Canada. A month after having olive oil with cannabis extract or alcohol or sugar water forced into their stomachs for half a year, the rodents refused to run through a maze for mere sugared rat food. So "it was necessary to substitute chocolate ice cream as the reward before the animals would perform satisfactorily," Kevin O'Brien Fehr and Harold Kalant related (1976).

At the end of three weeks of training, the scientists gave the rats, twenty-two in number, a dozen graded maze problems. The cannabis and alcohol groups both scored significantly more errors than the controls.

Then they trained the same rats to walk on a moving belt over an electrified grid; any rat that left the belt got a shock. Compared with controls, the alcohol group spent significantly more time, and the cannabis group somewhat more time, getting shocked.

One year after the drug treatment ended, the investigators implanted electrodes in three brain sites of each surviving rat, five animals. The brain-wave recordings of the marijuana rats showed, they said, epilepticlike abnormalities in the hippocampus—"irregularly occurring high-voltage sharp waves." The learning impairment seemed to be "due to residual cellular change."

The doses were large but produced intoxication that jibed with clinical accounts of very heavy cannabis smoking and alcohol drinking in various countries, according to the researchers.

Later, using the same substances, same doses, and more rats (thirty), they repeated the six months of stomach-tube treatment and the moving belt test, with a month's rest intervening. Cannabis and alcohol groups both did significantly worse than controls, Mrs. Fehr and Kalant reported (1979).

One and two months after treatment ended, they introduced a mouse into each rat's cage for up to ten minutes. Significantly more cannabis rats than control rats killed mice. Alcohol rats came in second, not quite significantly. An analysis of the belt scores showed the killers to be notably dumber than the nonkillers for unknown reasons. The authors saw changes in brain functioning. (One may speculate that cannabis made the rats more aggressive—or more hungry.)

When the mouse tests ended, the experimenters again implanted electrodes in the rats' brains (eight sites in each group) and charted brain waves. The same abnormalities appeared, as before, in the cannabis group's hippocampal tracings. This time they turned up also in the hippocampal and cortical tracings of the alcohol rats.

The scientists viewed the combination of electrical changes and stupidity on the moving belt test as "consistent with other evidence of learning impairment in animals with hippocampal lesions" (injuries). The hippocampus (a ridge along each lateral ventricle) is said to be essential for the formation of memory.

The doses in the above experiments included 20 mg/kg of THC and 6 gm/kg of ethanol. Control rats received sucrose solution equal in calories to the alcohol.

The earlier tests used eight rats in the cannabis group, six in the alcohol group (four died), and eight controls. All were males weighing about 120 grams. In the maze, given twelve problems (twenty trials maximum per problem), control rats averaged 87 errors; cannabis rats, 107; ethanol rats, 102. Surviving animals (two cannabis, two alcohol, and one control) were given EEGs. Sites studied were anterior neocortex, dorsal hippocampus, and mesencephalic reticular formation.

The later belt tests used ten rats in each of three groups, all young adult, 100-gram males. Cannabis, alcohol, and control rats took 9, 10, and 5½ days, respectively, to reach criterion (no more than 1 percent of the time off belt per two-minute test). The mouse-killing scores for cannabis, alcohol, and control rats, respectively (four trials each), were 7-4-1 after a month and 8-3-1 after two months.

Seven cannabis, six control, and five ethanol rats were given EEGs the second time, 2½ months after the end of drug treatment. Sites added were septum, mammillary bodies, amygdala, and thalamic nuclei. Each rat had electrodes in three sites, but sites varied from one animal to another.

"The most striking finding was the presence of irregular high-amplitude spike-like waves in the hippocampal tracings of the cannabis rats, and in both the cortical and hippocampal tracings of the alcohol rats." There appeared to be "a tendency toward slowing of the basic wave pattern in cortical and limbic system leads in both ethanol and cannabis animals."

In three earlier maze experiments, hungry rats that were force-fed 10 mg/kg of cannabis extract made, compared with olive-oil controls:

1. About 30 percent more errors after one dose (trained a day before treatment).

2. About 85 percent more errors after two weeks of treatment (trained in the second week of treatment).

3. About the same number of errors after thirty, sixty, or ninety days of treatment (when trained a week after treatments).

Total number of rats in each experiment: eighteen, ten, and thirty, respectively.

The experimenters, of the University of Toronto and Addiction Research Foundation of Ontario, recorded that "no residual impairment was found at a THC dose of 10 mg/kg daily for 3 months." Doubling that dose kept rats intoxicated for four hours after each dose but in good general health. The ethanol dose, which would be "lethal in humans," hit the rats harder than did the cannabis but was "fairly well tolerated." Brain weights did not differ.[35]

Two Soviet psychiatric academicians fed immense doses of cannabis resin to twenty-two dogs and reported severe damage to the essential parts of the brain, in a publicized study (1971, 1972). In both acute and chronic tests the resin killed or grossly harmed the animals. The pair observed radical changes throughout the dogs' brains, in the centers regulating consciousness, bodily systems, reflexes, senses, and coordination. But the size of the doses—as great as two or three ounces—and the study's shortage of data and avowed propaganda purpose cast doubt on its scientific value.

In the chronic cases and worst acute cases, microscopic examination showed nerve cells to be corrugated, with broken-down nuclei and various symptoms of degenerative change. In the majority of those cases, the degenerative processes ended in the death of nerve cells. Structural changes in blood vessels of the brain distinguished the acute poisoning. A. I. Durandina, senior lecturer in psychiatry of the Kirghiz Government Medical Institute, and V. A. Romasenko of the Institute of Psychiatry, Academy of Medical Sciences of the U.S.S.R., reported in a quarterly of the United Nations Division of Narcotic Drugs.

They did not indicate potency or list experimental results by dose. One or two acute doses varying from 1.5 to 4.08 grams per kilogram of body weight were administered to fourteen adult and young dogs weighing 5.3 to 21 kg. In the chronic treatment, doses of 0.5 to 3.0 g/kg were fed daily for up to ten weeks to eight adult dogs weighing 12 to 21 kg.

The acute poisoning induced stimulation alternating with depression, or depression alone. The chronic poisoning caused permanent or intermittent depression culminating in prostration. Both regimens caused "toxic encephalopathy" or dysfunction throughout the brain. If a dog survived acute treatment, the symptoms abated in two days. In both acute and chronic poisoning—even if the dosage is increased slowly—"the compensatory adaptive functions may become deranged and the animal may die." How many dogs died was not made clear.

The experimenters said they had undertaken a maiden study of cannabis growing in the Soviet Asian republic of Kirghiz to investigate the possible disorders caused by its resin, to compare them with those of "Indian hemp"—they said both had the same behavioral and neurological effects on animals—and to use the information for health education and the prevention of addiction. Although lately banned, "Cannabis has grown wild in Kirghiz from time immemorial" and was cultivated until 1964.[36]

*   *   *

While the U.S.S.R. strictly prohibits nonmedical drugs, drug abuse there has become a major medical and social problem, according to Boris M. Segal, substance abuse chief at the Veterans Administration Hospital, Montrose, New York. Hashish, popular in the southern regions, he said, generally is considered dangerous by Soviet physicians, of which Dr. Segal was one. He reported (1981) observing organic damage in the cerebral cortex, subcortical ganglions, and cerebellum of rats after chronic hashish intoxication (at more moderate doses than the dogs got).[37]

Now we return to marijuana-smoking monkeys and the work in New Orleans. A score of them got "stoned" in experiments throughout the 1970s at Tulane University.

The monkeys got that way promptly, although they had no more desire to smoke pot than the Indian monkeys had. They would sit and "stare blankly into space. You could stick them with pins or put your finger in their mouths without concern, and this is impossible with normal rhesus monkeys as they are rather hostile animals," said Dr. Robert Galbraith Heath.

But the behavior of intoxicated monkeys was only a small part of the trove of knowledge Dr. Heath was questing. He wanted to know also what took place in their brains as the drug hit, what would happen when they took it again and again—and, of course, what could be inferred about humans.

In the context of his research since the 1950s, Heath was after the inside story of the brain. Looking into the workings of the brain deep below the surface, he hoped to correlate brain activity and behavior.

Heath was a professor and since 1949 the chairman of the Department of Psychiatry and Neurology at Tulane University School of Medicine. His interest, however, was more than academic. As a psychiatrist and neurologist, he had been concerned with causes and cures for various disorders of the mind and nerves. At the university's psychiatric-neurological clinic, patients suffering severe psychosis, epilepsy, pains of cancer, and so on, began in 1950 to undergo an unusual type of treatment. It involved direct stimulation of the brain by small electric charges, or, in some cases, by chemicals.

By stimulating particular parts of the brain, doctors could drastically change moods, emotions, and physical sensations of patients, for better or worse.

Stimulation of one particular place, "the septal region"—deep in the front part of the brain, within the limbic system—immediately relieved mental distress and physical pain and created a state of pleasure. Occasionally it brought a sexual feeling.

The electrical method entailed surgery to implant electrodes. Besides giving patients relief, it enabled the doctors to get information on the functioning of the patients' brains that could not be obtained with the conventional scalp recordings of brain waves, although those were taken too.

On four occasions, in 1970, Heath gave a chronically depressed, young drug abuser a marijuana cigarette to smoke while recording impulses from sites in the inner brain and cortex and on the scalp. He instructed the patient to push a button—thereby marking the graph paper—when he experienced a "rush" from the marijuana.

The mood changes began within three to five minutes after the first deep inhalation of smoke. Marijuana turned on the brain's pleasure circuit. As the euphoria began, the recording pen responded. "High voltage slow-wave activity" (one to three cycles per second) "appeared in the septal leads" (recordings). This electrical activity coincided with the patient's behavior under the influence of the drug. It became most pronounced when he was "highest."

During the "rushes," which came and went for up to an hour, his behavior matched the oft-described overt effects of marijuana: he smiled broadly, sometimes giggled, and told how good it felt, displaying "silliness, flight of ideas, and obviously shortened attention span, with varying degrees of impairment of thinking." (He said, however, that on a few occasions marijuana had made him depressed.)

As for brain recordings, only septal changes—"high voltage, slow-wave activity"—ever accompanied marijuana smoking in this patient. Scalp recordings showed minimal or no changes.

The joints smoked by the patient each contained 1½ grams of marijuana with 2½ percent THC.

Peaks of euphoria came in waves of thirty seconds to one minute, interspersed with plateaus of thirty seconds to two minutes when his mood remained higher than it was before smoking began. The intermittent euphoria lasted forty-five minutes to one hour. After that, his feeling of well-being continued for two hours, slowly diminishing.

"When the 'rushes' subsided, the high-amplitude 1 to 3 Hz activity in the septal leads disappeared and was replaced by more rhythmical, lower amplitude 5 to 7 Hz activity also focal in the septal leads."

After deep inhalation of a tobacco cigarette, there were no behavioral changes; recordings resembled his usual recording during periods of alertness, except for more low-voltage fast activity.

After intravenous injection of 15 mg of methamphetamine, the patient felt good and became talkative and recording changes were minimal (there was low-voltage fast activity).

After drinking six ounces of whiskey with as much water, he was more euphoric and talkative and plainly "a little 'high' "; changes in recordings were insignificant.

A report on this patient said (1972) that sixty patients had been studied by deep-electrode techniques in the Tulane laboratories since 1950. The method, Heath acknowledged (1964), was impractical and unjustified in any but a few severe psychiatric cases. But he hoped to see the "knowledge obtained from these experiments" applied to the curing of psychiatric disorders. It would involve "manipulation of the basic regulators of behavior, pain and pleasure. . . ." He looked for a nonaddicting compound that would induce pleasure and heighten, not reduce, awareness.[38]

As Heath defined the "septal region," it is "in the vicinity of the nucleus accumbens at the base of the anterior horn of the lateral ventricle rostral to the anterior commisure (15 mm in man and 7 to 8 mm in the rhesus monkey)."[39]

Marijuana at first served as just another technique—along with stimulation and so forth—for probing the pleasure centers of patients, Heath told us in an interview (1980).

". . . We had even back twenty years ago reported on the effects of cocaine and Demerol and opiates on the brain. . . . So when marijuana became available and popular and people were using it, we had another tool, essentially, in our hands for demonstrating the correlation between pleasure and what went on in the brain. And we got curious, particularly when we began seeing patients who seemed to be suffering effects from its use in our clinic and the same from the long-term effects.

"That's when we got into the monkey studies after that. We wondered if it would eventually do some damage, or whether you could use it without ill effects for long periods of time. We went into it with an open mind."

Heath had begun making deep-brain recordings of people smoking marijuana when the Campbell "cerebral atrophy" report issued and came under attack.

"We chose to work with monkeys because there had been criticism of the early human studies," Heath recalled (1980). "The critics said, for example, that the human subjects might have become psychotic and developed brain changes even if they had not used marijuana, and that everyone who used marijuana probably used other drugs, including alcohol, as well, and that they, not marijuana, were responsible for the undesirable effects. . . . Using monkeys, we circumvented these criticisms. Further, we were able to invoke exact controls in the monkeys, a species close to man insofar as central nervous system is concerned."[40]

Knowledge, not therapy for patients, became the primary goal. The subjects, not being human, could be experimented on freely and then could be killed for microscopic brain examinations. Monkeys resemble humans the most closely of any animal group except the great apes.

So Heath requisitioned six rhesus monkeys from the university's vivarium. By surgery, they installed electrodes in eight sites in the monkeys' heads. The animals rested for three weeks.

For the smoking, Heath and group designed and built their first device, variations of which would follow. A monkey sat restrained in a chair, a plastic box over its head. Marijuana (2¼ percent THC) burned in a pipe attached to the box. Air came through another opening. Each test lasted only five minutes. No one knew just how much drug a monkey took in.

Within one to three minutes after the monkeys started receiving the fumes, their behavior began to change. Within five more minutes they were sitting in a semistupor and staring blankly at the walls, their mouths ajar, pupils dilated, reflexes slowed. They ignored hand clapping, clasping of their limbs, and even jabbing with pins.

Brain waves always corresponded to the behavioral changes. Active marijuana "consistently induced distinct recording changes in recordings from the septal region, occasionally accompanied by changes in . . . the cerebellum . . . thalamus, hippocampus and . . . cortices." These remained distinct for at least half an hour, taking about an hour more to return to normal. Increases in pulse rate (50 to 100 percent) accompanied the changes.

Neither inert marijuana, tobacco, alcohol, nor (except for two monkeys) amphetamine induced significant changes in the brain waves, although alcoholic injections sickened the monkeys and made them plainly drunk.[41]

In short, the changes corresponded to those in the human subjects, impelling Heath to carry the monkey experimentation further. Animal studies usually serve as advance models for human studies. In this case, it was the other way around.

Next time, monkeys would be tested for six months, with more elaborate gadgetry. Those monkeys that had electrodes and wires in their heads (eight animals) would have fifteen sites recorded at once, and computers later would analyze the electrical changes. Cameras were rigged to take videotapes showing zigzagging brain waves and the reacting monkey on the same, split screen. And the scientific crew had redesigned the smoking device so that an electric motor pulled the smoke through a respirometer, pouring the smoke from given quantities of marijuana right into a monkey's nose. (The use of the respirometer was adapted from an elaborate human experiment in Chicago, by Renault et al., 1971, described in our heart section. Again humans pave the way for animals.)

The monkeys, numbering ten, formed four groups: (1) "heavy" smoking: three times daily, five days a week, (2) "moderate" smoking: twice a week, (3) inactive-marijuana smoking: same schedule as "heavy," and (4) not smoking but injected with THC once daily, five days a week.

Of the monkeys with deep electrodes, four smoked the active marijuana (two on each schedule) and, with each smoke, "distinct alterations were seen in recordings from specific deep sites of their brains— the most consistent changes occurring in the septal region, hippocampus, and amygdala. . . .

". . . These are brain areas where activity has been correlated with various specific emotional states."

While this went on, scalp EEGs of those same four monkeys showed "no consistent or notable changes." Nor did such changes appear in scalp EEGs of two monkeys that lacked implanted electrodes and underwent the "heavy" smoking schedule.

The two monkeys smoking inactive marijuana showed no visible changes, either in brain recordings (deep and surface) or in behavior— "suggesting that what we found was directly related to the active ingredients in the marihuana." Confirming that point, THC injected into two deep-electrode monkeys caused the kind of brain-wave and behavioral changes that the active marijuana had caused, but they came quicker and hit the monkeys harder.

Those were the "immediate" effects, taking place only during intoxication. After about three months, however, the active-marijuana smokers with deep electrodes and the injected monkeys began to show certain "persistent" effects: brain-wave changes in the three above-mentioned regions. The changes (beginning after two months in the THC-injected monkeys) persisted at least through the weekend, when no drugging took place. "They were present on the Monday morning following and we have let them go as long as five days and these effects were still present," Heath testified. He called the finding "evidence of irreversible alterations in brain function."

Complications arose. First, two of the animals died, after 3½ and 5½ months of "heavy" marijuana smoking. (One had deep electrodes; the other did not. Cause of death: respiratory complications.) Then came a crisis relating to dosage.

Heath summarized his monkey work in testimony before the Senate Judiciary Committee in 1974. He did not go deeply into the matter of dose, but he did say that a "moderate" monkey's level nearly equaled that of a person who smoked three average marijuana cigarettes per day. He added that in the future, if funds were provided, monkeys would be tested at a lower dose level, one representing human smokers of three to five marijuana cigarettes a week.[42]

Later in the same day's session, Julius Axelrod was asked whether his cannabis research tied in with Heath's. He responded with criticism.

He said Heath's doses equaled the smoking of 90 to 100 marijuana cigarettes a day, and he wondered whether the finding of irreversible harm to the brain was caused by the large amounts given the monkeys. The amount of drug entering the body is fundamental to pharmacology, he said. Tiny amounts of a poison may have no effect; large amounts of a supposedly safe compound may be toxic.

Axelrod thought the experiment would be better performed with various doses, from small to large, to see what level produced the irreversible effects.[43]

The challenging of his dosage was to lead Heath to emphasize the matter of dosage in subsequent marijuana work for the rest of the decade. He soon carried out a study of "light" usage (three monkeys, two with implanted electrodes, received daily doses one-tenth of the "heavy" dose), detecting no notable changes in recording or behavior, either immediately or after six months of smoking. Later he tested the smoking equipment, finding it inefficient, and replaced it with a third apparatus;

changed his method of figuring equivalent dosage and began using blood level of THC as a basis; and undertook a similar study of more monkeys.

Heath's ultimate position on the disputed doses was that they approximately equaled those of human marijuana smokers (gauged by THC in the blood, rather than marijuana burned): it turned out—by virtue of the machine's inefficiency—that the monkeys had received much less smoke than even he had thought.

> R. Keith Stroup, director of the National Organization for the Reform of Marijuana Laws, circulated a memorandum declaring that "the average dose level used by Dr. Heath was the equivalent of from 600 cigarettes per month (20 per day) to 7,200 per month (240 per day)." He called the Heath research useless.[44]
>
> Heath indicated that he had chosen a human dose of 300 grams of hashish a month (per Tennant and Groesbeck's report of GIs abroad, 1972) as the basis for the monkey dose.[45] He then doubled the figure to allow for loss of smoke in the machine and tripled the product to correspond to a human-to-animal conversion theory (Freireich et al., 1966), reducing the resulting amount to mg/kg. So a single monkey dose used 0.82 of a gram of 3-percent-THC marijuana.[46] Later he found that a man smoking a pipe captured one-fourth of the THC in marijuana while the machine delivered only a twenty-ninth of the THC in the starting material.[47] And a single smoke starting with 0.82 of a gram of marijuana induced a monkey plasma level that "approximated plasma levels induced in human subjects who smoked an average-sized joint (0.8 to 1.2 g of marijuana containing 3.0% delta-9-THC)."[48]
>
> Heath said (1974) that when the monkeys with bipolar electrodes implanted deep in the brain were regularly exposed to marijuana, "at both moderate and heavy dose levels, persistent—perhaps irreversible—alterations developed in brain function at specific deep sites where recording activity has been correlated with emotional responsivity, alerting and sensory perception."[49] The changes, he wrote (1980), involved "increased spiking with slow-wave activity," particularly in the septal region, hippocampus, and amygdala."[50]

After spending half a year as captive cannabis consumers, the main group of monkeys rested for eight months. Through that entire drug-free period, the abnormal brain waves in those three deep sites persisted in monkeys that had received sizable drug doses, at least in those with equipment to pick up the waves. Ordinary scalp recordings never picked them up. Monkeys with deep electrodes had scalp electrodes too, so a direct comparison could be made.

Still later, Heath monitored an additional pair of monkeys in the newest smoking machine for eight months. During that time, one smoked a joint a day (containing six to seven milligrams of THC) five days a week; the other smoked double that amount. Results resembled the earlier ones. The marijuana affected the same deep-brain sites in the same way. There were the immediate changes; then persistent changes developed, in the heavier smoker after two months and in the lighter smoker after three months.

With an electron microscope, Heath and group examined thousands of cells in six monkeys' brains. The animals included three from the first long-range study (one "heavy" smoker, one inactive-marijuana smoker, and one injected monkey) killed at the end of the eight-month rest period; one from the last long-range study (a lighter smoker) killed after two months' rest; and two monkeys that never had been used before.

Doctors Jon W. Harper and William A. Myers, colleagues in Heath's department, worked on these studies with him, but we will quote Heath.

"We did not see any changes on the light microscopy, but on electron microscopy there were some striking changes," he said (1980 testimony). Those changes appeared in all of the three animals that had been exposed to THC, whether by smoking or injection. Nothing changed in the inactive-marijuana smoker or the two undrugged monkeys.

The doctors discovered three basic types of change in the brain tissues.

First: "changes at the synapse. This is where one neuron [nerve cell] connects to the next one to create the reverberating circuits that make the brain function . . . whatever the function is: behavior or perception or motor activity. . . ."

They found "a widening of the synaptic cleft, the cleft between the two cells, the connecting link. There were deposits of a radiopaque material [one that X-rays cannot penetrate] in that cleft. The vesicles which contain the chemicals which, at the end of one nerve, are released when the signal is going to the next one, those began to clump, showing evidence of pathology [diseased condition]. . . .

"Secondly, we had major changes in substance within the nerve cells known as the rough endoplasmic reticulum. These are constituents which are thought to have something to do with memory. This was disintegrated and disorganized.

"The third major change was in the nuclei of the nerve cells. There was a deposition of a protein material called an inclusion body. This appeared in a significantly high percentage of regions examined in these animals.

"What do all of these changes mean? . . . They are changes that have been reported in human beings in association with a variety of conditions: with viral diseases, with exposure to toxic agents such as carbon tetrachloride, and some of these changes have been reported with the aging process.

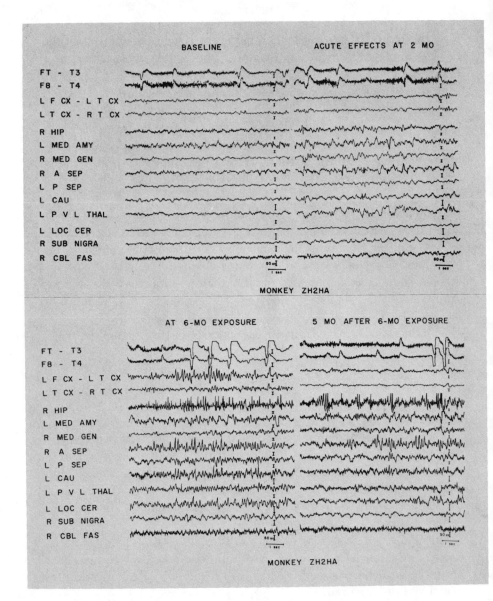

Recordings of brain waves from one of the Heath monkeys before marijuana treatment (baseline) and three times afterward. The second record (acute effects) represents the brain activity ten minutes after the latest exposure to marijuana smoke following two months of such treatment: waves from deep-brain sites are generally slower and sharper. Two days after half a year of the treatment (at six-months exposure), persistent effects, which began after three months of exposure, are graphed: again there are generalized slow waves but with greater spikes. Finally (five months after six-months exposure ended), effects persist in deep-brain regions, most *conspicuously in the hippocampus. The upper four lines are scalp record-ings. The lower ten are deep-brain recordings. (Abbreviations, top to bot-tom: frontal cortex to temporal cortex, right anterior temporal to right midtemporal cortex, left frontal cortex to left temporal cortex, left tem-poral cortex to right temporal cortex, right hippocampus, left medial amygdala, right medial geniculate, right anterior septal region, left pos-terior septal region, left caudate, left posterior ventrolateral thalamus, left locus ceruleus, right substantia nigra, and right fastigial nucleus of cer-ebellum.)*

"They definitely indicate that the brain . . . had structural impair-ment or damage.
"We considered this to be permanent. . . ."[51]

In making their microscopic tissue studies of the structures of monkey brains, the doctors viewed photographic prints of hundreds of neurons from each site (for example, a total of 600 prints of synapses, magnified 39,000 times), measuring synaptic clefts and densities of organelles (specialized parts of cells) and counting inclusion bodies in nuclei. They compared samples from the drugged and un-drugged animals, making statistical analyses. By significant margins, the former had wider synaptic clefts, lower densities in the rough endoplasmic reticulum, and more nuclear inclusions than the latter.

For the studies of synapses and organelles, septal and hippocampal parts "were selected for detailed, time-consuming ultrastructural study because the septal re-gion and hippocampus were two of the three brain sites that showed the most consistent lasting changes in recordings. . . ." (The ultrastructure is the ultimate physical and chemical organization of protoplasm.)

For the examination of the nuclei, they viewed nerve cells from seven brain sites: the septal region, posterior ventral lateral thalamus, hippocampus, amyg-dala, fastigial nucleus, caudate nucleus, and motor cortex.

The nature of the pathological changes were the same at all sites studied, but the degree of change varied to some extent. It was "most pronounced in the septal region, next . . . in the hippocampus and amygdala, and least . . . in the cor-tex."[52]

Heath et al. concluded that "the physiologic changes we previously reported in monkeys exposed to marijuana correlate with the ultrastructural changes."[53]

*   *   *

A committee of the Institute of Medicine (National Academy of Sciences) studying cannabis noted in *Marijuana and Health* (1982) that "at least one of the changes noted, clumping of synaptic vesicles . . . is a normal variant in the syn-aptic morphology of axon terminals in mammalian brain . . . and does not rep-resent a pathological change" (citing J. C. Sipe and R. Y. Moore, 1977).

The committee considered the structural studies to be methodologically flawed. While the material was evaluated double-blindly after electron micrographs were made, the fixation, tissue preparation, and photography appeared to be done without those safeguards against bias. Further, the reports of brain-cell changes were based primarily on examination of two limited brain areas in three treated monkeys.

The committee could make no definitive interpretation but added that "the possibility that marijuana may produce chronic, ultra-structural changes in brain has not been ruled out and should be investigated."[54]

At Davis in northern California, again the brains of rhesus monkeys were scrutinized. This time the monkeys survived. Dr. John P. Mc-Gahan (1981) subjected them to CAT scans, and some differences emerged between monkeys chronically given THC and untreated monkeys.

Over a year earlier, the animals had completed either long-term (three to five years), short-term (two to ten months), or no treatment with THC, fed to them in their food. The doses were said to correspond to the amount of THC consumed by chronic marijuana smokers.

Scanned for possible enlargement of the ventricles and the cisternae (certain cavities and spaces in the brain), the short-term and untreated groups did not differ. There did appear to be enlargement in some (but not all) of those places in the long-term group, compared with the untreated group.

Twelve monkeys participated, four to a group. Two radiologists made the measurements without knowing which monkeys were which.

The data suggested "that delta-9-THC may cause enlargement of the frontal horns and bicaudate distances of the brain when administered orally on a long-term basis to rhesus monkeys."[55] Enlargement of the spaces implies atrophy or wasting away of the brain tissues.

> The monkey's daily oral dose, 2.4 mg/kg, was said to equal the smoking of a daily 3 percent-THC marijuana cigarette by man, allowing a human-to-monkey conversion factor of three and another factor of three to correct for lower blood levels of THC from ingestion than from smoking.
>
> Dr. McGahan, M.D., has been with the Department of Diagnostic Radiology, University of California at Davis.

Ethel N. Sassenrath, who had used those same monkeys for reproductive and behavioral studies with L. F. Chapman and other associates, commented (1983): ". . . It would appear to be wishful thinking to assume these brain effects would be limited to monkey primates and not human primates . . . [and that] there is some 'safe' lower level of chronic drug intake at which nothing detrimental happens. Given the extremely long persistence of this drug in body tissues, especially fatty tissues like the brain, it is reasonable to expect that low levels of exposure over long enough periods of time will have detrimental effects similar to those of higher levels of drug intake—it will just take longer."[56]

"These changes in brain structure in the long-term, THC-treated monkeys were of particular interest since they had persisted for more than a year after cessation of drugging," Dr. Sassenrath told us (1983). "At the time these brain scans were made, these monkeys were caged individually and appeared to respond normally to the limited stimulation of their environment. However, during the course of their previous long-term drug treatment, they had been group-caged and had shown subtle but significant changes in their social behavior within their living groups.

"In general, after the first three or four months of daily drugging, they became less responsive to the critical tranquilizing or sedating effects of the drug and gradually became more irritable, especially at times of disturbance or stress. They no longer engaged in play behavior with cagemates and spent more time sitting alone. Under conditions of extreme stress, such as introduction to unfamiliar cagemates, they became highly aggressive, causing pronounced stress-related hormonal changes and behavioral responses in the *undrugged* cagemates. Relative to normal social behavior for this species, the THC-treated monkeys were less affiliative or friendly, and less adaptable to psychosocial stress.

"These were the same long-term, THC-treated monkeys which were shown later to have enlarged ventricles, suggesting drug-related cerebral atrophy or cell death."

THE
MIND

1

High-Mindedness: Studies of Cannabis Intoxication

• "A group of my friends . . . while not using any other drug, just mar- ijuana . . . claimed or acted as if they could fly. And they played this little game, taking a running start from one end of this long living room of mine and then they were going to crash out of the window—from, I guess, a fourth story I lived on—and fly . . . like Batman or Superman or whatever. And I was very frightened by that.

"I don't think I happened to be stoned at the time, so I stood up on the couch in front of the window to sort of ward them off so they wouldn't do this. And I remember being struck.

"But all they had that particular time was marijuana." —Nathan (ex- user)

(More in Supplement, G-1.)

Moreau, Paris, France, 1845:

"There is not a single elementary manifestation of mental illness that cannot be found in the mental changes caused by hashish, from simple manic excitement to frenzied delirium, from the feeblest impulse, the simplest fixation, to the merest injury to the senses, to the most irresist- ible drive, the wildest delirium, the most varied disorders of feelings." Thus did French psychiatrist Jacques-Joseph Moreau liken the two states in his book *Hashish and Mental Illness; Psychological Studies.*

Moreau based his treatise on travels in the Near East and experiments in which he and his students ate hashish, in the form of a greenish paste. (He used the word "hachisch" to refer to the drug-type cannabis plant as well as to a "greasy extract" of it with "a very nauseating taste.") The dose had to be at least the size of a walnut for results, he said.

Moreau believed that psychiatry could benefit from the experiments because hashish gives people the power to study in themselves the men- tal changes of insanity. Because of hashish's property of keeping con- sciousness intact, one could record all of his impressions while his fac- ulties disintegrated. In modern fashion, Moreau used varying doses and control groups and spoke of the importance of suggestibility and setting.

An unnamed person who took hashish for the first time (evidently a woman) presented Moreau with notes written shortly after her fit, Moreau wrote, and he used them in his book. "It tasted horrible" but with difficulty she swallowed the paste. Then she burst out with laughter while at dinner; stood with a spoon as though about to duel some candied fruit; saw that her brother, atop a piano, had a forked tail ending with three lanterns; cried, "Why do you nail down my limbs? I feel as if I am turning into lead"; fell down and was helped to her feet; picked up a small stove to dance the polka with it; imitated several actors; and visualized herself at the opera ball.

Then she choked, suffocated, and fell into a bottomless shaft; felt millions of insects eating her head; sent for an obstetrician to have him deliver a female insect of seven little creatures; saw the guests of a dinner she attended five years earlier; saw her son, with white and pink wings, flying in the sky, surrounded by other winged children; was carried along the Seine River by a fairy; wanted to swim but began to drown; screamed and was rescued by a friend; declared that her child did not belong to her; and in a café saw a rat running in a man's head and swelling to enormous size. "I cannot describe the thousand fantastic ideas that passed through my brain during the three hours that I was under the influence of the hashish."

Moreau concluded that all forms of delirium, madness, hallucinations, and so forth, originated in an identical mental change he called "manic excitement." Hashish creates this psychic factor, creating a "sleepless dream" in which the imaginary and reality are mingled and the clearest consciousness cannot distinguish them.

It seemed to him that the drug acted directly on the mind without affecting the organs, which he saw as true of mental illness.

Moreau set forth eight groups of mental phenomena encompassed by hashish intoxication:

1. Initial joy without reason, giving way to calm and peace of mind.

2. Excitation and inability to direct one's thoughts; a torrent of strange ideas, emphasizing the past; the slightest interference breaking the sequence of thoughts; contradictory passions and moods, happy to sad; groundless suspicions becoming certainties; the mind exaggerating everything.

3. Errors of time and space; time dragging; forms expanding or contracting.

4. Hearing becoming keen; music exciting fiery emotions, happy or sad.

5. Fixed ideas or delusions—as of persecution—when the delirium has progressed to advanced stages.

6. Apparent damage to the emotions; the sound of bells, for instance, precipitates a feeling of terror.

7. Irresistible impulses and urges—for example, a yen to jump out of a window—particularly if the dose is strong.

8. Illusions and hallucinations.

After eating hashish, Moreau stared at a picture and said, "I do not like horses that kick, even in a painting. That one [pointing] kicked me." Laughter greeted his words. "My illusion was nothing more than a dream, but a dream as swift as a thought and provoked by an external cause, a sensory impression . . . a true manifestation of mental illness."

Moreau administered hashish to several mental patients and reported some apparent recoveries but, aside from calling attention to the "prophylactic action of a substance that could offer valuable therapeutic resources," he drew no precise conclusion.[1]

*   *   *

Much later (1934) a New York psychiatrist, Walter Bromberg, smoked two reefers within forty minutes and felt "a sensation as though the top of the head were lifted, accompanied by optic images of skulls and skeletons." His head felt alternately light and heavy. He imagined his legs lengthening and his arms rising.

He recorded dizziness, confusion, and constant loss of memory. Minutes seemed to go on for hours. Reality felt like a dream. He described hunger, difficulty in thinking of needed words, then garrulousness, a fit of laughter, long lapses of time, and rapid arrival of new thoughts.

The imagery stood out clearly and sharply, "yet I know there is no change."[2]

Ames, Cape Town, South Africa, 1958: In a hospital ten medical interns—including the investigator, Frances Ames—took pills of resinous cannabis extract and observers took notes on their reactions. Symptoms started abruptly, came in waves, and varied with individual personality and temperament, but included in all cases "a curious disturbance of consciousness," disordered time perception, difficulty in immediate recall, and mood changes, the researcher reported. She placed symptoms in the categories below.

Thought disorders: Several described their thought processes as "fragmented." Often subjects could not sustain conversations unless reminded of what had been said. Several felt they were thinking better but kept forgetting what they were thinking about.

Disordered time perception: During the first few hours, brief periods seemed immensely long (except that one subject, overdosed, at first felt that time was passing incredibly quickly; later it went agonizingly slow).

Mood changes: Usually they felt mild euphoria and talked excitedly, often suddenly laughing without explanation.

Hallucinations: Six saw changing figures and colors when they closed their eyes, and six felt strange things happening to their bodies (ribs sticking through their flesh, teeth turned to plastic, body twisted, body rocking and spinning, and so forth).

Delusions: Several became suspicious and fearful of hospital personnel.

Visual disorders: To four, people looked like cardboard, an observer like an Egyptian pharaoh, eyes like oranges, or a face like "an alabaster tortoise."

Detachment and depersonalization: Often personality seemed split or mind separated from body. Some felt they were observing themselves, as in a movie. At times when the observer would become concerned about a symptom (such as a sustained heart rate of 140), the subject would be detached and unconcerned.

"G., while complaining bitterly of painful muscular spasms, burst out laughing." Another begged to end the experience because everything had become unreal and terrifying—"This is like schizophrenia." A third said later, "The outstanding psychic experience was a loss of feeling real. . . ."[3]

In another South African study, Morley, Logie, and Bensusan (1973) presented 150 *dagga* (cannabis) smokers with a questionnaire listing 134 subjective effects and asking them whether each was ever the feature of a "high." Not only did some subjects contradict others, but subjects contradicted themselves. For example, 72 percent checked "more talkative" while 70 percent checked "less talkative."

Other percentages: "Less noisy/boisterous," 68%; "more noisy/boisterous," 37%. "Increased mental efficiency," 55%; "decreased mental efficiency," 53%. "Increased mental activity," 82%; "decreased mental activity," 41%. "Feel happy," 88%; "feel depressed," 33%. "Makes drowsy," 87%; "keeps awake," 47%. "Extroverted," 61%; "introverted," 58%. "Increases desire for food," 88%; "decreases desire for food," 35%.

One subject tried to explain: "I found it very difficult to answer these questions. Dagga has different effects at different times. . . . Sometimes I find it hard to sleep; sometimes I can't stay awake. It depends on me personally at different times and also on the strength of the hash and quantity smoked."[4]

Isbell et al., Lexington, Kentucky, 1967: Soon after the isolation and identification of THC in the cannabis plant, Dr. Harris Isbell and others demonstrated its marijuana like effect on the mind. Some forty prisoners got THC to drink or smoke (together with tobacco cigarettes).

Without being told at first that the drug resembled marijuana, they all found it similar, at least in smaller doses. Mood consistently changed, usually becoming euphoric. "Other changes included alterations in sense of time and visual and auditory perception (usually described as keener)."

Large doses produced "marked distortion in visual and auditory perception, depersonalization, derealization and hallucinations, both auditory and optical," in most subjects. The experimenters established that THC was a drug that mimicked psychoses and that such effects depended on dose.[5] Moreau had determined as much for hashish over a century earlier.

*   *   *

Weil, Zinberg, and Nelsen, Boston, 1968; also Weil and Zinberg, 1969: Boston University School of Medicine was the scene of "the first attempt to investigate marihuana in a formal double-blind experiment with the appropriate controls," according to the experimenters (Dr. Weil, then newly graduated from Harvard medical school; Dr. Zinberg of Harvard; and Judith M. Nelsen of Boston University).

The subjects were nine young men who never had smoked marijuana before, though all smoked tobacco, and eight young chronic users of marijuana (sex not mentioned). Given small or larger doses of confiscated marijuana to smoke, all chronic users became obviously "high," in the judgment of the experimenters, who had seen many in that condition; but only one of the hitherto inexperienced subjects had a definite "marihuana reaction," except that some of them noticed that "things seemed to take longer."

Yet marijuana seemed to have more impact on the minds of the "naive" subjects, as judged by the results of psychological tests (given fifteen and ninety minutes after the smoking of active and inactive marijuana). These subjects registered significant losses in a test of "cognitive function" (digit-symbol substitution test: substituting symbols for numbers) and a test of "muscular coordination and attention" (pursuit rotor test: touching a moving spot with a stylus). In most cases losses varied with dose.

Performances of chronic users did not change or even improved a little with marijuana (a result of practice?). The researchers cautioned, however, that the study was not designed for comparison of the two groups; experimental conditions were not the same.

In their "Conclusions" they did make comparisons between the two groups: Marijuana, smoked in a fairly pleasant setting, affects them subjectively and objectively in opposite ways.

The first paragraph of their report stated: "The study was not undertaken to prove or disprove popularly held convictions about marihuana as an intoxicant, to compare it with other drugs or to introduce our own opinions." They wanted "simply to collect some long overdue pharmacological data."

However, in their "Discussion" they said: "Our observations, that the chronic users after smoking marihuana performed on some tests as well as or better than they did before taking the drug, reinforced the argument advanced by chronic users that maintaining effective levels of performance for many tasks—driving for example—is much easier under the influence of marihuana than under that of other psychoactive drugs." (But an end note in tiny type said, "The influence of marihuana on driving skill remains an open question of high medico-legal priority.") Also: "Lack of any change in pupil size of subjects after they had smoked marihuana is an enlightening finding especially because so many users and law-enforcement agents firmly believe that marihuana dilates pupils."

Among other "Conclusions": it is feasible and safe to study marijuana on human volunteers in a laboratory; marijuana smoking does not change sugar levels, dilates eye blood vessels, and does not change respiratory rate; and in a neutral setting the effects of an inhaled dose "appear to reach maximum intensity within one-half hour of inhalation . . . and to be completely dissipated by 3 hours." Under "Results," however, "observable effects . . . were maximum at 15 minutes after smoking" and "largely dissipated 3 hours after the end of smoking." And "Chronic users showed a small but statistically significant increase in respiratory rate after smoking, but we do not regard the change as clinically significant."

The researchers commented on "the fact that marihuana appears to be a relatively mild intoxicant in our studies. If these results seem to differ from those of earlier experiments, it must be remembered that other experimenters have given marihuana orally, have given doses much higher than those commonly smoked by users, have administered potent synthetics, and have not strictly controlled the laboratory setting." The Boston investigators said that ingestion seemed to cause more powerful effects than smoking, on the basis of what users reported. (The opposite has come to be accepted as fact.) Their own dose, in a total of two cigarettes, was half a gram (low) or two grams (high) of marijuana said to contain 0.9 percent THC.[6]

Time magazine's version of the above quotation: "The drug, the investigators concluded, 'appears to be a relatively mild intoxicant, with minor, real, short-lived effects.' " In a full page on the study, it said the findings "confirm some popular ideas about marijuana's effects and expose others as completely false."[7]

The study, as covered by the news media, was cited for years as evidence of marijuana's mildness by people wishing to liberalize the marijuana laws.

Those high on marijuana forget from moment to moment what is being said. The marijuana may interfere with the retrieval of information from immediate-memory storage in the brain, said Weil and Zinberg (1969). They looked into the subject of memory after studying the speech of those smoking marijuana. And they had delved into speech after puzzling over the way subjective and objective mental effects differed. How can you tell if a person is "high"? The only way is "for him to tell you so—hardly a satisfactory criterion for psychopharmacologists." They sought a specific, consistent change in mental function as an index.

Users, even those quite experienced, would report difficulty talking to others when high—perhaps not making sense, forgetting what they were talking about, and saying "crazy things." So looking to speech as a possible index of intoxication, the researchers gave each subject a tape recorder and asked him to talk for five minutes about "an interesting or dramatic experience," both before and fifty minutes after a smoke of marijuana. (Presumably the subjects were the ones in the 1968 study.)

Marijuana did not distort individual words and sentences. But judges could usually tell the "before" from the "after" (except for the naive subjects on low doses) from "subtle speech retardation." Scores, in various categories (such as narrative quality, coherence, unity, thought completion, and being aware of a listener) generally dropped after smoking, particularly in chronic users.

An example: Before smoking, one subject told a rambling but integrated story of a protest demonstration. After the smoke, his talk became incoherent. He babbled about the experiment and the room and quoted irrelevant poetry.

The problem, said Weil and Zinberg, is that "a high individual appears to have to expend more effort than when not intoxicated to remember from moment to moment the logical thread of what he is saying." They suspected "an actual change in brain function" rather than merely a change in motivation. One forgets what he has said or will say, going off at tangents because he has forgotten the line of thought.

Marijuana seemed to interfere with "ultra-short-term (or immediate) memory . . . memory over the past few seconds. . . . The interference seems to be with retrieval of information while it is in an immediate memory storage; once it passes into the next (recent memory) storage, it again seems to be easily accessible to consciousness."[8]

☆   ☆   ☆

Melges et al., Palo Alto, California, 1970: Strong marijuana extract drinks induced "temporal disintegration"—inability to coordinate a series of mental operations needed to reach a goal—in eight graduate students. Stemming partly from impairment of immediate memory, the disintegration was associated with disorganized speech and thinking.

Subjects had taken different drug doses and set to work at arithmetic tasks, reciting their mental operations aloud. For instance, one might be assigned the number 113 and asked to subtract 7 and add 2 repeatedly until reaching 48. All doses impaired performance, in terms of time spent or number of mistakes; and the higher the dose, the worse the score and the more hours of impairment.

With increasing doses came (a) progressively more mistakes in the "serial" or "working" functions of immediate memory—as one student said, "I'd forget which number I just did or what I was supposed to do next"—and (b) progressively more errors in reaching the goal, subjects passing over it or forgetting it entirely.

In a simpler memory test, repetition of numbers, while the drug impaired short-term memory, impairment did not vary with dose. In a third test, subtraction of sevens, the drug made no difference. In this and the main test, long-term memory appeared intact, judged from the fact that errors of subtraction and addition did not increase.

Incoordination of recent memories with intentions may partly explain the speech disorganization under marijuana, according to Doctors Melges and Tinklenberg and fellows. Said another student: "I can't follow what I'm saying . . . can't stay on the same subject . . . I can't remember what I just said or what I want to say . . . because there are just so many thoughts that are broken in time, one chunk there and one chunk here."

If immediate memory breaks down, so does speech; the person loses his train of thought, and "loose associations" emerge. "Lack of goal-directedness and loose associations were common in the speech patterns of our subjects when they were under the influence of THC."

> The team, associated with Stanford University School of Medicine and the nearby Veterans Administration Hospital, administered 20 to 60 milligrams of THC per milliliter of ethanol, diluted in water, or at other times cannabinoid-free placebos, in double-blind experimentation.[9]
>
> In another experiment by Melges et al. (1974), using alcohol and smoked THC, "temporal disintegration" correlated with "delusional-like" thinking.[10]

Abel, Berkeley, California, 1970, and Toronto, Canada, 1971: Psychologist Ernest L. Abel studied marijuana and memory through word tests of men and women familiar with the drug. Specifically he performed the following three experiments:

A. He tested eight subjects when sober and when intoxicated. After reading a ghost story, they had to write down as much as they remembered of the story, using exact words if possible. When high, they were worse at reproducing either words or ideas.

But did marijuana prevent information from entering the brain, from entering the memory-storage place, or from being retrieved?

B. Abel had forty-nine subjects memorize word lists when sober, smoke marijuana or tobacco cigarettes (falsely claimed to have been dipped in THC) or not smoke at all, then try to recall the words and also try to select the words from larger lists mixed with new words. No significant differences among the three groups showed up on the recall test. Likewise, on the recognition test, the groups identified about the same number of correct words, although those on marijuana accepted the most incorrect words as well.

That eliminated the possibility that marijuana influenced memory-retrieval processes, by Abel's interpretation.

C. Finally he gave ten subjects marijuana to smoke and then word lists to memorize and recall. On another occasion they took the test without marijuana. All remembered fewer words with marijuana than without.

Interviewed after the tests, many subjects said that upon smoking marijuana they could not concentrate long enough to perform at their best. This might explain why marijuana hindered memory, Abel said. "In not being able to concentrate, subjects cannot rehearse. As a result, information cannot be transferred to permanent memory."[11]

* * *

Clark, Hughes, and Nakashima, Salt Lake City, 1970: Dr. Lincoln D. Clark and others in the psychiatry department at the University of Utah College of Medicine tested eighteen sober men, who never had used marijuana, on their time of reaction (to colors), recent memory (of numbers), time estimation, hand steadiness, and silent reading and comprehension. A week later they had the subjects swallow marijuana extract and take the tests again.

Scores changed for the worse in all categories. The "psychedelic" substance had "significant effects on complex reaction time (largely through sporadic impairment of vigilance), recent memory, recall and comprehension of written information, and accuracy of time estimation." Hands became significantly less steady too. Errors in estimating 15, 90, and 180 seconds "were striking," increasing with the time interval; subjects overestimated 180 seconds by more than five times, never underestimating it.[12]

* * *

Klonoff, Low, and Marcus, Vancouver, Canada, 1970: Professors of psychiatry and neurology administered thirteen tests (with thirty-two variables) to eighty-one volunteers, all experienced marijuana smokers, "to determine the effects of low and high doses of [smoked] marijuana on neuropsychological functioning and . . . on learning."

Both doses generally impaired all mental processes tested—"concept formation, memory, tactile form discrimination, and motor function"—but the high dose impaired them more extensively. (The low dose adversely affected seven tests and twelve variables; the high dose—not so high by more recent standards—so affected eleven tests and twenty-eight variables, somewhat fewer in a retesting.) Men and women scored about the same. The volunteers, described as educated people, comprised forty-three women and thirty-eight men.

Professor Harry Klonoff and colleagues postulated a temporary "drug-related effect on the individual's central integrative processes." Interference with such brain functions may have hindered recall, hence learning.[13]

* * *

Harshman, Crawford, and Hecht, Los Angeles, 1976: Marijuana may alter the relative roles of the right and left cerebral hemispheres, according to psychologists of the University of California at Los Angeles. (The cerebrum, the largest part of the brain, is composed of two hemispheres, which are connected by a band of nerve fibers. Normally each hemisphere specializes in a different type of activity. It is believed that generally—at least in a right-handed male—the left side controls spoken and written language, reasoning, analysis, and calculation, while the right side handles space, images, patterns, and nonverbal ideas.)

Richard A. Harshman and the others gave twenty psychological tests to twenty-five male subjects in both the intoxicated and the nonintoxicated state (with about two weeks intervening). Marijuana intoxication impaired verbal and analytic tasks but often facilitated nonverbal and holistic tasks (that is, tasks emphasizing whole pictures). With mixed tasks, results were mixed.

They said the results supported their hypotheses that the process of getting high on marijuana involves (1) shifting into a new "cognitive style," that is, basic mode of thinking, and (2) decreasing the participation of the left hemisphere while increasing the participation of the right, in cognitive activities (those concerning the process of knowing). Why marijuana should do this, they did not know.[14]

2

In The Long Run: Studies of Chronic Use

• "*I began smoking dope (hash-ish) in Europe almost three years ago. For the first 1½ years, I smoked almost daily 1 bowl of dope in the evening being stoned 1½ to 2½ hrs. During that time I cannot recall any mental detereation or indolence, I was active as before But at the halfway point, I came into contact with people that smoked 3,4,5 bowls a night, and as you may know, when at first I declined a second bowl they hassled me and me being and idiot and a nice guy (I didn't want to ruin their nightly parties, ha! peer pressure) I submitted to the second & third & forth bowls. And so for the next year & half I noticed myself sliding downhill and because of this and did nothing about it.*

"Upon returning to the U.S. I experienced no pschological withdrawal symptoms, but I still am feeling the effects of the dope in lack of motivation, shortness of attention span, and a frustrating, extremely frustrating inability to comprehend

"I have been home for one month and during that time I took a full battery of (timed) aptitude tests, while taking these tests I felt the frustration of not comprehending what I was reading or looking at. The outcome of these tests were as I thought they would be. A definite decrease in all areas save general mechanical reasoning which as before seems to be my forté. My IQ dropped 119 to 100 20 pts, space relations went down considerately, my mathematical ability dropped some .30 points. . . . I only answered 52 of 80 question on the Mental Ability test, of these .52 answered 47 were correct.

". . . I am interested to know what coarse to follow to once again attain my former abilities." —Robert of Boston (in a letter)

(More in Supplement, G-2.)

Chopra and Chopra, Calcutta, India, 1939; also Chopra and Jandu, 1976: Observing 1,238 "hemp-drug addicts" in India, the Chopras reported that the drugs affected the mental faculties of the majority. They saw "evidence of gross injury to the central nervous system"—mainly insanity or immorality—in 3 percent and "minor changes"—uncontrollable emotions, slight impairment of judgment or memory, dirty or lazy habits, irritability, and/or sleep problems—in 51 percent.

The sleep problems included disturbed sleep (nights shortened, often by dreams), 12 percent; and insomnia, 6 percent (the majority being neurotic individuals who had taken drugs to help their insomnia).

The Chopras did not attribute the changes entirely to the hemp-drug habit. Many of those observed were "persons with neurotic tendencies" and the drugs "enhanced the preexisting nervous defects."

As R. N. and G. S. Chopra saw it, "Mental injury is more likely to occur in the case of those individuals who take large doses and for prolonged periods."[15]

Thirty-seven years later a report by G. S. Chopra and B. S. Jandu, in Calcutta, demonstrated that proposition. The pair interviewed 275 chronic cannabis users and their relatives, friends, and employers. They reported that those lacking "initiation, motivation, and interest in their work and family" and exhibiting "emotional immaturity, low frustration tolerance, and failure to assume responsibility" were much more likely to be older individuals who had used the drug longer and took larger doses. In total, 30 percent showed "behavioral changes" and 11 percent "amotivational syndrome" (presumably caused by the drug).

In the opinion of Chopra and Jandu, cannibis caused "no or little" structural changes in the brain but apparently changed the sensitivity of brain cells or altered their functioning.

Chopra informed the New York Academy of Sciences, "The intensity of the chronic effects of marijuana usage, as observed in India and Africa, has not been reported by Western observers" because of milder preparations used in the West.

> Chopra and Jandu had statistically divided the total into four groups according to daily dose, which correlated with duration of use and also with age. A set of fourteen pertinent symptoms varied in frequency 5½ times from lightest to heaviest group. Duration of use varied from two to twenty-seven years, age from seventeen to forty-eight, and dose from 40 to 350 mg of THC daily.
>
> Their report stated, "The individuals studied were apparently healthy persons with little or no apparent personality problems and no history of mental disorder or neurosis." However, the paper in large measure was "based on a study of 200 cannabis dependents that took place from 1963 to 1968."[16] Articles by Dr. G. S. Chopra (1971) and Chopra and Smith (1974) described a study of 200 patients of the Addiction Research Clinic, Calcutta, seen between 1963 and 1968 for "acute toxic psychosis" following the reported use of cannabis preparations. Two-thirds of them (132 patients) had histories of personality or psychiatric disorders, which in 10 cases included "overt psychosis," while only 34 percent (68) had no such histories, according to the latter article.[17]

Soueif et al., Cairo, Egypt, 1960–80: "The Egyptian Study" was a psychological examination of 1,103 long-term, regular hashish users and 994 nonusers, all males.

In the most important part of the study, standard tests of mental functioning were administered to 850 prisoners serving time for using cannabis and 839 nonusers imprisoned for other offenses.

Twelve of sixteen tests showed differences between users and nonusers. As described by Professor M. I. Soueif, chairman of Cairo University's psychology and philosophy department and the head of the research team throughout most of the years, the results included these, among others:

"A. Takers were definitely slow on tests used for the assessment of speed of very simple motor tasks. . . .

"B. They did also poorly on a test measuring speed and accuracy of visual discrimination. This test requires a good deal of attention.

"C. Takers were definitely below the average for their comparable non-takers on tests for hand-eye coordination with and without speed being explicitly emphasized in the instructions.

"D. We also found that on some tests of immediate memory . . . especially those requiring some kind of mental reorganization of the test material . . . cannabis takers were very low performers.

"E. Cannabis takers tended to overestimate distances of moderate lengths. However non-takers tended to underestimate such distances." (So testified the professor in 1974.)

"On estimation of time (short periods of three minutes each) we did not find any reliable differences" (he wrote, 1980). This result was not typical; intoxicated users usually overestimate time.

Relatively speaking, cannabis impaired mental functioning in edu-cated people more than in uneducated people, in urban subjects more than in rural ones, and in younger subjects more than in older ones, the research team noted.

In response to three special questions, more "heavy" takers than "moderates" said they slept badly, lay awake long before falling asleep, and woke up very early in the morning without being able to go back to sleep.

Asked at a London cannabis conference how long a period elapsed between cessation of drug use and testing, Professor Soueif explained that "we were pretty sure that some of those prisoners didn't stop taking cannabis while they were in prison. So they might have been using cannabis the day before they were tested."

The prisoners took twelve standard tests with sixteen variables. For example, the assessment of immediate memory used two parts of the Wechsler-Bellevue intelligence test. A subject repeated digits forward and backward. The first part showed no difference, but in the second, users' performances dropped far below those of the controls.

The Bender Gestalt test measured hand-eye coordination and memory for de-signs. A subject copied geometric designs, then drew them from memory; accu-racy, not speed, counted. "And in both cases the users gave a very bad perfor-mance compared with that of the controls.

"Thus our users were very poor performers compared with matched controls, on tests assessing speed and accuracy of psychomotor performance, changing mental set and various aspects of memory."

Those who took opium as well as cannabis amounted to 31.5 percent of the users. They did better than the cannabis-only users on three tests, worse on two, and no differently on eleven.

The hashish users nearly always smoked it, usually with a water pipe, some-times in cigarettes. The first group of users studied, 215 ordinary citizens in Cairo, took it twelve times a month. The next group, 40 villagers, took it eight times monthly. The prisoners used to take it sixty-six times a month.

Chemical analysis of seven pieces of confiscated hashish determined its THC content to range from 1.9 to 3.6 percent, averaging 3.1 percent.

The dose per session ranged from 0.21 to 2.5 grams (6 to 75 mg of THC). The majority consumed about one gram of cannabis a session (about 30 mg of THC).

Ages of the users averaged thirty-nine, ranging from fifteen to fifty. The investigators found in general that the more often a subject took the drug, the younger he had been when he started taking it.

To try to reconcile conflicting studies of cannabis users, Soueif et al. formulated this hypothesis: "Other conditions being equal, the lower the non-drug level of proficiency on tests of cognitive and psychomotor performance, the smaller the sign of function deficit associated with drug taking."

In other words, illiterates have less to lose from use of cannabis than educated men. Also, rural and older men, normally scoring lower than urban and younger men, respectively, have less to lose than the urbanites and young ones. Soueif said the Egyptian tests confirmed the hypothesis for the three variables of literacy, urbanism, and age. He recognized, though, that the hypothesis needed empirical examination and did not know if it would work in other cultures and among other types of subjects (for example, females, who in Egypt rarely used cannabis).

History records the introduction of cannabis into Egypt around the middle of the twelfth century, though some writers claim evidence that it existed there 3,000 years ago or more. It was prohibited in 1879. In 1957 a committee launched an investigation of its chronic consumption, sponsored by Egypt's National Centre for Social and Criminological Research. The first report, an Arabic book, came out in 1960. The first English paper appeared in 1967 (in the United Nations *Bulletin on Narcotics*, which also published six related papers, 1971–77).[18]

Kornhaber, New York, 1971: Psychiatrist Arthur Kornhaber, writing to a medical journal, said an eighteen-month experience with fifty outpatients, thirteen to eighteen, led him to believe that marijuana "exercises a toxic effect upon the developing nervous system."

In addition, he wrote, the drug fosters a regression from logical thought to fantasy and magical thinking, "has a long-term depressant effect . . . impairs the learning ability and judgement of the young by its harmful effect upon attention span and ability to concentrate," facilitates passive and dependent ways from which youngsters find it hard to emerge, and turns them away from reality toward an inactive peer group.

The condition resembles common adolescent turmoil, but marijuana "locks" the developing youth into it, wrote Dr. Kornhaber. "He psychologically remains an adolescent, and a seriously disturbed adolescent."

The fifty patients each had smoked marijuana at least twice daily, four times weekly, for a year. Many used other drugs too. At the start of treatment most felt pot was "harmless."

Marijuana, said the doctor, had dramatically affected school performance and commonly initiated this sequence of events:

"1. Decrease in concentration and attention span; increase in daydreaming, fantasy, and withdrawal.

"2. Decrease in personal hygiene, physical exercise, and logical thinking processes.

"3. Increase in school absence, cutting classes, and problem behavior.

"4. Search for a peer group with similar problems."

He mentioned only one therapeutic prescription: a wristwatch for youngsters complaining of time disorientation. Inattention to time led to sacrifice of planning and vocational goals for "immediate gratification of impulse or desire." Many also reported depressive symptoms, including "constipation, and day-night reversal in sleeping patterns."

Many symptoms abated and many patients "with underlying depressive and behavioral symptoms improved in school performance, concentration, and mood four to six weeks after" quitting marijuana, and they quit their peer groups too. (The number of such patients was not mentioned.)

Dr. Kornhaber concluded that cannabis "provokes an organic brain syndrome" but that the brain "shows marked functional improvement upon cessation of the drug action."[19]

✻ ✻ ✻

Rubin and Comitas, Jamaica, 1975, and associated investigators: Nineteen standard intelligence, neuropsychological, and other tests brought out no substantial differences between thirty chronic *ganja* smokers and a comparable group of "nonsmokers" on the island of Jamaica. No evidence emerged that long-term use of cannabis had produced any intellectual or ability deficits.

The exams were administered in a hospital at least forty-eight hours after the start of a smoke-free period. They comprised the Wechsler Adult Intelligence Scale, a personality test, two verbal tests, and fourteen neuropsychological tests measuring motor abilities, sensory perception, memory and attention, and concept formation. Admittedly, "These tests are not culture free, but since the primary concern was to determine differences between the smokers and non-smokers, this was not considered a limiting factor, on the assumption that any cultural bias in the test items would be similar and consistent for both groups."[20]

Satz, Fletcher, and Sutker (1976) disagreed with this reasoning, noticing "many items that were culturally biased against native Jamaicans," for "if the tests were too difficult for both groups, which might be expected for rural disadvantaged groups . . . depressed performance levels would mask possible differences between groups." They further assailed the study for statistical shortcomings, inadequate testing of memory and personality, and other problems, declaring nevertheless that "the Jamaica Project stands as a landmark study on the long-term effects of chronic cannabis usage."[21]

Forty-five professionals acted as staff and consultants for the Jamaica project, including Robert M. Knights of Carleton University, Ottawa, Canada, who analyzed the results of the psychological testing.

He said (1976) that exotic studies might be irrelevant to North American society, with users largely under thirty, often social dropouts, using multiple drugs. The Jamaican subjects were laboring men in their midthirties who smoked marijuana to spur themselves to heavy work. He suggested that drug tolerance might have been a factor in the results. Studies of long-term users seem to rule out intellectual damage of great magnitude but not necessarily "subtle deleterious effects," Knights said.[22]

As noted in Part I, many of the "nonsmokers" had consumed cannabis preparations themselves.

Not only could Rubin and Comitas see "no evidence of any causal relationship between cannabis use and mental deterioration, insanity, violence or poverty; or that widespread cannabis use in Jamaica produces an apathetic, indolent class of people," they gave it good marks for providing "an adaptive mechanism by which many Jamaicans cope with limited life chances in a harsh environment."

One part of the Jamaican study measured production and movements of four smokers during agricultural labor in fields before and after smoking. The calculations disclosed that marijuana smoking resulted in less production per unit of time with more movements and a greater expenditure of energy to work a given acreage.

Nonetheless, most smokers felt that marijuana energized them and made them work better. And the authors of *Ganja in Jamaica*, while finding the "behavioral changes" significant over extended periods of time, declared in their final summary that the smoking reinforced "social cohesiveness during work in group situations" and that "heavy use of *ganja* does not diminish work drive or the work ethic."[23] (But, we would add, it can diminish work.)

In psychiatric examinations, Beaubrun and Knight (1976) discerned no significant differences in work record, particularly job stability, as disclosed in narrated life histories and psychiatric questionnaires, but they added: "It may be that a difference could have been demonstrated if our sample had included intellectual workers or white-collar workers of any kind, but in a sample made up mainly of fishermen, subsistence farmers, and unskilled or partly skilled manual workers from villages where there is relatively little mobility, such differences were not detectable."[24] (Continued in 3, this section.)

Williams et al. had noted earlier (1946), "Marihuana smokers claim that smoking marihuana increases their productive activity, interest in work, and artistic ability. . . . No such effects were observed" in a U.S. Public Health Service study in Lexington, Kentucky, of six men who for thirty-nine days could smoke unlimited amounts of marijuana. (Its potency was unknown, but the subjects—prisoners serving time for federal marijuana violations—pronounced it "good weed.")

One subject, given a work assignment, lost interest and quit early in the experiment. Another, who styled himself a painter in oils, brought some artwork that he planned to complete during the study, but he abandoned it the first day. A musician had intended to do a good deal of practicing, but he did almost none.

Initial exhilaration and euphoria changed in several days to "general lassitude and indifference which resulted in carelessness in personal hygiene and lack of productive activity."

Administered before the smoking period and on the third day after smoking ended, the MacQuarrie Test for Mechanical Ability showed an improvement where speed alone was the factor but loss in accuracy where coordination and manual skill were necessary; the Seashore Measure of Musical Talents indicated no improvement in musical ability, although subjects felt it had occurred; and the Stanford-Binet test demonstrated impaired intellectual functioning.[25]

Stefanis et al., Athens Greece, 1976, 1977: Comparing forty-seven long-time hashish smokers with forty men who smoked no cannabis, investigators in Greece turned up a "higher incidence of personality disorders, unemployment, and prison sentences in the group of chronic users."

The users, men who had smoked hashish an average of nearly three times a day for twenty-three years, had "a high incidence of psychopathology": 38 percent (eighteen) of them suffered some type of mental problem, compared with 18 percent (seven) of the controls. (Twelve cases of psychopathology in users were identified as "personality disorders," which included five of the "antisocial type." Nonusers had three personality disorders, none antisocial. Three users were diagnosed as suffering "paranoid schizophrenia," not apparently linked to their smoking.)

In a psychiatric journal article (by-lined by five M.D.s), Professor Costas Stefanis of the University of Athens and his associates declared it impossible to determine whether chronic hashish smoking *caused* or *resulted from* the personality disabilities.[26]

In a book, some of them suggested that personality disorders, not cannabis, probably caused the other problems. Among the problems: 43 percent of the hashish smokers (twenty), though just 15 percent of the nonsmokers (six), lacked jobs. Only 26 percent of users (twelve) against 63 percent of nonusers (twenty-five) were skilled workers.

Cannabis violations had imprisoned over half of the smokers (twenty-five) and only one who didn't use hashish (but who sold it). Three-fifths of users (twenty-nine) versus one-fourth of nonusers (ten) had served time for noncannabis crimes.

Only 55 percent of users (twenty-six) but 95 percent of nonusers (thirty-eight) had been soldiers. Cannabis use, like mental disorder, exempted men from military conscription in Greece.[27]

*   *   *

Carter and Doughty, Costa Rica, 1976, and associated investigators: A two-year study of chronic marijuana smoking in Costa Rica's capital city of San José uncovered a number of differences between users and nonusers—notably in employment problems and trouble with the law—but none that would persuade two anthropologists that marijuana "seriously interferes with an individual's functioning as a normal, productive member of society."

Meanwhile, a battery of neuropsychological, intelligence, and personality tests revealed to psychologists "essentially no significant differences" between forty-one users and forty-one nonusers.

The anthropologists, William E. Carter and Paul L. Doughty of the University of Florida, observed that 37 percent of the users but no nonuser had been sentenced to a reformatory, and that users changed jobs more often than nonusers, were more likely to work part time, were unemployed more often and longer, had fewer raises and promotions, and were more likely to engage in illegal activities, be arrested and jailed, and get involved in legal entanglements.

They felt that marijuana did not cause those differences but stemmed from society's response to delinquency, which in turn originated in childhood deprivation, unhappy home lives, weak families, sibling rivalry, early entry into street life, etc. (But most subjects believed their childhood and home life were satisfactory and some began smoking before leaving home.) The social scientists blamed the trouble with the law on police harassment of marijuana smokers.

They added, "If marijuana usage leads to poorer social adjustment, irresponsible behavior and lack of motivation, one would expect that the heavier the usage, the greater such problems would be. The opposite however is the case. The heavier the usage, the more stable is the employment record . . . the fewer are the periods of unemployment . . . the shorter are these periods of unemployment."

Carter and Doughty heard a good deal of case evidence for "the buildup of tolerance." Experienced users described in detail how they learned to handle the drug. "The heaviest user averages forty marijuana cigarettes per day and yet manages a very successful business with eight employees."

The smoking of marijuana "was not shown to result in behavior that impaired the individual's ability to function as a regular member of the society.

". . . The basic problem derived from marijuana usage is police harassment and possible imprisonment. Secondary problems are the financial drain caused by the cost of an illegal substance and the type of peer group with which one associates when he engages in illegal behavior." Generally they learned of very few adverse effects of marijuana smoking during the two years. None of the users reported hallucinations, "though many did report a panic reaction known locally as 'white death.' " It depended not on dose but on the "physical and psychologic state of the victim." A high-sugar drink brought swift recovery. Highly experienced users never suffered from "white death."

The Costa Ricans did not seem to acquire the "high" of American users. They said marijuana smoking helped them to sleep, increased their appetite, improved sex, or helped them to work better, more often than they cited mirth or euphoria as effects of the drug.

They averaged seventeen years' experience and ten cigarettes per day (about 40 mg of THC), less than their Egyptian, Indian, or Moroccan counterparts (consuming 60–90 mg). The cigarettes each contained about 200 mg of marijuana and varied in THC content from 1.3 to 3.7 percent.

The anthropological portion of the study included 84 users and 156 nonusers the first year and subgroups of 41 and 41 the second.[28]

The psychological part, directed by Satz (University of Florida), included twelve tests. Only one technically significant difference emerged between users and nonusers, a liberalism-conservatism factor on a personality test. There were no major differences between high and low users (more or less than seven joints a day). Low users performed higher than controls on an information test, while controls had a higher object-assembly score.[29]

The Center for Latin American Studies at the University of Florida conducted the study for the National Institute on Drug Abuse.

Three who worked on the Costa Rica project, Fletcher (Texas Research Institute of Mental Sciences), Satz, and Carter, reviewing it and other foreign studies for a law quarterly (1978), made this frank acknowledgment: "The possibility that more subtle deficits in higher cortical functions are associated with chronic cannabis use cannot be excluded on the basis of cross-cultural studies reviewed in this paper. Such deficits, if real, may have a very low frequency of occurrence and may be difficult to detect. In this respect, no cross-cultural study has addressed satisfactorily a similar problem common to cancer research. Lung function tests, in the absence of prospective studies, often reveal no differences between cigarette users and nonusers. This finding is deceptive, however, because many subjects afflicted with cancer because of chronic tobacco use may have already died."[30]

*   *   *

Petersen, in Maryland (1979), raised the question of whether different inhalation patterns—the smoke perhaps not being inhaled as deeply or held in the lungs as long as among American users—might explain "the relatively benign consequences of chronic cannabis use found in the Jamaican, Greek, and Costa Rican studies. . . ."[31]

Cohen, in Los Angeles (1981), said of the three studies: "The sample size was small and sick people were excluded, the very group that would have been most important to study." The Costa Rican investigation seemed to him the most flawed. Citing the two anthropologists' conclusion that cannabis did not destroy motivation, "despite these obvious social deviances"—employment and legal problems—he called it "a tribute to their ability to confirm a preconceived notion."[32]

Mendhiratta, Wig, and Verma, Punjab, India, 1978; also Wig and Varma, 1977: Cannabis has been smoked in a pipe or drunk as a beverage in India for centuries and a multitude of Indians consume it daily. "Although in recent years many of the Indian States have totally banned all products of cannabis, the wild growth of the plant is so common that it is virtually impossible to eliminate the habit, which has considerable social sanction," wrote Mendhiratta and colleagues.

Punjab state in northern India was the scene of two studies comparing a total of seventy-three long-term, habitual users with thirty-six nonusers on psychological tests. The users had not taken their drug for at least twelve hours. Notable differences emerged in fifteen measures.

Psychiatrist Mendhiratta, psychiatry professor Wig, and clinical psychologist Verma tested fifty who had used cannabis for at least four years and twenty-five nonusers, all from the city of Amritsar. They found the cannabis users "to react more slowly, to be poorer in concentration and time estimation, to have higher neuroticism and greater perceptuomotor disturbance." In eight of nine tests, smokers scored worse than nonusers. Cannabis drinkers did worse than nonusers in five of the nine tests.

Wig and psychiatry professor Varma, using eight (largely different) tests, examined twenty-three users who had taken cannabis for at least five years and eleven nonusers, all from the cities of Chandigarh or Jullundur. Users did worse than nonusers in six tests, suffering in intelligence, memory, time perception, and otherwise.

> In both studies, subjects were men from poor socioeconomic groups, working as gardeners, sweepers, laborers, and the like.
>
> Half of the fifty users in the Mendhiratta study drank an average of 14 grams a day of *bhang* (cannabis leaf), about 1 percent THC; while half smoked an average of 5 grams a day of *charas-ganja* (combination of resin and flowering tops), about 3 percent THC. Twenty-three had used cannabis for four to ten years, twenty-seven for longer periods. Controls had never used it.
>
> Forty users and twenty-one controls smoked tobacco. Twenty-two users and one control had used opium occasionally (monthly or so). Nine users and one control drank alcohol more than weekly, none daily.
>
> Sixteen users and three controls suffered at least minor neurotic problems; in five users the symptoms were severe enough to constitute "depressive neurosis."
>
> The Speed and Accuracy test (in which a subject crosses certain designs) was

the only one showing no difference between controls and others. In addition, *bhang* drinkers did no worse than controls in Recognition, Pencil Tapping, and Size Estimation. Controls fared better than charas-ganja smokers in those three tests plus Digit Span (backward), Time Perception, Reaction Time, Bender Visuo-Motor Gestalt, and Maudsley Personality Inventory.[33]

Wig-Varma's users by definition consumed an estimated minimum of 50 mg of THC daily in *bhang* or *charas*. Residents of Chandigarh (thirteen users, seven controls) were hospitalized for twenty-four to forty-eight hours there at the Postgraduate Institute of Medical Education and Research (with which Wig, Varma, and Verma were associated). Jullundur subjects were not hospitalized.

Users scored worse than controls on two IQ tests (Raven's and a Wechsler adaptation), a memory scale (Wechsler adaptation), Bender, Speed Marking, and Time Perception. Differences were insignificant in Color Cancellation and in H-marking.

Of 139 users in a demographic study, 95 had taken cannabis for more than ten years, 39 of them for more than twenty years, and 7 for more than forty years. The majority were illiterate or literate without schooling; only six had completed high school.[34]

An account of this study appeared in a Swiss journal one year before publication of Mendhiratta's article in a British journal, although the latter was submitted four months earlier, in 1976.

Schaeffer, Andrysiak, and Ungerleider, unspecified locations, 1981: A trio of researchers from the University of California, Los Angeles, reported observing a certain religious sect that smoked huge cigarettes or pipefuls of tobacco mixed with strong marijuana continuously throughout the day as a religious sacrament.

The three would not name the sect or say just where their observations took place except that it was "in both a Southern state and a Caribbean island." They said they administered a variety of standard neuropsychological tests to seven men and three women.

They could discover "nothing . . . that might suggest impaired mental functioning due to brain or cerebral dysfunctioning resulting from heavy and prolonged use of ganja" (a term used in India and Jamaica). The subjects smoked constantly, even while taking the tests, and not even temporary declines in mental functioning showed up. The explanation lay, perhaps, in "the development of tolerance to one or more of the constituents of cannabis." An analysis of urine samples (Emit Cannabinoid Assay) confirmed the presence of cannabinoid.

Every day the sect members used two to four ounces of the mixture, half tobacco and half cannabis—analyzed by the researchers at 8 percent THC. The members had smoked it for an average of seven years, ever since taking up the religion. The ten were all U.S.-born-and-raised Caucasians, aged twenty-five to thirty-six, working largely in agriculture and business, and leading "active and spiritually oriented lives."

None of the results of seven tests—measuring intelligence, learning, memory, and verbal, nonverbal, and general intellectual functioning—indicated "impairment of cognitive functioning." IQ scores (averaging 128 on the Wechsler scale) ranged from "superior to very superior."

While the IQ scores were high and other test scores normal, one could speculate that the subjects might have done even better without cannabis, as the investigators pointed out. They obtained early school IQ scores for two subjects and these compared closely to the recent scores. They could not locate any nonusers in the same environment for comparison as "all church members continuously smoked ganja."[35]

Did the smokers get high? What were the physical effects—heart rate, for one? Did the smoke affect the experimenters? Where, when, and by whom were the observations made? What was the sect—was it the Ethiopian Zion Coptic Church, of Jamaica, with members in Florida (publicized by "60 Minutes" on CBS-TV in 1979)?

The report raised many questions, and we addressed a series to Jeffrey Schaeffer (Ph.D., assistant clinical professor, Department of Psychiatry and Biobehavioral Sciences, UCLA School of Medicine). But he indicated that he and associates (Therese Adrysiak, registered nurse, and Professor J. Thomas Ungerleider, M.D.) would give no further information besides name and rank; it could not enhance "the scientific value of our work."

Others had questions too. A medical publication noted, "The authors did not report on other problems associated with marijuana use, including lung damage or hormonal abnormalities," and contended that the smallness of the sample and the shortage of before-and-after comparison flawed the study.[36]

The ten were not compared with nonusers in either of the two areas. Since location is obscured, other investigators cannot easily follow up or repeat the research.

The year before its publication, Dr. Ungerleider, a member of the erstwhile National Commission on Marihuana and Drug Abuse, 1970–72, had told a Senate committee investigating the health consequences of marijuana, "As you hear the various allegations and research reports, put them in perspective. . . . Ask the right questions. In other words, be skeptical.

"In research, remember . . . the number of subjects, preferably humans, is important and that double-blind procedures are vital . . . as is the use of a control group or the patient as his own control. In addition—and this is extremely important—research, to be valid, must be able to be duplicated by other investigators without vested interests at other research centers."[37]

3
Out Of Their Minds:
Cannabis And Psychic Illness

• *"I was living in kind of a commune in Bremerton, Washington. Somebody brought this seventeen, eighteen-year-old man, probably a serviceman home on leave. He was telling about his Vietnam experience, how he had gotten real high. He hadn't been back long, maybe a couple days.*

"Somebody had some really incredible pot, probably Mexican, and so we smoked this joint of really good pot and we all got really stoned. It's a little psychedelic. There are colors. The colors are changing. It has a very definite spirit. Everyone can feel it—except this young man. He had maybe one full hit and started another.

"At first I thought he was having an epileptic fit. His body was reacting like . . . [grand] mal. We asked his friend, 'Is he epileptic?' His friend said he wasn't. All of a sudden he didn't know where he was. He was crying, and this was a very real thing. Eventually he had a very bad sobbing fit and like amnesia: 'Where am I?' He was very confused. His eyes were flickering, his eyeballs were jumping, and his body was shivering like he was cold.

"We got him calmed down, tried to tell him he was real high. Everyone was very loving toward him. A man who was older and more experienced took him out and talked to him again. We kept him for a couple of hours and gave him coffee. Then he left with his friend. They said he was welcome. He never came back." —Alice (chronic user)

(More in Supplement, G-3.)

Indian Hemp Drugs Commission, 1893–94: "The popular idea that the use of hemp drugs may induce insanity can be traced back for many centuries," said the commissioners studying the effect of cannabis preparations on the people of India to determine whether the substances should be banned. They had delved into the question of insanity because, they said, it was the most often heard aspect of the subject.

The commission found enough instances to accept it as "reasonably proved, in the absence of evidence of other cause, that hemp drugs do cause insanity." But it also pointed to overblown statistics from asylums arbitrarily blaming the drugs for cases of other or unknown causes.

The commission studied 1,344 admissions to the asylums of British India during 1892, gathering personal and family histories on each. Whereas 16.5 percent of the cases had been officially attributed to hemp drugs, the commission found that in only 7.3 percent of them might the use of hemp drugs be reasonably regarded as a factor in causing the insanity—4.5 percent if one eliminated "mixed" cases (those with other contributing causes, such as other intoxicants, heredity, diseases, or grief).

"Over and over the statistics . . . have been referred to in official documents or scientific treatises," reported the commission, but it deemed those figures "absolutely untrustworthy." They represented guesses by police or medical officers ignorant of hemp drugs and often pressed by superiors to list causes. Even authors on insanity disagreed on causes, and asylum superintendents usually had scant experience in the field. One superintendent said it was traditional practice "to enter hemp drugs as the cause of insanity where it has been shown that the patient used these drugs. I cannot say precisely why. . . ." Cross-examination showed that doctors largely ignored the causes of mental patients' ailments.

The commission noted that hemp intoxication had been mistaken for insanity in some cases, causing men to be held in asylums. In other cases "men who committed offences, especially crimes of violence, under the influence of hemp drugs have been acquitted on the ground of insanity," though they would have been convicted had the intoxicant been alcohol.

It pointed out that *ganja* intoxication produced an unbalancing of the intellect and a mental condition similar to insanity—"often that strange mixture of apparent clearness with manifest derangement of thought which is found in insanity but not usually in alcoholic intoxication."

Analyzing the symptoms in the ninety-eight cases it connected to hemp drugs (involving only one female, a prostitute), the commission could find no typical set of symptoms that would determine a given case to have been caused by drug use. It did establish that in most cases "The type of hemp drug insanity is mania . . . acute or chronic." However, the majority of medical witnesses who had studied the subject could cite no typical symptoms in "hemp drug mania" to distinguish it from mania of other causes. The outcome of long drug use, it differs from mere "hemp drug delirium," a condition of wild frenzy with transitory mania brought on by a heavy binge, which (by the commission's classification) in turn overshadows simple "hemp drug intoxication," a temporary delirium with hallucination and merriment from a single large dose.

Any injurious effects on the mind stemmed not from "moderate use of hemp drugs"—except in quite exceptional cases involving marked neurotic predisposition—but from "excessive use." Such use "intensifies mental instability. It tends to weaken the mind. . . . It appears that the excessive use of hemp drugs may, especially in cases where there is any weakness or hereditary predisposition, induce insanity. It has been shown that the effect of hemp drugs in this respect has hitherto been greatly exaggerated, but that they do sometimes produce insanity seems beyond question." Similarly, any moral and physical problems lay only in "excessive" use.

The commission never explained where one drew the line between "moderate" and "excessive" use.

Climaxing a voluminous report, it found the total prohibition of the hemp plant and its narcotics to be neither necessary nor expedient and advocated a policy of control, restriction, and taxation.

Two of the seven members dissented, placing much more stock in the veracity and expertise of police and medical authorities. They believed *ganja* (stronger marijuana) and *charas* (cannabis resin) to be sufficiently detrimental to warrant their prohibition. One calculated that 209, two-thirds, of the medical witnesses had pronounced "the moderate use of ganja and charas to be deleterious" in general. But the dissenters looked kindly on *bhang* (milder marijuana) and favored not only its continued legality but its exemption from taxation.[38]

*   *   *

Bromberg, New York, 1934, 1939: Presenting case studies of eleven patients hospitalized for psychotic reactions to cannabis, Dr. Walter Bromberg, the senior psychiatrist of a New York psychiatric hospital, divided the cases into three categories: (1) "acute intoxications," (2) "emotional reactions to the intoxication features," and (3) "toxic psychosis due to admixture of drug effects and basic psychosis (manic-depressive, schizophrenic, etc.)."[39]

Later (1939) Dr. Bromberg described and classified thirty-one cases of "insanity following the use of marihuana (marihuana psychosis) observed at the Bellevue Hospital . . . (1) acute intoxication, lasting from hours to days (fourteen cases), and (2) toxic psychoses, lasting from weeks to months (seventeen cases); often the toxic picture was superimposed on a basic functional mental disturbance, such as schizophrenia."

He commented that the basic personality of the smoker appeared to be vital in the development of the psychosis, for many people used the drug without developing "an observable mental condition."[40]

Similarly, the New York Mayor's Committee on Marihuana reported (1944): "The conclusion seems warranted that given the potential personality make-up and the right time and environment, marihuana may bring on a true psychotic state."

This conclusion followed the development of such a state in three subjects after ingestion of marijuana concentrate—shortly after, for an epileptic man (nonuser) and a woman with a history of heroin addiction (nonuser); and two weeks after, for a man with a "prepsychotic personality" (occasional user).

Besides those three, six others (three nonusers and three occasional users), five of them male, responded to the consumption of marijuana concentrate with "psychotic episodes," lasting three to ten hours. Dr. Samuel Allentuck wrote that they exemplified "acute marihuana intoxication in susceptible individuals which comes on shortly after the drug has been taken and persists for several hours. The main features of the poisoning are the restlessness and mental excitement of a delirious nature with intermittent periods of euphoria and an overhanging state of anxiety and dread."

The nine were among seventy-seven subjects, all but five of them prisoners.[41]

*   *   *

In an experiment on prisoners at Lexington, Kentucky, to compare the effects of THC and LSD, ten subjects started but two of them dropped out on experiencing "psychotic reactions" after smoking tobacco cigarettes injected with THC. Isbell and Jasinski reported (1969) that both drugs in general caused "distortions, alterations in mood and, with the higher doses, hallucinations," although LSD was about 150 times as potent. Those who developed tolerance to LSD gained no tolerance to THC.[42]

Keeler, Reifler, and Liptzin, and other investigators, various locations, 1968–76: "For a month I can feel high even though I haven't done any smoking," says Betty, who has smoked marijuana for ten years and keeps attempting to quit. Pilot Ted tells of similar experiences.

Once thought to be a phenomenon tied to LSD, the "flashback"—a return of the effects of a drug after it has supposedly worn off—is now known to be possible, though not common, among those taking just marijuana. Flashbacks can occur among casual users as well as habitual users. And apparently marijuana sometimes sets off "acid" flashbacks among LSD consumers. Take these five studies:

• Keeler and other North Carolina psychiatry professors described recurring reactions in four men, aged twenty-one to twenty-three, who had taken only marijuana (1968). About four marijuana cigarettes provoked confusion, disorientation, panic, and hallucinations in one man, who thereupon had similar experiences for three weeks without smoking. He was hospitalized and his symptoms abated in several days.

Another smoked about a dozen joints in a week, and intoxication kept returning for the next (smokeless) week, setting off extreme anxiety. A third, smoking less than two joints, thought his fingernails heavy, his throat covered with fuzz, and the air heavy to his lungs and arms; these delusions came and went for two days. A fourth, smoking more than three joints, saw objects sparkling and rippling; the experience returned the next day.[43]

• How marijuana triggered a repetition of a frightening LSD "trip" in an eighteen-year-old college freshman was described by Doctors Favazza and Domino in Michigan (1969). The patient, with no history of mental problems, had regularly smoked marijuana without adverse reactions. When he tried LSD, for hours he hallucinated that he was dead and in hell, his room boiling, his friends crazy, and the world being destroyed.

Three months later the youth took marijuana for the first time since the LSD, and he experienced a two-hour rerun of the LSD horror. In addition, he imagined friends tormenting him by reading his mind and, for five days, felt animal claws dug in his back, a cloud in his head, and continuous wind on his face. For three weeks he was too frightened to sleep. When he lay down, he saw bloated faces and monstrous clocks pointing their hands at him. He also suffered distorted vision and frequent panic. Obtaining psychiatric help, he was found to be basically normal, given a tranquilizer, and advised to take no more mind-altering drugs.

The doctors advised victims of frightening LSD experiences to give up all hallucinogens, including marijuana.[44]

• Lackland Air Force Base, Texas, had 431 basic trainees who admitted drug abuse before entering the service in 1969. Five percent of them avowed using marijuana alone, and 5 percent of those experiencing flashback phenomena reported marijuana to be their only drug.

Medical Corps Captain Blumenfield (1971) considered 94 (22 percent) of the 431 trainees to have had flashback experiences: 83 with LSD, alone or with other drugs; 5 with marijuana alone; 5 with amphetamine or barbiturate only; and 1 after another hallucinogen only.[45]

• Brown and Stickgold of Los Angeles (1974) described thirteen cases of self-diagnosed marijuana flashbacks (reported to a midwestern drug hot line) to familiarize doctors with the notion of flashbacks and "to suggest that this may be an authentic phenomenon."[46]

• Stanton and associates in Philadelphia (1976), analyzing questionnaires from 877 GIs in Vietnam who had used marijuana and 241 who had used "acid" (LSD or STP), told of 12 cases of flashbacks attributed to marijuana and 57 attributed to acid. The groups overlapped somewhat, but 9 of the 12 people reporting marijuana flashbacks avoided acid. Four of the 12 used only marijuana.

The heaviness of marijuana use did not appear to be an important factor in determining marijuana flashbacks. Only five who experienced the marijuana flashbacks were considered "habitual" users (200 times or more). Similarly, the extent of acid use did not correlate with the occurrence of acid flashbacks. But acid users who reported flashbacks also reported significantly more use of marijuana than those who did not report flashbacks. The finding (while it did not prove what caused what) jibed with the Favazza-Domino anecdote in which marijuana triggered a flashback to a previous LSD experience. Just why this should happen, or why any other flashback occurs, is the subject of various theories, both psychological and physiological.[47]

* * *

Talbott and Teague, Vietnam, 1969, and others: A nineteen-year-old U.S. soldier on guard duty was offered a share of a joint and thereupon smoked his first marijuana. Then the soldier who had furnished it reportedly told some children he was "Ho Chi Minh" and fired his weapon near them. The young guard asked if he was really Ho Chi Minh and the other displayed a T-shirt showing that name. Thereupon the guard panicked and shot him fatally in the chest. Entering the base camp, he announced that he had killed the North Vietnamese leader and displayed the shirt to prove it. He felt he was a hero.

Two psychiatrists found him to be suffering from an acute toxic psychosis. After a short hospitalization, he began to show grief and depression about the events. No further symptoms appeared in the next several months. On first smoking the joint, said the patient, he experienced throat irritation, the urge to cough, sensations of choking, and some tingling in his extremities.

In another case, a second lieutenant and registered nurse, twenty-six, smoked his first joint, suffered a burning, choking sensation in the throat, and later fled in terror from a bar, fearful that the "nationals" meant him harm. In a third case, a private, twenty-four, who had smoked a pipeful of "strange-tasting tobacco," thought his mind was split into two parts, good and evil; he feared he would kill someone or be killed; he believed he was dead and saw clouds pulling him up or bright lights coming toward him from the clouds.

Psychiatrists Talbott (of New York) and Teague (of Los Angeles) who served in Vietnam with the U.S. Army, 1967–68, cited these histories as three of twelve cases of a "clinical syndrome of acute psychosis" associated with marijuana smoking. Whereas some observers considered it a combat reaction precipitated by cannabis, the pair believed that its development directly and essentially involved cannabis, although environmental stresses might worsen the symptoms. In each case the patient had just tried marijuana for the first time. Toxic psychosis with physical symptoms characterized each case, and each cleared up in a short time.

Each patient showed "impaired cognitive functioning"—that is, disorientation, severe forgetfulness, confusion, difficulty in concentration, and disjointed thinking that strayed from the subject. All patients had changeable emotions, and all exhibited "marked anxiety and fearfulness" (although a tabular breakdown of symptoms indicated just six as "anxious"). Ten displayed paranoid symptoms with delusions. Two patients had psychiatric histories while the rest did not evidence preexisting personality disorders. Symptoms lasted one to three days in ten cases; a week in one case; and eleven days in another case, involving a suicidal patient.

"Initially the first [six] patients hospitalized were treated with moderate doses of phenothiazines and soporifics. In addition they received individual as well as group therapy. It soon became apparent that the phenothiazines were doing more for the therapist and the ward personnel than for the patients. Following this realization no drugs were used."

"Physicians in Vietnam have been impressed by the severity and frequency of adverse reactions to smoking Cannabis derivatives," Talbott and Teague informed American doctors. In potency the tropical Vietnamese marijuana eclipsed the product normally sold at home. Moreover, about half of the cannabis contraband seized in Vietnam contained opiates; hence marijuana there was "likely to produce a much stronger effect," they added, without elaborating.[48]

In two 1968 surveys, other medical corps officers in Vietnam compared a total of 96 psychiatric patients with 372 other patients, and in each case a larger proportion of the psychiatric patients than the others admitted using marijuana in that country.

> The mental hygiene patients were interviewed and the others were queried by questionnaire. The percentages admitting the use of marijuana in Vietnam:
> Postel: 56% of 50 mental patients and 34% of 104 surgical patients.
> Casper, Janacek, and Martin: 52% of 46 mental patients and 36% of 268 dispensary patients.[49]

*   *   *

Another psychiatrist who served in Vietnam, 1967–68, Dr. H. Spencer Bloch, reported: "Brief psychotic episodes, usually with predominantly paranoid symptoms, are a syndrome that psychiatrists and other physicians in Viet Nam have come to associate with marijuana usage there, although such syndromes are reported only infrequently with marijuana usage in the United States."

While the syndrome had not been subjected to analytic research, "any unusual symptom complex developing in previously healthy (though often character-disordered) men has come to make physicians in Viet Nam strongly suspect marijuana usage."[50]

*   *   *

Dr. Edward Colbach, who headed a psychiatric facility there, 1968–69, associated marijuana with "ineffectiveness, panic states, and psychoses."[51]

Weil, several U.S. cities, 1970: Over a two-year period, in connection with cannabis experiments (Boston) and hospital practice (San Francisco), Dr. Weil interviewed hundreds of users and saw and treated "many adverse reactions" to the drug. While most users suffer mild ill effects such as "nausea, headache and transient paranoia," he said, marijuana causes a minority of users serious mental disorders.

In those without histories of mental disorder who never took other mind-altering drugs, he observed the following three types of ailment:

A. *Panic reactions*—More than three-fourths of all of his cannabis cases (number unspecified) were reactions in which the victims felt they were dying or losing their minds. "Patients may be depressed, tearful, withdrawn or agitated but they are not disoriented and do not hallucinate." Such a reaction might be rare in a community accepting marijuana, but at a rural southern college (Weil wrote in Virginia) one-quarter of those first trying the drug might become panicked.

Panic states (which Weil felt were often incorrectly diagnosed as "toxic psychoses") could always be ended by simple reassurance by the doctor that nothing was seriously wrong. "If the doctor approaches the patient as a psychiatric emergency (by administering tranquilizers or urging hospitalization), he will often prolong the panic by inadvertently confirming the patient's fears of a mental breakdown." (But later Weil said that sedation might be desirable in cases of "extreme agitation.")

One example given involved a medical student, twenty-four, who smoked "a lot of marijuana—stronger than I've ever had" at a party in San Francisco. The next morning he suffered an acute anxiety attack and felt he was losing his mind. Tranquilizers from two medical residents did not help but reassurance by a physician did.

Most victims were novice users, often older or ambivalent about trying the drug.

A New York housewife, thirty-seven, who never had taken cannabis before, let her fifteen-year-old daughter persuade her to "turn on" by eating candy made with hashish. Within an hour the mother felt her heart racing and feared she would have a heart attack. She lay down. Dizzy and flushed, convinced she was poisoned, she had her daughter call the family physician, who told her to take a taxi to an emergency ward. There he found her in a state of nervous collapse with a pulse of 140. He injected her with a sedative and had her hospitalized. She remained agitated and depressed for four days and was discharged on the fifth day. The daughter, by the way, had eaten three times as much candy and had "a good time" lasting about six hours.

B. *Toxic psychoses*—These are "acute brain syndromes . . . temporary malfunctions of the cerebral cortex due to the presence of toxins [poisons] in the body; they disappear when the toxins disappear." Weil saw ten such cases from eating of cannabis but none from smoking.

Symptoms "closely resemble the delirium of high fever. Patients are disoriented, confused and frequently prostrate. Hallucinations, both auditory and visual, are common." The psychoses end by themselves. Weil advised physicians that no matter how serious a reaction should appear, "the world literature on cannabis does not report a single fatal case due to the dose." (But see "The Heart and Circulatory System," 3, on cannabis fatalities.)

An example of this psychosis: One evening a law student, twenty-four, who smoked marijuana daily, took a half-inch cube of hashish, powdered it, mixed it in coffee, and drank the mixture. In forty to sixty minutes he grew "higher" than ever, sickened, confused, and unable to understand what people were saying or what was happening. Lying in misery, "I saw crawling patterns on the walls and heard very unpleasant voices calling me." He had "horrible nightmares" and in the morning felt exhausted. "I ached all over and had a headache and hangover for a day and a half."

C. *Simple depressive reactions*—Marijuana might provoke acute depressions, usually in new users. Weil saw twenty such cases and all ended spontaneously. They resembled "transient neurotic depressions." He said the patients mainly were "obsessive-compulsive persons who were ambivalent about trying the drug or who invested the decision to experience marijuana with great emotional meaning."

In people with no history of mental disorder who took hallucinogens (not counting marijuana) he observed two other forms of adverse reaction to marijuana. It precipitated (1) eight cases of a recurrence of hallucinogenic symptoms, and (2) an unknown number of delayed psychotic reactions to the hallucinogenic drugs.

Lastly, in people with histories of psychosis, he observed five cases of nonhospitalized schizophrenia patients in whom marijuana set off psychotic reactions, suggesting that "the drug might be capable of precipitating true psychotic breaks" in those with low threshholds for psychosis.[52]

*   *   *

Kolansky and Moore, Philadelphia, 1971, 1972: Two psychiatrists in separate private practices described fifty-one patients of theirs (1965–71) who all demonstrated adverse psychological effects that began with the start of the cannabis habit and in most cases disappeared after they gave it up.

Claiming to have discovered a specific marijuana syndrome (a uniform and unique set of symptoms), announcing a correlation between the symptoms and the frequency and duration of smoking, and speaking of possible biochemical and structural changes in the brain, the two stirred widespread controversy with articles in *JAMA, The Journal of the American Medical Association.* In the absence of psychiatric examinations, Doctors Kolansky and Moore refused to accept the commonly held belief that large numbers of young people smoked marijuana without problems.

In 1971 they described twenty male and eighteen female patients, aged thirteen to twenty-four (1965–70), whose psychiatric problems began shortly after they began to smoke marijuana, except in eleven patients with "mild anxiety or occasional depression." The patients smoked only marijuana. The doctors did not include patients who had serious psychological problems before they began smoking or who used other drugs. Usually one psychiatrist saw a patient. In addition a clinical psychologist tested about one-fourth of the patients.

Most of the thirty-eight patients had smoked marijuana twice a week or more, two or more joints each time. They "consistently showed very poor social judgment, poor attention span, poor concentration, confusion, anxiety, depression, apathy, passivity, indifference, and often, slowed and slurred speech." Other common symptoms were "an inability to bring thoughts together, a paranoid suspiciousness of others, and a regression to a more infantile state." Cleanliness, grooming, dressing, and study or work habits all suffered; some patients used to have bad habits in these respects before smoking but afterward these became accentuated.

Formal neurological examinations were not made, but a few patients who smoked four or five times weekly for many months displayed "gross indications of neurologic impairment."

Eight of the patients, with no personal or family history of mental problems, reacted to cannabis by becoming psychotic. Four attempted suicide—a seventeen-year-old girl while smoking marijuana and in a euphoric state; a boy, seventeen, who thought he was the Messiah; a girl, sixteen; and a boy, fourteen.

The other four included a man of twenty-four, who thought that his friends wanted to kill him and take his wife, that he had developed a superior intellect at the expense of his sex life, and that he was the first member of a new "super race." A young man, twenty, fancied himself in charge of the Mafia and a potentate of the Ku Klux Klan and began gathering weapons and training dogs to attack. A youth of nineteen believed that he had superhuman mental powers, could control animals, and (he too) was the Messiah. An eighteen-year-old thought he was a guru and, eventually, the son of God. Psychotic symptoms went away in all but the last patient, who moved to the West Coast and continued an "unproductive, aimless life."

As psychotic patients withdrew from marijuana, those who had been smoking for a shorter time gave up their delusions relatively quickly, but "these patients seem to be left with a residual of some memory difficulty and impairment of concentration. One patient has shown this for two years. . . ."

Eighteen patients, fourteen male and four female, aged fourteen to twenty, were not grossly disturbed but fit in "borderline states" with "evidence of ego decompensation . . . disturbance in reality testing, memory, social judgment, time sense, concept formation, concentration, abstract thinking and speech production." Each underwent academic decline and a feeling of isolation. Twelve of them were on trial for marijuana possession. Besides the other symptoms, they had trouble putting thoughts into words and might substitute memorized phrases (eight patients); they relied on grandiose fantasies as defenses against anxiety and gave way to impulses at the cost of others' feelings (four patients); and/or they underwent "periods of depersonalization when *not* under the influence of the drug. They felt that they were watching themselves and others interreact, as if in a dream" (three patients).

Thirteen unmarried females, aged thirteen to twenty-two, had symptoms similar to those of the above eighteen plus an "unusual degree of sexual promiscuity . . . sexual relations with several individuals of the opposite sex . . . same sex . . . both sexes" and sometimes even "both sexes on the same evening." None were promiscuous before taking up marijuana and all lost inhibitions after short smoking periods. Seven became pregnant, one several times, and four developed venereal disease. All thought of suicide and three attempted it. (One was the girl of seventeen listed also among the psychotic patients.) The thirteen cases showed marijuana loosening the superego, said Kolansky and Moore (both affiliated with the child analysis division, Philadelphia Association for Psychoanalysis).

They were struck by marijuana's accentuation of "the very aspects of disturbing bodily development and psychological conflicts which the adolescent had been struggling to master . . . the inconsistencies of behavior, the lack of control of impulses, the vagueness of thinking and the uncertainty of body identity." While the adolescent struggles "to master new physical, intellectual, and emotional strengths, he is hampered by marihuana. This leads to further anxiety."

Their impression was that their study demonstrated the "possibility that moderate-to-heavy use of marihuana in adolescents and young people without predisposition to psychotic illness may lead to ego decompensation ranging from mild ego disturbance to psychosis.

"Clearly, there is, in our patients, a demonstration of an interruption of normal psychological adolescent growth processes following the use of marihuana; as a consequence, the adolescent may reach chronological adulthood without achieving adult mental functioning or emotional responsiveness."[53]

By 1972 Kolansky and Moore had developed a belief in "a specific pathological organic response in the central nervous system" to cannabis, "identified by a group of uniform symptoms common to all which seem unrelated to individual psychological predisposition."

They described thirteen adults, aged twenty to forty-one (their patients, 1969–71), who had smoked cannabis intensively (three to ten times weekly) for sixteen months to six years. All demonstrated symptoms that "began with cannabis use and disappeared within 3 to 24 months after cessation of drug use."

They contended that the chemical effect of the drug on cerebral functioning, rather than purely psychological factors, was primary. They saw no difference in the symptoms of adolescent and adult chronic cannabis smokers.

Having regularly smoked three to ten or more times a week, the patient was apathetic and sluggish in mind and body, and usually unkempt and without goals. Though he boasted emotional maturity and insight, questioning of his new ways easily disrupted his "pseudoequanimity." If anyone threatened his cannabis supply, "the peaceful facade quickly gave way to irritability or outbursts of irrational anger." Most patients looked thin and older than they were. Often they felt tired, sleeping by day and awake at night. Headaches were common.

"The symptoms of mental confusion, slowed time sense, difficulty with recent memory, and the incapability of completing thoughts . . . seemed to imply some form of organicity either of an acute biochemical nature as noted in cases with shorter histories of cannabis use or, one might hypothesize, structural encephalopathy [brain damage] when found in cases with prolonged heavy marihuana use," wrote Kolansky and Moore. They grouped the thirteen cases in three categories:

"1. Biochemical Change." Less use of cannabis; symptoms gone within six months after drug use ended.

"2. Biochemical Change With Suspected Structural Change." Chronic intensive use of cannabis; no symptoms found after nine months. (The reason for the suspicion was not spelled out.)

"3. Biochemical Change With Possible Structural Change." Chronic intensive cannabis use; residual symptoms present nine months or more after drug use ended.

They maintained that they had established "a definite correlation between the presence of symptoms and cannabis use."

They described personality and occupational deterioration in nine men (advertising executive, architect, real estate agent, tree surgeon, veteran, and four teachers) and four women (dental assistant, housewife, social worker, and student). One man was an English professor who smoked marijuana daily for four years, encouraged students to smoke it during class "to think more clearly," and thought he was the reincarnation of Hamlet, conversing with his dead father during night walks on campus. Eventually he left his job, wife, and children. Joining an Eastern religion, he slowly gave up marijuana and improved mentally, although one year after quitting he still had difficulty with memory, concentration, and speaking. At thirty-eight, he looked fifteen to twenty years older.[54]

The news media reported the 1971 article in detail with commentary from professionals skeptical that the case histories had incriminated marijuana. Some questioned whether the thirty-eight cases were representative. But even skeptics agreed the report was a warning signal to be taken seriously.[55]

It attracted two letters to the AMA journal. Dr. Doris H. Milman of Brooklyn, New York, wrote that many physicians were unaware of marijuana's adverse effects because they did not think to make the association. Were they "as aware and keenly observant as Dr. Kolansky and Dr. Moore, the documentation of the dangers of marihuana would be more than sufficient to satisfy the sceptics."[56]

Dr. Victor M. Benson of Redondo Beach, California, wrote that "the basic deficiency of this paper is its lack of a control group." The authors had failed to consider numerous adolescent psychotics who never used drugs, he said.[57]

In publishing the second article, *JAMA* editorialized: "Spokesmen who espouse tolerance toward 'occasional' or 'moderate' use of marihuana should be mindful of the possibility that, for whatever reasons, occasional may become 'frequent' and moderate may become 'intensive,' with forbidding consequence. . . .

"If marihuana ever were given the same legal status as alcoholic beverage, nothing could be said except 'Buyer beware.' "[58]

In a 1975 commentary in the AMA journal, Kolansky and Moore went beyond merely raising "the possibility" of brain damage. ". . . We presumed that with intensive cannabis use, biochemical and structural changes occurred in the central nervous system."[59]

> Among three physicians writing to the journal in response to the second article, one from New Hampshire denied that the patients might have suffered "permanent structural changes in the cerebral cortex" because the majority regained their mental functions. Another, from Washington, D.C., disputed the claim of a unique, stereotyped syndrome of uniform symptoms because all of the case reports did not contain thirteen symptoms listed as features of the syndrome. A third, from San Diego, said a statement that symptoms of all patients "disappeared within 3 to 14 months after cessation of drug use" contradicted a case description of a teacher, twenty-five, who "left town before we could determine the presence or absence of symptoms after six months."[60]

Tennant and Groesbeck, West Germany, 1972: "Hashaholics"—that's what some U.S. soldiers in Europe were called. Hashish was cheap and they smoked mammoth amounts of it. They burned it several times a day, usually in pipes and often mixed with tobacco.

Medical corps officers who treated GIs for respiratory troubles stemming from hashish told of psychiatric and neurologic problems it had precipitated as well. Of a group of 720 hashish smokers who visited the U.S. Army Hospital in Würzburg, Germany (1968–71), nearly half, 328, suffered from serious mental ills.

Two thirds of these mental patients (218) had acute or persistent psychoses—with disorientation, hallucinations, delusions, paranoia, and so on—which in many cases required hospitalization. The majority of them took other mind-altering substances besides hashish.

The remaining third (110) were strictly "hashaholics," living in a perpetually stoned state, consuming 50 to 600 grams a month (about 2 to 21 ounces). They exhibited "apathy, dullness, and lethargy . . . impairment of judgment, concentration, and memory . . . intermittent episodes of confusion, and inability to calculate . . . poor hygiene . . . slightly slowed speech." Many had lost interest in their appearance, proper eating, and personal affairs—often enmeshing themselves in legal or social trouble.

Majors Tennant and Groesbeck followed nine of them before, during, and after periods of severe hashish abuse, lasting up to two years. The above symptoms developed after two or three months of smoking. After quitting hashish, six of the nine soldiers regained their faculties. "Three of the nine patients, however, exhibited intermittent residual symptoms analogous to those of organic brain disease . . . intermittent periods of memory loss, confusion, and inability to calculate and concentrate. Episodes lasted from several hours to days, and sometimes hospitalization was required due to extreme confusion. With passage of time, these intermittent episodes became less severe and less frequent."

Twenty-three others quit hashish. Even after being "detoxified," 10 of them continued to exhibit the same symptoms shown by the above three. The remaining 78 (of the 110) continued smoking until discharge from the army—which in 70 cases came prematurely because the soldiers could not function.

Simultaneous abuse of hashish and alcohol and/or other drugs resulted in acute psychosis in 85 cases (hashish used three to seven times a week, 10 to 50 grams a month) and persistent schizophrenic symptoms in 112 others (hashish used several times daily, 25 to 200 grams a month); the 112 patients all were sent to the United States for long-term psychiatric hospitalization. Eighteen acute psychotic cases (occasional use, under 25 grams a month) and three schizophrenic reactions (three to seven times a week, 10 to 50 grams a month) occurred with hashish use alone; the 21 patients required brief hospitalizing.

The eighteen included five novice users who suffered "panic reactions characterized by a feeling of impending death and/or loss of mental function . . . resolved with reassurance and mild sedation" plus thirteen with toxic psychosis resulting from smoking a large amount of hashish—usually 5 to 30 grams—within a few hours. The main clinical findings of the toxic psychosis were "disorientation, delusions, anxiety, depersonalization, and confusion"; "paranoia and hallucinations" appeared in most cases. The symptoms disappeared in three days after treatment with antipsychotic agents like Thorazine.

The 110 in the chronic intoxicated state took monthly between 50 and (rarely) 600 grams of hashish, which, according to Tennant and Groesbeck, had a THC content of 5 to 10 percent. On the basis of 10 percent THC this dose range would equal between 500 and 6,000 one-gram marijuana cigarettes with 1 percent THC— or about 17 to 200 a day.

Figures presented by Dr. Tennant at a Senate committee hearing in 1974 indicated that about an eighth of drug hospitalizations in ten U.S. Army, Europe, hospitals through 1971 and half of 1972 (657 of 5,093) were for adverse reactions to hashish; and that of 5,044 GIs in Germany anonymously surveyed in 1971, 35 percent reported taking hashish there, 25 percent taking two or more illegal drugs, and 15 percent using hashish at least weekly.[61]

Beaubrun and Knight, Jamaica, 1972; also Knight, 1976: "Three subjects from one area of Jamaica reported a first-time visual and auditory hallucination of a little lady dancing toward them in a fear-provoking experience that sounded like an initiation rite. The experience seemed to be exciting as well as frightening, but the subjects knew that they had only to hold their ground and open their eyes wide for the vision to disappear. They seemed to feel that they were being tested, and one subject said that his mother had told him that if his mind were not strong, he would go mad."

The three beheld this vision upon their first use of *ganja*. They numbered among thirty Jamaican cannabis smokers and thirty controls given psychiatric examinations by Michael H. Beaubrun and Frank Knight of the psychiatry department at the University of the West Indies.

Altogether ten smokers reported having had hallucinatory experiences, compared with two controls. Of the smokers, "more than half" (the number was not mentioned) had these experiences only once, when they began taking the drugs as youngsters.

One man from each group had a personal and family history of mental illness. "The smoker had been hospitalized for a schizophreniform illness that might have been provoked by heavy cannabis use." Eight smokers had histories of mental illness in their families, compared with two controls. Given such family histories, the fact that the smokers themselves showed little mental illness suggested to Beaubrun and Knight "that cannabis smoking may play a role in preventing psychosis in predisposed individuals."

Four smokers and three controls had past problems of alcoholism, while respectively seven and three gave family histories of alcoholism. Beaubrun and Knight stopped short of constructing a theory that cannabis prevents alcoholism, but they did point out that two smokers reported they had reduced their alcohol intake and "seemed to relate this to cannabis use."

Little or no differences between the two groups emerged in tests of neuroticism, extroversion, and childhood deprivation. The smokers impressed the staff in the hospital where they were examined as more "affable and popular," but they seemed motivated to prove that their habit was not harmful. No mental abnormalities transpired from examinations. No one avowed taking any drug besides cannabis, outside of alcohol and tobacco.[62]

The results of the controlled studies did not agree with clinical observations. In 1976 Knight told a scientific conference in New York, "Clinical observation suggests that cannabis is implicated in some types of psychiatric disturbances." Figures that he cited from six Jamaican hospitals—where *ganja* smoking figured in scores of diagnoses a year—

"lend support to the idea of causation of illness or modification of existing illness" by cannabis.

For instance, of seventy-four males admitted in one year to the psychiatric unit at the University Hospital of the West Indies, twenty-nine, or two-fifths, had a history of cannabis usage. Ten of them were diagnosed as suffering from "ganja psychosis." The diagnosis for four others was "marijuana-modified mania."

"Ganja psychosis" is a term used by psychiatrists and nurses in Jamaican psychiatric units to describe "disturbed, sometimes aggressive, behavior after several days of unaccustomed cannabis use" (either first-time use or the taking of a larger dose than ever before) with "schizophrenic features" and persistence for several weeks after supposed elimination of the drug from the body.

In explaining the variance between the results of the controlled Jamaican studies and the clinical observations, Knight said he considered such a discrepancy inevitable. He explained that the thirty smokers tested for any permanent effects from cannabis "are really in a different category from those in whom clinical observation incriminates cannabis as a cause of psychiatric illness and adverse psychologic effects." Of the many who expose themselves to the drug, only a few—presumably those with "constitutional liability"—fall into the latter category.

"In considering the carefully controlled studies on long-term use, the question could arise as to the status of these users; whether, in fact, the samples may be biased from the beginning because the subjects chosen could be seen as the *survivors*, as it were, of many years of cannabis use."

Of 223 patients admitted for functional psychoses to the psychiatric unit of Jamaica's Cornwall Regional Hospital in twelve months, 54 patients or 24 percent had a history of cannabis usage, which according to Knight was "a contributory factor." Meanwhile at three other Jamaican rural general hospitals, cannabis smoking was held to be a contributory factor in a total of 57 or two-fifths of 144 cases of psychosis. Of 106 males admitted (nearly consecutively) to Bellevue Psychiatric Hospital in Kingston, 26 were heavy *ganja* smokers (smoking at least daily) while 7 were light users.

Symptoms appearing to be part of schizophrenia stemmed from cannabis in so many cases that the provisional diagnosis of "schizophreniform reaction" came into frequent use at Cornwall Regional Hospital, where 37.5 percent of patients so diagnosed in a twelve-month period had a history of cannabis use, Knight said.[63]

*   *   *

In the Greek study (1976) the absence of any diagnosis of organic psychosis, after thorough mental, neurological, and brain tests, made it clear to the investigators that such dementia was "not a usual accompaniment of high-dose, chronic hashish use."

Three cannabis users (6 percent), and no nonusers, did prove psychotic, suffering "paranoid schizophrenia" (unrelated to fear of arrest for hashish possession). For two of them it developed after they took up hashish smoking. Because they showed no clinical signs different from those of schizophrenia, the researchers could draw "no conclusions" as to the existence of a specific cannabis psychosis.[64] In addition, the smokers described occasional panic reactions during their long-term use.[65]

* * *

Whether cannabis triggers true psychosis and, if so, whether it does so just in those predisposed to mental ills was argued at the New York Academy of Sciences (1976). G. S. Chopra described experiments in India: "We had certain individuals suffering from toxic psychosis due to hemp abuse, and they had the disease for about one month and . . . it subsided. When we asked the patients to take hemp again, the psychosis appeared again." That demonstrated a specific psychosis precipitated by hemp drugs.

When Dr. Chopra listed symptoms such as confusion, disorientation, aggressiveness, and talkativeness, Dr. Costas Stefanis said, "In that sense, every marijuana smoker has an organic psychotic syndrome . . . whenever he is intoxicated. . . ." The smoker is bound to have some consciousness disorders, disorientation, and other manifestations. But as for a steady mental condition resulting from chronic use, "we didn't find any such evidence" in studies of Greek hashish users.

Dr. Reese T. Jones of San Francisco said, "From our experience, almost anybody given the right dose and in the right setting can exhibit . . . a schizophrenia-like set of symptoms." But there is a predisposition in some people. In one abnormally sensitive subject, "Every time we tried to exceed a fairly modest dose of cannabis . . . which was tolerated by all of our other subjects, this young man would develop delusions, disturbed aspect, and visual distortions."[66]

PART III

CANNABIS
AND SOCIETY

THE CHANGING SCENE

"The whole climate around drugs has changed tremendously since I was involved with them. I started smoking marijuana in 1963 and I stopped in 1966. . . .

"I was at Harvard and it was something that was extremely exotic. I sort of thought this might be a scene like Baudelaire and Rimbaud and those French poets and it was just a sort of crème de la crème of Bohemian intelligentsia or something that would do something like this. . . . That's what I figured I was, and my friends. And, sure enough, most of the other students thought we were a little odd. Somehow it got tied in with certain things connected with personal appearance. I grew a mustache when I was a sophomore and I figured that made me look more like some distinguished poet or artist or something. And my classmates thought it was shocking, most of them. . . . I was the first member of an athletic team to have a mustache. . . .

"Timothy Leary was there then. He was just getting going and I didn't know him. . . . I wasn't part of his group, maybe just very much on the fringes. I knew a few people that knew him, but my involvement with drugs is very different than his. I thought he was very silly, talking about the spiritual value of LSD or whatever. I thought that was a lot of nonsense.

"My own opinion was that I was doing this as an escape. I didn't like reality very much and I wanted to get away from it. And I figured it probably wasn't a very good thing to do, but I had—thought I was having fun, and the alternative of hard work was so distasteful . . . that's one of the things that motivated me. And for somebody to come along and claim that there was some transcendent value in this seemed absurd to me even being stoned. But that's not to say there weren't a bunch of people around at that time who sincerely felt that they were doing something that was going to expand their consciousness. And, of course, once you get your mind distorted by drugs, then you can believe just about anything. . . .

242

" 'Course it's a little hard to distinguish now between what was purely marijuana thinking and what might have been influenced by, let's say, LSD or something else, because I mixed all these things together after a certain point. But I started out with just marijuana, and I would say, looking back on it, that marijuana is the most dangerous of all the drugs that I got involved with because it was one which you could believe was harmless. You took LSD: you knew you were doing something very powerful to your brain, and unless you were a certain type of kook, you wouldn't want to do it too often. It was just too powerful. Marijuana, on the other hand, you'd do it and you'd think it was fun or 'neat' . . . something that made you feel good. . . .

"We were out, graduated from school, and now these friends of mine had moved into a sort of seedy apartment [in Cambridge, Massachusetts], which we thought was exquisitely rustic and beautiful or whatever, and I remember one evening they put on this Beatles record and we'd all light up. And I noticed all the other houses in this kind of rundown, bohemian area of town, the lights—you'd see the lights flicking on and off; you'd hear the same Beatles record. You'd know that they were getting stoned.

"Across the street, down the street—everybody was doing it. . . . They were all listening to the same music and all playing the same games and it was all the same. It was conformity. . . . That was really just about the first thing that made me realize that I had really been fooling myself. Because I thought this whole business was so original and so special, and then to realize that everybody else was thinking he was doing the same thing, each one thinking that they're unique. I really began to think, 'Hey—wait a second—what on earth are you doing? '

"I also felt ashamed of myself for not having done any better. I didn't feel quite so guilty about the academic thing. I did manage to get myself into graduate school. But I had been a member of this athletic team. I played squash and I really, really loved the game and I could have been a lot better at it, but I wasn't. I just sort of slipped and slipped and then—the Harvard team had been undefeated for about four years and I lost the deciding match in this really close match against Princeton, and, you know, I'd been stoned the night before. . . .

"One of the key things that made me feel differently after three years of fooling around with marijuana was (after I had gotten off of it and had moved out to Berkeley from Cambridge) . . . to see how everybody was now taking drugs. And kids twelve or thirteen, or maybe fourteen or fifteen or whatever, would be walking down the street looking like dead fish—I mean really looking drawn, pale, bad skin coloring, their eyes just looking terrible, dirty, having lost self-respect, having lost their energy, *magnetism, whatever you want to call it, kind of bloom-on-the-peach feelings just totally wiped out. And you'd see these old cadavers of thirteen or fourteen walking around, but they would be saying the same kinds of things I used to say: 'Oh, wow, look at that! Oh, far out! Isn't that beautiful?' And they apparently would be feeling exactly the kind of lovely, mellow stuff that I had been feeling, but looking at them was really frightening."* —Nathan (ex-user)

1

Smokers

"Expand your consciousness," urged drug proponents on the campus of the University of California at Berkeley, across the bay from San Francisco. The use of mind-altering drugs as a major movement began there early in 1965, as did the student protest rage of the sixties. Drugs and protests went together. Marijuana became a symbol of opposition to "the Establishment" generally or the escalating conflict in Vietnam specifically. A student could march, picket, or even burn his draft card and still make no dent in world events. But he could take drugs and see instant changes.

"Tune in! Turn on! Drop out!" so-called drug priest Timothy Leary exhorted the students from the steps of the campus administration building. The use of marijuana, LSD, and other illegal drugs was advocated in the campus newspaper, the *Daily Californian*; in "underground" newspapers; in handbills; and through unauthorized loudspeakers in the noon hour.

The drug revolutionists embraced a far-flung and ancient product and practice. Hemp had been cultivated, processed, eaten, drunk, and smoked in numerous societies for ages and still was, although much of the world officially scorned the nonmedical use of the species' drugs. Cannabis smoking, then largely restricted to men of certain subcultures, encompassed young and old devotees and a variety of purposes besides euphoria. The new movement, while limited to young people aiming at "getting high" (philosophical and political rationalizations aside), took in females and before long attracted such a multitude of followers as to win for the practice a degree of social respectability.

> Tracing the cannabis plant to ancient civilizations of the Old World, in *Ganja in Jamaica* (p. 9), Rubin and Comitas discern marked sociocultural differences in the plant's uses—industrial, magicoreligious, medicinal, dietary, and psychoactive. Among Jamaican laborers, they write (p. 166), "Ganja serves multiple purposes that are essentially pragmatic, rather than psychedelic. . . . They express social rather than hedonistic motivations for smoking." These include: being energized for their arduous labors, bolstering their health, promoting peer group relations, and enhancing religious and philosophical contemplation.

In the midsixties Berkeley probably had a greater proportion of its population smoking marijuana than any other city in the United States.

Professor Hardin B. Jones took a survey in his class on drug abuse on the Berkeley campus in 1971, and three-fourths of the male students and half of the female students smoked marijuana. On the average, males did it every day and a half; women, every two days.

In 1972 while an initiative referendum to legalize marijuana lost in California as a whole by a margin of two to one, in Berkeley over 70 percent of the voters cast favorable ballots.

The drug movement spread. Gallup polls indicated that 5 percent of college students had tried marijuana by 1967. The figure ascended to 22 percent in spring of 1969 and 42 percent by the following fall. It rose to 51 percent in 1971 and 66 percent in 1978.[1]

A student from Oregon State University transferred to the University of Alaska, where he was the only marijuana smoker in his dormitory; by the time he finished his courses, he boasted, he had "turned on" his whole floor.

Researchers in Boston, searching the student population for experimental subjects who never had smoked marijuana, needed to spend nearly two months interviewing prospects before they found nine young men who qualified.[2]

From colleges, marijuana spread in epidemic fashion into high schools, junior highs, and even elementary schools, public and private.

Nationwide surveys of some 17,000 high school seniors in about 130 schools, sponsored by the National Institute on Drug Abuse (NIDA), recorded that 47 percent had used marijuana at least once by 1975, and 60 percent had done so by 1979. The number of daily users among the seniors rose from 6 percent in 1975 to a peak of 11 percent in 1978, dropping to 10 percent (1979), 9 percent (1980), 7 percent (1981), and 6 percent (1982 and 1983).[3]

In 1968 (in the first of ten annual surveys conducted by the county and financed by NIDA) 45 percent of twelfth graders in San Mateo County, California, adjoining San Francisco, reported smoking marijuana at least once in the preceding year; by 1977 the figure climbed to 65 percent. Seventh graders (not polled in 1968) went from 11 percent in 1969 to 23 percent in 1977. Those using it at least weekly in 1977 amounted to 4, 11, and 34 percent of the seventh, eighth, and twelfth grades, respectively.[4]

In 1981 in Berkeley 9 percent of fourth graders surveyed said they had tried marijuana, 54 percent had drunk beer, and 30 had drunk hard liquor. Among sixth graders, 32 percent had tried marijuana; 46 percent, beer; and 55 percent, hard liquor.[5]

Elsewhere in the region a mother reported at a parents' meeting how her kindergarten child en route to school was stopped by older children and offered marijuana. And a teacher informed us that six pupils in her grade school were sent home in one week for "coming to school stoned." One was a kindergartner.

The practice spilled over to the population at large. In a national survey of general households (also sponsored by NIDA) the number of young adults saying they had used marijuana in the last month rose from 17 to 35 percent between 1971 and 1979 while the comparable figure for all other adults, twenty-six and older, increased from 1 to 6 percent. (The former group peaked in 1979, the latter in 1982. More in Supplement F.)[6]

Marijuana users tended to smoke it more and more frequently. "During the early seventies at our marijuana research project we defined a heavy user as one who smoked three times a week or more. This was a generally accepted definition in those days," said Dr. Sidney Cohen of Los Angeles (at a Maryland conference, 1981). "In our more recent studies heavy usage was redefined as daily use. . . . It may become necessary to split this category into heavy (1–3 joints a day), very heavy (3–9 joints a day), and extra heavy (10 or more a day)."[7]

Not only have the numbers of users, frequency of use, and ages of smoking populations changed, so have the places where smoking is done. The haze and odor from hundreds, if not thousands of joints have accompanied rock concerts for years. Marijuana smoking of late has gone on more openly on streets and in parks, theaters, public buildings, transportation vehicles, and even schools. A graduate student in Pomona, California, had a classmate "who smokes grass during class. He says it makes him think better." New York's Staten Island Ferry banned smoking of all kinds because marijuana had become prevalent on the boats and passengers were complaining.[8]

According to a 1979 government estimate (by NIDA) 55 million Americans over age twelve had smoked marijuana at least once and 23 million were current users. Diverse sources (Drug Enforcement Administration and *High Times* magazine) estimated the country's 1979 outlay for illegal drugs—mostly marijuana, but secondarily cocaine—at $50 billion. The government estimated later (1982) that 20 million Americans were consuming marijuana, perhaps 35 million pounds annually.[9]

Surveys find previously low-use groups "catching up" with high-use groups. Marijuana no longer is used mainly by white, middle-class college students. Statistically females are approaching males, the South is nearing the rest of the United States, and lower-population areas are drawing near the metropolitan areas. Marijuana takes in all classes, regions, ethnic groups, occupations, and to some extent even ages. Occasional stories about senior citizens growing or selling cannabis hit the news media. A marijuana lobbyist said, "I've smoked marijuana with cops, lawyers, district attorneys, legislators—you name it."

Twenty-six members of the U.S. House of Representatives admitted having smoked marijuana, of 101 who answered a *Playboy* poll in 1978.[10] Meanwhile, in California's capital of Sacramento, several legislators were gathering in an apartment weekly to smoke marijuana. And in San Francisco in 1979, an arrest for possessing cannabis plants ousted a state Court of Appeal justice. (He said they belonged to his wife.)

Marijuana has gone to work at assembly lines, construction sites, and offices from Wall Street to Silicon Valley. The press has tied it to industrial accidents and botched jobs. Workers at some places smoke with the boss's tacit approval. Sometimes the boss does it too.[11]

These objects, depicted in two advertising leaflets of a Los Angeles company, are all pipes. The leaflet at the right says, "Stop losing half your high with this zero loss pipe. You reclaim smoke normally lost into the air. All smoke is automatically pumped into wine-filled cooling chamber. We highly recommend a cheap, sweet-fruit wine. Light-up by hand the regular way, then just flick the switch." The ads don't mention marijuana but do offer a "hash-oil water pipe" (transparent bottle at left). The vertical cylinder is a bright red "bong."

2

Reefers

George Washington grew cannabis on his plantation. The cannabis was of the fiber type, then better known as hemp. An important crop in the American colonies, it ended up as rope, twine, paper, or canvas. The word "canvas" comes from "cannabis."

During World War II the government encouraged the planting of hemp for rope. After the war the need for the crop dwindled. Hemp growing wild in fields and parks and beside roads remained undisturbed until the 1960s. Maps of areas where cannabis could be found were distributed among collegians. A Nebraska Highway Patrol lieutenant testified before a congressional committee: "To date in 1969 we have documented eighty-one arrests of people from outside of Nebraska who have come in to harvest the marijuana that is growing here."[12]

The THC content of the wild plants varied from 0.02 percent to 0.5 percent—and the latter was considered a good grade at the time.

Imports from Mexico, trickling in during the latter sixties, swelled in the early seventies. The marijuana had a THC content of 1 percent to 2 percent. Material with a THC content of 3 percent to 5 percent soon followed from Mexico, South America, and Jamaica.

Marijuana smokers aimed at finding "good pot," meaning the most potent available. It came from the tropics. Smugglers sneaked in such choice variations as "Acapulco Gold," "Colombia Buds," "Jamaican Gold," "Maui Wowie," "Panama Red," and "Thai sticks" (dried buds bound onto bamboo sections). Colombia took over the lead from Mexico and went on to furnish the bulk of the marijuana in the United States.

From the start, individual Americans replanted the seeds and grew their own. Some saw this occupation as the way to riches. Amid the seventies a potent product called "sinsemilla" entered the market, produced in remote areas mainly in the region north of San Francisco. In 1984 it retailed in California for around $200 an ounce. Its popularity boosted an illegal botanical to a lofty position among the crops of the Golden State.

In the earlier years of the drug movement (as Professor Jones noted) one's first reefer did not normally intoxicate one. It was usually so mild

The cannabis plant, which probably originated in Asia, is a fast-grow-
ing, herbaceous annual, propagated by seed. Cannabis sativa and the hop
plant make up the family Cannabaceae. Cannabis normally is dioe-

cious, that is, an individual plant is either male or female, unlike many other species in which each flower produces both pollen and seeds. The flowers are small and typically green, greenish-yellow, or (in the male) white. Wind carries the pollen to females, which produce small, hard, one-seeded fruits. Cannabis leaves are distinctive, commonly with five, seven, nine, or other odd numbers of saw-toothed leaflets, arranged palmately, like fingers of a hand, dark green on the upper side and lighter on the lower. They may measure two to ten inches in length at maturity. Minute hairs, including cystolith and resin-secreting hairs (the latter most dense on female tops) characterize cannabis. Let alone, male plants usually wither upon shedding pollen; female plants can grow until seeds mature. Odors vary. Hemp fiber comes from the stem, in the fibrous type of plant; seeds have served for bird and human food and for oil to make paint, soap, etc.; resin that rubs off the plant becomes hashish; and flowers, small stems, and leaves are used for marijuana. The drawings depict (1) the flowering shoot and leaves of the male plant; (2) the male inflorescence, flower cluster, and (3) detail; (4) the female inflorescence and (5) detail; (6) the fruit; and (7) the seed. (Reprinted, with permission, from Cannabis and Health, *edited by J. D. P. Graham, copyright 1976 by Academic Press [London] Ltd.)*

that it took additional exposure for the brain to accumulate enough drug. Later on, "highs" commonly went with first joints.

The Marihuana Project at the University of Mississippi (under NIDA contract) has been analyzing samples of confiscated cannabis since 1972, when marijuana contained an average of 0.4 percent THC. The percentage rose yearly to 3.1 percent in 1982—more than a sevenfold increase.

Up to the midseventies, the strongest marijuana yet analyzed at the Mississippi laboratory—a sample from Brazil—possessed a THC content of 6 percent.[13] By 1983, that was the average percentage of THC in over a hundred samples of home-grown sinsemilla, and marijuana with double that potency had shown up on occasion. (More in Supplement, B.)

> Sinsemilla (from the Spanish: without seed) consists of the tops of female plants that the grower has kept from pollination by prematurely harvesting male plants. Energy that would have been devoted to seed production has gone into the making of more bracts and bigger plants. Some are huge, but height as such has nothing to do with potency. The sinsemilla process is not an American innovation; the Indian Hemp Drugs Commission essentially described it in 1894.
>
> Growers in northern California plant cannabis in the spring and harvest it in the fall, four to six months later. By then it may be as high as twenty feet. Under

some other conditions, a cannabis specimen may grow only as high as a house plant.

Traditionally growers prefer female cannabis plants over the male, although male plants can be just as psychoactive. Analyses by several investigators show the same cannabinoids in similar ratios and amounts in both plant genders. But since the female grows for a longer time than the male, the female will have more foliage and top, hence a greater yield of cannabinoid per plant. It will have more resin too, although THC content does not depend on resin.

The concentration of cannabinoid in a given plant increases in this order: roots and seeds, thick stems, thin stems, large leaves, small leaves, flowers, and bracts (Doorenbos et al., University of Mississippi, 1971, and Fairbairn, University of London, 1976).[14] Of course the fiber type of cannabis plant is low in THC. Cannabidiol (CBD), nonpsychoactive compound, is its predominant cannabinoid. The pattern reverses in the drug type. Some identify an intermediate type, with THC and CBD in close to equal amounts.

Colombia, which took over the lead from Mexico, accounted for about three-fourths of the marijuana in the United States in 1980. Mexican, Jamaican, and domestic marijuana, in that order, followed in close competition. As of 1982, Colombia provided possibly 70 percent of the marijuana consumed by Americans.[15]

3

Attitudes

In the beginning there was hemp and it was used just for manufacturing, at least in the United States. Some medicinal use of the "Indian" variety followed. Changes began about 1900 when itinerant Mexican workers brought their weed and their smoking habits into the southwestern border states of the U.S. About a decade later, coming from South America and the Caribbean, the practice entered the southeastern part of the country via New Orleans.

In the Southwest, resentment toward the newcomers led some authorities to blame marijuana for inciting them to violence. U.S. troops returning from Mexico were reportedly found smoking it on duty. In New Orleans, where it became associated with black jazz musicians and places of ill fame, safety and health officials crusaded against what they considered a dangerous narcotic. The ethnic association—Mexican to the west or Negro to the east—tinged the opposition to cannabis even after it spread to other groups. The practice was linked also to "immoral" elements.

State laws to ban marijuana began in 1914 in Louisiana, Maine, and Massachusetts. Half of the states passed such statutes by 1930, when the Federal Bureau of Narcotics started. People then smoked marijuana in the major American cities, yet as ethnic minorities and bohemian types they were outside of the mainstream of American society and their number was small. Few Americans even knew what marijuana was. Even the bureau, under Harry J. Anslinger, paid little attention to it at first. After local police expressed concern, the bureau issued warnings and per-suaded Congress to enact the first federal restrictions on the drug. The Marihuana Tax Act of 1937 discouraged the medical use of cannabis, which had declined anyway. The state antimarijuana laws, by then on the books of all of the forty-eight states, exempted medical use. The penalties generally increased with heroin penalties.

In the year of the tax act, Texas made the unlawful possession of any "narcotic drug," including marijuana, punishable by a minimum of two years in prison and a maximum of life imprisonment for the first of-fense, regardless of the amount possessed. (The law was repealed in 1973 and replaced with a misdemeanor statute.) Among other tough states: Missouri threatened a life sentence for possession, second offense. Mis-souri and Louisiana had a death penalty for selling marijuana to a mi-nor, first offense. That crime, second offense, could bring death in Georgia. In Illinois, life imprisonment was mandatory for selling mari-juana, second offense. Such heavy artillery was not usually rolled out for small-timers involved only in marijuana offenses.

Violent crime was the main concern. Police had attributed rapes and murders to marijuana and the press featured that angle in crime stories. Warnings issued from moralist groups about the curse of the "killer weed" or "assassin of youth," which began with addiction and ended in death. The 1936 film *Reefer Madness*, depicting people quickly driven to in-sanity and violent crime by marijuana cigarettes, symbolizes the alarm of that era. Narcotics Commissioner Anslinger and his bureau freely re-leased stories of brutal offenses committed by marijuana smokers. While accepting the view that the drug had the quality of inducing aggression and violence, he believed (in those early years) that "the marijuana ad-dict" did not go on to opiates or cocaine. (He was wrong on both scores, as shown in "Crime" and "Other Drugs.")[16]

The federal government, until 1970, never prohibited marijuana but imposed requirements of taxes and paperwork. Of course, one who conformed to the fed-eral law opened himself up to state prosecution if his business with marijuana was not legitimate.

The Marihuana Tax Act of 1937 subjected violators to a maximum penalty of five years imprisonment, a $2,000 fine, or both. A 1956 amendment imposed a prison term of two to ten years for the first offense, five to twenty years for the second offense, and ten to forty years for the third offense; in addition, a fine of up to $20,000 could be imposed for any violation.

Taxes were payable yearly ($1 by producers, doctors, researchers, or instructors, $24 by importers, manufacturers, or compounders; and $3 by others dealing in or giving away marijuana) and at each transfer ($1 per ounce by the marijuana recipient if an annual registrant, $100 per ounce if not, the transferor being equally liable for an unpaid tax), except for doctors (who still needed to record transfers) and pharmacists. Books and records had to be kept by taxpayers, and official order forms had to be made out for each transfer and retained two years by both the transferor and transferee, subject to inspection.

"Marihuana" meant all parts of the Cannabis sativa plant, growing or not, including resin and seeds, or any product or derivative, except for mature stalks, sterilized seeds, or fiber or other products from the mature stalks or oil or cake from the seeds.[17]

Another federal law pertaining to marijuana had been enacted in 1929 to establish two "narcotic farms for the confinement and treatment of persons addicted to the use of habit-forming narcotic drugs who have been convicted of offenses against the United States, and for other purposes." Among the substances specified were "Indian hemp and its various derivatives, compounds, and preparations. . . ."

At the start of the marijuana surge of the sixties, national concern about drug abuse focused on heroin. Controlled scientific studies of cannabinoids were just beginning. Plainly, though, people were not going mad, murdering, or dying from marijuana. Students defended the herb. Siblings and friends listened and sympathized. Parents were confused, fearful of the drug and its felonious status, but loath to see youngsters imprisoned for an act that looked as innocent as their own drinking.

Reform groups sprang up, the National Organization for the Reform of Marijuana Laws (NORML), based in Washington, D.C., being the most effective. Its financial supporters have included the Playboy Foundation, which in 1970 put up the money to start the organization, and *High Times* (a slick, prodrug magazine born in 1974).[18]

In 1970 the United States enacted the Comprehensive Drug Abuse, Prevention and Control Act. Setting up five classifications, it placed marijuana, heroin, and LSD in Schedule One—drugs with no medical use and high potential for abuse, requiring strict security. However, it reduced unauthorized possession of small amounts from a felony (more than one year's imprisonment) to a misdemeanor (one year or less), and it abolished mandatory jailing.

The act also established the National Commission on Marihuana and Drug Abuse for the purpose of making a one-year study. The thirteen-member (Raymond P.) "Shafer Commission" published its findings in three volumes in 1972.

While acknowledging possible health hazards of long-term, heavy use of cannabis, the commission observed no such pattern in the United States, where most experience was with low doses of weak preparations. Given "little proven danger of physical or psychological harm from the experimental or intermittent use" of marijuana, the commission could not consider it a major public health concern. It saw no trend to more intensive use and no chance of marijuana leading to other drugs.

The report introduced the term "decriminalization" to characterize the commission's main proposal for reforming the Marijuana Laws: Eliminate criminal penalties for possession of small amounts for personal use but subject any material possessed in public to immediate seizure as contraband. (More often "decriminalization" is used to mean a sharp reduction in penalty for a criminal act, a reclassification from a felony to a misdemeanor or lesser violation. "Legalization" means the elimination of all penalties.) In public, possession of more than one ounce or use or distribution would be a criminal offense punishable by a $100 fine.

How did the proposal to permit some possession jibe with the nation's obligation under the Single Convention on Narcotic Drugs, of 1961, which bound signatories to make the unauthorized possession of marijuana a punishable offense? Under the commission's interpretation, possession for personal use and not sale could be permitted.

The commission's report said its "partial prohibition scheme" would symbolize society's continuing discouragement of marijuana.[19] What the report did was encourage promarijuana lobbyists, who relied heavily on it in lobbying efforts at state legislatures across the country.

Among arguments of those pushing to decriminalize or to legalize marijuana completely: Everyone has a right to do his own thing. Marijuana is harmless, a soft drug. The older generation has its alcohol—let the younger generation have its pot. The laws against marijuana make criminals of young people and cause them much more harm than marijuana itself. Police are locking up vast numbers for committing a victimless crime.

In California, where citizens may initiate legislation, a group gathered signatures for a ballot measure to legalize marijuana for everyone eighteen and over. A medical doctor at a forum to debate it (Berkeley, 1972) called marijuana "innocuous and nontoxic" and declared, "We don't care if anybody smokes grass, but we do care if people go to jail for it. . . . An individual has the right to maintain whatever state of consciousness he chooses and to do whatever he pleases with his body."[20] (After the measure's defeat in 1972, efforts to put it on the ballot again failed repeatedly.)

Opinion did not necessarily divide along "liberal" or "conservative" lines. Among those in the latter camp, Senator Barry Goldwater came out for decriminalization in 1969. And an issue of William F. Buckley, Jr.'s *National Review* bore the cover heading "The Time Has Come: Abolish the Pot Laws."[21] (Buckley admitted trying marijuana—"on my boat, outside the three-mile limit," and it "didn't do a thing for me.")[22]

A call for legalization appeared also in *Licit and Illicit Drugs*, a 623-page report by the independent and normally nonpolitical Consumers Union.[23] Among other groups endorsing marijuana law reform were the American Medical Association, the National Council of Churches, the American Public Health Association, and the National Education Association.

Going against the tide of opinion, in spring of 1974 Mississippi Senator James O. Eastland's Committee on the Judiciary held hearings on cannabis's "impact on United States security." Witnesses were scientists from the United States and abroad and officials, and the hearings concentrated on possible injury to the body, mind, or armed forces from the smoking of marijuana or hashish.[24] The press largely ignored the hearings.

In the fall of the same year, Iowa Senator Harold E. Hughes, chairman of the Subcommittee on Alcoholism and Narcotics, conducted hearings with the opposite slant. For openers he noted that columnist Ann Landers, the attorney general, and the *Washington Post* all had spoken lately for marijuana reform, and that the U.S. attorney for the District of Columbia had stopped prosecuting those possessing small amounts. Witnesses urged abolition of criminal penalties for personal use and possession (Dr. Thomas Bryant, M.D., president of the Drug Abuse Council, created by the Ford Foundation to evaluate public policy) or at least elimination of jail terms (Dr. Jerome H. Jaffe, M.D., Columbia University psychiatry professor).

Committee member Jacob K. Javits, senator from New York, had served with Hughes on the Shafer Commission and with Hughes introduced a bill to legalize personal use and nonprofit sale. It bothered Javits that "Last year approximately 420,000 Americans were arrested for the possession, sale, or use of marijuana—most of them between the ages of eighteen and twenty-five without a previous arrest record."[25]

The official National Institute of Mental Health, in *A Family Response to the Drug Problem* (1976 booklet), knew of no evidence of damage to body organs from cannabis and offered among the most serious effects the fact that "you can get arrested for using it."[26] *Handbook on Drug Abuse*, published by NIDA and the White House Office of Drug Abuse Policy for policy makers and professionals (1979), said that "in light of the research . . . and in light of the continuing increase in prevalence of marihuana use, it seems to be counterproductive to maintain its status as an illicit drug."[27]

Oregon, in 1973, was the first state to eliminate jail as a penalty for the private possession of marijuana. Possession of up to one ounce (about twenty-five to thirty cigarettes) became a "violation" with a top penalty of a $100 fine. Ten other states followed suit between 1975 and 1978: Minnesota, Alaska, Ohio, California, Maine, Colorado, North Carolina, Mississippi, New York, and Nebraska, in that order.[28]

Ultimately all states except Nevada removed from their lists of felonies the possession of a small amount of marijuana; and all states including Nevada eliminated mandatory jailing for such offense.

Attitudes of three successive presidents reflected the shifting opinion. Nixon opposed decriminalization. Ford professed an "open mind." Carter recommended federal decriminalization.

Dr. Robert DuPont, chief drug abuse adviser of Nixon and Ford, and later the director of NIDA, said at a 1974 NORML convention that "the benefits of deterrence are available at a lower social cost than the current criminal sanctions." That year at a press conference and a Senate hearing he admitted having smoked marijuana several times "out of curiosity" between 1960 and about 1965. In 1977 he told the Psychiatric Institute Foundation, "Decriminalization of marijuana possession makes sense on economic and humanitarian grounds." He expressed impatience at the hesitation of Congress and most states to enact it, and he even advocated eliminating felonious penalties for personal growing of cannabis.[29]

Dr. Peter Bourne, Carter's chief drug adviser, strongly advocated decriminalization. A disclosure that he himself had used cocaine forced his resignation in 1979.

During the drug boom, "head shops," stores specializing in paraphernalia for marijuana smokers, sprang up throughout America, particularly near colleges. Stores could legally sell rolling papers, "roach clips," "stash cans," "bongs," a variety of pipes from glass tubes to sculptured hookahs, fantastic posters, colored lights, incense, and other accessories of the so-called drug culture.

Drug-related merchandise spread to other stores and included items geared to children—bags of practice "grass," T-shirts, and comic books—and a profusion of books on growing, smoking, and cooking with marijuana. Meanwhile, drug messages emerged from movies, TV shows, and rock-and-roll music.

John Lennon of the Beatles expressed the prevailing sentiment by calling marijuana "a harmless giggle."

Police told *The New York Times* (1983) that 800 stores in New York City—often doubling as drug-paraphernalia, candy, record, or tobacco shops—were selling marijuana to anyone walking off the street. The city's special narcotics prosecutor commented, "They're taking over our neighborhoods, and no neighborhood in New York City is immune to them any longer." Law enforcement officials said they had been unable to close those "smoke shops" because of lenient marijuana laws, cutbacks in the police force, and unwillingness of judges to send the dealers to jail.

✻ ✻ ✻

As the seventies drew to a close, increasingly pessimistic reports in the news media about marijuana and health, coupled with antidrug organizing by parents of the nation worried about their children's habits, put the brakes on the movement toward legalization.

Preparing a special television program on marijuana legislation in 1979, the Public Broadcasting System could not locate a single member of Congress, in either the House or the Senate, who would go on television in favor of further decriminalization.[30]

Lee Dogoloff, who succeeded Bourne as presidential drug adviser, said to us (1980) that while he opposed jail for personal possession, "there is no way of reducing criminal penalties and at the same time getting across the message of increased health concern. What this basically says to the average person is you have reduced your penalties because you have reduced your concern. This is the issue I think we failed to recognize. . . .

"As we in the White House began to recognize this aspect, we talked a lot less about the issue of decriminalization. We no longer questioned whether marijuana was harmful or not; we knew that it was. That was my feeling. I changed my focus in '79 when I saw the survey of high school seniors showing that in '78, 59 percent of the seniors had tried marijuana and one in nine used it daily. . . .

"What we have in the country today is a de facto decriminalization, with the consensus in practice, if not in the law, of not putting people in jail for simple possession. The challenge remains, however, how to get a clear message across to the American people on the real health hazard potential associated with marijuana use. . . .

"My notion is to have an alternate group of sanctions that are enforced in a consistent basis for simple possession of small amounts of marijuana, such as fines, community service, parent involvement, education."

Dogoloff said that NORML's alarm about huge numbers of people arrested for marijuana possession had haunted him. So investigators checked and learned that in nearly all cases police had arrested the people for other offenses and in the process discovered marijuana on them. The idea of police spending their time and resources hunting marijuana smokers has provided a popular argument against the laws.

Another federal drug spokesman, Dr. Jack Durell of NIDA (then acting deputy director), said at a 1980 press conference, "We are quite convinced that marijuana is a harmful and unsafe drug, especially for children. Most of the material distributed to the public about the health risks of marijuana over the last six to eight years has been very scientifically cautious. The public likely is not getting the message about the hazards of marijuana use.

"Consequently the federal government has now decided that in terms of material on marijuana for the public, it is better to emphasize the hazards, that it would be better to put the burden of proof on those who are alleging marijuana is safe. . . . We are revising much of our popular literature to make it clearer and less ambiguous."[31]

Testifying before a congressional committee in 1981, Carlton E. Turner, by then President Reagan's drug policy adviser, was asked his response to the widespread call for legalization. He said that more than 100,000 young people required hospital attention each year because of drugs, 60,000 of them because of marijuana. Legalization would not solve those problems and would create new ones, he said. "I would hate to see us going down the same road as we have gone down with alcohol and some of the other drugs on the market."

While continuing to be "deeply disturbed" about opiate problems, he expressed equal concern about other drugs. "For the past decade much of our effort has been focused on opiate problems. However, we are now seeing the effects of the widespread use of other drugs. These drugs, once considered soft and less dangerous, are now creating acute and chronic problems for the well-being of our people."[32]

Ronald Reagan, having vetoed decriminalization bills when governor of California, carried the same attitude to the White House. He declared (1982), "We intend to mobilize all our forces to stop the flow of illegal drugs into this country, to erase the bogus glamour that surrounds drugs, to let our nation's kids know the truth, and to brand drugs such as marijuana for exactly what they are: dangerous."[33] His wife, Nancy, made the curbing of juvenile drug abuse her special project as First Lady.

Dr. DuPont, who advocated decriminalization so strongly when director of NIDA, reversed his position and became president of the American Council on Marijuana and Other Psychoactive Drugs, Inc., a group opposing such drugs. (In 1983 its name was changed to the American Council for Drug Education, Inc.) He said talk of marijuana's safety made him "sick," predicted "horrendous" consequences to the body, and called it more dangerous than tobacco or alcohol (1978). He opposed further decriminalization (1979) and charged that marijuana "poses the single biggest new threat to our nation's health" (1980).[34]

The marijuana views of Dr. Sidney Cohen, professor of psychiatry at the University of California at Los Angeles, have reflected the national shifts. He testified at a congressional hearing in 1979 that before the 1960s, he accepted the scientific opinions of the day, namely that "prolonged use may result in mental deterioration, a fact known for centuries in Egypt and the Orient," and that cannabis was believed to be "a breeder of crime and violence"—he was quoting a 1941 textbook on therapeutics.

In the 1960s he revised his opinion and wrote and spoke of cannabis as "a trivial weed." In the seventies "my impressions about the harmfulness of marijuana have changed again; and this latest shift has been brought about by emerging research reports, including my own, and by an unhappy change in the street scene . . . younger and younger children becoming involved, increased numbers who smoke daily, and often many times a day, and a much more potent product ranging from 5 to 7 percent THC readily available from Colombia, Thailand, and from our own country. . . . This heavy use by increasingly younger persons make the marijuana issue a whole new ball game."[35]

Other physicians have switched their views in late years. Dr. Harvey Powelson changed earlier. He was the psychiatric director at the student health center in Cowell Memorial Hospital, University of California at Berkeley, when the campus newspaper printed this headline: " 'Legalize Pot, Down with Acid' Says Cowell Psych." The story had him calling marijuana harmless. "There is no evidence it does anything except make people feel good. It has never made anyone into a criminal or a narcotics addict."[36]

Interviewing about 200 students a year, he "gradually learned to pick up subtle but important signs of the mental changes in marijuana users": impairment in judgment, memory, and logic, and ultimately delusional and paranoid thinking. "I became convinced that my original opinion about the harmlessness of marijuana was wrong." When he made public his changed attitude in 1970, in local press interviews, he quickly lost friends and acquired foes on the promarijuana campus.

The reformers too have shifted, as the scientific evidence has come in. At first they called marijuana completely harmless. Then they pronounced it no more harmful than alcohol. Later they cautioned that marijuana could affect the unborn child, as any drug could. Still later they advised that it might hinder adolescent development.

Keith Stroup, director of NORML, said on TV (1978), "There is a tendency on the part of young people today to underestimate the potential for harm from psychoactive drug use. . . . There is no such thing as a totally safe drug, and I don't think marijuana is going to be the first. It should obviously not be a daily habit" or indulged in before school or study.[37]

Gordon W. Brownell, the organization's West Coast coordinator, said (1981), "NORML is strongly opposed to kids under the age of eighteen using marijuana or any drug." The group was warning also of a risk to heart and lung patients. And Brownell remarked to a newspaperman, "I no longer believe in the peace and love syndrome that I felt ten years ago," that "the more people who turned on to grass, the better society would be."[38]

The Drug Abuse Council stated in a 1980 report, "Enough is now known to warrant considerable caution with its use, particularly heavy use; use by pregnant women and by adolescents should be avoided."[39]

In the 1975 survey of high school seniors, 43 percent of them saw "great risk" from regular marijuana smoking. The number holding that opinion dropped to 35 percent in 1978. Four years later 60 percent of the 1982 class attributed "great risk" to regular smoking.

"This is a dramatic change . . . during a period in which a substantial amount of scientific and media attention has been devoted to the potential dangers of heavy marijuana use," the surveyors commented. In the '83 class, 63 percent held that view, while one in eighteen was smoking marijuana daily.[40]

In trying to answer the question "What are the health implications of marijuana use for Americans?" NIDA published a 1980 summary of research findings entitled *Marijuana and Health* that could be interpreted (per one headline writer) as "A grim report on pot."[41] Yet the report displayed scientific restraint—something its predecessors had done to a greater extent. This could be misinterpreted, its writer (Dr. Robert C. Petersen) regretted: "Despite our increasing knowledge, much remains to be learned about the effects of chronic use. Unfortunately, our present limited knowledge is often interpreted as indicating that marijuana is 'safe.' "

"While all of us would wish for greater certainty in this area, such certainty is not yet possible," said the report. "The American marijuana experience has been of brief duration. It is comparatively recently that significant numbers of individuals have been using the more potent cannabis now available on a daily basis. As our experience with tobacco and alcohol demonstrates, it frequently requires many years of use by large numbers for long range effects of a drug to become apparent. While there are cultures in which cannabis use has been traditional for many years, the drug is often used differently, and traditional users rarely include women or the very young."

The forty-eight-page 1980 *Marijuana and Health* was the eighth and last in a series of reports by the Secretary of Health, Education, and Welfare to Congress and the people. Mandated by Congress, they began in 1971 (and were issued annually through 1977 as *Marihuana and Health*).[42]

*   *   *

In 1982 the National Academy Press published a 188-page *Marijuana and Health*, prepared by a special, twenty-two-member committee of the Institute of Medicine in a fifteen-month study, supported by a contract with the National Institutes of Health. Dr. Arnold S. Relman, editor of *The New England Journal of Medicine*, was the chairman.

This report, in conclusion to its general summary, said: "The scientific evidence published to date indicates that marijuana has a broad range of psychological and biological effects, some of which, at least under certain conditions, are harmful to human health. Unfortunately, the available information does not tell us how serious this risk may be.

"Our major conclusion is that what little we know for certain about the effects of marijuana on human health—and all that we have reason to suspect—justifies serious national concern. Of no less concern is the extent of our ignorance about many of the most basic and important questions about the drug. Our major recommendation is that there be a greatly intensified and more comprehensive program of research into the effects of marijuana on the health of the American people."

Federal support for cannabis research was fairly steady in dollar terms through the 1970s, although declining in terms of inflation. The support for such research—much less than support for tobacco research—averaged a little over $4 million annually in fiscal years 1977 to 1979, NIDA (created in 1972) accounting for four-fifths of the total.[43] The main federal support program began with a little over $1 million for a score of projects in the 1967–68 fiscal year.[44]

NIDA's budget for fiscal 1983 included $4.6 million for cannabis research—grants or contracts for thirty-eight projects—out of $43 million for all types of drug research.

The total federal budget for drug abuse programs in fiscal 1983 approached a billion dollars, including about $700 million for drug-law enforcement. Enforcement funds rose annually from fiscal 1979 to 1983, particularly in the first three years. Funds for the other programs, both treatment and prevention (including NIDA), changed little from fiscal 1979 to 1981 but sank in 1982 and plummeted in 1983.[45]

*   *   *

The number of technical articles, reports, and books on cannabis was due to approach 10,000 by the end of 1984. The total (excluding popular literature and works on industrial hemp) includes 1,860 before 1964 (listed by Eddy), 3,045 between 1964 and 1974 (listed by Waller et al.), 2,670 between 1975 and 1979

(Waller et al.), and 433 in 1980 plus 400 to 500 new works a year (according to the Research Institute of Pharmaceutical Sciences, University of Mississippi).[46]

✢   ✢   ✢

In a 1983 Gallup youth survey, teenagers ranked marijuana as the most serious school problem. Thirty-five percent considered it a "very big" problem and 23 percent a "fairly big" one. Thirteen percent admitted having driven cars "when high from smoking" marijuana, 10 percent "after drinking too much." Thirty-five percent of the teenagers called "drug abuse" the biggest problem facing their generation. Next came "unemployment," 16 percent.[47]

DRIVING

※   ※

- *"I liked to drive when I was high. It gave me a neat feeling—the dancing lights and the compensations you have to make for time and distance. . . . I drove slowly. I was extra cautious when driving high. It was a real challenge."* —John (ex-user)

- *"I used to drive after smoking marijuana—very slowly. I became supersensitive to the fact that I was in a car and stoned. . . .*
  "My reaction time was slower. The traffic lights looked brighter, and I would focus on the traffic lights instead of what it means. I was very easily distracted." —Anna (ex-user)

- *"I drive all the time when I'm stoned. I find I'm a lot more cautious."* —Millie (chronic user)

- *"Yes, I drove both while smoking and soon after smoking marijuana. It was hard. I had to keep on my toes a lot more. I had to really concentrate. Time was hard judging. You think you'd be further away from stop signs than you are. . . .*
  "I know a girl who got into a car accident from pot and alcohol. It was on an icy road. Her car was a write-off. She got cut up with glass." —Steve (ex-user)

- *"I'm a carefuler driver when I'm on pot. I get in the slow lane."* — Alice (chronic user)

- *"I did drive . . . under marijuana influence . . . and it certainly had an effect that can cause danger in driving, in my opinion . . . distortion of perception and depth and time . . . particularly at nighttime. . . .*
  "Say you come to a light . . . and you want to stop behind that car. So normally you have a kind of coordination that allows you to see the

264

amount of time that it would take you to brake . . . and this gets kind of distorted." —Hiram (ex-user)

● *"I used to smoke and drive. That's pretty hard to do. Now I'll smoke a joint and drive afterwards, which sometimes is nice. It makes you more aware of the cars. You're more cautious. Your reflexes are about the same. Maybe a little slower, but not much. . . .*

"One friend of mine got into a wreck on the freeway. He wasn't smoking while driving but he had some before driving, but nobody got hurt. He was with his wife. He smashed into the back of another car. He was stoned, so I don't think that helped matters." —Charlie (chronic user)

● *"I've probably driven more stoned than I have straight. I tend to drive too fast any time, but when I'm stoned I tend to be more careless. I've come close to having accidents quite often, but I still do it. It worries me. A lot of things worry me about smoking marijuana."* —Betty (long-time user, trying to quit)

● *"I never had an accident. If anything, sometimes it improved my driving because I was so conscious of the fact. I had to be a good driver.*

"Everybody drives stoned. I've only met one pot smoker in my whole life who refused to drive stoned. He got into several accidents, when not stoned.

"I know of a couple people who had accidents when stoned. A guy was on a highway, approaching a road ramp. He hit his brakes and the car skidded. Another, a friend, went through a stop sign and had a collision." —Bert (chronic user)

● *"I found it very difficult to drive autos at night. I would hallucinate— seeing people running into the road. . . .*

"I did have a lot of car accidents around the time I was smoking a lot. I wasn't actually stoned when I drove. Maybe it was a general lack of caution and awareness. I wasn't a very good driver. I'd say every summer I bashed in a separate fender." —Kathy (light user, former heavy user)

● *"Yeah, I drove. At first I wouldn't have done that, because I was afraid. But then later I would drive without hesitation when I was stoned. With the sense of time being slowed down, I felt I was a safer driver."* —Gregory (occasional user, former chronic user)

● *"Once I smoked a bunch of pot and went with my four best friends on a bike trip. . . . My legs were heavy and it was hard to pedal. I crashed.*

I was unconscious. The girl behind me said I fell over the front of the bike. I broke my collarbone and really smashed up my face. . . . I have never driven a car. . . .

"One friend who crashed while skiing under pot was really stoned. He spent about a year in a body cast. Another friend wrecked a guy's car while under the influence of pot and alcohol." —Janet (ex-user)

• *"My parents were in bed one night and it was after midnight. They heard a crash and a car was in their living room. They lived at the end of a street in a wealthy Chicago suburb. Some kids had been coming down the street at high speed and bounced off a tree and the front end of the car went through the front wall of the house.*

"My family came out to help them. They were two teenage boys, brothers. I don't think they had a scratch on them. The kids seemed dazed. We all assumed it was from the accident. Then a family member who was visiting saw what appeared to be marijuana cigarettes in the vehicle and pointed it out to the police. While the police discussed whether there was probable cause to search the car, the marijuana disappeared.

"We didn't pursue the matter because the kids were the children of people in our church, friends of ours. The family took care of the damage." — Michael

Who, me? (Giggle.) *Don't be silly, officer.* (Giggle.) *I haven't drunk a drop all day.* (Giggle. Giggle.)

1

Under the Influence

It was a hazardous experiment. But two university students in Miami decided to try it one evening in the late sixties.

One of the students, an occasional user, smoked marijuana and then got behind the wheel of a car. The other student sat beside him in front. A tape recorder lay between them and the driver, Arnold, talked as he drove. Sometimes his friend, Richard, made an observation. The talk went like this:

ARNOLD: I am presently now stoned from what I consider were two to two and a half good joints of marijuana. I just noticed that I forgot to turn my lights on and I was backing up. I am now pulling out. Richard, please keep the tape recorder running. I'm very serious about that. Going now?

RICHARD: Yeah, tape recorder's working.

ARNOLD: I'm very worried at this time, especially that the tape may not work. I would not like the total opportunity to be a failure.

I now feel my head vibrating in between two or three different people. I forgot to look one way when I rounded that corner. I went into third gear very, very poorly, possibly the worst I've done in my entire life.

I am coming to a stop sign, and for some reason I feel maybe I won't be able to stop. It's difficult to force my foot down to the floor on the brake. It seems as though both my feet are riding on cushions, the cushions between my feet and the brake pedal.

I am going to make a right turn. . . . Very worried because cars in both directions. I have the radio on because I enjoy the radio playing. Cars keep giving me signals to turn off my high beam, which I have done. I feel as though I'm being wafted, and I'm only going twenty miles an hour. Isn't that a great word, "wafted"? Being "wafted."

I feel as though I'm rising high in my seat. The lane seems quite wide enough but the car cannot go fast enough, and it appears miles to the next stop. I seem to have different—I seem to sway back and forth across the road. Richard, am I swaying or driving badly? Will you describe my driving?

RICHARD: Right now you're staying close to the center of the road.

You're shifting slightly towards the center and you keep correcting.

ARNOLD: Yeah, it's sort of as though I take too long to correct—isn't it?

RICHARD: Yeah.

ARNOLD: I'm going too slow.

RICHARD: Definitely don't have a proper control of the vehicle.

ARNOLD: It seems exactly right when you say that. I will now bring myself down, and it's really not difficult to keep myself down [sober]. A car in my rear has its brights on and it's almost blinding me.

RICHARD: Even though Arnold believes he is down, he's still swaying quite a bit and has not increased speed to any great—he's still going between twenty and twenty-five.

Take a left.

ARNOLD: I know. I know I take a left. Don't worry about my direction. My car seems to be swaying into the lane. You can really get it driving, as people have said previously.

The light change is absolutely beautiful.

RICHARD: Took him four to five seconds to realize the light had changed to green.

ARNOLD: Are you kidding.

RICHARD: No. . . . How long do you think you've been driving, Arnie?

ARNOLD: Oh, about fifteen minutes.

RICHARD: You've been driving two minutes.

ARNOLD: Oh, God, two.

RICHARD: Wait till you get on the expressway.

ARNOLD: Is that timed to my watch, by the way?

RICHARD: Yes.

ARNOLD: Oh, great, if that's what it's going to be like. Fantastic. Richard is down, by the way. I want to remind you all.

RICHARD: I haven't taken anything except something to clear——

ARNOLD: Very poor perception of the car passing on the right.

RICHARD: You want to go south now on Ninety-five.

ARNOLD: Yup. Very poor perception—nearly ran into that car, Richard, whether you know it or not.

RICHARD: I know.

ARNOLD: I'm amazed that they don't pick up more stoned drivers. I worry about being in the correct gear, more than usual. I'm very frightened of cars passing me. I just did a totally mechanical action. I don't know why I did it. I just feel as if I could lift my foot off the brake and just go screaming around the world.

Oh—watch that dog!

RICHARD: That was a rag in the middle of the road.

ARNOLD: Wow! [*Laughing. Singing along with radio in snatches.*]

RICHARD: We're now going on to One ninety-five, heading south, the Miami Gardens Drive.

ARNOLD: Well, a great place to go, but I feel I cannot handle this curve much longer, 'cause I feel like I'm going around the edge of a teacup, and I hate going around the edge of a teacup in a car. It's like I'm going to roll right off. It's like I'm way up on top of the world. I'm really frightened up here—I'm so very high. [*Singing with radio again.*] Oh, it's like going straight down.

RICHARD: Arnie's only traveling forty, whereas most other traffic is traveling sixty.

ARNOLD: You know something: it was like going straight downhill. [*The road was actually flat.*] Like you know something? I don't know where the last four seconds went to. From the time I came off the hill to here, I do not know where that time has gone to. Like all of a sudden I was in the middle of——

RICHARD: How far ahead of you do you think the car is in front of you?

ARNOLD: I can't drive, Richard. I'm going off the road. I can't drive.

RICHARD: Okay. How far ahead do you think it is? Arnie is going off the road now slowly, and I'll resume driving for him.

ARNOLD: Let me explain something. I was upside down driving and it's happening again. I've got to say something: I cannot possibly drive now, no matter what anyone does to me, because I am driving on my head. You know, driving is not good when you are upside down, folk, and us. I have to get off the road. My God! What was happening? I'm a little too high.

RICHARD: Do you want me to drive?

ARNOLD: No. Wait a second. Let me hold on. I've got to breathe. I mean, I want to drive some more, Richard. Like I really can't. Like wow! I really can't drive whatsoever. I was driving on my head. Like I just didn't know what was happening. You know, I overload. I just remember, overload. I was driving along and all of a sudden I was absolutely upside down and I was falling off the front of the car, and I really didn't know what to do.

RICHARD: Here comes a state trooper.

ARNOLD: Amazing. [*Laughing.*]

RICHARD: Yeah, here he comes.

[*At this point, they pull to the side of the expressway. A patrolman approaches. They get out of the car and tell him they have just arrived in town, the driver was tired, and they stopped to change places. The car has an out-of-state license plate. "Okay," says the patrolman, and he goes on his way.*]

ARNOLD: Like we were just approached by a highway patrolman and he stopped us—and like I can't drive whatsoever. And if I continue to drive, I'm going to kill both of us.

It's amazing. I was driving and—Richard, don't overshift—and virtually upside down, and I didn't know what to do, and it was like—oh——. It was just—it was disastrous.

Have you ever been in Funland Park? You probably never have been, but if you ever get there, there's this ride like a dive-bomber, and when you're in it—oh, Richard, stop the car. I think he did something to it. I think the car's broken, folk. I bet the fan belt.

RICHARD: If we go off the expressway again, that highway patrol is going to bug us again.

ARNOLD: Okay. Just take it very slowly. If that's the fan belt, it could ruin my car. I bet my fan fell off.

(End of tape.)

*   *   *

The marijuana brought hallucinations, distortions, distractions, and difficulty in braking—but no staggering, no breath odor, and no slurred speech.

"Now if this had been somebody with a three-tenths alcohol, that officer could have spotted it," commented Dr. Joseph H. Davis, medical examiner of Dade County, Florida. "But here's a kid who's 'upside down' and the officer can't even tell when he's 'upside down.'

"This is one of the big dangers of this stuff on the highway. So if it comes to carte blanche legalization-commercialization and we turn this loose on the highways, we're wiped out."

In a tape recording of a similar test, made a bit later in the same city, three young men ride in a car after all of them took marijuana. All are high. The driver finds it hard controlling the car. It overruns a lawn and a passenger decides to get out of the car while it moves along the highway. The other two, stuffed with "grass," think this a big joke and laugh uproariously as the occupant is starting to open the door. (Fortunately he never makes it out.)[1]

Questionnaires from Klein, Davis, and Blackbourne (1971) asked Florida college and university students to rate themselves on driving ability under the influence of marijuana. Most of 156 former, infrequent, or weekly users indicated that the drug worsened their ability—specifically to judge time, distance, and speed; to respond to an emergency; and to control a motor vehicle. Of 100 who smoked more often than weekly, only a minority felt that marijuana hurt any of those abilities, except that 54 found it harder to judge time. Those heaviest users had been stopped by police a lot more often than the others (who in turn were stopped much more often than a comparison group of 247 nonusers) but police did not necessarily arrest those they had pulled over. Said one user, "Well, I was stoned and a cop stopped me because there were three people in the front seat of my sports car. . . . He didn't know that I was stoned. He was dumb because I was really wrecked."[2]

While *dagga* (cannabis) intoxication seemed to make time pass more slowly for 77 percent of 150 drivers and nondrivers polled in South Africa, 73 percent of those responding (about three-fourths of the 150 responded to this question) felt that the drug made them drive slower. In view of the first answer, Morley, Logie, and Bensusan (1973) discounted the second, because "what to the subject may seem a snail's pace could just as easily be a dangerously high speed." Only two-fifths of the respondents indicated that *dagga* worsened their motoring.[3]

A stoned driver's assertion that a drug doesn't hinder his driving, or even helps it, need no more be taken at face value than a drunk's insistence that he can drive superbly even though he cannot walk a straight line.

The man who made the following statement was a twenty-eight-year-old physician.

"I often drive my automobile when I'm high on marijuana and never have had any actual problems doing so. But I do have some purely subjective difficulty, which perhaps you'll understand. My reflexes and perception seem to be okay, but I have problems like this: I'll come to a stop light and have a moment of panic because I can't remember whether or not I've just put my foot on the brake. Of course, when I look down, it's there, but in the second or two afterwards I can't remember having done it. In a similar way, I can't recall whether I've passed a turn I want to take or even whether I've made the turn."[4]

He thinks he never has any real driving problems, yet he cannot even remember whether he pressed the brakes or made a turn.

Those we interviewed split evenly on whether marijuana hindered or actually helped driving. Either way, no past or present user refused to drive because of marijuana intoxication.

Among 246 driver-licensed college students in Canada, most drinkers and the majority of marijuana smokers admitted having driven while intoxicated. Three times as many drove when under the influence of alcohol as drove when high on marijuana. They were surveyed by Smart of the Addiction Research Foundation in Toronto (1974), who calculated three times as many alcohol-driving occasions as marijuana-driving occasions in one year. Each group admitted getting into a few accidents while intoxicated, and the accident rate for each group was the same.[5]

Advocates of the legalization of marijuana and those opposing it agree on one proposition: A driver under the influence of marijuana should not be allowed to drive. There is a "legitimate public interest in prohibiting such conduct," a California group promoting legalization said in campaign literature.[6]

"Influence," however, is open to differing interpretations. For one thing, how long does it last?

A research group (University of Michigan Institute for Social Research) interviewed 3,731 seniors in 131 high schools throughout the country. About half indicated that they had used cannabis in the past twelve months. They were asked: "When you take marijuana or hashish, how long do you usually stay high?" Approximately 47 percent of these users replied that they stayed high for one to two hours; 39 percent, three to six hours; and 5 percent, seven to twenty-four hours. At the extremes, about 8 percent indicated they usually did not get high, while 0.6 percent told the pollsters that they remained high more than 24 hours![7]

The hallucinations of the "upside down" driver came immediately after smoking marijuana. But sometimes the hallucinations are delayed.

Here is an experience described by a patient during psychiatric treatment for anxiety and depression. A youth of nineteen, he had no history of psychosis. He said he had used marijuana and hashish for about a year, two or three times a week. He had tried other drugs but had taken none for a week before this experience. At about 11:30 on a clear night, he was driving with a girl friend:

"And then I saw the teacup on the road. . . . It was a real teacup, a cup and saucer. It was pink and it had blue flowers on it. I had seen a picture of one like it when I was a little kid, in a book I used to have. . . . It was on the road right in front of me and there were about six people in it. . . . They were just sitting there, riding down the road. . . . It was going real slow and we were going real fast. . . . We were right behind it and I was going to crash into it. . . . I went off the road. . . .

"When I went off the road it wasn't there anymore, so I go back on the road again. . . . I was going about sixty-five, maybe, and after that I didn't go any faster than thirty or forty, 'cause like I was afraid to, 'cause like I didn't know, like these big black bars kept on being in front of the car and they would just like lift up into the air and there were all these different flashing lights and everything. . . . Just all these things were there that I knew weren't there really. . . .

"I thought I would never get home, thought for sure I would get in some kind of accident. . . . And then there were like airplanes swooping down at the car and all kinds of stuff like that. . . . Like these things, like there was nothing there at all I could have misconstrued as a tea-cup. It was just empty space."

The case was reported by a Philadelphia doctor, who also reported comparable experiences of two other young male patients, each of whom had taken marijuana or hashish nearly every day for two years. Each had taken other drugs, including occasional LSD, and the doctor suspected that the LSD was responsible for the illusions. But cannabis was the last drug each had taken, maybe eight to ten hours before the incident.

One of them, aged twenty-two, said, "I was driving down the street, turning, making a left. . . . Suddenly, zing, it's like there was a car in front of me. . . . I saw headlights, like for a flash, and like I slammed on the brakes and almost went over the curb, and then I realized it wasn't anything."

The story of the other young man, aged twenty, was similar, although the doctor thought he had experienced a prolonged afterimage rather than a hallucination: "I made a right-hand turn, and the car behind me made a turn, and I always look in the rear-view mirror to see if the car was there, and I looked back onto the road. . . . There was a car dead in front of me, and I jammed on my brakes and there was nothing there. . . . Oh, that happens a lot."[8]

It has been shown that the "flashback"—a sudden return of the drug reaction many hours, days, or weeks after the taking of the drug—can occur in some users of marijuana alone. There is also some evidence that marijuana may trigger "acid flashbacks" in some people who have already taken LSD.

*   *   *

William Pollin, director of the National Institute on Drug Abuse, has called it an "alarming danger" that some of the deterioration in perception or performance resulting from marijuana may persist after the user no longer feels high. Hours after the feeling of intoxication has gone, one's ability to drive or fly may remain impaired, although the cannabis taker does not realize it when entering a car or a cockpit.

Dr. Pollin, in Senate testimony, also said: "Because the ages of peak marijuana use coincide with those of peak driving accident rates, and such accidents are the principal cause of death and injury in adolescents and young adults, the impact of marijuana on driving is an important public health issue. There is good evidence that marijuana use, at typical social levels, impairs driving ability. Studies . . . tend to show significant performance and perceptual deficits related to being high. . . ." He added that the bulk of marijuana users questioned admitted driving sometimes while stoned and that marijuana use in combination with alcohol was quite common, magnifying the risk of accidents.[9] (Two Canadian studies were sources for his estimation.)[10]

If it's true that the majority of adult users with cars drive while high, it would be paradoxical if the majority of them considered it detrimental to do so. Yet that opinion is what hundreds in that category expressed when polled in different parts of the United States.

Of 588 adults (eighteen and over) who had tried marijuana 100 or more times, 61 percent believed that "getting really high on marijuana would cause a person to drive less well." And 51 percent of the 588 believed it because "it happened to me." Less experienced users were more likely to hold that view of marijuana's effect on driving, not so often on the basis of firsthand experience but more often because "it happened to someone I know."

> Among 730 adults who had used marijuana three to ninety-nine times, 76 percent felt that getting "really high" (taking more than "one or two puffs") shortly before driving would cause one to drive worse than he usually does. For 42 percent of the 730, the belief stemmed from firsthand experience.
>
> Of 317 adults who had tried marijuana once or twice, 85 percent believed it worsened driving—20 percent from personal experience.
>
> Among the total of 4,099 adults polled, 2,464 had never taken marijuana and 84 percent of them held that view.
>
> The National Institute on Drug Abuse conducted this ninth annual national survey on drug abuse in 1979.[11]

One result of decriminalization may have been to put more intoxicated drivers on the roads. Figures from the California Department of Justice (furnished at our request) suggest this.

Effective in January, 1976, California reduced penalties for possession of marijuana from a felony to a misdemeanor handled by a citation. That year the number of arrests throughout the state for driving under the influence of drugs jumped 48 percent from the previous year. (In 1975 the number had risen only 8 percent from the year before.) Meanwhile, arrests in California for "drunken driving" rose only 7 percent in 1976. (In 1975 they had risen 11 percent.) The drugged-driving totals remained elevated in the years following. (See table 2.)

TABLE 2

ARREST OF DRIVERS

Arrests Throughout California by All Law Enforcement Agencies on Two Kinds of Charge During Five Years. (Note the increased number of people apprehended for driving while under the influence of a drug in 1976, the year that marijuana was decriminalized.)

	1974	1975	1976	1977	1978
Driving under the influence of drug (both misdemeanors and felonies, adults and juveniles)	3,250	3,522	5,224	5,910	6,975
Driving under the influence of alcohol, or an alcohol-drug combination (both misdemeanors and felonies, adults and juveniles)	208,918	231,862	247,698	272,068	282,413

Sharpening the picture is a similar California statistic broken down into adults (eighteen and older) and juveniles. In the six months following decriminalization (January through June, 1976) arrests for driving under the influence of drugs rose about 46 percent for adults and 71 percent for juveniles, compared with the first half of the previous year.[12]

We consider alcohol a greater overall problem on the road than marijuana—but only because so many more people drink alcoholic beverages than smoke marijuana. An official estimate of adult Americans placed the ratio of drinkers to marijuana smokers at seven to one. Even among young adults through the age of twenty-five, alcohol won in popularity by more than two to one. Of course many combine the two intoxicants, but when arrests or accidents result, police are likely to report only the "drunken driving."

In some ways, driving under marijuana's influence is a more ticklish problem. It is harder to detect. The effects of cannabis are subtle, complex, and less popularly known. Its lethal possibilities are too little appreciated, even by those who understand what it means to operate a car while drunk.

> A 1979 report to the president by the Strategy Council on Drug Abuse estimated that of 30.6 million Americans eighteen to twenty-five, 21 million drank alcohol while 8.3 million used marijuana or hashish.
> Among 117.3 million Americans twenty-six and over, 63.4 million drank alcohol while 3.8 million used marijuana or hashish—a ratio of about 17 to 1.[13]

2

Researching Stoned and Drunken Drivers

The scientific studies of cannabis and driving have included:

A. Experiments, ranging from laboratory tests of skills assumed to be important in motor vehicle operation to real street driving of real cars. They usually have tested subjects under intoxication, sometimes from alcohol as well as from cannabis.

B. Surveys, covering driving populations, accident victims, and/or arrested motorists. Chemical tests may or may not have been used.

Laboratory experiments may use driving simulators. A subject sits in a mock car, viewing moving road scenes and operating a steering wheel, accelerator, brake pedal, and so on in response to the pictured situations.

Climaxing one of the earlier experiments, Alfred Crancer, Jr., and others in the State of Washington (1969) announced that they had determined the effect of a "normal social marihuana high" on simulated driving performance among experienced smokers.

Before the tests, thirty-six subjects each took three treatments on different days: smoking marijuana, drinking alcohol, or just sitting. Subjects accumulated more accelerator, brake, signal, speedometer, and total errors when intoxicated from cocktails than when sober. When high on marijuana, they made only more speedometer errors (failure to monitor the meter). Neither alcohol nor marijuana affected steering.

How valid was the marijuana-alcohol comparison? The marijuana seems to have been weak, while the enormity of the cocktails took them out of the "social" category. The testers held back from assuming that a person doing all right on a driving-simulating machine would necessarily do well on the road.

Nevertheless, marijuana advocates proceeded to use the Crancer experiment as supposed proof of the drug's innocuousness on and off the road and the "fact" that alcohol is worse than marijuana.

Less often quoted was a survey of drivers by Crancer and Quiring (1968) in which users of illegal drugs were shown to have higher accident rates and higher rates of reckless-driving, negligent-driving, and hit-and-run violations than the general driving population of Seattle. Among them were seventy-nine marijuana users, who had a two-fifths higher accident rate.

The researchers suggested that knowledge of drug arrests would help predict driving performance and could well be used to restrict or suspend licenses.

The simulated driving experiment, of the Washington State Department of Motor Vehicles, used seven female and twenty-nine male drivers, who each smoked two marijuana cigarettes totaling 1.7 grams. The potency was not reported. They took the first of three simulator tests half an hour after they finished smoking. They also took alcohol mixed in orange or tomato juice, enough to raise the blood concentration above 0.10 percent. A subject weighing 150 pounds, for instance, received the equivalent of about seven ounces of 86-proof liquor—seven times the strength of the standard bar drink.

A Breathalyzer reading tested concentration about an hour after drinking began; most subjects finished drinking in half an hour. Heart acceleration served to check the subjects' own statements that they were high on marijuana but figures were not reported.

Tripling the marijuana dose for four of the subjects did not substantially change the scores. Four additional subjects who, unlike the thirty-six others, never before had smoked marijuana, took the simulated driving test before and after smoking and showed negligible changes in scores. The extra results led to the statement that "impairment in simulated driving performance apparently is not a function of increased marihuana dosage or inexperience with the drug."

Crancer et al. felt that "because the simulator task is a less complex but related task, deterioration in simulator performance implies deterioration in actual driving performance. We are less willing to assume that nondeterioration in simulator performance implies nondeterioration in actual driving."[14]

* * *

The Canadian Commission of Inquiry Into the Non-Medical Use of Drugs reported (1972) that the alcoholic dose in Crancer's study was relatively high, raising blood alcohol levels to 0.11 percent. Further, while a substantial amount of marijuana was smoked, the potency was questionable, and "in another laboratory, marijuana from the same supply was found to be much weaker than originally estimated."[15]

Caldwell et al. (1969) and Rodin et al. (1970), all in Detroit, reported that marijuana from the National Institute of Mental Health was supposed to contain 1.3 percent THC but two independent laboratories, to which they had sent the marijuana for assay, placed the THC contents at 0.5 percent and 0.2 percent. They speculated that the marijuana may have deteriorated when they stored it at room temperature instead of refrigerating it.[16]

Kalant in Toronto wrote that "many marihuana users have a bias against alcohol. . . . Was it not possible for them to deliberately do badly on the simulated driving test in the alcohol trials?"[17]

* * *

The Crancer and Quiring survey of records considered 302 licensed drivers in the files of the Seattle Police Department who had been arrested and charged with drug offenses. They compared them with 687,228 licensed drivers of the same sex and age groups for number of accidents, number of violations, and types of violations, 1961–67.

The accident rate was 57 percent higher for "dangerous drug" users, 39 percent higher for marijuana users, and 29 percent higher for narcotic users. Rates for the first group and a combination of all groups were statistically higher than the control population. Each illegal drug group had statistically higher traffic violation rates than the control population. And only 11 percent of male drug users had records free of accidents or violations in that period, compared with 42 percent of the male population.[18]

In Denmark, Rafaelsen and colleagues (1973) also employed a simulator after feeding cannabis resin baked in cakes or alcohol mixed in juice to eight young men, both nonusers and (not heavy) users of cannabis. The resin, in all doses, greatly expanded estimates of time and distance. It also increased brake-time (except in the smallest dose) as well as start-time and variations in speed (at the highest dose). Alcohol increased brake-time and gear changes.

The researchers explained why part of the study used only seven subjects: one man, stoned on cannabis, "violated 8 out of 10 red signals without activating the brake pedal, let alone making a full stop."

"Objective" estimates of time and distance ("How long and how far do you really *think* you have been driving?") increased as much as 75 to 85 percent. "Subjective" estimates ("How long and how far do you *feel* you have been driving?") increased up to 225 to 300 percent (the highest being an estimate of time interval at the top dose).

The cannabis doses were 200, 300, and 400 mg of resin containing 4 percent THC. Alcohol was served in one dose of 70 grams in 500 milliliters of juice. Each subject consumed both a cake and a drink, but one or the other was a placebo. Subjects were tested at weekly intervals before and after consumption. Ole J. Rafaelsen (professor of biological psychiatry) et al. allowed half an hour more for the cannabis to take effect than the alcohol and tested the subjects when they seemed to reach peak intoxication.[19]

In still another simulated driving experiment, psychology professor Herbert Moskowitz and associates in Los Angeles tested the performance of twenty-three pot-experienced male college students on a complex, computerized simulator. Smoking of marijuana just before the testing had no effect on their control of the mock automobile, compared with their performance under a placebo (impotent marijuana). But the smoking did lead to significant impairment when it came to an added visual task (operating levers in response to green or amber lights).

Insofar as marijuana impairs driving ability, said a journal report of Moskowitz's (1976), it seems to do so by interfering with the processes of perception and attention needed for safe control of a vehicle, rather than by affecting the "motor" skills involved in car handling.

Indeed, other experiments of his (1972–74), using twelve or twenty-three male subjects, had demonstrated marijuana's impairment of vision, hearing, and reaction. Smoking impaired outer vision (subjects counting blinks of light), increased the apparent movement of lights in the dark, decreased the ability to detect sounds (tones and numbers), and delayed reactions to sounds and lights—to the lights in proportion to dose. Alcohol, in other experiments by Moskowitz and others, decreased perception of sounds and peripheral lights when a subject's attention was divided (by a central blinking light or by noise bursts) but not when attention was concentrated. Marijuana lessened such perception under both conditions, more so when attention was concentrated.

Moskowitz and associates (1981) noticed that marijuana smoking deteriorated the ability of fifteen subjects to deal with simulated curves, winds, and emergencies during a mock automobile drive lasting forty-five minutes. Marijuana—particularly the higher of two doses—made it hard for them to keep in their lanes, stay at a constant speed, and maintain a distance behind a vehicle. The sudden appearance of a roadway obstacle brought seven "crashes" at the lower dose and twice as many when the dose was doubled. In contrast, smokers of inactive marijuana had two "crashes."[20]

> "Since tracking is an important component of driving, this is clearly an important finding," Moskowitz wrote in a monograph, referring to results of an experiment by Manno and coworkers in Indianapolis (1970). Among tasks, given by the Manno group to twelve male volunteers, four of whom had used marijuana before, was the following of a moving target on a pursuit meter. Each of two doses (2.5 and 5 mg of THC) grossly impaired performance about equally. The combination of marijuana and alcohol (to a 0.05 percent blood level) resulted in poorer performance than marijuana alone in only one of four test patterns.
>
> "When questioned whether they thought marihuana was a stimulant or a depressant," Manno et al. wrote of the subjects, "the consensus was that it stimulated them 'mentally' while depressing them 'physically.' "[21]

The first of several prominent sets of Canadian experiments on marijuana and driving was conducted by the official Commission of Inquiry Into the Non-Medical Use of Drugs, also called the Le Dain Commission (1972).

Upon taking alcohol or either of two doses of marijuana or placebos (nonalcoholic drinks or THC-free marijuana), sixteen subjects motored repeatedly through a mile course. Both the alcohol dose and the higher dose of cannabis resulted in "poorer car handling performance." Cars hit more poles and cones than normally. The commission also observed tendencies to rough handling from alcohol and marijuana, particularly the former, and slower speeds from marijuana.

> The major changes took place in tests immediately after smoking or drinking. Four female and twelve male drivers taking placebos averaged thirteen hits per lap. In the alcohol or higher cannabis condition, the average number of hits rose to seventeen. Three hours later, the number of each decreased to near normal and handling and speed were normal.
>
> The Clyde Mood Scale indicated a decrease in clear thinking as a result of alcohol and the higher dose of cannabis.
>
> The commission was vague as to the subjects' experience with marijuana, but apparently most were familiar with it.
>
> The marijuana doses gave 21 and 88 micrograms of THC per kilogram of body weight. The ethanol dose produced an average blood level of 0.07 percent, described as the equivalent of three cocktails.
>
> In three other experiments by the commission:
>
> • Alcohol and the upper cannabis dose resulted in substantial increases in error scores by twenty-two male subjects using a tracking device.

• Twenty physical, mental, and subjective tests on fourteen male subjects uncovered no qualitative or quantitative differences between marijuana and pure THC.

• Marijuana made five male subjects less accurate in identifying a visual signal (a brief outage of a light). The commission interpreted the effect as a decrease in attention. It correlated with feelings of "highness." [22]

A drinker downs two or three cocktails. The alcohol in his blood remains within the legal range. Now what happens if he takes a drug on top of it and gets behind the wheel of a car?

To get the answer, the Insurance Bureau of Canada commissioned two experiments in Ontario in 1973. It publicized them heavily.

Each of sixteen medical students took marijuana or a medicinal pill together with screwdriver cocktails—just enough alcohol to bring the blood level to 0.06 percent (below the legal maximum). The first experiment measured reactions on a tracking machine. The second used a car equipped with special instruments and a computer to score drivers' performances on 8.5 miles of highway (a new road, not yet open to the public, with traffic lights, oncoming cars, and a half-mile of obstacle cones added).

On the tracking device, alcohol at a blood concentration of 0.06 percent (a legal level) plus smoked marijuana caused more impairment than did alcohol alone at 0.10 percent (an illegal level). The same was true for combinations of alcohol and antihistamine, tranquilizer, or sedative.

In the actual driving, the combination of alcohol and marijuana produced extremes in all five measures of performance: the slowest reaction to a traffic light, the least accurate stopping, the most oversteering, the slowest speed, and the worst scores in the obstacle course. The other drug categories were alcohol alone, alcohol with tranquilizer, and alcohol with antihistamine.

Compared with placebo (orange juice, sugar pills, or marijuana without THC), all treatments increased total response time on a Stressalyzer. A subject tested on this device aligns a pointer over a target by moving a steering wheel. These are maximum percentages of increase, in ascending order: alcohol plus codeine (painkiller or cough medicine, 30 mg), 12 percent; alcohol alone (at 0.06 percent level), 12 percent; alcohol alone (at 0.10 percent level), 14 percent; alcohol plus diphenhydramine (antihistamine, 50 mg), 16 percent; alcohol plus cannabis (three half-gram cigarettes, 1 percent THC), 16 percent; alcohol plus diazepam (tranquilizer, 5 mg), 17 percent; and alcohol plus phenobarbital (sedative, 32 mg), 18 percent.

In the real-driving experiment, codeine and phenobarbital were not used. Computer failure lost half of the obstacle scores, but all of the other scores represented statistically significant changes from the subjects' performances under placebos.

Eight subjects participated in each experiment, all males except for two women in the driving tests. All had used marijuana in the past. The subjects in the tracking tests were described as drug-free at the time of the experiment as verified by urine screening. Nucro-Technics Laboratories of Scarborough, Ontario, conducted the research, the first part in Toronto and the second part in Ottawa. The legal alcohol blood level there was 0.08 percent.

Two separate teams conducted the two experiments, and their reports contrasted in tone. In reporting on the tracking experiment, R. Burford et al. concluded: "These levels of impairment are clear threats to automotive safety. Greater attempts must be made to inform the public and government agencies . . . that meaningful interactions occur at such low levels of pharmacological intervention." In a report on the real-driving experiment, hardly going out on a limb, Alison Smiley et al. said: "The results of this experiment show that alcohol alone and in combination with other drugs affects driving performance in different ways. . . . Further research in this area will be needed before the manner in which driving behaviour is affected by a drug can be related to the physiological action of that drug."[23]

In Vancouver, Canada, stoned men and women drove about seventeen miles along city streets during peak traffic. It was an experiment, of course. An examiner sat in the front seat and watched. The subjects were tested also on a traffic-free driving course.

Each subject was scored on driving ability before and after smoking a marijuana cigarette, of lower or higher potency. Scores following the smoking declined for many drivers—as many as three-fifths of the drivers tested on the streets. The stronger cigarette (mild by latter-day standards) brought down more scores than did the weaker.

To psychiatry professor Harry Klonoff, who conducted the study, it was plain that the smoking of marijuana had "a detrimental effect on their driving skills and performances," more so on city streets than in the restricted driving area.

On the streets, marijuana caused major deterioration in judgment, care, and concentration. Intoxicated drivers missed traffic lights and stop signs, passed other vehicles without exercising caution, dealt poorly with traffic, and ignored pedestrians and stopped cars.

A number of drivers apparently had the "capacity to compensate," especially after the weaker dose. Thus some drivers' scores remained essentially unchanged and the scores of a few even improved.

Subjects on the course numbered sixty-four, of whom thirty-eight also drove in the street tests. All had used marijuana occasionally.

The design of the experiments aimed to minimize the danger through the professional screening of drivers, observers in the cars, dual controls (which needed to be used three times on the streets), and so on. Klonoff (1974) pointed out other common conditions, not built into the experiment, that might have worsened the results, such as higher doses, fast speeds, and the use of alcohol in combination with marijuana. Nearly two-thirds of his subjects admitted having driven soon after consuming alcohol in combination with marijuana.

His recommendation: "Driving under the influence of marijuana should be avoided as much as should driving under the influence of alcohol."

Following are results by percentage (and number) of drivers:
Course:
Decline—low, 33% (7); high, 55% (12).
No change—low, 43% (9); high, 31% (7).
Improvement—low, 24% (5); high, 14% (3).
Streets:
Decline—low, 42% (8); high, 63% (12).
No change—low, 26% (5); high, 21% (4).
Improvement—low, 32% (6); high, 16% (3).

Each active marijuana cigarette weighed 0.7 of a gram and contained 0.7 percent or 1.2 percent of THC.

On the course, forty-three men and twenty-one women had to negotiate a zig-zag obstacle route, back up, turn a corner, stop suddenly on cue, and go through (or around, if the car did not fit) tunnels simulated by cones. A subject ran the course twenty times, smoking marijuana or placebo once before the last five runs. The scoring allowed for normal improvement from learning during practice runs.

Accordingly, mean scores on the course worsened 29 percent for the low-dose drivers and 54 percent for high-dose drivers.

Thirteen women and twenty-five men took the street test, 16.8 miles, basically the official driving test for the Province of British Columbia, in an average of forty-six minutes. Each had two weekday, daylight trials (a week apart), smoking placebo before one and active marijuana before the other.

The experiments also monitored heart rate (through cardiograph transmitters). The mean rate during sobriety was one-quarter higher on the course than on the streets, and marijuana increased each group's rate one-quarter.

Ages of the sixty-four volunteers ranged from nineteen to thirty-one. The subjects were relatively well educated and averaged seven years of driving experience.[24] All used marijuana infrequently at modest doses, took hardly any other drugs, and were "reasonably well integrated emotionally," said a letter (1982) from Dr. Klonoff, Ph.D., head of The University of British Columbia's psychology divison.

3

Accidents Will Happen

Few students of the subject of intoxicants and traffic safety now doubt that marijuana, like alcohol, can exert detrimental influence. Just how detrimental is debatable. The debate pits optimists ("it's much less of a problem than alcohol") versus those on the pessimistic side ("but who needs any new problems?").

Yet there can be no question that some drivers who met their ends on the highway would be alive were it not for marijuana.

At 4:10 one morning, a divorcée of twenty-five, dressed only in see-through pajamas, went driving in the rain on a major Florida highway. Her car left the road and rolled over, killing her. On her record were three traffic convictions. Blood alcohol was negative. An investigator recognized a strong smell of marijuana in her apartment, and the manager had seen her "higher than a kite" (presumably not long before the accident).[25]

This lone anecdote may not prove any case. But the studies that we now will describe, most of them based on chemical test evidence, link cannabis to a fourth of some 2,300 drivers in fatal and nonfatal accidents.

As 267 motor vehicles took the lives of drivers, passengers, or pedestrians in the Boston area during a 2½-year period (1971–74), a five-man study team of Boston University's law school investigated the marijuana usage of the driver "most responsible" for each accident. Interviews and records divulged that 121 of the drivers—45 percent—smoked marijuana and that 43—16 percent—had been under its influence at the time of the accident. Thirteen of the 43 had taken just marijuana within four hours of the accident; the remaining 30 had taken marijuana with alcohol—or, in five of the cases, marijuana with alcohol and another drug. The 30 were among 122—46 percent—under alcoholic influence.

The 267 drivers had a third higher percentage of marijuana smokers than a "control sample" of 801 Boston area drivers, which the team assembled at random and interviewed during the next two years. In each group, the marijuana smoker was more likely than the nonsmoker to drink alcohol often, to be a problem drinker, to have been treated for a psychological problem, and to have made a suicide attempt.

Most of the marijuana smokers among the "controls" (all but thirty) answered questions on their reactions to marijuana intoxication. The majority found it *easier* when high "to make foolish or impulsive decisions" (while driving), 76 percent; and "to be distracted" (from driving), 65 percent. Further, the majority found it *harder* when high "to make sudden physical movements" (such as braking or turning), 74 percent; "to remember things" (such as car instruments or road directions), 73 percent; "to make sudden decisions" (for instance, in response to traffic lights or danger), 71 percent; and "to concentrate on a job or project" (like a driving task), 60 percent. Fifty-four percent considered it more difficult to drive during marijuana intoxication than during sobriety; 38 percent saw no difference; and 8 percent said driving during intoxication was easier.

> Of the 801 drivers, 34 percent (272) smoked marijuana. These controls, never involved in a fatal motor vehicle accident, approximately matched the 267 drivers in place of residence; age, nearly all being under forty; and sex. Women made up 9 percent of smokers and 11 percent of nonsmokers among the 267.
>
> In a report to the sponsoring National Highway Traffic Safety Administration, the authors, Sterling-Smith and Graham, tended to be statistically conservative. For instance, they did not rank with the 43 marijuana-influenced "most responsible" drivers 18 other drivers suspected of being under the influence. Moreover, although 19 (7 percent) of the 267 and 49 (6 percent) of the 801 had used marijuana once or twice in the past year, they entered the nonsmoking columns. Most smokers in each group used marijuana weekly or more often.[26]

When he was a medical corps officer in the U.S. Army, Europe (1968–72), Forest S. Tennant, Jr., "saw many [motor vehicle] accidents that appeared to be related to hashish consumption." Most of the mishaps were minor, Dr. Tennant, from Los Angeles, testified before a Senate committee (1974), but these were two tragic cases from his files:

"1. K.S., under the influence of hashish, drove his motorbike under a truck and decapitated himself. His roommate said he made a usual practice of smoking hashish while riding his motorbike.

"2. A 2½-ton truck carrying several soldiers drove over a cliff while attempting to make a turn. Eight soldiers were killed. My investigation revealed, via information from soldiers who were not killed, that the driver smoked two pipe-bowls of hashish about one hour before driving."[27]

*　*　*

Coroners and medical examiners throughout the United States sent specimens of blood, urine, bile, and swabs from 710 fatally injured drivers to the Midwest Research Institute in Kansas City, Missouri. There

E. J. Woodhouse (1974) analyzed them for forty-four commonly abused drugs by a variety of methods.

A test for contact with marijuana gave positive responses for 38 percent of the cases. That is, close to two out of every five drivers had handled the drug and presumably used it. The test examined the alcoholic washes of face and fingers (by thin-layer chromatographic and colorimetric methods). According to other tests, 58 percent of the drivers had drunk alcohol, 47 percent to the point of being legally drunk, and 13 percent were on prescription drugs.[28]

* * *

Kier in Colorado (1974) studied a dozen consecutive motorists injured in one-vehicle accidents and admitted to the emergency room at Denver General Hospital. From the test of lips and hands that he had devised, five showed signs of marijuana (one of them with an opiate), six showed alcohol, and one showed opiate (alone).[29]

* * *

On an English highway one afternoon in 1975, a nineteen-year-old driver of an MG, evidently crossing double white lines while passing, crashed head on into a truck. He was killed; the truck driver was unhurt. Inspection of the car revealed packets of cannabis leaf and a special smoking pipe beneath the seat. A postmortem examination showed no evidence of disease and no alcohol in blood or urine. Tested by a new English method, both fluids showed an exceedingly high concentration of THC and metabolites. The coroner recorded a verdict of accidental death. The victim had been a railway signalman.

"Cannabis, like alcohol, produces euphoria and impairs judgment. There can be little doubt, therefore, that it contributed to the accident in the present case," wrote J. D. Teale and colleague (1976).

"Its current social acceptability and ease of use makes cannabis, as the present case exemplifies, a potentially dangerous drug, not only to those actually using it, but to others as well. This is emphasised by the victim's occupation as a railway signalman."

Sixty-six more blood specimens from fatally injured motorists (fifty-four car drivers and twelve motorcyclists) arrived in 1976 and 1977 at the University of Surrey's biochemistry department, mostly from coroners in England and Wales. Six of the sixty-six—9 percent—contained cannabinoids. (Three of these samples came from car drivers and three from motorcyclists.) Only one of the six contained alcohol. Teale and five others (1977) claimed a method "permitting the rapid routine screening of samples." That, together with another method (high-pressure liquid chromatography), gave specific THC measurements, they said.

In one of the cases, a twenty-year-old male fell off a motorcycle and was run over by a following car. The victim carried cannabis in a pocket. At about 8:30 P.M., half an hour after the accident, a blood sample was obtained. It showed no alcohol or other drug but did contain rather low levels of cannabinoid. The Teale group found it "difficult to relate" a THC-cannabinoid level "with a degree of intoxication" without knowing the time and amount smoked.[30]

☆   ☆   ☆

A dozen teenagers, fourteen to nineteen, were riding in a fast-moving compact pickup truck on a winding country road near Crofton, Maryland, bound for a party at Patuxent River Park on the evening of April 23, 1979. The truck, a 1978 Ford Courier, was speeding far past the limit of twenty-five miles per hour. Passengers yelled to its eighteen-year-old driver to "slow down!"

At about 9:15, approximately a mile from their destination, the vehicle missed a left curve. It skidded, careened on its two right wheels, sideswiped three trees about seven feet from the pavement, and rolled over, ending upside down on the road.

The accident took the lives of ten of the riders, killing seven of them instantly. One passenger suffered serious injury but survived. The driver-owner was only slightly injured. Seven of the victims had been riding in the rear (including the one surviving passenger) and three in the cab.

Behind the wheel was an uninsured young man, a carpet cutter, a high school dropout with "family problems" who periodically stayed away from home for several days. He had been cited for speeding a year earlier. On the day of the accident, he said, he loitered around a bowling alley on the Fort Meade military base and drank four beers.

He admitted being a user of marijuana, PCP, and cocaine but claimed to have last used any of these, marijuana, the night before. However, five teenaged witnesses saw him smoking marijuana at various times and in varying amounts on the day of the accident. Their statements proved that he had smoked "an appreciable amount of marijuana" that day, the National Transportation Safety Board reported. He took a blood test but no analysis was performed for cannabis. (The alcohol content of his blood was 0.06 percent five hours after the accident. At the time of the accident, it probably had been below the 0.15 percent level at which Maryland law deemed a driver "intoxicated" but above the 0.10 percent mark of most other states.) The safety board did not determine exactly how the marijuana affected this driver but commented, citing scientific literature, "it is known that high risk-taking behavior is frequently associated with alcohol and marijuana intake."

The board found the probable cause of the disaster to be "high speed, reckless driving of a vehicle by a driver who was under the influence of alcohol and marijuana." Investigators had estimated from scuff marks that the truck had been going between sixty-four and seventy-eight miles per hour. The fact that passengers rode in the open bed contributed to the tragic consequences, the board added. Its report went to high school driver-education instructors throughout the country. This was the first accident that the board ever blamed, at least in part, on marijuana.[31]

"I would consider it an emerging and increasing problem," John Keryeski, investigator in charge of the accident, said to us. Alcohol used to be the single substance problem in traffic safety and still remains the most important, he said. "But recent research indicates that there is an increasing problem of drug use in accidents."

The driver? Convicted on ten counts of manslaughter, he received a sentence of probation, community service, and a suspended license.

*   *   *

A car moving rather speedily left the road and hit a tree in North Carolina, killing the vehicle's sole occupant. Analysis of a blood sample (by a new method developed in that state) eliminated the possibility of alcohol but indicated that the driver had used cannabis shortly before the accident. He became one of 340 victims of fatal one-car crashes tested for THC over a two-year period (1978–80) by the state's Office of the Chief Medical Examiner and the University of North Carolina's pathology department.

But few of the cases showed the influence of marijuana so clearly. Six percent of the 340 samples contained THC; that is, at least twenty-one of the drivers had smoked marijuana (or taken cannabis in another form) shortly before their accidents. Of these, fifteen also had an illegal level of alcohol in their blood (0.10 percent or more); three showed a little alcohol; and the other three (including the car-tree accident victim) had no alcohol at all. Blood of two-thirds of the 340 killed (or surviving less than an hour) contained alcohol in excess of the legal limit.[32]

*   *   *

Testing for ninety drugs, public and private investigators examined 401 drivers and 83 pedestrians fatally injured in traffic accidents in Ontario, Canada, during a twelve-month period (1978–79). They detected thirty-four drugs (not counting alcohol), of which cannabis was the most common. Twelve percent of the victims evidenced cannabinoids in urine or blood. Next came salicylate (7 percent), diazepam (3 percent), and codeine (2 percent). Cannabis users included 48 drivers and 11 pedestrians, with only one female in each category. Of these 59 victims, 41 had also drunk alcohol, 17 showed only cannabinoids, and just one had cannabinoids in combination with drugs other than alcohol (codeine and diphenydramine).

The investigators expressed concern that cannabis might be a threat to traffic safety, particularly in combination with alcohol.

The Traffic Injury Research Foundation of Canada, in Ottawa, and the provincial government of Ontario, in Toronto (Centre of Forensic Sciences and Office of the Chief Coroner), jointly made the investigation, financed by Research on Drug Abuse, Health and Welfare Canada. Limited to drivers and pedestrians over thirteen who died within an hour after impact and could supply both blood and urine specimens, the study included about a third of a year's total of traffic deaths in Ontario.

The rate of cannabinoid detection was nearly the same for both the (48) drivers and (11) pedestrians. The ages of these victims ranged from fifteen to forty-two, averaging twenty-two. They included 46 percent of the 129 victims with drugs (not counting alcohol). Cannabinoids could be detected in blood (as well as urine) in only 16 of the 59 cases. In the remaining 43 cases, signs of cannabis appeared only in the urine.

Toxicologist George Cimbura et al. commented (1980): "It is unlikely that behavioural impairment from the use of cannabis existed in these victims [the forty-three] at the time of the crash. This reduced the proportion of cases with potential cannabis impairment to 3%, sufficient, however, to justify some concern."

They seemed to be most conservative in this assessment. In a preliminary experiment (by Cimbura et al., 1979) in which ten subjects each smoked four marijuana cigarettes, blood levels of THC (which never rose high and could not be detected in one case) were disappearing two hours after smoking. Many marijuana smokers remain high considerably longer than two hours.

Fifty-five percent of the victims were found to have consumed alcohol. Alcohol alone was found in 41 percent; and alcohol combined with drugs, 14 percent. Twelve percent of the victims showed drugs without alcohol.

Pointing out that in fourteen of the sixteen cases where THC appeared in blood the victims had also drunk alcohol, the authors of the report declared that "the issue of cannabis-alcohol interactions would seem to be of substantial importance, both for future research as well as for traffic safety in general."

While they could not establish direct causality, they concluded that "there is still cause for concern that drugs may represent a threat to traffic safety. Of particular concern are cannabis and diazepam [Valium] which were found with sufficient frequency to warrant study on a priority basis."[33]

According to writer Peggy Mann (1983), over seventy research studies have shown the driver-impairing effects of marijuana.[34]

In a 22-minute documentary film, "Danger Ahead: Marijuana on the Road," with Jason Robards (produced by the National Association of Independent Insurers, 1981), a young man says: "I have been in person-ally, what I can remember, six different auto accidents because we were too stoned to know what we were doing, and there was one in particular where we had sideswiped a car and it ran off the road into the ditch and it flipped over and we just kept going. It scared us, you know, and we just flew, and we found out later that the lady was hospitalized for quite a few weeks and everything. It was just all a big joke to us."

Pictured in a wheelchair in the same film, a young woman describes a party and its aftermath. ". . . It was out in the country. . . . There was a lot of pot—just all kinds of pot. A guy was . . . dealing it out. . . . I got so loaded that I don't remember too much of it. . . . I was in my own world. The next thing I knew . . . we were on motorcycles. I was with a friend. . . . We were holding hands . . . and we came to a corner . . . right in front of a light. . . . We were supposed to be going thirty-five miles and we were going seventy. . . . He went off one way and I went off another way into the field. They say that he will never walk again. I was lucky that I have a fifty-fifty chance. . . . I almost died four times. I didn't realize what was going on for two weeks—I was in a coma. Now that I look back through it all, I think, 'Why was I ever so stupid?' "

4

California's Quest

Using a new test based on a goat serum, the State of California analyzed blood samples of 1,792 drivers for the presence of THC during an ex-perimental project (1976–79). The samples came from motorists whom the California Highway Patrol had stopped because of aberrant driving or had found to be involved in accidents. Ages averaged thirty-two and ranged from fourteen to eighty-eight. Six out of seven were males.

The results of the survey suggested that at least 15 percent of "im-paired" operators on California's highways possessed THC in their sys-tems. They had smoked marijuana either by itself or, more often, in combination with alcohol or other drugs. All of such drivers in the sur-vey flunked a standard roadside sobriety test (except for accident victims not given the test).

California justice officials described the project as the first in which a large number of impaired drivers were chemically tested for THC. They pointed out that the resulting figures could be considered quite conservative (for reasons we will go into shortly). Thousands of statistics came out of the study; we present just a few.

Fifteen percent of drivers with more than the legal limit of alcohol also exhibited THC. (Nine of every ten blood samples secured throughout the state by highway patrolmen evidenced excessive alcohol.) Of drivers in the study who did not violate the alcoholic limit, 17 percent showed THC. Less than a fifth of the below-limit drivers had no alcohol at all, and 24 percent of these had THC. An eighth of drivers in fatal accidents (4 of 32) and a seventh of drivers in nonfatal accidents (70 of 508) displayed THC.

The arrests and accidents occurred in forty-one of California's fifty-eight counties, and the incidence of THC by county varied from 7 percent in Butte County to 38 percent in Calaveras County. They did not generally include the populous Los Angeles and San Francisco areas (the latter being the birthplace of the hippie movement and the marijuana surge of the sixties).

"The lack of a testing procedure has allowed the marijuana user freedom to drive while under the influence of marijuana, thereby creating a potential traffic safety problem," said a report of the California Department of Justice (which conducted the study for the National Highway Traffic Safety Administration of the U.S. Department of Transportation). "Other studies have proven that marijuana impairment while driving does occur and is dangerous. . . .

"It's been very clearly established that marijuana impairs a wide variety of functions that are important with respect to safe driving and this impairment occurs at low delta-9-THC levels." Without reliable enforcement, driving while under the influence of marijuana will "probably increase as the drug becomes more widespread in its use."

The majority of motorists arrested for alcoholic driving are convicted, largely because of chemical tests, but fewer drug-driving arrests hold up in court, because of the lack of supporting laboratory evidence. For example, in California from 1978 through 1980, two out of every three motorists charged with driving under the influence of alcohol were convicted, but only two out of every five charged with driving under the influence of a drug were convicted (based on statistics of the California Department of Motor Vehicles, including both misdemeanors and felonies).

Accompanying the large-scale study was an experiment to relate blood levels of THC, policemen's ratings of subjects on sobriety tests, and the subjects' evaluations of their own fitness. It was part of an effort by the state justice department to design a prototype for a program of mass marijuana detection.

In the city of Palo Alto, fifty-eight paid volunteers smoked marijuana. At intervals they yielded blood samples and uniformed officers of the California Highway Patrol gave the roadside sobriety tests. The tests require standing on one foot, reciting the alphabet, touching index finger to nose without looking, and so on.

The experiment linked THC with "significant driving impairment" and proved the drug takers to be poor judges of this impairment. Except at the start, most subjects thought themselves more capable of driving than the sobriety tests or blood analyses indicated.

Five minutes after smoking ended, nearly all of the stoned subjects admitted that they were in no condition to drive, and patrolmen agreed. Half an hour after smoking, about a fifth of them evaluated themselves as fit to drive, but none passed the sobriety tests, while less than a third of the subjects had negative blood analyses (no THC). Two hours later, all but three considered themselves fit for driving, but only two out of every five passed the sobriety tests, while the blood of two-thirds was negative. In other words, though hardly any subjects felt weakened in their mental faculties two-and-one-half hours after smoking, the patrolmen rated the majority as so impaired in mental ability that they would be dangerous on the road. By this time, however, the blood test no longer detected the THC in many of these impaired subjects. (See figure 1.)

During the large-scale study too, it often happened that a driver would fail the roadside sobriety test but the blood test would not pick up THC or alcohol. At the same time, the driver might admit smoking marijuana or the officer might find it on him. This may explain the paradox: THC declines rapidly in the blood, quickly going to the brain and elsewhere in the body; by the time the officer can get the suspect a blood test, the THC may have dropped below the measurable level. The method of analysis used, though practical and inexpensive, was not ultrasensitive. So a driver in whom it did measure THC may have taken a high dose, perhaps a relatively short time before the testing.

Add to this the facts that only about two of every five arrested in the state agreed to give a blood sample and that tens of thousands of traffic accidents of unknown origin occur annually in California alone—and you can reasonably assume that marijuana plays a greater part in the impairment of drivers than the study indicated.

California has one-tenth of the nation's licensed drivers, yet in one year it made three-tenths of the total impaired-driving arrests in the country (266,000 out of 887,000 in 1976 for driving while intoxicated from alcohol or drugs or for reckless driving). If the 15 percent figure applied, about 40,000 arrested drivers in California were driving at least partly under the influence of marijuana. The 1,792 samples included 540 drivers in accidents, of whom 14 percent showed THC. (In some cases, patrolmen submitted samples of more than one driver in an accident.)

In that year 18 people in California died and 1,368 were injured in accidents attributed to drugs (without alcohol) while 478 died and 18,975 were injured in accidents of unknown origin. The unknown-origin figures represented respectively 11 and 7 percent of all traffic deaths and traffic injuries in the state for the year. In a health department report (1977) Epstein speculated that "some percentage of fatal and injury accidents of unknown origins could be related to psychoactive drug use." [35]

A curious statistic (reported to us by the driving study's principal investigator) tends to support this statement. Arrests in the state in 1977 included about 7,000 for reckless driving, but the year saw about ten times as many convictions on that charge. Many of the convictions for reckless driving represent drivers arrested on

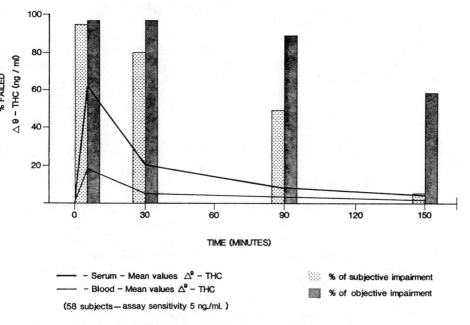

TIME (MINUTES)

——— – Serum – Mean values Δ^9 – THC   ⋯ % of subjective impairment
——— – Blood – Mean values Δ^9 – THC   ▓ % of objective impairment
(58 subjects — assay sensitivity 5 ng./ml.)

Figure 1. Impairment of Drivers and THC Blood Levels

This combination of graphs illustrates the impairment of 58 subjects by marijuana as well as the blood levels of THC in those subjects, all drivers, at Palo Alto, California. The light gray bars represent the percentages of subjects who felt impaired 5, 30, 90, and 150 minutes after completion of smoking. The dark gray bars represent the percentages that state patrolmen found to be unfit to drive at those same times. The lines symbolize the concentrations of THC in blood serum (heavy line) and in whole blood (thin line) at the same times, as measured by the Los Angeles radioimmune assay of Gross et al. using hydrogen-3 and goat serum. (Reprinted, with permission, from the *Journal of Forensic Sciences*, vol. 28, no. 4, October, 1983. Copyright, ASTM, 1916 Race St., Philadelphia, PA 19103.)

suspicion of drunken driving; when little or no alcohol shows up in analyses, prosecutors reduce the charges in plea bargains.

Of a year's blood samples secured by highway patrolmen at hospitals or clinics, about nine-tenths had alcohol above the legal limit, and the study randomly surveyed 765 of them; the remaining 1,027 comprised all of the available samples from drivers with less alcohol than the limit. (The 15 percent figure representing the impaired motorists with THC is weighted in accord with the makeup of the sample.) Those with no alcohol at all numbered 185.

The California Highway Patrol administered sobriety tests to 1,385 of the motorists (omitting 407 accident victims but including 31 others in accidents). Only four drivers, none with THC, passed the sobriety tests.

The study omitted city jurisdictions, which have their own procedures, and omitted breath and urine samples. A motorist whom an officer arrests on suspicion of driving under alcoholic influence must take a test or lose his license for six months but can choose the type of test. A state law, effective in 1982, makes an alcohol level of 0.1 percent or above firm proof of intoxication, instead of just a presumption that the defendant could counter by other evidence.

The experiment on fifty-eight subjects, male and female, young and middle-aged, was designed by Dr. Leo E. Hollister, who conducted it in 1978 at the Veterans Administration Hospital in Palo Alto. They smoked ad lib, the majority stopping at one cigarette (18 mg of THC). They were asked periodically how stoned they felt and whether they considered themselves fit to drive. Meanwhile, patrolmen gave sobriety tests and decided whether each was under the influence of the drug. At five minutes and thirty minutes after the completion of smoking, the officers rated all of the subjects but one as impaired. (He said he never inhaled the smoke and did not become high.)

Five minutes after smoking, the mean THC level stood at 62 ng/ml in serum or 18 ng/ml in blood. In the large study the mean level in blood was 9 ng/ml.

The figures are expressed in nanograms (U.S. billionths—1,000,000,000ths— of a gram) per milliliter (thousandth of a liter).

The concentration of THC is greater in serum than in whole blood because serum excludes the red blood cells, which THC does not enter.

The principal investigator was Victor C. Reeve, managing criminalist in the Forensic Services Bureau, Division of Law Enforcement, California Department of Justice, Sacramento. Robert W. Drake, bureau chief, was the project director, and Stanley J. Gross, M.D., director of the Radioimmunoassay Laboratory, White Memorial Hospital, Los Angeles, was a coworker.

Once aware of the goat-serum method, a radioimmune assay developed by Dr. Gross and associates, the state officials checked it against the established method, gas chromatography/mass spectrometry, at laboratories in Ohio and Missouri. The methods correlated except that at low levels the Los Angeles assay sometimes gave false positives and negatives, according to Reeve. He presumed the threshold of accurate measurement to be 5 ng/ml.

Associated Press in Los Angeles (1977) quoted researchers as announcing the first practical test for measuring the level of marijuana in the blood. James R. Soares of Los Angeles said, "At the moment, it's a test that has to be done in the lab, but it's one that conceivably could be refined into a roadside test. . . . It'll tell you how much is in the bloodstream, and allows easy processing of large numbers of samples." Reeve then said that the technique was "quantitative and quite specific, but it's still in the pioneering stages" and not usable in courts.

The "Executive Summary" of the California study also sounded optimistic, describing "a specific, sensitive and inexpensive test capable of analyzing a large population of hemolyzed blood samples for THC." [36]

Reeve indicated to us, however, that the high hopes had not wholly materialized. Because of the test's lack of total accuracy at low levels, it cannot alone serve as legal evidence. "At least two independent analytical methods are required. Radioimmunoassay screens promising samples for delta-9-THC and gas chromatography/mass spectrometry confirms the presence and level of delta-9-THC."

Laws against drugged driving go largely unenforced. This will continue to be the case, it appears, until cannabis tests join the routine alcohol tests used by law enforcement agencies. A policeman may sniff a marijuana smoker and watch him fail a sobriety test, but convincing a court requires positive evidence that the driver took a drug and drove while under its influence.

Cannabis's nature raises special problems. The telltale breath and slurred speech of the drunk are no clues in cannabis detection. And in seeking a chemical aid to enforcement of laws like the California statute that declares, "It is unlawful for any person who is under the influence of any drug to drive a vehicle," researchers have run into a biochemical barrier. Cannabis is unlike alcohol, whose level in the blood closely reflects intoxication. A reading of the blood level of THC, the chief psychoactive ingredient of marijuana, may not reflect the mental state of the user (figure 2).

Jack, a "social" marijuana smoker, lights a joint. Before he finishes "toking," the THC peaks in his blood and he feels the first mental surge. The THC in his blood declines rapidly as Jack's "high" reaches its peak. Within an hour, Jack feels able to drive. But a sobriety test would show otherwise. Much of the drug has permeated his brain as well as other fatty tissues and organs, for THC is highly soluble in fat, unlike water-soluble alcohol, which soon leaves the body.

The THC in Jack's blood dropped very sharply within half an hour after he smoked, continuing to decrease gradually. A few hours after the smoking, the THC has reached quite a low level. For practical purposes Jack may be back to normal. Or he may still be under the influence of the drug. After he feels that he has "come down," to some extent the drug still may be altering his perception, dulling his reflexes, and distorting his judgment. Merely measuring the THC blood level does not indicate what goes on in his brain.

For a month or more, traces of the drug remain in the fatty components of cells, gradually returning to the bloodstream and getting excreted. Even if Jack is not among the few experiencing "flashbacks" or suffering psychotic reactions, the question can be raised as to whether the drug has somewhat dulled the edge of his mental ability during its weeks in the brain. If he smokes often, his brain may never be free of cannabinoid. The character of the cannabinoids ideally calls for a test to measure them in the human brain.

A possible way out of the difficulty emerged from a second California study (1980–84). In a further attempt to advance toward a program for catching drugged drivers through chemical evidence, the state's justice

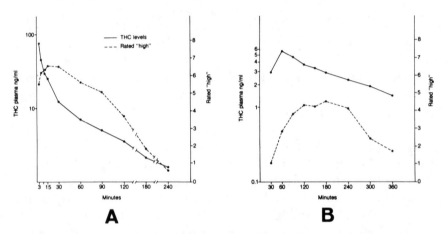

Figure 2. Levels of THC and Intoxication After Smoking and
Ingestion

To what extent does the concentration of THC in the blood reflect the degree of intoxication? And, in those respects, how does smoking differ from ingestion? In a joint American-Swedish study conducted by Dr. Leo E. Hollister, M.D., eleven young male volunteers who all used marijuana (but not for at least 72 hours) had their blood tested and rated their intoxication on a scale of 0 to 10 at the Veterans Administration Hospital at Palo Alto, California. Note that after smoking of marijuana (19 mg of THC) plasma concentration of THC reached a peak within three minutes and then declined rapidly; but the peak "high" came later and declined more slowly (A). After consumption of THC (20 mg) in a chocolate cookie, plasma concentration peaked much lower and later than after smoking and declined relatively gradually, while the "high" took still longer to peak and never quite reached the height associated with smoking but stayed elevated longer (B).

The relation between concentration and intoxication varied in different individuals and even in the same individual at different times. ". . . It seems evident that one will not be able to make the neat correlations between plasma concentrations of THC and intoxication that have been made in the case of alcohol." (Courtesy of *The Journal of Clinical Pharmacology*; published August–September, 1981.)

department conducted a set of experiments involving actual driving by eighty-four young men, paid volunteers. Among notable results, the study shed more light on alcohol-marijuana combinations and looked at a possible way to estimate the time when a suspect smoked marijuana.

The California Highway Patrol Academy near Sacramento was the scene. Most subjects smoked marijuana cigarettes or drank screwdriver cocktails or did both. Those not taking both drugs consumed THC-free marijuana cigarettes or simulated cocktails or both. Then they piloted cars equipped with video cameras and computing devices through skill-testing courses, urban-type streets, and an extended rural drive, as state examiners in the cars made observations. The subjects took sobriety tests and of course had their blood tested.

"The combined effects of marijuana and alcohol produced by far the greatest decrement," said Victor C. Reeve, the principal investigator in this study and the previous one. "The alcohol would tend to remove inhibition. Mixed in with time distortion effects, it led to worse performance." Those given cocktails drank enough to bring their blood levels to 0.06 to 0.08 percent, below the legal limit. Those who smoked marijuana and drank alcohol too generally drove "as though they were substantially over point one percent," the level at which California law presumes a driver to be under the influence.

The alcohol-only and combination groups tended to use the accelerator excessively. The marijuana-only drivers tended to drive slower—except when the speedometers were covered up, when they generally went faster than the alcohol group (the combination group going fastest). With the guidance of the speedometer, the marijuana drivers slowed down consciously. From what the marijuana smokers said, it appeared that the marijuana instilled in some a fear of the people observing them while others wished to demonstrate that their drug was harmless. Drivers taking marijuana alone or on top of alcohol generally became disoriented on an S-curve and would either go off the road or into imaginary oncoming traffic.

While most cars of course are equipped with working speedometers, "With marijuana, I think there is a tendency to let the mind wander. If a person is letting his mind wander when driving, he could easily miss getting the feedback from the speedometer and find himself going at a higher speed than normal," Reeve pointed out. At the opposite extreme is the slow driver, who can still be a reckless driver. "You can be driving slowly but weaving out of your lane onto oncoming traffic, stopping in the middle of the freeway, going slow in the fast lane, going out of control on curves, striking another car and going on your way. . . ." Reeve drew his examples from observations at the closed driving course and documented instances involving driving by marijuana smokers.

When drivers in the study drank and smoked, in most cases the alcohol effect tended to predominate. Sometimes the marijuana effect dominated. Thus the combination group took the longest to complete an obstacle course yet made the most errors.

The second study tried out two similar methods of cannabinoid measurement, adding a more sensitive method from North Carolina to the

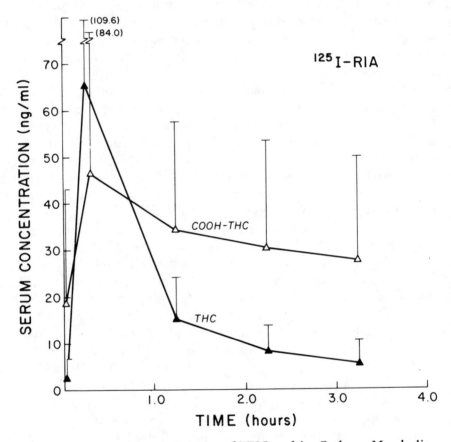

Figure 3. The Diverging Courses of THC and its Carboxy Metabolite

The two sloping lines represent the mean concentrations of THC and its 9-carboxylic acid metabolite (COOH-THC) at intervals in the blood serum of eighty-four subjects following marijuana smoking near Sacramento, California. (The vertical lines indicate ranges.) The ratio of the two compounds may be useful in estimating the time elapsed since smoking. Measurement was by the North Carolina radioimmune assay using iodine-125 and rabbit serum. (Reproduced from the *Journal of Analytical Toxicology* by permission of Preston Publications, Inc.; published March/April, 1983.)

one used in the first study. The latter study also added another compound to be measured: the 9-carboxylic acid metabolite formed out of THC (carboxy for short). The course of carboxy in the blood differs from that of THC. Carboxy peaks at a lower level but declines more gradually. When the THC drops to a level too low to incriminate one, the carboxy will be substantially higher (figure 3). The ratio of carboxy to THC appears related to the elapsed time since smoking. Knowledge that someone smoked marijuana within X hours could someday serve as evidence in court—at least where a suspect's blood contains an amount of alcohol that has not quite exceeded the limit.

The original hope was that this study would present the criminal justice system with a scale for relating blood levels of THC—and THC plus alcohol—with driving impairment, but marijuana displayed its baffling complexities. Reeve commented during our interviews: "It's taken thirty years and hundreds of thousands of documented observations correlated with blood alcohol level to draw the line at point one percent as legally impaired. Now to get to the same state of affairs with a much more complicated drug or mixture of drugs like marijuana, it's going to take some time—and it may never be realized as definitely as with alcohol."

As a start, Reeve came up with this rough rule of thumb. When the carboxy level in plasma is lower than the THC, smoking occurred less than an hour ago. If the carboxy level is a little higher than the THC, smoking was done about an hour ago. And if the carboxy level is four to six times as great as the THC level, it means that two to four hours have passed since the smoking.

Each sample was tested by two radioimmune assays. Samples yielding positive or contradictory findings were retested by a third method: gas chromatography/mass spectrometry. The three methods produced different values for given samples. The assay from Los Angeles used in the previous study gave the lowest readings while a comparable method from North Carolina gave the highest—often four or more times as high as the lowest.

Urine was tested first to make sure the subjects were free of drugs. Three were not and were eliminated from the study, two for taking cocaine and one for taking amphetamine during the driving tests. (Mechanical failure lost more results. The original roster stood at 100.) Subjects were men, aged twenty-one to thirty-five. Each received one of four treatments: three cocktails (alcohol adjusted according to subject's weight) plus placebo marijuana; a marijuana cigarette of 2 percent THC plus a simulated cocktail; alcoholic drinks followed by marijuana; or double placebo. The doses of alcohol and marijuana were chosen to represent "moderate" consumption by contemporary standards.

By the end of 3½ hours of driving tests, a majority of the combination subjects, about half of the alcohol subjects, and a minority of the marijuana subjects were impaired, based on sobriety tests. The duration of the overall impairment surprised Reeve.

Combination subjects, whether fast or slow, usually drove the worst. Going through an obstacle course, for example, the double placebo group finished in the shortest time; then came the alcohol, marijuana, and combination groups, in that order. Placebo had the least errors, marijuana was next best, alcohol was third, and combination had the most errors.

In the extended drive, two miles in length, the alcohol drivers finished first; next and about equal were the marijuana and combination groups, while placebo took the longest. A patrolman following in a car indicated that he would have stopped the placebo, marijuana, alcohol, and combination groups about a seventh, a third, half, and three-fifths of the time, respectively (for going too fast or too slow, weaving, or going off the road). He and other observers did not know to which treatment condition a driver belonged.

The driving experiments were conducted in 1980 and 1981. Statistical evaluation continued into 1984. (First publication in a scientific journal was in 1983. Two journal articles on the previous study followed.)[37]

*   *   *

Soares and Gross (1976), in the anatomy department at the University of California (Los Angeles) School of Medicine, had pointed to the possibility of determining the time of smoking. They gave occasional users marijuana cigarettes and with their new assay separately measured both THC and C-THC (11-nor-9-carboxy-delta-9-THC) in body fluids. They found that plasma and urine C-THC "remains elevated long after delta-9-THC became scant or undetectable."

After one cigarette, THC peaked soon and became almost undetectable an hour or two afterward in plasma; C-THC persisted for several hours. After three consecutive cigarettes, plasma THC faded after four hours but C-THC was going strong after forty-eight hours.

Gross et al. (1978) commented: "Thus, forensically" (with respect to legal proceedings), "the most interesting cannabinoid is delta-9-THC, which persists in blood for a period most likely to correlate with behavioral impairment. Metabolite(s) such as C-THC in the absence of delta-9-THC would point to a nonintoxicated marihuana user. The divergent pattern of delta-9-THC and C-THC in blood might allow assessment of recent versus distant exposure to marihuana."[38]

5

The Development of Chemical Testing

"There is no chemical test for marijuana," a highway patrolman informs us with assurance, and we have heard other law enforcement men say this. If they mean that there is yet no practical, roadside device that can instantly prove a person to be under the influence of cannabis, they are right.

Numerous chemical tests for marijuana do exist, however. Such tests have been around since the sixties, mostly little known outside of scientific circles. The most precise techniques require sophisticated equipment and high skill. While simpler and cheaper methods abound, there is no consensus on the reliability of any that could be used in traffic cases.

The tests serve the functions of (a) detection or (b) measurement, or both. For example, a certain urine test will determine whether a person's system contains any cannabinoid, without saying which one or how much; it may register positive for days or weeks after marijuana smoking. Another kind of test can specifically identify THC or another cannabinoid and measure its concentration in the blood.

Reviewing the scientific literature before 1974, a lecture in Belgium, published in a Yugoslav journal, told of about forty different methods proposed for cannabis detection or measurement. They began with a simple breath test (in which cannabis turned a chemically treated paper blue, but sometimes so did tobacco), included tests of teeth, fingers, and saliva (swabs or mouthwash acting on sheets or solutions), and reached heights of sophisticated instrumention in the measurement of minute amounts of drug in blood plasma.[39]

At first, scientists had relied on radioactively labeled THC—which they supplied—to trace cannabinoids in the human system. Obviously such a technique could serve just for research.

Using a combination of elaborate processes—gas-liquid chromatography and mass spectrometry—and experimenting on three cannabis smokers, a Swedish group announced "the first method to identify and accurately measure non-labelled delta-1-THC [same as delta-9-THC] in the plasma of persons who have smoked cannabis" (Dr. Stig Agurell, of Stockholm's Karolinska Institute, and others, 1973).[40] This method, with refinements, remained the only one universally accepted by scientists at the time of this writing. It can measure minute quantities of THC—sometimes in blood for days after smoking. But it takes a fairly long time, "is very expensive and requires large amounts of blood or urine and is therefore unsuitable for clinical use" (J. D. Teale, 1974).

A North Carolina laboratory, Research Triangle Institute, may rate credit for developing the same process independently at about the same time as the Swedes (even a little earlier when it comes to acid metabolites). Published articles on cannabinoid assays from both labs date to 1970. Monroe E. Wall of the Carolina group says that "three laboratories in the world developed these methodologies more or less simultaneously." The third was that of Raphael Mechoulam at Hebrew University in Israel.

The principle of using antibodies to seek out cannabinoids in bodily fluids entered early in the 1970s, although the use of antibodies in detecting other chemicals began more than a decade earlier.

Scientists at the University of California, Los Angeles, reported (1972) a complicated fluorescent method, which became (1974) "a simple rapid radioimmune assay for delta-9-THC utilizing goat antiserum," (later to be put on the market by Immunalysis Corp., Glendale, California). And a group in Guilford, England, announced (1974) a similar technique of its own. Each "radioimmune assay" combined anticannabinoid serum with a radioactive tracer to detect and measure cannabinoids in blood plasma or urine. ("Radio" refers to radioactivity; "immune" to the immune system, creating antibodies in reaction to specific invading substances; and "assay" to analysis.)

A different kind of cannabinoid-antibody method, Emit (an acronym for "enzyme multiplied immunoassay technique") went into commercial production in 1980. Developed and patented by Syva Company in Palo Alto, California, the test could quickly detect—but not measure— THC metabolites in urine (based on changes in enzyme activity). It was tried out in California prisons, where an official credited it with helping to reduce the use of marijuana. Portable Emit kits were introduced in the armed forces to screen for cannabinoids and played a part in turning the tide there. A competing urine screening kit has been marketed by Collaborative Research in Massachusetts. Roche Diagnostics in New Jersey was reported readying a urine screening test, Agglutex THC, for marketing.[41]

A monograph on the measurement of cannabinoids in humans, issued by the National Institute on Drug Abuse (NIDA) in 1976, contained a dozen papers on pertinent research projects at ten laboratories from Sweden to California. They "delineate the tremendous progress that has been made over the past few years . . . in this difficult area of research," commented the editor, Robert E. Willette of NIDA's research division.

"We have now reached a stage in the search for and development of such methods that many of them can now be employed in a routine manner. . . .

"The road to acceptable methods has been long and arduous. Early attempts continued to suffer from lack of adequate sensitivity. It was eventually learned, as the studies on the composition of marihuana and the metabolism of its constituents progressed, that the problem of detecting any specific cannabinoid in the body after use would be an extremely difficult task."

The rapid distribution and metabolizing of THC made its measurement a major challenge, Willette said.

He placed the methods in three categories: immunoassays (increasingly used, fast, suitable for screening many samples, but often lacking specificity), chromatography (an older technique, applied in new ways to measure low levels of drugs and metabolites) and mass spectroscopy ("the method of choice in terms of sensitivity and specificity" but not ideal for routine screening because of "size, cost, and complexity").[42]

NIDA's then director, Robert L. DuPont, noted in a foreword that investigation of a number of serious social and health problems, the chief one being the effect of marijuana smoking on driving, had awaited refinements in techniques of cannabinoid measurement. "Thus, we can begin to establish specific correlations between cannabinoid levels and driving impairment. This information is necessary in order to build marihuana into the highway safety campaign now largely restricted to alcohol."[43] (Such correlation was still eluding research workers eight years later.)

Declaring in 1977, "The greatest concern I have about this drug—and marijuana is an intoxicating drug—is in its potential effect on automobile accidents in this country," Dr. DuPont announced that "I am placing a priority on the development of a simple marijuana-detection test, similar to those presently used to detect alcohol, which can be used at the site of an accident."[44]

In 1981 members of the anatomy department at the University of California, Los Angeles, School of Medicine reported developing a small device in which police could obtain breath samples of drivers suspected of being under the influence of marijuana. Essentially a plastic box, it could not instantly analyze the samples. In experiments, samples were positive for THC for two hours after a smoke.[45] The device remained in the experimental stage at last check.

*   *   *

The Swedish technique, gas-liquid chromatography and mass spectrometry, could measure levels as low as 0.1 to 2 ng/ml, depending on processing, Agurell et al. reported (1979). They said studies in many laboratories showed that immediately after the smoking of a few milligrams of THC, "plasma levels of 50–200 ng/ml are reached." They drop within an hour to 5–10 ng/ml, in four hours to 1–5 ng/ml, and in twenty-four hours to 1 ng/ml or less.

When Agurell et al. (1976) had three cannabis users each smoke a cigarette containing 10 mg of THC, the peak levels appeared to be 19–26 ng/ml, reached in about ten minutes.

There appears to be "a good relation" between the high feeling and the THC blood level, Agurell said (1979), but "some psychomotor functions are affected longer than the plasma levels would indicate."

In addition to use in legal cases, he wrote, plasma-level determinations may be important for clinical diagnosis of cannabis intoxication, study of drug interaction, and safety if THC is used medically. And "Since cannabis has effects on time perception and short-time memory, and has been implicated as a cause of road traffic accidents," epidemiological studies of drivers would also be important. For such studies (but not for legal purposes) urine screening with less specific methods would be enough.[46]

*   *   *

Dr. Wall, vice-president for chemistry and life sciences at Research Triangle Institute, Triangle Park, North Carolina, stressed the absence of a direct correlation between measurable levels of THC and degrees of intoxication, when we conversed with him:

"Within five minutes after you smoke a standard reefer, your blood level will be at a maximum and, depending on the potency of the reefer, whether you're an experienced smoker, and how deep you inhale—all these variables—you could have one hundred to two hundred nanograms per milliliter in the blood at that point.

"However, the intoxication level lasts about three hours after that, so a person can be high but the blood level by that point will be down to four or five nanograms per milliliter. There is not a direct correlation between the level of delta-9 and the degree of intoxication."

Wall, also an adjunct professor at the medical school of the University of North Carolina, referred to experiments he had done with animals.

"In rats, for example, it turns out that the parent drug goes into the brain early, within a few minutes after you inject into the tail vein of a rat. And then it stays at a constant level in the brain for several hours before dropping off. It stays up at that constant level, but if you analyze the blood of the rat, you'll see it's down to a low level and yet, you see, it stayed at a constant level up in the brain.

"I don't believe that an analysis can give you any reliable indication of the degree of intoxication unless you've got it at a fairly early stage."

*   *   *

In 1967 da Silva, in a Brazilian university publication, claimed a "very efficient" verification of cannabis inhalation in blood, saliva, and urine of both "addicts and individuals exposed to an atmosphere contaminated by smoke from the drug." But other chemists have tried and failed to confirm his work.[47]

*   *   *

Hollister et al. (1972) administered oral doses of THC to human subjects in Palo Alto, California, and for four days afterward recovered from their urine an undetermined amount of what appeared to be cannabinoids. They found no pure THC. They used the processes of thin-layer chromatography, gas-liquid chromatography, and mass spectrometry.[48]

*   *   *

The chromatography isolates each chemical compound and the mass spectrometry identifies each.

Essentially chromatography is a process of separating compounds by allowing a mixture of them to seep through an absorbent substance. Diffusing at different rates, the compounds can then be collected individually.

Once each compound is separated, the mass spectrometer comes into play. Accelerating the molecules through an electromagnetic field, it fragments them into charged particles and separates these according to mass. By either visual analysis of the fragmentation pattern or computer reconstruction, the experienced operator determines the molecular formula of the compound.

*   *   *

In the THC test of Kier Laboratories in Denver, the lips and hands of a subject, alive or not, are swabbed with a cotton-tipped stick. Chemical treatment and processing by thin-layer chromatography produce a pink spot on a special strip if results are positive.

If lips show marijuana, then hands are tested. "An ideal positive test" shows a measurable amount of THC from the lips plus a trace of THC on one hand—the right, if the subject is right-handed—but none on the other hand, Lawrence G. Kier said. Subjects who attended "pot parties" but denied smoking "did demonstrate positive tests on lips, right and left hands—all of equal intensity."

Kier tested volunteers, who smoked gram joints of "good grass," immediately after smoking and six, twelve, and twenty-four hours after. Only the immediate and six-hour tests gave positive results.[49]

*   *   *

The Emit Cannabinoid Assay is designed to detect in urine primarily two metabolites of THC (11-nor-delta-9-THC-9-carboxylic acid, and 11-hydroxy-delta-9-THC). Syva Company announced (1980, 1981) that the test could detect 50 ng/ml or more of them 95 percent of the time, did not need a highly skilled technician, and took a minute or (in a portable version) a minute and a half for a reading.

Syva came out with the Emit assays in 1972. Seven types of drug, including opiates and cocaine, could be detected. The company then developed the cannabinoid assay with the aid of a grant from the National Institute on Drug Abuse. Marketing offices for this and other Syva products opened in seven countries besides the United States.

Detection of a drug is based on the level of enzyme activity, which is directly related to the concentration of drug in the urine specimen.

The person testing the urine combines it with (a) antibodies from sheep, (b) cannabinoid molecules coupled with enzyme, (c) chemicals that react in the presence of the enzyme, and (d) water.

The antibodies, being specific for cannabinoids, will immediately bind with any cannabinoid originally present in the specimen as well as with the enzyme-labeled cannabinoid that is added. In effect, the two forms of cannabinoid compete for antibody space.

The enzyme exerts a catalytic action on the added chemicals. It does so even though coupled with the cannabinoid but not when also bound to the antibody. The more cannabinoid originally present in the specimen, the more enzyme is free to act, and hence the greater is the chemical reaction.

A spectrophotometer measures this chemical activity (by the opaqueness of the solution). High activity means the specimen had cannabinoid. (Some test machines indicate a positive or negative result by printing " + " or " − ".)[50]

*   *   *

We summarize the main steps in devising and using a radioimmune assay. The laboratory analyst:

1. Injects an animal with the substance to be assayed (let us say THC).
2. Lets the animal naturally develop specific antibodies (to THC).
3. Bleeds the animal and extracts those antibodies.
4. Combines the antibodies with a radioactive tracer.
5. Mixes them with the human blood (or other fluid) to be tested, letting them bind with any of the suspected substance (THC) in that blood sample.
6. Chemically pulls from the mixture those radioactively tagged antibodies that do not participate in the reaction.
7. Counts the radioactivity (per volume) in the blood sample. The count cor-

responds to the concentration of the substance (THC) in the blood. (Substitute urine, etc., as the case may be.)

*   *   *

The Los Angeles radioimmune assay of Dr. Gross and collaborators, used in the California driver studies, was designed to measure THC or metabolite specifically—in plasma, urine, or saliva—although not in the most minute amounts. The radioactive marker was hydrogen-3 (tritium).[51]

Using a sheep antiserum, J. D. Teale and others in the Division of Clinical Biochemistry at the University of Surrey, England, put together an assay that measured at least 6 ng/ml of THC together with metabolites—in blood or urine—though not THC specifically. They claimed for it considerable sensitivity as well as simplicity and low cost. It too used hydrogen-3.[52]

Then, by use of rabbit antiserum, another hydrogen-3 method to measure cannabinoids in body fluids was devised primarily by Collaborative Research, Inc., Waltham, Massachusetts, with federal support. The company has packaged it as a kit for sale, stating, "This RIA [radioimmune assay] measures as little as 0.3 nanograms of the broad spectrum of cross reacting cannabinoids. Ideally suited to the detection of trace amounts in urine, the Collaborative Research system provides a simple method of large scale screening for THC abuse."[53]

Cooperating groups in North Carolina later developed a rabbit-serum method using iodine-125 as the radioactive marker to measure THC alone or individual metabolites of THC in blood. It was perfected by the North Carolina Office of the Chief Medical Examiner and the University of North Carolina School of Medicine, following work by the Research Triangle Institute.[54] Used in the later State of California study, it measured concentrations in serum down to 2 ng/ml.

*   *   *

Arthur J. McBay, who as chief toxicologist for North Carolina's Office of the Chief Medical Examiner, helped develop his state's radioimmune assay, has been skeptical about talk of cannabic danger. In various writings over the years, he expresses doubt that marijuana is a driving hazard.

McBay points out that THC concentrations in victims' blood are usually small and that most accident victims who smoked marijuana also drank alcohol. He can find almost nothing written on the effects of alcohol-drug combinations on driving but says, "Intuition leads us to believe that the other drugs won't favorably improve the ability of the driver influenced by alcohol." He figures that the state of marijuana intoxication—"relaxation, euphoria . . . altered perception of distance and time, impaired memory of recent events, and impaired physical coordination"—lasts only "about an hour or two." He writes, "No deaths have been attributed to smoking marihuana" and "the drug is relatively safe."[55]

Concerning the small concentration of THC in victims' blood, we note that research, including work by McBay, shows rapid decrease on intoxication. Regarding alcohol, Canadian and California studies indicate a potentiating effect of marijuana. On the duration of intoxication, we refer to the high school survey in which about 45 percent of smokers stayed high more than three hours. As to marijuana's safety, the studies summarized in this section—including one by McBay's office—lead us to the opposite conclusion.

AVIATION
AND
OTHER TRANSPORTATION

※   ※

• "Marijuana smoking is quite widespread in the airline industry. I have a couple of American Airlines pilot friends who smoke it. . . . I had a good friend who was flying for Delta and smoked marijuana. He was killed in an aerobatic accident in Florida. . . . A pretty prominent flying instructor at Oakland airport was killed a few years ago testing a home-built airplane. He used to smoke grass all the time and fly. . . . I'm a former airline pilot. I've flown for three airlines in California. . . . I smoked marijuana heavily for years, five or six times while flying. . . .

"When we flew stoned, depth perception was really altered and it was very hard to concentrate. . . . One time we were coming back from Los Angeles and we'd gotten stoned and the fog came in, and on making the instrument approach in San Francisco, I found that it was very, very hard to maintain my scan pattern on the instruments. I'd start fixating on one instrument and say 'Gee, that's a pretty instrument.' So everything would be fine on that one instrument but everything else was going to hell. After that, my friend and I looked at each other one night and said, 'Hey, this is crazy.' We decided that there was no way that we could effectively fly an aircraft in a safe manner and get stoned. . . .

"I think there's definitely a hangover from marijuana, just kind of a lethargy and sluggishness. If you smoked a lot of grass one night, the next day you're not going to be quite as sharp as if you hadn't. For the next day or two, you just don't think as clearly as if you hadn't been smoking. It's enough to make a difference if you get into a critical situation. . . .

"One afternoon I was coming back from Oregon with friends in a small plane. I was just flying along at about twelve thousand feet and all of a sudden I felt like I had just smoked a joint. I was getting very high and *very confused and I started getting very scared because I didn't know what was happening. I put on the oxygen and that tended to calm me down a bit. . . . I had stopped smoking marijuana months before. . . .*

"I think that it's probably a growing phenomenon, that you're going to have more and more airline pilots these days who have smoked marijuana, just because the young people that they've hired on have been exposed to it. . . . At Trans-West [defunct cargo airline] we had about thirty pilots and copilots and all of them except two smoked grass. Pilots were actively smoking it, not while they were flying, but on their time off and when they were on layover in Salt Lake City or Seattle or Phoenix or something. At Valley [defunct California passenger airline] we had twelve pilots. I'd say at least half smoked marijuana." —Ted (ex-user, except for an occasional puff)

• *"I'm a private pilot. I've owned my own plane. I've done a bit of non-scheduled flying, clandestine trips back and forth from Canada to Mexico, flown a little pot up and down the coast. I've smoked grass since about 1964. I'm a fairly heavy user. I smoke it two or three times a day. . . .*

"I have a lot of friends who smoke grass and fly, but not at the same time. One is in commercial aviation. He's a captain for Western Airlines. He allows eight hours before he's gonna fly. He's more of a social user, one to three times a week. . . .

"I've tried to fly with pot a couple times and I don't recommend it. . . . A couple years ago I took a young lady up at a little country airport in Oregon. We took off at sunset and shared a joint and landed about half an hour later. I was very ill at ease. I couldn't hardly wait to get the thing back on the ground. I had some difficulty landing. It was far down the field, for one thing. I was going a little too fast and I tried to hold the plane down and it bounced up. It was just sloppy handling of the equipment. . . . When you're landing, it's very critical that you have the feel of the aircraft. . . . With grass, you kind of lose your touch a little. . . . You're making the flying job more difficult. . . .

"I think for ten or twelve hours there are slight residual effects. . . . Once I had smoked some sinsemilla bud the night before and got up early next morning and made a flight in my own plane. I was by myself. A couple thousand feet over the Sierra Nevadas in Oregon I got into some really serious turbulence. I got kind of disoriented and kind of paralyzed. The turbulence was so bad that I froze up. I was afraid I would forget something that would kill me. I managed to get down okay and I didn't hurt the plane none, you know, but there were a couple sticky moments. I didn't check my weather like I should have. I got a little loose and care-

less. I feel if I had not been smoking the night before, my mind would have worked better." —Harry (chronic user)

• "*I was really wiped out . . . and tried to do simple mathematic calculations. . . . Going up to fourteen thousand, five hundred . . . I found myself sitting there, looking at the scratch paper, trying to figure out what I was doing. . . .*

"*The thing that was scary to me . . . I would perceive noises different. . . . If I let my mind think about it for a minute, I could fantasize noises that I was used to listening to but they're for some reason sounding different . . . a different vibration in the engine . . . a change in a hum. . . . You're always listening for a different noise you want to correct. You don't want to be taken by surprise up in the air. . . . Marijuana intensified my anxiety. . . .*

"*I know half a dozen pilots that it doesn't bother. . . . They do smoke pot and indulge in other drugs, including alcohol and cocaine, while they're flying. . . . Probably half the pilots I've known in the last six or eight years have smoked pot when they've flown. . . . Four are commercial. . . . They've been in smaller commuter airlines. . . . They've progressed on to other jobs. . . .*

"*I've got a lot to come home to and I feel that will lessen my chances of coming back home.*" —George (chronic user)

• "*I know three men who fly for three separate commercial airlines and they all smoke [marijuana]. . . . They smoke fairly regularly, three or four times a week. I also know an air controller who smokes and I have a couple of friends who are flight attendants who smoke [marijuana]. . . .*

"*One of the pilots is a good friend of mine. . . . There's a fairly short period of time that elapses between the time he's high and the time he has to go to work. . . . Usually whenever he comes over, he and my old man get high . . . three or four times a week. He's high a lot. He drinks too. I've seen him more than just socially high. He uses coke [cocaine] too.*" —Anna (ex-user)

1

Smoky Skies

The flight from Kahului on the Hawaiian Island of Maui to Honolulu on the Island of Oahu is only a hundred miles. Commercial passenger planes have made it hundreds of thousands of times without a fatal accident.

At 2:30 P.M. Saturday, March 14, 1981, a single-engine, Piper Cherokee airplane took off on such a flight. All of its four seats were occupied. Michael David Lewis, thirty, of Paia, Maui, a flight instructor with about 2,500 hours of piloting experience, was flying the plane, which he had borrowed. His passengers were three Maui women, aged twenty-seven, twenty-five, and twenty-four. According to a friend's later account, they were going to attend a bridal shower in Honolulu.

The pilot radioed his last message, giving his location, thirteen minutes after takeoff. At 3:15 P.M., not having received an expected position report on the hour, the Honolulu Flight Service Station initiated search and rescue procedures, and soon after 4:00 the Coast Guard launched a search mission from Oahu. At 7:15 an Aloha Airlines passenger plane picked up a signal from an emergency locating transmitter on Molokai, an island best known for its leper colony. Twelve hours later, coast-guardsmen in a helicopter spotted airplane wreckage on a remote, fern-covered, steeply sloping ridge overlooking the Wailau Valley at the rugged eastern end of the elongated, sparsely populated island.

"It looks like the plane hit a finger of the [Kolo] ridge . . . and went between two trees, which sheared off both wings," said a police sergeant, one of six members of a recovery team that descended from a hovering army helicopter to the crash scene. The plane had crashed near the top at about 2,500 feet, its fuselage sliding nose-first about 300 feet down.

They found two bodies inside the cabin, one just outside, and the fourth about 150 feet above. The helicopter evacuated the bodies, along with a damaged transponder from the plane that could not be turned off and was putting out a constant distress signal. Two days later another helicopter removed the wreckage. Government investigators found no evidence of mechanical failure and returned it to its owner on Maui.

The crash scene also had yielded an assortment of drugs, including marijuana, cocaine, and various pills; drug paraphernalia; and a nearly empty bottle of vodka. Further investigation revealed that the youngest victim, from Wailuku, Maui, had a record of drug dealing. And a registered nurse from Maui said she had flown with Lewis and on several occasions he smoked marijuana while flying.

A chemical analysis for alcohol and various drugs turned up no alcohol and just one drug in the pilot's blood: cannabis. The women's blood specimens proved positive for cannabis as well as alcohol. (Analysis by gas chromatography and mass spectrometry at an eastern laboratory showed two nanograms of "marijuana constituents" per milliliter of blood in the pilot's specimen, more in the passengers' specimens.)

The then Hawaii regional flight surgeon, Dr. Casimer Jasinski, reported that Lewis appeared to be "a drug abuser and a kind of a free spirit. He liked to fly into scenic, narrow valleys on Molokai for the fun of it. . . .

"The pilot's judgment must have been markedly impaired from the marijuana and he was unable to exit the valley," the flight surgeon said in his report. The probable cause, in his opinion, was "poor judgment from marijuana intoxication."[1]

A comparable mishap had occurred in a rural, sugar-raising area near the town of Waipahu in the interior of the island of Oahu on May 23, 1968. It was a dry, sunny, cloudless Thursday morning as Albert J. Rutland went up for a solo flight in a single-engine, Cessna 150 airplane belonging to his flying school. A twenty-six-year-old Vietnam veteran and California native, lately of Honolulu, Rutland had been studying flying under a government veterans program. He had eighty hours of flying experience, held a private license, and intended to be an airline pilot.

He may have been practicing a maneuver. In any case, at 9:45 A.M. eyewitnesses observed the plane suddenly plummeting in a spin, its pilot making no apparent attempt to recover control. It crashed into a sugar cane field, digging a large hole in the ground. When plantation workers and police reached the scene, they saw the wreckage of a demolished little airplane and the lifeless body of the young pilot.[2]

"We searched through the aircraft and searched in his pockets and we found marijuana cigarette roaches, two or three butts that had been recently smoked, in the ashtray of the aircraft. Also we found seeds in his briefcase and a pipe and cigarette paper and all the other paraphernalia that goes along with the leaves," Dr. Jasinski recalled for us. "I actually took the seeds, with the permission of our local security division chief, and I planted them in my office and, sure enough, it grew out—a marijuana plant. After it got a few inches, high enough so we could see it was marijuana, we of course destroyed it then."

Investigators checked the plane and determined that nothing had gone wrong mechanically. From all of the evidence, the cause seemed obvious to the doctor: "This guy was flying solo and apparently he was out there just enjoying himself with his marijuana smoking and apparently became so overjoyed about it that he didn't care what was happening and he got himself into some unusual attitude and got into a spin and just spun right in."

Those were the only two well-documented marijuana-caused accidents coming to the attention of Dr. Jasinski (flight surgeon for Hawaii, 1964–82, formerly a military flight surgeon and a Navy pilot). "We had some others that we suspected but there was no proof. Frequently they crash in the ocean and we never find anything."

✻   ✻   ✻

Having found out that marijuana smoking was "not an uncommon practice among pilots, some of whom reported that they have flown aircraft while 'high' on marijuana," a group connected with the medical school of the University of California at San Diego sought to test marijuana's effects on flying ability.

Janowsky, Meacham, and others tested ten certified pilots (seven professionals and three private fliers) on their ability to operate an instrument-flight simulator while intoxicated from marijuana. All had smoked marijuana "socially" for several years. (At the time of the study, seven smoked it three times a week or more; three smoked it less often.)

The test covered four consecutive four-minute "holding patterns," including operations encountered in instrument flying (such as straight and level flight, turns, maneuvers, and radio navigation). Two of the patterns incorporated altitude changes, and all included a little "turbulence," so that the pilots needed to manipulate the controls continually. The tasks demanded high skill as well as coordination, short-term memory, concentration, and orientation in time and space.

Before being given marijuana, the pilots practiced operating the simulators and performing the four flight sequences. When they had become proficient, two tests were conducted, one week apart. The first time, half smoked marijuana (2 percent THC) in pipes while the other half smoked placebo (inactive) marijuana for ten minutes. The second time, the groups switched, the former smoking placebo and the latter smoking active marijuana.

The experimenters videotaped each pilot's sixteen-minute performance just before the smoking as well as after the smoking, analyzing them at brief intervals. They calculated deviations in altitude, direction, and radio navigation.

Half an hour after the smoking of active marijuana, the performance of all ten pilots decreased in all measurements. They made twenty-nine "major errors." After smoking placebo marijuana, they made four. "Major errors" were defined as deviations that could have dire consequences, for example, getting lost, running out of fuel, stalling, and greatly changing altitude or direction. ("Minor errors" numbered forty-five with active marijuana and seven with placebo. The study was "double blind.")

Marijuana had caused major impairment in:

A. Short-term memory and sense of time. "After smoking the active marijuana, the pilots often forgot where they were in a given flight sequence or had difficulty recounting how long they had been performing a given maneuver, in spite of the presence of written instructions and a stopwatch."

B. Concentration and attention. A pilot would become preoccupied with one task to the exclusion of others or might even daydream. After a momentary lapse in attention, several pilots lost their orientation in time and space and then would oversteer to try to make up for tasks they had ignored.

Six of the pilots were also tested two, four, and six hours after smoking each type of marijuana. Two hours after the smoking of active marijuana, their flying ability had improved but still was below standard. At four hours the performance of all six had returned substantially to what it was before they smoked. Flying performance remained fairly consistent over the six-hour period after placebo-smoking.

The researchers cautioned that "more subtle effects, detectable with more sophisticated equipment, may conceivably persist for longer periods of time" than four hours. They pointed out that the test was easier than actual flying. (It did not measure several necessary tasks or consider the possibly aggravating effects of pressure changes. Also, the pilots performed memorized sequences with instructions in front of them, rather than taking instructions from an air traffic controller.)

"We believe that the performance of a pilot under these circumstances would be even more adversely affected by marijuana intoxication than in our experimental setting," wrote David S. Janowsky, M.D., professor of psychiatry, and others (1976).

Most of the pilots could distinguish the active marijuana from the placebo. They rated the test harder and their performance worse under intoxication.[3]

*   *   *

Millions of people in America use marijuana. Among them may be "people you and I are depending on to fly an airplane or drive a bus or perform our surgery," Dr. Harvey Powelson, psychiatrist of Berkeley, California, has pointed out.

He told us that he once had a young patient who smoked marijuana regularly and who was learning to fly. In describing his experiences in the air, the latter mentioned that he was learning to fly "blind," by use of instruments. On his second attempt, he was approaching the airport and something went wrong with his instruments. At this point, he had a pecular reaction, namely, a complete lack of fear. His fearlessness pleased him.

When Dr. Powelson heard this, he thought, "I would certainly not want to be flying in an airplane whose aviator was not frightened when the instruments went blank."

Ultimately, he learned, the patient made an error in judgment while piloting a light plane. It crashed, killing him and two companions.

The psychiatrist used to have another patient who worried him because he worked as an airplane mechanic, checking instruments on airplanes going from Alaska to Japan. He used marijuana and cocaine. For many months, until he left the job, he went to work high and his supervisor never knew it.

The mechanic just wanted to stay "stoned." He concisely expressed his attitude about checking instruments: "I don't give a s − − −!"

Dr. Powelson has observed in his clinical work that regular marijuana users gradually tend toward the "not caring" state illustrated by that airplane mechanic.

"I would think certainly in a professional like an airline pilot one would expect that his first concern should be for his fellow workers and his passengers. It is my experience, which I could substantiate with many, many cases, that marijuana users develop an attitude of not caring for anyone but themselves."

He has called marijuana dangerous to aviation, and other critical occupations, for these additional reasons: It remains in the brain for weeks or months, active all that time. Meantime it warps judgment and distorts reality, unbeknown to the user or his associates. Marijuana intoxication measurably slows reflex time and hinders coordination and other nervous system responses. And, combined with alcohol or other drugs, marijuana evokes strange and unpredictable effects.

*   *   *

Was it unique for the airplane mechanic to go to work under the influence of drugs?

A California director of the alcoholic abuse program of the International Association of Machinists and Aerospace Workers, a labor union that takes in airline ground personnel, said to us: "I think it's a very small problem in the airline industry. Very few people would smoke it on the job. I've never seen anybody use marijuana on the job or even in uniform. I don't worry about it."

Nor did it concern him that "I've run across people [in the union] who have had it in their possession" and that "As far as smoking it at home, it's a common thing in our industry and in other industries. I've been told by a lot of people that they use it at home."

*   *   *

At Los Angeles in 1981 maintenance mechanics on the night shift of a major commercial airline were observed going to work under the influence of some drug and remaining that way. Urine screening disclosed significant amounts of cannabinoid in eleven employees and they were suspended.

> Dr. Sidney Cohen made the case known at a 1982 symposium in Alexandria, Virginia. He told also how marijuana smoking during lunchtime and breaks by employees of a subcontractor for space and missile guidance systems marred production until they were discovered and fired.[4]

The Wall Street Journal reported (1983) that many air traffic controllers "have been users of mind-altering drugs, including marijuana, hashish and cocaine, and that many still are—although FAA officials and controllers alike have tried to keep the problem quiet." Interviews revealed controller students stoned in class, controller trainees sitting at their radar screens "totally lost," and even experienced controllers too drugged to function, making wrong decisions and causing "near-tragedies."

A former Baltimore-Washington controller, fired for striking, said his crew used to pass around joints after work, and he guessed that at least half of the controllers whom he had met throughout the country smoked marijuana. Known users of illegal drugs may be but are not necessarily fired and some have even been rehired, including a former heroin pusher, the newspaper reported.[5]

*   *   *

"From time to time I hear of people doing it, and my reaction is to say 'You're nuts,' " pilot Ted said. Over a period of several months, he had done that "nutty" thing himself—smoked marijuana while flying.

"When I was in high school, I never even had heard of marijuana. The first time I ever smoked it was in 'sixty-five. Ironically it was a pilot friend of mine who first turned me on to marijuana. He was a flight instructor at the time. It was a novel experience and at first kind of nice. There was a period of years when I was smoking it every day. . . .

"I guess it was 1970 and I was twenty-one when this friend introduced me to the small cargo airline that he was working for. I started flying as his copilot. He was really into marijuana, and one day he surprised me. I'd smoked grass with him before, but not flying. We were on our way to Sacramento and right after takeoff from San Francisco, he pulled out a joint. So we got high and the weather was clear and we landed. We had no problem, other than the fact that it made the airplane seem noisier and the trip seem longer. . . .

"Once when I was stoned, I made what I thought was a beautiful landing at Burbank in a Beech D-18 at about 2:00 A.M. Then all of a sudded I looked down and we were up in the air about twenty feet and almost stalling out. I hadn't realized that I had too much air speed and I relaxed the forward pressure on the stick and the airplane just took off again and we didn't even notice it at first. It was a scramble to get the power on and go around again and make another landing. . . .

"If you had to get on instruments, you'd be really in trouble, because your scan pattern is pretty much destroyed. There are several instruments you have to look at and your eyes scan over the instruments in a certain pattern. So you might maintain your airspeed but your altitude would vary. Or you might maintain your altitude but then your magnetic heading would vary. . . .

"I certainly wouldn't want to be riding in an airplane when the pilot's stoned. I just think that it could be potentially very dangerous. If you had an engine going out or a fire or something like that, you'd have difficulty dealing with it. You might tend to panic more than if you weren't stoned. In a routine flight, when you don't have any bad weather and everything's working properly, you'd probably get away with it. You may have to concentrate more on landing. We have a saying, 'Once you get it off the ground, you don't have to worry about it—until you land it.' When it comes to the landing, depth perception is affected."

One night in 1978 (the year he left commercial aviation when his employer went out of business) Ted was captaining an air express plane going from Los Angeles to Phoenix. "I had a copilot who wanted to smoke a joint. I said 'Well, go ahead.' The guy had a hard time maintaining his altitude."

Even if the marijuana is not smoked in the air, the residual effects could make it hazardous, he said. "I wouldn't even try smoking it the day before flying. In a routine flight, you probably wouldn't run into any trouble. But if you had an emergency arise, where you got into a bad storm or something and had to work at controlling the aircraft, then definitely it could affect your performance."

Note too the possibility of a flashback, which aviator Ted encountered once while flying. He had stopped smoking marijuana months before, but evidently enough drug remained in his brain to make him suddenly "very high," throwing him into a panic.

In addition to all the marijuana-smoking pilots, "there are also a lot of alcoholic pilots. They manage to cover it up somehow." An alcohol hangover, like a marijuana hangover, produces "definitely a lessening of your senses." Tobacco cigarettes also diminish the senses, said Ted, who smokes them. "When I was flying for Trans-West, I gave up cigarettes for a while because we were flying at night. Definitely the cigarettes affect your night vision."

Ted no longer likes marijuana. He gave it up around 1974 except for an occasional puff at a party. "After a while I realized that this stuff can be quite damaging, just from the lethargy it produces."

☆　☆　☆

Marijuana smoker Harry, fifty, has been piloting light planes now and again for thirteen years, when not working at his white-collar job—and usually when not under the acute influence of the drug. He explained what's wrong with it:

"Like any dangerous machine, an airplane requires constant attention and monitoring to make sure that something doesn't go wrong. . . . You've constantly got to be watching altitude and course and oil pressure and everything else. . . . Flying is something that requires intense attention to detail. The pilot looks like he's relaxed when he's sitting there but he's watching two dozen things. . . . You're up there all the time violating the law of gravity. It's only possible when ten thousand interlocking pieces all work properly and your judgment and skill are all working for you. Any one thing can negate all of that. You never can tell when some emergency is gonna come up there. It's just not the sort of thing that anyone with any brains is gonna do while stoned. . . . I think it's highly dangerous."

He thought a moment and interjected, "Actually, I drive a car frequently. . . . It can be considered a piece of dangerous equipment. . . . I don't mind smoking a little grass when I'm driving up and down the freeway." He rationalized it with the explanation that driving does not require the intensity of flying.

"I know one guy that drinks a lot while he flies. You never could tell. He's a private pilot, a rancher. He takes a case of beer with him and drinks while he flies. . . . A lot of guys come back from a holiday weekend or something and they've got something in them—one or the other or both—and sometimes don't make it. . . . I see a lot of young longhairs taking pilot's lessons. They'll probably be the ones. . . . Only a damn fool is gonna smoke this stuff and fly."

Of course many a pilot does smoke the stuff and does fly—including Harry.

*   *   *

Zsa Zsa and Eva played major roles in an experiment at the Federal Aviation Administration's Civil Aeromedical Institute in Oklahoma City in 1975 to find out whether increases in altitude changed marijuana's effect on behavior. It was the only experimental study pertaining to cannabis and flying known to be conducted by the U.S. government. The subjects were adolescent, female baboons.

Psychologists trained the animals to match colors by pressing keys. Different colored lights illuminated each of two keys. If a baboon pressed the one that matched a sample color, which changed periodically, she automatically received a banana pellet. The apes went through 4,320 trials in an altitude chamber at different simulated altitudes. They would begin a day's session two hours after consuming a sweetened, orange-flavored drink. The drink sometimes contained THC, in one of four doses, and at other times had no THC.

Without the drug, the baboons completed all of the trials, regardless of altitude. With the drug, although they could finish nearly all trials at ground level and at 1,250 feet, at 8,000 or 12,000 feet they could complete only a fraction of them (as few as 7 percent at 12,000 feet) except at the lowest dose.

Without the drug, the high altitudes reduced the baboons' speed of response to three-fourths of the ground-level speed. The two lower doses of THC either did not affect or increased the response speed (relative to the nondrug condition). However, the two higher doses greatly slowed down the animals at the higher altitudes. Neither altitude nor drug had any effect on accuracy. The apes knew their colors.

The experiment appeared to demonstrate that increased altitudes, with the resulting decreases in oxygen, could magnify effects of marijuana.

"The implications of the present research to the aviation community seem obvious," said Mark F. Lewis and colleagues (1976). "Clearly, a failure to execute a required behavior or a reduction in the speed of performing complex judgmental or memory tasks can lead to aviation accidents."

The four THC doses were 0.25, 0.5, 1, and 2 mg/kg. Mean percentages of trials completed were respectively 100, 67, 56, and 12 percent at 8,000 feet; and 100, 31, 49, and 7 percent at 12,000 feet.

Respective mean response speeds, figured as percentage of response speed at ground level, were 77, 94, 47, and 49 percent at 8,000 feet; and 104, 69, 45, and 2 percent at 12,000 feet. The drugless response speed at each higher altitude came to 73 percent of the ground-level speed.

The baboons got nineteen out of every twenty responses correct with or without drug and regardless of altitude. There were ninety trials a session.

As several researchers had shown in the case of alcohol, this study demonstrated "that hypoxia can also potentiate the effects of delta-9-THC," Lewis et al. wrote. (They referred to the presumed lowering of the oxyhemoglobin level with increase in simulated altitude.)[6]

Dr. Lewis described the background of the baboon study. He said (in 1981, after being transferred from research to data services) that he had been studying drugs affecting pilots, found little information on marijuana, and suggested a symposium on the aeromedical effects of marijuana. One was held in 1972. Results of the symposium and papers presented were published.[7] None of the studies dealt directly with aviation. The panelists recommended that the Federal Aviation Administration itself engage in research. A research program was begun but ended within a couple of years when a new federal air surgeon with new priorities took over in 1975.

The ten pilots in the human flying experiment worked simulated equipment, of course, for it would be too dangerous to send them up stoned. Not even Eva and Zsa Zsa went into the air in that condition.

But two amateur fliers of northern California rushed in where scientists feared to tread. The pair tried an "experiment" to investigate flying while one engaged in his "particular vice." At least they had enough sense not to engage in it together. One time George flew "wiped out" on marijuana and friend Len was "straight." Another time they switched roles, except that Len took cocaine. We spoke with George, who described his experience:

"We went to different altitudes and tried to do simple mathematic calculations. . . . When you're flying you have to do navigation and there are certain things you have to figure out from time to time . . . your time of arrival, your fuel. . . . We tried it at different levels because the higher you go, there's less oxygen. . . .

"It was possible to do it at the five-thousand-foot altitude, through some force of concentration to stay on it. . . . But going up to fourteen thousand, five hundred really, really slowed things down. I found myself sitting there, looking at the scratch paper, trying to figure out what I was doing. . . .

"When you go up that high without being stoned, you get a little high.

. . . Smoking pot just intensified the euphoric, giddy feeling where you didn't give a f——— what you were doing, so to speak. It could be a dangerous situation. . . . I did keep the plane straight and level and I did bring it down, but I was no longer interested in what we went up to do. . . . I decided from this experiment that I wouldn't do it by myself. . . .

"I've only landed and taken off once or twice stoned, when I was doing this experiment with my friend, but I didn't trust myself. I didn't trust myself. I didn't like it. It wasn't pleasant. I had to really work. Flying for me is a pleasure."

George called himself "a pothead from way back," having indulged in products of the cannabis plant for fifteen years, since his college days. He had logged 1,200 hours in ten years of private flying.

He flew and smoked one other time, on a pleasure trip. After half a joint, "I had to concentrate on not listening to the noises because I'm sort of a mechanic. I'm a car mechanic. I do minimum maintenance on my own aircraft. There are so many things that can go wrong—all those many parts—and my mind would run wild with the possibilities. . . .

"Driving a car, if I'm really whacked out, I can hear wheel bearings going out or a bearing in the drive shaft or a knock, or I'll feel a flat tire, and I'll pull off the road and get out and walk around—and there's absolutely nothing wrong with the car. In an airplane you don't have that option. . . .

"So I don't smoke pot when I fly. . . . I can smoke pot in the evening at home, rest for eight or ten hours, and then fly the next day, but I won't smoke or drink the same day."

George recounted an experience as a jet plane passenger at a Morocco airport that recalls the incident (related by psychiatrist Powelson) in which a marijuana-smoking student pilot felt no fear when his instruments failed aloft.

"We were revving up the engines, ready to go. The guy had just released the brakes and we were starting our takeoff roll. One of the right engines blew up, the wing caught on fire, and it was completely full of people. People were screaming and crawling over the seats and fighting each other, trying to get out of the plane before it blew up.

"I was so bombed—I'd been smoking hash and eating hash, which is made from the marijuana resin—it didn't bother me at all. My friend and I stood up; I reached for the overhead rack and got my camera bag and my *Playboy* out of the seat pocket in front of me, just like a slow-moving movie, and made my way to the back."

*   *   *

A search of the records of the National Transportation Safety Board retrieved data on sixty civil aviation accidents reported to involve marijuana in some way during a period of four years and one month (1976–80). Twenty of them were fatal, taking twenty-nine lives. In most cases investigators found marijuana aboard, anywhere from a butt in an ashtray to 15,000 pounds.

The last of these was typical. On the afternoon of Sunday, October 19, 1980, a Piper plane carrying one occupant and 450 pounds of marijuana crashed into trees in isolated woods 9½ miles north of Weeki Wachee, Florida. The impact tore the plane into pieces and killed the pilot, William E. Wilson, forty-one, of Nogales, Arizona, who may have had about 600 hours of flying experience. He was believed to be trying to land on a road.

Wilson had rented the plane the day before from a Lakeland, Florida, flying service, "to fly some friends around the state." Actually, according to charts and notes, he flew to Jamaica and back via Cuban air space, with no flight plan. Nothing in the wreckage suggested any cause of the accident. A toxicological analysis of blood and urine failed to detect alcohol or any of various drugs—but no test was made for marijuana.

*   *   *

Dr. Lewis, who conducted the baboon experiment, wondered (a) whether the pilots were using marijuana, and (b) whether the marijuana at those altitudes might have given off some kind of fume that reached the pilots.

"We don't know how much of a problem it is. We have not looked for information. Therefore we don't have it," Lewis said. "My feeling is, if there was no serious interest in the problem before we did the paper that demonstrated the altitude effect, there should have been after the fact."

As the problem has intensified throughout the country and driving studies have illuminated the role of marijuana in the operation of surface motor vehicles, the response of the Federal Aviation Administration (FAA) has been sluggish.

"I'm not aware of any progress in ten years as far as accumulated data or research in the aviation field. It's not recognized as a problem. So there is no real concerted effort to look or study," said Dr. J. Robert Dille, chief of the Civil Aeromedical Institute, Oklahoma City.

"We haven't identified it as a problem," said Dr. U. A. Garred Sexton, western regional flight surgeon, Los Angeles. He was much more concerned with amphetamines, narcotics, and alcohol, particularly alcohol.

Can aviation tolerate marijuana? Views differ. The current tests for cannabis did not suit Dr. Sexton. He wanted a test that would show "a dose-effect relationship, and so far we don't have any."

Dr. Delbert J. Lacefield, chief FAA toxicologist, Oklahoma City, said, "In certain cases, I'm sure that just depending on the normal skill of the pilot and experiences and the circumstances that he's in and things like that, that it doesn't take much to take off the fine edge that allows him to fly safely. I know that pilots can really have a pretty large performance decrement and still manage to fly the plane and get it off the ground. You may have a guy who has lost a little of that fine edge, and if all of a sudden he develops a mechanical problem . . . weather . . . he can't handle it. . . . So you've got to look at each individual case."

His impression was that the effects of one or two joints were "pretty brief. . . . The pilots that we really worry about are those guys that leave their office on Friday and they fly someplace for a weekend or something and they may spend the whole weekend high on drugs or drunk . . . the pilot who during the course of a day may repeatedly smoke marijuana or something like that . . . the long-term chronic effects. . . ."

Another regional flight surgeon, whom we will call Smith, considered the demands of an airplane inconsistent with any marijuana use at all. Pointing to the persistence of cannabinoids in the brain and other fatty tissues, he said, "There's a drug effect between the times when the people are subjectively high."

He felt that the use of any stimulant or drug by a pilot must diminish his performance. "If he's a coffee user, an alcohol user, a drug user, it automatically has an effect on safety." The burning of tobacco cigarettes produces carbon monoxide, which affects the brain and heart, he added.

"You don't smoke marijuana and fly," said Dr. Smith. "The demands of the cockpit are so unforgiving and so refined compared with the demands on the interstate truck driver or the ordinary Joe who drives his Toyota down the road."

Drugs might be responsible for some aircraft accidents officially laid to "an error in judgment" when the cause cannot be pinned down, he said. Failure of a test to detect THC in the blood would not absolve cannabis. "Was the guy stoned when he did his preflight planning two days earlier?" The surgeon would like all fatal accidents in a five-year period to be studied to learn how many of the pilots had histories of drug habit.

Still another flight surgeon, whom we will call Johnson, considered the problem of marijuana usage in aviation worse than it looked. "The standard toxicology study looks for carbon monoxide, barbiturates, and alcohol, and sometimes a drug scan. Some of the later techniques for identifying marijuana aren't that prevalent countrywide, so it kind of falls through the cracks. . . . There's bound to be more of it than we're aware of. . . .

"From the standpoint of flying, any marijuana present in the system would be disqualifying. It would be illegal for a pilot to fly with the presence of any marijuana actively circulating in his system. . . . If you could just get a trace of cocaine, or PCP, or heroin, or marijuana or something like that in the blood specimen or tissue specimen of a pilot, in the strictest legal sense, he wouldn't be legal to hold his medical certificate and fly. . . . You just don't smoke pot and fly—period."

Are there more pot-caused accidents than have come to light? Dr. Johnson said, "If you translate what's known in moving vehicles on the ground, it's bound to be happening. . . . There are circumstances in flight where an airplane is not forgiving. You can't pull over to the side, get out, and kick the beast. . . . You're up there and someone's got to get it down. . . . Those accidents usually come out, when they can't find out anything, as an error in judgment. Case closed. . . . There's just a great big hole there."

＊　＊　＊

Following these (telephone) interviews, we wired the federal air surgeon, H. L. Reighard, to ask: "Is marijuana a problem in aviation?" and "Is the FAA doing anything about it?" The reply to the first question was not a clear yes or no.

"With the widespread use of marijuana in our society and known effects on performance, the possibility that aviation safety is affected exists," the air surgeon wrote back after reviewing the matter with his professional staff at the Office of Aviation Medicine in Washington, D.C. "Unfortunately, quantification of cannabinoids in body tissue is far more difficult than with such drugs as alcohol."

What was the FAA doing? Its Civil Aeromedical Institute planned to get equipment for analyzing cannabis, if finances permitted. Then research studies on the relation of cannabis to accidents would be possible. Current simple detection methods, measuring cannabinoids in urine as long as a week after use, were not enough to connect the drug to a loss in flying ability and a resulting aircraft accident, the letter said. It cited the federal regulation prohibiting anyone from working as an aircraft crew member "while using any drug that affects his faculties in any way contrary to safety." Since cannabis is an illegal drug with "known behavioral and psychological effects," this regulation adequately covers it.

So the FAA recognizes the possibility that marijuana is affecting aviation safety but is not sure. Nevertheless, the remark about the federal regulation acknowledges that working aboard an aircraft while using cannabis is "contrary to safety." A question that the regulation does not answer is, what constitutes "while using" cannabis? Does a crew member have to be caught smoking a joint in an airplane to be considered in violation? We requested but did not receive clarification on this point (and numerous related factual questions). It appears (from the letter, with its remarks about urine testing, and from other documents) that the FAA would not tolerate smoking of marijuana by a pilot in an aircraft but might tolerate it off the job.

The crew member could not be subject to "drug dependence," under the provision of another federal regulation: An applicant for a medical certificate must have no such medical history or clinical diagnosis. How do they usually find out? Through chemical analysis? No—by asking him! A medical questionnaire (which fliers complete at periodic medical examinations) asks, "Have you ever had, or have you now, any of the following?" and one item to be checked yes or no is "any drug or narcotic habit." Needless to say, not many marijuana smokers check yes. Some rationalize that it's not a "drug," others that their smoking is not a "habit."

Regulations or no regulations, a number of licensed pilots in all categories have had known histories of drug dependence. And innumerable others who regularly and covertly dim their senses with drugs fly overhead.

The text of the letter from the federal air surgeon (April 8, 1982) follows:

"Your message of March 30, 1982, with questions related to the effects of cannabis and aviation safety has been reviewed in the Federal Aviation Administration (FAA) Office of Aviation Medicine.

"With the widespread use of marijuana in our society and its known effects on performance, the possibility that aviation safety is affected exists. Unfortunately, quantification of cannabinoids in body tissue is far more difficult than with such drugs as alcohol. Simple detection methods of cannabis metabolites are readily available and will yield positive results from the urine as long as a week after the smoking of a single marijuana cigarette. A positive test by this method is not necessarily indicative of use within the previous few hours and does not provide evidence of recent intoxication as a breath test does for alcohol. Therefore, the detection of cannabis metabolites in body tissue, cannot simply be correlated to a performance decrement resulting in an aircraft accident. With the development of more readily available quantitative methods and of studies of human performance related to specific tissue concentrations of cannabinoids, the true relationship of aircraft accidents to the use of marijuana can be determined.

"The Code of Federal Regulations, Title 14, Part 91.11, specifically states that no person may act as a crewmember while using any drug that affects his faculties in any way contrary to safety. Since cannabis is a drug with known behavorial and psychological effects, and since the use of cannabis is illegal by federal statute, the FAA feels that this regulation adequately covers the use of cannabis and performance as a crewmember.

"You may be interested to note that the Civil Aeromedical Institute (CAMI) Aviation Toxicology Laboratory currently plans to procure the required equipment for the quantitative analysis in the near future, fiscal constraints permitting. Research studies to determine the relationship of cannabis to performance decrement resulting in the cause of accidents will then be possible.

"Thank you for your interest in aviation safety."

* * *

The letter left many questions unanswered and raised others, and so we telephoned for clarification. An aide of the air surgeon asked that we put our inquiry in writing. We sent a letter with fifteen questions, touching on the strictness—or laxness—of the FAA toward marijuana-smoking pilots and drug smugglers, on the FAA's interest—or lack of interest—in studying marijuana matters, on the possibility of drug tests for crewmen, and so on.

We never received a reply.

* * *

Federal aviation regulations require that "No person may act as a crew-member of a civil aircraft . . . while using any drug that affects his faculties in any way contrary to safety." In addition, no pilot may allow "a person who is obviously under the influence of intoxicating liquors or drugs (except a medical patient under proper care) to be carried in that aircraft" (Section 91.11).

Nor may anyone "operate a civil aircraft within the United States with knowledge that narcotic drugs, marihuana, and depressant or stimulant drugs or substances . . . are carried in the aircraft" except as authorized by Federal or State statute or agency (Section 91.12).

"No person who is convicted of violating any Federal or State statute relating to the growing, processing, manufacture, sale, disposition, possession, transportation, or importation of narcotic drugs, marihuana, and depressant or stimulant drugs or substances [nothing is said about use] is eligible for any certificate or rating under this part [for pilot, flight engineer, or flight navigator] for a period of 1 year after the date of final conviction" (Sections 61.15 and 63.12). Presumably after a year the drug criminal is eligible again to fly.

An applicant for a medical certificate must have "No established medical history or clinical diagnosis of . . . 'drug dependence' . . . a condition in which a person is addicted to or dependent on drugs other than alcohol, tobacco, or ordinary caffeine-containing beverages, as evidenced by habitual use or a clear sense of need for the drug" (Sections 67.13, 67.15, and 67.17).[8]

* * *

In 1975 Federal Air Surgeon Reighard acknowledged that thirty-three airmen "are known to have been certified after careful evaluation in spite of a history of drug dependence or drug addiction." Those with first class, second class, and third class certificates (airline transport, commercial, and private, respectively) numbered one, eleven, and twenty-one. He did not include licensees who used drugs once or "experimented" with them.

The information had been compiled at the request of an Illinois pilot. He was concerned about drug usage in his industry, particularly by two fellow pilots at American Airlines. One left the drug scene in time. The other got fired for marijuana use; but in arbitration by the airline, the Allied Pilots Association, and a referee, he won reinstatement (1974) because of improper intrusions into his private life to gather evidence. The panel did not restore back pay, commenting, "The use of mind-altering drugs about which so little is known (unlike alcohol) is wholly incompatible with a pilot's responsibility for the lives and safety of those on board his aircraft."

2

Two Train Wrecks

Going at full throttle, the Conrail train with forty-three freight cars sped east toward Philadelphia. In its diesel locomotive were the engineer and conductor—the latter inexplicably manning the controls. Never once had he slowed the train since it left the station near Pottstown, Pennsylvania, at 4:55 that Monday morning, October 1, 1979, picking up thirty-seven cars loaded with anthracite coal.

At about 5:14 A.M. the unauthorized operator disregarded a wayside signal to slow down. He made two street crossings at Royersford without blowing the whistle as required, and then he raced through a stop signal. He even ignored the explosion of torpedoes, explosive charges warning of obstruction ahead. A brakeman had placed them on the track to warn of a freight train stopped for a signal half a mile ahead. En route to the waiting train's caboose, the brakeman saw the approaching train, lit a red flare, and waved it to signal "Stop!"

Flashing amber lights on the standing caboose should have been visible to the pair in the locomotive as their engine rounded its final curve at about 45 miles per hour.

The joyride ended violently at 5:16. At maximum power, the locomotive crashed into the rear of the standing train. The collision killed the conductor, Anthony J. Dobin II, twenty-eight, and the engineer, Francis R. Thompson, twenty-four, casting their bodies 50 and 150 feet respectively from the point of impact as it demolished their engine. It also derailed the front train's caboose and 20 of its 115 freight cars, spilling tons of coal and causing an estimated total of $562,000 damage to equipment, cargo, and tracks.

Providentially, there were no injuries to ten other train employees: two in the caboose of the rear train, seven in locomotives of the front train, and one outside—the brakeman, who may have saved his own life by remaining outside to signal.

On the morning before, the four crewmen of the rear train, including the two surviving brakemen, had come from Philadelphia to Bethlehem. Riding then in the caboose, the conductor confided to the rear brakeman that the engineer was making his last round trip in his present assignment, soon to be displaced for lack of seniority. They were close friends and he, the conductor, intended to join the other.

After spending the afternoon and evening at a motel, the crew took a taxi to the Conrail engine house at Bethlehem, where their shift would begin at 1:00 A.M. The engineer seemed listless and fatigued, "not his usual talkative self," according to the rear brakeman. The latter and the taxi driver both heard the conductor tell the engineer, "Let's get high."

With the conductor operating, the crew rode together in the locomotive's cab to the Allentown Yard. There the conductor ordered the head brakeman to ride in the caboose with the rear brakeman. The head brakeman objected strongly, for a rule required him to ride in the locomotive, but he did as told. Evidently the conductor did not want the brakeman watching him on the way to Philadelphia. The conductor, who had begun as a trainman with the Penn Central in 1973, was not a stickler for railroad rules; his record bore suspensions and reprimands for violations.

Following the accident, a toxicologist analyzed blood, urine, and tissues of the two victims. The only stimulant, intoxicant, or poison to turn up in either victim's samples was cannabis—in the conductor's. Measured by an array of sophisticated techniques, it appeared in sufficient concentrations (in the blood: some five nanograms of THC and an equal amount of its carboxylic metabolite) to indicate that the conductor could have smoked a marijuana cigarette within two hours of the accident, according to the laboratory report (by Toxicon Associates, Willow Grove, Pennsylvania).

When investigator John A. Rehor of the National Transportation Safety Board discussed the evidence with the toxicologist, "what we had found fit very nicely into the behavioral pattern that we would have expected" (Rehor told us). The failure to respond to all of the danger signs "would be indicative of somebody who really was under the influence of delta-9-THC."

For the safety board, "this was a landmark case," as the investigator pointed out. It established the use of marijuana alone as a probable cause of a transportation disaster. The Maryland highway accident of April,

1979, that took ten teenaged lives had been traced by the board to alcohol plus marijuana ("Driving," 3).

In its report on the train wreck, the board concluded that "the conductor probably smoked a marijuana cigarette" aboard the engine. "The concentration of the active constituent of marijuana and its metabolite in his system probably modified his behavior to the degree that he did not respond to danger warnings."

The board determined the probable cause of the accident to be the failure of the conductor, "who was operating the train without authority and under the influence of marijuana," to comply with signals and stop the train. (The conductor's failure to let the head brakeman perform his duties in the locomotive and to see that a capable engineer operated it contributed to the accident, the board added. In addition, it urged the Consolidated Rail Corporation to supervise night crews, and, for the ninth time since 1973, called for an automatic device to stop a train at a stop signal if the engineer fails to do so.)[9]

While this was the first train wreck that the safety board officially laid to marijuana, it was not the first rail accident in which the question of marijuana came up.

*   *   *

In the heart of Chicago's Loop at 5:27 during the late-afternoon rush on Friday, February 4, 1977, a rather crowded, eight-car Lake–Dan Ryan elevated train slowly rounded a curve and struck the rear of a six-car Ravenswood train stopped ahead of it.

The front car of the Lake–Dan Ryan train rocked slowly from side to side and moved slightly back. Then came an electrical arc flash and a loud report as the car plunged to the street twenty-one feet below. The next three cars turned over slowly and they too toppled off the elevated structure, hitting the street.

The accident killed 11 people and injured 268.

The first and third cars landed on their right sides; the second and fourth cars each came to rest with one end against the elevated structure. Some passengers left the cars unaided through end doors or broken windows. Rescuers helped the others out through doors, windows, or openings torn in the car bodies. Property damage was estimated at $1.2 million. (By 1984 legal judgments and settlements amounted to $4 million; a few cases were pending.) The impact pushed the Ravenswood train about twenty-five feet. The Ravenswood had been stopped between stations (Randolph-Wabash and State-Lake) because a red flashing signal in the cab indicated a train ahead.

The disaster was the worst in the history of the Chicago "L," which

Aerial view of the Pennsylvania train wreck. In terms of this picture, the wayward train was going from bottom to top. The arrow points to the remains of the cab of the demolished locomotive. Other parts of the locomotive are at the extreme top to the left. The caboose it hit is seen at the bottom to the right of the tracks. (Courtesy of the National Transportation Safety Board and the photographer, Tom Kelly of Sanatoga, Pa.)

began operating in 1892. (The Loop around the central city was completed in 1897, two years after conversion from steam to electricity.)[10]

On the evening of the accident, a policeman reported finding at the scene four hand-rolled marijuana cigarettes in a small envelope in a shoulder bag belonging to the motorman.

Shortly thereafter the envelope and contents disappeared. After a night of searching, four investigators sorting victims' belongings in a sporting goods store across the street located the evidence. It had been placed in a passenger's attaché case by mistake. A test five days later verified that the cigarettes were marijuana joints. But now it would be "a very tricky legal problem" to prove ownership (said a deputy police superintendent), notwithstanding an additional discovery: marijuana residue in the motorman's bag.

The motorman consented to submit blood and urine samples. The National Transportation Safety Board had them analyzed, and the blood showed no signs of alcohol, barbiturates, or amphetamines; it was not checked for cannabis. The urine was another story.

A urine sample went to North Carolina for cannabis analysis at Research Triangle Institute. Chemist Monroe E. Wall, vice-president, looked for the cannabis metabolite 9-carboxy-THC acid (converted from THC by liver enzymes) because "a lot of research work done in my laboratory has shown that in the urine of people who smoke marijuana you inevitably find some. . . . We're the group that has synthesized it," he informed us.

"We did the analysis and we found a very small amount. . . . It was getting close to the limits of our test [two nanograms per milliliter] but unmistakable." Wall had received only one sample and never was told when it was taken, so he could not pinpoint the time of smoking or amount smoked. "Say he was a chronic user. You might see it in his urine a week later. This stuff takes many days to clear altogether. . . . You cannot make any conclusion from one sample, unless it's zero or very high."

Called to Chicago to testify at a hearing of the safety board in March, Wall described the finding and said it showed only that the man had taken marijuana at some time in the recent past. It could have been just before the crash or several days before. Wall likened the accuracy of his method—gas-liquid chromatography with mass spectrometry—to that of fingerprint analysis. A chart displayed the mass spectra produced by the analyzed compound and by a known sample of the metabolite; the peaks matched perfectly. The testimony evoked extensive press coverage, including a streamer headline across the front of the *Chicago Tribune*, announcing that " *'L' driver had smoked pot*. . . ."[11]

A urine sample also went to the Walter Reed Army Institute of Research, Washington, D.C. Dr. Leo Kazyak testified that he failed to detect cannabinoid but the mass spectrometer used was due for an overhaul and the sample was small. "A second test, performed after the laboratory's instruments were recalibrated, detected the presence of THC" (acid), the safety board later reported.

The motorman, Stephen Martin, 34, showed up at the hearing on crutches. He had been hospitalized for six weeks, suffering a broken pelvis and internal injuries.

> Martin testified that when his train was at the Randolph and Wabash station, just before the critical curve, he could not see the Ravenswood train. He assumed that it was at the next station, State and Lake, because it had been one station ahead of him at the previous two stops.
>
> He admitted that a red light had flashed in his cab at the Randolph-Wabash station. He said that it meant to go no faster than 15 miles per hour. Actually, the light meant to stop—a train is stopped ahead—and wait for permission to proceed (and the posted speed limit at the curve was 10 miles per hour).
>
> Martin testified that he left the Randolph-Wabash station on minimum power, possibly 10 to 12 miles per hour, and coasted into the curve (to the left) at perhaps 8 to 12 miles per hour. Standing in the curve was the Ravenswood train.
>
> The motorman said, "As I entered the curve, I began to stand up, and that is when I first saw the Ravenswood train. I immediately went to three points brake [normal maximum grip]. The train did not respond. When I got to—I don't know how close I was to the Ravenswood train, I went to brake four [full emergency], and right after I went to brake four, I had the impact."
>
> Asked whether his train had sufficient distance to stop on three points of brake, he said, "I felt assured that I was at least two and a half car lengths away from the train before I struck it."
>
> Tests conducted by the safety board and officials of the Chicago Transit Authority two days after the accident had found the brakes to have been in working order.
>
> The motorman did not recall landing on the street. After the collision atop the elevated structure, "my train was careened over to the side. I remember seeing part of the structure sliding past me, as I looked out of the motorman's cab window. I worked myself into the small of the seat . . . made the sign of the cross and covered up. I believe I must have blacked out. . . . Witnesses have told me that I was thrown from the train and I came through the windshield of the train I was operating."

The whole matter of marijuana was disposed of in twenty-three words. Hubert Jewell, the safety board's principal investigator, asked, "Did you at any time during the day of February 4th, prior to your accident, smoke a marijuana cigarette?"

"No, sir, I didn't," replied Martin.

Not another question on the subject arose in two days of testimony. Ten questioners inquired, not only about the motorman's understanding of safety rules and the events of the tragic day, but into his state of mind, physical condition, outside activities, and eyeglasses, and whether he ate breakfast and dinner, had enough heat in his cab, spoke to passengers, was taking medication (no) and so on and so forth. And Kay Bailey, who presided, asked if he smoked "regular cigarettes" (yes), which brand (he said "mostly O.P.'s . . . other people's"), and whether he was smoking one at the time of the accident (no).

On the Friday of the accident he arose at 10:00 A.M. and started work at 1:38 P.M., he said. He had been off the day before, but "I don't feel it's necessary for me to divulge to this committee what I did that day."[12]

> The Illinois Institute of Technology made a mathematical study of the conditions and estimated the speed at impact to have been less than ten miles per hour. "This was a slow-motion crash in which nobody should have been killed," David Young, *Chicago Tribune* transportation editor, told us (1984). He pointed to reports of survivors that they could barely feel the collision and remained standing immediately thereafter. It was the plunge to the street that caused the deaths and the host of injuries. Several rail specialists whom Young interviewed propounded the theory that the train had fallen off the elevated structure because the motors remained in power after the rail collision and the resulting engagement of anti-climbers encouraged the train to jackknife horizontally.
>
> The safety board reported, "It is unlikely that an eight-car train that entered the curve at from 8 to 10 mph could coast completely through the curve. Therefore, it is logical to assume that at some point, propulsion power was reapplied to maintain the train's speed. If power was being applied at the time of the impact, it more readily explains the heavy electrical arc that was reported."[13] It would account also for witnesses' observations of increasingly violent rocking of the train for several seconds before it left the tracks. So most likely the motorman was applying the propulsion power and not the brakes at the time of the rail collision and continued doing that for seconds after the impact.

His record (introduced at the hearing over the objections of the Amalgamated Transit Union) showed a history of rules violations since 1970, producing suspensions and citations: running red lights, speeding, improper use of brakes, improper display of front lights, passing by stations, failing to stand at curves, reading while operating his train, etc. One of the red light violations caused a derailment in 1974. About three months before the fatal accident, the motorman was suspended a day for refusing to give a urine sample during a physical examination. "This would seem to confirm later evidence at the hearing that Martin used marijuana," the *Chicago Tribune* commented editorially.[14]

The transit authority's general manager, George Krambles, said rule violations caused the crash. Kay Bailey, vice-chairman of the safety board, found nothing to contradict the authority's finding of human error. She said evidence on marijuana was inconclusive because it was not proved that the motorman had smoked it on the day of the collision.

"We never could make an issue of that with any definitive proof," investigator Jewell later recalled. The problem, he said to us, was that the drug found could not be related to the time of use. "They can now do a blood analysis. They have improved the technique. At that time it was a relatively new scientific approach. . . ."

In recent years the Chicago Transit Authority has been testing operators for cannabis; urine sampled during annual physicals is screened routinely and blood is tested in the event of serious accident or suspicious behavior.

Exactly six months after the accident, the transit authority fired motorman Martin. (Thereupon the union filed a grievance!)

Nearly ten months after the accident, the safety board issued its report. It determined that "the probable cause of this accident was the failure of the motorman to exercise due care in meeting his responsibilities in the unauthorized operation of the Lake–Dan Ryan train into a signal block occupied by the standing Ravenswood train, at a speed that was too fast to stop after the operator sighted the standing train."

It mentioned the police finding of marijuana (police did not testify but were queried by board investigators) and the laboratory results, and stated: "The extent that the motorman may have been under the influence of marijuana at the time of the accident could not be determined by tests. Because of the nature of THC and its behavior in a human body, tests could conclude only that the operator had ingested marijuana at some time before the accident. There is no scale available to relate levels of THC or [to?] its effect on the behavior of the individual."[15]

But *why* had the motorman failed to "exercise due care"? Tests proved that he had taken marijuana (or some form of the drug). When and how much? How often did he use it? Were there no other witnesses who knew of his drug usage? What were marijuana joints doing in his bag in the cab of the train? Why wasn't he confronted with the police finding?

Marijuana may have made the crucial difference in this train wreck as it assuredly had in the Pennsylvania one. Both were similar, rear-end collisions. The drug can extend the senses of time and distance, distort perception, stymie memory, dull reflexes, and allay fear of danger. And, while the case may not have involved peak intoxication, the effects of cannabis can be remarkably persistent in some people. Some stay "stoned" far longer than others; and as long as the substance lingers in the brain, it poses a potential problem.

How many train engineers, plane pilots, bus operators, and vessel captains, let alone drivers of cars and trucks, skirt the brink of disaster in an "altered state of consciousness"? The spotlight needs to be cast on a too-little-known threat to transportation safety.

After the above was written, there occurred another fatal train accident with a possible drug link, this time in Queens, New York City.

A head-on collision of two Amtrak passenger trains on an elevated track leading to the Hell Gate Bridge brought death to a passenger and injuries to 115 other people on Monday, July 23, 1984. W. Graham Claytor, Jr., Amtrak's president, said the likely cause was an error by a signal operator, who failed to stop a northbound train from proceeding on a track occupied by a southbound train. Claytor added that "very minute" amounts of marijuana and cocaine had been found in the man's urine. The sample was said to have been taken three hours after the accident and analyzed by a commercial laboratory under contract to Amtrak.

John J. Riley, head of the Federal Railroad Administration, said, "I'd be extremely surprised if drugs turn out to be a factor." His agency had been pushing for stricter and more uniform drug and alcohol testing of railway workers. It had proposed (a) requiring a railroad in any major accident to take all employees involved to the nearest medical facility as soon as possible for mandatory blood and urine sampling, (b) requiring preemployment tests, and (c) authorizing periodic screening of employees.[16]

THE
NONSMOKER

꽃   꽃

- *"I hate to go to parties where marijuana is being smoked. It makes me feel yuk. The smell makes my stomach upset. My head feels like I'm drunk."* —Thelma (high school senior and nonuser)

- *"I had a contact high this afternoon, and it was miserable. We were on a porch outside at lunch hour. It was well ventilated. Three people smoked marijuana, and I experienced a contact high for about thirty minutes. I experienced the same reaction as when I was high."* —Rosemary (ex-user)

- *"I'll never be in the same room or near anyone [smoking marijuana] for that reason. Any small amount definitely does affect me. The last time I noticed that feeling that some of it had got into me was when I went to a reggae concert. . . .*
  "I saw a boy, two or three . . . in Vancouver. The mother was eighteen and smoked pot. The kid was very, very quiet. He wasn't rambunctious like most babies. He was spaced out. It was very hard to communicate with him." —Steve (ex-user)

- *"My son went to a friend's home and saw the mother blow marijuana smoke into her two-year-old baby's mouth to make it stop crying.*
  "I heard of another mother who used a power hitter to get smoke into the mouth of her fifteen-month-old baby when it was fussing from teething." —Charlene (New Hampshire mother)

- *"I've heard of people who've blown smoke into others' nostrils and given the others a high. . . . It was sort of a trick."* —Edward (ex-user)

• *"Luckily since I was on campus [in Florida] . . . I didn't have to associate with riffraff, except once my girl friend took me to some local townspeople to buy some [marijuana]. . . . They were smoking in close proximity to their nine-month-old son. On my questioning, they said in their opinion their baby would suffer no ill effects from breathing the smoke.*

"I think that was pretty horrid. I think it would slow down the baby's acquisition of knowledge by dampening the baby's natural activity. Marijuana encourages a laid-back feeling, and a baby in its first year learns more than adults learn in twenty years. It's very important that they be seeking out new information. I think it would have effects on the baby's intelligence." —Kathy (light user, former heavy user)

• *"One time I was getting high in a car with the windows rolled up [while someone else smoked marijuana]. There were two little kids in the car and I really think they got a buzz out of it. When we got out—we were in the mountains—they were going nuts running around."* —Millie (chronic user)

• *"One of my customers at the restaurant once, his daughter was crying, and it seemed to me he was smoking marijuana at the time—at that very time. . . . He took his daughter down to the rest rooms after she was crying—and she was a year and a half—and when she came back, she wasn't crying anymore. . . .*

"You can definitely be affected by it [someone else's smoke]. . . . I've felt it really strongly. I feel like, wow, I'm starting to fall asleep, or I'm starting to feel sick, or starting to feel light-headed. . . . I really try my hardest just to get away from it." —Lewis (ex-user)

• *"I'm one of those people who are irate against cigarette smokers. I have my nerve. . . .*

"I know there are a lot of hippie parents that get their kids high. . . .

"You can't be in a room of pot smokers and not get high, if the room is real closed up." —Alice (chronic user)

• *"As to being next to someone who was smoking: I would actually get more of a headache than I would get the effect of it."* —Quentin (ex-user)

• *"Standing in line to see Star Wars, people up ahead of us were smoking dope and it gave me a headache, and this was even outside."* —Nathan (ex-user)

• *"I have to smoke it [to get high]. But I get a little nauseated."* —Janet (ex-user)

• *"I know of a few [nonsmoking] people who are allergic to pot smoke. They get sneezing attacks and stuffed noses."* —Bert (chronic user)

• *"One of my brothers still lives at home, and he's very susceptible to contact highs. I won't smoke around him. I've seen him get very stoned— almost out of his mind—from being in contact with marijuana smoke."* —Betty (long-time user, trying to quit)

1

Involuntary Smoking

In 1972 U. S. Surgeon General Jesse L. Steinfeld issued *The Health Consequences of Smoking* and disclosed to the public that tobacco smoke, from the standpoint of the nonsmoker, is more than just annoying: it is harmful. His successors followed up with additional information on this theme.

The reports cited studies of smoke-filled rooms in which carbon monoxide levels exceeded legal limits for air pollution, even with lots of ventilation. In normal people the smoke can temporarily change their vital signs and impair their ability to see, hear, think, and react efficiently. To those suffering from heart or lung disease, it can be dangerous. The studies found that the smoke coming from the lighted end of a cigarette has higher concentrations of many irritating and hazardous substances than does the smoke inhaled by the smoker, that large numbers of the population experience physical irritation from smoking, that infants of smoking parents are more likely to have bronchitis and pneumonia— and on and on.

Studies on involuntary smoking—also called passive smoking or secondhand smoking—number in the hundreds.

The largest and most important of these, a study of 91,540 nonsmoking wives, aged forty and above, came out of Japan in 1981 (part of a larger health study of 265,118 men and women). During fourteen years 174 of the women died of lung cancer, and "Wives of heavy smokers were found to have a higher risk of developing lung cancer than wives of non-smokers," reported Dr. Takeshi Hirayama, a physician heading the epidemiology division of the National Cancer Center Research Institute in Tokyo.

Compared with a household in which the husband never smoked or occasionally smoked, the risk to the wife was twice as great if he smoked twenty or more cigarettes a day; and it was 1.6 times as great if he smoked between one and nineteen cigarettes or had given up smoking.

"The effect of passive smoking was around one-half to one-third that of direct smoking," Dr. Hirayama added. The passive smoking seemed also to bear on deaths from emphysema and asthma, although the relation to smoking was statistically significant only for lung cancer.[1]

Studies in Greece by Trichopoulos et al. (1981) and in Louisiana by Correa et al. (1983) also suggested statistical links between lung cancer and passive smoking of spouses' cigarettes, although Garfinkel (1981) detected scant relationship upon analyzing American nonsmoker statistics.[2]

> Over a dozen studies signify more respiratory illness and less lung capacity in children of mothers who smoke than in children of nonsmoking mothers. In one such study (1983) medical researchers periodically examined 1,156 youngsters in East Boston and inferred that maternal smoking held down lung growth in children. Results of pulmonary function tests as adjusted by interview data implied to Tager et al. that "after five years, the lungs of nonsmoking children with mothers who smoke grow at only 93 per cent of the rate of growth in nonsmoking children with mothers who do not smoke. . . ." They reckoned the detriment enough to predispose the handicapped ones to obstructive airway disease in adult life.[3]
>
> The 1984 surgeon general's report on *The Health Consequences of Smoking* let it be known that cigarette smoking at typical levels "can make a significant measurable contribution to the level of indoor air pollution"; smoke chemicals enter the systems of involuntary smokers (nicotine metabolite has been measured in their urine), altering lung function in chronically exposed adults and children, increasing objective measures of eye irritation, and so forth.
>
> Surgeon General C. Everett Koop, at a press conference in May, 1984, called the evidence of harm from passive smoking "very solid." The Tobacco Institute pointed out that not all authorities agreed.

Now, what about marijuana? "In the case of marijuana, this [passive smoking] takes on particular significance because of the ability of the agent to cause psychotropic effects and to alter heart rate," wrote Phillip Zeidenberg, New York research psychiatrist and Columbia University professor, in cooperation with a Paris chemistry professor and a Columbia colleague (1977). Marijuana, said their report, often is smoked in closed, poorly ventilated rooms because it is illegal and cannot be smoked in public. (But increasingly it *is* smoked in public!)

Stories of nonsmokers becoming intoxicated by social contact with smokers had been common. Professionals had attributed "contact highs" to the power of suggestion. Dr. Zeidenberg and his associates, however, documented a case of an experimental subject who did not smoke marijuana himself but experienced a "high" by being in a group of marijuana smokers. He was proved to have cannabinoid in his system.

Five habitual marijuana smokers were admitted to a locked hospital ward in 1975 and directed to smoke for three weeks, in an experiment to test marijuana's effects on various biological and psychological functions. One nonsmoking volunteer, a foreign student, was assigned to live with them but to smoke only inactive joints. He was supposed to serve as a check against any possible "hospitalism" effect—but the plan backfired because he was housed in the same quarters as the smokers.

After mingling with the smokers for two weeks, the nonsmoker reported dizziness and slight nausea. His pulse raced and eyes reddened. He felt "high." He chose to leave the smokers and shift to the other end of the ward.

Thinking that the placebo cigarettes had been accidentally contaminated with active material, the experimenters sent some of them back to the National Institute on Drug Abuse, which had provided all of the marijuana, to be analyzed. They contained no cannabinoid.

Urine specimens taken from the student once or twice a week showed substantial amounts of cannabinoid. The cannabinoid began to appear one week after the onset of smoking in the ward and reached a peak at the time that he reported a "contact high," at which time the doctors noted the rapid pulse and red eyes. (The peak was 260 nanograms per milliliter, assayed by "gallium chelate formation.") For weeks after he began to avoid the other smokers, the drug slowly left his body, presumably as released from fatty tissues. The pattern indicated "true passive marijuana intoxication."

The student was not the only one suffering from secondhand marijuana smoke. Numerous staff members who observed the subjects smoking complained of discomfort and they too experienced nausea, speeding heart, and inflamed eyes. Eventually the scientists had to set up a closed-circuit television system to observe the smokers.

"If marijuana smoking is legalized," Zeidenberg and colleagues climaxed, "special precautions may have to be taken to protect individuals from passive absorption of cannabinoids."[4]

Unfortunately, legalization is not necessary for marijuana to be smoked openly. In states where decriminalization is in effect, the weak "parking ticket" laws are usually ignored by police and prosecutors and hence by the smokers themselves, who have become increasingly bold in public places.

Nonsmokers are subject to more than the physical hazards and subjective discomforts of breathing secondhand smoke as such. Cannabis smoking can entail involuntary intoxication, with all that implies in terms of safety and well-being.

Millions are allergic to tobacco smoke. Similarly, there are those who show special sensitivity to cannabis smoke. The reaction can be unusual. A northern California woman, whom we will call Dorothy, suffers a delayed sickness after passive exposure to the smoke, the same reaction she experienced on the few occasions when she actively smoked. She tells this story:

"I had never smoked marijuana until I was thirty-five. . . . It was just a quirk that I should meet people who got involved in this. They were very artistic-type people. . . . I was curious and also the people I was associating with were very involved in it, and they did persuade me too. They thought I was quite old not to have experienced it. They said that it would feel good, that you'd feel floaty, that it would make you feel relaxed. . . .

"I only smoked it for a matter of three or four months. Maybe I had five experiences with it. One of those occasions I smoked hashish, which cost two hundred dollars for one of those little cubes, so it was fairly good stuff, but I didn't get high at all. . . . The people who were with me were experiencing some kind of high, but I wasn't. I never did get high. I was with people who were using it all day long, and so I was smoking it all day long, and the only effect that I got was an extremely raw mouth and fever blisters appeared on my lips. And since I don't smoke cigarettes, I didn't enjoy any of it. . . .

"Every time I smoked it, I would become sick in twenty days . . . nausea and light-headedness. . . . So I stopped smoking marijuana and I also stopped being around it, because I found that even being in the same room with people who are using it, I will be affected with a similar reaction. . . . It's happened three times. . . . I don't have the reaction immediately, but twenty days later I have a whole day of light-headedness and nausea, and it lasts for one day. It's real uncomfortable. . . .

"It took me a while to convince the people I was around at that time that either they would have to go into another room to smoke or I would have to leave, because I wasn't going to knowingly make myself sick. . . . It was my first experience with people who were involved in drugs, and it didn't take me very long to realize that I just don't have a whole lot in common with people who need to have artificial highs. I prefer more natural kinds of experiences."

Was she sure about the time interval? "I would look at the calendar and see when I was around the people, and it was twenty days!"

A friend of Dorothy's also is sensitive to secondhand marijuana smoke: "My girl friend finds that when she's around it, it bothers her. She gets a contact high and then she gets nauseous immediately."

2

Other Hazards

"Sex act sparked hotel fire," shouted a front-page banner headline. The actor was a twenty-three-year-old busboy arrested following a fire that took eight lives at the Las Vegas Hilton in February, 1981. According to a detective's affidavit, the busboy said he had started the fire "by touching the drapes with a marijuana cigarette while he was engaged in homosexual activity. . . ." By substituting "Pot joint" for "Sex act," the headline would have made more sense. The excuse never made any sense. A year later the accused was convicted of arson and eight counts of mur-

der and sentenced to life imprisonment without parole.[5]

But the story points to another side of the marijuana problem. Marijuana joints, like commercial cigarettes, can spark fires, and fire is the primary hazard that nonsmokers face from smokers in general. Smokers and their cigarettes constitute by far the greatest single source of fatal fires in the United States.

The intoxicating character of marijuana and the addition to the smoking population of millions of marijuana smokers—children among them— may have widened the danger.

> Careless smokers have long led in causes of fires.[6]
>
> The National Fire Protection Association reported that in the period 1971 to 1978 cigarettes were to blame in the two leading scenarios—ignition of upholstery and bedding at home—for U.S. fires killing one or two people, accounting for 32 percent of the deaths and an equal percentage of the fatal fires. Third, with less than 4 percent of such deaths and fires, came highway crashes igniting fuel tanks. Cigarettes were responsible for five of the top sixteen scenarios. (One- and two-fatality fires accounted for most fire deaths, 87 percent of 8,621 deaths in 1978.)[7]
>
> Cigarettes also took the first two places—also upholstery and bedding—on a list of ignition scenarios for multiple-death (three or more) fires in residential properties, 1971 to 1980, accounting nationally for 25 percent of the total deaths and the same percentage of fires. Again the third scenario—heat from solid-fueled equipment—covered less than 4 percent of comparable deaths and fires. Five of the top fifteen scenarios involved cigarettes. Butts commonly ignited homes, apartments, hotels, rooming houses, institutions, and so forth.[8]

✻   ✻   ✻

> In fire-conscious San Francisco, whose official seal depicts a phoenix arising from flames, three fire officers shared with us their thoughts on the marijuana matter.
>
> A lieutenant described the scene of a fire in a housing-project apartment. Partially clad, a woman was collapsed on a sofa, a man in an armchair, as two types of smoke competed for space. A marijuana joint had fallen from her hand and ignited a rug. "The two of them were spaced out when we got there. They were in never-never land. There was no reflex." Both were hospitalized and recovered—from drug overdose.
>
> "Anything that alters a person's thinking naturally is going to indirectly be the cause of fires, whether it's alcohol, heroin, cocaine, or marijuana," said another lieutenant.
>
> "There's no doubt in my mind that it will be a cause," said a battalion chief. "In the act of smoking the reefer, you've got the potential for fire in one act, the smoking and the intoxication."

The drug user's habit may be imposed on the nonuser in diverse ways, sometimes unintentionally. Smoking of marijuana by pregnant and nursing mothers can affect their offspring. As animal and human studies demonstrate, cannabinoids are transmitted across the placenta and through the milk. At other times the imposition on the nonuser is quite intentional.

In mid-1983 a group of clerks and secretaries organized, as a morale builder, a potluck breakfast at the Dade County courthouse, Miami. During the second hour some of the breakfasters began complaining of nausea, dizziness, and sweating. Ambulances came and victims were carried out of the courthouse on stretchers. Altogether twenty-two people went to three hospitals. The trouble traced to brownies containing marijuana, the contribution of a twenty-eight-year-old clerk. Police arrested him.[9]

Six months later in Monterey Park, Los Angeles County, the same kind of pastry caused an uproar at a Thursday evening dance class for senior citizens. Members lost their balance and complained of feeling giddy and ill. Five elderly people, suffering from nausea and dizziness, were taken to hospitals, three of them admitted. A man of seventy-one said "everything was kind of fuzzy" as he drove home that evening, and a truck honked at him as he passed through a light—"right away I wasn't sure whether the light was red or green." The dance instructor and his roommate admitted baking the brownies, laced with marijuana, and were booked on felony charges of tampering with food. They said, "We meant no harm. We thought it would loosen them up a bit."[10]

Ex-marijuana smoker Nathan describes an incident during his university days at Harvard in the midsixties when he smoked marijuana habitually:

"My roommate wasn't interested in turning on at all. He was practically a saint to put up with me doing it. He was very tolerant, but he was just not interested. He was interested in studying. In fact, he was president of Phi Beta Kappa, straight A average, Latin orator, and all the rest of it.

"Two or three of us, we kept telling him that it was so great and he really ought to try it, and he said no—he wasn't interested. He wasn't putting us down; he just wasn't interested himself. And one night we decided it would be a great lark to grab him and throw him on the floor and sit on him and stick a lighted joint in his mouth and make him smoke it.

"And, you know, actually what stopped us was that in the course of this wrestling match, a floorboard or something had a great, huge sliver, about three inches long, that went into his foot. I think it landed under his nail or something. And that was so painful and so obvious that we desisted from trying to make him smoke the thing. I think we actually did get it into his mouth and he had to inhale a little bit, but it didn't have any effect and then this thing happened, so we kind of called it off and helped him get the sliver out of his foot."

DEPENDENCE

1

Is It Addictive?

We wondered why the young woman with whom we spent the day sightseeing in southern California kept absenting herself every couple of hours, for about ten minutes each time.

"I'm addicted to marijuana," she finally admitted. "I'm physically addicted to it."

Addicted? But conventional wisdom has it that marijuana is nonaddictive, or at most psychologically habit-forming.

When he used to smoke marijuana, Nathan "didn't want to admit it, but there would be times when I felt almost desperate to get it." After a couple of years of smoking, "I'd go looking around for people in the campus . . . who I knew who might have some marijuana . . . especially in the evening. . . . Obviously, there was the alternative of studying all these different courses. . . . And I'd feel this compulsion that I had to instead get stoned. . . . So I'd go to one person. If they didn't have it, I'd be frustrated. Go to somebody else. If they didn't have it, I'd be frustrated. . . .

"Those feelings that I had at that time were so strong and I was so irritated, I can see now it was physical addiction. My palms started to get sweaty, I was extremely nervous and irritable, and I was really, really bothered."

Betty, a long-time marijuana smoker who would like to quit, said, "It's addictive. It's something I can't do without. . . . It's like an alcoholic. I'm irritable unless I get my high." Chronic users Charlie and Millie also thought they were addicted to marijuana. He said, "You stop for a couple of days and the following days you feel kind of down. . . . It makes you kind of mad because you want it and you can't get it." She said, "I don't think it's an addiction I couldn't break. I think I'm more addicted to cigarettes."

Alice, also a chronic user, acknowledged a habit but no addiction, because "I've gone without marijuana. The worst symptom I've ever incurred is sleeplessness. Also a little edginess . . . aggression. . . . I'm dependent on pot to relax me in the evenings." Ex-users Rosemary, Joe, Anna, and Pierre doubted that it was physically addictive. Pierre knew high schoolers who "could smoke every fifteen or twenty minutes practically all night long. I would consider it a habit, a psychological addiction." Former regular users Janet and Quentin denied having had even a habit.

Said Fred, a New York drug-treatment worker who used to smoke cannabis heavily (and later graduated to heroin), "When you start smoking marijuana . . . you get this euphoric effect. . . . Everything seems funny. You look at someone's face and you just start laughing. . . .

"After a while those things stop happening. You're so used to smoking it that it's just part of a normal daily function. You get up in the morning to smoke a joint because after a while you become sort of like psychologically dependent on it. You don't feel you can function without the use of it . . . interact with people. . . ."

With heavy smoking, "you're in a daze. You really don't want to be bothered. You lack a lot of motivation. You just hang around and smoke pot," Fred said.

Cecilia, a nonuser, said, "The two men that I have been with that liked marijuana . . . could not have a good time without it. . . . I lived with one of them for a year and a half and he told me, 'If you really knew me without a drug, you wouldn't like me.' . . . He was almost alone in lovemaking. It wouldn't have mattered who I was because he was in his own, magic, marijuana bubble. And if people say it isn't habit-forming, they're out of their minds. . . . He always had a habit. He wanted it around all the time. . . . It's like taking a tranquilizer when you're going through a very difficult, anxious time . . . to make you not feel. Grass makes you not feel. . . .

"When we were traveling, he didn't have any drugs at all. . . . He went through really great mood swings . . . from being practically manic to down in hell. . . . He wasn't wonderful . . . but he was better as a human being when he had a lot of grass. It was like something was amiss in his chemistry and grass added that missing link."

*   *   *

Walton (1938) cited several observers who recognized a physical basis for the cannabis habit, among them Lipa in Egypt (1908), Iglesias in Brazil (1918), Kerim in Turkey (1930), and Skliar and Iwanow in Russia (1932). The last pair, studying twenty-eight *anasha* (cannabis) smokers, listed withdrawal symptoms that sometimes included pain, vomiting, sweating, fear, and depression; the symptoms disappeared when the drug was taken.[1]

Two physicians, writing to two British medical journals, described withdrawal symptoms among Indians (1949) and South Africans (1971) craving cannabis when deprived of it during expeditions. In each case only a small number of each group suffered the symptoms.

• J. D. Fraser told of Indian troops sent abroad. Nine who had long smoked *ganja* ("the flowering and fruiting heads of the female plant") displayed irritability, culminating in outbursts of violence and "acute psychotic episodes." They begged for the drug, fought for ordinary cigarettes, acted filthily, sometimes hallucinated, and grew emaciated.[2]

• A. D. Bensusan recounted a desert trip in which marijuana smoking was prevalent among young adults. As supplies diminished, three males and two females developed "anxiety symptoms and restlessness coupled with acute abdominal cramps, nausea, sweating, increased pulse rate but no rise in temperature, low blood pressure, and muscular aches." Later he realized that the disappearance of symptoms coincided with the arrival of more marijuana. Elsewhere he saw two similar cases.[3]

The World Health Organization's bulletin (1965) set forth the generally accepted view: "Absence of physical dependence" and "no characteristic abstinence syndrome." Committees of the American Medical Association and the National Academy of Sciences (1968) accepted the "fact that no physical dependence develops with cannabis . . ." (but still considered the drug "dangerous"). And the British government's Advisory Committee on Drug Dependence (1968) stated: "Unlike heroin, cannabis does not cause physical dependence and withdrawal effects do not occur when its use is discontinued."

In 1964 drug advisers of the World Health Organization (WHO) recommended substituting the term "drug dependence" for the terms "drug addiction" and "drug habituation." Writing for WHO (1965), four physicians declared it scientifically unsound to maintain a single definition for all forms of drug addiction/habituation. A feature common to all of these conditions is "dependence, psychic or physical or both." To speak of "drug dependence of this or that type" is more illuminating. "Drug dependence of the cannabis type" has these three characteristics: "moderate to strong psychic dependence on account of the desired subjective effects. . . . Absence of physical dependence, so that there is no characteristic abstinence syndrome when the drug is discontinued. . . . Little tendency to increase the dose and no evidence of tolerance."[4]

The AMA-Academy of Sciences committees emphasized, "Many stimulants are dangerous substances although they do not cause physical dependence." In this category they placed cannabis, which in many countries of chronic heavy use, such as Egypt, Morocco, and Algeria, "has a marked effect on reducing the social productivity of a significant number of persons."[5]

The British advisory committee was satisfied, as was nearly all "informed opinion," that tolerance and physical dependence did not develop, although its report took note of contrary reports from abroad. (Concerning the Skliar-Iwanow account from Russia, "There seems . . . doubt as to whether opium and cocaine may have been mixed with the cannabis in 'anascha.' ") The bulk of users continue because they enjoy it, "but if they decide to give it up they do not usually experience difficulty," and the use of cannabis by itself "does not appear to impair the subject's efficiency," said the advisers, accepting most arguments of the cannabis movement (but not favoring legalization).

In the United Kingdom, where hashish then was stronger than America's marijuana and more commonly used than marijuana, the Ministry of Health had listed 82 hospital admissions for "drug addiction" involving cannabis during 1966 (a year when convictions for cannabis offenses rose nationally from 626 to 1,119). The advisory committee checked further data on 79 of the admissions that left the evidence of cannabis addiction "inconclusive or irrelevant" in 42 cases while in the other 37, other drugs might also have been used.[6]

Rubin and Comitas (1975) denied that their *ganja*-smoking subjects in Jamaica suffered withdrawal symptoms or showed signs of severe dependence during a week's abstention in a hospital. But one heavy user reported much discomfort for at least a day whenever he discontinued smoking, and interviews elicited quotations like these:

- "If I don't get a draw in the morning I can't feel good."

- "You can give me a spliff every 15 minutes. I feel dead if I don't get a smoke."

- "I can't do without my smoke."

- "When I don't take a draw I feel out of myself."

- "I am like a fish out of water" (when no *ganja* is available).[7]

The late Professor Hardin B. Jones called dependence on cannabis "both chemical and psychological." It is "chemically addictive" in view of two factors: tolerance (diminished effects of a drug after repeated doses) and withdrawal symptoms (discomfort when a drug is given up). The symptoms are relatively mild—they may include only brief irritability, restlessness, and sleeplessness—because THC accumulates in the body and leaves it slowly. The narcotics, on the other hand, leave the body rapidly. "The psychological addiction may be the more difficult of the two to break," he wrote (1978). "In recent years I have seen more and more cannabis users who are unable to stop without help."[8]

Experiments by the late Dr. James Olds of the California Institute of Technology (1956) illustrate the persistence of the drive for pleasure. Electrodes were implanted in animals' brains and connected to current that they could activate themselves. They would press the pleasure lever—rather than food and water levers—for hours, until they dropped from exhaustion. The studies gave rise to a theory of "pleasure" and "punishment" centers in the brain's limbic system.[9]

* * *

Robert G. Heath, psychiatrist-neurologist of Tulane University, has been concerned about the social consequences of obtaining "pleasure that is disassociated from the performance of a task." Pleasure and pain are the basic moving forces in behavior, as he sees it. If "by puffing on a joint or by popping a pill" people can get the pleasures of food or sex or sports, the results can be malnutrition, nonpropagation of the species, or physical deterioration. And if drugs replace the apprehension associated with preparation for an examination or an important job, academic failure or loss to society can follow. (Heath expressed these ideas at the 1981 Southeast Drug Conference at Georgia State University, Atlanta, and elsewhere.)

Withdrawal symptoms appeared in subjects who had been given frequent doses of THC or cannabis extract by mouth for five to twenty-one days in San Francisco. They had received "modest doses" (10 to 30 mg of THC) every three or four hours, remaining continuously intoxicated, Dr. Reese T. Jones, M.D., of Langley Porter Neuropsychiatric Institute reported (1979, 1980).

Tolerance developed rapidly to many psychological and physiological effects. Following the sudden withdrawal of THC or cannabis extract, the symptoms appeared. Fifteen subjects given only cannabidiol suffered no symptoms. Altogether 120 paid volunteers, all males and all experienced cannabis smokers, were tested in a hospital research ward over several years.

The withdrawal syndrome—which varied with the dose, frequency, and length of intoxication—had "many similarities" to that produced by "modest doses of sedative hypnotics." Deprived suddenly of THC, subjects reacted with "irritable and angry mood, disturbed sleep, restlessness, decreased appetite, increased perspiration, chills and feverish feeling, nausea and other abdominal distress, tremulousness, weight loss, salivation, tremor, body temperature increase," etc. The symptoms began a few hours after the last dose and generally disappeared in three or four days.[10]

* * *

Dr. Lester Grinspoon, Harvard psychiatry professor and writer on drugs, said: "Cannabis is not physically addictive. Something resembling mild withdrawal symptoms has been reported in laboratory animals given enormous doses of THC for a long time and even in human beings in a laboratory situation; but as a clinical phenomenon in ordinary recreational use a cannabis abstinence syndrome simply does not exist, even among Jamaicans who use up to 420 milligrams of THC a day."

As for the common statement that cannabis creates a psychological dependence, "almost any habit that satisfies a need or desire" can be so described. Some dependencies are trivial or benign. "The significant question is whether the habit does any harm to the individual or society. One test of this . . . is whether the person who has the habit wishes he could give it up but feels unable to do so. Marijuana users rarely feel that way; they usually state they can take the drug or leave it and they do not feel tormented craving in its absence."

> Dr. Grinspoon saw little evidence of "pharmacological tolerance" outside of the laboratory. While he did acknowledge "behavorial tolerance," compensation for high-dose intoxication, he knew of no reports of a need to increase doses to regain the original euphoria or prevent depression.
>
> In a general defense of cannabis before a Senate committee (1980), he pronounced it "remarkably safe" compared with many legal substances. "On the evidence now available, chronic use of cannabis does no serious damage to the body or the mind."[11]

Long-term, heavy hashish smokers in Egypt (1980) underwent changes in mood and personality when deprived. Although 83 percent of some 1,100 smokers considered themselves good-humored when drugged, only 8 percent so described themselves when deprived. Only 9 percent avowed being impulsive and rash when drugged, but 43 percent were that way when lacking the drug. Negativism or contrariness rose from 14 percent under the drug to 42 percent on deprival. With the drug, 72 percent were docile; without it, 30 percent. When drugged, 2 to 4 percent had frequent conflicts with people at work, friends, or family; but without the drug, 39 to 48 percent had such conflicts (more often at home than at work).[12]

> It is "universal" for cannabis-dependents—or alcoholics or narcotic addicts—to become hostile toward anyone trying to deprive them of what they crave, Dr. Harvey Powelson, psychiatrist of Berkeley, California, said in an interview. When he switched his opinion and began arguing against marijuana at the University of California, "people physically threatened me and shouted at me. The situation was sometimes riotous."

Julia Ross, director of the substance abuse program at the Counseling Center of the Henry Ohlhoff House in San Francisco (1981), called marijuana "physically addictive. We have seen men in our residential program go through prolonged periods of insomnia, cold sweats, and rushes of anxiety." In her nonresidential program she was seeing more and more children who would start marijuana and escalate quickly to huge amounts. "Within weeks getting high is all that matters to them."[13]

Lots of marijuana regulars cannot work or sleep without their joints and are "just about frantic when they can't find any roaches" (joints or butts), said psychologist Joe Reilly of San Francisco (1981). They cannot abstain for even a day. Some of them can easily limit their use of tobacco, alcohol, and coffee, but not pot. They are miserable in settling "far below their real potential" and often suffer troubling mental symptoms from their drugging. The marijuana abusers he works with range from "street people" to schoolteachers and lawyers, demonstrating that "there is no typical pot-head."[14]

*　　*　　*

"Marijuanics" are the counterparts to alcoholics. Two medical doctors used the term and sought to describe the syndrome of "marijuanism."

• Dr. J. M. Scher of Chicago (1970) estimated that 10 to 20 percent of users fit that category. Patients were visiting him in increasing numbers for relief of marijuana habits. They did not necessarily relate their symptoms to their smoking, but on questioning he discovered that such a patient "smokes more or less continuously throughout the day or night or both. . . ."

The typical patient was twenty to thirty years old. He had smoked marijuana for at least five years, "socially" at first, experimenting with other drugs but giving them up. He suffered headaches, vague physical discomforts, weakness, uneasiness, reduced creativity and effort, periods of intensified insecurity, an increasing sense of aimlessness, decreasing pleasure and satisfaction from life, and progressive loss of interest in sex. Marijuana gave less pleasure than before but he could not quit voluntarily. When he did stop smoking, the headaches grew worse and pains developed elsewhere.[15]

• According to Dr. Stanley R. Dean, Florida psychiatry professor (1980), the typical "marijuanic" smokes several joints at a stretch several times a week and tends to abuse alcohol and other drugs as well as cannabis. He becomes addicted in his late teens, drops out of college, changes jobs often, and does not marry or have sustained friendships.

He shows most of these symptoms: anxiety and panic reactions, especially on withdrawal; disorientation and emotional and sensory distortions; short- or long-range memory impairment; partial or total blackouts; physical symptoms: headaches, insomnia, coughing, nausea, vomiting, tremors, general malaise; withdrawal distress but reluctance to admit it; need for marijuana on awakening or before a task; marijuana binges, with or without other substances; inability to give up cannabis no matter what trouble it causes; arrests, accidents, fights, and hospitalizations while "stoned"; lying, irresponsibility, stealing; apathy, depression, hostility, guilt; disruption of family, friendship, and life goal; and moral and ethical unconcern.[16]

As director of an outpatient program for adolescent drug abusers at Minnesota's Mayo Clinic, Dr. Robert G. Niven learned that symptoms of marijuana dependence paralleled those of alcoholism. The user increases doses, uses the substance alone, does it surreptitiously, takes it to treat symptoms, blacks out, undergoes a personality change when intoxicated, cannot control the amount used, is preoccupied with it, uses it at inappropriate times, and takes it even at the cost of adverse consequences.[17]

"Don't think that marijuana is too minuscule, that it isn't a drug problem," said actress Mackenzie Phillips on the Dick Cavett TV show (1981), "because there are people who smoke marijuana all day long and never get out of bed. They just constantly smoke marijuana." She likened the problem to narcotic addiction and considered it nearly as "damaging." Mackenzie had become a cocaine addict and her father, musician John Phillips, a heroin addict. Each started with marijuana.

2

Getting Hooked and Unhooked

Like other dependencies, the marijuana habit is a lot easier to start (although some have to work at it) than to stop. Here is how a few started:

Steve, ex-user: "All my peers were doing it. . . . They said it was fun and all right, so I tried it. . . . Nothing really happened until several tries later . . . in a neighborhood park. Friends told me to take a big breath and hold it in."

Alice, chronic user: "My best friend, who belonged to the ―― church, asked me if I wanted to smoke marijuana. I didn't know what it was. I said, 'Oh, sure.' I didn't want her to know she was more sophisticated than me. Then we spent that summer getting high and fat."

Pierre, ex-user: "It was introduced to me by a close friend, one whom I admired. He had trumpeted its virtues to me, and since I trusted his judgment, I thought, 'Well, maybe there's something to it.'"

Betty, chronic user: "My big brother had just gotten out of the service and come home from Vietnam. We were bored one afternoon. He had a silly grin on his face and said, 'C'mon. Let's go up to my room.' He had lots of very strong, Vietnamese dope with him. He pulled it out of his duffel bag and said, 'Have you ever tried any of this stuff?' There's something about your big brother asking you. I trusted him.

"We smoked five pipefuls. I got very giggly. I remember my lips turned numb. I got very high. I stayed that way the whole day, about five hours. I was real gone."

Often the hooked have a yen to hook others.

Quentin, ex-user: "We tried to get some new people—just basically at high school parties—to try this new stuff. We wanted to get women up there for sexual purposes. . . . They were in the seventeen to twenty year age range."

Steve: "I would tell people it was 'a very neat thing to do. . . . You're not cool unless you smoke this.'"

Alice: "I think I only seduced one person. She was my oldest friend, and innocent. She grew up in the suburbs while I grew up in the city. We were fifteen. I took her to Hollywood and told her I was going to show her some hippies. I showed her hippies—my friends."

Janet, ex-user: "My best friend turned my little sister on. She was fourteen."

The unhooking comes in diverse ways.

Rosemary, ex-user: "I suffered paranoia. . . . I was nervous, unsure of what I was saying or thinking, and I would lose confidence, but I kept on smoking it because of the peer pressure. I explained my problems to a friend of mine and she said, 'Don't smoke it anymore,' and I quit. It was just overcoming the power of habit. I'd never considered stopping."

Quentin: "The Vietnam war's over. Your nerves come back to normal. I don't need it. How'd I quit? Just strictly cold turkey. Just said, 'I don't need it anymore,' told my friends who smoked it a lot my experiences, and asked them when I go to a party don't give the stuff to me anymore. And everyone has cooperated."

Janet: "The very last time I smoked pot, it was my first date with a new guy. He bought a pint bottle of Jack Daniel's. I drank most of it. One of his friends asked me if I wanted to smoke pot. I did and got really, really sick on the street in San Francisco outside some rock club. . . . I just didn't smoke it again."

Steve: "When my mom found out I was smoking, she kept giving me information that she had, and a lot of it was confirming suspicions that I had. . . . A month or two later, a teacher overheard another kid saying, 'Steve is into a lot of hard drugs.' The teacher told my parents. I had a long talk with them. Everything combined in that one day. . . . For the first couple months after I quit, I had a craving for it."

Donna, ex-user: "First I decided it cost too much and I wasn't going to spend the money. Then after I was away from it, my energy level picked up so much and I got just so much more done and slept better and just all the way around felt better."

*   *   *

Alice, who boasts of having been one of the early hippies during the midsixties, knows of "a lot of hippie parents that get their kids high."

A girl, ten, asked a lecturing doctor whether marijuana could have harmed her. "I was given pot by my parents when I was six. Three cigarettes a day or more."[18]

Ex-marijuana smoker Anna knows a man "whose little boy is five and smokes occasionally."

Upon discovering that their children use marijuana, parents typically are upset. They may blame themselves, not realizing that it can happen in every kind of family. What should they do? There seems to be no answer for all cases. Some parents act sternly, others softly. Either way, some juveniles abandon drugs and others don't.

Two girls on two coasts began smoking marijuana at thirteen. Their parents reacted much differently. Yet the results do not differ much.

• One was Millie in New Jersey: "At first when they found out, they were really upset. They asked me how they failed as parents. They didn't really punish me in any way. . . . Now they take it real well. They gave me permission to smoke pot in the house. . . . I think my parents are great."

Eleven years later, Millie, a switchboard operator, smokes nearly every day. In her school and college days, she did it mainly on weekends. "Today I had three bongs so far," she said with a slur on the Monday we last spoke with her.

• The other was Alice in Los Angeles. Her mother demanded that she desist and barred the drug from their house. Since the woman smoked tobacco cigarettes, to the girl it seemed hypocritical to ban her type of cigarette. Alice continued smoking, and at fifteen she ran away to a commune in the suburbs, waiting two days before phoning her distraught parent.

At twenty-nine, Alice smokes marijuana daily. Her consumption rose over the years. As a waitress, she was "always high." Now employed in an office, she waits until after work. She visits her mother occasionally and "I don't smoke pot, out of respect."

A mother herself, Alice admits that "if my daughter was doing the things I was doing, I'd be scared witless." (Actually, she used a word rhyming with "witless.")

*   *   *

For parents who want their children to give up marijuana, nineteen-year-old Steve (who smoked it—as many as 30 joints a week—between ages fourteen and seventeen) offered this advice:

"Definitely take an interest. Don't pass it by as an adolescent thing they might grow out of. It's definitely an addiction that takes a major effort to get out of. It's not something that can be grown out of naturally.

"The big mistake is to treat it as a bad thing—'You're a naughty boy for smoking pot.' It should be treated as a problem, a disease that has to be dealt with. When a parent tells a kid it's bad, the kid often says, 'She's just sounding off. I won't have her tell me what to do.' They have to be careful not to use scare tactics—say, 'Oh, you're going to get warts on your face!'—but very reasonable, objective information. There has to be an attitude that the decision has to be from the kid himself. It can't be the parent just telling him what to do.

"The parent has to take a very encouraging stance, that 'it's much nicer when you're off the drug. You have a lot more opportunity and potential within yourself.' It's really a fine line between helpful and overbearing. They really have to stick to the helpful side.

"You've got to give the kid objective information along with the encouragement, reminding the kid what the information says, because it takes a while for the information to sink in. Make sure it's objectively written . . . [not] just another fanatic person trying to persuade people to his views. . . .

"The best thing they can do is educate themselves and attempt to educate their children. Remain very open to the children's point of view. At the same time, let the children know their point of view. Keep it in the framework that both have an opinion."

*   *   *

Dr. Harold M. Voth, senior psychiatrist of The Menninger Foundation, Topeka, Kansas, gave considerably different advice (1980). He urged any parents of a marijuana-smoking child to keep the child away from marijuana and smoking friends, to conduct periodic searches, and to believe only the evidence and not promises. Meanwhile, he said, they should help the child find gratifying activities to substitute for the drug habit and find life goals to supplant the aimlessness into which users drift.

"Look your child squarely in the eye and tell him clearly and without the slightest equivocation that you are going to stop his use of marijuana." The battle that the parents wage against their child's sickness, unlike other battles, has no loser. "Your victory is also your child's victory," the doctor declared in a booklet.

To send the child to a mental health professional or hospital probably would be useless, except in the event of a suicide attempt—Dr. Voth advised—although counseling or psychotherapy may help him after he has been drug-free for at least three months. The parents can better interpose a "brick wall" between the child and marijuana. It is up to them to manage his life when he cannot adequately do so. They must never appear to reject him.

"Tell your child that you are taking more responsibility for the way he lives because you love him. . . . Nothing works better than parental interest, encouragement, wisdom and love."[19]

* * *

To get teenagers off marijuana, pediatrician Ingrid L. Lantner, of Cleveland, Ohio, (a) tells them what marijuana does to their bodies and brains; (b) asks them to compare favorite activities when high and when free of drug; (c) urges a small group desiring to quit to meet each week informally; (d) advises parents to do everything possible to keep their children away from the drug, even admitting them to rehabilitation centers if necessary; and (e) recommends physical exercise and nutritious food to counteract the inadequate, high-sugar intake of marijuana regulars.[20]

* * *

Private programs to deal specifically with marijuana dependency began in 1978. New York had Potsmokers Anonymous and San Francisco had the Marijuana Intensive. Both were still going strong in 1984. The first, patterned after Alcoholics Anonymous, aimed to get smokers to quit. The goal of the latter, a four-week course, was to "regain control" over consumption, not necessarily to give it up. (Drug counselor Julia Ross of San Francisco insists, on the basis of her experience, that only complete abstinence can defeat any "drug addiction," including "marijuana addiction.")

☆   ☆   ☆

"All those years we were just going through hell. I didn't know pot could do this," said Patricia, a mother in a San Jose, California, suburb. She described to us marijuana's impact on her son, Ken, and her efforts to get him to quit.

Ken began smoking at thirteen. It took Patricia and her husband, Norman, six months to find out. Later they learned that Ken's friends smoked marijuana and so did the parents of one of them. Over a three-year period, Ken displayed erratic behavior, a bitter personality, hatred for adults, and even violence.

"I have holes in the walls . . . where he knocked his fists. . . . He became violent with us physically, pushing and shoving us around if we tried to discipline him in any way. . . . One day Ken got violent with a teacher at school.

"He was really dirty looking, didn't want to wash his hair or take a bath . . . had the manners of an animal . . . was tired all the time . . . couldn't communicate with us. It was hard for him to study, couldn't communicate, forgot.

"He lied to us all the time and stole, just small things. He ran away from home a few times . . . would crawl out of the window in the middle of the night to go to parties. I would wake up . . . and find him gone."

They called the police many times. An officer would talk with Ken, to no avail. The parents could have placed him in reform school, but they wanted to handle the problem at home.

"I thought the more knowledge I had, the more I could handle him, so I went to the Parents Who Care workshops, drug council meetings . . . wherever there was a meeting . . . about once a week. I would tell Ken each time I went . . . 'I won't be home tonight. I'm going to . . . a drug meeting.' . . .

"When Ken's grades were slipping . . . my husband tutored him every night. It was really hard, as marijuana really affected his memory. He repeated a year of math because he couldn't think. Norm would tutor him one night. The next day Ken would forget it and Norm would have to tutor him again. His thinking would be fuzzy for five days after he had a hit."

A drug counselor said, "You may get Ken to cut back on his marijuana . . . but you will never get him off completely." Patricia could not accept that. She told Ken, "You're getting off." He said, "Mom, I'll never be able to quit. I'll have to have it at least once a week." She insisted, "You're going to quit it completely, and that's it."

Patricia told his teachers, his pediatrician, and her own close friends, "My son's on pot. Please help me." They all talked to Ken, encouraging him to quit marijuana. Ken did not know that Patricia had coached them.

She offered him a dollar for each day that he went without marijuana. If he smoked, she marked the date on a calendar in his room. She would say, "Hey, Ken, you haven't had a hit for one week. . . . Isn't that great?" Or else, "Oh oh, you've been on pot. You don't get your dollar today." She would then remind Ken what marijuana did to him.

"I got so I could tell immediately when he had a hit. . . . His eyelids would drop. . . . Pot smokers have . . . a drawn look to their faces. The muscles are dropped. It's hard for them to smile. Bloodshot eyes. . . . Sometimes unsure of walking. . . . Very different behavior. . . . Very relaxed. . . .

"He was a burnout for the last three months of his smoking. He had three or four hits a day. He was at his lowest when he started coming off. It's like living with an alcoholic. They just get down so far in the gutter, and he was way down."

Ken kept saying he couldn't quit. Patricia kept saying, "Yes you can. . . . I care for you. . . . I love you." She ordered him to change friends and (on the advice of a parole officer) forbade him to learn to drive until he had been off marijuana for a year.

At sixteen Ken quit. At seventeen he attended a rock concert in the Oakland Coliseum and emerged reeking from marijuana. Ken said he could not turn it down. "Everybody was smoking. They were passing it around from everywhere." He stopped going to rock concerts.

Ken was eighteen when Patricia rhapsodized, "It's almost miraculous. . . . He has a beautiful personality and he's getting A's and B's in school. He's in football, wrestling . . . has a beautiful group of friends now. He didn't grow during the time he was on pot. The doctor expected he would be about five feet, six, and now he's five feet, ten and a half or eleven."

As for the pot-smoking pals Ken used to hang around with: "One kid is in Juvenile Hall. Another is in a school for slow learners. Another has run away from home. One just comes home, takes a hit, doesn't even listen to music, just stares at the ceiling for hours on end."

Patricia continued going to drug meetings—to learn about cocaine and discuss it with Ken. "Ken told me the other day that he did buy some white stuff once that was supposed to be cocaine but it wasn't. It was soda—thank goodness."

One day in May, Ken gave Patricia a homemade greeting card. It said, "Happy Mother's Day to a great mom who helped a lot. You're always around when bad things happen and when I need your help. I'm very grateful to have a mom like you."

3

Handicapped Kids, Divergent Doctors, And Organized Parents

At one o'clock one September night in 1980, federal and state investigators swooped upon a San Francisco pier and arrested fifteen men and a woman as they were loading $40 million in Columbian marijuana from two vessels (one of them President Franklin D. Roosevelt's former yacht) into a truck labeled "Crippled Children's Society of America."

Probably nothing could have been further from the minds of those mobsters than the welfare of children, crippled or otherwise. Indeed, according to a number of doctors, the juvenile abuse of that smuggled commodity does much to create mental if not physical cripples. We quote three psychiatrists:

• "Adults are always saying, 'Well, it's not such a bad thing. I just get high for a couple of hours and I don't see any bad effects,'" said Dr. Jerry Cowan, psychiatrist at the Walnut Creek (California) Hospital for treatment of drug dependence. However, in his patients, half of them adolescents, the less mature the person's nervous system, the greater and longer lasting are the effects of marijuana.

In adolescent patients who have regularly smoked marijuana several times a week, marijuana has destroyed motivation (he said to us). And marijuana tends to perpetuate existing problems, such as depression, emotional immaturity, or learning disabilities; to impair their judgment; and to dull their reflexes. It can take months to restore their mental functioning.

• Dr. Mitchell S. Rosenthal, president of the New York drug treatment center Phoenix House, also observed a more far-reaching effect on younger smokers than older ones. "At a time when youngsters need to be mentally acute, to learn and to grow, to expand their intellectual horizons, marijuana shortens attention span, reduces performance level, and disrupts memory," he said (1979).

"When they need most to grow psychologically, they are pushed back toward infantilism by self-absorption and the need for instant gratification. When they need to learn how to cope with their emotions—with anger, with pain, and with distress—they are copping out. . . . When their concerns should be long-range, their time frame is shrunken."

As a consequence, Dr. Rosenthal predicted "a growing population of immature, underqualified adults, many of whom will be unable to live without economic, social, or even clinical support. We will have, in time, an unmanageable number of emotionally, or socially, or intellectually handicapped citizens. This, I believe, is too high a price to pay for the extension of smoking privileges to those who can handle it without demonstrable ill effects."[21]

• Dr. Voth, the Kansas psychiatrist, said (1981), "I am completely convinced that anyone will be harmed eventually if marijuana is used for a prolonged period of time and heavily. I believe emotionally unstable and immature individuals are most vulnerable."[22]

* * *

The medical community, like the community at large, includes in its vast membership a number of alcoholics and drug addicts. Some doctors not only condone the use of marijuana, they smoke it themselves. A psychiatrist we interviewed said that five marijuana-smoking physicians had been among his patients.

Steve recalled that while dependent on marijuana he went to a psychiatrist who said "that maybe I needed it as an escape. . . . He was very respectful of the dependence. . . . He brought up that he smoked it. . . . He didn't think it was any detriment."

Anna, another former user, said that her obstetrician-gynecologist "was at my house one night and he got a call on his beeper while he was smoking marijuana, and he had to go to the hospital and it couldn't have been more than twenty minutes away."

An Atlanta high school principal sent a drug-taking boy to a psychologist, who reportedly advised the boy, "There's nothing wrong with grass. Just don't smoke it in that man's school." In the same city, public "experts" lectured parents of drug-taking juveniles on the "responsible use" of marijuana by teenagers, and a pediatrician reportedly told one such couple, "Your biggest danger is in overreacting. Be glad it's only marijuana."[23]

* * *

A U.S. government-sponsored symposium in Maryland (1981) asked, "Does moderate marijuana use produce behavior problems in adolescents . . . ?" Donald Ian Macdonald, a Florida pediatrician, objected to the word "moderate"—it implied acceptance of the widely held but unproven belief that "a certain amount of mind alteration is OK," whereas "for adolescents, use of any psychoactive agents, even prescribed, may be dangerous." Their immaturity makes them "extremely susceptible to infection" with a "progressive disease" that afflicts millions of youngsters: chemical dependence. Living in a society in which "doing drugs" has become the norm for adolescents makes the "disease" so infectious, Dr. Macdonald said.

Adolescents' use of psychoactive drugs, including alcohol, leads to a "clear-cut and easily recognizable syndrome of behavior and emotional change." No matter why youngsters start experimenting with such drugs, once they start using them to feel good at times of stress, the illness has snared them, said the pediatrician.

Dr. Macdonald, of Clearwater, Florida, then president of the Florida Pediatrics Society, said that studies isolating the behavioral effects of marijuana ignored the fact (based on surveys, including one he made of 104 adolescents treated for chemical dependency) that "well over 95% of pot-smoking youngsters drink and vice versa. Effects on behavior are probably synergistic. This is not to say that such things as amotivation, short-term memory loss, and paranoia may not be more specifically marijuana-related."

He advised pediatricians to give all adolescents urine tests for cannabinoids at regular annual examinations. If chemical dependency is diagnosed, "The pediatrician must be aware of the importance of drug-free treatment and the frequent need for at least temporary removal of the child from his environment."

The disease, he said, progresses in four stages (described by Millard Newton of Straight, an adolescent drug-treatment program in St. Petersburg, Florida).

1. "Learning the Mood Swing." The adolescent is offered alcohol or marijuana by a friend or sibling. He usually tries both. He proceeds to regular use at parties or during weekends, returning to normal when the drug wears off.

2. "Seeking the Mood Swing." He has an urge to beg or buy drugs to reach euphoria more often, especially when there is stress. Behavior starts changing. Activities are dropped or slowed. Friends change. Hangovers and falling performance cause more stress, which the adolescent treats with more drugs—and he is hooked.

3. "Preoccupation With the Mood Swing." He smokes marijuana daily and directs all activity toward the next high. Behavior has deteriorated and there are usually problems of school, family, sex, and the law. Dealing or stealing is common.

4. "The Burnout." He constantly searches for chemicals just to avoid pain. There is no euphoria. The youth is out of school, worth little to employers, unwanted by family, and suffering chronic fatigue and coughing and usually mental symptoms.[24]

✻   ✻   ✻

Heavy users of marijuana, constantly stimulating their brains artificially, ultimately lose their capacity to feel good in natural ways, psychiatrist Powelson said
in our interview. "There is a physiological principle that if you stimulate something artificially long enough, it loses its capacity to respond to subtle stimuli. . . . I work with drug users all the time. They have lost their capacity to get
pleasure from anything but the grossest kinds of stimuli . . . violent or extreme. . . . They really have to be stimulated to get any kind of kick out of anything. . . . You deaden yourself. You choose death when you choose drugs."

At the same symposium, Dr. David E. Smith, founder and director
of the Haight Ashbury Free Medical Clinic (in the San Francisco section associated with the early days of the hippie movement), said, "We
view the compulsive and chronic use of marijuana, like chronic alcohol
use, especially by the very young, to be counterproductive and unhealthy, both to the culture and to the individual. . . . However, such impairment occurs only in a very small and susceptible segment of adolescent marijuana users" and is not the inevitable result of chronic use.

From Dr. Smith's paper: In 1967 to 1981 the clinic saw more than half a million patients, of whom nine-tenths (mean age twenty-one) had tried marijuana.
Comparing it with other drugs, from alcohol to heroin, "We found that marijuana . . . has a relatively low abuse potential." A major concern is the potential
for lung disease. Moreover, combination with alcohol or other drugs substantially
increases marijuana's potential for acute toxicity or overdose.
    In the fourteen years they saw thirty cases of adolescents (mean age sixteen)
who developed chronic or "psychological toxicity," with school and family difficulties and impairment in learning ability. Half showed an underlying depression. None showed abstinence symptoms "other than some anxiety and desire to
return to the use of marijuana . . ." In some young people heavy daily use seems
linked to an "amotivational syndrome"—decreased desire to work, compete, or
face normal challenges, and perhaps a learning disability—but not to brain damage.
    The professional "hard line" on marijuana has slighted the proven dangers to
youth from alcohol and tobacco. All scientific indicators demonstrate that "alcohol produces far more damage . . . in adolescents than does marijuana. . . ."[25]
    In a group discussion, Dr. Smith denied "that all marijuana use brings about
a dependency syndrome." He knew of "a fair number that have gotten into meditation, exercise, and stopped their use of marijuana. It was a phase in their lives."
On the other hand, "many come to me with marijuana dependency problems."
The population of problem smokers probably parallels the alcoholic population.[26]

Still another participant at the symposium, Dr. Lantner, the Ohio
pediatrician, stated that "a typical syndrome slowly develops in all the
regular users," even weekend smokers. Because symptoms are related to
dose and time, it may take nearly a year to notice the gradual changes
in a weekend smoker, Dr. Lantner said. She reported gradual "deterio-

ration" in patients of hers who smoked "moderately"—two to five joints per week.

When schools began to refer to her increasing numbers of teenagers, who suffered persistent lethargy and problems of social adjustment, it puzzled her—until in 1978 a patient described symptoms he and friends had developed from chronic, heavy marijuana smoking, the pediatrician said.

Having followed fifty patients who smoked marijuana—some who had no prior history of maladjustment and whose symptoms abated when they quit marijuana—and having interviewed many smoking nonpatients, she listed several "reliable symptoms of marijuana intoxication: a lack of motivation with a concomitant slacking off of school performance, dropping out of extracurricular activities, and perceptible changes in personality." Short-term memory and concentration are impaired, hindering schoolwork. Abstract thinking and hence mathematical work particularly suffers.

Chronic users, additionally, often abandon or compromise life goals, are estranged from their families, change moods suddenly, and feel irritability, hostility, paranoia, loneliness, isolation, and depression. They have suicidal tendencies. Often they have poor self-image and diminished interest in personal appearance. Sometimes there are sexual problems. Eating and sleeping habits change. They complain of tiredness and coughing, often of chest pains.

The younger the user, the more serious are the consequences, she said. And in individuals with preexisting emotional or personality problems, marijuana may trigger latent psychotic conditions, which "may explain the increasing number of irrational acts and violent crimes of our present-day youth."[27]

When a couple giving their daughter a barbecue party for her thirteenth birthday in an Atlanta suburb realized that she and her friends, eleven to fourteen, had turned it into a pot and alcohol party, they got together with parents of the other children. About thirty organized a group that was unusual for the time—1976—consisting of parents of drug-taking children.

In those days drug-abuse counselors were telling them not to worry, because "marijuana isn't addictive" and "kids will experiment." Their libraries' marijuana collections were sparse. Books said "that we should do nothing, that the drug was harmless, and that the only problems were with parents who put too much pressure on children. . . . None of this correlated with the deterioration of personality and physical condition that we were seeing with our own eyes in our children," Marsha Manatt, mother of that thirteen-year-old girl, said to us. (She told the story also in a booklet, *Parents, Peers, and Pot.*)[28] The sole useful source available to parents then was an article for doctors by Hardin B. Jones,[29] she said.

Since then, thousands of community parents' groups have sprung up in the United States to help deal with the problem of drug abuse by juveniles. Membership has ranged from a handful of families to hundreds of them. The groups have been instrumental in checking the movement toward legalization and shifting concern to the effects of cannabis on health.

Each parents' group works in its own way toward a common goal—drug-free youth. One primarily offers moral support and education to parents of drug dependents. Another crusades to drive drugs and pushers out of the schools. Still another lobbies for legislation: for instance, to prohibit the sale of drug paraphernalia. Some of the groups involve youngsters as well as parents.

Two national parent organizations are PRIDE (Parents Resources and Information on Drug Education) of Atlanta, Georgia, and the National Federation of Parents for Drug-Free Youth (NFP), of Silver Spring, Maryland. PRIDE, a drug information and education center, was founded in 1978 by Dr. Manatt and Dr. Thomas J. Gleaton, Jr. (both educators at Georgia State University). In 1980 Gleaton and others initiated the formation of NFP, an umbrella organization. By 1983 it counted some 4,000 member groups.

☆   ☆   ☆

In all regions of the United States parents personally concerned about drug abuse donate their efforts to the antidrug cause. One who has fought for years against marijuana is Dottie Kellner of Thiensville, Wisconsin. Mrs. Kellner and women she organized have issued literature, sent innumerable letters, and bought books for libraries, and—though "a shy person by nature"—she has bared her soul in the press, in public talks, and in testimony before legislative bodies. A traumatic episode got her started. This is her account:

"Our son was a friendly, happy-go-lucky, well-adjusted kid until he was seventeen. Then his personality seemed to change. He gradually developed mood swings, lack of drive, irritability, quite often temper tantrums.

"As an example, he would play rock records real loud. We would ask him to turn the music down, in a nice way, and he wouldn't do it. We would tell him again and then he would get mad. He even hit my husband one time. He had never been that way before. . . .

"We were concerned about the drug situation from the time it began to surface here around 1968. But we didn't find any evidence that Larry used drugs.

"One night in 1971 Larry broke down and cried and complained there was something wrong with his head. He told us then that he had been smoking pot for the past three years, since he was seventeen. A friend started him on it during his last year in high school.

"He couldn't seem to reason, to think things out. He couldn't anticipate or come to logical conclusions. He would talk round and round in circles. He got arrested several times for speeding because he couldn't judge how fast he was going. He got into an accident once.

"I looked into drug literature but there wasn't much available on marijuana at the time. The literature I could find and even the drug experts I consulted said marijuana was harmless. One counselor we approached advised 'responsible use' of marijuana. . . .

"Larry was committed twice to a mental health institute, four months each time. He went through a series of group therapy sessions with us and with groups at the institute. He was always heavily medicated. They didn't seem to know how to help him or us. It was like the blind leading the blind. We didn't know what to do, how to handle it. We didn't want to get so tough we alienated Larry and drove him away. On the other hand, we wanted to be tough enough.

"Sometimes Larry would quit pot and then go back. We were never quite sure, because he lied. When they're on the stuff, they're such convincing fibbers. That's one of those things about it. Another thing, it is addicting; I don't care what people say.

"Along with pot, Larry started drinking and using some uppers and downers. He would drink a whole bottle of booze without vomiting it up.

"The last three years of his drug use were really bad. He was depressed and had lost all of his confidence in himself. His mental maturation was stifled. He just couldn't think straight. . . .

"The second time he was out of the hospital, he went to the Milwaukee Area Technical College to take courses toward his goal to be a chef, but he just couldn't concentrate, so he quit. Then he worked in his dad's office. . . . He just couldn't handle it. His memory was real bad.

"In 1974 we went out of town, my husband and I, on business. We had a foreign student living with us. The student came home one afternoon at three o'clock and found Larry dead. He had shot himself with a rifle. He was twenty-three years old.

"Larry left a note. He wrote he just didn't feel he would ever be able to function right again. . . .

"Looking back, Larry's depression started with the use of marijuana. He could never seem to lift himself out of the depression. He never had any zip to do anything. . . .

"Today so much is known about marijuana. Why isn't this information getting to the public—especially the youth—before it's too late?"

Following is a list of national organizations or agencies to combat drug abuse that offer information to the public. (The addresses and telephone numbers were current in summer, 1984.)

American Council for Drug Education, 6193 Executive Boulevard, Rockville, Maryland 20852; (301) 984-5700 (founded in New York in 1977 as the American Council on Marijuana and Other Psychoactive Drugs).

Committees of Correspondence, P.O. Box 232, Topsfield, Massachusetts 01983; (617) 774-2641.

Families in Action, Suite 300, 3845 North Druid Hills Road, Decatur, Georgia 30033; (404) 325-5799.

National Clearinghouse for Drug Abuse Information, Room 10A-43, 5600 Fishers Lane, Rockville, Maryland 20857; (301) 443-6500 (for free publications of the National Institute on Drug Abuse, sent by third-class mail).

National Institute on Drug Abuse (NIDA), Prevention Branch, Room 11A-33, 5600 Fishers Lane, Rockville, Maryland 20857; callers in Maryland, Hawaii, or Alaska: (301) 443-2450; in all other states, toll-free number: (800) 638-2045 (for technical assistance to groups, schools, and state and local governments in planning programs for drug abuse prevention).

NFP, Suite 16, 1820 Franwall Avenue, Silver Spring, Maryland 20902; toll-free number: (800) 554-KIDS (will put parents in touch with local parent groups).

PRIDE, Suite 1216, 100 Edgewood Avenue, Atlanta, Georgia 30303; toll-free number: (800) 241-7946.

＊　＊　＊

Typical of local and regional antidrug groups are Californians for Drug-Free Youth (Sacramento and Los Angeles), Florida Informed Parents (Tallahassee), Hampshire Informed Parents (Amherst, Massachusetts), Ohio Federation of Families for Drug-Free Youth (Columbus), Others (Boise, Idaho), Parents Who Care (Mountain View, California), Texans' War on Drugs (Austin), and Unified Parents of America (Atlanta).

Youngsters themselves have been organizing, forming such groups as Florida Informed Teens (Pinellas Park), Kids Against Drugs (Ketchikan, Alaska), Prevention Using Student Help (Council Bluffs, Iowa, and Indianapolis and Zionsville, Indiana), Youth Against Drug Abuse (Millard, Nebraska), and Youth to Youth (Columbus).

Pharmacists Against Drug Abuse (founded by McNeil Pharmaceutical executives in Spring House, Pennsylvania, in 1982) has mounted a national campaign, utilizing drugstores to distribute folders on illicit drugs and instructing druggists further on the subject so that they in turn can enlighten the public informally or through formal lectures.

Service/benevolent organizations have adopted drug abuse projects. From their Illinois headquarters in 1983, both Lions International and the Benevolent and Protective Order of Elks launched programs of drug education for juveniles, leaving it to individual Lions clubs and Elks lodges to adapt the programs to their communities.

＊　＊　＊

Listed below, by author, are some books suitable for the layman that deal with juvenile drug abuse. (All were being sold in 1984 by PRIDE or Committees of Correspondence, some by other groups as well.)

Dorothy Cretcher, *Steering Clear: Helping Your Child Through the High-Risk Drug Years,* Winston Press, Minneapolis, 1982.

Richard A. Hawley, *The Purposes of Pleasure: A Reflection on Youth and Drugs,* Independent School Press, Chagrin Falls, Ohio, 1983; and *A School Answers Back: Responding to Student Drug Abuse,* American Council for Drug Education, Rockville, Maryland, 1984.

Curtis L. Janeczek, *Marijuana: Time for a Closer Look,* Healthstar Publications, Columbus, 1980 (for junior high and high school students; illustrated with color cartoons).

Donald Ian Macdonald, *Drugs, Drinking and Adolescents,* Year Book Medical Publishers, Chicago, 1984.

Marsha Manatt, *Parents, Peers, and Pot,* NIDA, 1979; and *Parents, Peers, and Pot II: Parents in Action,* NIDA, 1983.

Peggy Mann, *Twelve Is Too Old,* Doubleday, New York, 1980 (a novel).

*   *   *

A monthly magazine for teenagers that specializes in problems of drugs, alcohol, and tobacco is *Listen,* P.O. Box 7000, Boise, Idaho 83707; (208) 467-7400.

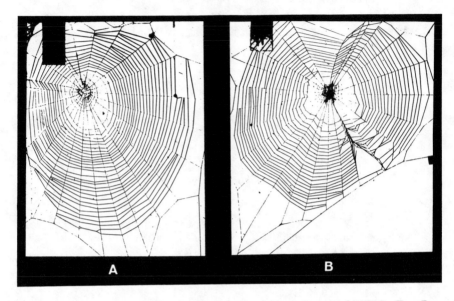

Oh, what a bungled web weaves he who tries to live with THC. Dr. Peter N. Witt (M. D.) of North Carolina is known for experiments in which he gave spiders dozens of drugs and observed their webs. Different drugs resulted in webs with varied shapes and aberrations. Using twenty-seven different measures, he would compare a web before and after drug application and also compare it with an undrugged spider's web. "No other drug showed the complete spectrum of changes in all twenty-seven measures that THC showed, however there were overlaps," he wrote us. THC-webs showed some resemblance to webs produced under the influence of strychnine, for example, being less elongated and rebuilt less often. THC approximately halved the number of webs, Witt recalled. Repeated treatment increased the effects. After withdrawal, the webs returned to normal. "We offer no explanation in terms of central nervous system function," said Witt. The photos show (A) the web of a typical Araneus diadematus subject fed sugar water and (B) a web by the same spider—pictured in the center of the web—after five treatments with THC in sugar water. (The THC, 600 mg/kg given each two days, was a water-soluble variation prepared by W. B. Dewey and Louis S. Harris.)

CRIME

---

* "I think marijuana does bend one's ethics, especially when one is young, because morals is so tenuous. . . . It encourages one's tendency to be a little reckless. I know a guy who burglarized someone's apartment after smoking pot." —Kathy (light user, former heavy user)

* "Most people have a built-in moral resistance. And what marijuana did for me was it broke it. It started to take my moral pattern of my value system and break it down. . . . You lose a sense of values. . . . I was ready to do whatever would excite me or stimulate me. . . . I became very selfish, very self-centered. . . .
   "After I got into drugs and marijuana, I would take things. I would steal things. If something was left out and I wanted it, I would take it. I did some really terrible things. . . . I remember I pulled down aerials of cars. . . . I just tore them down for the sake of destruction. . . . I had no regard for people's property or feelings. I would just say, 'Well, if I want something, I want it, and if they don't like it, it's too bad.' . . .
   "I did have fear of the law. . . . I think that was one of the things that kept me from smoking more marijuana than I did . . . I was really, really afraid of getting caught." —Lewis (ex-user)

* "He was always an honor student until that time. It took three years for me and my husband to recognize he was using pot. A friend turned him on. All his group of peers used pot. He changed from being loving and open to being withdrawn and self-centered. He was careless and left marijuana papers around, so we found out. . . . He had real trouble with his memory. He couldn't tell jokes because he couldn't remember them.
   "He got into other drugs: uppers, downers, PCP, Quaaludes. He would steal, at first from his sisters, and he dealt. He got arrested for stealing. He and some friends went to another town and stole tires and brought

369

them home in my car and left them in the driveway. It was as if he couldn't make the connection between stealing and hiding the evidence. The judge ordered him to go to jail for two years or to treatment. He went to a treatment center." —Viola (mother of an ex-user)

• "*There was a place in the sidewalk that had a hole and had one of those yellow flasher signs, you know, that yellow light going on and off, and I kept tripping over that as I'd come home from one or another party or, you know, constant round of getting stoned, freaking around. So one night I thought, 'I'm just going to take this thing home with me, and besides it'll be a nice thing to set up in the living room. To have that nice yellow light going on and off—wouldn't that be cool?' . . .*

"*So I picked it up and brought it home, and who happened to be coming out of the door of the dormitory at that time of two in the morning but one of the [Harvard] campus police? And, of course, what I was doing was I was stealing city property or whatever. I mean, anyway, I had stolen this flasher thing off of a hole in the sidewalk and got kind of hauled in for it. . . . I had to talk to the house master or assistant dean or whatever. . . . He pointed out to me . . . 'That place isn't terribly well lighted. It's there to protect people so they don't fall into that hole.' And my reaction was, 'Well, I tripped over the flasher sign, so it was the real menace . . . and anybody that's foolish enough to walk in a hole, that's just 'cause they're dumb.'. . .*

"*But, I mean, my thinking was so distorted. I mean, how could I be so wrong? . . . And the fact that I was stealing, I mean, that didn't enter the picture at all. . . . And I can see where a person would, and many people have, had just such a perspective who did things that were a lot worse in the way of crimes, felonies, et cetera. . . .*

"*The combination of marijuana and alcohol made me do some things I couldn't believe that I would ever or could ever do . . . and usually didn't remember. . . . One was throwing beer bottles at my friends. . . . I remember one night being under that kind of condition . . . and I was doing something that the police were suspicious of . . . and I heard one of them say to the other, 'Watch out for him. He hit so-and-so'—you know, one of their fellow policemen—'the other night.' . . . There were things that people told me I did, like in the middle of winter throwing myself into the gutter and drinking out of puddles. . . .*

"*I belonged to a sort of fraternity-like club. . . . In the upstairs part of this clubhouse-type thing there was this case of cigars and this other guy and I went up. We each wanted a cigar and there was only one last cigar of this kind left so we both began kind of friendly tussling over it, and I had gotten stoned before I had gone over there and then was pretty drunk in addition . . . and I guess I sort of threw him through a door. . . . I don't remember doing that or how I did it exactly, but I do remember seeing him on the floor in the next room with his wrist cut to pieces and bleeding. . . . Of course he had to go to the hospital and have a lot of stitches and he couldn't use his hand for a couple of months. . . . Perfectly nice guy. We were friends, and I mean I hadn't felt, as far as I remember, angry. . . . I wanted that cigar and that's all I knew. . . .*

"I think alcohol has that violent thing associated with it to start with. But there's something that is an added disorientation that comes with marijuana, besides which it softens the hangover and . . . you can take more alcohol." —Nathan (ex-user)

1

Studies From Several Lands

Crime and cannabis have long been linked, at least in many minds. A form of each are even related in etymology: "Assassin" traces to the Arabic "hashshashin," literally meaning hashish addicts. The word has been applied in Arabic to Moslem sectarians "who used to intoxicate themselves with hashish or hemp, when preparing to dispatch some king or public man" (according to the *Oxford English Dictionary*, although some dispute this). The Assassins were a secret order of fanatics that murdered Christian leaders at the time of the Crusades.

Does cannabis lead to crime? The question must be qualified. Obviously, as long as growing, selling, or possessing the plant or the drug remains illegal, the commission of any of these acts is technically a crime. (Possession of a small amount of marijuana constitutes a minor offense in most states.)

For now, let us exclude the cannabis laws—and the felonious activities connected with cultivation, smuggling, and selling—and find out whether the use of the drug bears any relation to the commission of nondrug crimes. Following are several diverse studies, stories, and theories from the 1890s to the 1980s.

*　*　*

The Indian Hemp Drugs Commission (1893–94) gained the impression, from testimony, that "the connection between hemp drugs and ordinary crime is very slight indeed" and that "it is but rarely that excessive indulgence in hemp drugs can be credited with inciting to crime or leading to homicidal frenzy." Examining the records of twenty-three cases in which hemp drugs supposedly caused "homicidal frenzy," the commission found a true connection in only four of those cases.

Popular condemnation of the drugs stemmed in part from the presence of proportionately more "bad characters" among consumers than among the general population; but then most hemp drug consumers belonged to the poorer classes, to which those characters belonged, said the commission's report. Habitual use of the drugs further impoverished users, tempting them to steal, but so might any unwise expenditure. Some criminals and thugs no doubt used the drugs to fortify themselves for premeditated crimes and beatings, the report added.

372

Sometimes the drugs had a sedative effect, but a number of witnesses spoke of habitual use causing irritability. "Undoubtedly, the excessive use does in some cases make the consumer violent." All in all, "the tendency of the drugs often seems to be to develop or bring into play the natural disposition of the consumer, to emphasize his characteristic peculiarities, or to assist him in obtaining what he sets his mind on." If he wants to rest and is let alone, he will remain restful, but if he is naturally excitable or ill-tempered or if one disturbs or crosses him, he might become violent. So said the commissioners.[1]

*   *   *

"Loco Weed, Breeder of Madness and Crime," read a feature headline in the *New York Mirror*. Psychiatrist Walter Bromberg (1934), who cited the story, deemed its slant wrong inasmuch as users were basically psychopathic and antisocial types to begin with. "The anti-social, aggressive and sadistic elements of the personality uncovered by the drug are responsible for crime rather than any specific, crime-producing properties of marihuana," he wrote. The weed was an angle favored by police-beat reporters of the day.

Based on routine interviews with marijuana-experienced felons during some five years in a New York court's psychiatric clinic that he headed, Bromberg (1939) found "negative connection with major crime . . . no positive relation between violent crime and the use of marihuana . . . no cases of murder or sexual crimes due to marihuana." Of sixty-seven felons who said they used marijuana, forty-six were convicted on drug charges during that time, twenty-one on other charges from larceny to murder. "In only nine cases of the sixty-seven was the criminal record found to commence with a drug charge, indicating that there was not in those cases a close relationship between drugs and the beginning of a career of crime."[2]

*   *   *

Chopra and Chopra in India (1939) played down the part of hemp drugs in violent crime—"they may actually act as deterrents"—but Chopra, Chopra, and Chopra (1942) pointed to various crimes in which "a single ganja or charas smoke was responsible for a heinous crime."

While referring to instances in which addicts committed criminal acts of passion or premeditation, the first work (by the two Chopras) denied that such cases necessarily proved any definite relation between the drugs and crime. It echoed points raised by the hemp drugs commissioners: so many consumers were criminals because most belonged to poorer classes, which used the drugs; the drugs were not wholly to blame if financial pressure led addicts to steal; the drugs tended to bring out the user's true character.

The two Chopras said nomadic thieves and robbers used the drugs before committing their crimes. As for premeditated violent crimes, hemp drugs in some cases might actually act as deterrents because one of their major actions, unlike alcohol's, was to quiet and stupefy the taker. "The result of continued and excessive use of these drugs is to make the individual timid rather than lead him to commit a crime of a violent nature."

Furthermore, "Hemp drugs have not been used for suicidal or homicidal purposes in the same way as opium." However, "Children are sometimes decoyed and offered sweetmeats containing hemp drugs to make them insensible and rob them of their ornaments."

Of 1,238 in their series of hemp-drug addicts, 16 percent were convicted of a crime (half of them once and half more than once). They mentioned that the conviction rate was higher than the rate in the general population but failed to specify the latter.[3]

A 1942 article by the three Chopras (Colonel Sir Ram Nath Chopra, M.D., and Gurbakhsh S. Chopra, authors of the 1939 book, plus I. C. Chopra) reiterated the foregoing and added: "The use of hemp drugs if pushed further than the stage of light depression of higher centres may produce confusion of mind and restlessness. Intellectual impairment as well as disorientation may show itself in various ways, such as weakening of moral sense, habit of telling lies, prostitution, theft, etc."

The addict might become egotistic and unreliable and resort to theft and unnatural sex perversions, they said. Sometimes the drugs "may release subconscious impulses and lead to violent crime."

Indulgence in the drugs would often result in illusions, delusions, and hallucinations. In susceptible individuals these might resemble paranoid conditions.

"Delusions of a persecutory nature and sexual infidelity are dangerous and frequently lead to homicidal crimes, the power of discrimination being lost through a lack of control over the higher centres. Inquiries in various jails and mental centres revealed that in quite a number of cases, simple indulgence even in a single ganja or charas smoke was responsible for a heinous crime." They cited neither cases nor figures.[4]

* * *

The belief that marijuana smoking directly caused crimes was popular when the New York Mayor's Committee conducted its investigation (1944). But when the committee asked federal, state, and local law en-

forcement officers for their opinions, "In most instances they unhesitat-
ingly stated that there is no proof that major crimes are associated with
the practice of smoking marihuana. They did state that many marihuana smokers are guilty of petty crimes, but that the criminal career
usually existed prior to the time the individual smoked his first marihuana cigarette. These officers further stated that a criminal generally
termed as a 'real' or 'professional' criminal will not associate with marihuana smokers. He considers such a person inferior and unreliable and
will not allow him to participate in the commission of a major crime."[5]

* * *

Professor C. G. Gardikas, head of the Greek Criminal Services, expressed a contrasting opinion. He had followed 379 hashish users caught
by the law. After starting to use hashish, he said, the majority changed:
either they became habitual criminals or vagrants, or, if criminals already, they became more hardened. He blamed it all on hashish, offering no clear evidence, only this theory:

Hashish intoxication, he said in a 1950 paper, leads to crime and violence by transforming one's personality, making "a lazy, unstable (thereby
vagrancy, thefts), contentious, excitable, suspicious coward . . . a fearful feeling to attack is created (thereby illegal carrying of arms, as-
saults)." The hashish habit leads to crimes also in that chronic abuse
results in serious psychoses, he said, giving even less evidence.

Gardikas said that between 1919 and 1950 the Greek Criminal Services examined 379 individuals sentenced for or caught using hashish publicly. He divided them into three categories:

A. One hundred seventeen who never had been arrested before but afterwards
turned into habitual criminals, with propensities toward: violent crimes exclu-
sively, 33 percent; crimes of violence and dishonesty, 39 percent; and crimes of
dishonesty, particularly theft and fraud, 28 percent.

B. Fifty-three who never had been arrested before but later got arrested for hashish
use again, hashish smuggling, or vagrancy, but for no other crimes.

C. Two hundred nine who were criminals before starting hashish; three-quarters of them continued as criminals, the degree of criminality remaining the same
in eighty-two and intensifying in seventy-five.

Gardikas gave no evidence of cause and effect and no case studies, except for
police records of five men, spanning between seven and thirty-two years (two in
category A, three in C); average age at first arrest was twenty.[6]

Pharmacologist James C. Munch, member of the Advisory Committee of the Federal Bureau of Narcotics for twenty-five years, drew from
the bureau's files outlines of sixty-nine cases of crimes occurring "after

use, and under influence, of marihuana" between 1921 and 1964. They included beatings, bigamy, reckless driving, rape, robbery, and twenty-seven homicides.

Examples: In 1937 a New York marijuana pusher, thirty-nine, fatally shot his roommate while both smoked reefers, hiding the body in a trunk. He was quoted as saying, "I was fearless after smoking marijuana cigarettes but would not have done this without marijuana." The same year seven youths pulled thirty-eight holdups in central Ohio while under the influence of marijuana. The following year a St. Joseph, Missouri, man, thirty-seven, smoked two marijuana cigarettes and raped his seven-year-old daughter. And in 1943 a hotel bellboy, twenty-seven, bit a sailor on a street in Oklahoma City, hit a boy, grabbed the gun of a guard in the federal building and shot him to death, and went off singing down the hall. Next morning he remembered nothing.

"This objective evidence supports published statements of the association between the use of marihuana and various types of crime," Dr. Munch wrote for a United Nations periodical, 1966. (How objective was the bureau's evidence is open to question. Bromberg, 1939, had found no cause to link the first killer to marijuana.)

> Munch said in a letter (1980) that the accuracy of the case reports was "authenticated by MDs and coroners prior to use."
>
> In his paper, he called the sixty-nine cases typical of marijuana crimes, but he did not say how the cases had been selected and how common they were. Nor did he say whether alcohol or other factors could have been involved. The summaries are sketchy; some lack places or dates, some do not specify how marijuana was involved, and two cases are from Mexico. One report, from 1953 (giving no location) has a man attempting to rob a diner after smoking sixteen marijuana cigarettes.[7]
>
> The case of the man who killed his roommate and put the body in a trunk had been described by Bromberg (1939), who said that examination in the New York court's psychiatric clinic (where Bromberg was chief psychiatrist) and investigation by the probation department failed to indicate the culprit's use of marijuana or any other drug. The victim was addicted to heroin.[8]
>
> Dr. Munch, Ph.D., of Silver Spring, Maryland, pharmacologist for government and industry, former professor at Temple University, and author of *Bioassays, A Handbook of Quantitative Pharmacology* (1931), died in February, 1981 at eighty-five. He devised canine tests of cannabis potency.

During a year as an army psychiatrist at the Long Binh stockade in Vietnam (1968–69), Dr. John K. Imahara conducted fifty-four sanity-board hearings into violent crimes. In interviews, thirty-five of the prisoners (nearly two-thirds) admitted using marijuana at some time or another, and thirteen (nearly a fourth) admitted using marijuana "at or near the time of the crime."

He described two such cases to illustrate "the close connection" between the crime and the use of marijuana. In each case a soldier had taken a smoke, heard an imaginary voice, picked up and fired a weapon, and then put it down and rested calmly.

One assailant, twenty-three, had been deteriorating mentally for a month with heavy use of marijuana. Obeying a "voice" after smoking one day, he took a pistol and shot and wounded a lieutenant colonel he had never seen before. The young man was treated in Japan for psychosis considered to have been precipitated by marijuana.

The other assailant, twenty-one, who had been drinking, was picked on and hit by a man bigger than him. Angered several hours later on seeing the latter lying in the barracks, he went outside and smoked a joint to calm down. Instead came confusion and a "voice" (an experience that marijuana had evoked twice before). It said to get even. Returning to the barracks, he picked up a rifle and shot the man to death. He was found sane and tried for murder.

Marijuana smoking among general prisoners in the stockade appeared no more prevalent than among other soldiers. In questionnaires to 246 consecutive incoming prisoners, 38 percent admitted having used marijuana and 16 percent admitted regular use of it. Similar surveys of surgical and medical patients in 1968 had drawn very similar results.[9]

*   *   *

Some two decades after the Gardikas work, another Greek professor renewed talk of a fear-aggression syndrome but laid it not to intoxication from hashish but to withdrawal from hashish by the chronic smoker. Wrote C. J. Miras: "There is definitely a dependence risk, although much less serious than with the opiates. The chronic hashish smoker"—when puffing periodically on a water pipe—"is usually quiet, lazy, slow-going, a coward, seeking to avoid trouble. But in abstinence he becomes excited and dangerously aggressive."

Describing adverse mental responses to cannabis, Professor Miras included "the panic reaction between periods of intoxication, with fears of being spoken about or assaulted." Later, in a scientific discussion, he said, "Some of these patients show pure panic reactions and pure fear. We have had a number of cases of people who assault other people because they thought they looked at them in a strange way."[10]

*   *   *

Among the hashish-smoking American soldiers in Germany described by Dr. Forest S. Tennant, Jr., (1974) were many who got into hashish dealing or other illegal activity to support their habits. Rarely did soldiers chronically intoxicated from alcohol commit violent crimes though they were constantly in other trouble, he said.

In one of several cases of violence from his own medical records, "Three soldiers under the influence of hashish, raped a fifteen-year-old dependent girl. All three soldiers blamed the incident on hashish."

The worst of the cases he encountered was a grisly murder involving both smoke and drink: "J. M., under the influence of unknown quantities of alcohol and hashish, took an axe and killed his German girl friend by literally chopping her into several pieces. The following morning he claimed he did not remember the incident."

In another cannabis-alcohol case, after consuming hashish and strawberry wine, S.G., considered by superiors to be a model soldier, one evening stole several soldiers' belongings, including stereo sets and watches. The next morning he said he did not remember the episode. He returned the loot to the owners.

Hashish caused most of the violence indirectly. Dr. Tennant told of an army building called "Smoky Barracks" because it had become so well known as a place for hashish transactions. Many violent acts occurred there related to hashish dealing. Five or six soldiers evidently conducted the operation.

"Failure to pay a drug bill for as little as ten or twenty dollars resulted in violence. Since I was the surgeon who had to care for the victim of the violence, I became involved and knowledgeable. The usual violent act was a 'blanket party' which occurred when the attackers would find the victim asleep. They rolled him up in his blanket like a hot dog and physically assaulted him with fists and clubs. On two occasions soldiers were thrown from a two-story window because they failed to pay a hashish bill, and in one instance a soldier's wife was beaten for a deficit of sixty dollars."

He said that some fights between black and white GIs in Germany that were labeled "racial incidents" were really fights over control of the local hashish franchises.[11]

* * *

B. P. Sharma, head of psychiatry at a Katmandu hospital, discerned "no difference in crime rate" between 266 heavy users and a matched group of nonusers in Nepal (1975). As he saw it, "Criminal activities commonly stem from aggressive trends, sexual urges, self-assertion and ambition, but such traits are almost unknown among cannabis users."

Sharma nevertheless had little good to say about the users, men who took cannabis thrice daily and had taken it for at least two years. They had "a poor work record" and were aloof from their families, "untidy, unkempt, slovenly and slow . . . morbidly jealous," with "no ambition. . . . Users are thought of as persons of rather low calibre." Using the same material as in India, they usually smoked it in funnel-shaped clay pipes.

Their median age was thirty-seven and they ranged in education from illiterate (seventy-three) to university graduates (nine). Controls were men of comparable education and age. Sharma did not describe his method of investigation.[12]

In a nationwide survey (1974–75) 2,510 men aged twenty to thirty answered questions about their drug usage and commission of crimes. While the resulting statistics did not establish that marijuana led to crime or vice versa, they demonstrated a clear relationship between the use of marijuana and criminal acts (if the men polled told the truth).

The percentages of those who had committed auto theft, breaking and entering, armed robbery, shoplifting, theft from a person, and issuing bad checks were far higher among 1,382 young men who had used marijuana than among 1,128 who never had used marijuana. Just how high the crime figures went depended on the extent of marijuana use. "Heavy" users always reported more offenses than any other subgroup of users.

For example, 3 percent of those who never had used marijuana admitted auto theft; 8 percent of the marijuana users admitted it. Among "experimental," "light," "medium," and "heavy" users, 4, 6, 9, and 12 percent, respectively, admitted auto theft.

Similar strong associations transpired when it came to criminal arrests (nontraffic), juvenile court appearances, crime convictions, and serving of sentences. More marijuana users than nonusers had experiences in each of these legal situations, and again the prevalence was related to the extent of use. (The charges were not mentioned.)

Two-thirds of the young men themselves said that drugs had caused their legal problems. However, the late sociologist John A. O'Donnell of the University of Kentucky, and others, discussing the survey for the National Institute on Drug Abuse (1976), said that "if there is a casual connection between drug use and criminal behavior, it is not a simple one," and that factors of age, education, ethnic grouping, and urbanism added complications.

Following are the respective percentages of the 1,128 who never used marijuana and 423 "experimental," 231 "light," 227 "medium," and 501 "heavy," users who admitted each of seven offenses. (A zero signifies less than half of one percent.)
Armed robbery—0, 1, 2, 2, and 4%.
Bad checks—1, 2, 3, 4, and 7%.
Breaking and entering—6, 10, 10, 20, and 27%.
Forgery of prescriptions—0, 0, 0, 4, and 4%.

Illegal gambling—1, 4, 2, 5, and 6%.
Stealing (face to face)—1, 3, 3, 3, and 9%.
Shoplifting—29, 50, 52, 56, and 64%.
More "heavy" marijuana users reported committing those crimes than did users of "other drugs." Those who admitted auto theft constituted 11 percent of 845 users of "other drugs." Other such percentages: armed robbery, 3%; bad checks, 6%; breaking and entering, 24%; forgery of prescriptions, 4%; illegal gambling, 4%; stealing (face to face), 7%; and shoplifting, 62%. (Of course, some used both marijuana and "other drugs": cocaine, opiates, psychedelics, sedatives, or stimulants.)

For those who used marijuana, some began using it before the first criminal act; others committed the first criminal act before starting marijuana. Marijuana came first in the majority of cases of armed robbery, operating gambling, and check forgery. In most cases of auto theft, breaking and entering, and stealing from a person, marijuana came first if they started using it before age seventeen but the crime came first if they began use after turning seventeen.

Academics from the University of Kentucky, Lexington, and the University of California, Berkeley, designed and coordinated the study. The Temple University Institute for Survey Research, Philadelphia, and its staff of 138 interviewers gathered the data in 1974 and 1975 from men who were aged twenty to thirty in 1974.[13]

An Egyptian team, headed by M. I. Soueif, Cairo University psychology professor, polled 2,008 men, mostly prisoners, and examined the criminal records of 1,011 of the prisoners.

The records showed no significant relation between cannabis and criminal activity, except a possible reverse relation: 6 percent of users and 14 percent of nonusers had criminal records before their latest arrest. The polls did not wholly support this trend, however.

Thirty prisoners who had been convicted for noncannabis crimes but who took the drug were asked: "Did you commit many offenses when you were under the effect of hashish . . . when you were craving for hashish . . . or neither?" Eleven said they committed them when influenced by hashish; six, when craving; and thirteen, under neither condition.

All those interviewed were asked these questions: "Would you spend time and effort to do a job thoroughly or just do it the easiest way if nobody would uncover the defects?" More users than nonusers indicated they would do the inferior job.

"If someone were blamed for your mistake, would you admit it or let it pass?" More users than nonusers said they would let it pass.

"Do you think that hashish takers have more criminal tendencies than nontakers?" Few takers but the majority of nontakers said yes.

Chronic takers reported mood changes when deprived of the drug. They became ill-tempered, less docile, more impulsive, negative, and quarrelsome.

Of the 2,008 interviewed, 1,689 were prisoners. The 1,011 prisoners whose records were checked comprised 553 users serving time for cannabis-related offenses and 458 nonusers imprisoned for other crimes. The nonusers slightly exceeded users in the number of offenses committed.

Soueif told a symposium on drugs and criminality, in Brazil, 1976, that "within the prison population, we could not establish a significant association between criminal behavior and cannabis taking. Indeed, if anything, we may talk about an inverse relationship." Phrased another way, they found that "our convicted takers were less criminal than the convicted criminals." Was this a meaningful comparison? At least two studies were needed, he indicated: (1) "comparing convicted takers with free takers" and (2) "comparing free takers with free controls."

Replies to polls by users and nonusers, respectively, by percentage:

Would not do a good job—prisoners 6% (of 850 users) and 2% (of 839 nonusers); free citizens 18% (of 204 users) and 3% (of 115 nonusers).

Would not admit their mistakes—prisoners 14% and 8%; free citizens 22% and 8%.

Believe that cannabis takers have more criminal tendencies than nontakers—prisoners 6% and 61%; free citizens 21% and 68%.

Those answering the last question affirmatively agreed that users, by and large, tended more than nonusers to engage in bribery, forgery, shady business, and rape, but not robbery, violence, or murder.[14]

2

The "Drug Culture" and The Law

" 'My son is not involved in any of this. . . . I asked him right before I came—"You aren't using drugs, are you?" and he looked me right in the eye and said, "No" ' . . . A tall man . . . turned to the objecting mother . . . and said, 'I hate to disillusion you, but your son sells pot to mine in the woods behind my house. They like to get high before catching the schoolbus.' "

The above is an excerpt from a booklet published by the National Institute on Drug Abuse (1979). About thirty parents in a neighborhood of an Atlanta suburb are meeting to discuss a recent discovery: Guests at a girl's thirteenth-birthday party in a local backyard had not come simply to consume hamburgers and Cokes.

Soon the neighborhood parents realize not only that illegal substances and drug trading have become part of juvenile life but that their kids have had a well-organized subculture in which deception and larceny have played parts.

"A fifth grader regularly shoplifted marijuana rolling papers from the corner variety store. A tall 10th grader made fake IDs and bought pop wines from careless supermarket clerks. An angelic-looking 12-year-old, with pigtails and braces, shared her generous allowance with her friends, so they could have a ready supply of marijuana. An eighth grader supplied eyedrops from his father's pharmacy so his friends could 'get the red out' before going home to supper."

At the same meeting, a man who ran a gift shop bitterly complained about a lot of shoplifting by junior-high students. "Those punks have no respect for the law," he declared. He did not consider it relevant that the shoplifters aimed mainly at his stock of paraphernalia for the illegal use of drugs.[15]

*   *   *

"I saw decent youngsters turning into con artists who would lie, steal, or convert their friends to drug use to get money for their next joint," wrote Dr. Frederick W. Lundell, psychiatrist. He was describing "marijuana casualties" he saw as director of the mental assessment and guidance clinic at the Montreal Children's Hospital in the late 1960s. "And in the emergency department of the hospital I saw teen-agers brought in by police, either aggressive and violent, or withdrawn and rambling incoherently—so stoned on marijuana that they appeared psychotic."

He said the marijuana users all were deficient in concentration, comprehension, and short-term memory and suspicious to the extent of paranoia, and "showed a pronounced tendency to act out their rebellious feelings in flamboyant gestures such as shoplifting and vandalism."

Dr. Lundell (1980) followed 100 cases and discovered that one in four had graduated from marijuana to harder drugs.

Among his later patients was a girl of seventeen who had forged checks on her father's bank account and hocked a ring of her mother's. Her well-to-do parents could not understand why she needed money. She admitted that she had been smoking marijuana since she was twelve and was heavily indebted to pushers. Her parents sent her far away to a treatment center.[16]

*   *   *

Can marijuana intoxication directly affect one's sense of right and wrong? Several marijuana-experienced men and women whom we have interviewed believe that it can. "Marijuana can lead to a breakdown of morals," says Ira, a convicted drug pusher. When high, Pierre could condone thoughts that normally he would "consider immoral" and Carol's "moral perception just went out the window." The three are speaking in a sexual context, but three others are talking about theft. "Marijuana does bend one's ethics," user Kathy says, telling of one who broke into an apartment when under the drug's influence. Lewis remembers that marijuana tore down his moral resistance and as a result "I would steal things." And Nathan describes how marijuana distorted his thinking so that "the fact that I was stealing . . . didn't enter the picture at all." If he wanted something, he simply took it. With alcohol added, the taking sometimes became violent.

> In 1980 the *Boston Globe* sponsored a poll of 400 residents of that city and suburbs on eleven questions of ethics and morals. Ethical strictness appeared related to age. For instance, these are the respective percentages of the under-thirty group and the forty-five to fifty-nine group who found some actions "seriously wrong": cheating on taxes, 46% and 62%; letting a sales clerk undercharge one, 52% and 73%; padding expense accounts, 61% and 91%; making long-distance personal calls on company time, 66% and 84%. Research Analysis Corp., Boston, conducted the poll by telephone.[17]
>
> Citing the poll, columnists Glen and Shearer sought to explain what they saw as the dwindling ethics of the " 'Me' Generation." As possible causes, they suggested increased competition, society's appreciation of achievement over character, and too little time spent by parents with their children. They did not mention drugs.[18]

The lax attitude of the "drug culture" toward law and the underworld environment in which the drug trade is conducted also need to be considered. A neophyte's casual entry into the drug world—made especially easy by the softening of the cannabis laws—can introduce him to other forms of illegality and foster the attitude, "If you can break one law, you can break another." The marijuana smoker that Kathy mentioned who committed the burglary apparently saw no distinction. Probably few smokers will turn to burglary. But it's an easy move from buying marijuana (usually a misdemeanor, in small quantity) to selling it (a felony).

"I know a lot of people who have gone into selling marijuana to support a pot habit," says ex-user Rosemary. "Probably about twenty percent sell. It's very common for people to sell pot. I could find about sixty people I could buy pot from."

A majority of the scores of marijuana users and ex-users that we interviewed indicated fear, at some time, of getting caught by the police.

If anyone felt any guilt, it was for yielding to a bad habit. Not a single one expressed the slightest guilt about breaking the law. When we raised the question, those saying anything more than no volunteered comments like these:

Anna, age thirty-three, ex-user: "I think that's one of the least considerations that people go through."

Bert, twenty-one, chronic user: "I can't see doing it or not because it's against the law."

Janet, twenty-seven, ex-user: "I never really thought of it as being illegal."

Millie, twenty-two, chronic user: "No. It never crosses my mind. I don't know why it should."

Steve, nineteen, ex-user: "Never. In fact, that made it more exciting, doing it illegally."

We asked also whether they had ever felt any qualms about their involvement in the drug scene or the people with whom they had to associate. A few were bothered that those selling them the dope were not kind or generous people. A few indicated occasional fear. Not one showed any concern that marijuana purchases helped organized crime or that he was dealing directly or indirectly with smugglers, racketeers, and perhaps killers.

One of those interviewed, Pete, a heavy user and marijuana advocate, objected to "the capitalist attitude of the dealers. They're heartless. . . . I've been ripped off a lot of times, because it's a black-market situation. . . . I'm not into heavy dealing but I know a lot of people who are, and they nearly always have a gun. . . . I get real scared of them."

Another, Joe, a user and former pusher, occasionally had cold feet when meeting with his sources of supply in New York City. "I thought there were some pretty weird people—crazy, dangerous, paranoid. Some had guns."

Still another, Ira in California, not only dealt with gangsters but had even gloried in his underworld associations.

After using marijuana sporadically for years, Ira began taking it habitually in college. Sinking grades forced him to drop out. At eighteen he became a dealer in cannabis, cocaine, and other drugs and an intensive, daily marijuana smoker. He observed his nineteenth birthday by taking peyote, brooding over the "dishonesty" of his girl friend, and attempting suicide by swallowing large amounts of hashish, hashish oil, and LSD, but, he said, "My religion pulled me through." Then began two years as a cocaine addict.

Ira was arrested twice. He spent a month in jail for felonious possession of hashish. A 3½-month term plus three years' probation for possessing cocaine for sale ended a three-year career as a drug pusher in 1979. The next year he gave up drugs entirely.

Once a strong advocate of marijuana and other "God-given drugs," he now takes the equally strong opinion that marijuana has been proven physically harmful and that the drug culture, of which it is part, is "destructive to society." Concerned about others following his path to addiction, he not only opposes legalized marijuana but would even outlaw hard liquor.

"What I felt then was, 'That's their problem, not mine,' and that's what everybody feels that smokes weed. . . . It's not just drug values, but it's the whole moral breakdown."

He regrets the drug years—particularly the blowing of nearly $20,000 in inherited money on cocaine and the waste of time meant for education—although he insists that THC and LSD gave him lasting power of "telepathic communication through time and space with people on TV" and he admits that he enjoyed his criminal life.

"I was making money, and everyone wanted to see me because I had all the dope. It was easy to make friends, and you were a sought-after person. It was easy to be important, which I really wasn't," Ira said.

"I got to be a gangster. I got to be with gangsters. It was fun. I was doing something that nobody else could do. It was like Mr. 007 and nobody knew what my underworld life was and everybody was bad and I was one of them, you know. It was kind of fun in the sense that I was always running away from the cops and I was involved in this whole invisible world that nobody else was aware of. I'd walk down the street and see Joe Gas Station or Joe Grocer, and here's me—I'm Joe Dealer, with all these people. They'd bump off a friend, or something like that, if I wanted them to. It was a sense of power and camaraderie that I couldn't find anywhere else. . . .

"Once I felt this guy ripped me off. I knew some people and they knew some people and they said, 'Well, if you want something done, just let me know.' So I could have had somebody really messed up or even killed if I wanted, but I never went that far."

A friend of Ira's once came to his room unexpectedly with a stranger who wanted to buy a large amount of amphetamine. Soon two other men Ira had never seen, who were to supply the drug, barged in. His room had been chosen as a meeting place.

"All of a sudden this one little guy pulls out this big .45 and tells the guy to lie spread-eagle on the bed, and they searched him and he had a little .25 caliber, and they said, 'We're gonna take you out and see if people know you, and if they don't know you, that's the end of the line for you, buddy.'

"This was kind of a shock to me, you know, to have like 'Mannix' or like '[Hawaii] Five-O' going on in my bedroom. To have people that you don't even know and all of a sudden have guns popping out, people ready to kill each other when they think some guy's a narc, isn't really that unusual in some circles. . . .

"The friend of mine told me that the guy called the next day looking for his gun. I don't think they wasted [murdered] him. . . .

"Among the marijuana growers, up in the mountains, it's not unusual for them to have people with shotguns keeping guard. If you got too close or you're doing the wrong thing or you look suspicious, you get blown away.

"In anything the underworld is involved with, illegal activities like that, murder is often a cure-all, you know, to prevent somebody from going to jail. It's not unusual.

"I almost got wasted myself once—because somebody thought that I was a snitch—by some people that had just come in from out of town. They were called in, most likely, to waste me, but they were convinced by people that cared about me and knew that I wasn't a snitch and that it wasn't the right thing to bump me off."

Ira chuckled.

*   *   *

What marijuana had done to the paradisaical wilderness of the Hawaiian Islands by the 1980s occupied editorial writers there:

". . . Marijuana-growing has turned some formerly idyllic hiking areas in the Islands into places that are no longer safe. Several killings have been attributed to growers trying to protect their crops by force." —*Honolulu Star-Bulletin*

"Innocent hikers and hunters on public trails, not to mention in remote areas, have faced armed men, menacing guard dogs and the unexpected danger of booby traps near marijuana plants. Several missing persons may have been victims of pot-related violence. Helicopters have been fired upon.

"All this takes place both on public property and private land that doesn't belong to the marijuana growers, and in some places it is not safe for the public or property owners to go unarmed and alone. Some property owners are intimidated.

"The fact is that marijuana is much more than the 'harmless' drug or lucrative cash crop many perceive. It is also a source of growing violence in the countryside and a financially attractive distribution activity for organized crime in the cities." —*Honolulu Advertiser*

Both newspapers favored a continuation of strong action by law-enforcement authorities against the growers and their crops.[19]

A heroin addict may spend \$50 to \$500 a day for the drug (depending on the heaviness of his habit and the number and potency of his "fixes"). Where does he get the money?

Some researchers have related a majority of major crimes to drugs.[20] It is well known how theft stems from heavy narcotics by providing addicts with the means of financing the habit. Less appreciated is marijuana's connection to those drugs. We examine this next.

OTHER DRUGS

※   ※

• "When I started marijuana I was thirteen and I'm twenty-nine now. . . . I've taken LSD, heroin, speed, reds, Seconals, yellows, downers, mushroom, peyote, Quaalude, belladonna, PCP, THC. I was the true product of my era. I tried everything. . . . There was a time when if someone said it was a drug and got you high, I'd try it. . . .
"I did heroin for a period of six or seven years. I never was addicted. A man I was dating, I think he was trying to get me high on purpose."
—Alice (chronic user)

• "I've done just about everything except heroin, tried it anyway: speed, downs, cocaine, hallucinogens, peyote, mushrooms, mescaline . . . I guess just to do it, just to try it, a new experience. . . .
"I know a few people who tried heroin, about twenty. One or two shot. I guess if they hadn't started marijuana, they never would have tried heroin." —Millie (chronic user)

• "I had a lot of psilocybin mushrooms, a fair bit of LSD, a few times cocaine . . . all after marijuana . . . mainly hearing about them from friends, what a far-out thing it is to do." —Steve (ex-user)

• "Cocaine came around. I used it in the service simply because I thought it would be a better high." —Quentin (ex-user)

• "Around 'sixty-three, 'sixty-four I started smoking pot. . . . We would get together on a Friday night and everybody chip in a dollar and buy a 'nickel bag' and we would all stay high Friday night. At that time for $5 you could get about twenty, twenty-five joints, and today I think you get two or three joints. . . .
"I smoked a lot of marijuana, and I can say for myself that just the indulgence in marijuana on a daily basis sort of put me in a trend where

387

drug use was part of the day and eventually led on to other types of drugs. . . .

"*I had used so much marijuana that I got tired of it. It wasn't doing anything for me anymore. I just kept on smoking and smoking and I said, 'There has got to be a better way to get high,' so I just started taking amphetamines. From amphetamines, I graduated to barbiturates and tranquilizers; and from barbiturates and tranquilizers, I graduated to heroin.*

"*I am not saying that all people who use marijuana take the same course, but that's exactly what happened to me. I just tried to relieve one boredom by substituting another type of drug and getting a different kind of a high. Before I came into . . . [a New York treatment center in 1969] I was addicted to heroin and barbiturates, so I had a dual habit. . . .*

"*I stole from my folks. Anything I could get my hands on, I stole. I hocked their wedding rings. TVs went. At one time I even planned a burglary for my own apartment but I never pulled it off. I had hit rock bottom. I had been arrested. I really didn't have any money for drugs. I was out there hustling every day. I caught hepatitis twice. I was really on skid row. I was a real bum.*" —Fred (ex-user and drug-rehabilitation worker)

• "*It used to be half a joint or a couple of hits to get me high. Now it usually takes a whole joint and I have to smoke strong dope. If I smoke just average, it doesn't do a thing for me. It was usually Mexican and Vietnamese, the majority Mexican. Mexican dope is generally average. Now I smoke Colombia or sinsemilla . . . very intense, resinous dope. . . .*

"*I had been using speed and acid and alcohol before I used marijuana.*" —Betty (long-time user, trying to quit)

• "*It takes more pot to get me really stoned to the point where I like getting stoned. I definitely don't get as high. The quality has deteriorated. Recently, three weeks ago, I smoked very good pot, $180 an ounce. Two hits and I was seeing God. . . .*

"*Tobacco after smoking pot is a bit of a lift. Marijuana and alcohol, when I first did it, provided complete euphoria. It eliminated all inhibitions. Now I find the combination makes me tired. . . .*

"*I've had hash, Thai stick pot, Quaalude, Valium, LSD, mushrooms, mescaline, cocaine.*" —Bert (chronic user)

• "*All I ever smoked was cheap Mexican weed. It probably went from a couple of joints a week to five joints a day at the peak, in the middle of the two and a half years. It required more to get high. Then it began to make me so paranoid and uncomfortable later, I went down to two joints. . . .*

"*Once I smoked opium in a joint. It reminded me of my earliest pot. A couple times hash. Hash made me vomit. Once PCP. I was deceived. I did not know what angel's dust was. It was in a joint. A boyfriend was eager for me to smoke it. I remember feeling pleasant and my boyfriend crying on the street, definitely psychotic.*" —Rosemary (ex-user)

• "*I tried most drugs. I tried heroin. I knew a user and wanted to see what it was like. Acid a few times. Mescaline I used regularly for a couple of years, five or ten times a year. There were a couple of years when I used cocaine maybe once every two weeks, and there were three or four years when I took peyote half a dozen times a year. I also tried ups and downs . . . and speed . . . and I smoked hashish. . . . Alcohol came first. Pot came before the others. . . . I smoked it for twelve years, sometimes once or twice a week, sometimes as much as once or twice a day. There were some long periods I was stoned at least some of the time every day.*" —Joe (ex-user)

• "*When I was in college I used every drug imaginable: marijuana; speed; Dexedrine and amphetamines; diet pills to stay up when I had to do papers; then I smoked marijuana to go to sleep, or sometimes straight speed; different little specialty pills . . . capsules that asthmatics take . . . heroin—I would snort it. I went on one little spree with it that lasted three months or so . . . belladonna, acid, mescaline, mushrooms. . . . I went to school in Virginia. The thing there was syrup with codeine. . . . Marijuana came before the other drugs. . . . Tobacco and drinking socially came before marijuana. . . . I preferred to smoke marijuana and drink at the same time. . . .*

"*I know people who were addicted to other drugs, a couple to heroin. I'm sure they started on marijuana, but I don't think marijuana was responsible.*" —Anna (ex-user)

• "*I started marijuana at eleven. . . . The smell of the smoke nauseated me. I wasn't too into it, but I did it. I liked being high. . . . I also took downers and uppers. . . . I sort of liked the zonked-out feeling. . . . Hashish . . . mostly I'd want to sleep. . . . LSD . . . codeine . . . speed. I snorted cocaine a few times. . . .*

"*I nearly always took marijuana and cigarettes. . . . I discovered if you take a deep toke on a joint and then take a puff on a cigarette, you get this weird instantaneous buzz that lasts a second or two, like when*

*you lost your stomach on a roller coaster. . . . I was heavy into alcohol
and pot for a while. Usually I got sick."* —Janet (ex-user)

● *"I started marijuana when I was seventeen and a half. . . . I've used
LSD and took my first at nineteen. A girl on campus had some pills she
called THC. I bought them for fifty cents apiece. After I took it, I discovered it was LSD. . . . I've taken a few Quaaludes and amphetamines in my lifetime. I started cocaine when I was 21, three years ago.
It's been six months since I've had any. . . .*

*"There are certain people who are drug-prone. They want to take drugs
to escape from reality. Marijuana was the first drug they tried and they
did move to harder narcotics. It's not that marijuana isn't satisfying. If
you're searching for a real escape, marijuana won't, or will provide it only
for a short period of time."* —Kathy (light user, former heavy user)

● *"I've smoked a lot of weed in my day. . . . I first tried marijuana in
the sixth grade. . . . Through dealing, I met a group of people who got
high all the time, and that's what I started doing. . . . I stayed at a
friend's house and he was into shooting up drugs and stuff like that, and
I wanted to try it. I wanted to try all the drugs. I'd tried mushrooms
. . . depressant . . . sniffing lacquer. . . . So I got into heavier drugs
and started shooting up cocaine. I was on cocaine for about two years,
using on the average twenty-five dollars a day. . . .*

*"You're exposed to that kind of situation where other drugs are preva-
lent and you can't say that using marijuana doesn't somehow lead to
using harder drugs, because everybody feels that using drugs is okay. Su-
perficially people will say 'don't abuse drugs,' but—face it—there are many
people in society that can't help themselves. . . . The other drugs are
available in that type of society . . . so 'why not try something else?'
. . . Once you're introduced to that culture, all the bars are down. . . .
Some people have an addictive personality . . . like me. I got stuck on
cocaine. Maybe they'll get stuck on heroin or opium or something like
that."* —Ira (ex-user and former pusher)

1

The Stepping-Stone Theory

"One of the public's greatest fears about marihuana is that its use will lead to the use of other drugs (the 'stepping-stone' theory). This appears to be a myth." A sociology textbook made that statement (1973) without offering any documentation.[1]

Once prevalent, the stepping-stone theory fell out of favor with academics amid America's big drug boom. They paid little heed to studies showing relationships between marijuana and other drugs, such as the following two studies from the 1960s.

In "the first attempt . . . to describe the drug use of a normal population" (1967), interviews and record checks of 235 black St. Louis men disclosed that almost half—109 men—had used drugs of abuse: marijuana, barbiturates, amphetamines, or opiates. All but six used marijuana—"it served as the introduction to drugs for most of those who went on to other drug use."

Professors Robins and Murphy (both of the psychiatry faculty of Washington University School of Medicine) thought it "surprising" that as many as 33 men, 14 percent, had records of selling, using, or possessing narcotics. Twenty-eight of them had tried heroin, all but six becoming addicted to it. (The 235 men, aged thirty to thirty-five, had been chosen from school records.)

What did not surprise them was that 21 of 28 men who tried heroin—three-quarters—had used marijuana first; four men took up both drugs in the same year; two started marijuana later; and only one never took marijuana. "This is in keeping with the commonly held belief that marijuana is a stepping stone to heroin, although it must not be forgotten that half of the marijuana users never used any other drugs."[2]

* * *

Records of 2,213 opiate addicts admitted to hospitals in 1965 revealed a close association between marijuana and opiate use among residents of sixteen states, the District of Columbia, and Puerto Rico. John C. Ball (government sociologist and University of Kentucky professor) and two others so reported in a law journal (1968).

Four-fifths of the addicts in those locations, including the most heavily populated areas, had used marijuana. A typical sequence of events, as far as interviews with 337 of the patients determined, was (a) start of marijuana smoking at age seventeen, (b) arrest at nineteen, and (c) start of heroin at twenty.

In twelve other states, mostly in the Southeast, only one-quarter of 390 opiate addicts studied used marijuana. Rather than heroin, theirs were legally manufactured drugs such as morphine and paregoric, not secured from underworld sources of supply. The remaining twenty-two states had few addicts.[3]

*   *   *

Marihuana: A Signal of Misunderstanding, it was called, aptly describing the signal sent to the American public in 1972 by the National Commission on Marihuana and Drug Abuse (the Shafer Commission). The publicity given to the commission's recommendation that the private use of marijuana be legalized overshadowed its cautionary advice about the hazards of prolonged smoking.

The report recognized that marijuana usually preceded heroin, that most heroin addicts had taken marijuana first, and that heavy marijuana smokers often used other drugs, but it "emphasized that the overwhelming majority of marijuana users do not progress to other drugs."

It pronounced false the viewpoint that drug abusers start with a "soft" drug such as marijuana and "progress" to harder drugs. Alcohol and cigarettes—the argument went—are really hard drugs themselves, and the pattern is to start with these and go in many ways from there.[4]

Such redefining of terms hardly solved any drug problem. The questions remained: Does marijuana somehow encourage a move to narcotics that are universally recognized as strongly addictive and tied to crime? Would elimination of marijuana prevent addiction to those other drugs?

*   *   *

Professor Hardin B. Jones, of the University of California at Berkeley, made three surveys of multiple drug use, two of them among male students there and one in the military.

• The first (1971) covered 400 students, of whom 280 regularly smoked marijuana. Two-fifths of those smokers, 118, had taken heroin or another opiate one or more times. Of the 120 who never had used marijuana, not one ever had tried an opiate.

• Next, of 367 heroin addicts studied in the U.S. armed forces at different world stations (1971–73), 363 had used marijuana before starting heroin. Only four began heroin without having first tried marijuana.

• In the final survey, of 150 marijuana smokers and 48 nonsmokers (1975–76) only those who had smoked marijuana went to other illegal drugs—about a quarter of them to opiates, nearly half to cocaine, and more than half to LSD. In addition, substantially larger percentages of marijuana users than nonusers smoked tobacco and drank coffee, alcohol, and even tea.[5]

* * *

Twenty-two percent of the chronic hashish smokers studied in Egypt admitted using opium also (1971). The longer a man had taken hashish or the heavier his hashish consumption had grown, the more likely he was to have added opium to his drug menu. A jaggedly soaring line of a graph symbolized the progression from a small fraction of hashish takers in the early years of use to a majority after thirty years of use. About a third more "heavy takers" (over thirty hashish doses monthly) than "moderates" liked opium.

The Egyptians also found that cannabis takers far exceeded nontakers in attachment to alcohol, coffee, tea, and tobacco. Professor M. I. Soueif suggested (1974) that "cannabis taking may be viewed as part of a broad need or urge for any chemical agent that would affect the central nervous system, either by arousal or by inhibition. . . ." Furthermore, an increasing attachment to cannabis facilitates a procession to "harder drugs," whether through "pharmacological" or "psychosocial mechanisms."[6]

* * *

In Seattle, Carlin and Post of the University of Washington's psychiatry department (1971) interviewed 106 adult male marijuana users about their drug experiences. Three-fourths reported taking psychedelic drugs (LSD, mescaline, or both; the number of "trips" varied from one to hundreds); three-fifths took amphetamines; 27 percent had "experimented" with opium; and 6 percent had "experimented" with either heroin or morphine.

Carlin and Post did not see fears about "graduation to addicting narcotic drugs" materializing, but it did appear to them that "if one is a regular user of marihuana, one is likely to go on and at least experiment with other more powerful psychedelic drugs."[7]

* * *

Psychiatrist Lester Grinspoon of Harvard University is among those who have denied any causal relationship. He and others consider the stepping-stone theory an example of a logical fallacy: thinking that one event caused another because one followed another.

If there is any relation between marijuana and heroin, wrote Dr.

Grinspoon (1971), it may be explained by the "fact" that laws equating the two—and entailing contact with the underworld for purchase of marijuana—make it relatively easy for marijuana users to be persuaded that heroin is no more dangerous. But, he added, one need not have to go so far: ". . . Doubtless they all drank milk, ate food, read comic books, wore clothes and rode bicycles before they used either cannabis or heroin, yet, so far as I know, no one has maintained that any of these activities lead to cannabis or heroin use."[8] (If, however, surveys demonstrated not only that the vast majority of heroin addicts started with milk but also that milk drinkers turned to heroin in far greater numbers than nondrinkers, then we might expect to hear talk about milk leading to heroin.)

Pointing out the fallacy of *post hoc, ergo propter hoc* (after this, therefore because of this), David F. Duncan of the School of Public Health, University of Texas, Houston, also included milk in his argument: "If heroin addicts tend to come from populations in which marijuana use is widespread (as it is among young people in many parts of the world today), then we can expect many heroin addicts to have experienced marijuana smoking. By the same light, if heroin addicts came from populations in which milk is commonly consumed, most heroin addicts will have drank [sic] milk prior to their first use of heroin."

Duncan's comments, in a British journal (1975), followed a description of two series of interviews with heroin addicts. First, sixty inmates of an unnamed prison in the U.S. South were asked, "What was the first illegal drug you used?" The majority—thirty-seven—replied "speed," that is, amphetamine. Barbiturates were next—twenty-three prisoners. Later, in an unnamed southern U.S. city, Duncan asked nineteen rehabilitation patients to give the order in which they first used seven types of drug. His list included alcohol, and fourteen patients numbered it first. Marijuana was the leading second drug (six patients). In each survey, only two subjects reported marijuana as the first drug used. The results tied in with the Ball study, in which the Southeast fell below other regions in marijuana use by opium addicts.[9]

*   *   *

"The belief that young people begin on marijuana and proceed step by step through harder drugs to heroin addiction is hoary with age," commented Dr. Norman E. Zinberg, Boston psychiatrist, in a popular psychology magazine in 1976. Rejecting that belief as nonsense, he cited the Duncan and Carlin-Post studies and reports of commissions.

He said the Carlin-Post study "specifically discounted the notion that such [marijuana] users develop an interest in other drugs, particularly opiates." (But most of those studied had taken other drugs, especially LSD and amphetamine.) And Duncan's "definitive study . . . shows—it does not simply indicate—that marijuana use does not lead to heroin use." (However, is it definitive for regions other than the South?)

" . . . Marijuana is a remarkably innocuous substance," Dr. Zinberg wrote, denying any link with motivation, chromosomes, the brain, psychosis, immunity, crime, general health, or sex.[10]

Earlier in 1976 the report on the nationwide survey of 2,510 young men and drugs had come out. It presented facts like these:

• Of all those surveyed, 148 took heroin. All of the heroin takers except two also used marijuana. Put another way, 11 percent of the 1,382 marijuana users also took heroin while less than two-tenths of one percent of the nonusers of marijuana did.

• Nine out of every ten of those dual drug takers had consumed marijuana first; 7 percent tried heroin first; and for the remaining 3 percent, the order could not be determined.

• One-quarter of marijuana users and almost no nonusers took cocaine; 96 percent of the dual users had started marijuana before starting cocaine.

• One-third of marijuana users and 4 percent of nonusers also took opiates (besides heroin); marijuana came first in 77 percent of the dual-use cases.

• Two-fifths of marijuana users and almost no nonusers consumed psychedelics; 80 percent of the psychedelic users had first smoked marijuana.[11]

Two of those who carried out the survey continued to analyze the data and reached a conclusion six years later on the relation of cannabis use and heroin use. Reviving the stepping-stone theory, Kentucky sociology professors O'Donnell and Clayton argued that "marijuana use is a cause of heroin use in the U.S. . . . ." They marshaled additional statistics, derived from the survey:

• The more times a young man had smoked marijuana, the more likely he was to have taken heroin. One-third of the 1,000-time smokers consumed heroin. Of those who had used marijuana 1 to 9 times, only 1 percent also had used heroin; 10 to 99 times, 4 percent; 100 to 999 times, 12 percent; and finally, 1,000 times or more, 33 percent. Three-fifths of the heroin takers had smoked marijuana 1,000 or more times.

• The top heroin addicts were also in the top marijuana category. Of eighteen men who had taken heroin 1,000 or more times, fifteen also had taken marijuana 1,000 or more times (two, 100 to 999 times; and one, 10 to 99 times).[12]

• Cocaine followed the same pattern: the greater the use of marijuana, the greater the likelihood of cocaine too being used. Only one cocaine user had not tried marijuana. Among those who had smoked marijuana 1,000 times or more, three-quarters had used cocaine too. (Data on cocaine was furnished by Professor Clayton, 1982).

That a "new government-funded study" linked marijuana with "harder stuff" received conspicuous albeit sketchy press coverage (via testimony of Dr. William Pollin, director of the National Institute on Drug Abuse, before a Senate committee, 1981).[13]

O'Donnell (now deceased) and Clayton summarized their case as follows. Marijuana use is a cause of heroin use because:

"1. Marijuana use and heroin use are statistically associated.

"2. Marijuana use precedes heroin use, not invariably, but in the vast majority of cases; and

"3. The association has not been shown to be spurious."

They rebutted the argument that drinking of alcohol or smoking of tobacco is the real culprit, not marijuana. Marijuana is a better predictor of other-drug use; the statistical associations are stronger, whether number of users or extent of use is considered, they said. The sample of young men had many who avoided marijuana but few who shunned tobacco and fewer nondrinkers.

Illustrating how overwhelming was the rejection of the stepping-stone theory in the social-scientific community, they cited nine sociology textbooks, 1971–75. Each treated lack of causal relation as almost a self-evident fact, needing no documentation.

According to some writers, to say that the use of one drug "causes" the use of another, you must demonstrate that nearly every user of drug A proceeds to drug B. Obviously, this did not happen to most of the young men. Only one marijuana user in four proceeded to cocaine and only one in ten went on to heroin. By the above standard, marijuana use did not cause heroin use.

O'Donnell and Clayton wondered if such writers denied "that cigarette smoking is a cause of lung cancer, on the grounds that only a minority of smokers develop the disease?"

They suspected that the denial of causality expressed a political rather than a scientific viewpoint of social scientists: possibly the sociologists (at least those active in the drug field) had reacted against the arguments of law enforcement officials that the progression from marijuana required severe penalties for marijuana possession.

The two researchers endorsed the sociologists' soft approach while chiding them for perhaps letting "debater's blindness" obscure the "basically correct premise." In fact, they climaxed their paper with a 180-degree shift in argument. As a possible solution to the heroin addiction problem, they suggested "a legal supply of marijuana"! Their thought was to eliminate the need to enter the drug subculture, wherein heroin is found. They were not yet ready to advocate such a policy, inasmuch as nobody fully understood how marijuana use led to heroin use.[14]

Certainly a multiplicity of illegal drugs are available in the drug subculture. Although signs indicate a modest decrease in heroin usage as the law has grown softer on marijuana users, the use of cocaine has soared. (For example, it tripled in ten years through 1982 in polls of young adults—more than one out of four having used it.)[15] If marijuana were completely legalized, we would expect a significant percentage of the new, legal users eventually to seek out "better highs."

> The survey of young men showed that 100 percent of marijuana users and 94 percent of nonusers drank alcohol; 94 percent of marijuana users and 81 percent of nonusers smoked tobacco. Alcohol nearly always came before marijuana; tobacco was not so studied.
>
> Whereas 11 percent of the marijuana users moved to heroin, only 6 percent of alcohol drinkers and 7 percent of tobacco smokers (and nearly no nonusers of those substances) used heroin. Three-fifths of the tobacco smokers and about as many of the alcohol drinkers used marijuana. About one-quarter of the non-smokers of tobacco and a twenty-fifth of the nondrinkers used marijuana.[16]

"There are no reports of a need to increase the dose to recapture the original euphoria or prevent a relapse into misery," Dr. Grinspoon said (1980).

"Recreationally, I have not seen—and I think most people would agree that there is not—a tolerance. And with respect to animals, one has to be careful about what one extrapolates from animals," he testified.[17]

Our interviews and a number of human studies, however, show smokers growing increasingly tolerant to marijuana as their consumption increases. When the dose remains constant, the effects diminish. When subjects can smoke as many marijuana cigarettes as they want, they generally keep increasing the number. Take these three experimental studies, each of male marijuana users smoking ad lib for weeks after a nonsmoking period.

• Williams and others (Lexington, Kentucky, 1946) studied six subjects who averaged about ten marijuana cigarettes on the first of thirty-nine days of smoking. The number of reefers climbed, with fluctuations, going to twenty or more some days and exceeding fifteen at the end. Physical tolerance developed. For three weeks, pulse would speed after smoking, then it stayed about normal.[18]

• Jack H. Mendelson, M.D. (Boston, 1974) reported that twelve "casual" users averaged 2 marijuana cigarettes per day at the start and rose gradually to 3 per day, jumping to 6 on the final, twenty-first day. Fifteen "heavy" users started at 3½ a day and gradually went up to 6½— 15 on the last day. While doses climbed, the heavy users continually rated themselves less "high" and the heart did not race as much.[19]

• Nowlan and Cohen (Los Angeles, 1977) observed thirty men smoking for sixty-four days. Except for the "light" smokers, who stayed at about two joints a day, the quantity of marijuana smoked generally rose as the weeks went on. ("Low moderate" smokers increased their average daily consumption from three to five cigarettes; "high moderate," from five to seven; and "heavy," from seven to nine). Meanwhile, the "high" feelings became lower and the heart sped less.[20]

✳   ✳   ✳

"The use of marijuana can become a stepping-stone to other drugs for rather simple reasons," said Dr. Robert G. Heath, the Tulane University brain researcher (1978). "Use of pleasure-inducing agents tends to lead to increased desire for the pleasure derived. This leads to increased use and, often, increased dosages.

"Marijuana doesn't supply the brain with the fundamental chemicals that produce pleasure, but it stimulates other chemicals in the brain that do so in turn. And with protracted stimulation, these other chemicals are used up or lose their strength. So, to maintain the pleasure feeling, the system needs to be stimulated more strongly. This can lead to the selection of something stronger to do the job."[21]

Britain's Advisory Committee on Drug Dependence reported (1968): "Unlike the 'hard' drugs such as heroin, cannabis does not produce tolerance. Consuming the same, sometimes even a smaller, amount of cannabis continues to produce the original effect."[22]

The notion of so-called reverse tolerance was advanced in days when half-percent marijuana was considered strong and a joint a week was categorized as regular usage. The neophyte needed several exposures before his brain accumulated enough THC to give him his first "high"; it took less smoking for him to get high again. Ultimately regular tolerance developed.

One social researcher who has rejected the stepping-stone theory—"too simplistic and based on faulty logic"—is Denise Kandel (Columbia University and New York State Psychiatric Institute). She has denied that one drug "causes" the use of another, although her research demonstrated that one type of drug usually would follow another in a definite sequence, marijuana preceding the so-called "harder" drugs.

The core of the research was a survey of 8,000 students from eighteen high schools in New York state (1971–72) through questionnaires. Each was questioned twice; some were queried a third time, after graduation.

A key point was designation of tobacco cigarettes and alcoholic beverages as drugs. By this terminology, marijuana is not the first step in drug abuse. "The legal drugs"—taken by four-fifths of the teenagers studied—"are necessary intermediates between non-use and marijuana. . . . A direct progression from non-use to illegal drug use practically never occurs."

Accordingly, Dr. Kandel set forth four distinct "stages of drug use" by adolescents: (1) beer or wine, (2) hard liquor or cigarettes, more often the liquor, (3) marijuana, and (4) other illicit drugs. The other illicit drugs usually follow a sequence of (a) pills, (b) psychedelics, such as LSD, (c) cocaine, and (d) heroin.

Through questionnaires to subjects' parents and, in some cases, friends, she came up with these "predictors" of three of the stages: *Hard liquor*—minor delinquency, high sociability with friends, and parents and peers who drink it. *Marijuana*—beliefs favoring it, standards unlike adults', minor delinquency, and peers who use it. *Other drugs*—poor relationship with parents, parents and peers who use various legal and illegal drugs, psychological distress, and somewhat more deviant behavior. (The importance of each factor varies with the individual.)

While the data showed a clear sequence of drugs, they did not indicate that any drug necessarily led to any other drug. "Many adolescents stop at a particular stage and do not progress further; many regress to lower drugs."

The trouble with the stepping-stone theory, in her opinion, is this: "The fact that 100% of heroin users have had experience with marijuana does not mean that the reverse is true and that 100% of the marijuana users will end up using heroin" (1979).[23]

We don't know of anyone who says the reverse is true. Plainly it is not. But this fact should not invalidate the theory.

Let us imagine a series of five stepping-stones leading to a little island in the middle of a stream. Everyone visiting the island steps on the five stones. But not everyone stepping on stones visits the island; some step upon only one or two or three stones, enjoy the view, and turn back.

All five stones are necessary, however, for those going all the way.

Alcohol and cigarettes could be two such stepping-stones. (We do not dispute those who emphasize their dangers.) Marijuana could be another.

✻　✻　✻

Senators at two hearings listened to personal accounts of childhood drug abuse from rehabilitated addicts. Ron was fifteen when he testified in 1983 before a Senate appropriations subcommittee: "When I was eleven, everyone in school was getting high. I didn't know anybody that didn't do it. I was stealing, failing in school [parochial school in New York City] and getting in trouble all over the place. I stole from anybody I could." Ron had begun smoking marijuana at the age of seven. He graduated to alcohol, cocaine, and peyote.[24]

Jeff, aged twenty-five, of southern California, had testified in 1980 that "I started smoking pot when I was nine in New York. I said I would never ever do any other drugs." By the age of twelve he had taken LSD, cocaine, and nearly everything else the "drug culture" offered. The taking of marijuana and other drugs was rebellious, but at the same time it had "a lot of acceptance and peer pressure" behind it. Leaving bad company and moving to a wealthier environment in California did not help; things were worse. "I have shot heroin. . . . In 1979 I spent $30,000 on cocaine. . . . I have taken pills day in and day out." He said decriminalizing marijuana put an official OK on it, inevitably meaning that "drug abuse of other kinds will follow. This is not only from my own experience. I am a very average case of drug abuse in schools."

His brother and two sisters also suffered addiction to other drugs after starting with marijuana. Treatment rehabilitated the four.[25]

In a letter to the presiding senator, Jeff wrote that a decade earlier his best friend "was smoking pot that wasn't satisfying enough anymore. He decided to shoot (mainline) heroin, which he had tried a few times prior to this. He took too much, the result was death. . . . I could write of many examples resulting in death. . . . The truth in this matter of smoking pot is that out of literally hundreds of adolescents and adults I have encountered personally, I have not met one person involved that has not gone on to try at least some other kind of drug whether it be uppers, downers, heroin, angel dust, and most of all cocaine and Quaaludes."

✻　✻　✻

A grim picture of drug addiction emerged from a three-show series on Dick Cavett's television program featuring popular musician John Phillips and his actress daughter Mackenzie Phillips (together with psychiatrist Mark S. Gold, who was treating them at a New Jersey hospital). Father and daughter were recovering drug addicts. Independently, he had become hooked on heroin, she on cocaine. The family blew "millions" on drugs. Aside from shooting the drugs into their bodies, nothing in the world mattered to them—not love, not food, not even survival. She married because her husband could get cocaine for her. Seeing themselves deteriorate and people they knew die from drugs made no difference.

Portions of the TV conversation follow.

CAVETT: Legalization of marijuana?
MACKENZIE: No.
CAVETT: For a time the idea was very fashionable.
JOHN: I believed in it.
MACKENZIE: I did too. I disagree now. . . . I started with marijuana. He started with marijuana.

JOHN: There are lots of people who smoke marijuana . . . and they go no further, and they can handle it. There are lots of other people who start with marijuana [and] end up being drug addicts. . . .

It was in the early sixties I started smoking marijuana, then hallucinogens in the sixties . . . then cocaine in part of the seventies. And then around 'seventy-six it [heroin] also caught up with me. I'm living proof that the domino theory works. You know: one drug to the next, to the next, to the next, to the next. . . .

If I smoked marijuana, I wouldn't really be satisfied. I'd have to smoke something else. It would just be the whole circle over again . . . in record time.

Mackenzie elaborated (at the Southeast Drug Conference, Atlanta, just after the TV taping, 1981): "During the last four years I've gone from smoking marijuana to taking Quaaludes, to snorting cocaine, to injecting cocaine, and to injecting cocaine every five or ten minutes. . . .

"I started to get into drugs when I was sixteen. . . . I thought I was too successful and too together to let drugs take over my life. . . . I was partying with people who used drugs, and everyone seemed to be smoking grass and . . . snorting cocaine. . . . Mainly I just wanted to fit in with the group. . . . At first I just used them socially. . . . The drugs blocked out the other problems . . . just as long as I took them. . . . I rapidly went from grass to coke to needles. I needed more and more just to break even. . . . I didn't want to work to get a high; coke was easier. . . ."

2

Interaction

Most of the research that we cite elsewhere deals with cannabis alone. In actuality indications are that relatively few chronic marijuana smokers stay with marijuana alone, at least in the United States. From the start, a partnership of marijuana and alcohol or tobacco is common. The move to other street drugs does not necessarily mean that the drug dependent gives up marijuana. He may return to it from time to time or intersperse marijuana among the other drugs.

To predict how a confirmed drug taker will react in body and mind at different times to all of the changing combinations and permutations of abused chemicals may never be possible. Researchers have studied the effects of cannabis or THC with a variety of drugs, however, in humans as well as in animals.

Exploring the effects on the central nervous system, the scientists have observed interactions between marijuana or THC and alcohol or any of a number of drugs: sedatives, hypnotics, stimulants, and opiates. The effects of combinations of drugs often exceed those of any individual drug. Sometimes the effect of a combination is greater than the sum of the parts or different from the effect of any individual drug.

Human research has been more limited than the animal studies and by no means has it covered all possible combinations, doses, and sequences of cannabis and drugs of abuse. Two drugs may interact at one combination of doses but not at another, or in one order or time sequence but not in another. Then too, marijuana tends to persist in the system, and much remains to be learned about the effects of chronic use of cannabis and other drugs. What is known about marijuana may be the tip of an iceberg headed for a massive impact on body, psyche, and society.

A review of the scientific literature on the effects of cannabis in combination with alcohol or other drugs, by a Buffalo drug researcher in a monograph of the National Institute on Drug Abuse (1980), ended with 160 citations. A summary of some of the experiments follows.

Alcohol—Cannabis and alcohol (ethanol) are the most common combination. In rodents the acute effects of the two together in depressing central nervous system activity are greater than those produced by either drug alone.

In human studies too, the use of alcohol together with smoked marijuana at common doses can produce more marked effects than either drug alone on perception, movement, and higher mental functioning.

Not only does tolerance develop to each substance alone, but exposure to one often makes rodents more tolerant to the other. Inquiries into such cross-tolerance in man are inconclusive.

Sedatives, hypnotics, and opiates—Many investigators demonstrate that cannabinoids enhance the depressant effects of sedatives and hypnotics on rodents' central nervous systems, prolonging drug-induced sleep. Combinations of THC and phenobarbital, chlordiazepoxide (Librium), ethanol, or PCP at highest doses cause a greater depressant effect on measures of conditioned behavior and vital signs that any individual component. THC lightens morphine withdrawal but increases aggressive behavior in morphine-dependent rats.

In man, marijuana added to oral secobarbital has a more depressant effect than either drug alone on steadiness and motor and mental activity. Injection of THC added to injection of pentobarbital induces more profound mental effects, including hallucinations and great anxiety, than one drug alone. Similar enhancements are seen in oxymorphone and diazepam. THC treatment increases the life of pentobarbital and antipyrine.

Stimulants—In rabbits, THC and amphetamines are sometimes additive, sometimes antagonistic. Acute doses of cocaine, caffeine, and apomorphine all reverse THC's depression of activity in rabbits.

Human research shows interactions between cannabis and amphetamines at higher doses, inducing a greater than additive increase in intensity and duration of the "high" and an increase in blood pressure.

Medicines—Aspirin prolongs the presence of THC in the blood and increases the levels of THC in the brains of rats. Phenylbutazone (analgesic drug) increases THC levels in the brain and liver.[26]

Note the warning of Beaconsfield et al. (1972) that treatment with atropine (antispasmodic and anesthetic) or an anesthetic containing epinephrine could enhance and prolong a patient's marijuana-induced tachycardia for "a dangerously long period."

* * *

The British advisory committee, doubly mistaken on tolerance, erred a third time by stating: "When combined with another drug, cannabis in man does not cause this to exert an effect quantitatively greater than that which would result from the use of that drug alone in the same dosage."[27]

THE
MILITARY

1

Drugs and Nukes

That the development of nightmarish weapons by rival powers has brought the world's inhabitants to the brink of destruction is generally agreed. This would be the case even if those manning the instruments of mass lethality possessed the very clearest of heads. Now what if those heads are befogged by drugs?

This is more than a theoretical possibility. News media and congressmen have picked up many warning signals over the years.

A petty officer on a nuclear-powered aircraft carrier has shipmates who handle nuclear weapons and are "doing one drug or another." A navy man caught smoking marijuana is assigned to guard nuclear weapons. An ex-addict says that as a military policeman in Germany he sold drugs to men handling atomic weapons. Marijuana smoking goes on in the reactor room of a nuclear submarine. A sailor talks of drug offenses by nuclear technicians and a radiation accident in a harbor. Atomic weapons guards in Germany are disqualified for drug abuse, while marijuana smoking prevails in a nuclear missile outfit there. A Strategic Air Command officer is convicted of selling marijuana and LSD; a senator raises the specter of atomic bombers being flown by drugged pilots; the SAC commander reveals a problem of drug abuse among bomber crew members, atomic maintenance personnel, and others; and air force leniency toward marijuana smoking nuclear weapons personnel disturbs congressmen. And at a Missouri base for the launching of intercontinental nuclear missiles, hundreds of air force men are charged with marijuana offenses; at least three are officers, including a captain commanding a missile silo. (More detail on these items will follow shortly in small type.)

Murphy's Law (in its popular form) says: "If anything can go wrong, it will." Atomic devices can and do.

The defense department admitted in 1976 that 27 major nuclear weapons accidents had occurred in the armed forces of the United States. A Swedish estimate placed the number of U.S. nuclear weapons accidents, major and minor, at 125 through that year.[1]

Could drugs have played any part?

Inasmuch as thousands of servicemen in the nuclear weapons program are caught with drugs every year, the idea is not too farfetched. Neither is the possibility of guards, valuing drugs above duty, allowing

405

hostile elements access to atomic hardware or material. Or nuclear bombers being operated by crewmen under the influence of drugs, setting off a Dr. Strangelove–type catastrophe.

Our discussions of cannabis and transportation are pertinent here. Every day the military moves hundreds of nuclear bombs, transporting them routinely between, through, and over cities in America and abroad by ships, barges, helicopters, trains, trucks, and even mobile homes. "A nuclear weapons accident is most likely to occur during transportation, when the device is most vulnerable to collision, carelessness or terrorism," according to investigative reporter David Kaplan.[2]

As for drugs and nuclear weapons, Stan Norris of the Center for Defense Information, Washington, D.C., gave us his outlook: "It's a serious problem and the military knows it's a serious problem. It tries to do something about it, but it's only probably marginally successful in these attempts to isolate who it is and shift him to another job." The marijuana smoker may be caught, "but then the guy they replace him with does the same thing."

Can you sketch a scenario in which drugs could result in a nuclear weapons accident? we asked. Norris responded, "I see the major problem in handling them, transporting them—let's say on a ship, taking them off . . . on . . . moving them from one place on the ship to another place . . . something happening. . . . They have a crane and they're taking a missile off and misjudge what they're doing and they drop the damn thing and it splits apart."

Kaplan's response to the same question: "Nuclear weapons have to be transported from ship to ship, from ship to land, and from land to air, and there's a series of critical movements in which absolute security is demanded. If there isn't this absolute security, if there isn't coordination on the part of all personnel involved, someone could screw up. . . .

"One of these guys is on dope, and through errors in judgment a nuclear weapon falls fifteen, twenty, thirty feet onto concrete on a naval station's wharf. It's accidentally dropped from a crane or a helicopter, or it's banged into a truck. You have a detonation of the conventional high-explosive trigger, like TNT, thereby dispersing plutonium—according to one federal study—over an area as wide as seventy square miles."

Steve Talbot, who investigated the matter of military nuclear accidents for a documentary on KQED-TV in San Francisco, answered us in this way: "In a situation where someone was actually in control of a nuclear weapon in a silo someplace, if people there were under the influence of drugs, of course that could be potentially catastrophic."

The following are extracts from broadcast interviews, personal conversations, press stories, and congressional documents.

• *Petty officer on a nuclear-powered aircraft carrier:* "I know friends of mine on the ship who handle weapons, nuclear weapons at that, who are doing one drug or another."

TV reporter: "They handle nuclear weapons?"

Petty officer: "Nuclear weapons, yes. That can be very dangerous."

TV reporter: "What percentage of the guys on the *Enterprise* are going to be involved with drugs, would you guess?"

Petty officer: "I would say 65 to 70 percent." . . .

TV reporter: "Sailors in Alameda [California] said most drug use is out to sea and it consists of powerful Asian marijuana, cocaine, and even heroin. Not only are the sailors using these drugs, many sell large quantities back in this country, and I was told tonight the whole drug scene is so widespread that no crackdown can stop it."[3]

• *Steve Talbot of KQED-TV, San Francisco:* "Two people talked to me who at one time were guarding nuclear weapons. . . . They were on board a naval weapons ship ferry. . . . This one guy had been caught smoking marijuana. . . . He got in some trouble because of drug use and even after that episode was assigned to guard nuclear weapons. . . . He continued to use marijuana, although he never said he was under the influence or used it while on duty. . . .

"He was sort of taking the job seriously. He was sort of saying, 'Look, here I am, a guy who used drugs, and they still assigned me to guard these weapons.' So he was critical of the navy's own procedures. And then he went further and said, 'There are rules not to smoke cigarettes around nuclear weapons. Guys do smoke cigarettes around nuclear weapons. There's a two-man rule that two people have to be guarding them at all times. Often it's just one person.' " (From a conversation, 1982.)

• *Staff assistant for the defense subcommittee, House appropriations committee:* "I had one guy call me one day from out of the blue. Refused to give his name. He said that he had been a military cop for an army security unit in Germany (he was out of the army now), that he had been hooked on drugs himself, that he'd gotten off them fortunately, but that he had been a pusher. He had contacts in the army's drug search-and-seizure type of teams, so that he knew pretty well when they were coming around, and he was selling to people handling nuclear weapons.

". . . Our investigators . . . have too many independent reports of the same sort of stuff going on." (From a conversation, 1981.)

• *David Kaplan, Center for Investigative Reporting, Oakland, California (in a radio interview):* "As a lot of people recognize, drugs are a problem in the military, and some of the people who had worked aboard U.S. Navy submarines told us how they would go to the reactor room to smoke marijuana because it's the only room in the submarine with adequate ventilation.

"So you could imagine what kind of problems this sort of thing would bring. A Poseidon submarine . . . has enough atomic firepower aboard to incinerate 160 Soviet cities and these guys are getting stoned. . . ."[4]

• A sailor caught smoking marijuana aboard the Polaris missile submarine *Thomas Jefferson* told of widespread drug abuse aboard the subs and said, "The navy is covering up a drug scandal." He also disclosed an incident in which the sub accidentally discharged sixteen gallons of radioactive water into the harbor at Charleston, South Carolina.

The sailor, Gary Anderson, was introduced to drugs the day after reporting on board and "caught smoking red-handed" a year later in the lower level missile compartment, fined $500, demoted, and ordered off sub duty. His and others' testimony implicated twenty-seven crewmen; thirteen were disciplined and fourteen cleared.

He charged that lower ranking seamen would be dismissed for drug offenses while nuclear reactor or missile technicians, whose skills were in demand, got off easier. Further, "I was told on at least three occasions by officers ranging in rank from chief warrant officers to lieutenant that 'We don't care if you smoke. Just don't get caught.' "[5]

• "The U.S. Army has disqualified 33 military policemen from guard duty at a nuclear weapons depot for reported drug abuse . . . in Germany . . . at the Miesau Ammunition Depot. . . . The Army feared the MPs had been smoking hashish while guarding the atomic weapons. . . . Most of the 33 men have been reassigned to other camps in Germany."[6]

• "The 1st Battalion 81st Artillery shows what's happening to the U.S. Army here in Germany. . . . Drug use is increasing at an alarming rate in the unit, which is a nuclear missile outfit. Battalion officers and noncoms estimate that from 50% to 80% of the battalion's 1,600 men smoke marijuana, some while on duty."[7]

• ". . . A Strategic Air Command officer was convicted of selling marijuana and LSD at a California air force base. . . . Three other SAC flight officers . . . were cleared. . . . The Pentagon statement was in response to remarks . . . of Senator Thomas J. Dodd (Democrat of Connecticut) during a drug-abuse hearing where he raised the spectre of nuclear bombers being flown by pilots under the influence of drugs."[8]

• General Richard Ellis, commander of the Strategic Air Command, revealed in 1981 a problem of drug abuse and alcoholism among nuclear missile security guards, B-52 bomber crew members, maintenance personnel dealing with atomic weapons, and other SAC members—as reported by Representative Joseph P. Addabbo, chairman of the House defense subcommittee, at a hearing he conducted four months later, in June, 1981.

Colonel Wade S. Gatling, deputy chief, Human Resources Development Division, Air Force Headquarters, said at the hearing that "the air force has a program referred to as the Personnel Reliability Program [for] individuals who are directly affiliated with the nuclear program. The air force presently has about 53,000 individuals in this kind of capacity. During fiscal year 1980, about 1.8 percent of that 53,000 were removed permanently from the program because of drug involvement [close to 1,000]. That sounds small, but we take no comfort in the 1.8 percent. Any kind of involvement in this PRP program is, of course, too much."[9]

• "Probably the single most disturbing piece of information provided to the committee from the Air Force was the issue of the lenient first-time marijuana offender policy. As it relates to the [nuclear weapons] Personnel Reliability Program, the Air Force presented the following interpretation [to the House Select Committee on Narcotics Abuse and Control, 1978]:

"The decrease in the number of cannabis disqualifications in calendar year '76 was due, in part, to a more flexible disqualification policy when first-time use or experimentation is involved. The revised policy gives the commander the option of not permanently disqualifying a first-time marijuana user (experimenter)." Drug disqualifications totaled 1,970 in 1975 and 1,474 in 1976, cannabis figuring in 70 and 73 percent of the cases, respectively.[10]

The air force's "first-time marijuana abuse policy" by which a marijuana abuser may be put back to work was reaffirmed by Colonel Gatling at the 1981 hearing.[11]

During 1981 the armed forces disqualified 1,700 people from duty in the nuclear weapons program because of drug abuse and 660 more for alcohol abuse, John H. Johns, deputy assistant secretary of defense, drug and alcohol abuse prevention, reported to the House defense subcommittee, 1982.[12]

• The Daily Star-Journal of Warrensburg, Missouri, reported in July, 1979: "More than 80 enlisted men at Whiteman Air Force Base—including some who work with Minuteman missiles—are being investigated for use or sale of marijuana. . . ."

In the ensuing months of 1979, the official total of marijuana defendants increased periodically, reaching 236, including 2 officers (the newspaper reported); unofficial sources placed the total higher. The air force sent some to a rehabilitation center at Wichita, Kansas, subjecting the others to discharge, court martial, or administrative action.

Marijuana charges were lodged against sixteen more personnel at Whiteman base in 1980 and ten more in 1981. In May, 1984, police in nearby Warrensburg arrested an air force captain for possession of the drug. He was relieved of duty as commander and member of a two-man operational crew for the Minuteman ICBM.

* * *

Drugs could render civilian nuclear equipment vulnerable too. At the San Onofre nuclear power plant in southern California, a group of former workers admitted in 1981 that after smoking marijuana they did shoddy repairs to the steam generator of a nuclear reactor.[13] In 1983 at the same plant, twenty-one security officers were suspended from their jobs after urine testing indicated noticeable THC levels.[14] Also in 1983, present and past plant employees told the Los Angeles Times that the use of illegal drugs, including marijuana and cocaine, had been widespread among craftsmen who built, maintained, and repaired the plant's three reactors.[15]

Twenty-three people, among them thirteen working at the Diablo Canyon nuclear plant site on the coast of central California, were charged by San Luis Obispo County authorities with selling marijuana, hashish, cocaine, and amphetamine on and near the site (the San Francisco Chronicle reported, December 7, 1983). They included construction and power workers and security guards. The plant had been under construction for some fifteen years, never in operation. Owner Pacific Gas & Electric Company had recently received approval from the Nuclear Regulatory Commission to load uranium in its reactors in preparation for tests. On August 10, 1984, the NRC voted to permit full operation of the plant.

2

Vietnam

Quentin, who smoked marijuana for six years, started in 1971 and joined the navy six months later. There he began smoking it more and more often. It was potent Vietnamese marijuana.

"Paranoia," which the smoke had instilled in him during civilian days, pursued him in the military. "Being in a very secretive operation, being in intelligence, you worried about your clearance and everything else. The other people around me didn't, though.

"By getting to Vietnam, then it was already plentiful, and I used it almost every day as a, you might say, tension easer, to get me ready for combat flights. . . .

"It cost, when I started in high school, about twenty-five cents a joint. In Vietnam you could get a dozen for ten cents or supply the rolling papers to the person you were buying it from and they'd do it for you. . . . Sometimes we would make it in Vietnam as a nice little sauce to put on your chicken that you were cooking. . . .

"Cocaine came around. I used it in the service simply because I thought it would be a better high. . . .

"You could buy drugs on board ship fairly easily from the guys that went to the mail runs that went ashore. They could get just about any kind you wanted. The navy did not approve of drug use, but in a combat situation, especially out on a carrier, not on the front-line units, they really wouldn't care too much if it made you do your job all right. . . .

"There was never anything put on my health record or personnel record. . . . It was just treated nonchalant. 'Everybody does it'—that sort of thing."

*   *   *

For years the armed forces generally ignored their drug problems. This certainly was the case in Vietnam.

Two U.S. Army surveys, each of about 1,000 men, found that half of the enlisted men in a replacement battalion and two-thirds of those in an airborne group, had smoked marijuana in Vietnam. In each survey, three out of ten were smoking it heavily or habitually.[16]

At the peak, in 1971, 69 percent of about 14,000 GIs surveyed admitted having smoked marijuana in Vietnam, and 28 percent avowed having first smoked it in Vietnam. The prevalence of marijuana smoking nearly matched that at the University of California at Berkeley, where 71 percent of students surveyed in 1971 by Professor Hardin B. Jones acknowledged having tried marijuana. But the marijuana in Vietnam was much stronger.

Also powerful was the Vietnamese heroin—nine-tenths pure. (On U.S. streets the "smack" or "horse" may contain as little as 1 percent heroin.) A far greater proportion of Americans in Vietnam—more than a third of the GIs—took this powerful heroin than took the weaker junk in the United States. A fifth of the soldiers became addicted to narcotics, mostly heroin.

Military leaders paid little attention to the profuse consumption of marijuana, amphetamines, and barbiturates, but when drug usage culminated in heavy heroin addiction, they took heed and instituted a program of urinary testing for heroin (as Professor Jones related).[17] The technology for urinary testing for marijuana did not yet exist.

A woman journalist reported buying vials of heroin in a dozen conspicuous places within a few minutes—even just outside of the headquarters of an American general, where children sold them at a stand nearly every day for three dollars per vial the size of a salt shaker. GIs usually would "snort" it (push it into the nostrils and inhale) or smoke it.

As for cannabis, it grew wild and abundantly. Disguised as regular cigarettes, pot was peddled on Saigon street corners or taken to men in the front lines by civilians, occasionally by other soldiers driving army trucks. Some smokers played hippie roles, wearing beads, displaying "psychedelic" posters, and playing "acid rock."

A belated treatment program went into effect and the word "crackdown" began to figure prominently in news stories from Vietnam after the U.S. forces' commander, General Abrams, ordered officers to help combat the use and traffic in drugs, including marijuana, in 1971.

While heroin use did abate, marijuana use remained heavy. Notwithstanding directives from the top, lower down, at battalion and company level, officers often looked the other way.[18] Few understood the effects of marijuana (although some factual information was available to commanders).

Any officers or "noncoms" who tried to crack down on marijuana faced trouble. A marine sergeant's objections to marijuana smoking infuriated men under his command to the point where one tried to murder him. He testifed (at a Senate subcommittee hearing) that he had survived twenty months of combat in Vietnam without seeing any troops use drugs. When he returned in 1968, he saw his men smoking marijuana to the extent that they "couldn't do their jobs . . . they were useless." His attempts to curb the drug resulted in legal frustrations, open threats on his life, and hatred by troops. One night a private rolled a hand grenade under his bed. It exploded, causing him extensive internal injuries.[19]

Professor Jones said (to another Senate subcommittee), "The officers I talked to in Vietnam were worried about cannabis because they suspected that this may have been a part of some of the terrible events such as the murdering of officers." (The euphemism for it was "fragging," from fragmentation.) ". . . All of the officers were uptight about this situation because they didn't know when it might be their turn.

"The incidence wasn't so great that it would be likely to induce a neurosis in the officers, but it was great enough to worry about, and they knew that this kind of event was not associated with the heroin user, but rather with the cannabis user, and also the amphetamine user. But the amphetamine user also had to be a cannabis user, and the tie between these two is very, very great."

He testified that records of thousands of cases showed that the average amount of a drug used increased with the length of time it was used. With boredom, ready availability, and peer reinforcement, the beginning cannabis user abroad would progress more deeply into drugs. All of the hundreds of heroin addicts he had interviewed (including eighty-eight servicemen in southeast Asia) had used cannabis before heroin.[20]

✻   ✻   ✻

Dr. Joel H. Kaplan, who as a major commanded a neuropsychiatric team in Vietnam (1968–69) reported on some of the problems. In a year his team saw about 4,000 outpatients, of whom three-fourths were drug abusers; meanwhile, half of 500 hospital patients abused drugs. They took mainly marijuana but also opiates, amphetamines, LSD, glue, and other substances.

Vietnamese "papasans" or "mamasans" running opium dens would start the incoming soldiers on marijuana. Then they would get them to smoke "OJs" (opium-laced joints). Finally they would graduate the GIs to opiate injections. "We had many OD's [overdose victims] brought into the emergency rooms . . . comatose from drugs or dead on arrival."

A helicopter commander called marijuana smoking a tremendous problem in his unit. He could walk around and find pot hidden in many places. The abusers included pilots as well as crewmen, gunners, corpsmen, and ground personnel.

Dr. Kaplan reported seeing many cases of toxic psychosis in Vietnam and said that many of the soldiers likened the experiences to LSD "trips." Most had to be flown abroad. Often used heavily, marijuana could also cause men to become fearful and paranoid "and led in a number of cases to acts of violent crimes."

Kaplan told of these two cases in which marijuana severely—perhaps tragically in one case—impaired a soldier's performance: One soldier was on guard duty near the demilitarized zone and smoked marijuana during the evening. Suddenly he decided to make peace with the Viet Cong. He took his shoes off and tried to cross the barbed wire. Friends brought him back and he was removed from guard duty.

Another soldier, normally an excellent "point man" (scout), began to use marijuana before going on patrols and also in the field. One morning, after getting "stoned" the previous night, he missed an ambush and four fellow soldiers were killed. Depressed and guilt-ridden, he felt the drug had caused him to miss the ambush.

Kaplan noted that soldiers could react in different ways. A soldier smoking marijuana away from the stresses of battle might feel a sense of euphoria. "The same soldier who has been in combat, who is suspicious of the people living in the area, not knowing how to distinguish a South Vietnamese from a Viet Cong, seeing his fellow soldiers being killed, watching young children destroy themselves by blowing up G.I.s with them, will have paranoid feelings, become frightened under the drug and become more angry and vengeful."

Soldiers often claimed that they would give up drugs when they returned home. But Kaplan told of many cases of "soldiers coming to us shortly before the end of their tour in desperate need, crying for help because they were not able to stop the use of drugs. There were cases of soldiers who signed up for a second tour because of the readily available drug supply throughout Vietnam."

He said the army at first did not discharge men for drug addiction—it waited till they got into enough trouble to be kicked out—nor did it even approve drug treatment. Kaplan's detachment set up an unofficial, voluntary program. Few soldiers ever had been told about the dangers of drugs or had seen any doctor for their drug problems.[21]

Finally, the army instituted a program granting immunity to drug dependents who turned themselves in for treatment.[22]

Other psychiatrists who served in Vietnam traced impairment and even tragedy to marijuana. Doctors Talbott and Teague told how a young sentry, reacting to his first joint, thought a fellow soldier was Ho Chi Minh and shot him to death.

Dr. John K. Imahara described two cases in which young soldiers smoked joints and, impelled by "voices," committed shootings, fatal in one case. He included these among thirteen violent crimes in Vietnam associated with the use of marijuana close to the time of the incident. He said the bulk of soldiers using marijuana regularly would develop an "amotivational syndrome" that would no longer permit them to function effectively.

Psychiatrist Edward Colbach did not come across any "sensational" marijuana cases in a year in Vietnam. But "marijuana was associated with ineffectiveness, panic states, and psychoses." And four of five studies that he reviewed indicated that the soldier smoking it "tends to have more disciplinary problems" than the soldier avoiding it.[23]

*   *   *

Ex-user Quentin says he did his navy job exceedingly well despite his taking of drugs. Some servicemen, however, have told much different stories.

An anonymous army man, wearing dark glasses, testified at a Senate subcommittee hearing in 1970: He had received two purple hearts in Vietnam. While under the influence of marijuana, he fired his rifle at what he imagined were enemy soldiers, thus revealing his position.

Another witness, masked, said that in Korea he had nearly run over some fellow soldiers with a tank he was operating while on marijuana. A former sailor, also masked, said he started smoking marijuana at a California base and that he used drugs while working as a jet airplane mechanic.[24]

One press account told (rather vaguely) of four GIs smoking marijuana who depinned a grenade in their midst for fun. It exploded, killing two of them. Another time some pot smokers were said to have exposed themselves in combat to watch incoming tracer rounds. A medic who tried to save them died from gunfire. The news story quoted unnamed military authorities who felt that the enemy was encouraging marijuana distribution among GIs as a weapon.[25]

Another instance of passivity in the face of violence—indeed, esthetic appreciation of war—comes out of a work by John Steinbeck IV. Poetically he described an experience in which he sat with soldiers on a Vietnam mountaintop. Intoxicated on marijuana, they watched a shelling. "The beauty of all that gunpowder was almost too much to bear," he wrote.[26]

It became clear that marijuana was not necessarily an instrument of "peace and love." Peter Lemon, a young man who insisted he was antiwar, won America's highest military honor, the Congressional Medal of Honor, for heroism in Vietnam. One night in 1970, in an army support group, he had used rifle, machine gun, and hand grenades to smash an attack; fought hand to hand; and made a rescue before collapsing from three wounds. Interviewed the next year, he admitted that he was "stoned on marijuana" that night.[27]

While passivity and lack of motivation may accompany cannabis in many takers, the use of the drug by some men to fortify themselves for war or homicide has been talked about since the Dark Ages. Thus old Hindu literature and folk songs refer to *ganja* and *bhang* beverages being drunk by soldiers and heroes. It is said that "the Rajput warriors . . . used to indulge in bhang so that any nervousness present might be banished, and a feeling of determination created either to win or die on the field of battle."[28]

3

Probing High And Low

It was the evening of May 26, 1981, and the *Nimitz* had been at sea for eleven days. She was the largest warship afloat, a thousand-foot, nuclear-powered aircraft carrier, believed to carry at least a hundred atomic weapons.[29] The *Nimitz* had served as the launching platform for the ill-fated mission to Iran (April, 1980) and would so serve in a skirmish that would down two Libyan planes (August, 1981). But her most infamous experience was fated to occur about seventy nautical miles north-north-east of Jacksonville, Florida.

About 200 men were busy in night operations and airplanes were landing and taking off. At 11:51 P.M. one landing plane (an EA-6B electronic warfare jet attached to a marine early warning squadron) hit a helicopter, touched down and struck a plane, then slid into three other planes, exploding and bursting into flames. The mishap killed fourteen men—three in the plane and eleven in the deck crew—and injured possibly forty-eight. It damaged or destroyed a score of planes. It was called America's worst peacetime accident on a carrier.

Three weeks later Congressman Joseph P. Addabbo (Democrat of New York), chairman of the defense subcommittee, House appropriations committee, made the nightly TV network news when he announced that his staff had heard that a majority of the fatal victims on the *Nimitz* had drugs in their systems and that he would conduct a hearing two days hence about drugs in the military in general and on the *Nimitz* in particular.

He wrote to the navy secretary, John F. Lehman, Jr., asking him to forgo the "intense secrecy" and release results of his investigation. Lehman wrote back the next day that the air crew showed no drugs, that to imply a connection with drugs would "deprecate the heroic efforts of a fine crew of a proud ship," and that if the congressman had to conduct hearings on drug abuse in the military, he should ignore the *Nimitz* incident.

The next day Lehman wrote again, in a more cooperative vein, with this information: Six of twelve urine samples tested from the victims showed cannabinoid. No sample was available on a thirteenth. (A fourteenth was lost at sea.) Three of the six showed peak readings (more than 75 ng/ml on the Syva Cannabinoid Assay, verified on a mass spectrometer). No alcohol was found. The data merely showed that the deck crewman—not the flight crew—had used marijuana at some time. "It does not establish in any way that any of these men were in the least impaired in the performance of their duty."[30]

In the hearing that began the following day, Lieutenant Commander David Michael Kouns, chemist heading the Navy Drug Testing Laboratory, said that the drugs could have been taken roughly between six hours and ten days before the accident, although the peak reading for three victims suggested "heavy use, or recent use . . . within a six-hour period."[31]

Vice Admiral Wesley McDonald, deputy chief of naval air operations, testified that all of the fatalities and injured victims on the aircraft carrier had support functions in the operation and were not directly involved in the landing of the airplane. The navy's official position was that illicit drugs had nothing to do with the accident or casualties. But only the dead were tested.[32]

Of 447 punishments aboard ship in the first third of 1981, 124 related to drugs. Yet the *Nimitz* (from inspections in November, 1980) had received an overall grade of "outstanding" for drug and alcohol abuse control.[33]

> The subcommittee asked the defense department whether any drugs or alcohol had been found in the systems of military aviators involved in plane crashes in five years (1976–81). A different type of answer came back from each armed service.
>
> The air force: No illegal drug contributed to a fatal accident. Medication may have contributed to five fatal accidents since 1974.

The army: There were six drug cases—half involving marijuana (drugged pilots at the controls in two cases)—plus an alcohol case.

The marines: In 3½ years eight cases of drug abuse involved aviators and flight officers, none contributing to a major mishap and only one to a minor mishap (hard landing); refined drug-testing procedures were not available before 1978.

The navy: In rare instances alcohol was found; in one pilot (not in control), cocaine.[34]

Later the committee staff reported learning from navy sources that 15 to 20 percent of the navy's major aircraft accidents in 1979 appeared to involve alcohol and hangover effects.[35]

While the congressmen accepted the official position on the *Nimitz*, they did not so readily accept the Pentagon's approach to drug use in the armed services. A $489,224 survey conducted for the Department of Defense in 1980 pointed up the problem.

Burt Associates of Bethesda, Maryland, had given multiple-choice questionnaires to about 20,000 servicemen—representing 1.9 million—in installations worldwide. The forms listed nine types of abused drug. It turned out that 36 percent of the servicemen had used at least one of them in the last twelve months, 27 percent in the last thirty days. The results for "any drug use" barely topped those for "marijuana/hashish"— 35 percent in twelve months and 26 percent in thirty days—which indicated that nearly all drug abusers smoked cannabis, whatever else they took. (They also abused amphetamines, cocaine, hallucinogens, barbituates, tranquilizers, opiates, PCP, and heroin, in about that order.)

The Marine Corps led in drug abuse. Its marijuana/hashish smokers made up 47 percent (twelve months) and 36 percent (thirty days) of those surveyed. Next: navy, 42 and 32 percent; army, 37 and 28 percent; and air force, 22 and 14 percent. Those who used marijuana or hashish weekly or more during the last thirty days came to 29 percent of the marines, 24 percent of the navy, 23 percent of the army, and 10 percent of the air force.

One in five junior enlisted personnel (E1-E5) was "high while working" during the last twelve months—navy, 26 percent; marines, 25 percent; army, 21 percent; and air force, 8 percent. Many indicated they had missed all or part of some days' work or noticed their performances lowered because of drugs. From acknowledged behavior and symptoms during twelve months, the surveyors regarded one in twenty-five junior enlisted personnel as "drug dependent"—army, 5 percent; marines, 5 percent; navy, 4 percent; and air force, 1 percent. Fifteen percent of these personnel were drunk while working during the last twelve months.

A majority of servicemen aged eighteen to twenty-five—52 percent—admitted using marijuana or hashish in the last twelve months, 40 percent in the last thirty days (8,224 sampled). Comparative figures for civilians eighteen to twenty-five were

418   CANNABIS AND SOCIETY

54 percent and 42 percent (2,022 sampled, source of the sample not cited). Within thirty days, amphetamine use was higher among those young servicemen than among civilians (10 percent compared with 4 percent); cocaine use by those servicemen was slightly lower (7 percent and 10 percent); and use of hallucinogens (5 percent), barbiturates (4 percent), tranquilizers (3 percent), and heroin (1 percent) were equal. Current drinkers of alcohol amounted to 84 percent and 82 percent, respectively. Only one in every fourteen of the servicemen worldwide failed to respond.[36]

Some reasons given by the defense department for the better air force record: It has the oldest and best educated personnel with the largest proportions of married people and women. Age, education, marital status, and sex were cited as four determinants of drug-alcohol abuse accepted by social scientists.[37]

The survey prompted several measures by the Pentagon, Brigadier General William C. Louisell, then deputy assistant secretary of defense for drug and alcohol abuse prevention, testified at the hearing. They included a statement of policy declaring, "Alcohol and drug abuse is incompatible with the maintenance of high standards of performance, military discipline and readiness." (Yet the navy secretary had stated that the marijuana smokers on the *Nimitz* were not necessarily "in the least impaired in the performance of their duty.") Other steps included a requirement of instruction in abuse prevention for all servicemen, improved drug intelligence, upgrading of rehabilitation and treatment, protable urinalysis kits for remote locations and aboard ships, and a "joint" project with the National Institute on Drug Abuse to survey substance abuse among dependent students.

The Department of Defense was spending about $100 million a year and had 3,900 people working on the problems of drug and alcohol abuse, General Louisell said.

"I commend you on that effort," said Representative Addabbo. But his group and others had held hearings on military drug use since the early 1970s. "Why is it taking the military so long to realize that there is a problem and to do something about it?"

The general replied that a number of military drug programs had a long history, and he told of some progress since the last comparable survey, 1974.

The navy had a different slant: "The Burt survey opened our eyes. We recognized we had an increasing problem, an increasing trend toward drug abuse in the navy and we set about doing something about it," said Captain Leo A. Cangianelli, assistant for drug and alcohol abuse for the deputy chief of naval operations.

They had devoted most effort to treatment and rehabilitation. Now the tendency would be "towards a get-tough attitude" and more "drug enforcement and education and prevention." They were buying portable urinalysis kits to test for cannabinoids and they were adding additional dogs to sniff out drugs (except LSD). In the past the inability to detect the main drug abuse, cannabis, had been a stumbling block. The kits represented a breakthrough.

There were limitations, the officers explained. If urinalysis identified a drug user—even on duty—the evidence could not be used to take any judicial action against him, though he could be given education or treatment. In addition, the armed forces had to grant honorable discharges to members ousted for drug and alcohol abuse. (Six months later the Defense Department changed these rules.)

Representative Jack Edwards (Republican of Alabama) asked, ". . . Are we concerned if somebody wanted to get out of the service they could go smoke a little pot, get caught a couple of times and get out?"

General Louisell replied, ". . . Is it possible to drug your way out of the service? Certainly it is."

In 1979 Brigadier General Joseph Lutz (then director of human resources development for the U.S. Army) had told a congressional task force on military drug abuse: "We have accepted the fact that alcohol and drug abuse problems are endemic to our society."

"I hope that is not the creed of the military at this time," Representative Addabbo said, asking General Louisell to comment.

"In the DOD policy directive we are stony-faced and intolerant. There is no place in the armed forces of the United States for drug abuse and related activities," said the general.

However, the services made it clear that they did not customarily either punish or discharge men solely for drug abuse. Even in the Strategic Air Command, "Each case is carefully and thoroughly evaluated to determine the appropriateness of rehabilitation and retention. In all cases, necessary duty limitations are involved to ensure nuclear surety," said a written Pentagon statement. (We assume that this means drug abusers are kept away from atomic weapons.)

Did they really want to weed out all drug abusers? Military lawyers were looking at ways to use urinalysis as an enforcement tool. But General Louisell saw a mixed blessing:

". . . Looking at the prevalence of the use of marijuana, it is fairly high. We would be faced with a rather enormous problem. We have to look very judiciously at how that policy for the use of urinalysis to detect marijuana is going to be used so that we do not decimate the force. . . ."

Asked later about recruiting policy, he said, "we have a mechanism in place to not induct drug or alcohol-dependent individuals. . . . but we do accept people with some incidental history of the use of light drugs. . . .

"We just have to accept the reality that there is a very high expectation that approximately 65 percent of the individuals who walk into a recruiting station would have used marijuana in the last year. To reject them out of hand would cause quite a problem manning the force."

He added that "there is a strong feeling that the casual use of light drugs, marijuana, is an adolescent phenomenon" that tends to disappear in time with age.

Rep. Jamie L. Whitten (Democrat of Mississippi), chairman of the full Committee on Appropriations, thought "the reason the services have let this situation get worse and worse . . . is that they are not being very careful who they recruit in the first instance." Taking issue with the attitude that "We are no worse than the rest of them," he said, "a man in a key place may have all the rest of his associates depending on his actions. . . . You have been comparing yourself with the average in society. I hate for you to have to fall back on such weak reasoning."[38]

A 1979 army report indicated that those who used marijuana or hashish before they joined the army accounted for four-fifths of the current marijuana-hashish abuse among first-term soldiers.[39]

*　*　*

Three weeks after the hearing, news media reported that unannounced urine tests of some 2,000 enlisted men at naval bases in San Diego and Norfolk, Virginia, had uncovered cannabinoids in roughly half of the sailors. Admiral Thomas B. Hayward, chief of naval operations, was described as shocked and alarmed and ready to take punitive action against drug abusers.[40]

The new measures met with some resistance. A few petty officers assigned to investigate drug abuse aboard ships informally told the subcommittee that "they are not receiving command support for their efforts . . . that command officers are not eager to see them initiate investigations because it would not go well on performance records," Representative Addabbo said.[41]

Later he quoted an officer on the *Nimitz* as saying, "We don't care what those smart-aleck congressmen do. We will do what we want. We are cutting in half our drug investigations, our tests."[42]

When we called a subcommittee aide, he said: "I was just on the phone to someone in the navy a few minutes ago. I heard a rumor that some dogs that they use for drug searches had disappeared over the side of a ship and I was trying to get him to confirm it. He said he heard the same rumor and so far he hadn't been able to pin it down, that nobody had reported it. But he said it's not the kind of thing that a ship CO would report right away because he wouldn't be too proud of it. . . .

"The biggest cost of those dogs is security for them. They'll be killed; they'll disappear; the handlers are in danger. The new [$3,000] urinalysis kits that are going out on some of these ships and in some of the troop units end up being damaged mysteriously. People that have to handle them feel threatened. There are real problems out there."

* * *

Congressmen were covering the matter of military drug abuse from A to Z. Three months after Addabbo's hearing, Representative Leo G. Zeferetti (also a New York Democrat) conducted a similar hearing through his Select Committee on Narcotics Abuse and Control.

Representative Glenn English (Democrat of Oklahoma) emphasized that the U.S. taxpayer was being asked to spend in five years about $1.5 trillion for defense. This would include a lot of sophisticated hardware and those using and maintaining it "have to be alert and have their faculties about them at all times. . . . We simply cannot afford the type of drug abuse problem in the military that presently exists."

The committee's Task Force on Drug Abuse, headed by English and Congressman Benjamin A. Gilman (Republican of New York) had just surveyed 1,906 military personnel: soldiers and some airmen in Germany and sailors and marines with the Mediterranean fleet and stationed in Italy. Among reported results, 42 percent of sailors, 38 percent of soldiers, 24 percent of marines, and 5 percent of airmen admitted smoking marijuana or hashish during working hours in the last month; 52 percent of sailors on the carrier *Forrestal* admitted this. Majorities of sailors and soldiers admitted some cannabis use in the month.

Dr. John F. Beary III, M.D., new (two months) assistant secretary of defense for health affairs, said that the committee's study, not being random, scientifically fit "the eighth-grade level—if that." It bothered him that a CBS-TV reporter "took the handout like he was your PR man . . . and put across to the public last night the impression that 50 percent of the navy are potheads." He approved of the worldwide Burt survey.

The critique provoked English. Didn't the witness know that the General Accounting Office had criticized the company and survey because Burt's vice-president had worked in the Pentagon's Office of Drug and Alcohol Abuse prevention before joining Burt? Better to spend his time solving the drug problem than criticizing the committee and press, etc.

"We can't manage without data," Beary said. "The only data we have is in the Burt report and we plan to do a study like that and improve on it every couple of years." He said Burt's was a random survey. "If you walked into the area where all of the drug abusers were sitting you would find a biased sample."

English said, "We were taken to those locations by the U.S. officers in charge and I sincerely doubt they are going to take us to the location where all the drug abusers hang out."

Beary did not minimize the marijuana problem. He said drug-education programs would stress newly recognized chronic health effects of cannabis.

"Early in the seventies there was an impression among many young people that this was a benign drug which had some short-term effects but that the long-term effects weren't a problem. However, current research shows reason for concern in that regard," said Beary. He specifically cited as examples memory impairment, presence of cancer-causing ingredients, and fetal loss.

General Louisell said most servicemen rated the treatment program as "fair to excellent." Nonetheless, figures he secured at committee request showed some 46,000 servicemen discharged for alcohol and drug abuse in six years, 1975–80. (The 1980 figures: army, 2,864; air force, 1,708; navy 736; marines, 187.)

Rear Admiral Paul J. Mulloy (a month in his job as director of the navy's Human Resources Management Division) reported that both the chief of naval operations and the secretary of the navy had issued messages to naval officers to get serious about curbing drugs. He said the navy was adding many more urinalysis kits and drug dogs, bringing the total of the kits to 103 (and the dogs also to 103, according to Captain Cangianelli in the previous hearing) in 1983.

Representative Zeferetti said the committeemen felt that the problem had to be faced in recruitment as well as in all phases of the service with effective education, training, and effort.[43]

> Addabbo (participating in the narcotics committee's questioning, although not a member) asked Major General Mary E. Clarke, director of U.S. Army Human Resources Development, about recruitment policy. She said "the army authorizes limited or experimental preservice use of cannabis. . . . However, dependence on marijuana or a court conviction or juvenile court adjudication for selling or trafficking in marijuana is a nonwaiverable disqualification for appointment or enlistment. Any use of cannabis immediately preceding the application for the army is disqualifying and a waiver will be required prior to enlistment."
>
> Addabbo suggested that recruiters, under pressure to meet their quotas, might look the other way. "Are any tests given?"
>
> "No, sir, because we have had none to test for cannabis up to this point." Ad-

dabbo said urine testing at the preinduction physical could detect marijuana use and possibly tell when it was used. General Clarke said it was up to the doctor to make the determination. How? "The only way he can tell that is by asking the young man."

"If the young man says, 'I am not an addict. I was nervous, so I smoked one just before I got here,' so we now put him into the service and we find him as one of the statistics we have been reading about today. Is that correct?"

"I would say that was possible, sir."

Later, in an intense grilling of the general, Addabbo brushed off her denial that the army approved of soldiers smoking marijuana on duty, and angrily charged that the services were "condoning drug use," and even implied that they winked at marijuana smoking near nuclear weapons.[44]

In 1978 the same Select Committee had crossed the Atlantic for a hearing into drug abuse by GIs in West Germany. Meeting in Stuttgart, Congressman English presiding, the members quizzed enlisted men and officers. The enlisted men did not fear to be identified. Some of the questions and replies of various witnesses follow.

A private, asked whether there was much more drug abuse in Germany than among troops in the United States, said, "Yes, there is. Over here the hashish is a lot more stronger than marijuana and it is a lot easier to get than marijuana. . . ." *What about drugs like heroin—are they more used here?* "Yes, because the soldiers over here are being pressured, tension, you know. . . . They go ahead and start off with hashish and then they want to go on to something stronger, so they just keep on going on to something stronger so when they do go back to the states, they are already on it." *How many in your unit use hashish?* "I would say, in our whole unit, battalion unit, there are at least 600 of us, male and female. I would say from 300 to 400 would use drugs."

Do you observe any drug trafficking in the barricks? (Sergeant:) "I've seen it done." *Does it include the sale of heroin?* "Yes, sir."

How often? (Private:) ". . . Hashish and heroin, more or less you have that every week."

Have you observed any narcotic usage out in the field? (Sergeant:) "Yes, I have. Quite a bit. . . . Heroin; guys will be smoking hash, popping pills." *While they are out on field training?* "Yes, sir."

How secure do you feel knowing that you have people who are—— (Sergeant:) "I don't." (Private:) "Not too secure."

Of those you know, how many use hashish and other drugs? (Another sergeant:) "I would say approximately 80 percent use hash and approximately 10 percent use the harder drugs or speed." *Are they using hash on duty?* "Some of them on duty, yes." *What is the attitude of officers about smoking hashish on duty?* "They feel more or less the general consensus is that it is socially acceptable." *And you disagree?* "I don't feel that any combat troop I may have to crawl under a foxhole with some day when somebody is shooting at me should be using any kind of narcotics." *Do you think soldiers can do the job when they are regular or social users of hash?* (A third sergeant:) "Personally, no. Anytime that you've had anything that's changing the way your brain functions, you don't function the same way." *Have you observed results of drug abuse among combat soldiers in training?* ". . . Accidents . . . fights, things of that nature."

How soon after you entered your unit here in Germany were you asked to buy drugs? (Another private:) "Five minutes, sir." *By an enlisted man or a noncommissioned officer?* "A noncommissioned officer, sir." *Did you accept or decline?* "I accepted, sir." *Were you pressured into using other drugs?* "Heroin, yes sir. . . . You have people coming to you all the time, pushing it on you."

When all of you came over, did you get any drug orientation? (Three enlisted men:) "No, sir."

Had you used narcotics before you came into the service? A private, eighteen, formerly a heroin addict and pusher, answered, "I smoked marijuana occasionally." *What caused you to use heroin?* "Peer pressure. . . . When you first come to Germany, among the soldiers that have been here longer . . . you ain't nothing but a piece of s——, and my feelings were if maybe I do blow with them or smoke a bowl with them or get drunk with this man that maybe he will accept me." *Were lack of recreation or inability to speak the language factors, as some have said?* "All of it together because you couldn't leave the barracks, and the barracks is the main spot where the drugs are."

Would it make any difference if a drug abuser knew he would be out of the army if caught using any kind of illegal drug? (Sergeant major:) "Would that soldier going out of the Army still have the benefit of an honorable discharge? . . . If a guy wants to get out and knows he is going to have all these benefits, he will use drugs." *Suppose he knew that he would not have an honorable discharge and not have Veterans Administration benefits—would this affect his use of drugs?* "I think you would have the best deterrent that you could ever devise."[45]

*   *   *

Investigators of the defense subcommittee secured an estimate from the U.S. European Command that "the equivalent of about four U.S. combat infantry battalions assigned to Europe were lost because of drug abuse," Representative Addabbo announced (1981).[46] A subcommittee staff report pictured the defense department as tolerant of the use of drugs.

In response to the revelations in Germany, the defense department had taken action primarily against opiates, barbiturates, and amphetamines. Data on drug use in the U.S. Army in Europe show "we had a large measure of success in our attack on hard drug use," John H. Johns, deputy assistant secretary of defense for drug and alcohol abuse prevention (General Louisell's successor) informed congressmen in 1982. The rate for opiates dropped from 360 positive laboratory findings per 10,000 tests in 1978 to 25 in 1981. "Only cannabis and alcohol remain at a persistently high level."

Johns denied any tolerance of cannabis by the military—which classifies all illegal drug use as abuse regardless of the effects on performance and which in 1981 took 650,000 urine samples and formally identified 75,000 servicemen as drug or alcohol abusers. Many smokers, he said, think the only effect of cannabis is a brief "high," ignoring "the strong evidence that impairment persists, often in very subtle but dangerous ways."

The Court of Military Appeals, reversing earlier decisions to the contrary, had recently provided legal weapons against drugs. It permitted positive urinalysis findings to be "used as evidence in actions under the Uniform Code of Military Justice when constitutional safeguards are followed. Urinalysis results can also be used as a basis for characterizing discharges as less than honorable" (Johns said). In an earlier helpful decision, the court had held drug abuse by servicemen off post to be a punishable military offense.

A remaining legal problem involved the mail. It was a major drug-smuggling device, and (Johns said) "our law enforcement activities have been hampered by U.S. Postal Service regulations which require search warrants for inspecting mail for drugs, such warrants to be issued by federal judges or magistrates." This left the mail inviolable aboard ships and overseas.

The defense department and the postal service soon reached an agreement empowering commanders to act as federal magistrates in remote locations.

Johns, a former career officer, said "punitive measures alone will never solve the alcohol and drug abuse problem"—he called alcohol abuse by far the most serious type of substance abuse. "As with any form of widespread misconduct, the sanctions to modify that conduct must come from within individuals themselves and from peers in their day-to-day living." Besides educating personnel, each service had programs under way to develop pride and professionalism, better discipline, and stronger cohesion.[47]

The defense department was trying to improve the quality of noncommissioned officer leadership, create wholesome barracks living for junior enlisted personnel, make available organized activities that would attract the single person living in barracks, and provide tough entrance training with more emphasis on attitudes and values.[48]

A Pentagon directive in March, 1983, backing up a memorandum to commanders fifteen months earlier, set forth the legal rules for urine testing. They were explained to us this way: In a general inspection, testing an entire unit, a commander can use any positive findings in disciplinary proceedings. But if he just singles out an individual for testing, a positive finding can be so used only if there is probable cause (some other evidence of drugs). Without probable cause, it still can be the basis for ordering treatment and rehabilitation.

*　　*　　*

Chats with enlisted men of the Naval Air Station at Alameda (next to Oakland), California,—a site of nuclear bombs—reflected tightening (1982). Petty officers seemed impressed by a closed-circuit TV tape of the chief of naval operations saying he was tired of seeing stoned sailors and would back up any efforts to scuttle the drug scene.

"Some commands have been real strict. It hasn't been bad lately," said a boatswain on an oiler. "I was on a destroyer. You'd go back on the fantail and see guys smoking marijuana all the time. They'd see you coming and they'd toss the butt overboard. There wasn't anything you could do. . . . Now they have urinalysis."

A young sailor on a supply ship said, "They're really getting tough. A couple days ago a chief petty officer on our ship was busted for smoking marijuana. He got demoted from E6 to E5, lost $630 a month pay for two months, and got forty-five days confinement and forty-five days hard labor. . . .

"At every port they bring the dogs on. In Karachi they gave everyone a strip search. At other ports, you had to pick a card. If you got a face card, you were searched. . . . There haven't been any urine tests yet. . . . There are a lot of places to get drugs. Thailand is a good place. . . . It's easy to get them. Just ask a prostitute. She'll have some for you. . . .

"I won't smoke it. I have a job to do. Some guys can function with it. Other guys can't function at all. . . . Down in the boiler room you mess up one valve and you can kill everyone. . . . I won't let anybody down there who's on drugs."

Over a bottle of beer in a bar, a sad-faced young marine from an aircraft carrier told a tale of what he felt to be a miscarriage of justice: "This guy got busted coming on ship with six Thai sticks. He was an E2. He said another guy, an E4, gave it to him. It cost the E4 $275 and thirty days restriction, he was busted from E4 to E3, he lost his secret clearance, and he's getting kicked out of the Marine Corps.

"I was the E4."

What's the truth?

"It was the truth, but they didn't have any evidence," he protested bitterly. "I've been in three years, five months. The E2's been in a year," he added, to emphasize the weakness of the case. After that, the marine said, he decided to give up marijuana, even though "I think it's pretty good myself."

*   *   *

The navy in 1982 conducted surprise urine tests of 2,300 sailors in San Diego and Norfolk again, a year after the first such tests had shown cannabinoid in half of the sailors. This time about one-fifth showed signs of marijuana use. A spokesman said that commanding officers had been instructed to "use any legal way to identify those using and trafficking in drugs" and that "use of undercover agents and informers was encouraged." Congressman Addabbo wrote a letter congratulating Admiral James D. Watkins, chief of naval operations, and his predecessor, Admiral Hayward, on the results.

As for the *Nimitz* crash, a drug—but a legal drug—may have played a part. The spokesman said the main cause appeared to be pilot error brought on partly by increased psychological stress: the pilot was low on fuel, weather was poor, and he had missed a landing attempt on a previous pass. But his blood contained a high level of brompheniramine, an antihistamine, which "may have degraded the pilot's skills needed for a night landing."[49]

*   *   *

In summer of 1983 the defense department released the results of another worldwide survey, conducted the previous year by Research Triangle Institute of North Carolina. Based on questionnaires completed by about 22,000 personnel, 17 percent had used marijuana or hashish in the past thirty days, 24 percent in the past twelve months, and 40 percent in their lifetimes. In the past thirty days, 19 percent had taken "any drug" nonmedically while 9 percent took "any drug except marijuana."

Compared with the survey made two years earlier—when 26 percent admitted smoking cannabis in the past thirty days—this survey showed statistically significant declines. Presumably the declines were genuine. We trust they did not simply reflect an increased reluctance of servicemen to admit that they used illicit drugs.

Nearly 27,000 questionnaires had been administered in group sessions or mailed to selected personnel. This time the army led in cannabis use. The percentages for the past thirty days and the past twelve months, respectively, were: army, 24% and 31%; marines, 17% and 26%; navy, 13% and 26%; and air force, 10% and 14%.

Among junior enlisted personnel (E1 to E5) in the past thirty days 23 percent had used marijuana or hashish—one-fourth of these smoking it twenty or more times in the month—and 12 percent had used another nonmedical drug. In twelve months 12 percent of those personnel had been high from some drug while working and drugs had caused loss of productivity for 14 percent. Forty percent of them lost productivity because of alcohol.[50]

*   *   *

A Pentagon health official said (in December, 1983) testing of urine and informing troops that the testing was taking place and that no illegal drugs would be tolerated had made a difference. Roughly three million urinalyses were planned for the fiscal year ending September 30, 1984, about half by the navy. An army alcohol and drug consultant explained that each service, in its marijuana testing, decided for itself how to test and utilize the results. The army, for instance, mostly used two tests (screening by radioimmune assay and confirming positive samples by gas-liquid chromatography). A commander could test a whole unit or just suspects and had a further option of action: fining, reduction in rank, or (on a second offense by a junior enlisted man) a recommendation of discharge.

*   *   *

In December, 1983, a federal law was enacted to outlaw in the military all drugs illegal in civilian life. Until then, drug use and sale had not been specifically prohibited in the Uniform Code of Military Justice but could be prosecuted as a violation of regulations or breach of order and discipline. Consequently, offenders might be treated unequally.

MEDICINE

1

Marijuana for Therapy: Opposite Views

A smiling man in a white coat with a stethoscope around his neck extends a hand containing three small, slim objects. "Could marijuana be the next wonder drug?" asks a headline alongside the cover illustration. Just below, recalling the snake-oil ads of the last century, New Times magazine goes on: "Forget the scare headlines. Among other things, grass is good for: pneumonia, diphtheria, typhoid, tuberculosis, glaucoma, menstrual cramps, ennui, cancer, burns, bed sores, staphylococcus, making love, pain, drug withdrawal, headaches, psychotherapy, anxiety, epilepsy, aggression, battle shock, asthma."

The article inside acclaims any hint of "positive medical effects" as "unbiased research" while dismissing suggestions of "hazards of its use" as "rumors and half-truths." (Yet it fails to show that marijuana cures any of the above maladies, even "making love.")[1]

At the other extreme we find Dr. Robert L. DuPont, Jr., saying, "I think it is impossible to understand the 'medical uses of marijuana' issue unless you realize this is a screen for legalization and permissiveness about marijuana." To deal with the question of whether marijuana is good for this or that condition misses the point, according to Dr. DuPont (former director of the National Institute on Drug Abuse).

He denies that marijuana can ever be an effective treatment for any condition. "It would be as if we told people who were suffering from strep throat or pneumococcal pneumonia that they should go out and eat bread mold because it contains penicillin." He begrudgingly allows that if any constituents of marijuana or synthetic analogues prove useful in medical treatment, they may be used, but he is "very skeptical" that this will happen.

In a later statement urging state legislators to oppose bills to make marijuana available as a "medicine," DuPont—who used to champion decriminalization—says, "For years 'decriminalization' was the stalking horse for the marijuana lobby. Today 'medical uses' has become the symbol behind which the pro-pot activists are marching." Good medical research into "possible medical uses" goes on and federal laws provide the mechanism for making cannabis or its purified components available "when and if any medical uses are identified," Du Pont continues. Passage of state laws "are widely interpreted by the public, especially by youth, as a signal that pot is 'okay' or, even worse, that it is 'healthy.' "[2]

Logically, the use of cannabinoids for specific medicinal purposes should provide no more justification for the marijuana habit than the medical use of an opium derivative like morphine as a painkiller or sedative should justify the opium smoking habit. Still, there is good reason for DuPont's suspicion. Marijuana activists have indeed undertaken a promotion of what might be called innocence by association.

This is substantiated by the founder of the lobby himself. In a 1979 interview, an Atlanta university newspaper asked R. Keith Stroup, chairman of the board of the National Organization for the Reform of Marijuana Laws, "How is NORML utilizing the issue of marijuana treatment of chemotherapy patients?" Stroup replied, "We are trying to get marijuana reclassified medically. If we do that, (we'll do it in at least 20 states this year for chemotherapy patients) we'll be using the issue as a red herring to give marijuana a good name. That's our way of getting to them (new right) indirectly, just like the paraphernalia laws are their way of getting to us."

> Stroup seemed to label all those opposed to legalized marijuana or legal drug equipment as "new right." Actually, they cut across a wide spectrum of ideology. Stroup expected to win the battle for legalization "the slower way, state by state, legislature by legislature," and not rely on the courts to take care of "the drug problem" (the laws against drugs). In a possible hint of things to come after the legalization of marijuana, he said the Alaska Supreme Court lacked "political courage" in refusing in 1978 to okay cocaine on "privacy" grounds.[3] (The court, in 1975, making the essence of a legislative decision, had ruled that marijuana was not enough of a public health and welfare problem to breach an individual's "privacy," that is, to outlaw marijuana smoking at home.)[4]

The *New Times* article appeared in 1974. As of this writing in 1984 there have been hundreds of medical investigations in which cannabinoids have been given to thousands of patients and the only "positive medical effect" on which the medical profession tends to be agreed was not mentioned in the magazine. It is the curbing of nausea and vomiting in patients receiving chemotherapy for cancer. Some studies with capsules of THC or artificial cannabinoids show relief for a limited number of patients who are not helped by standard antinausea medicines. Hardly any of the published research on this matter has dealt with marijuana, and few professionals expect marijuana to become the medicine of choice.

There are several reasons for physicians to be hesitant about marijuana.

• When a drug has enough side effects to fill a volume, a responsible doctor will not prescribe it when safer alternatives exist. The hazards are accentuated when the substance is customarily taken in a manner unlike that of any medicinal drug. The risks of damage to the lungs and other vital organs and to the immune system must be carefully considered before a patient is ordered to start smoking.

It would be particularly ironic to condone smoking in connection with cancer therapy when so many cancer cases are, by scientific consensus, caused by smoking. The smoking has been of tobacco products. But the likelihood is emerging that other forms of smoking are carcinogenic too.

Recent medical observations have hinted at the possibility that nicotine can benefit sufferers of ulcerative colitis. If this is so, would it make any sense for a physician to prescribe cigarettes when medicinal nicotine is available in another form?

• By medical standards, it may be impossible to control the dose. Smoking the marijuana in different ways, people take it in different amounts. Moreover, cannabis has long been "notorious for its chemical variability and its easy deterioration."[5] No two batches of crude marijuana contain the same proportions of chemicals; even samples taken from the same plant at 8 A.M. and 10 A.M. differ; and burning produces chemical changes that vary with temperature, which depends on many variables in the plant and paper (according to Carlton E. Turner, who directed the Marihuana Project in Mississippi for ten years).[6]

Dr. Sidney Cohen (of UCLA) remembers a dusty bottle of cannabis extract on the shelf of a pharmacy where he worked in the late twenties and early thirties. "The only time it was opened was to pour a few drops into the store's own remedy for corns—to color it green." Physicians neglected the drug because batches differed widely "from practically inert to so strong the doctor would think twice about prescribing it." It had a poor shelf life, becoming nearly inactive in a few years, and because of its near insolubility, "doctors could not predict whether a given patient's body could absorb it."[7]

• Smoke of any kind in a health institution can be detrimental to patients, particularly those suffering from respiratory or cardiac disease. The effects of the fumes on medical staffs, as well as the rights of nonsmokers, patients, and others, also need to be considered. While the smoke may relieve nausea in some, paradoxically the smoke sickens others. Nobody, least of all any seriously ill patient, should be subjected to such distress.

A final point could be the most important. Cigarette smoking plays the primary role throughout the nation in causing fatal fires. The smoking of reefers by drowsy patients could enlarge the danger.

2

Perspective, Historical And Medicinal

The medicinal use of cannabis since ancient times and the drug's prominence in folk medicine of different cultures have been described by writers repeatedly. China looms large in the histories—or mythologies—although books do not concur on the details. Recorded Chinese medical use of cannabis may have begun about 200 B.C. when the physician Hoatho supposedly used it, mixed in wine, as an anesthetic in surgery; or almost 2000 B.C. when advocated as a sedative and all-around medication by the "mythical" emperor and pharmacist Shen Nung; or about 2700 B.C. when the same "legendary" emperor indicated its use for female weakness, gout, rheumatism, malaria, beri-beri, constipation, and absentmindedness. (In these three examples, the more recent the book, the more ancient its version.)[8]

Visiting China in 1979 A.D., drug-plant scientist Carlton E. Turner learned that cannabis had no place in formal medical institutions there.[9] Of course antiquity and popularity scarcely guarantee medical worth, otherwise hospitals could well hire medicine men to offer incantations.

"One need not take too seriously the anecdotal accounts of its use for many purposes in China or by the Hindus in the pre-Christian millennia . . . and by the Arabs," wrote J. D. P. Graham of the Welsh National School of Medicine. "Its occasional use in Western medicine dates back to the mid-nineteenth century and may be in part attributed to O'Shaughnessy" in India. Drawing from traditional Indian medicine, O'Shaughnessy gave the drug to patients suffering seizures and rheumatism, concluding that it helped some in relieving pain and relaxing muscles in spasms.

Reynolds (in England's *Lancet*, 1890) rated cannabis extract a useful medicine for fits, neuralgia, migraine, and psychosomatic disorders, though not for rheumatic conditions. American textbooks recommended it to calm restless patients, to give to incurables, and sometimes for menorrhagia. The variations in potency and irregularity in absorption, hence uncertainty as to the best doses, and delay in the onset of positive effects reduced the popularity of cannabis (Dr. Graham said). Then came a variety of better medicines—morphine, aspirin, chloral, barbiturate, and tranquilizers—and the inclusion of cannabis in the list of drugs deemed by the world community to require legal restrictions.[10]

The U.S. pharmacopoeia last listed cannabis ("the dried flowering tops of the pistillate plants of *Cannabis sativa*") in 1936. That year's epitome of the pharmacopoeia and national formulary described the drug for physicians thus: "A narcotic poison, producing a mild delirium. Used in sedative mixtures, but of doubtful value. Also employed to color corn remedies." Cannabis was out of the next pharmacopoeia, 1942.[11]

> The 1937 U.S. dispensatory said: "Cannabis is used in medicine to relieve pain, to encourage sleep, and to soothe restlessness. We have very little definite knowledge of the effects of therapeutic quantities, but in some persons it appears to produce a euphoria and will often relieve migrainic headaches. One of the great hindrances to the wider use of this drug is the great variability in the potency of different samples of cannabis which renders it impossible to approximate the proper dose of any individual sample except by clinical trial. Because of occasional unpleasant symptoms from unusually potent preparations, physicians have generally been overcautious in the quantities administered. The only way of determining the dose of an individual preparation is to give it in ascending quantities until some effect is produced." (The book suggested using a fluid extract—powdered cannabis in solution, four-fifths alcohol—three times a day, starting with two or three minims.)[12]

*　　*　　*

In 1980 a symposium on "Therapeutic Progress in Cannabinoid Research" (sponsored by Pfizer Central Research) drew some 175 scientists to the University of Connecticut at Groton to present about sixty research papers. Raphael Mechoulam, professor of medicinal chemistry at the Hebrew University, Jerusalem, led off with an overview. (In 1964 Y. Gaoni and he had announced the first isolation of an active constituent of cannabis—THC—and the determination of its structure.)

Enumerating eighteen medicinal uses of cannabis in folklore based on the crude plant, plus ten possible therapeutic properties studied in fifteen years aside from the cannabis "high," Mechoulam called it ridiculous on the face of it to consider cannabis a medicinal drug. A "cure-all" is not a medicine. "Modern therapeutics aims at specific targets, or closely related ones. Pharmacologic activity other than the desired one is considered a 'side effect.' "

There is some hope, however, he said. The isolation and identification of THC and over sixty other natural cannabinoids make it possible to distinguish among cannabinoids.

Most of the drug activities discovered in cannabis repose in THC. It possesses numerous properties that, individually, would be medically useful.

However, "This wide scope of effects caused by THC eliminates it as a major potential drug. The exception may be in fields where at present no other drugs are available. The only use I can foresee is an antiemetic [vomit-preventing] drug during chemotherapy and on radiation therapy."

THC is not ideal even for this specific purpose. It does not appear to curb the severe vomiting caused by some anticancer drugs (cis-platinum compounds) and sometimes it causes psychotic reactions, particularly in elderly patients.

But fortunately THC is not the only cannabinoid with important properties. Cannabidiol, which is not very toxic and does not seem to be psychoactive, has shown antiepileptic activity in animals. Mechoulam wanted cannabidiol to be thoroughly investigated for neurologic activity; epilepsy, spasticity, migraine, and neuralgia have been mentioned as being influenced by cannabis. It would probably need to undergo "molecular modifications and manipulations" to find the best drug for the given purpose.

The development of the cannabinoids in medicine, Mechoulam said, depends largely on separating the psychoactive activities from the other activities. His laboratory has been doing such work, and experiments on rhesus monkeys suggest that new, pain-killing cannabinoid drugs, without psychic effects, are possible by "synthetic modification."[13]

☆   ☆   ☆

To determine whether the ancient use of cannabis to relieve pain had any scientific basis, a St. Louis team (Hill et al. at Washington University School of Medicine, 1974) performed an experiment on twenty young men experienced in marijuana smoking. Before and after they smoked official reefers, electric impulses of different strengths were applied to their fingers and pain thresholds recorded. It was a method that earlier had verified the pain-killing effects of morphine, aspirin, and codeine.

Marijuana not only failed to lessen pain, it increased it. Sensitivity to painful as well as nonpainful stimulation increased and tolerance for pain decreased, obviously "casting doubt on the usefulness of marihuana as an analgesic drug."[14]

Further pain studies, both of women and men, yielded different results. In Iowa City, substantial oral doses of THC alleviated cancer pains in seven of ten mature patients, to a greater degree than placebos, while causing mental clouding and drowsiness (Noyes et al., 1975). Volunteers in Calgary, Canada, could tolerate somewhat more pressure to the thumb after breathing active marijuana smoke (through a special device) than after inhaling placebo fumes; the effect was slightly greater for fifteen users than for sixteen nonusers (Milstein et al., 1975). And among fourteen confined users smoking ad libitum for weeks in New York City, marijuana apparently decreased pain for the heavier smokers while increasing it for the more moderate smokers (Clark et al., 1981).[15]

3

Formalities

Besides being subject to strict controls of the Drug Enforcement Administration under the Controlled Substances Act (1970) cannabis and cannabinoids fall under other U.S. laws when it comes to possible medical use, primarily the Federal Food, Drug, and Cosmetic Act (1938) as amended, the same law that governs any newly developed drug. It authorizes tests of a "new drug" on people after the Food and Drug Administration (FDA) finds that animal studies indicate reasonable safety, approves plans for the testing, and grants an Investigational New Drug exemption (IND).

In 1983 there were seventy-nine active IND studies of THC and cannabis for therapy. Those dealing with nausea and vomiting from cancer therapy numbered fifty-three (including chemotherapy, fifty-one, and radiotherapy, two); intraocular pressure or glaucoma, thirteen; spasticity, including multiple sclerosis, eight; anorexia and weight loss, three; and miscellaneous syndromes, two.

The Food, Drug, and Cosmetic Act prohibits the introduction into interstate commerce of any drug without the FDA's approval of a New Drug Application. Approval requires proof of safety, effectiveness, proper manufacturing, and compliance with various standards. "Safe" means that benefits outweigh risks.

In 1983 Unimed Inc. of Somerville, New Jersey, filed a New Drug Application for THC. Eli Lilly and Co., Indianapolis, had an application on file for the synthetic variation nabilone. Both were under review in 1984.

Dissatisfied with the status of cannabis and THC for therapy under federal law and prodded by marijuana lobbyists and allies, half of the fifty states had enacted legislation on the subject by 1980, thirty-three states by 1983; New Mexico was first, in 1978.[16] Some of the state laws conflicted with federal law and regulations by providing for medical treatment instead of research or by authorizing the use of confiscated marijuana—which could place participants in direct violation of U.S. criminal law. Some bore the contradictory aims of research and treatment. For example, the California law, enacted in 1979, was intended to provide "compassionate access" to the very substances being "researched."

After nearly six years of research by different investigators into THC's quality as an antiemetic, the FDA made some changes in 1980. It okayed a program of federal distribution of THC capsules to approved states by the National Cancer Institute (NCI). Under the program, THC would remain an "investigational" drug but would enter a category of NCI's permitting broad distribution of a drug shown to be effective and safe for physicians to administer but not yet commercially available. Note that paradoxically THC—being under the most stringent controls of the Controlled Substances Act, as was marijuana—legally was unsafe with no accepted medical use and available only for research.

The U.S. Department of Health and Human Services issued a news release headed, "FDA Approves Wider Use of THC for Aid to Cancer Patients," telling how about 4,000 doctors could now prescribe THC pills to patients. It did not sound very investigational.

If the government seemed a bit confused, the news media compounded the confusion. They generally failed to make it clear that a single component of marijuana was being distributed under the program, not marijuana itself (although a limited amount of marijuana went to individual researchers and states conducting separate antiemetic research). Headlines suggested that "Pot as Medicine" was now legal or that patients could take "Pot for Cancer" and news stories continually referred to "legal marijuana." These gave rise to erroneous notions among the public that marijuana was legal or even that it could cure cancer.

The American Medical Association, in a report stressing marijuana's hazards, futilely recommended that states enacting medical-use laws heed federal requirements, carry out true research, and not permit medical use of marijuana and THC outside of clinical investigation.

The Controlled Substances Act, applying both to interstate and intrastate commerce, established five "schedules" of substances, each with a separate set of controls. Schedule I imposed the most severe controls, Schedule V the least. A Schedule I drug—with high abuse potential, no accepted medical use, and lack of safety—is available only for research. A Schedule II drug—with high potential for abuse, which may lead to severe dependence, but with an accepted medical use—is available on prescription. Congress initially placed cannabis and cannabinoids under Schedule I. The law has procedures for rescheduling, which may be activated "on petition of any interested person." The secretary of the Department of Health and Human Services (HHS) makes a recommendation to the attorney general. The latter, through the Drug Enforcement Administration (DEA), makes the final decision but must accept the medical and scientific evaluations of HHS (or, in effect, FDA).[17]

The National Organization for the Reform of Marijuana Laws (NORML) has sought to remove cannabis and its components from control or move them to a less strict schedule. In 1972 it first petitioned DEA's predecessor, the Bureau of Narcotics and Dangerous Drugs. NORML's petition was rejected three times through 1979. (In 1978 an FDA advisory committee recommended rescheduling THC and cannabidiol to Schedule II but was overruled by the secretary of HHS.) NORML appealed each time to the U.S. Court of Appeals, which ordered hearings by DEA (1974), medical and scientific recommendations by HHS on cannabis and THC (1977), and consideration by HHS of new evidence on medical uses (1980). After a review of evidence and a hearing, HHS recommended to DEA that cannabis and its resin remain in Schedule I but opened the door to a Schedule II placement of THC if and when the FDA approved a New Drug Application for its marketing (1982).[18] The matter was pending in summer, 1984.

*   *   *

Of twenty-five states enacting statutes on medical use of cannabis or THC by 1980, officials in twelve secured federal approval for clinical research trials: Arkansas, California, Colorado, Florida, Georgia, Illinois, Louisiana, Michigan, Nevada, New Mexico, Oregon, and Washington. The rest were Alabama, Iowa, Maine, Minnesota, Montana, New York, North Carolina, Ohio, Rhode Island, South Carolina, Texas, Virginia, and West Virginia.

In the next three years, eight more states enacted such statutes. Only Arizona, Tennessee, and Wisconsin secured federal approval. The others were Alaska, Connecticut, Hawaii, New Hampshire, and New Jersey.

All of the federally approved state programs dealt with the antiemetic matter. In addition, as of January, 1983, state glaucoma programs existed in Florida, Georgia, Minnesota, New Mexico, and Washington (the only state with such a program in January, 1980).

The laws of Alaska, Arkansas, Connecticut, Hawaii, Illinois, Montana, New Hampshire, North Carolina, Oregon, Virginia, and Vermont provided for medical treatment with marijuana or THC.[19]

Two physicians, from the FDA and the National Institutes of Health, noted in the AMA journal that the legislation had caused a lot of confusion among patients, doctors, scientists, state and federal bureaucrats, and the press. Misconceptions were prevalent that marijuana was a proven remedy for glaucoma as well as cancer side effects and that it was now a prescription drug in the states concerned. Patients were asking doctors for marijuana.

"We believe that state-by-state drug-specific legislation makes no sense from a practical or even theoretical point of view. Where an attempt is made to approve a drug by state law, circumventing the usual scientific requirements, protection afforded the public by federal and state health regulatory bodies may be lost. These kinds of decisions should be made by public health officials on the basis of safety and efficacy considerations and not made by legislators. Such legislation represents to the public that these substances are safe and effective and, by imparting an official governmental stamp of approval, undoubtedly increases the demand for these substances."[20]

The concept of legislating for a specific drug, particularly on a state-by-state basis, did not begin with cannabis. When the FDA declined to approve the use of Laetrile for cancer, the legislatures of more than half of the states adopted legislation to legalize Laetrile therapy before NCI agreed in 1978 to study the drug.[21]

* * *

Following a five-to-four decision of its Oncological Drugs Advisory Committee, the FDA approved (1980) a program permitting broad but controlled distribution of THC. It would enable cancer patients to "fill prescriptions" (to quote an HHS news release) at hospital pharmacies approved by the Drug Enforcement Administration (DEA).[22] NCI would supply the pills free. Doctors and pharmacies could charge the patients for services.

NCI would classify THC as an Investigational Agent in Group C—a compound that has been demonstrated by research studies to be effective in disease care, that is safely administered by cancer specialists without requiring hospital care, but that is not yet commercially available.[23]

At the same time, however, THC remained legally a controlled substance in Schedule I, one with "a high potential for abuse . . . no currently accepted medical use . . . [and] lack of accepted safety . . . under medical supervision." As such, it was not a prescription drug (as the FDA's chief counsel had indicated to lawyers the year before).[24]

NCI officials acknowledged that THC was made "a modified Group C drug in an effort to extend its antiemetic benefits to the cancer patient population at large who are resistant to standard antiemetic therapy." They described how participating physicians might write "Research Orders for Medication" for patients.[25]

FDA interprets "accepted medical use" as referring to the approval of a new drug application. "Accepted" means accepted by the FDA.

* * *

When it comes to apparent contradictions, the California experience is illustrative.

Dow and Meyers (executive secretary and member, respectively, of the Research Advisory Panel administering the California therapeutic cannabis program), acknowledged that California's legislation had "two partially conflicting objectives," to provide cancer patients with "compassionate access" to the controlled drugs and to conduct research into them. California's program provided for THC pills for patients unresponsive to standard antiemetics plus marijuana to hospitalized "adults," age fifteen and older. The marijuana patients did not have to have taken any other antiemetic and they could smoke up to eight cigarettes a day.[26]

The panel reported that in 1980, the day after the FDA approved California's therapeutic program, word came that the National Institute on Drug Abuse (NIDA) would not supply any THC or marijuana. The panel considered ways to get THC and drew up a plan for securing confiscated marijuana and manufacturing it into cigarettes, which would conform to state law (but violate federal law). Appeals to the agencies went unanswered, and "it was not until the Panel enlisted the help of U.S. Senator Alan Cranston, U.S. Congressman Henry Waxman and State Senator Robert Presley [who had initiated the state legislation] that the federal agencies began to communicate." Surgeon General Julius Richmond transferred responsibility for supplying THC and marijuana for use in antiemetic programs from NIDA to the National Cancer Institute and California ultimately got its drugs.[27]

Budgetary considerations figured in NIDA's hesitation. California had overestimated its needs by tenfold on the basis of oncologists' initial enthusiasm at a time when the cannabinoids were thought to be something of a panacea. The logic of having a cancer agency rather than a drug abuse agency in charge doubtless was a factor in the transfer of responsibility.

*   *   *

In Congress the possible therapeutic use of marijuana and even heroin (proposed for terminal patients by the National Committee on Treatment of Intractable Pain) came up at a hearing of the House Committee on Narcotic Abuse and Control (1980). Three laymen, who as patients had smoked it illegally, pleaded for legal marijuana. Three physicians agreed that THC was an effective antiemetic for some cancer patients but were uncertain on the value of marijuana. Two doctors testifying on glaucoma research could not come to any conclusion on marijuana's worth.

Bureaucratic processes bothered both physicians and congressmen. When Dr. Solomon Garb of Colorado testified that it took him seven months to get THC, despite full cooperation of all government agencies involved, it upset the presiding congressman, Stephen L. Neal (Democrat of North Carolina), who said, "Just about any high school kid in America can go out and get marijuana in an hour, and yet you, who want to do research that will help people who are experiencing severe suffering and pain . . . it takes seven months to get it. . . . That doesn't make very much sense to me." Dr. Richard Crout, director of the FDA's Bureau of Drugs, said procedures were streamlined and it no longer took so long.

The public confusion between restricted medical use and indiscriminate legalization, and between THC and the crude drug with hundreds of components and variable content, distressed Congressman Billy L. Evans (Democrat of Georgia). When a therapeutic-use bill passed in his state, misinformation abounded to the point where "some of the law-enforcement people in seizing marijuana wanted to know if they should turn this over to the local drugstores for administration." Dr. Marvin Snyder of the National Institute on Drug Abuse said children and parents were calling him up and saying, "What's wrong with marijuana? It cures cancer."[28]

*   *   *

These are some examples of press confusion. A headline and lead:
"*Legal marijuana capsules on way to 4 cancer victims.*
"Santa Fe, N.M.—Capsules containing federally grown marijuana were en route to four cancer patients yesterday under provisions of a pioneering New Mexico law aimed at easing side effects of chemotherapy."[29]

(The capsules actually contained synthetic THC for a state-sponsored antie-

metic study, although New Mexico received marijuana too for the purpose.)
Two California headlines:
"Pot—a New Prescription for Cancer?" [30]
"Pot for cancer available." [31]
(Marijuana, or more often THC alone, is not "for cancer" but for curbing nausea and vomiting in some patients taking anticancer drugs.)

* * *

The American Medical Association toughened its position on marijuana by ratifying a report that recommended fines large enough to deter personal use, vigorous prosecution for trafficking, and the banning of drug-paraphernalia shops.

Drawn up by a six-man panel headed by Dr. Joseph H. Skom of Chicago, the report gained the approval of the AMA's House of Delegates, meeting in San Francisco in December, 1980.

It began: "It is perhaps ironic that concomitant with emerging therapeutic possibilities for cannabis and its constituents, new evidence has appeared that marijuana is hazardous to health.

"On the one hand, we are at the threshold of providing symptomatic relief to some patients who suffer extreme nausea from cancer chemotherapy and for whom existing anti-emetic agents are ineffective. On the other hand, we face the growing prospect of an appreciable number of marijuana users incurring physiological and psychological impairment."

Citing effects on brain function, driving, reproduction, lung, heart, and mind, the report called marijuana "a dangerous drug." [32]

4

Sickening Situation

The introduction of a chemical weapon to the war on cancer created a new problem for many victims: nausea, retching, and vomiting. These side effects can occur several times an hour for twelve to twenty-four hours and create dehydration and weight loss, among other medical problems. In extreme cases they have persisted for as long as three days and led to ruptures and fractures. Feeling the cure to be worse than the disease, some suffering patients have chosen to give up treatment altogether. [33]

While dozens of antinauseants are on the market, only a few (the phenothiazines) have been proven in clinical trials to be effective against the side effects of anticancer drugs, but not in all patients. The National Cancer Institute estimated that of 200,000 people undergoing chemotherapy for cancer in a year, 50,000 suffered nausea and vomiting problems not helped by conventional drugs.[34]

In 1971, as Dr. Emil Frei III of Boston later recounted, he and other physicians discovered that several teenaged leukemia patients taking anticancer drugs at M. D. Anderson Hospital and Tumor Institute in Houston, Texas, appeared to be complaining less about the usual nausea, vomiting, and malaise. On questioning, the patients said that one of them had discovered that smoking marijuana prevented extreme symptoms and that the others had tried it too with like results.[35]

Later at Sidney Farber Cancer Institute in Boston, Dr. Frei collaborated with oncologist Stephen E. Sallan and psychiatrist Norman E. Zinberg (1975) in an experiment with THC capsules and placebo capsules (sesame oil), given two hours before and two and six hours after chemotherapy. Patients reported the results by questionnaire the next day.

The patients, most of whom had not responded to standard antiemetics, reported an antiemetic effect in fourteen of twenty three-dose courses (complete in five, partial in nine). Placebos never were effective. Of sixteen male and female hospital inpatients given THC, thirteen experienced "highs," during which they did not vomit. Reported side effects, besides one to five hours of intoxication, included sleepiness and, in two cases, mental effects. Some patients reported a lessening of the antivomiting effects with repeated doses. The doctors pronounced THC effective.[36]

W. Regelson at the Medical College of Virginia and others (1976) independently tested THC for nausea and vomiting on twenty-two cancer patients, failing to demonstrate a clear-cut effect on the basis of the patients' own evaluations. (It was part of a broader study in which THC acted as a tranquilizer for the majority and checked weight loss but had little effect on pain. Information that marijuana smoking reduced radiation sickness was credited to B. Clarkson, 1971.)[37]

In 1979 three more reports of cancer patients—in Maryland, Minnesota, and North Carolina—given THC for relief of nausea and vomiting appeared in the same issue of a medical journal. Results differed, but so did the design of each experiment, the age of patients, and possibly the points of view of the experimenters.

• Dr. Alfred E. Chang and seven others by-lined a report of fifteen inpatients at the National Cancer Institute, Bethesda, Maryland. Patients were scheduled for five trihourly THC capsules (or sesame oil placebos) beginning two hours before chemotherapy. Anyone vomiting despite the pill switched to smoking a special marijuana cigarette—not a regular reefer, but an inert one injected with THC.

Responses of fourteen of fifteen patients ranged from "fair" to "excellent," based on a nurse's rating. The greater the blood-concentrations of THC, the fewer the incidences of nausea and vomiting. The cigarettes generally delivered more THC than the pills, but "many patients complained of the adverse taste of smoked marijuana, which induced nausea and vomiting in a few instances." The main side effect was sedation; occasional rapid heartheat, dizziness, and mental episodes were reported. After half a year the group conducted a new set of trials on the same patients, and the drug was less effective.[38]

• The (Rochester) Minnesota project studied 116 outpatients receiving chemotherapy at the Mayo Clinic. Whereas the median age of patients was twenty-nine in Boston and twenty-four in Maryland, it was sixty-one in this study. Dr. Stephen Frytak and nine others compared oral THC, the standard agent prochlorperazine (Compazine), and a placebo (sugar pill).

THC (taken two hours before and two and eight hours after chemotherapy) proved superior to placebos but no better than prochlorperazine. Side effects from THC involving the central nervous system were much more frequent and severe than from the prochlorperazine. (After the first day, ten patients on THC and five on the other drug withdrew from the study because of intolerable effects.)[39]

• Dr. John Laszlo of Duke University described a study of forty-one patients unresponsive to standard antiemetics who received THC (beginning eight to twelve hours before chemotherapy). "We found surprisingly good results in more than two thirds of the patients," he said, and he pleaded for reclassification of THC and distribution to physicians. (An overlapping 1980 report by Lucas and Laszlo on fifty-three patients recorded no nausea and vomiting in ten, at least 50 percent improvement in twenty-eight, and no results in fifteen. Toxic reactions were "generally mild" except in nine; four patients quit THC therapy.)[40]

Penta, Poster, and others of the National Cancer Institute reviewed thirty-four studies (1963 to 1980) in which some 2,200 cancer patients received twenty-five different antiemetics. The use of conventional antiemetics was "of marginal value." In fourteen studies with prochlorperazine, for example, it was "effective" in ten, "not effective" in four. Among the studies were nine using THC and three using nabilone, an artificial cannabinoid. THC was "effective" in all but one (Frytak); nabilone was "effective" in all.

Patients received THC (in various dose schedules, often 10 or 15 milligrams each time, depending on body-surface area) at fixed intervals, before and after chemotherapy. In five studies THC's antiemetic activity was associated with the feeling of a "high" (not so in Frytak's). Garb and coworkers prevented that sensation by administering THC with prochlorperazine.

Aside from the intoxication, the most commonly reported side effects of THC have been sleepiness, dry mouth, incoordination, dizziness, mental depression, and low blood pressure when patients stand. Less often patients have complained of visual distortions, hallucinations, and other effects on the central nervous system. Heart effects have not been reported often. Nabilone usually has produced side effects akin to those of THC but without intoxication.

> Among the nine THC studies reviewed by Penta, Poster et al. (besides those of Frei, Chang, Frytak, and Laszlo) were two from 1979, by Kluin-Nelemon and Ekert, and three from 1980, by Sallan, Garb, and Orr, trying it on a total of 230 patients. Three nabilone studies of 159 were made by Herman (1977), Nagy (1978), and Herman (1979).[41]
>
> Eli Lilly and Co., Indianapolis, the developer of nabilone, withdrew it from clinical trials when it produced unexpected seizures and deaths in dogs. An editorial in *The New England Journal of Medicine* urged the company to reverse its decision. It did.[42]

Testing 214 patients in Los Angeles, Dr. J. Thomas Ungerleider and colleagues (1982) determined THC and prochlorperazine to be equally effective in reducing nausea and vomiting, based on patients' self-ratings. They were equally effective even among patients who had obtained no relief from prochlorperazine in the past (a fifth of the subjects).

> THC caused more side effects, including dizziness, mental clouding, and space-time distortion, but for some reason those who experienced some of the side effects benefited more from THC than from the other drug. Neither the factors of age, marijuana use, attitude toward marijuana, nor ability to identify the antiemetic received in this double-blind study had any bearing on whether THC helped a patient. Most patients preferred whichever drug helped them and side effects did not influence choice. Three-fifths went into the study with a positive attitude toward marijuana, one-third with a positive attitude toward prochlorperazine.
>
> The fact that those who failed before on prochlorperazine did just as well on it as on THC in this study, led Ungerleider et al., of UCLA Center for the Health Sciences, to suggest "the importance of a regularly administered dosage schedule." Three-fourths of the subjects had taken prochlorperazine before, but mostly as needed and not on a regular schedule. A participant in this study received both drugs, each given orally in four doses starting an hour before chemotherapy, then every hour. Prochlorperazine dose was 10 mg. THC dose was 7.5 to 12.5 mg,

depending on body surface area. Half men and half women, subjects ranged in age from eighteen to eighty-two, mean of forty-seven.[43]

• "It's really great. I couldn't handle chemotherapy without it."
• "I didn't like the spaced-out feeling it gave me—and I won't use it anymore."

These are characteristic of comments that cancer patients jotted down on their report forms after taking antiemetic treatments in California's official THC-marijuana program. In 1980 the state launched the program for cancer patients not helped by standard antiemetics. Combining research and treatment, it has been carried out by more than 200 cancer specialists in twenty-two counties. Near the halfway point in an eight-year project, about 1,800 patients—three-fifths of them women—had participated. Physicians had prescribed marijuana cigarettes for about 100, THC capsules for the rest.

Gordon J. Dow, executive secretary of the state's Research Advisory Panel, the agency charged with conducting the investigation, summarized for us the results so far: "THC has been helpful to a significant number of patients receiving chemotherapy who weren't helped by ordinary agents. About 60 percent of patients get a good result. Among them are patients who would have given up potentially life-saving chemotherapy had it not been for THC. But it doesn't totally eliminate all nausea and vomiting; it does not help some patients at all; and some don't like it.

"By working on the dosage regimen, we've come up with a low-dose, cumulative exposure method that makes THC more tolerable to the patient in terms of side effects."

Dr. Dow provided figures. One set, taking in 482 patients, compares the effectiveness of THC and a patient's previous antiemetic (usually prochlorperazine) where the patient was treated with the same anticancer agent each time. With THC, 75 percent felt less nauseous and 73 percent vomited less, while 9 percent suffered more nausea and 14 percent vomited more. Respectively 16 and 13 percent felt that THC had the same effect on those symptoms as other antiemetics.

Anticancer drugs vary in the severity of the nausea and vomiting they produce, and THC did not work equally well with all of those drugs. Among fifty-six patients undergoing therapy with CMF, a drug combination carrying moderate side effects, physicians rated THC overall as "moderately effective" or "very effective" in thirty-seven cases (66 percent). THC received those ratings for only thirteen (38 percent) of thirty-four patients taking a combination of drugs known for severe side effects, Dacarbazine and Adriamycin.

At the THC doses tried, effectiveness in curbing nausea and vomiting appeared to have nothing to do with dosage. Dosage did have a bearing on side effects—the smaller the dose, the fewer the side effects. When the project began, "we were getting side effects that were intolerable." About a year later they reduced the dose by a third and the unpleasant reactions diminished. In both cases a THC capsule would be taken every four hours, starting six hours before therapy (and continuing for twenty-four to forty-eight hours as needed). In the third year the dose was halved and the first capsule given twenty-four hours in advance of therapy. Side effects lessened again.

The three successive doses of THC were 7.5, 5.0, and 2.5 mg/m^2 (milligrams per square meter of body surface area).

These are examples of the relation between side effects and dosage: The medium dose brought moderate or severe symptoms of dizziness to 24 percent and of anxiety to 10 percent (of 224 patients). The low dose caused a moderate or severe degree of dizziness in 17 percent and of anxiety in 4 percent (of 134 patients).

Those patients not hospitalized obtained THC or marijuana cigarettes at participating pharmacies on prescriptions of oncologists. At midyear, 1984, marijuana results were too few for tabulation. Doctors and patients did not often choose the cigarettes over the capsules. Beginning in 1984, patients participating in the program no longer had to have failed antiemetic treatment; they needed only to have been receiving anticancer treatment known to cause nausea and vomiting.

California's Research Advisory Panel of nine members, mostly physicians and pharmacologists, was formed by the state legislature in 1968 to further marijuana research. Supervision of research projects on the treatment of narcotic addiction later became part of its job. In 1979 the legislature directed the panel to conduct a four-year "program for the investigational use of cannabis and its derivatives," specifically as an antiemetic in cancer treatment, with clinical trials that would allow oncologists to distribute the substances "on a compassionate basis to seriously ill persons not responding to conventional treatment." In July, 1984, the state extended the program through 1988. It also mandated a comparable program of cannabinoid trials for certain glaucoma patients not helped by standard treatments.

*   *   *

Poster, Penta et al. (1981) asked "why more attention has not been given to marijuana cigarettes, because they have produced effective blood levels more reliably than the oral form." (They cited only the Chang study.)

Their first answer was that "this route may not be acceptable to the patient population at large for reasons such as unfamiliarity with smoking and the adverse taste of smoked marijuana." Besides, they added, smoked marijuana "can result in airway destruction and compromise the immune status of the lung. Both of these situations would be detrimental to the already compromised cancer patient." Despite these damning comments about marijuana smoking, they allowed that it "may be a viable and effective alternative" to pills for a subgroup of patients and this needs to be studied.[44]

Chang et al. were not set on smoking, a method they considered unsuitable for nonsmokers. They commented, "Clearly, an alternative parenteral drug route needs to be established if THC is to have wide clinical acceptability"; that is, there should be a means of administering the drug outside of ingestion and smoking.[45]

* * *

At the hearing of the House narcotics committee, Dr. Garb, clinical professor of medicine at the University of Colorado, suggested the possibilities of a suppository and an aerosol, pointing out that some patients did not do well either on marijuana cigarettes or on pills.

Dr. Garb had tested some fifty patients, mostly with THC capsules, and a handful with standard marijuana cigarettes supplied by the National Institute on Drug Abuse, containing about 18 mg of THC. "Altogether I have used the marijuana cigarettes on five patients, in situations in which they could not retain any more of the oral THC. In two of the patients it was helpful. In three, it wasn't." Nonsmokers did not benefit.

With cigarettes, "You don't know how much of that 18 milligrams actually gets in the patient, how much gets into the room, and so on."

When he gives a patient a 5 mg capsule, "I know that the patient is getting exactly five milligrams . . . whereas when I give the patient the cigarette . . . one patient may smoke the cigarette in such a way as to only get one milligram into his lungs, and the other one may get 10 milligrams."

Among other problems of smoking, "it's quite a difficult thing in a ward of any hospital, really, to have a patient start smoking marijuana cigarettes. That smells up the whole place. You want to have somebody watching them so they don't start a fire, and things like this."

Should there be additional research on marijuana?

"I believe that the research should be focused on the constituents. I don't think we're ever going to get an answer working with a crude mixture of an unknown number of substances. I think what we have to do is get one constituent down at a time and test it properly and scientifically, and this cannot be done overnight."

Representative Neal was familiar with tobacco studies: "Tobacco was assumed to be a very simple substance when people first started looking at it. They found, though, that there were some nine, I believe, active alkaloids, nicotine being one of them, and that it is a very complex plant. They have been doing research on it for decades now and finding it is increasingly complex."

This reminded Dr. Garb of "the situation we had about 30, 40 years ago with the digitalis glycosides. . . . Some patients were getting digitalis leaf. There were problems with it because one batch was quite different from another, and it took many, many years to develop the purified glycosides which most doctors would use today."[46]

* * *

Both smoking and intravenous administration "tend to produce too severe a degree of intoxication and too short a span of action for any sustained use," said Dr. Leo E. Hollister, director of psychopharmacology research, Veterans Administration Hospital at Palo Alto, California, at the Connecticut symposium (mentioned in this section, 2).

"Oral administration is somewhat more suitable, although absorption is erratic, in the sense that effects are sustained longer and are not as severe. This route would be most applicable if one could predict in advance the span of time during which the effects were desired and if the desired effect could be obtained with relatively low concentrations of the drug," Dr. Hollister said.[47]

Among other findings presented at the symposium were the following three sets on THC, followed by three dealing with the synthetic cannabinoid levonantradol, made by Pfizer of Groton, Connecticut:

• Dr. James A. Neidhart et al. in Columbus, Ohio, found the tranquilizer haloperidol and THC equally effective in controlling nausea and vomiting in fifty-two patients, but THC produced more side effects.[48]

• Dr. Garb learned from his clinical studies that the combination of THC and prochlorperazine (Compazine), a phenothiazine, blocked some cannabinoid side effects. He added that possible interactions of cannabinoids and anticancer drugs, both useful and harmful, needed exploring.[49]

• Dr. Donald L. Sweet at al. in Chicago gave outpatients (median age fifty-one) THC at six relatively low doses at eight-hour intervals starting a day before therapy. Nausea went away in two, decreased in eighteen, and increased in two. THC seemed "a toxic but transiently effective antiemetic." It caused "a disturbing number" of mental reactions. Effectiveness diminished with repeated administration. Four patients quit THC because mental effects interfered with their work. "It is our suspicion that the therapeutic index of THC is extremely narrow. Before THC is hailed as the panacea of antiemetic therapy, additional and carefully controlled studies are in order," the Sweet paper ended.[50]

• Two related studies in Boston and Durham, North Carolina (Dr. Carol M. Cronin et al. and Dr. John L. Laszlo et al.) tested levonantradol on patients who did not respond to conventional antiemetics. Of those getting injections, twenty-five of twenty-eight achieved a partial or, sometimes, complete response; of those taking capsules, eighteen of thirty-three were helped. Many of THC's mental side effects were present. They bore no relation to effectiveness. Levonantradol, incidentally, has pain-killing activity twelve to thirty times greater than morphine by various tests, they said.[51]

• Dr. Robert B. Diasio et al. studied twenty-seven hospital patients in Richmond (Virginia) and Baltimore who took levonantradol for severe vomiting problems. It appeared to be "a relatively well-tolerated oral antiemetic that deserves further evaluation."[52]

• Dr. Manfred E. Heim et al. in Mannheim, Germany, studied twelve hospitalized patients, calling levonantradol "a potent antiemetic drug" whose use on outpatients "is complicated by a high incidence of side effects."[53]

Whether toleration of the side effects differs more in the patients or in the experimenters is a question we will not attempt to answer.

✳   ✳   ✳

During another antiemetic study, testing marijuana on cancer patients taking chemotherapy and radiation treatment, Ungerleider et al. (1982) discovered that the cigarettes provided by the National Institute on Drug Abuse were contaminated with pathogenic bacteria. Examining six marijuana cigarettes from three separate lots, they identified substantial numbers of *Klebsiella pneumoniae*, *Enterobacter agglomerans*, group D *Streptococcus* (enterococcus), *Bacillus* species, and *Enterobacter cloacae*. Treatment with ethylene oxide or with high-dose radiation killed the bacteria.

The researchers pointed out that anticancer treatments impaired the antimicrobial defenses of the lung, which "may be further compromised in patients who smoke marihuana." (They cited studies by Huber, Tashkin, and others). Thus they advised the sterilization of cigarettes used by cancer patients.[54]

* * *

Could the tendency of cannabinoids to interfere with the vital biochemical processes of cells be utilized against cancer itself?

Faculty members at the Medical College of Virginia discovered in 1973 that when they transplanted lung cancer cells into mice, treatments with delta-9-THC by stomach tube or injection usually would retard the cancer for a while, in comparison with its progress in untreated mice.

The discovery came as a surprise. Doctors Albert E. Munson and Louis S. Harris had been thinking about the effects of the drug on the immune system. "We thought that if the compound suppressed the immune system we should see an increase in tumor growth. Essentially we found that it inhibited tumor growth," Dr. Munson recalled (1983).

They and colleagues also tried delta-8-THC, cannabinol, cannabidiol, and scores of other cannabinoids, both natural ones and artificial analogues. The first two worked but the third stimulated tumor growth instead of slowing it.

"One problem that became apparent following the use of the active cannabinoids was the diminution of activity with time and repeated medication," said a 1976 report. The inhibition of tumor growth was marked at first but only temporary. In about three weeks the tumors would grow rapidly. The tolerance effect of cannabinoids proved much greater than that of standard antitumor drugs, Dr. Munson said (1983).

The net result was an extension of survival time, at most about the same as some standard antitumor agents afforded. The National Cancer Institute repeated some of the experiments, obtaining similar results, and the investigations ended. Cannabinoids "never gave a big enough effect," said Dr. Harris, the college's pharmacology and toxicology chairman (1983).

Besides testing hundreds of mice, over a four-year period, the Virginians performed numerous *in vitro* experiments. THC markedly depressed the production of DNA and RNA by isolated lung cancer and leukemia cells, as measured by the absorption of radioactive thymidine and uridine, respectively.

Harris, Munson et al. (1974–76), describing the initial mouse experiments, reported that when mice inoculated with lung cancer cells were treated daily for ten straight days with delta-9-THC by lavage, tumor growth usually was retarded. The degree of retardation, ranging from 30 to 75 percent, depended on dose, 25 to 100 mg/kg. Delta-8-THC had an even greater effect, and cannabinol too was effective, although the least so, but the tumors in mice given cannabidiol grew

45 percent larger than those in control mice. Extensions of survival time ranged from 22 to 36 percent. The cannabinoids did not inhibit leukemia in mice.[55]

Note that in experiments elsewhere (by Szepsenwol and by Cottrell and Vogel) rodents developed cancer after long-term treatment with marijuana smoke condensate or cannabinoids. Anticancer drugs paradoxically have been found to be carcinogenic in the long run and this may be true of cannabinoids too.

5

Shall The Eyes Have It?

Some glaucoma patients swear that marijuana saved their sight. Some doctors believe them. We heard a physician on a popular medical radio program denouncing the government's failure to free marijuana for eye patients but adding that they knew what to do.

In general, however, the medical profession is not convinced.

Glaucoma is a condition in which fluid pressure builds up within the eye, usually from obstruction of drainage canals. If it is not treated, by drugs or surgery, ultimately the pressure can damage the optic nerve and lead to permanent blindness. Glaucoma has been responsible for something like a seventh of new blindness cases in the United States.[56] Standard medications usually can keep it well under control.

Los Angeles physicians Hepler and Frank discovered a relation between marijuana and intraocular (inside-the-eye) pressure. In a letter to the American Medical Association journal in 1971, they reported examining eleven normal, mostly young subjects before and one hour after the smoking of a water pipe. Intraocular pressure substantially decreased in nine of the eleven. In further smoking studies with normal subjects, eye pressure remained lowered for periods up to 5½ hours. While the pressure would not stay down for good, the temporary lowering effect occurred repeatedly for up to three months.[57]

Hepler, Frank, and Petrus later tested twelve glaucoma patients. Eye pressure dropped for a few hours in ten of them after either smoking of marijuana or swallowing of THC capsules.[58]

Meanwhile, at the University of the West Indies in Jamaica, Lockhart and others tested forty patients with glaucoma and forty with normal intraocular tension before and after the smoking of tobacco cigarettes and cannabis cigarettes. Neither form of smoking had any effect on eyes of normal patients. Each affected glaucoma patients—in a different way. Eye pressure dropped after cannabis. After tobacco it rose and then returned to the original level.

> After cannabis, in the Jamaica tests, the pressure dropped on average more than a third in each eye in about eighty minutes, staying low for the two hours of the test. After tobacco the pressure rose a third in the right eye in fifteen minutes and a sixth in the left eye in thirty minutes, returning to the original level in two hours.[59]

*   *   *

> Among many to repeat and vary the experiment, Cooler and Gregg in North Carolina reported eye pressure dropping in nine of ten normal subjects in response to intravenous injections of THC while blood pressure dropped markedly in two of the subjects.[60]

One of Dr. Hepler's subjects at the University of California at Los Angeles was Robert Randall from Washington, D.C. A glaucoma patient, he parlayed his ailment into nationwide prominence, calling himself the country's only legal marijuana smoker in talks, TV shows, and interviews.

He had been among millions of illegal marijuana smokers when he decided in 1973 that only marijuana gave him relief from glaucoma, evidenced by absence of "halos" (multicolored circles around lights, forming with increase in eye pressure). He began growing cannabis plants himself but police discovered them and charged him with the felony. However, he won an acquittal on the extralegal grounds of "medical necessity."

That was 1976, when Randall became the sole subject of what the government considered a research project and he considered therapy. Whatever it was, it got him seventy marijuana cigarettes a week through his eye doctor. When the doctor moved away to North Carolina in 1978 and the government agencies required his new physician to file for a new permit, Randall sued them. They soon settled out of court and set up an arrangement whereby he could fill prescriptions for marijuana through a federal pharmacy. He scoffed at the government's insistence on calling it research: "They can call it 'Fred' as long as I get the marijuana. To me it's treatment."[61]

His first ophthalmologist was John C. Merritt. In an affidavit to help Randall in his lawsuit, the doctor called marijuana "safe and effective" medication for Randall, taken with two conventional drugs (Glaucon and Phospholine Iodide), and he stated that his studies on other glaucoma patients confirmed marijuana as "effective and safe" in reducing intraocular pressure.[62]

By 1980, after three years of research into the subject, Dr. Merritt presented a rather different slant. A report in the journal of the American Academy of Ophthalmology described a study he conducted of eighteen glaucoma patients given marijuana to smoke. In sixty to ninety minutes came decreases in both intraocular and blood pressure. Sinking of blood pressure was the most serious side effect. This, together with racing of the heart, palpitations, and mental changes, occurred so often as to rule out the routine use of marijuana in the general population, Merritt and associates reported. Nine patients never had used marijuana before. Because of anxiety, they suffered more severely from the side effects than the patients who had used marijuana, although the latter also experienced those effects.

Two cases were cited. A man of twenty-eight who never had used marijuana sat and smoked a reefer. In ten minutes his heart rate fell and his blood pressure became inaudible. "He became pale, cold, and sweaty as a result of the sudden decrease in blood pressure." Eye pressure also dropped. He lay down and blood pressure and eye pressure both rose. When a daily marijuana smoker, aged thirty-one, smoked one cigarette, nothing happened. On the next day he smoked two and "he became nauseous, light-headed, cold, sweaty." The same pressure events occured to him as to the other man. Both had experienced typical symptoms of fainting.

The article ended: "It is because of the frequency and severity with which the untoward events occurred that marijuana inhalation is not an ideal therapeutic modality for glaucoma patients."[63]

Before a congressional committee, Dr. Merritt described his research, with the aid of slides. Asked by a member whether it indicated that marijuana was useful or not useful, he replied that "it indicated that marijuana does lower the pressure, and if you use the reasoning that lowering the pressure helps the glaucoma, yes, then it's helpful; but I want to reemphasize that it has an inordinate amount of cardiovascular side effects in this population described."

The doctor would not recommend marijuana for elderly glaucoma patients, the population most at risk of having both glaucoma and heart disease.

Then too, he pointed out to the congressmen, his were single-dose studies. The marijuana lowered eye pressure for five or six hours. "The real issue is: Does the marijuana repeatedly lower the intraocular pressures?" He had no data to answer the question. (Nothing was said about his "research" with Randall, lasting about fourteen months.)[64]

Merritt described "exciting research" on THC eye drops, which lowered eye pressure in both glaucoma patients and normal lab animals. A drop placed in one eye reduced pressure in both eyes. A strong drop worked no better than a weak one. Further work was needed to identify the best cannabinoid and put it in a practical form. He said investigators should be given numerous cannabinoids and different marijuana varieties to study.[65]

Another professional witness had words of caution. Carl Kupfer, director of the National Eye Institute, emphasized the fact that in patients smoking marijuana "there was not only a decrease in the intraocular pressure, the pressure in the eye, but also a decrease in the systemic blood pressure. Now this is extremely important because we know that it is necessary for the optic nerve to be properly nourished, and the optic nerve is the nerve that connects the eye with the brain, enabling us to see.

"For the optic nerve to be properly nourished, there must be an adequate amount of blood flowing to that nerve at all times, so that if we have a drug that both lowers intraocular pressure as well as blood pressure, we may be interfering with the supply of blood to the optic nerve, and therefore even though the pressure in the eye may decrease, such a patient will not be protected against losing visual function from the glaucoma process."[66]

One eye doctor who denied any use for marijuana or THC in eye treatment was Dr. George L. Spaeth, professor of ophthalmology, Thomas Jefferson University (Philadelphia), and director of glaucoma service at Wills Eye Hospital.

In a letter to the House Select Committee on Marijuana Abuse and Control, he described a study of five glaucoma patients he conducted with Dr. Kenneth Benjamin. They put THC eye drops in one eye, placebo drops in the other eye. There were small decreases in intraocular pressure. Because the decreases were about equal in both eyes and no general effects were felt, "it seems highly likely that the decreases in intraocular pressure was a response to the testing situation, and not to the use of the THC." Three patients developed superficial keratitis (inflammation of the cornea) and three (the same three?) suffered "severe discomfort."

Reviewing research on smoking and THC administered by mouth or injection, Dr. Spaeth said that a person who wanted to keep eye pressure down would have to use THC four times a day. This would imply a continuous "high" and low blood pressure.

"One of the hardest things to get across to patients, physicians and legislatures is the goal of the treatment in glaucoma. The goal of the treatment is not to lower intraocular pressure. The goal of the treatment is to prevent the progressive damage to the optic nerve that is characteristic to glaucoma. Lowering intraocular pressure in itself does not achieve this goal. For example, if medication lowers intraocular pressure but also lowers blood pressure an equivalent amount, the blood flow to the optic nerve is decreased, eliminating any beneficial effect from the lowering of the intraocular pressure."

He gave the example of clonidine, developed in Germany to treat high blood pressure. It was found to lower intraocular pressure when given as eye drops. But studies by Helimann showed that while lowering eye pressure, it also caused a worsening of the glaucoma because it lowered blood pressure more than it lowered eye pressure.

Numerous medications lower eye pressure but are not clinically useful for glaucoma, he said. Alcohol lowers the pressure, but a patient would have to remain drunk for it to work. Local colchicine greatly lowers eye pressure but makes the eye red and inflamed.

Spaeth saw no reason for further research into marijuana or THC for the eyes, and he said that the heads of three university ophthalmology departments with whom he had just met agreed with him. He did favor work to achieve chemical modifications of THC that would make it better tolerated and more effective for eye drops.[67]

*   *   *

Two chemical modifications of THC were tested, on otherwise healthy patients with high intraocular pressure, by Tiedeman, Shields, and others (1981). Consuming single capsules, sixteen patients at Duke University took one of the drugs, BW29Y, while twenty-eight at Ohio State University took the other, BW146Y. The first did not work. The second, which unlike the other—and unlike THC—was soluble in water, did lower intraocular pressure, without blood pressure changes in most patients. Three in the latter group suffered declining blood pressure, one of them fainting. Their eye pressure did not go down.

In studying any new drug proposed for the treatment of glaucoma, they pointed out, it is not enough to demonstrate that eye pressure goes down without side effects. Success ultimately depends on the extent to which the drug prevents visual loss. While existing antiglaucoma medicines do control glaucoma (at least in part) by lowering eye pressure, currently accepted thinking is that if a drug lowers eye pressure but decreases blood flow to the optic nerve head, it may not help and could harm it. A more complete evaluation would require optic nerve data, determine whether side effects would continue over the long range, and consider the possibility of eye drops.[68]

What are the long-range effects of cannabis smoking on the eyes? Two reports in journals of ophthalmology (1974 and 1977) apply here. They described opposite findings as to intraocular pressure. Each connected the use of cannabis with a pattern of symptoms.

• First, Shapiro in Switzerland told of observing in more than 350 cannabis-smoking patients a consistent pattern of ocular manifestations including low intraocular pressure, photophobia with blepharospasm (abnormal intolerance of light with involuntary tight contraction of eyelids), congestion around the cornea, and often marked visibility of corneal nerves.

Distant vision needed correction in all cases. Near vision at examination always was good, except that many patients claimed problems in near vision at other times, "and indeed they were incapacitated just after using these drugs by their inability to read." Intraocular pressure averaged around 10 to 12 millimeters of mercury. (Precise figures were not given.) Each of the patients had been seen at least once since 1968.[69]

• A study in Costa Rica of thirty-nine chronic users (cannabis smokers for ten years or more) included several eye tests. The subjects probably did little or no smoking for at least ten hours before the testing. The smoking group as a whole had slightly higher intraocular pressures in seventy-eight eyes than a matched nonsmoking group. The chronic users also showed lower visual acuity (ability to read letters of different brightness) and slightly smaller pupil diameter, and in addition they exhibited greater light sensitivity and formation of tears.

The investigators (including Dawson of the University of Florida and Costa Rican colleagues) observed that all of those trends in the chronic users paralleled symptoms known in eye disease.[70]

Supporting a congressional bill to make it simple for doctors and hospitals to obtain marijuana, The New York Times stated (1983) that "in the case of several illnesses, marijuana is the therapeutic drug of choice. It reduces nausea for patients undergoing cancer treatment, for instance, and arrests developing blindness in glaucoma victims."[71]

Dr. Bruce E. Spivey of San Francisco, executive vice-president of the American Academy of Ophthalmology, responded that the academy's drugs committee knew of no clinical evidence of benefit from marijuana in the long-term treatment of glaucoma and advised keeping marijuana a Schedule I drug. He said there were new, more effective ways of treating glaucoma, adding:

"It is true that marijuana can decrease intraocular pressure temporarily in some cases. But to maintain lowered pressure could require a patient to smoke more than 2,100 marijuana cigarettes a year. Keep in mind that most cases of glaucoma require lifetime, daily treatment. So a patient might need to smoke six marijuana cigarettes a day because the pressure-lowering effects last only three to four hours.

"Consumption of this quantity of marijuana could lead to significant psychological and physiological changes in the user, including impairment of ocular motor coordination."[72]

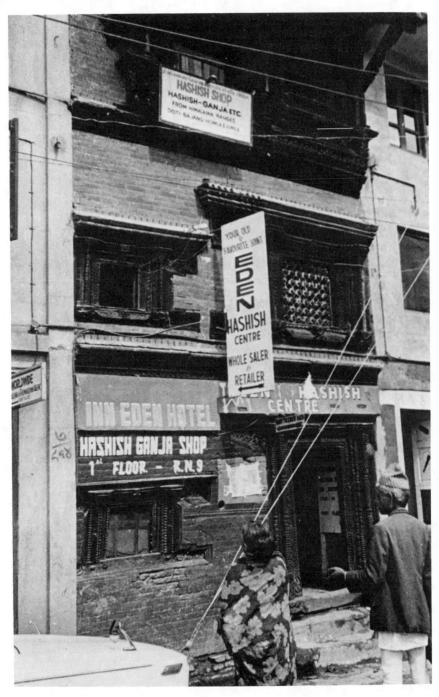

A hashish shop on the main square in Katmandu, Nepal.

The late Professor Hardin B. Jones took this picture when he and his wife, Helen C. Jones, visited Nepal in March, 1973. The next summer the Nepalese government—distressed that local young people had begun imitating western visitors in the smoking of cannabis, a socially unacceptable practice—ordered the closing of all marijuana-hashish shops and restaurants. The restaurants had served food and beverages laced with cannabis. This is Mrs. Jones's story: "As we were walking in the main square early one evening, the proprietor stood in the door of his shop and motioned for us to enter. We were hesitant but he said we could just come and look. We cautiously entered the door and wound up two flights of narrow, dark stairs, passing small, smoke-filled rooms as we went up. The smoke was so thick, we could barely make out young men sitting or lying on benches or on the floor and smoking, mainly from water pipes. At the top of the winding stair was a small room lined with shelves stocked with jars, like candy jars, containing various grades of marijuana (cannabis flowers, leaves, and stems). Cakes of hashish (cannabis resin) were stacked on shelves or stored in jars. Hashish came in a variety of sizes and shapes: sticks, bricks, spheres, discs, cylinders, hexagons, and granules. The color varied from amber to ebony, the consistency from that of hard wax to that of putty. The proprietor proudly held up a jar oozing with a dark, greenish brown, viscous liquid: hashish oil. We only looked. We did not buy."

COMMENTARY

It's amazing how many people we encounter who are fully aware that tobacco smoking can lead to fatal disease but who have the notion that marijuana smoking is an innocuous diversion. "It's harmless" is a phrase we have heard innumerable times. Sometimes we've even heard the non sequitur, "I don't smoke. I only smoke pot."

Such people know that the smoking of tobacco cigarettes causes lung cancer. Many also may be aware of its role in heart attacks, strokes, emphysema, and a host of other ills. Some may even recognize its designation by the surgeon general and other medical authorities as the chief preventable cause of death in America. However, they have been taken in by the myth that somehow you can pour cannabis smoke into your system day after day, year after year, with impunity; that while it may be hazardous to inhale the products of combustion of any other substance, *Cannabis sativa* somehow is an exception.

On the basis of research trends, we expect that it will ultimately prove at least as harmful as *Nicotiana tabacum*. Although it's proper for scientists to wait until "all the facts are in" before closing the books, by the time a consensus is reached it could be too late for some marijuana users.

That habitual marijuana smoking endangers the lungs and respiratory system already appears to be scientifically established. The immediate effect of smoking an isolated joint is a deceptive expansion of the air passages. An extended period of such smoking, though, can bring about the reverse effect. Heavy, prolonged cannabis smoking, particularly in combination with tobacco, has produced ominous tissue changes in some human smokers as well as in test animals.

What scientific researchers have not done is follow certain smokers over many years. Some, however, have treated rodents with cannabic substances for long periods of the animals' lives, and cancer has been discovered in the lungs and other organs.

Starting in the latter 1980s, we predict an increase in the rate of lung

458

cancer among middle-aged people, representing the marijuana epidemic that began in the midsixties. Those smoking both tobacco and marijuana probably are most at risk.

Long-range studies of cannabis and the heart are in short supply. While evidence of damage to the normal heart is wanting, it has been shown that a dose of marijuana usually increases the work of the heart and distorts the blood pressure. This plainly poses a threat to patients with cardiovascular problems. Those with normal hearts must consider how long they can overwork their hearts without paying a price.

Remember that subjects selected for most scientific studies of cannabis have been young and apparently healthy. Anyone who may have been seriously harmed by cannabis probably would not be studied.

Many effects are not immediately apparent. For instance, there is evidence that cannabis can affect sex hormones and sperm in men; cause a wide variety of reproductive problems, including the death of fetuses, when taken by pregnant female animals; and, when used by childbearing women, even affect their offspring.

While studies conflict on whether cannabis and cannabinoids depress the immune system, damage genetic material, and harm brain tissue, certain disturbing cellular and chemical trends have been demonstrated. Accumulation in the cells and tissues is cause for concern.

Studies of cannabis and the mind have been abundant. Most of them have dealt with "acute" effects, the immediate reactions to intoxication. The temporary disabling effects of cannabis and its main mind-altering ingredient, THC, on brain activity—perception, learning, thought, emotion, coordination, judgment—have been chronicled repeatedly and these often are spectacular. Few dispute them or deny that marijuana can trigger mental illness in susceptible individuals. (Even small doses can do this.) There is less agreement on long-range consequences. Nevertheless, possible harm to the developing nervous system and mind of the child has even some marijuana partisans concerned.

We have shown that the impact of cannabis on the mind sometimes—no one knows how often—is reflected tragically in auto smash-ups, plane and train accidents, and use of weapons by transiently deranged individuals. The phenomenon of passive intoxication of nonsmokers breathing smokers' fumes conceivably broadens the problem. Moreover, burning plus inebriation add up to fire danger. And the outcome of drug use by those connected with nuclear equipment or weapons could be catastrophic.

A new look needs to be taken at the old theories—prematurely discarded—of marijuana leading to other, narcotic drugs and to crime. The stepping-stone theory has some scientific support. And if marijuana leads to narcotic addiction—a known cause of crime—then marijuana's link to crime follows logically.

People often take their habits to work with them. Industry and labor should consider whether marijuana affects the quality and quantity of production and the safety of workers.

* * *

We have avoided the expressions "soft drugs" and "hard drugs." Cannabis is harder than many think and it has become harder over the years. The contemporary illegal market commonly offers foreign and domestic marijuana with THC content of around 5 percent—at least ten times as potent as the home-grown weed available when the fad exploded in the sixties.

Neither do we speak of "recreational drugs." We don't fathom the concept of swallowing pills for entertainment, breathing in toxic chemicals for fun, or contorting one's mind for amusement. Wholesome, healthful pleasures are abundant. A world of natural delights is out there.

For simplicity's sake, we have referred to the consumption of illicit substances as drug "use." It should be called drug "abuse." The legitimate function of a drug is to alleviate illness or suffering. Cannabis—or, more likely, synthetic cannabinoids—may have limited medical use, taken in prescribed doses for specific purposes. We hope so. Society deserves it, and the classification of its useful derivatives with other medicines could help to strip cannabis of myth and mystique.

All drugs have side effects, and cannabis is no exception. The youth focusing on the pleasurable effects does not worry about the price he may have to pay in the future, any more than the legendary Faust dwelled on the little matter of accounting when he made that business deal with Mephistopheles. He probably won't notice all of the mental and physical changes in himself—until he has quit. The penalty may depend on how heavily he's drugged himself and his personal constitution.

Aggravating the problem are the notions prevalent in our contemporary culture, and exaggerated in the "hip" subculture, that (1) for every ill there's a pill, (2) the world owes me a perpetual "high," and (3) only "now" counts. Of course it's normal to avoid pain and seek pleasure. Marijuana, bathing the brain in instant pleasure, may offer a momentary escape from problems. Unfortunately, it solves none. And a surfeit of this unearned pleasure may ultimately result in a dulling of the senses and a withdrawal from normal life.

"You hear a lot about . . . marijuana. Nothing! Nothing! *Alcohol* is America's drug problem," declared a physician on a popular medical radio program not long ago. While drinking is more widespread than marijuana smoking, America has become aware of the former problem and is learning to deal with it. Marijuana dependence—among millions of adults and children—is a problem that has intensified because it has been denied. (After writing the above, we heard the same radio doctor say: "When we start talking about drug abuse, everything pales by comparison: *cigarettes*—that's this nation's number-one health problem right now." We share both of his concerns.)

Of late many states have toughened their drunken driving laws. Paradoxically, as increasing scientific information has emerged about the hazards of cannabis, the marijuana laws have been weakened. While drunks are picked up on the street without public uproar, those burning marijuana in public are, in many places, ignored or at most served with parking-type tickets. Yet marijuana partisans—just as they have done since the sixties—still plead for young people who supposedly are hounded and arrested in vast numbers simply for possessing bits of marijuana.

At one time many indeed were arrested when found in possession of marijuana, and some of the penalties used to be too harsh for the crimes committed. Of course, such people knew the law and willfully violated it. There are worse things than an arrest—a wasted life, an undeveloped mind, a dissipated body, and the endangering of the public.

Those who lamented that "the marijuana laws are making criminals of our children" may well have helped turn many of those young people into prisoners of drugs.

If the felony laws were too tough, various states went to the opposite extreme. The consequence may have been to encourage cannabis use further, for the message of decriminalization is that marijuana is okay. The wishy-washy statutes have confused even the police. We stopped a patrol car to complain about some marijuana smoke on the street. "Don't you know? It's legal now," said the uniformed (and uninformed) driver, and with that he sped off.

The effort of knowledgeable groups like the American Medical Association to warn against habitual marijuana smoking may be futile when the law (which differs confusingly from state to state) pulls in an opposite direction.

*   *   *

Advocates of legalization emphasize that marijuana is not so serious a problem as alcohol and tobacco—as though three wrongs make a right.

We question whether marijuana—which combines noxious features of the other two substances with some of its own—actually is softest on the system. Its THC clings to the brain and other organs for weeks, whereas a drink of alcohol can wash from the body in an hour. The smoking of marijuana entails all of the risks to the lungs incurred from tobacco smoking, adding the hazards of THC. The absence of health statistics on smokers of an illegal drug precludes a really meaningful comparison.

Some people, on grounds of personal liberty, propound an inalienable right to grow and burn cannabis. But what about the rights of those who do not want to be subjected to added pollution and involuntary drugging?

Many call marijuana activity "victimless crime." But research is indicating more and more that society is the victim.

In the increasingly competitive and severe milieu of today, it appears to us that the rational course is to protect one's health, safety, and mental sharpness to whatever extent possible. This would seem to serve the interests not only of personal well-being but of the world's effort to extricate itself from its predicaments.

Instead, we find millions in the prime of life risking body, mind, and future in their pursuit of chemical happiness, while serious voices appeal for the legalization of a substance shadowed by scientific findings.

If we end up finding marijuana cigarettes neatly packaged at each smoke shop and check-out counter, let's hope that the packs at least are appropriately labeled. They might say:

**Warning: The Weight of Evidence Shows
That Marijuana Smoking Is Dangerous
to Your Health and to Our Society.**

SUPPLEMENT

A

Distribution of THC from a Marijuana Cigarette

This figure shows the average distribution of delta-9-THC from marijuana cigarettes in studies at the Batelle laboratories, Columbus, Ohio,
using a machine to simulate smoking by experienced smokers. Half of
the THC was burned up (pyrolyzed); 6 percent left the burning end as
"sidestream" smoke; 21 percent lodged in the butt; and the remaining
23 percent emerged in the "mainstream" smoke, which a smoker would
inhale (according to data from Foltz et al., reported by Truitt, 1971).
The marijuana in a typical joint may weigh a gram, 1,000 milligrams
(mg). If its THC content is 1 percent, it contains 10 mg, of which the
theoretical smoker would take in 2.3 mg if he smoked the entire cigarette. Since THC accumulates in the butt, the last in a group sharing a
joint receives much more THC per puff than the first one (Dr. Reese
T. Jones, 1980). (By permission of *Pharmacological Reviews.*)

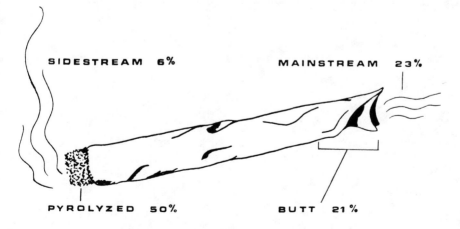

B

THC Content of Confiscated Cannabis Samples

(As analyzed by the Marihuana Project, Research Institute of Pharmaceutical Sciences, University of Mississippi, under contract with the National Institute on Drug Abuse, 1973 through March 31, 1983; dash indicates no analyzed sample)

Form	Highest and Lowest Percentage of Δ^9-THC	Average (arithmetic mean) Percentage of Δ^9-THC (by dry weight)				Total Number of Samples
		1973	1982	1983	All analyzed samples	
Marijuana (broken down below)	13.6% and a trace (less than .0095%)	0.7%	3.1%	5.6%	2.5%	2,096
Loose plant material (including reefers)	13.6% and a trace	0.8%	2.6%	4.8%	1.8%	1,249
Kilobricks	3.1% and .03%	0.2%	—	—	0.6%	577
Buds	11.3% and .24%	—	5.3%	5.7%	3.2%	153
Sinsemilla	12.6% and .19%	—	7.1%	8.4%	5.9%	104
Thai sticks	8.9% and .05%	—	4.6%	—	1.8%	13
Hashish	27.7% and a trace	1.0%	2.4%	8.3%	2.8%	439
Hash oil	43.2% and .70%	16.1%	21.6%	34.0%	21.2%	131

C

Chemical Structures of Cannabinoids

(From Institute of Medicine, *Marijuana and Health*, 1982)

Δ^9-THC (delta-9-tetrahydrocannabinol), which is the same as Δ^1-THC, has an empirical formula of $C_{21}H_{30}O_2$ and a molecular weight of 314. Cannabidiol has the same empirical formula and the same molecular weight. Cannabinol has an empirical formula of $C_{21}H_{26}O_2$ and a molecular weight of 310. Two prominent metabolites of Δ^9-THC are 11-nor-Δ^9-THC-9-carboxylic acid and 11-hydroxy-Δ^9-THC.

Δ-9-THC

Cannabinol

Cannabidiol

11-hydroxy-Δ-9-THC

D

Chemical Constituents of Cannabis Preparations

(Based on a table by Carlton E. Turner, 1980, and information from the Marihuana Project, University of Mississippi, 1984)

1. Cannabinoids: *62 known*
   a. Cannabigerol (CBG) type: *6 known*
   b. Cannabichromene (CBC) type: *4 known*
   c. Cannabidiol (CBD) type: *7 known*
   d. Δ^9-Tetrahydrocannabinol (Δ^9-THC) type: *9 known*
   e. Δ^8-Tetrahydrocannabinol (Δ^8-THC) type: *2 known*
   f. Cannabicyclol (CBL) type: *3 known*
   g. Cannabielsoin (CBE) type: *3 known*
   h. Cannabinol (CBN) type: *6 known*
   i. Cannabinodiol (CBND) type: *2 known*
   j. Cannabitriol (CBT) type: *6 known*
   k. Miscellaneous cannabinoids: *14 known*
2. Nitrogenous compounds: *20 known*
3. Amino acids: *18 known*
4. Proteins, glycoproteins, and enzymes: *9 known*
5. Sugars and related compounds: *34 known*
6. Hydrocarbons: *50 known*
7. Simple alcohols: *7 known*
8. Simple aldehydes: *12 known*
9. Simple ketones: *13 known*
10. Simple acids: *20 known*
11. Fatty acids: *12 known*
12. Simple esters and lactones: *13 known*
13. Steroids: *11 known*
14. Terpenes: *103 known*
15. Noncannabinoid phenols: *20 known*
16. Flavonoid glycosides: *19 known*
17. Vitamins: *1 known*
18. Pigments: *2 known*

Total number of compounds found in the cannabis plant or its preparations to date: 426.

E

Marijuana and Tobacco Reference Cigarettes: Analysis of Mainstream Smoke

(From Institute of Medicine, *Marijuana and Health*, 1982)

	Marijuana Cigarette (85 mm)	Tobacco Cigarette (85 mm)
A. Cigarettes		
Average weight, mg	1,115	1,110
Moisture, percent	10.3	11.1
Pressure drop, cm	14.7	7.2
Static burning rate, mg/s	0.88	0.80
Puff number	10.7	11.1
B. Mainstream smoke		
I. Gas phase		
Carbon monoxide, vol. percent	3.99	4.58
mg	17.6	20.2
Carbon dioxide, vol. percent	8.27	9.38
mg	57.3	65.0
Ammonia, μg	228	199
HCN, μg	532	498
Cyanogen $(CN)_2$, μg	19	20
Isoprene, μg	83	310
Acetaldehyde, μg	1,200	980
Acetone, μg	443	578
Acrolein, μg	92	85
Acetonitrile, μg	132	123
Benzene, μg	76	67
Toluene, μg	112	108
Vinyl chloride, ng[a]	5.4	12.4
Dimethylnitrosamine, ng[a]	75	84
Methylethylnitrosamine, ng[a]	27	30
pH, third puff	6.56	6.14
fifth puff	6.57	6.15
seventh puff	6.58	6.14
ninth puff	6.56	6.10
tenth puff	6.58	6.02
II. Particulate phase		
Total particulate matter, dry, mg	22.7	39.0
Phenol, μg	76.8	138.5

	Marijuana Cigarette (85 mm)	Tobacco Cigarette (85 mm)
o-Cresol, μg	17.9	24
m -and p-Cresol, μg	54.4	65
Dimethylphenol, μg	6.8	14.4
Catechol, μg	188	328
Cannabidiol, μg	190	—
Δ⁹-Tetrahydrocannabinol, μg	820	—
Cannabinol, μg	400	—
Nicotine, μg	—	2,850
N-Nitrosonornicotine, ng[a]	—	390
Naphthalene, μg	3.0	1.2
1-Methylnaphthalene, μg	6.1	3.65
2-Methylnaphthalene	3.6	1.4
Benz(a)anthracene, ng[a]	75	43
Benzo(a)pyrene, ng[a]	31	21.1

[a] Indicates known carcinogens.
SOURCES: Hoffmann et al., 1975, 1976; Brunnemann et al., 1976, 1977.

F

Percentage of Americans Using Drugs of Abuse

(Issued in 1983 by the National Institute on Drug Abuse, based on the National Household Survey on Drug Abuse conducted by the George Washington University Social Research Group; dash indicates "not available"; stars indicate "less than one-half of 1 percent")

LIFETIME PREVALENCE OF DRUG USE: 1972–82 (at least tried once)

	Youth: age 12–17						Young Adults: age 18–25						Older Adults: age 26 +					
	'72	'74	'76	'77	'79	'82	'72	'74	'76	'77	'79	'82	'72	'74	'76	'77	'79	'82
Marijuana	14.0%	23.0%	22.4%	28.0%	30.9%	26.7%	47.9%	52.7%	52.9%	59.9%	68.2%	64.1%	7.4%	9.9%	12.9%	15.3%	19.6%	23.0%
Hallucinogens	4.8	6.0	5.1	4.6	7.1	5.2	—	16.6	17.3	19.8	25.1	21.1		1.3	1.6	2.6	4.5	6.4
Cocaine	1.5	3.6	3.4	4.0	5.4	6.5	9.1	12.7	13.4	19.1	27.5	28.3	1.6	.9	1.6	2.6	4.3	8.5
Heroin	.6	1.0	.5	1.1	.5	**	4.6	4.5	3.9	3.6	3.5	1.2	**	.5	.5	.8	1.0	1.1
Nonmedical Use of:																		
Stimulants	4.0	5.0	4.4	5.2	3.4	6.7	12.0	17.0	16.6	21.2	18.2	18.0	3.0	3.0	5.6	4.7	5.8	6.2
Sedatives	3.0	5.0	2.8	3.1	3.2	5.8	10.0	15.0	11.9	18.4	17.0	18.7	2.0	2.0	2.4	2.8	3.5	4.8
Tranquilizers	3.0	3.0	3.3	3.8	4.1	4.9	7.0	10.0	9.1	13.4	15.8	15.1	5.0	2.0	2.7	2.6	3.1	3.6
Analgesics	—	—	—	—	3.2	4.2	—	—	—	—	11.8	12.1	—	—	—	—	2.7	3.2
Any Nonmedical Use	—	—	—	—	7.3	10.3	—	—	—	—	29.5	28.4	—	—	—	—	9.2	8.8
Alcohol	—	54.0	53.6	52.6	70.3	65.2	—	81.6	83.6	84.2	95.3	94.6	—	73.2	74.7	77.9	91.5	88.2
Cigarettes	—	52.0	45.5	47.3	54.1	49.5	—	68.8	70.1	67.6	82.8	76.9	—	65.4	64.5	67.0	83.0	78.7

CURRENT DRUG USE: 1972–82 (consumed in the month before interview)

	Youth: age 12–17						Young Adults: age 18–25						Older Adults: age 26 +					
	'72	'74	'76	'77	'79	'82	'72	'74	'76	'77	'79	'82	'72	'74	'76	'77	'79	'82
Marijuana	7.0%	12.0%	12.3%	16.6%	16.7%	11.5%	27.8%	25.2%	25.0%	27.4%	35.4%	27.4%	2.5%	2.0%	3.5%	3.3%	6.0%	6.6%
Hallucinogens	1.4	1.3	.9	1.6	2.2	1.4	—	2.5	1.1	2.0	4.4	1.7	—		**	**	**	**
Cocaine	.6	1.0	1.0	.8	1.4	1.6	—	3.1	2.0	3.7	9.3	6.8	—		**	**	.9	1.2
Heroin	**	**	**	**	**	**	—	**	**	**	**	**	—		**	**	**	**
Nonmedical Use of:																		
Stimulants	—	1.0	1.2	1.3	1.2	2.6	—	3.7	4.7	2.5	3.5	4.7	—	**	**	.6	.5	.6
Sedatives	—	1.0	—	.8	1.1	1.3	—	1.6	2.3	2.8	2.8	2.6	—	**	.5	**	**	**
Tranquilizers	—	1.0	1.1	.7	.6	.9	—	1.2	2.6	2.4	2.1	1.6	—	**	**	**	**	**
Analgesics	—	—	—	—	.6	.7	—	—	—	—	1.0	1.0	—	—	—	—	**	**
Any Nonmedical Use	—	—	—	—	2.3	3.8	—	—	—	—	6.2	7.0	—	—	—	—	1.1	1.2
Alcohol	—	34.0	32.4	31.2	37.2	26.9	—	69.3	69.0	70.0	75.9	67.9	—	54.5	56.0	54.9	61.3	56.7
Cigarettes	—	25.0	23.4	22.3	12.1	14.7	—	48.8	49.4	47.3	42.6	39.5	—	39.1	38.4	38.7	36.9	34.6

G

Quotations Continued from "The Mind"

1

- *"It was last New Year's Day. I was at a friend's house . . . under the influence of alcohol, mushrooms, and marijuana. . . . I secreted myself in the bathroom. . . . I felt that I might be sick. . . . It was late . . . about 3 A.M. . . .*

"She had a shell in the bathroom . . . and I noticed that under the influence, the shell had the markings of a rattlesnake and that it seemed to move. . . . I was laughing hysterically . . . and I was thinking about the ways I could have humiliated my employers in the past, my professors, and people in authority. . . . Then I became very melancholy and began to think about friends I'd known in the past who'd died . . . and I started to cry and I began to think about the meanings of brotherhood . . . and I cried because my brother didn't love me, my own brother. . . . I actually believed that the Marxist-Leninist dialectic was the Mylanta bottle in the cabinet. . . . This went on for about three hours [in the bathroom]. . . .

"Oh, it wasn't a hallucination . . . . It was what you'd call free-form thinking. I never actually hallucinated. . . .

"I had a girl friend who thought . . . that her passage into the next world was imminent [after she had smoked marijuana]. She was lying on the floor waiting for the Reaper. This is also in a bathroom during a party . . . . She eventually came off it, but she was very depressed . . . hours afterwards. . . .

"Your mind is so active. It's almost as though one hemisphere of your brain that you've never used before suddenly activated. You're too distracted to concentrate on mundane things. I don't think a person could type very well, for example, or file papers in a cabinet. . . .

"It produces sort of nonlinear thinking. . . . You can't go from point A to point Z without hitting all the points in between. I mean you just want to go everywhere. . . .

"It seemed like the first time I took it [marijuana, with no other drug]

too there was a euphoria in the beginning and then a sadness in the end. I think I began by laughing and then crying." —Edward (occasional user)

• *"When I'm straight, I have a great memory. When stoned, I'm very forgetful. . . .*
"Time slows down. Things just seem to take forever. . . .
"I get a little paranoid. I tend to hibernate. I don't leave the house. 'Nobody loves me'—that sort of thing. . . .
"It either makes me ecstatic or depressed, but then when I'm straight, I'm manic-depressive anyway, so it just amplifies that personality." —Betty (long-time user, trying to quit)

• *"I remember the night I first felt the effects. I was fifteen. It was Easter vacation in 1971 and I went with a friend to her parents' home. Two brothers next door shared three joints with us. They were rolled from toilet paper. We smoked outside. The boy who rolled it said he worshiped the moon. We came in and giggled and I felt I was in a surrealistic picture. I tried to read a book and kept reading and rereading the same line. The high lasted three hours. We were in adjoining twin beds. She became very frightened and kept saying, 'Oh, what if I die in my sleep? What will happen to me?' She commented that she looked like Mickey Mouse. I said I thought so too. . . .*
"With marijuana I felt slightly distanced from the mundanity of life. Also I found I was capable of great introspection. Coke and M&Ms tasted wonderful. . . .
"It does elongate time. One loses hold of one's internal clock.
"I used to have confusions. I used to do silly things.
"I was generally an unhappy person and focused on it when high. . . .
"The thing about people who are high all the time: You sit around having wonderful insights about yourself but you sit around, not doing anything about it.
"There was a certain amount of paranoia.
"I became slightly more introverted.
"It generally encouraged laziness about taking care of myself and my activities. It encouraged irresponsibility and living in a fantasy world. Procrastination. You couldn't write a paper or study. The mind finds it hard to stay focused. I couldn't read when alone. . . .
"At the time I didn't realize that some of my lazy ways were due to it. It's not a drug that takes its toll on the body the way other drugs do. It takes its toll on the mind but at the same time it hides its action from the mind so the mind isn't aware it's being tampered with." —Kathy (light user, former heavy user)

- *"I started in 1969 in South Dakota. I was eighteen and driving for a combine crew in a wheat harvest. I had read a lot about it and had never even seen it and I was in a bar and there was a band and I talked to the guys. One of them, his brother was in Vietnam and brought him marijuana. I urged him to let me have some. He sold me eight dollars' worth, which now would be worth about eighty dollars.*

"I went home to my trailer and rolled three joints, smoked them all, and nothing happened. The very next day I rolled three joints and smoked them and I was blown away—giggling, loss of consciousness. After that, it was never such a strong experience. Since then I've been a chronic smoker. . . .

"It enhances my hearing and my sensitivity and gives me more intellectual activity. It's often a source of inspiration for creative thought processes. . . .

"Now I'm just doing telephone sales, looking for a better job."
—Pete (chronic smoker and marijuana advocate)

- *"I started smoking about seventeen years ago. I was about twenty-one. I was a waitress trying to be a student. . . . In Manhattan I fell in love with my first lover, and he turned me on to weed. . . . I remember we used to sit and smoke at one house I used to visit. They'd just pass the rolling joints and we'd smoke all night long, one right after another, maybe eight hours.*

"One time I was sitting there smoking. He had a lot of hair and a beard. Suddenly his face changed to a bear. I ran out and walked the streets, laughing and crying. A friend had to pick me up.

"Another time I remember I was pretty high like that. They set a cup of coffee. I couldn't remember that I was supposed to pick up the coffee. I think I tried to lap it like a cat. . . .

"I have noticed that I may go into a room to get something when I'm high and forget exactly what it was I went in for. I tried to make out my check for my landlady and forgot her name. My memory, even when I'm not high, has been slightly reduced. . . .

"It really does affect my mood. I do get what I would call paranoid and schizophrenic. Socially if I'm sitting around with a bunch of people, whereas before I smoked I would be lively and in the conversation and interested, after I smoked I would get self-conscious and quit talking and probably leave or stay and be withdrawn.

"There have been times that I've been alone, just having thoughts go through my head—scary thoughts—hearing voices at times. . . .

"You think people are laughing at you, or think you're stupid, or are

just patronizing you, or making fun of you, or thinking bad thoughts about you. . . .

"A lot of times people will smoke weed to relieve their depression. It will for a short time. Then it will lower their blood sugar so eventually they'll feel worse and more depressed." —Rhoda (long-time user, trying to quit)

• *"Personally I couldn't concentrate on anything very well while I smoked it, which is why I quit. I couldn't do anything constructive. I'd just do it when relaxing or listening to music.*

"I was an honor student in college. I remember forgetting things occasionally. Sometimes I used to think marijuana affected my memory. . . .

"I could smoke two or three hits and I didn't get intoxicated but it put me in a mood where I would be lazy. I wouldn't want to go out and play racketball. . . .

"You can't really keep track of time. It magnifies your mood. If you're in a good mood, time will go quickly. If you're in a bad mood, time will take forever.

"With certain types of marijuana, I got hallucinations. If you looked into a shadow on the wall, you'd see a pattern. . . .

"It magnifies your mood. If you're in a bad mood where there's a lot of gossip, you'll get paranoid." —Alvin (ex-user)

• *"After I smoked pot I couldn't recall details or thoughts. I would say, 'That's really a cool thought.' Then I couldn't remember what it was I had thought was so intriguing. I felt stupid. I think I had convinced myself that I was stupid.*

"I felt paranoid, street-scared, scared to go out at dark. I would get insecure, though outwardly I would be 'ha, ha, ha, ha!'

"Loss of self-confidence: 'I'll never get anything done. I'll never amount to anything. All I do is go home and smoke pot.'

"Insecure about the social aspects: 'Nobody really likes me.' 'Why doesn't she invite me to the party?' 'She doesn't really care about what I'm saying.' Things like that. . . .

"I had a hard time concentrating. . . .

"I guess what made me decide that it wasn't for me: I got really depressed. I was depressed in the first place. Then when I smoked it, I got even more depressed. . . .

"No mental activity. I just sat around and smoked pot, sort of zombie-like. . . .

"Usually I had marijuana and cigarettes. If you take a deep toke on a joint and then take a puff on a cigarette, you get this weird instantaneous buzz that lasts a second or two. Like when you lose your stomach on a roller coaster. . . .

"I'm more introverted [after quitting marijuana]. It made you feel less inhibited. I don't have the crutch. It was more of a change right after I quit. Now I feel different about it. I've always been kind of a loner and I prefer to be by myself. I prefer to sit around and study math. . . .

"Once when I was stoned up, I hitchhiked from Seattle to Portland at 2 A.M. It was cold and I had on sandals and a shirt." —Janet (ex-user)

● *"During the time when I was an adolescent, it was a social thing. . . . I start using it now when I'm under stress. . . . For me it's a more effective high than alcohol. . . .*

"When I'm high, my thought processes tend to be more expansive. At this time, when I'm straight, I don't have much imagination. . . .

"I remember once being so high from marijuana, I thought I was on a carnival wheel when I was in a house with friends. I threw up.

"Even though I live that way, I feel very moral about drugs. I disapprove of people who use intoxicating substances. . . . Maybe I have guilt feelings." —Rita (chronic user)

● *"The good effects? Well, mainly heightened sensitivity in terms of eating, sex, listening to music. Any sort of entertainment, aural diversion seemed to be heightened. . . .*

"There were bad effects, more as I got older. Paranoia, without a doubt, to the point where I often created a lot of—as they used to say—bad vibes by being paranoid, especially if I'd see a police car or something. I'd imagine certain people who looked what I thought very straight, perhaps they were undercover police officers and were going to arrest us immediately. My friends didn't appreciate that and told me to relax. But ironically I was the only one of my immediate group that didn't have any run-ins with the police during the years that I was getting high. . . . I used to think that firemen and anyone who worked for the city was going to find out I was high and going to arrest me. Even the police tow trucks when they'd come, I'd think, 'Oh no. I'm gonna get arrested.' . . .

"Another bad effect was a sensitivity to pain. . . . I found that if I were to injure myself when stoned, it hurt intensely. . . .

"And any situation that required mental or physical effort when I was stoned was a most unwelcome interruption and caused me unhappiness in knowing that I had to deal with it. That was a problem because obviously life is full of situations like that, so for me, if I'm stoned, I can't

cope with them. . . . It could be anything. From the time I was living with my parents: run an errand, make the bed, do the laundry. . . . If it required some physical effort or if I was talking to someone, a person I knew was straight, like an adult, and had to deal with him to a certain extent, it was very hard. . . .

"During the entire time I was smoking marijuana, the ten years, there would be a short-term memory loss, the usual sensation of discussing something with somebody and then a few seconds later not remembering what it was you were saying. . . . When I wasn't under the influence, I had the problem to a lesser extent. . . .

"The thinking, when stoned, was very random, coming from all directions. . . .

"There was increased depression most times, unless I was involved in some kind of diversion, a film, a concert, sex. If I was just going through my normal routine and happened to be stoned, I'd be more upset with a situation that would upset me anyway, but I'd be more upset if I was stoned. . . . If you bring a predisposition to smoking marijuana, a good one or a bad one, it's going to be intensified for the most part. And so if I was depressed, which I tend to be sometimes—sort of a melancholy person—then it would become intensified when I was high. . . .

"When I had professional-type jobs, I never got high during working hours, at least as a rule—I may have violated it a couple of times—because it definitely interfered with my ability to work properly and work efficiently. . . . I've had jobs where I've gotten high. I once had a job delivering and setting up mattresses, box springs, and to relieve the boredom I'd get high with my partner. I was able to do the job because the job was so simple, but I definitely found that I had less strength to do it and the physical labor was much more taxing when I was high. . . . I once was playing volleyball in college when I was stoned. . . . I jumped into the air, exulting in a hard-fought point that we had won, and landed down and my ankle didn't support me—which might tie into losing physical strength when stoned—and my ankle buckled and I sprained it." — Pierre (ex-user)

• "When I started marijuana I was thirteen. . . . It was 1964. . . . We were kind of the first hippies. . . . I left home when I was fifteen and then I lived in a commune. We got high a fair amount. . . .

"I do think it has side effects that a lot of people overlook. I think it affects your memory. It's not necessarily a long-lasting effect. I know definitely that when people are high and they have to apply concentration and knowledge, it's a little difficult. I think it gets in some of those little labyrinths in the brain. . . .

"If I had to take some exams, I didn't smoke the whole day. I would say it will wear off within twenty-four hours. I don't know what the long-term effects are. . . .

"After you've had five or six joints, you're kind of a blob. It's hard for you to do things. You get tired and lazy and want to hang out. . . . It induces a lack of physical activity. . . .

"I've had to give up smoking pot when I've wanted to lose weight. It lowers your willpower in all things, to get accomplished what you want to get accomplished. I say I'll do this and this, and then I'll smoke a joint. . . .

"Different kinds of pot, they have their own character. Some pot makes you laugh. Some makes you laid back. Some pot has a touch of paranoia in it. . . .

"My will is real strong. . . . I love my mind. I may treat it shabbily from some other people's point of view." —Alice (chronic user)

2

● *"I started eleven years ago. I was thirteen. . . . The first time I quit was in '72 for about six months. I had a very bad acid trip so I decided to cool it for a while. Basically it was the same thing in '75. I just stopped using all drugs to clear up myself. In '72 I didn't feel that much of a difference, but in '75 I really did. I definitely felt a lot sharper. Clear head. . . . I have a degree in sociology. I'm a telex operator. . . .*

"I definitely think it affects your memory for sure. You just forget a lot of things. . . . It affects the short-term memory. Forgetting things you have to do or where you placed your keys. . . .

"I never hallucinated until I was in Hawaii and I got really good pot, just the feeling of walking on soft ground when it was hard, kind of like walking on a marshmallow when I was walking on the sidewalk. . . .

"I used to have feelings of paranoia. At times I felt very worried. I've run when I shouldn't have a few times. . . .

"It makes you hungry, tired a lot of times. Sometimes makes you laugh. . . .

"When I was in college I was stoned quite a bit. I liked reading stoned and doing my homework. . . . I get high every day.

"I used to get stoned every break and lunchtime. It just made the day feel longer. Now I prefer to have a joint when I come home from work. . . .

"Usually on Saturdays and Sundays when I wake up, it's the first thing I do. One thing I like doing stoned is doing my wash. I find I get stoned to do housework and things like that. . . .

"A bong is my favorite way. . . . I prefer hashish. . . . I don't think I'll ever stop. . . . Today I had three bongs so far. . . . I'm stoned now."
—Millie (chronic user)

● *"I ruined my mind with drugs. . . .*

"At the beginning of the 2½ years that I smoked pot, I would get sleepy or sit around and laugh with my girl friends. . . . It would make me very nostalgic for my childhood. Then it would make me giggly and laughy. My brain just flowed. I wouldn't really focus on anything. . . . In the middle, I could smoke pot and go to class or go out.

"It began to make me super-aware of my surroundings. I went through a long period of paranoia. I was physically nervous, uncomfortable, unsure of what I was saying or thinking, and I would lose confidence. But I kept on smoking it because of the peer pressure.

"When combined with other drugs, it caused great depression. . . .

"It would make a fleeting moment last a real long time. It would make me think I was thinking all those profound thoughts that I would later forget. . . .

"I used to bake it in brownies. The effect was more long lasting. I had a job as a waitress. Friday I ate a lot of the brownies. I was so stoned, Monday evening I went to work, I took the food out to the people before I took the silverware. I was so embarrassed, I quit my job. . . .

"The first person I encountered who didn't smoke pot was a friend at the university. He never told me why. I thought it was the strangest thing he didn't smoke. One day two of us were arguing over the division of a bag of pot. My friend said, 'Now you want to know why I don't smoke? It makes people petty. It brings out the worst in people.' . . .

"My brother is an acute alcoholic, and when he combines it with marijuana, it just worsens his behavior. He's a dangerous person to give pot to. He becomes violent. I knew another guy who got bad on pot and also drank." —Rosemary (ex-user)

● *"I didn't use marijuana as much as I did hashish. . . . I'm from the Middle East, and over there it's pretty abundant. . . . I started at a relatively late age. . . . At the age of twenty really I started using it on a regular basis and in large quantity. . . . There were periods that were daily. . . . About 3½ years ago I quit. I was twenty-six. . . .*

"It took some time before I could get high from it and then for about,

I'd say a year, it was really very, very pleasant . . . more than pleasant. And it ranged between, you know, kind of mild high . . . to a stage which is hallucinatory. . . .

"It was kind of a gradual decline, and after three years . . . there started coming feelings of anxiety and paranoiac feelings . . . you know, insane . . . people kind of plot something . . . talk about me behind my back . . . anxiety and tension and less and less of the pleasant feelings. . . . The pleasant effect was not so strong anymore. . . .

"There is a term among smokers which is called 'burning out' and I think that's what happened to me. . . . I did it so much and with such intensity for that three-year period that eventually it kind of, you know, stopped affecting me positively—just negative effects. . . .

"I was at university, college, and I'd say at that time when I was smoking heavily, it did affect my performance at school, my motivation . . . my motivation more than my ability to perform. . . . I was taking mathematics and after that I was taking philosophy and sociology. . . . About two years out of those three years that I used it pretty heavily, I really didn't do anything. I was kind of a hippie, so to speak. . . . I was enrolled in school, but I didn't do anything. . . .

"I know—especially in this country, and that amazes me—that a whole lot of people smoke while they do a lot of things. . . . I worked in a store. . . . Salesmen, including myself, sometimes got a little stoned . . . and, you know, continued to work. . . . I couldn't work the way I would want to. . . . I didn't feel good doing the work, you know. And I didn't feel good at being high. I was kind of torn between—you know, the moment I started getting high, I wanted to quit the situation of work, but I could not. I was at work, right? . . .

"The youngest person that I saw . . . in my country back in the Middle East, I'd say it was a teenager of about fifteen . . . but I know from reports here that young kids of seven, eight do it too. . . . It's bad for their socialization. . . . It tends to make people passive. . . . I don't even, you know, endorse so to speak, you know, drug use as a recreational thing for adults anymore. . . . In my country . . . not as much smoked as here. . . . The drug was present there for centuries I'd say. But the youth-oriented type of use, you know, started mainly in the sixties, you know, here in the United States and spread all over the world. . . .

"I don't regret that I did it. It certainly did a lot of good things for me . . . broadening my perspective, broadening my consciousness. I just became more aware of myself and problems that I had. . . . But one of the things that it does—again, I'm talking from my personal experience—it can disorient a person, because what it does show him is—many *times is relative to*—*the relativity of things in the world, the relativity of things in life. You know, many times it shows a person people and things the way they really are, and by that it strips from him the value system that was entrenched in him by socialization . . . and that brings a person to, you know, a lack of motivation."* —Hiram (ex-user)

• *"The good effects were social acceptance, lowering of inhibitions (which no longer occurs—in fact, there's a raising of inhibitions), a feeling of being different, an escape.*

"Bad effects: an intense hunger that was difficult to satiate; occasional headaches and eye aches; a feeling of being lazy, useless after coming down from pot, a slovenly, lazy, decadent feeling.

"After a year of heavy smoking, not only was my memory deterred, but I felt my reading speed was being influenced. . . .

"I got depressed when I was coming down from the pot. I also felt socially guilty because I felt kind of it was a shame. Young guys, good-looking guys, athletic guys, and we didn't do anything but hang around and get high. Before then, I had been an intense jock, very athletic. I was an all-American boy and I wasn't being very all-American.

"After being stoned, the only feeling of paranoia was that my father or big brother would find out. That was always a fear hanging over my head. . . . The feeling of paranoia is much worse now when I get home. I don't get high with a group of people. I don't feel it's comfortable. I do it mostly alone. . . .

"While stoned, I wasn't as willing to talk to women as when I wasn't stoned. It definitely wasn't a social lubricant. . . .

"I feel that at times I'm not as quick. My memory isn't as quick. My recall is not as quick. I'll forget to do the practical things in life. —Bert (chronic user)

• *"I can see the change that this has done to my own son. From a bright, neat, and ambitious boy, to a lazy (without the thought of tomorrow) dirty (bathing once a week or less from a daily bather) and the more torn and old the clothes are the better. From high fashion to thrift shop, patched and torn is just fine. Even though he is living where he wants, in the hills of Vermont . . . with his fresh air which he says he enjoys, away from the sounds of the city and the commotion of a busy life . . . then why, I ask do you still smoke pot three times a day. How do you convince a person they are ruining their mind. He used to play a beautiful, peaceful piano, now it's wild, and restless. When he smokes he's happy, and then the low, is very low, biting and a put down on everything in life.*

". . . He left college at 19 now he is 23. I'd do anything to help if

he'd let me, and if I knew the right thing to do." —Philadelphia mother (in a letter)

- *"I'm thirty-seven years old. I started kind of late . . . in 1970. My first experience was around 1969. My girlfriend was smoking marijuana, so she gave me a little bit. We were turned on and listening to the radio, some Charlie Mingus. It was just incredible the way the music sounded. I really did experience the drug that time. That was my first time of using it. I think it was a very potent weed. She gave me an ounce for a Christmas present right after that, on that same evening. I had no real interest in it, so I put it away. . . .*

"After I started teaching, I was spending some time with a woman and she liked to get high on liquor or wine mostly actually, and I remembered I had some pot around, so I got it out and started smoking it with her. I had these incredible experiences—I had about three or four of them— in which I would lose all sense of time. Time would seem to slow down and stop and I would lose any sense of where I was. I would go into a different state altogether.

"Often these were scary. I became very insecure and afraid, and the whole sense of reality changed enormously. But even when they were scary, they really intrigued me. I think I was real bored with the sense I had of what reality was and I wanted to explore what the drug made available to me, so I kept on smoking it.

"I had some incredible experiences. I remember going out after I had been smoking it—sounds and everything were different. I heard people coming down the sidewalk and I was real afraid because they would see me stoned out of my mind, so I hid behind a little bush.

"Most of what I enjoyed on grass was listening to music while I was stoned. For the first time I started being able to like rock music. I couldn't stand it before. . . . I used it on weekends. . . .

"My whole circle of friends changed. I started associating with other people who turned on. I was able to understand a lot of things that I had read which before had been opaque to me, such as certain systems of psychology. The idea of the unconscious began to take on some meaning for me. . . .

"I had mild hallucinations, like color enhancements, and I would close my eyes and see patterns. . . .

"Initially when I went out a few times when I was stoned, I would see policemen and I would be afraid they would come get me for some reason. I think it just enhanced or exaggerated a feeling that was already there. . . .

"I got to a place where I wanted to smoke it every night as a way of

relaxing and of just passing the time. I didn't like that. I didn't like to feel it was happening, but it was happening. I felt it increased my passivity. . . .

"I have smoked about twice in the last six months. I still get a feeling my mind expands. After having done a good bit of meditation, on grass I don't get much of a change of consciousness anymore." —Gregory (occasional user, former chronic user)

• *"I was sort of introduced to marijuana . . . when I was thirteen. . . . I felt immediately more like drunk . . . like I was walking on air, that first feeling. . . . I was laughing a lot. I couldn't look at anything without laughing and getting hysterical. I was embarrassed. I knew I was acting strangely, but I couldn't control myself. . . .*

"I had no unpleasant feelings that I can remember at all, except wanting to eat a lot of candy and things like that, and that wasn't even unpleasant. . . . I saw the unpleasantness in retrospect. . . . One of the things I really regret about the whole experience . . . [is mental] disorganization . . . memory sort of things definitely. . . .

"It breaks down your resistance. . . . You lose a sense of values. . . . I was ready to do whatever would excite me or stimulate me. . . . I became very selfish. . . . My highest grade, I think, in the time when I was most intensely involved in this drug thing was a D. . . . It didn't really bother me. . . . I was very antagonistic to anyone who wasn't within my own clique, and anyone who was in my clique if they weren't around, I would put them down." —Lewis (ex-user)

• *"Initially it was a very happy kind of feeling. That's why I enjoyed smoking at parties, places where I was there to have a good time. It was a very light kind of feeling.*

"For the entire time I smoked, depending on the situation, it kind of made me feel paranoid. From the beginning, it heightened feelings of insecurity that I already had. . . . There are delusions: people are talking about you. They're holding perfectly regular conversations and you think they're persecuting you. . . . The feelings of being paranoid began to get worse, and I think it was because I was smoking more potent weed.

"There was a great deal of mental confusion, being not able to just connect thoughts and maintain one clear line of thinking, instead,. getting locked into one little thought and getting deeper and deeper into it and losing perspective. Rather than seeing a whole room, you just see one isolated part of it. You get kind of fixated on one thing, a flower, a picture. Your perspective just gets warped, particularly if you're having a conversation with somebody. You may clue in on one particular thing

*they're saying and lose track of everything else. . . . I used to think
I was smarter when I smoked. I don't think that really means anything. . . .*

"*Sometimes there's depression. Again, things get out of perspective and
one fault becomes very, very big. Something that's very insignificant looms
very big and much worse than it is.*

"*I became much more withdrawn. I was already quiet and shy and
this made it worse. . . .*

"*In the early days I could go to bed and sleep it off. The older I got,
it seemed that I went to bed high and woke up high. . . . I was draggy
and groggy. It took a couple of hours to wear out. . . . I'd feel tired a
lot and draggy and not getting as much done. . . .*

"*I don't smoke at all anymore, but my husband does, two, three, or
four times a week. He seems normal. . . .* —Anna (ex-user)

• "*I started in 1966. I was a New York student, around eighteen. The
first time, I smoked a joint of pretty good pot. I was at home with some
friends, listening to music. I was listening to* The Rite of Spring *by Stra-
vinsky on the record player. It was frightening to the point where I wanted
to turn it off, but it didn't occur to me that I could do it. . . .*

"*I liked it. I found, particularly at the beginning, that I was more
open to new stimuli. It interfered with some of my usual patterns of looking at things. It made it possible to look at new things in a new way.*

"*There was occasional paranoia, an interruption of short-term memory, difficulty in concentration in certain types of detail work. In studying, I found I could do certain type of theoretical work fine stoned, but
I found I would make more mistakes in computation or in cranking out
details. . . .*

"*I took tests stoned and unstoned. If I were doing a paper on some
aspects of math or logic, my discrimination about technical detail was
not as high. I might come up with a theory that was wrong. There was
some step where I did not see a contradiction. I might do some of my
rough notes stoned and go over it when not stoned. Sometimes I found
errors, sometimes not. . . .*

"*Toward the beginning, time went slower. You had the sense that more
time had passed than actually passed. I can remember being in an ele-
vator and having a sensation that it was taking so long to go down that
it might go on forever. . . .*

"*You can react differently to the same batch if you're in a different
mood. If you're particularly jovial, it can make you more jovial. If you're
partly depressed, it can make you more depressed. . . .*

"*I stopped smoking for a year five years ago, smoked a couple years more, then quit. . . . There's a difference in the quality of thought. . . . There's a clarity that I have when I don't smoke that was lacking when I was smoking, and I'd say the type of clarity I'm talking about is to not have smoked pot for a month or two before the effects disappear. When you're smoking regularly when you're not high, there's still some residual effect."* —Joe (ex-user).

• *"Our problem is a college boy who had never used drugs before going away to school. It is now two years since he started college and apparently started using marijuana and hashish, possibly other drugs. We have been told by a practicing psychologist, an MD and a psychiatrist that there is absolutely nothing which can be done to help this son to stop the use of these chemicals even though:*

"1. He seems to have stopped growing emotionally.

"2. He has lost interest in just about everything.

"3. He has gone from a person of integrity and fundamental honesty to a person who is completely untrustworthy.

"4. He has gone from an open, communicative person to one who communicates hardly at all.

"We have read everything we can get on the subject, we have attended classes conducted for parents and we are told we must accept the situation. It does not seem possible there is no alternative." —Minneapolis mother (in a letter)

3

• *"I have a very good friend, my best friend from elementary school to college. She's nuts now. The weed itself didn't do that. She became schizophrenic. She began to hear voices. The pot made it worse. She could handle it when she wasn't smoking, but when she got stoned, it just took her out completely. Once she stopped, she went back to being normal.* — Anna (ex-user)

• *"Back in 1968–69 I became a steady user of marijuana, and I really thought it was wonderful stuff. . . . Things would pop into my mind that had happened a long time ago. . . . I thought it intensified—maybe it really did—my hearing ability. You think you're hearing more music than you did before. I would smoke two or three marijuana cigarettes a day. . . .*

"I thought it was great for about three years, and then I started to get

a very bad reaction. . . . It started to make me extremely nervous and jumpy. In fact, I would actually tremble and shake if it was really strong stuff. I would get terrible, negative feelings, like certain fatalistic feelings, like it's a terrible world, everything is closing in, everything is bad. I mean it was like I was allergic to it and my body or mind was telling me it was. . . .

"After a while I started to tell myself that all I was doing was sitting around and daydreaming with this crap. . . . And now it scares the hell out of me. . . . I have lots of friends who smoke it and they sit around and pass joints around and I'll take a puff once in a while, but if I really smoke, I get this reaction." —Oscar (former chronic user)

• *"There's a lot of paranoia. That's the only thing I don't like about it. After you smoke it sometimes, you just feel paranoid. Maybe if you see a police officer, you'll get kind of paranoid. Sometimes what people say to you. . . .*

"The only time I get kind of crazy is when I drink and smoke marijuana. A wild kind of feeling. You get loose and have funny thoughts. Sometimes you get violent on it. Maybe you have an argument and get kind of violent. It kind of takes over your mind." —Charlie (chronic user)

• *"For a month I can feel high even though I haven't done any smoking. The effects come on for a half-hour, maybe up to an hour at the longest. When I'm detoxing, I get a rush. It comes on you as though the being within your head is being pushed backwards. There's a zooming. It's quite exhilarating.*

"When you're detoxing and you're doing something and you get the rush, it's quite inconvenient. It's quite a dizzy and heady feeling. The rush is very intense and comes on very quickly. . . .

"The resin stays in your body. It does take that long. It's being cleansed out of your body. I spoke to others. It's very strange because you don't expect it." —Betty (long-time user, trying to quit)

• *"It's happened on several occasions, where I feel like I've just smoked a joint and I haven't. . . . It happened once while I was flying and it scared me to death."* —Ted (ex-user, except for an occasional puff)

• *"One of the things that happened . . . was seeing sort of yellow lights, halos or things like that around people, or sometimes their faces changing—that type of thing. . . .*

"One job I had after I graduated from college, in the summer, was the night shift in a meat-packing factory, and I wasn't using drugs any longer.

. . . It was a month and half after I stopped smoking marijuana, or something like that. . . . I started to have these kind of hallucinations that I was in hell. . . . I would see a man who was shoveling filler for hot dogs . . . into a vat or something and . . . I sort of had the feeling that I am in the Last Judgment and this is Charon mixing the hot dog filler by the river Styx." —Nathan (ex-user)

• *"It was good for relaxation, forgetting about problems and hassles, and a social tool. . . .*

"Among the bad effects: paranoia. . . . In the middle of my smoking period, I thought no one liked me and people just wanted to make fun of me and put me down. . . . The paranoia was still there, to different degrees, up to four months after I quit. . . .

"Plain forgetfulness, especially things I didn't want to do, chores around the house. My mom told me to do something; five minutes later I'd forget it. Reading books was very hard toward the last year of smoking, my last year in high school. I found myself reading over lines frequently. Memorizing the gist of a book was very hard. I would forget that very often. . . .

"Not real physical distortions, but colors and colored letters zooming off into space, and delusions of how people were perceiving me. . . .

"Depression too. At times it got pretty bad. I was pretty withdrawn. My parents noticed that especially during those four years. . . .

"During that period I felt it was okay to lie to my parents about smoking pot, and that extended to staying out late. I said I was at a friend's house and I'd stay out all night. Lying became perfectly okay. . . .

"I went to a psychiatrist for about six months. First he was thinking that maybe I needed marijuana as an escape. Then after I quit, he thought it was a very good thing because I was so dependent on it. . . . He was very respectful of the dependence. . . . He used it himself. . . .

"I know a friend who has gone psychotic as a result of a lot of drugs. He started with marijuana. He must have been thirteen or fourteen. He also started drinking and smoking. . . . He was paranoid and was hospitalized on and off for a few months. He's off it now and he's much better." —Steve (ex-user)

• *"I have a friend who is a severe schizophrenic who is all right until he smokes as little as 1½ joints of pot, and then he becomes so psychotic that he must be hospitalized.*

"He desires the pot as soon as he gets out of the hospital after a long stay, I believe to retreat to his world of unreality so as not to have to face the real world." —Louise (in a letter)

SOURCE NOTES

The notes for each section are independently numbered and listed.

I. Cannabis and the Body:

THE LUNGS AND RESPIRATORY SYSTEM

1. Harris Rosenkrantz and Robert W. Fleischman, "Effects of Cannabis on Lungs," in *Marihuana: Biological Effects*, p. 279, edited by Gabriel G. Nahas and William D. M. Paton, Pergamon Press, Oxford and New York, 1979.

2. Jerrold G. Bernstein, David Becker, Thomas F. Babor, and Jack H. Mendelson, "Physiological Assessments: Cardiopulmonary Function," in *The Use of Marihuana: A Psychological and Physiological Inquiry*, pp. 147–48, edited by Jack H. Mendelson, A. Michael Rossi, and Roger E. Meyer, Plenum Press, New York, 1974.

3. Hardin B. Jones and Helen C. Jones, *Sensual Drugs*, pp. 226–27, Cambridge University Press, 1977.

4. C. J. Miras, "Some Aspects of Cannabis Action," in *Hashish: Its Chemistry and Pharmacology*, pp. 37–53, edited by G. E. W. Wolstenholme and Julie Knight, J. & A. Churchill Ltd., London, 1965.

5. S. Agurell, I. M. Nilsson, A. Ohlsson, and F. Sandberg, "On the Metabolism of Tritium-Labelled Delta-1-Tetrahydrocannabinol in the Rabbit," *Biochemical Pharmacology*, v. 19, pp. 1,333–39, 1970.

6. H. A. Klausner and J. V. Dingell, "Studies on the Metabolism and Distribution of Delta-9-Tetrahydrocannabinol," *The Pharmacologist*, v. 12, p. 259, 1970.

7. J. Steve Kennedy and William J. Waddell, "Whole-Body Autoradiography of the Pregnant Mouse after Administration of 14-C-delta-9-THC," *Toxicology and Applied Pharmacology*, v. 22, pp. 252–58, 1972.

8. R. I. Freudenthal, J. Martin, and M. E. Wall, "Distribution of Delta-9-tetrahydrocannabinol in the Mouse," *British Journal of Pharmacology*, v. 44, pp. 244–49, 1972.

9. I. C. Chopra and R. N. Chopra, "The Use of the Cannabis Drugs in India," *Bulletin on Narcotics* (United Nations, Geneva), v. 9, pp. 4–6, 1957.

10. Gurbakhsh S. Chopra, "Studies on Psycho-Clinical Aspects of Long-Term Marihuana Use in 124 Cases," *International Journal of the Addictions*, v. 8(6), p. 1,016, 1973.

11. Indian Hemp Drugs Commission, *Report of the Indian Hemp Drugs Commission, 1893–94*, first of seven volumes, Government Central Printing Office, Simla, India, 1894; reproduced in *Marijuana Report of the Indian Hemp Drugs Commission, 1893–1894*, Thos. Jefferson Publishing Co., Silver Spring, Maryland, 1969.

12. R. N. Chopra and Gurbakhsh S. Chopra, "The Present Position of Hemp-Drug Addiction in India," *Indian Medical Research Memoirs* (Supplementary Series to the *Indian Journal of Medical Research*), Memoir No. 31, pp. 75–77, July, 1939.

13. Gurbakhsh S. Chopra, op. cit., pp. 1,015–17, 1,025–26.

486

14. U.S. Congress, *Marijuana-Hashish Epidemic and Its Impact on United States Security* (hearings before the Subcommittee to Investigate the Administration of the Internal Security Act and Other Internal Security Laws, Committee on the Judiciary, U.S. Senate, 93rd Congress, Second Session), p. 150, 1974.

15. Vera Rubin and Lambros Comitas, *Ganja in Jamaica: A Medical Anthropological Study of Chronic Marijuana Use*, pp. 84 and 115, Mouton & Co., The Hague and Paris, 1975. Also E. K. Cruickshank, "Physical Assessment of 30 Chronic Cannabis Users and 30 Matched Controls," *Annals of the New York Academy of Sciences*, v. 282, p. 162, 1976.

16. Rubin and Comitas, op. cit., chapters 6, 7, and 12, and appendix 3. Also Cruickshank, op. cit., pp. 162–67.

17. U.S. Congress, *Health Consequences of Marihuana Abuse: Recent Findings* (hearings before the Select Committee on Narcotics Abuse and Control, House of Representatives, 96th Congress, First Session), p. 18, 1979.

18. R. D. Magus and L. S. Harris, "Carcinogenic Potential of Marihuana Smoke Condensate," *Federation Proceedings*, v. 30, n. 2, p. 279, 1971.

19. John C. Cottrell, Seung S. Sohn, and Wolfgang H. Vogel, "Toxic Effects of Marihuana Tar on Mouse Skin," *Archives of Environmental Health*, v. 26, pp. 277–78, 1973.

20. D. Hoffmann, K. D. Brunnemann, G. B. Gori, and E. L. Wynder, "On the Carcinogenicity of Marijuana Smoke," *Recent Advances in Phytochemistry*, v. 9, pp. 63–81, 1975.

21. Cecile Leuchtenberger and Rudolf Leuchtenberger, "Cytological and Cytochemical Studies of the Effects of Fresh Marihuana Cigarette Smoke on Growth and DNA Metabolism of Animal and Human Lung Cultures," in *Pharmacology of Marihuana* (a monograph of the National Institute on Drug Abuse), pp. 595–612, edited by Monique C. Braude and Stephen Szara, Raven Press, New York, 1976. Also congressional hearings, 1974, op. cit., pp. 126–42.

22. M. Novotny, M. L. Lee, and K. D. Bartle, "A Possible Chemical Basis for the Higher Mutagenicity of Marijuana Smoke as Compared to Tobacco Smoke," *Experientia*, v. 32, n. 3, pp. 280–82, 1976.

23. Alton Ochsner and Michàel De Bakey, "Symposium on Cancer. Primary Pulmonary Malignancy," *Journal of Surgery, Gynecology, and Obstetrics*, v. 68, p. 435, 1939.

24. Associated Press, "Asbestos firm sues tobacco makers," *San Francisco Examiner*, September 18, 1980.

25. Congressional hearings, 1974, op. cit., pp. 288–314.

26. Forest S. Tennant, Jr., "Histopathological and Clinical Abnormalities of the Respiratory System in Chronic Hashish Smokers," *Substance and Alcohol Actions / Misuse*, v. 1, pp. 93–100, 1980.

27. Congressional hearings, 1974, op. cit., p. 75.

28. Ibid., pp. 61 and 70.

29. Louis Vachon, Muiris X. FitzGerald, Norman H. Solliday, Ira A. Gould, and Edward A. Gaensler, "Single-Dose Effect of Marihuana Smoke," *New England Journal of Medicine*, v. 288, n. 19, pp. 985–89, May 10, 1973.

30. Donald P. Tashkin, Bertrand J. Shapiro, and Ira M. Frank, "Acute Pulmonary Physiologic Effects of Smoked Marijuana and Oral Delta-9-Tetrahydrocannabinol in Healthy Young Men," *New England Journal of Medicine*, v. 289, pp. 336–40, August 16, 1973.

31. Idem, "Acute Effects of Smoked Marijuana and Oral Delta-9-Tetrahydrocannabinol on Specific Airway Conductance in Asthmatic Subjects," *American Review of Respiratory Disease*, v. 109, pp. 420–29, 1974.

32. Donald P. Tashkin, Bertrand J. Shapiro, Y. Enoch Lee, and Charles E. Harper, "Effects of Smoked Marijuana in Experimentally Induced Asthma," *American Review of Respiratory Disease*, v. 112, pp. 377–86, 1975.

33. Bernstein et al., op. cit., pp. 147–60.

34. Jerrold G. Bernstein, John C. Kuehnle, and Jack H. Mendelson, "Medical Implications of Marijuana Use," *American Journal of Drug and Alcohol Abuse*, v. 3(2), pp. 347–61, 1976.

35. Donald P. Tashkin, Bertrand J. Shapiro, Y. Enoch Lee, and Charles E. Harper, "Subacute Effects of Heavy Marihuana Smoking on Pulmonary Function in Healthy Men," *New England Journal of Medicine*, v. 294, pp. 125–29, January 15, 1976.

36. Donald P. Tashkin, Barry M. Calvarese, Michael S. Simmons, and Bertrand J. Shapiro, "Respiratory Status of Seventy-Four Habitual Marijuana Smokers, *Chest*, v. 78, n. 5, November, 1980. (Presented at the annual meeting, American Thoracic Society, Boston, May, 1978.)

37. U.S. Congress, *Health Consequences of Marihuana Use* (hearings before the Subcommittee on Criminal Justice, Committee on the Judiciary, U.S. Senate, 96th Congress, Second Session), pp. 110–20, 1980.

38. J. Hernandez-Bolaños, E. W. Swenson, and W. J. Coggins, "Preservation of Pulmonary Function in Regular, Heavy, Long-Term Marijuana Smokers," *American Review of Respiratory Disease*, v. 113, n. 4(2), p. 100, 1976.

39. J. C. Boulougouris, C. P. Panayiotopoulos, E. Antypas, A. Liakos, and C. Stefanis, "Effects of Chronic Hashish Use on Medical Status in 44 Users Compared With 38 Controls," *Annals of the New York Academy of Sciences*, v. 282, pp. 168–72, 1976.

40. Donald P. Tashkin and Sidney Cohen, *Marijuana Smoking and Its Effects on the Lungs*, p. 28, The American Council on Marijuana and Other Psychoactive Drugs, New York, 1981.

41. P. E. Roy, F. Magnan-Lapointe, N. D. Huy, and M. Boutet, "Chronic Inhalation of Marijuana and Tobacco in Dogs: Pulmonary Pathology," *Research Communications in Chemical Pathology and Pharmacology*, v. 14, n. 2, June, 1976.

42. Rosenkrantz and Fleischman, op. cit., pp. 279–99.

43. Steven L. Kagen, "Aspergillus: An Inhalable Contaminant of Marijuana" (letter), *New England Journal of Medicine*, v. 304, n. 8, February 19, 1981. Also John F. Turck, untitled news release from the Medical College of Wisconsin, same date.

44. Michael J. Chusid, Jeffrey A. Gelfano, Cathy Nutter, and Anthony S. Fauci, "Pulmonary Aspergillosis, Inhalation of Contaminated Marijuana Smoke, Chronic Granulomatous Disease," *Annals of Internal Medicine*, v. 82, n. 5, pp. 682–83, May, 1975.

45. Roberto Llamas, D. Robert Hart, and Neil S. Schneider, "Allergic Bronchopulmonary Aspergillosis Associated with Smoking Moldy Marihuana," *Chest*, v. 73, n. 6, pp. 871–72, June, 1978.

46. Congressional hearings, 1974, op. cit., p. 77.

47. Centers for Disease Control, "Salmonellosis Traced to Marijuana—Ohio, Michigan," *MMWR, Morbidity and Mortality Weekly Report*, v. 30, n. 7, February 27, 1981.

48. J. Thomas Ungerleider, Therese Andrysiak, Donald P. Tashkin, and Robert Peter Gale, "Contamination of Marihuana Cigarettes With Pathogenic Bacteria—Possible Source of Infection in Cancer Patients," *Cancer Treatment Reports*, v. 66, n. 3, pp. 589–91, March, 1982.

49. Carlton E. Turner, *The Marijuana Controversy*, p. 14, The American Council on Marijuana and Other Psychoactive Drugs, New York, 1981.

50. Committee to Study the Health-Related Effects of Cannabis and Its Derivatives (Arnold S. Relman, chairman), *Marijuana and Health*, pp. 186–88, National Academy Press, Washington, D.C., 1982.

51. Philip J. Landrigan, Kenneth E. Powell, Levy M. James, and Philip R. Taylor, "Paraquat and Marijuana: Epidemiologic Risk Assessment," *American Journal of Public Health*, v. 73, n. 7, July, 1983.

52. William E. Carter and Paul L. Doughty, "Social and Cultural Aspects of Cannabis Use in Costa Rica" in "Chronic Cannabis Use," *Annals of the New York Academy of Sciences*, v. 282, pp. 2–3, 1976.

53. D. Hoffmann et al., op. cit., p. 78.

54. Bernstein et al. (1974), op. cit., p. 148.

SEX, REPRODUCTION AND OFFSPRING

1. Erich Goode, "Drug Use and Sexual Activity on a College Campus," *American Journal of Psychiatry*, v. 128, n. 10, April, 1972.

2. Gurbakhsh S. Chopra and Balwant S. Jandu, "Psychoclinical Effects of Long-Term Mari-

juana Use in 275 Indian Chronic Users. A Comparative Assessment of Effects in Indian and USA Users," *Annals of the New York Academy of Sciences*, v. 282, p. 103, 1976.

3. C. Holden, "House Chops Sex-Pot Probe," *Science*, v. 192, p. 450, April 30, 1976.

4. Erich Bloch, Benjamin Thysen, Gene A. Morrill, Eliot Gardner, and George Fujimoto, "Effects of Cannabinoids on Reproduction and Development," *Vitamins and Hormones*, v. 36, pp. 203–58, 1978.

5. Robert C. Kolodny, William H. Masters, and Virginia E. Johnson, *Textbook of Sexual Medicine*, pp. 339–40, Little, Brown and Company, Boston, 1979.

6. Dioscorides and John Goodyer, *The Greek Herbal of Dioscorides*, p. 290, Hafner Publishing Co., 1959.

7. Galen, al-Antaki, and others quoted by Franz Rosenthal, *The Herb: Hashish Versus Medieval Muslim Society*, E. J. Brill, Leiden, Netherlands, 1971.

8. Indian Hemp Drugs Commission, *Report of the Indian Hemp Drugs Commission, 1893–94*, first of seven volumes, Government Central Printing Office, Simla, India, 1894; reproduced in *Marijuana Report of the Indian Hemp Drugs Commission, 1893–1894*, Thos. Jefferson Publishing Co., Silver Spring, Maryland, 1969.

9. R. N. Chopra and Gurbakhsh S. Chopra, "The Present Position of Hemp-Drug Addition in India," *Indian Medical Research Memoirs* (Supplementary Series to the *Indian Journal of Medical Research*), Memoir No. 31, pp. 79–84, July, 1939.

10. John Harmon and Menelaos A. Aliapoulios, "Gynecomastia in Marihuana Users," *New England Journal of Medicine*, v. 287, p. 936, November 2, 1972.

11. Idem, "Marijuana-Induced Gynecomastia: Clinical and Laboratory Experience," *Surgical Forum*, v. 25, p. 423, 1974.

12. Willard Cates, Jr., and James N. Pope, "Gynecomastia and Cannabis Smoking: A Nonassociation among U.S. Army Soldiers," *American Journal of Surgery*, v. 134, pp. 613–15, November, 1977.

13. Hardin B. Jones and Helen C. Jones, *Sensual Drugs*, pp. 132–35, Cambridge University Press, 1977.

14. U.S. Congress, *Marihuana-Hashish Epidemic and Its Impact on United States Security* (hearings before the Subcommittee to Investigate the Administration of the Internal Security Act and Other Internal Security Laws, Committee on the Judiciary, U.S. Senate, 93rd Congress, Second Session), p. 240, 1974.

15. Robert C. Kolodny, William H. Masters, Robert M. Kolodner, and Gelson Toro, "Depression of Plasma Testosterone Levels After Chronic Intensive Marihuana Use," *New England Journal of Medicine*, v. 290, pp. 872–74, April 18, 1974. Also congressional hearings, 1974, op. cit., pp. 117–26.

16. Jack H. Mendelson, John Kuehnle, James Ellingboe, and Thomas F. Babor, "Plasma Testosterone Levels Before, During and After Chronic Marihuana Smoking," *New England Journal of Medicine*, v. 291, pp. 1,051–55, November 14, 1974.

17. Robert C. Kolodny, Phyllis Lessin, Gelson Toro, William H. Masters, and Sidney Cohen, "Depression of Plasma Testosterone with Acute Marihuana Administration," in *Pharmacology of Marihuana* (a monograph of the National Institute on Drug Abuse), v. 2, pp. 217–27, edited by Monique C. Braude and Stephen Szara, Raven Press, New York, 1976.

18. Congressional hearings, 1974, op. cit., pp. 121–22.

19. W. J. Coggins, Edward W. Swenson, William W. Dawson, Alvara Fernandez-Salas, Juan Hernandez-Bolanos, C. Francisco Jiminez-Antillon, Joaquin Roberto Solano, Rodolpho Vinocour, and Federico Faerron-Valdez, "Health Status of Chronic Heavy Cannabis Users" in "Chronic Cannabis Use," *Annals of the New York Academy of Sciences*, v. 282, pp. 148–61, 1976.

20. U.S. Congress, *Health Consequences of Marihuana Use* (hearings before the Subcommittee on Criminal Justice of the Committee on the Judiciary, U.S. Senate, 96th Congress, Second Session), pp. 92–96, 1980. Also Susan Dalterio, Andrzej Bartke, and Denise Mayfield, "Delta-9-Tetrahydrocannabinol Increases Plasma Testosterone Concentrations in Mice," *Science*, v. 213, pp. 581–83, July 31, 1981.

21. Susan Dalterio, Fouad Badr, Andrzej Bartke, and Denise Mayfield, "Cannabinoids in Male Mice: Effects on Fertility and Spermatogenesis," *Science*, v. 216, pp. 315–16, April 16, 1982.

22. Hardin B. Jones and Helen C. Jones, op. cit., p. 121.

23. Kenneth C. Copeland, Louis E. Underwood, and Judson J. Van Wyk, "Marihuana Smoking and Pubertal Arrest," *Journal of Pediatrics*, v. 96, n. 6, pp. 1,079–80, June, 1980.

24. V. P. Dixit, V. N. Sharma, and N. K. Lohiya, "The Effect of Chronically Administered Cannabis Extract on the Testicular Function of Mice," *European Journal of Pharmacology* (Netherlands), v. 26, pp. 111–14, 1974.

25. Cecile Leuchtenberger, Rudolf Leuchtenberger, J. Zbinden, and E. Schleh, "Cytological and Cytochemical Effects of Whole Smoke and of the Gas Vapor Phase from Marihuana Cigarettes on Growth and DNA Metabolism of Cultured Mammalian Cells," in *Marihuana: Chemistry, Biochemistry, and Cellular Effects*, pp. 243–56, edited by Gabriel G. Nahas, Springer-Verlag, New York, 1976.

26. Wylie C. Hembree III, Philip Zeidenberg, and Gabriel G. Nahas, "Marihuana's Effects on Human Gonadal Function," ibid., pp. 521–32.

27. Wylie C. Hembree III, Gabriel G. Nahas, Philip Zeidenberg, and H. F. S. Huang, "Changes in Human Spermatozoa Associated with High Dose Marihuana Smoking," in *Marihuana: Biological Effects*, pp. 429–39, edited by Gabriel G. Nahas and William D. M. Paton, Pergamon Press, Oxford and New York, 1979.

28. Robert P. Walton, *Marihuana, America's New Drug Problem*, p. 156, J. B. Lippincott Co., Philadelphia, 1938. Also B. C. Bose, R. Vijayvargiya, A. Q. Saifi, and A. W. Bhagwat, "Chemical and Pharmacological Investigations of Cannabis Indica (Linn), Part I," *Archives Internationales de Pharmacodynamie et de Therapie*, v. 146, pp. 99–105, 1963.

29. C. J. Miras, "Some Aspects of Cannabis Action," in *Hashish: Its Chemistry and Pharmacology*, p. 37–53, edited by G. E. W. Wolstenholme and Julie Knight, J. & A. Churchill Ltd., London, 1965.

30. Juhana Idänpään-Heikkilä, G. Edward Fritchie, Leo F. Englert, Beng T. Ho, and William M. McIsaac, "Placental Transfer of Tritiated-1-delta-9-tetrahydrocannabinol," *New England Journal of Medicine*, v. 281, p. 330, August 7, 1969.

31. J. Steve Kennedy and William J. Waddell, "Whole-Body Autoradiography of the Pregnant Mouse after Administration of 14-C-delta-9-THC," *Toxicology and Applied Pharmacology*, v. 22, pp. 252–58, 1972.

32. R. I. Freudenthal, J. Martin, and M. E. Wall, "Distribution of Delta-9-tetrahydrocannabinol in the Mouse," *British Journal of Pharmacology*, v. 44, pp. 244–49, 1972.

33. T. V. N. Persaud and A. C. Ellington, "Cannabis in Early Pregnancy," *Lancet*, p. 1,306, December 16, 1967.

34. Idem, "Teratogenic Activity of Cannabis Resin," ibid., p. 406, August 17, 1968.

35. Frederick Hecht, Rodney K. Beals, Martin H. Lees, Hugh Jolly, and Patricia Roberts, "Lysergic-Acid-Diethylamide and Cannabis as Possible Teratogens in Man," ibid., p. 1,087, November 16, 1968.

36. Gerson Carakushansky, Richard L. Neu, and Lytt I. Gardner, "Lysergide and Cannabis as Possible Teratogens in Man," ibid., pp. 150–51, January 18, 1969.

37. Harris Rosenkrantz, "Effects of Cannabis on Fetal Development of Rodents," in *Marihuana: Biological Effects*, pp. 479–99, op. cit. Also congressional hearings, 1980, op. cit., pp. 88–92. Also personal letters and conversations.

38. David M. Grilly, Douglas P. Ferraro, and Monique C. Braude, "Observations on the Reproductive Activity of Chimpanzees Following Long-term Exposure to Marihuana," *Pharmacology*, v. 11, pp. 304–7, 1974.

39. Carol Grace Smith, Michael Timothy Smith, Norma F. Besch, Roy G. Smith, and Ricardo H. Asch, "Effect of Delta-9-Tetrahydrocannabinol (THC) on Female Reproductive Function," in *Marihuana: Biological Effects*, op. cit., pp. 449–67. Also congressional hearings, 1980, op. cit., pp. 70–77.

40. Carol Grace Smith, Ramona G. Almirez, Jeffrey Berenberg, and Ricardo H. Asch, "Tolerance Develops to the Disruptive Effects of Delta-9-Tetrahydrocannabinol on Primate Menstrual Cycle," *Science*, v. 219, pp. 1,453–55, March 25, 1983.

41. C. G. Smith, N. F. Besch, and R. H. Asch, "Effects of Marihuana on the Reproductive System," *Advances in Sex Hormone Research*, v. 4, pp. 273–94, 1980.

42. Congressional hearings, 1980, op. cit., pp. 77–83.

43. Mari S. Golub, E. N. Sassenrath, and Loring F. Chapman, "Regulation of Visual Attention in Offspring of Female Monkeys Treated Chronically with Delta-9-Tetrahydrocannabinol," *Developmental Psychobiology*, v. 14, n. 6, pp. 507–12, November, 1981.

44. R. C. Kolodny, J. E. Bauman, R. L. Dornbush, and S. R. Webster, "Chronic Marihuana Use By Women: Menstrual Cycle and Endocrine Findings," paper presented at the Second Annual Conference on Marijuana, American Council on Marijuana and Other Psychoactive Drugs, New York University, June 28, 1979. Also congressional hearings, 1980, op. cit., pp. 83–88.

45. Robert C. Kolodny, Phyllis Lessin, William H. Masters, and Gelson Toro, unpublished data, 1976, cited in *Textbook of Sexual Medicine*, op. cit., p. 337.

46. A. Jakubovic, T. Hattori, and P. L. McGeer, "Radioactivity in Suckled Rats After Giving 14-C-Tetrahydrocannabinol to the Mother," *European Journal of Pharmacology* (Netherlands), v. 22, pp. 221–23, 1973. Also P. L. McGeer and A. Jakubovic, "Ultrastructural and Biochemical Changes in CNS Induced by Marihuana," in *Marihuana: Biological Effects*, op. cit., pp. 519–30.

47. A. Jakubovic, R. M. Tait, and P. L. McGeer, "Excretion of THC and its Metabolites in Ewes' Milk," *Toxicology and Applied Pharmacology*, v. 28, pp. 38–43, 1974.

48. Fu-Chuan Chao, Donald E. Green, Irene S. Forrest, Joel N. Kaplan, Ann Winship-Ball, and Monique Braude, "The Passage of 14-C-Delta-9-Tetrahydrocannabinol Into the Milk of Lactating Squirrel Monkeys," *Research Communications in Chemical Pathology and Pharmacology*, v. 15, n. 2, pp. 303–17, October, 1976.

49. P. A. Fried, "Short and Long-term Effects of Pre-natal Cannabis Inhalation upon Rat Offspring," *Psychopharmacology*, v. 50, pp. 285–91, 1976.

50. P. A. Fried and A. T. Charlesbois, "Cannabis Administered During Pregnancy: First- and Second-generation Effects in Rats," *Psyiological Psychology*, v. 7, n. 3, pp. 307–10, 1979.

51. J. Szepsenwol, J. Fletcher, G. L. Murison, and E. Toro-Goyco, "Long Term Effects of Delta-9-Tetrahydrocannabinol in Mice," in *Marihuana: Biological Effects*, pp. 359–70, op. cit.

52. Congressional hearings, 1980, op. cit., pp. 92–96. Also Susan Dalterio and Andrzej Bartke, "Perinatal Exposure to Cannabinoids Alters Male Reproductive Function in Mice," *Science*, v. 205, pp. 1,420–22, September 28, 1979. Also Associated Press, Ann Arbor, Michigan, "Researchers say pot cuts sex drive in mice," *Oakland Tribune and Eastbay Today*, August 15, 1980.

53. P. A. Fried, "Marihuana Use by Pregnant Women: Neurobehavioral Effects in Neonates," *Drug and Alcohol Dependence* (Switzerland), v. 6, pp. 415–24, December, 1980; idem, "Marihuana Use by Pregnant Women and Effects on Offspring: An Update," *Neurobehavioral Toxicology and Teratology*, v. 4, pp. 451–54, 1982; idem, *Pregnancy and Life-Style Habits*, Beaufort Books, New York and Toronto, 1983.

54. Mario Perez-Reyes and Monroe E. Wall, "Presence of Delta-9-Tetrahydrocannabinol in Human Milk," *New England Journal of Medicine*, v. 307, pp. 819–20, September 23, 1982.

55. Ralph Hingson, Joel J. Alpert, Nancy Day, Elizabeth Dooling, Herbert Kayne, Suzette Morelock, Edgar Oppenheimer, and Barry Zuckerman, "Effects of Maternal Drinking and Marijuana Use on Fetal Growth and Development," *Pediatrics*, v. 70, n. 4, pp. 539–46, October, 1982.

THE HEART AND CIRCULATORY SYSTEM

1. J. Sterne and C. Ducastaing, "Les Artérites du Cannabis Indica," *Archives des Maladies du Coeur et des Vaisseaux*, v. 53, n. 2, pp. 143–47, 1960.

2. U.S. Congress, *Health Consequences of Marihuana Use* (hearings before the Subcommittee on Criminal Justice of the Committee on the Judiciary, U.S. Senate, 96th Congress, Second Session), pp. 6–7, 1980.

3. Reese T. Jones, "Human Effects: An Overview," in *Marijuana Research Findings: 1980* (Research Monograph Series 31), pp. 65–66, edited by Robert C. Peterson, National Institute on Drug Abuse, Rockville, Maryland, 1980.

4. Jacques-Joseph Moreau (de Tours), *Hashish and Mental Illness*, pp. 25–26, translated by Gordon J. Barnett, Raven Press, New York, 1973.

5. Accounts of Wood through Skliar and Iwanow reported by Robert P. Walton in *Marihuana, America's New Drug Problem*, J. B. Lippincott Co., Philadelphia, 1938.

6. R. N. Chopra and Gurbakhsh S. Chopra, "The Present Position of Hemp-Drug Addiction in India," *Indian Medical Research Memoirs* (Supplementary Series to the *Indian Journal of Medical Research*), Memoir No. 31, pp. 75–76, 78, 109–10, July, 1939.

7. Mayor's Committee on Marihuana, *The Marihuana Problem in the City of New York—Sociological, Psychological, and Pharmacological Studies*, pp. 51–64, Catell, Lancaster, Pennsylvania, 1944.

8. Frances Ames, "A Clinical and Metabolic Study of Acute Intoxication With Cannabis Sativa and Its Role in the Model Psychoses," *Journal of Mental Science* (South Africa), v. 104, pp. 972–99, 1958.

9. Harris Isbell, C. W. Gorodetzsky, D. R. Jasinksi, U. Claussen, F. v. Spulak, and F. Korte, "Effects of (—)-Delta-9-Trans-Tetrahydrocannabinol in Man, *Psychopharmacologia* (Berlin), v. 11, pp. 184–88, 1967.

10. Harris Isbell and D. R. Jasinksi, "A Comparison of LSD-25 with (—)-Delta-9-Trans-Tetrahydrocannabinol (THC) and Attempted Cross Tolerance between LSD and THC," ibid., v. 14, pp. 115–23, 1969.

11. Stephen Johnson and Edward F. Domino, "Some Cardiovascular Effects of Marihuana Smoking in Normal Volunteers," *Clinical Pharmacology and Therapeutics*, v. 12, n. 5, pp. 762–68, 1971.

12. Pierre F. Renault, Charles R. Schuster, Richard Heinrich, and Daniel X. Freemann, *Science*, v. 174, pp. 589–91, November 5, 1971.

13. Marc Galanter, Richard J. Wyatt, Louis Lemberger, Herbert Weingartner, Tom B. Vaughan, and Walton T. Roth, "Effects on Humans of Delta-9-Tetrahydrocannabinol Administered by Smoking," *Science*, v. 176, pp. 934–36, May 26, 1972.

14. Peter Beaconsfield, Jean Ginsburg, and Rebecca Rainsbury, "Marihuana Smoking: Cardiovascular Effects in Man and Possible Mechanisms," *New England Journal of Medicine*, v. 287, n. 5, pp. 209–12, August 3, 1972.

15. Mahendra S. Kochar and Michael J. Hosko, "Electrocardiograqhic Effects of Marihuana," *JAMA, The Journal of the American Medical Association*, v. 225, n. 1, pp. 25–27, July 2, 1973.

16. Samuel Vaisrub, "Cannabis and the Cardiovascular System," ibid., p. 58.

17. Kochar and Hosko, op. cit.

18. Wilbert S. Aronow and John Cassidy, "Effects of Marihuana and Placebo-Marihuana Smoking on Angina Pectoris," *New England Journal of Medicine*, v. 291, n. 2, pp. 65–67, July 11, 1974.

19. Jerrold G. Bernstein, David Becker, Thomas F. Babor, and Jack H. Mendelson, "Physiological Assessments: Cardiopulmonary Function," in *The Use of Marihuana: A Psychological and Physiological Inquiry*, pp. 147–60, edited by Jack H. Mendelson, A. Michael Rossi, and Roger E. Meyer, Plenum Press, New York, 1974.

20. Jerrold G. Bernstein, John C. Kuehnle, and Jack H. Mendelson, "Medical Implications of Marijuana Use," *American Journal of Drug and Alcohol Abuse*, v. 3, pp. 347–61, 1976.

21. Neal L. Benowitz and Reese T. Jones, "Cardiovascular Effects of Prolonged Delta-9-tetrahydrocannabinol Ingestion," *Clinical Pharmacology and Therapeutics*, v. 18, n. 3, pp. 287–97, September, 1975.

22. Adam Sulkowski and Louis Vachon, "Side Effects of Simultaneous Alcohol and Marijuana Use," *American Journal of Psychiatry*, v. 134, n. 6, June, 1977.

23. Joseph E. Manno, Glenn F. Kiplinger, Norman Scholz, Robert B. Forney, and Susan E. Haine, "The Influence of Alcohol and Marihuana on Motor and Mental Performance," *Clinical Pharmacology and Therapeutics*, v. 12, n. 2, part 1, pp. 202–11, 1971.

24. Robert Nowlan and Sidney Cohen, "Tolerance to Marijuana: Heart Rate and Subjective 'High,' " *Clinical Pharmacology and Therapeutics*, pp. 550–56, November, 1977.

25. Bertrand J. Shapiro, "Cardiovascular Effects of Marijuana," section of "Cannabis, 1977" (edited transcript of a UCLA Conference), *Annals of Internal Medicine*, v. 89, n. 4, pp. 544–46, October, 1978.

26. Arnold Gash, Joel S. Karliner, David Janowsky, and Charles R. Lake, "Effects of Smoking

Marihuana on Left Ventricular Performance and Plasma Norepinephrine," *Annals of Internal Medicine*, v. 89, n. 4, October, 1978.

27. Edward V. Avakian, Steven M. Horvath, Ernest D. Michael, and Samuel Jacobs, "Effect of Marihuana on Cardiorespiratory Responses to Submaximal Exercise," *Clinical Pharmacology and Therapeutics*, v. 26, n. 6, December, 1979.

28. U.S. Congress, *Marihuana-Hashish Epidemic and Its Impact on United States Security* (hearings before the Subcommittee to Investigate the Administration of the Internal Security Act and Other Internal Security Laws, Committee on the Judiciary, U.S. Senate, 93rd Congress, Second Session), p. 74, 1974.

29. Harris Rosenkrantz, "Marihuana and Cannabinoid Toxicological Manifestations in Man and Animal," in *Adverse Health and Behavioral Consequences of Cannabis Use. Working Papers for the ARF/WHO Scientific Meeting, Toronto, 1981*, edited by K. O. Fehr and H. Kalant, Addiction Research Foundation, Toronto, 1982.

30. U.S. Congress, *Health Consequences of Marihuana Use* (hearings before the Subcommittee on Criminal Justice of the Committee on the Judiciary, U.S. Senate, 96th Congress, Second Session), p. 21, 1980.

31. A. Heyndrickx, Ch. Scheibis, and P. Schepens, "Toxicological Study of a Fatal Intoxication by Man Due to Cannabis Smoking," *Journal de Pharmacie de Belgique*, v. 24, pp. 371–75, September–October, 1969.

32. C. Özen and H. Sözen, "Studies on the Problem of Asrar (marijuana) in Turkey and Oriental countries. A Case of Asrar (marijuana) Poisoning That Caused Death," *Istanbul Universitesi Tip Fakultesi Mecmuasi* (Bulletin of the Medical Faculty, Istanbul University), v. 32, pp. 543–62, 1969; cited by Şükrü Kaymakçalan, "Potential Dangers of Cannabis," *The International Journal of the Addictions*, v. 10, n. 4, p. 723, 1975.

33. Gurbakhsh S. Chopra, "Marijuana and Adverse Psychotic Reactions. Evaluations of Different Factors Involved," *Bulletin on Narcotics*, v. 23, p. 19, 1971.

34. S. Deakin, "Death From Taking Indian Hemp," *Indian Medical Gazette*, v. 15, p. 71, 1880; and G. F. W. Ewens, "Insanity Following the Use of Indian Hemp," ibid., v. 39, pp. 401–13, 1904; cited in *Marijuana and Health*, National Institute on Drug Abuse, Rockville, Maryland, 1972.

35. Indian Hemp Drugs Commission, *Report of the Indian Hemp Drugs Commission, 1893–94*, first of seven volumes, p. 224, Government Central Printing Office, Simla, India, 1894; reproduced in *Marijuana Report of the Indian Hemp Drugs Commission, 1893–1894*, Thos. Jefferson Publishing Co., Silver Spring, Maryland, 1969.

36. Gabriel G. Nahas, *Marihuana—Deceptive Weed*, p. 108, New York, Raven Press, 1973.

37. J. Gourvés, C. Viallard, D. Leluan, J.-P. Girard, and R. Aury, "Coma du au Cannabis Sativa," *Presse Medicale*, v. 79, pp. 1,389–90, 1971; cited by Kaymakçalan and by Nahas, op. cit.

38. Walton T. Roth, Jared R. Tinklenberg, Bert S. Kopell, and Leo E. Hollister, "Continuous Electrocardiographic Monitoring During Marihuana Intoxication," *Clinical Pharmacology and Therapeutics*, v. 14, n. 4(1), pp. 533–34, 1973.

IMMUNITY AND RESISTANCE

1. Susan A. Pratt, Theodore N. Finley, Morris H. Smith, and Aaron J. Ladman, "A Comparison of Alveolar Macrophages and Pulmonary Surfactant(?) Obtained from the Lungs of Human Smokers and Nonsmokers by Endobronchial Lavage," *Anatomical Record*, v. 163, pp. 497–508, 1969.

2. Philip E. G. Mann, Allen B. Cohen, Theodore N. Finley, and Aaron J. Ladman, "Alveolar Macrophages: Structural and Functional Differences between Nonsmokers and Smokers of Marijuana and Tobacco," *Laboratory Investigation*, v. 25, n. 2, pp. 111–20, August, 1971.

3. U.S. Congress, *Marihuana-Hashish Epidemic and Its Impact on United States Security* (hearings

before the Subcommittee to Investigate the Administration of the Internal Security Act and Other
Internal Security Laws, Committee on the Judiciary, U.S. Senate, 93rd Congress, Second Session), pp. 92–109, 1974. Also Gabriel G. Nahas, *Keep Off the Grass: A scientific enquiry into the
biological effects of marijuana,* ch. 13–14, Pergamon Press, Oxford and New York, 1979. Also
Gabriel G. Nahas, Daniel Zagury, and Iris W. Schwartz, "Evidence for the Possible Immunogenicity of Delta-9-Tetrahydrocannabinol (THC) in Rodents," *Nature,* v. 243, pp. 407–8, June 15,
1973.

    4. Nahas, op. cit. Also Gabriel G. Nahas, Nicole Suciu-Foca, Jean-Pierre Armand, and Akira
Morishima, "Inhibition of Cellular Mediated Immunity in Marihuana Smokers," *Science,* v. 183,
pp. 419–20, February 1, 1974. Also congressional hearings, 1974, op. cit.

    5. Jean-Pierre Armand, Joy T. Hsu, and Gabriel G. Nahas, "Inhibition of Blastogenesis of T
Lymphocytes by Delta-9-THC," *Federation Proceedings,* v. 34, p. 539, 1974.

    6. Gabriel G. Nahas, Akira Morishima, and Bernard Desoize, "Effects of Cannabinoids on Macromolecular Synthesis and Replication of Cultured Lymphocytes," ibid., v. 36, pp. 1748–52, 1977.
Also congressional hearings, 1974, op. cit.

    7. Congressional hearings, 1974, op. cit.

    8. Associated Press, "White Blood Cells Tested/Marijuana Found to Weaken Defenses Against
Sickness," *Los Angeles Times,* p. 1, January 26, 1974.

    9. Newhouse News Service, "Experts dispute claim that pot leads to illness," *San Francisco Examiner,* April 24, 1974.

    10. U.S. Congress, *Marihuana Research and Legal Controls, 1974* (hearings before the Subcommittee on Alcoholism and Narcotics of the Committee on Labor and Public Welfare, U.S.
Senate, 93rd Congress, Second Session), pp. 111–20, 1974.

    11. Alvin B. Segelman and Florence P. Segelman, "Possible Noninhibition of Cellular-Mediated Immunity in Marihuana Smokers," followed by answer of Gabriel G. Nahas, Nicole Suciu-
Foca, Bernard Desoize, Jean-Pierre Armand, and Akira Morishima, *Science,* v. 185, pp. 543–44,
August 9, 1974.

    12. Steven C. White, Steven C. Brin, and Bernard W. Janicki, "Mitogen-Induced Blastogenic
Responses of Lymphocytes from Marihuana Smokers," *Science,* v. 188, pp. 71–72, April, 1975.

    13. R. J. Lau, C. B. Lerner, D. G. Tubergen, N. Benowitz, E. F. Domino, and R. T. Jones,
"Non-inhibition of Phytohemagglutinin (PHA) Induced Lymphocyte Transformation in Humans
by Delta-9-Tetrahydrocannabinol (Delta-9-THC), *Federation Proceedings,* v. 34, p. 783, 1975.

    14. Hardin B. Jones and Helen C. Jones, *Sensual Drugs,* pp. 260–61, Cambridge University
Press, 1977.

    15. Melvin J. Silverstein and Phyllis J. Lessin, "Normal Skin Test Responses in Chronic Marijuana Users," *Science,* v. 186, pp. 740–41, November, 1974.

    16. Jones and Jones, op. cit., p. 237.

    17. Nahas, op. cit., pp. 156–57.

    18. B. H. Petersen, L. Lemberger, J. Graham, and B. Dalton, "Alterations in the Cellular-
Mediated Immune Responsiveness of Chronic Marihuana Smokers, *Psychopharmacology Communications,* v. 1(1), pp. 67–74, 1975.

    19. Arthur Fisher, "The Real Dope on Pot," in *Nature Science Annual,* p. 161, Time-Life
Books, New York, 1975.

    20. Gary S. Rachelefsky, Gerhard Opelz, M. Ray Mickey, Phyllis Lessin, Masahiro Kiuchi,
Melvin J. Silverstein, and E. Richard Stiehm, "Intact Humoral and Cell-mediated Immunity in
Chronic Marijuana Smoking," *Journal of Allergy and Clinical Immunology,* v. 58, n. 4, pp. 483–
90, October, 1976.

    21. Gabriel G. Nahas, Mark Davies, and Elliott F. Osserman, "Serum Immunoglobulin Concentration in Chronic Marihuana Smokers," *Federation Proceedings,* v. 38, p. 591, 1979.

    22. J. A. Levy, A. E. Munson, L. S. Harris, and W. L. Dewey, "Effects of Delta-8 and Delta-
9 Tetrahydrocannabinol on the Immune Response in Mice," *The Pharmacologist,* v. 16, p. 259,
1974. Also A. E. Munson, J. A. Levy, L. S. Harris, and W. L. Dewey, "Effects of Delta-9-
Tetrahydrocannabinol on the Immune System," in *Pharmacology of Marihuana,* pp. 187–97, edited by Monique C. Braude and Stephen Szara, Raven Press, New York, 1976. Also Fisher, op.
cit., pp. 161 and 164.

23. Carolyn Beach Daul and Robert G. Heath, "The Effect of Chronic Marihuana Usage on the Immunological Status of Rhesus Monkeys," *Life Sciences*, v. 17, pp. 875–81, 1975.

24. Gary L. Huber, Geneva A. Simmons, Carlton R. McCarthy, Mary B. Cutting, Raul Laguarda, and Wlademir Pereira, "Depressant Effect of Marihuana Smoke on Antibactericidal Activity of Pulmonary Alveolar Macrophages," *Chest*, v. 68, n. 6, December 1975. (Presented at the 40th annual meeting, American College of Chest Physicians, New Orleans, November 3–7, 1974.)

25. Gary L. Huber, Val E. Pochay, John W. Shea, William C. Hinds, Robert R. Weker, Melvin W. First, and G. Clinton Sornberger, "An Experimental Animal Model for Quantifying the Biologic Effects of Marijuana on the Defense System of the Lung," in *Marihuana: Biological Effects*, pp. 301–28, edited by Gabriel G. Nahas and William D. M. Paton, Pergamon Press, Oxford and New York, 1979.

26. Christopher C. Gaul and Alan Mellors, "Delta-9-Tetrahydrocannabinol and Decreased Macrophage Migration Inhibition Activity," *Research Communications in Chemical Pathology and Pharmacology*, v. 10, n. 3, March, 1975.

27. A. Chari-Bitron, "Effect of Delta-1-Tetrahydrocannabinol on Red Blood Cell Membranes and on Alveolar Macrophages," in *Marihuana: Chemistry, Biochemistry, and Cellular Effects*, pp. 273–81, edited by Gabriel G. Nahas, Springer-Verlag, New York, 1976.

28. Harris Rosenkrantz, "The Immune Response and Marihuana," ibid., pp. 441–56.

29. U.S. Congress, *Health Consequences of Marihuana Use* (hearings before the Subcommittee on Criminal Justice, Committee on the Judiciary, U.S. Senate, 96th Congress, Second Session), pp. 120–30, 1980. Also Selma Zimmerman, Arthur M. Zimmerman, Ivan L. Cameron, and Helen L. Laurence, "Delta-1-Tetrahydrocannabinol, Cannabidiol and Cannabinol Effects on the Immune Response of Mice," *Pharmacology*, v. 15, pp. 10–23, 1977.

30. Marsha Manatt, *Parents, Peers, and Pot*, p. 44, National Institute on Drug Abuse, Rockville, Maryland, 1979.

31. Frederick W. Lundell, "Marijuana Alert. II. Enemy of Youth," *The Reader's Digest* (Canadian), pp. 55–58, November, 1980.

32. Albert E. Munson and Kevin O'Brien Fehr, "Immunological Effects of Cannabis," in *Cannabis and Health Hazards* (proceedings of an ARF/WHO scientific meeting on adverse health and behavioral consequences of cannabis use), pages 339–40, Addiction Research Foundation, Toronto, Canada, 1983.

33. The Mayor's Committee on Marihuana, *The Marihuana Problem in the City of New York— Sociological, Psychological, and Pharmacological Studies*, p. 58, Catell, Lancaster, Pennsylvania, 1944.

34. M. G. Kew, I. Bersohn, and S. Siew, "Possible Hepatotoxicity of Cannabis," *Lancet*, pp. 578–79, March 15, 1969.

35. Forest S. Tennant, Jr., Merle Preble, Thomas J. Prendergast, and Paul Ventry, "Medical Manifestations Associated With Hashish," *JAMA, The Journal of the American Medical Association*, v. 216, n. 12, pp. 1,968–69, 1971.

36. Joel Simon Hochman and Norman Q. Brill, "Chronic Marihuana Usage and Liver Function," *Lancet*, pp. 818–19, October 9, 1971.

37. J. C. Boulougouris, C. P. Panayiotopoulos, E. Antypas, A. Liakos, and C. Stefanis, "Effects of Chronic Hashish Use on Medical Status in 44 Users Compared with 38 Controls," *Annals of the New York Academy of Sciences*, v. 282, pp. 168–72, 1976.

38. Max Fink, "Study of Long-Term Hashish Users in Greece: Summary and Discussion," in *Hashish: Studies of Long-Term Use*, p. 155, edited by Costas Stefanis, Rhea Dornbush, and Max Fink; Raven Press, New York, 1977.

THE CELLS AND CHROMOSOMES

1. U.S. Congress, *Marihuana-Hashish Epidemic and Its Impact on United States Security* (hearings before the Subcommittee to Investigate the Administration of the Internal Security Act and Other

Internal Security Laws, Committee on the Judiciary, U.S. Senate, 93rd Congress, Second Session), pp. 109–17, 1974.

2. Maimon M. Cohen, Michelle J. Marinello, and Nathan Back, "Chromosomal Damage in Human Leukocytes Induced by Lysergic Acid Diethylamide," *Science*, v. 155, pp. 1,417–19, March 17, 1967.

3. Richard L. Neu, Harold O. Powers, Saddie King, and Lytt I. Gardner, "Cannabis and Chromosomes," *Lancet*, v. 1, p. 675, March 29, 1969; idem, "Delta-8- and Delta-9-tetrahydrocannabinol: Effects on Cultured Human Leucocytes," *Journal of Clinical Pharmacology*, v. 10, pp. 228–30, 1970.

4. David Dorrance, Oscar Janiger, and Raymond L. Teplitz, "In Vivo Effects of Illicit Hallucinogens on Human Lymphocyte Chromosomes," *JAMA, The Journal of the American Medical Association*, v. 212, n. 9, June 1, 1970.

5. Douglas G. Gilmour, Arthur D. Bloom, Kusum P. Lele, Edwin S. Robbins, and Constantine Maximilian, "Chromosomal Aberrations in Users of Psychoactive Drugs," *Archives of General Psychiatry*, v. 24, pp. 268–72, March, 1971.

6. Santosh Kumar and K. B. Kunwar, "Chromosome Abnormalities in Cannabis Addicts," *Journal of the Association of Physicians of India*, v. 19, pp. 193–95, 1972.

7. Marigold J. Thorburn, "In Vivo Chromosome Studies in Cannabis Users and Controls," in *Effects of Chronic Smoking of Cannabis in Jamaica* (report by the Research Institute for the Study of Man to the National Institute of Mental Health), edited by Vera Rubin and Lambros Comitas, 1972.

8. E. K. Cruickshank, "Physical Assessment of 30 Chronic Cannabis Users and 30 Matched Controls," *Annals of the New York Academy of Sciences*, v. 282, p. 162, 1976.

9. Thorburn, op. cit.

10. Morton A. Stenchever and Marjorie Allen, "The Effect of Delta-9-Tetrahydrocannabinol on the Chromosomes of Human Lymphocytes in Vitro," *American Journal of Obstetrics and Gynecology*, v. 114, n. 6, November 15, 1972. Also congressional hearings, op. cit., pp. 84–92.

11. Morton A. Stenchever, Terry J. Kunysz, and Marjorie A. Allen, "Chromosome Breakage in Users of Marihuana," *American Journal of Obstetrics and Gynecology*, v. 118, n. 1, January 1, 1974. Also congressional hearings, op. cit., pp. 84–92.

12. W. W. Nichols, R. C. Miller, W. Heneen, C. Bradt, L. Hollister, and S. Kanter, "Cytogenic Studies on Human Subjects Receiving Marihuana and Delta-9-Tetrahydrocannabinol," *Mutation Research*, v. 26, pp. 413–17, 1974.

13. J. Herha and G. Obe, "Chromosomal Damage in Chronical Users of Cannabis: In Vivo Investigation with Two-day Leukocyte Cultures," *Pharmakopsychiatric*, v. 7, pp. 328–37, 1974.

14. Steven S. Matsuyama, "Cytogenic Studies of Marijuana," in *Marijuana and Health Hazards: Methodological Issues in Current Research*, pp. 17–24, edited by Jared R. Tinklenberg, Academic Press, New York, 1975. Also Steven S. Matsuyama, Fu-Sun Yen, Lissy F. Jarvik, and Tsu-Ker Ju, "Marijuana and Human Chromosomes," *Genetics*, v. 74 (part 2), p. s175, 1973; idem, "Chromosome Studies Before and After Supervised Marijuana Smoking," in *Pharmacology of Marihuana*, pages 723–29, edited by Monique C. Braude and Stephen Szara, Raven Press, New York, 1976.

15. Steven S. Matsuyama, Fu-Sun Yen, Lissy F. Jarvik, Robert S. Sparkes, Tsu-Ker Fu, Howard Fisher, Norm Reccius, and Ira M. Frank, "Marijuana Exposure in Vivo and Human Lymphocyte Chromosomes," *Mutation Research*, v. 48, pp. 255–66, 1977.

16. C. J. Miras, K. A. Kyrkou, and S. G. Markidou, "Chromosomal Abnormalities in Heavy Hashish Users," *Scientific Research on Cannabis* (international program of research pursuant to resolution 8 [XIV] of the Commission on Narcotic Drugs), n. 56, United Nations Secretariat, ST/SOA/SER.S/56, June 30, 1978. (A preliminary report on this research was presented at the Seventh European Congress on Cytology, 1977.)

17. Patricia A. Martin, Marigold J. Thorburn, and Sybil A. Bryant, "In Vivo and In Vitro Studies of the Cytogenic Effects of Cannabis sativa in Rats and Men," *Teratology*, v. 9, pp. 81–86, 1973.

18. Yugal K. Luthra, Harris R. Rosenkrantz, Neal L. Muhilly, George R. Thompson, and Monique C. Braude, "Biochemical Changes in Rat Brain After Chronic Oral Treatment with Can-

nabinoids," *American Chemical Society, Abstracts of Papers*, 162nd National Meeting (Washington, D.C.), Division of Biological Chemistry, paper 212, 1971.

19. Alexander Jakubovic and Patrick L. McGeer, "Inhibition of Rat Brain Protein and Nucleic Acid Synthesis by Cannabinoids In Vitro," *Canadian Journal of Biochemistry*, v. 50, n. 6, pp. 654–62, 1972. Also McGeer and Jakubovic, "Ultrastructural and Biochemical Changes in CNS Induced by Marihuana," in *Marihuana: Biological Effects*, pages 519–30, edited by Gabriel G. Nahas and William D. M. Paton, Pergamon Press, Oxford and New York, 1979.

20. Idem, "In Vitro Inhibition of Protein and Nucleic Acid Synthesis in Rat Testicular Tissue by Cannabinoids," in *Marihuana: Chemistry, Biochemistry, and Cellular Effects*, pp. 223–41, edited by Gabriel G. Nahas, Springer-Verlag, New York, 1976.

21. U.S. Congress, *Health Consequences of Marihuana Use* (hearings before the Subcommittee on Criminal Justice, Committee on the Judiciary, U.S. Senate, 96th Congress, Second Session), p. 130, 1980.

22. Congressional hearings, 1974, op. cit., pp. 341–44. Also Arthur M. Zimmerman and Selma B. Zimmerman, "The Influence of Marihuana on Eukaryote Cell Growth and Development," in *Marihuana: Chemistry, Biochemistry, and Cellular Effects*, op. cit., pp. 195–205. Also congressional hearings, 1980. op. cit., pp. 120–22 and 124–30.

23. Arthur M. Zimmerman, Hans Stitch, and Richard San, "Nonmutagenic Action of Cannabinoids in vitro," *Pharmacology*, v. 16, pp. 333–43, 1978. Also congressional hearings, 1980, op. cit.

24. Arthur M. Zimmerman, W. Robert Bruce, and Selma Zimmerman, "Effects of Cannabinoids on Sperm Morphology," *Pharmacology*, v. 18, pp. 143–48, 1979. Also Arthur M. Zimmerman, Selma Zimmerman, and A. Yesoda Raj, "Effects of Cannabinoids on Spermatogenesis in Mice," in *Marihuana: Biological Effects*, op. cit., pp. 407–18.

25. Congressional hearings, 1980, op. cit., pp. 127–30.

26. Ibid., pp. 122–27.

27. Congressional hearings, 1974, op. cit., pp. 109–17.

28. Akira Morishima, M. Milstein, R. T. Henrich, and Gabriel G. Nahas, "Effects of Marihuana Smoking, Cannabinoids, and Olivetol on Replication of Human Lymphocytes: Formation of Micronuclei," in *Pharmacology of Marihuana*, op. cit., pp. 711–22.

29. Akira Morishima, Richard T. Henrich, Jayashree Jayaraman, and Gabriel G. Nahas, "Hypoploid Metaphases in Cultured Lymphocytes of Marihuana Smokers," in *Marihuana: Biological Effects*, op. cit., pp. 371–76. Also congressional hearings, 1980, op. cit., pp. 122–27 and 131–39.

30. Ibid.

31. Ibid.

32. R. Dean Blevins and James D. Regan, "Delta-9-Tetrahydrocannabinol: Effect on Macromolecular Synthesis in Human and Other Mammalian Cells," in *Marihuana: Chemistry, Biochemistry and Cellular Effects*, op. cit., pp. 213–22.

33. Costas N. Stefanis and Marietta R. Issidorides, "Cellular Effects of Chronic Cannabis Use in Man," ibid., pp. 533–50.

34. Marietta R. Issidorides, "Observations in Chronic Hashish Users: Nuclear Aberrations in Blood and Sperm and Abnormal Acrosomes in Spermatozoa," in *Marihuana: Biological Effects*, op. cit., pp. 377–88.

35. Stefanis and Issidorides, op. cit.

36. E. W. Gill, W. D. M. Paton, and R. G. Pertwee, "Preliminary Experiments on the Chemistry and Pharmacology of Cannabis," *Nature*, v. 228, pp. 134–36, 1970. Also W. D. M. Paton, R. G. Pertwee, and D. Temple, "The General Pharmacology of Cannabinoids," chapter 4 in *Cannabis and Its Derivatives*, pp. 50–75, edited by W. D. M. Paton and J. Crown, Oxford University Press, 1972. Also congressional hearings, 1974, op. cit., pp. 75–76.

37. Michael F. Jacobson, *Eater's Digest, The Consumer's Factbook of Food Additives*, p. 27, Anchor Books, Doubleday & Company, Inc., Garden City, New York, 1976.

38. J. Szepsenwol, J. Fletcher, E. Casales, and G. L. Murison, "Experimentally Produced Synovial Sarcoma in Mice," *Federation Proceedings*, v. 42, n. 4, p. 1,022, 1983.

II. Cannabis and the Psyche:

THE BRAIN

1. William Pollin, statements on "Health Consequences of Marijuana Use" before the Select Committee on Narcotics Abuse and Control, House of Representatives, July 19, 1979, and the Subcommittee on Criminal Justice, Committee on the Judiciary, U.S. Senate, January 16, 1980, and on "Health and Educational Effects of Marijuana on Youth" before the Subcommittee on Alcoholism and Drug Abuse, Committee on Labor and Human Resources, U.S. Senate, October 21, 1981.

2. Reese T. Jones, "Human Effects: An Overview," in *Marijuana Research Findings: 1980* (NIDA Research Monograph 31), edited by Robert C. Petersen, National Institute on Drug Abuse, 1980.

3. U.S. Congress, *Marihuana-Hashish Epidemic and Its Impact on United States Security* (hearings before the Subcommittee to Investigate the Administration of the Internal Security Act and Other Internal Security Laws, Committee on the Judiciary, U.S. Senate, 93rd Congress, Second Session), pp. 142–46, 1974. Also Louis Lemberger, Stephen D. Silberstein, Julius Axelrod, and Irwin J. Kopin, "Marihuana: Studies on the Disposition and Metabolism of Delta-9-Tetrahydrocannabinol in Man," *Science*, v. 170, pp. 1,320–22, December 18, 1970. Also Louis Lemberger, Julius Axelrod, and Irwin J. Kopin, "Metabolism and Disposition of Delta-9-Tetrahydrocannabinol in Man," *Pharmacological Reviews*, v. 23, n. 4, 1971; idem, "Metabolism and Disposition of Tetra-hydrocannabinols in Naive Subjects and Chronic Marijuana Users," *Annals of the New York Academy of Sciences*, v. 191, pp. 142–54, 1971. Also Louis Lemberger, Norman R. Tamarkin, Julius Axelrod, and Irwin J. Kopin, "Delta-9-Tetrahydrocannabinol: Metabolism and Disposition in Long-Term Marihuana Smokers," *Science*, v. 173, pp. 72–74, July 2, 1971. Also David S. Kreuz and Julius Axelrod, "Delta-9-Tetrahydrocannabinol: Localization in Body Fat," *Science*, v. 179, January, 1973.

4. C. Anthony Hunt and Reese T. Jones, "Tolerance and Disposition of Tetrahydrocannabinol in Man," *The Journal of Pharmacology and Experimental Therapeutics*, v. 215, pp. 35–44, 1980.

5. Reese T. Jones, "Cannabis and Health," *Annual Review of Medicine*, v. 34, pp. 247–58, 1983.

6. H. E. Booker, C. G. Matthews, and W. R. Whitehurst, "Pneumoencephalographic Planimetry in Neurological Disease," *Journal of Neurology, Neurosurgery, and Psychiatry*, v. 32, pp. 241–48, 1969.

7. A. M. G. Campbell, M. Evans, J. L. G. Thomson, and M. J. Williams, "Cerebral Atrophy in Young Cannabis Smokers," *Lancet*, pp. 1,219–24, December 4, 1971; idem, same title (letter), ibid., January 22, 1972. Also Myrddin Evans, "Cannabis and Cerebral Atrophy," *Royal Society of Health Journal*, v. 94, pp. 15–18, February, 1974.

8. Editor, "Cannabis Encephalopathy?," *Lancet*, p. 1,240, December 4, 1971.

9. Mervyn Susser, "Cerebral Atrophy in Young Cannabis Smokers," ibid., January 1, 1972. Letters by others, same title, ibid., December 11, 18, and 25, 1971; January 15 and 22, 1972; and February 12, 1972.

10. Congressional hearings, 1974, op. cit., p. 118.

11. Ibid., p. 392.

12. D. Von Zerssen, K. Fliege, and M. Wolf, "Cerebral Atrophy in Drug Addicts," *Lancet*, p. 313, August 8, 1970.

13. Leo E. Hollister, Stephen L. Sherwood, and Audrey Cavasino, "Marihuana and the Human Electroencephalogram," *Pharmacological Research Communications*, v. 2, p. 307, 1970.

14. Ernst A. Rodin, Edward F. Domino, and James P. Porzak, "The Marihuana-Induced 'So-

cial High,' " *JAMA, The Journal of the American Medical Association*, v. 213, n. 8, p. 1,302, August 24, 1970.

15. Jan Volavka, Rhea Dornbush, Stanley Feldstein, Gloria Clare, Arthur Zaks, Max Fink, and Alfred M. Freedman, *Annals of the New York Academy of Sciences*, v. 191, p. 213, 1971.

16. D. R. Campbell, "The Electroencephalogram in Cannabis Associated Psychosis," *Canadian Psychiatric Association Journal*, v. 16, n. 2, pp. 161–65, April, 1971.

17. Vera Rubin and Lambros Comitas, *Ganja in Jamaica: A Medical Antropological Study of Chronic Marihuana Use*, pp. 107–10, Mouton, The Hague and Paris, 1975.

18. E. Barratt, W. Beaver, R. White, P. Blakeney, and P. Adams, "The Effects of the Chronic Use of Marijuana on Sleep and Perceptual-Motor Performance in Humans," in *Current Research in Marijuana*, pp. 163–193, edited by Mark F. Lewis, Academic Press, New York and London, 1972. Also Ernest S. Barratt, Wes Beaver, and Robert White, "The Effects of Marijuana on Human Sleep Patterns," *Biological Psychiatry*, v. 8, pp. 47–54, 1974.

19. Irwin Feinberg, Reese Jones, James M. Walker, Cleve Cavness, and Jonathan March, "Effects of High Dosage Delta-9-Tetrahydrocannabinol on Sleep Patterns in Man," *Clinical Pharmacology and Therapeutics*, v. 17, pp. 458–66, 1975. Also Irwin Feinberg, Reese Jones, James Walker, Cleve Cavness, and Thomas Floyd, "Effects of Marijuana Extract and Tetrahydrocannabinol on Electroencephalographic Sleep Patterns," ibid., v. 19, pp. 782–94, 1976.

20. I. Karacan, A. Fernández-Salas, W. J. Coggins, W. E. Carter, R. L. Williams, J. I. Thornby, P. J. Salis, M. Okawa, and J. P. Villaume, "Sleep Electroencephalographic-Electrooculographic Characteristics of Chronic Marijuana Users: Part I," *Annals of the New York Academy of Sciences*, v. 282, pp. 348–74, 1976.

21. John Hanley, Eleanore D. Tyrell, and Pierre M. Hahn, "The Therapeutic Aspects of Marihuana: Computer Analyses of Electroencephalographic Data from Human Users of Cannabis Sativa," in *The Therapeutic Potential of Marihuana*, pp. 187–204, edited by Sidney Cohen and Richard C. Stillman, Plenum Medical Book Co., New York and London, 1976.

22. Costas Stefanis, John Boulougouris, and Aris Liakos, "Clinical and Psychophysiological Effects of Cannabis in Long-Term Users," in *Pharmacology of Marihuana*, pp. 659–65, edited by M. C. Braude and S. Szara, Raven Press, New York, 1976. Also C. P. Panayiotopoulos, Jan Volavka, Max Fink, and Costas Stefanis, "Clinical Electroencephalography and Echoencephalography in Long-Term Hashish Users," in *Hashish: Studies of Long-Term Use*, pp. 59–62, edited by Costas Stefanis, Rhea Dornbush, and Max Fink; Raven Press, New York, 1977. Also Max Fink, "Study of Long-Term Hashish Users in Greece: Summary and Discussion," ibid., pp. 151–58.

23. Ben T. Co, Donald W. Goodwin, Mokhtar Gado, Michael Mikhael, and Shirley Y. Hill, "Absence of Cerebral Atrophy in Chronic Cannabis Users: Evaluation by Computerized Transaxial Tomography," *JAMA, The Journal of the American Medical Association*, v. 237, n. 12, pp. 1,229–30, March 21, 1977.

24. John Kuehnle, Jack H. Mendelson, Kenneth R. Davis, and Paul F. J. New, "Computed Tomographic Examination of Heavy Marijuana Smokers," ibid., pp. 1,231–32.

25. Hardin B. Jones, "The Dangers of Cannabis Smoking," *Australian Medical Association Gazette*, pp. 21–22, April 27, 1978.

26. U.S. Congress, *Health Consequences of Marihuana Use* (hearings before the Subcommittee on Criminal Justice, Committee on the Judiciary, U.S. Senate, 96th Congress, Second Session), pp. 258–73, 1980.

27. Indian Hemp Drugs Commission, *Report of the Indian Hemp Drugs Commission, 1893–94*, first of seven volumes, Government Central Printing Office, Simla, India, 1894; reproduced in *Marijuana Report of the Indian Hemp Drugs Commission, 1893–94*, Thos. Jefferson Publishing Co., Silver Spring, Maryland, 1969.

28. R. N. Chopra and Gurbakhsh S. Chopra, "The Present Position of Hemp-Drug Addiction in India," *Indian Medical Research Memoirs* (Supplementary Series to the *Indian Journal of Medical Research*), Memoir No. 31, pp. 105–19, 1939.

29. G. Joachimoglu and C. J. Miras, "Study of the Pharmacology of Hashish," *Bulletin on Narcotics*, v. 15, n. 3–4, pp. 7–8, July–December, 1963.

30. C. J. Miras, "Some Aspects of Cannabis Action," in *Hashish: Its Chemistry and Pharma-*

cology, pp. 37–53, edited by G. E. W. Wolstenholme and Jule Knight, J. & A. Churchill Ltd., London, 1965.

31. Beng T. Ho, G. Edward Fritchie, Patricia M. Kralik, Leo F. Englert, William M. McIsaac, and Juhana Idänpään-Heikkilä, "Distribution of Tritiated-1-delta-9-tetrahydrocannabinol in Rat Tissues After Inhalation," *Journal of Pharmacy and Pharmacology*, v. 22, pp. 538–39, 1970.

32. William M. McIsaac, G. Edward Fritchie, J. E. Idänpään-Heikkilä, Beng T. Ho, and Leo F. Englert, "Distribution of Marihuana in Monkey Brain and Concomitant Behavioural Effects," *Nature*, v. 230, April 30, 1971.

33. Hardin B. Jones and Helen C. Jones, *Sensual Drugs*, pp. 324–25, Cambridge University Press, 1977.

34. George R. Thompson, Marcus M. Mason, Harris Rosenkrantz, and Monique C. Braude, "Chronic Oral Toxicity of Cannabinoids in Rats," *Toxicology and Applied Pharmacology*, v. 25, pp. 273–390, 1973. Also Yugal K. Luthra, Harris R. Rosenkrantz, Neal L. Muhilly, George R. Thompson, and Monique C. Braude, "Biochemical Changes in Rat Brain After Chronic Oral Treatment with Cannabinoids," *American Chemical Society, Abstracts of Papers*, 162nd National Meeting (Washington, D.C.), Division of Biological Chemistry, paper 212, 1971. Also Associated Press, "Brain Damaged by Grass, Tests Show," *San Francisco Examiner*, p. 8, September 15, 1971. Also "Of Pot and Rats," *Time*, p. 71, September 27, 1971. Also Yugal K. Luthra and Harris Rosenkrantz, "Cannabinoids: Neurochemical Aspects after Oral Chronic Administration to Rats, *Toxicology and Applied Pharmacology*, v. 27, pages 158–68, 1974. Also Harris Rosenkrantz, Rosa A. Sprague, Robert W. Fleischman, and Monique C. Braude, "Oral Delta-9-Tetrahydrocannabinol Toxicity in Rats Treated for Periods up to Six Months," ibid., v. 32, pp. 399–417, 1975. Also Yugal K. Luthra, Harris Rosenkrantz, Irwin A. Heyman, and Monique C. Braude, "Differential Neurochemistry and Temporal Pattern in Rats Treated Orally with Delta-9-Tetrahydrocannabinol for Periods up to Six Months," ibid., pp. 418–31. Also Yugal K. Luthra, Harris Rosenkrantz, and Monique C. Braude, "Cerebral and Cerebellar Neurochemical Changes and Behavioral Manifestations in Rats Chronically Exposed to Marijuana Smoke," ibid., v. 35, pp. 455–65, 1976.

35. Kevin A. Fehr, Harold Kalant, A. Eugene LeBlanc, and George V. Knox, "Permanent Learning Impairment After Chronic Heavy Exposure to Cannabis or Ethanol in the Rat," in *Marihuana: Chemistry, Biochemistry, and Cellular Effects*, pp. 495–505, edited by Gabriel G. Nahas, Springer-Verlag, New York, 1976. Also Kevin O'Brien Fehr, Harold Kalant, and George V. Knox, "Residual Effects of High-dose Cannabis Treatment on Learning Muricidal Behavior and Neurophysiological Correlates in Rats," in *Marihuana: Biological Effects*, pp. 681–91, edited by Gabriel G. Nahas and William D. M. Paton, Pergamon Press, Oxford and New York, 1979.

36. A. I. Durandina and V. A. Romasenko, "Functional and Morphological Changes in Experimental Acute Poisoning by Resinous Substances Prepared from Yujnochuisk Cannabis (Part 1)," *Bulletin on Narcotics*, v. 23, pp. 1–7, October–December 1971; and "Functional and Morphological Disorders in Chronic Poisoning by Resinous Substances Prepared from Yujnochuisk Cannabis Resin (Part 2)," ibid., v. 24, pp. 31–37, January–March, 1972.

37. Boris M. Segal, "Hashish Use in Soviet Russia," in *Drug Abuse in the Modern World*, pp. 246–50, edited by Gabriel G. Nahas and Henry Clay Frick II, Pergamon Press, New York and Oxford, 1981.

38. Robert G. Heath, "Pleasure Response of Human Subjects to Direct Stimulation of the Brain: Physiologic and Psychodynamic Considerations," in *The Role of Pleasure in Behavior*, edited by Robert G. Heath, pp. 219–42, Hoeber Medical Division, Harper & Row, New York, 1964; idem, "Pleasure and Brain Activity in Man: Deep and Surface Electroencephalograms During Orgasm," *The Journal of Nervous and Mental Disease*, v. 154, n. 1, pp. 3–18, 1972; idem, "Marihuana: Effects on Deep and Surface Electroencephalograms of Man," *Archives of General Psychiatry*, v. 26, June, 1972, reprinted in congressional hearings, 1974, op. cit., pp. 369–82.

39. Congressional hearings, 1974, op. cit., p. 379.

40. Robert G. Heath, luncheon talk at the University Club, New York City, sponsored by the J. M. Foundation and the American Conference on Marijuana and Other Psychoactive Drugs, September 9, 1980.

41. Idem, "Marihuana: Effects on Deep and Surface Electroencephalograms of Rhesus Mon-

keys," *Neuropsychopharmacology*, v. 12, pp. 1–14, 1973, reprinted in congressional hearings, 1974, op. cit., pp. 356–69.

42. Congressional hearings, 1974, op. cit., pp. 49–70.

43. Ibid., pp. 145–46.

44. U.S. Congress, *Marihuana Research and Legal Controls*, 1974 (hearings before the Subcommittee on Alcoholism and Narcotics of the Committee on Labor and Public Welfare, U.S. Senate, 93rd Congress, Second Session), pp. 121–22, 1974.

45. Congressional hearings, 1974 *(Marihuana-Hashish Epidemic . . .)*, op. cit., pp. 382–83.

46. Robert G. Heath, "Cannabis Sativa Derivatives: Effects on Brain Function of Monkeys," in *Marihuana: Chemistry, Biochemistry, and Cellular Effects*, op. cit., pp. 510–11.

47. Robert G. Heath, A. T. Fitzjarrell, R. E. Garey, and W. A. Myers, "Chronic Marihuana Smoking: Its Effect on Function and Structure of the Primate Brain," in *Marihuana: Biological Effects*, op. cit., pp. 714–15.

48. Robert G. Heath, A. T. Fitzjarrell, C. J. Fontana, and R. E. Garey, "Cannabis Sativa: Effects on Brain Function and Ultrastructure in Rhesus Monkeys," *Biological Psychiatry*, v. 15, n. 5, pp. 662–64, 1980.

49. Congressional hearings, 1974 *(Marihuana-Hashish Epidemic . . .)*, op. cit., p. 61.

50. Heath, Fitzjarrell, Fontana, and Garey, op. cit., p. 675.

51. Congressional hearings, 1980, op. cit., pp. 243–58.

52. Jon W. Harper, Robert G. Heath, and William A. Myers, "Effects of Cannabis Sativa on Ultrastructure of the Synapse in Monkey Brain," *Journal of Neuroscience Research*, v. 3, pp. 87–93, 1977. Also William A. Myers and Robert G. Heath, "Cannabis Sativa: Ultrastructural Changes in Organelles of Neurons in Brain Septal Region of Monkeys," ibid., v. 4, pp. 9–17, 1979.

53. Heath, Fitzjarrell, Fontana, and Garey, op. cit., p. 688.

54. Institute of Medicine, *Marijuana and Health*, pp. 81–82, 89, National Academy Press, Washington, D.C., 1982.

55. John P. McGahan, Arthur B. Dublin, and Ethel Sassenrath, "Computed Tomography of the Brains of Rhesus Monkeys After Long Term Delta-9-Tetrahydrocannabinol Treatment," presented at the 67th Scientific Assembly and Annual Meeting of the Radiological Society of North America, Chicago, November, 1981.

56. Ethel N. Sassenrath, "Marihuana Update, 1983: Marihuana Effects on the Brain," address to the PRIDE West Coast Conference on Drug Abuse, San Francisco, February, 1983.

THE MIND

1. Jacques-Joseph Moreau (de Tours), *Hashish and Mental Illness*, translated by Gordon J. Barnett, Raven Press, New York, 1973.

2. Walter Bromberg, "Marihuana Intoxication. A Clinical Study of Cannabis Sativa Intoxication," *American Journal of Psychiatry*, v. 91, pp. 310–11, 1934.

3. Frances Ames, "A Clinical and Metabolic Study of Acute Intoxication With Cannabis Sativa and Its Role in the Model Psychoses," *Journal of Mental Science* (South Africa), v. 104, pp. 972–99, 1958.

4. J. E. Morley, P. Logie, and A. D. Bensusan, "The Subjective Effects of Dagga," *South African Medical Journal*, pp. 1,145–49, July 7, 1973.

5. Harris Isbell, C. W. Gorodetzsky, D. R. Jasinski, U. Claussen, F. v. Spulak, and F. Korte, "Effects of (—)-Delta-9-Trans-Tetrahydrocannabinol in Man," *Psychopharmacologia* (Berlin), v. 11, pp. 184–88, 1967.

6. Andrew T. Weil, Norman E. Zinberg, and Judith M. Nelsen, "Clinical and Psychological Effects of Marihuana in Man," *Science*, v. 162, pp. 1,234–42, December 13, 1968.

7. "The Effects of Marijuana," *Time*, p. 52, December 20, 1968.

8. Andrew T. Weil and Norman E. Zinberg, "Acute Effects of Marihuana on Speech," *Nature* (England), v. 222, pp. 434–37, May 3, 1969.

9. Frederick T. Melges, Jared R. Tinklenberg, Leo E. Hollister, and Hamp K. Gillespie, "Marihuana and Temporal Disintegration," *Science*, v. 168, pp. 1,118–20, May, 1970.

10. Frederick T. Melges, Jared R. Tinklenberg, C. Melvin Deardorff, Norma H. Davies, Richard E. Anderson, and Catherine A. Owen, "Temporal Disorganization and Delusional-Like Ideation," *Archives of General Psychiatry*, v. 30, pp. 855–61, June, 1974.

11. Ernest L. Abel, "Marijuana and Memory," *Nature* (London), v. 227, pp. 1,151–62, September 12, 1970; idem, "Marihuana and Memory: Acquisition or Retrieval?," *Science*, v. 173, pp. 1,038–40, September 10, 1971.

12. Lincoln D. Clark, Ronald Hughes, and Edwin N. Nakashima, "Behavioral Effects of Marihuana, Experimental Studies," *Archives of General Psychiatry*, v. 23, pp. 193–98, September, 1970.

13. Harry Klonoff, Morton Low, and Anthony Marcus, "Neuropsychological Effects of Marijuana," *Canadian Medical Association Journal*, v. 108, pp. 150–56 and 165, January 20, 1973.

14. Richard A. Harshman, Helen Joan Crawford, and Elizabeth Hecht, "Marihuana, Cognitive Style, and Lateralized Hemispheric Functions," in *The Therapeutic Potential of Marihuana*, pp. 205–54, edited by Sidney Cohen and Richard C. Stillman, Plenum Medical Book Co., New York and London, 1976.

15. R. N. Chopra and Gurbakhsh S. Chopra, "The Present Position of Hemp-Drug Addiction in India," *Indian Medical Research Memoirs* (Supplementary Series to the *Indian Journal of Medical Research*), Memoir No. 31, pp. 75–77, July, 1939.

16. Gurbakhsh S. Chopra and Balwant S. Jandu, "Psychoclinical Effects of Long-Term Marijuana Use in 275 Indian Chronic Users. A Comparative Assessment of Effects in Indian and USA Users," *Annals of the New York Academy of Sciences*, v. 282, pp. 95–108, 1976.

17. Gurbakhsh S. Chopra, "Marijuana and Adverse Psychotic Reactions. Evaluation of Different Factors Involved," *Bulletin on Narcotics*, v. 23, n. 3, July–September, 1971. Also Gurbakhsh S. Chopra and James W. Smith, "Psychotic Reactions Following Cannabis Use in East Indians," *Archives of General Psychiatry*, v. 30, pp. 24–27, January, 1974.

18. Committee for the Investigation of Chronic Cannabism, M. I. Soueif, chairman; A. M. El-Sayed, Z. A. Darweesh, and M. A. Hannourah, members, *The Egyptian Study of Chronic Cannabis Consumption*, National Centre for Social and Criminological Research, Cairo, Egypt, 1980.

19. Arthur Kornhaber, "Marihuana in an Adolescent Psychiatric Outpatient Population," *JAMA, The Journal of the American Medical Association*, v. 215, n. 12, p. 1,988, March 22, 1971.

20. Vera Rubin and Lambros Comitas, *Ganja in Jamaica: A Medical Anthropological Study of Chronic Marihuana Use*, p. 111 et seq. in chapter 9, Mouton & Co., The Hague and Paris, 1975.

21. Paul Satz, Jack M. Fletcher, and Louis S. Sutker, "Neuropsychologic, Intellectual, and Personality Correlates of Chronic Marijuana Use in Native Costa Ricans," *Annals of the New York Academy of Sciences*, v. 282, pp. 270–72, 1976.

22. Robert M. Knights and Mary L. Grenier, "Problems in Studying the Effects of Chronic Cannabis Use on Intellectual Abilities," ibid., pp. 307–11.

23. Rubin and Comitas, op. cit., p. 166 and chapter 5.

24. Michael H. Beaubrun and Frank Knight, "Psychiatric Assessment of 30 Chronic Users of Cannabis and 30 Matched Controls," *American Journal of Psychiatry*, v. 130, n. 3, p. 311, March, 1973.

25. Edwin G. Williams, C. K. Himmelsbach, Abraham Wikler, Dorothy C. Ruble, and Bolivar J. Lloyd, Jr., "Studies on Marihuana and Pyrahexyl Compound," *Public Health Reports*, v. 61, n. 29, pp. 1,069, 1,072, and 1,079, July 19, 1946.

26. Costas Stefanis, Aris Liakos, John Boulougouris, Max Fink, and Alfred M. Freedman, "Chronic Hashish Use and Mental Disorder," *American Journal of Psychiatry*, v. 133, n. 2, pp. 225–27, February, 1976.

27. Costas Stefanis, John Boulougouris, and Aris Liakos, "Incidence of Mental Illness in Hashish Users and Controls," in *Hashish: Studies of Long-Term Use*, pp. 49–53, edited by Costas Stefanis, Rhea Dornbush, and Max Fink; Raven Press, New York, 1977.

28. William E. Carter and Paul L. Doughty, "Social and Cultural Aspects of Cannabis Use in Costa Rica," *Annals of the New York Academy of Sciences*, v. 282, pp. 2–16, 1976.

29. Satz, Fletcher, and Sutker, op. cit., pages 266–306.

30. Jack M. Fletcher, Paul Satz, and William E. Carter, "Chronic Cannabis Use: Recent Cross-cultural Evidence from Costa Rica and Other Countries," *Contemporary Drug Problems*, p. 29, spring, 1978.

31. Robert C. Petersen, "Importance of Inhalation Patterns in Determining Effects of Marihuana Use," *Lancet*, pp. 727–28, March 31, 1979.

32. Sidney Cohen, "Cannabis: Effects Upon Adolescent Motivation," address to a "Work Group on Marijuana Abuse in Adolescence," Rockville, Maryland, June 3, 1981.

33. Sarabjit Singh Mendhiratta, N. N. Wig, and S. K. Verma, "Some Psychological Correlates of Long-term Heavy Cannabis Users," *British Journal of Psychiatry*, v. 132, pp. 482–86, May, 1978.

34. N. N. Wig and V. K. Varma, "Patterns of Long-term Heavy Cannabis Use in North India and its Effects on Cognitive Functions: A Preliminary Report," *Drug and Alcohol Dependence* (Switzerland), v. 2, pp. 211–19, May, 1977.

35. Jeffrey Schaeffer, Therese Andrysiak, and J. Thomas Ungerleider, "Cognition and Long Term Use of Ganja (Cannabis)," *Science*, v. 213, pp. 465–66, July 24, 1981.

36. Roger F. Lange, editor, "Does the IQ Go to Pot With Heavy Marijuana Smoking?," *Internal Medicine Alert*, v. 3, n. 15, p. 57, August 17, 1981.

37. U.S. Congress, *Health Consequences of Marihuana Use* (hearings before the Subcommittee on Criminal Justice of the Committee on the Judiciary, U.S. Senate, 96th Congress, Second Session), pp. 235–36, 1980.

38. Indian Hemp Drugs Commission, *Report of the Indian Hemp Drugs Commission, 1893–94*, first of seven volumes, Government Central Printing Office, Simla, India, 1894, reproduced in *Marijuana Report of the Indian Hemp Drugs Commission, 1893–1894*, Thos. Jefferson Publishing Co., Silver Spring, Maryland, 1969, chapters 12 and 13.

39. Bromberg, op. cit., pp. 303–30.

40. Idem, "Marihuana: A Psychiatric Study," *Journal of the American Medical Association*, v. 113, n. 1, pp. 4–12, July 1, 1939.

41. Mayor's Committee on Marihuana, *The Marihuana Problem in the City of New York—Sociological, Psychological, and Pharmacological Studies*, pp. 45–51, Catell, Lancaster, Pennsylvania, 1944.

42. Harris Isbell and D. R. Jasinski, "A Comparison of LSD-25 with (—)-Delta-9-Trans-Tetrahydrocannabinol (THC) and Attempted Cross Tolerance between LSD and THC," *Psychopharmacologia* (Berlin), v. 11, pp. 115–23, 1969.

43. Martin H. Keeler, Clifford B. Reifler, and Myron B. Liptzin, "Spontaneous Recurrence of Marihuana Effect," *American Journal of Psychiatry*, v. 125, n. 3, pp. 384–86, September, 1968.

44. Armando R. Favazza and Edward F. Domino, "Recurrent LSD Experience (Flashbacks) Triggered by Marihuana," *University of Michigan Medical Center Journal*, v. 35, n. 4, pp. 214–16, 1969.

45. Michael Blumenfield, "Flashback Phenomena in Basic Trainees," *Military Medicine*, pp. 39–41, January, 1971.

46. Alan Brown and Arthur Stickgold, "Self-Diagnosed Marijuana Flashbacks," *Clinical Research*, v. 22, n. 3, p. 316A, 1974.

47. M. Duncan Stanton, Jim Mintz, and Randall M. Franklin, "Drug Flashbacks. II. Some Additional Findings," *International Journal of the Addictions*, v. 11, n. 1, pp. 53–69, 1976.

48. John A. Talbott and James W. Teague, "Marihuana Psychosis," *JAMA, The Journal of the American Medicial Association*, v. 210, n. 2, pp. 299–302, October 13, 1969.

49. Wilfred B. Postel, "Marihuana Use in Vietnam: A Preliminary Report," *USARV Medical Bulletin*, September–October 1968, and Edward Casper, James Janacek, and Hugh Martin, "Marihuana in Vietnam," ibid., both cited by John K. Imahara, *The Prosecutor*, v. 7, n. 1, January–February, 1971.

50. H. Spencer Bloch, "Army Clinical Psychiatry in the Combat Zone—1967–1968," *American Journal of Psychiatry*, v. 126, n. 3, September, 1969.

51. Edward Colbach, "Marijuana Use by GIs in Viet Nam," ibid., v. 128, n. 2, p. 206, August, 1971.

52. Andrew T. Weil, "Adverse Reactions to Marihuana. Classification and Suggested Treat-

ment," *New England Journal of Medicine*, v. 282, pp. 997–1,000, April 30, 1970.

53. Harold Kolansky and William T. Moore, "Effects of Marihuana on Adolescents and Young Adults," *JAMA, The Journal of the American Medical Association*, v. 216, n. 3, pp. 486–92, April 19, 1971.

54. Idem, "Toxic Effects of Chronic Marihuana Use," ibid., v. 222, n. 1, October 2, 1972, pp. 35–41, October 2, 1972.

55. United Press International, " 'Real Evidence' of Harm In Pot Smoking Reported," *Oakland Tribune*, April 19, 1971. Also "Frequent Marijuana Smoking Is Harmful To Youth, Study Finds," *Wall Street Journal*, April 19, 1971. Also "Scientists Who Question the Pot Report," *San Francisco Chronicle*, April 27, 1971.

56. Doris H. Milman, "Marihuana in Adolescents," *JAMA, The Journal of the American Medical Association*, v. 216, n. 13, p. 2,145, June 28, 1971.

57. Victor M. Benson, "Marihuana 'Study' Critique," ibid., v. 217, n. 10, p. 1,391, September 6, 1971.

58. "Marihuana: Buyer Beware," ibid., v. 222, n. 1, p. 84, October 2, 1972.

59. Harold Kolansky and William T. Moore, "Marihuana. Can It Hurt You?," ibid., v. 232, n. 9, pp. 923–24, June 2, 1975.

60. Frederick P. Spin, William I. Bennett, and Joseph Stokes III, "Marihuana" (letters), ibid., v. 222, n. 11, p. 1,424, December 11, 1972.

61. Forest S. Tennant, Jr., and C. Jess Groesbeck, "Psychiatric Effects of Hashish," *Archives of General Psychiatry*, v. 27, pp. 133–36, July, 1972. Also U.S. Congress, *Marihuana-Hashish Epidemic and Its Impact on United States Security* (hearings before the Subcommittee to Investigate the Administration of the Internal Security Act and Other Internal Security Laws, Committee on the Judiciary, U.S. Senate, 93rd Congress, Second Session), p. 150, 1974.

62. Beaubrun and Knight, op. cit.

63. Frank Knight, "Role of Cannabis in Psychiatric Disturbance," *Annals of the New York Academy of Sciences*, v. 282, pp. 64–71, 1976.

64. Stefanis, Liakos, Boulougouris, Fink, and Freedman, op. cit.

65. Max Fink, "Study of Long-Term Hashish Users in Greece: Summary and Discussion," ibid., p. 154.

66. "General Discussion," *Annals of the New York Academy of Sciences*, v. 282, pp. 109–11, 1976.

III. Cannabis and Society:

THE CHANGING SCENE

1. George H. Gallup, editor, *The Gallup Poll: Public Opinion*, 1978, p. 166, Scholarly Resources, Wilmington, Delaware, 1979.

2. Andrew T. Weil, Norman E. Zinberg, and Judith M. Nelsen, "Clinical and Psychological Effects of Marihuana in Man," *Science*, v. 162, p. 1,236, December 13, 1968.

3. National Institute on Drug Abuse (NIDA) *Highlights From Student Drug Use in America, 1975–1981*, U.S. Department of Health and Human Services (HHS), Rockville, Maryland, 1981. Also Lloyd D. Johnson, Jerald G. Bachman, and Patrick M. O'Malley, *Drugs and the Class of '78: Behaviors, Attitudes, and Recent National Trends*, NIDA, U.S. Department of Health, Education, and Welfare, 1979; idem, *Student Drug Use, Attitudes, and Beliefs. National Trends 1975–1982*, NIDA, HHS, 1982. Also *Highlights From Drugs and American High School Students, 1975–1983*, NIDA, HHS, in press.

4. NIDA, "Summary Report—Surveys of Student Drug Use, San Mateo County, California," 1977.

5. Alcohol, Youth, and Drug Task Force Report to the Berkeley Unified School District, March 1, 1982.

6. NIDA, *National Survey on Drug Abuse, Main Findings: 1979* (also 1971, 1972, 1976, and 1977); and "National Household Survey on Drug Abuse," press release, April, 1983.

7. Sidney Cohen, "Defining Marijuana Use as a Clinical Problem Among Adolescents," presented to a conference of the American Council on Marijuana and Other Psychoactive Drugs, Bethesda, Maryland, May 4, 1981.

8. Mitchell S. Rosenthal, "Marijuana and Effects on Adolescents," presented to a symposium of the above group, New York City, June 28–29, 1979.

9. NIDA, "Drug Abuse Statistics 1979," press release; and telephone conversation, 1983. Also United Press International, "Task Force Seizes 6 Million Pounds of Pot," *San Francisco Chronicle*, February 5, 1982.

10. "High on the Hill," *Playboy*, pp. 176–77, November, 1978.

11. "How Drugs Sap The Nation's Strength," *U.S. News & World Report*, May 16, 1983. Also "Taking Drugs on the Job," *Newsweek*, August 22, 1983. Also Helen C. Jones, "On Marijuana Reconsidered," *Executive Health*, February, 1984.

12. U.S. Congress, *Marihuana* (First Report by the Select Committee on Crime), House of Representatives, 1970.

13. U.S. Congress, *International Narcotics Trafficking* (hearings before the Permanent Committee on Investigations of the Committee on Governmental Affairs, U.S. Senate, 97th Congress, First Session), testimony of Carlton E. Turner, 1981.

14. Norman J. Doorenbos, Patricia S. Fetterman, Maynard W. Quimby, and Carlton E. Turner, "Cultivation, Extraction, and Analysis of Cannabis Sativa L.," *Annals of the New York Academy of Sciences*, v. 191, p. 9, 1971. Also J. W. Fairbairn, "The Pharmacognosy of Cannabis," in *Cannabis and Health*, pp. 12–13, edited by J. D. P. Graham, Academic Press, London and New York, 1976.

15. *Federal Strategy for Prevention of Drug Abuse and Drug Trafficking, 1982*, p. 12, Drug Abuse Policy Office, Office of Policy Development, The White House, 1982. Also United Press International, op. cit.

16. David Solomon, editor, *The Marihuana Papers*, The Bobbs-Merrill Co., Indianapolis, 1966. Also Richard J. Bonnie and Charles H. Whitebread II, *The Marihuana Conviction*, University Press of Virginia, Charlottesville, 1974. Also Ernest L. Abel, *Marihuana: The First Twelve Thousand Years*, Plenum Press, New York, 1980.

17. *United States Statutes at Large*, chapter 553, v. 50, part 1, pp. 551–56, 1937; idem, chapter 39, v. 68A, pp. 560–68, 1954; idem, chapter 629, v. 70, pp. 567–71, 1956.

18. "Playboy Interview: Keith Stroup," *Playboy*, February, 1977.

19. National Commission on Marihuana and Drug Abuse, *Marihuana: A Signal of Misunderstanding*, U.S. Government Printing Office, Washington, D.C., March, 1972.

20. Mark Trautwein, "Experts in Clash Over Cannabis, Jones vs. Mikuriya," *Berkeley Gazette*, April 7, 1972.

21. Richard C. Cowan, "American Conservatives Should Revise Their Position on Marijuana," with commentary by Jeffrey Hart, James Burnham, and William F. Buckley, Jr., *National Review*, December 8, 1972.

22. "Marijuana: Seal of Approval," *Newsweek*, December 11, 1972.

23. Edward M. Brecher and the Editors of *Consumer Reports, Licit and Illicit Drugs*, Little, Brown and Company, Boston, 1972.

24. U.S. Congress, *Marihuana-Hashish Epidemic and Its Impact on United States Security* (hearings before the Subcommittee to Investigate the Administration of the Internal Security Act and Other Internal Security Laws, Committee on the Judiciary, U.S. Senate, 93rd Congress, Second Session), 1974.

25. U.S. Congress, *Marihuana Research and Legal Controls, 1974* (hearings before the Subcommittee on Alcoholism and Narcotics of the Committee on Labor and Public Welfare, U.S. Senate, 93rd Congress, Second Session), 1974.

26. FIND (Families Involved in Nurture and Development), A *Family Response to the Drug Problem. A Family Program for the Prevention of Chemical Dependence*, National Institute of Mental Health, Rockville, Maryland, 1976.

27. Robert L. DuPont, Avram Goldstein, and John O'Donnell, editors, *Handbook on Drug Abuse*, NIDA and Office of Drug Abuse Policy, Executive Office of the President, 1979.

28. The National Organization for the Reform of Marijuana Laws and the Center for the Study of Non-Medical Drug Use, "The Marijuana Laws, State and Federal Penalties," leaflet, May 1979. Also Richard Jay Moller, *Marijuana: Your Legal Rights*, Addison-Wesley Publishing Company, Reading, Massachusetts, 1981.

29. Robert L. DuPont, "Changing Perspectives on the Marijuana Controversy," address to the Third Annual Convention of the National Organization for the Reform of Marijuana Laws, November 14, 1974; idem, testimony at U.S. Congress hearing on *Marihuana Research and Legal Controls, 1974*, November 19, 1974, op. cit.; idem, address on "Marijuana—Our Next Step" to the Psychiatric Institute Foundation, Washington, D.C., February 4, 1977.

30. Idem, address on "Marijuana: A National Outlook" to the Second Annual Conference on Marijuana of the American Council on Marijuana and Other Psychoactive Drugs, New York City, June 29, 1979.

31. Jack Durell, remarks at NIDA press conference, May 8, 1980.

32. Congressional hearings, 1981, op. cit.

33. Federal strategy, op. cit., frontispiece.

34. Robert L. Dupont, quoted from the *Washington Post*, July 30, 1978, by *Consumers' Research Magazine*, p. 11, April, 1980; idem, address on "Marijuana: a National Outlook," op. cit.; idem, address on "Marijuana: The Medical and Societal Effects of Its Use and What Might Be Done to Confront This Epidemic" to the J. M. Foundation and the American Council on Marijuana and Other Psychoactive Drugs, New York City, September 9, 1980.

35. U.S. Congress, *Health Consequences of Marihuana Abuse: Recent Findings* (hearings before the Select Committee on Narcotics Abuse and Control, House of Representatives, 96th Congress, First Session), testimony of Sidney Cohen, 1979.

36. Laurel Murphy, " 'Legalize Pot, Down with Acid' Says Cowell Psych," *Daily Californian*, University of California, Berkeley, April 12, 1967.

37. NBC News Reports, "Reading, Writing, and Reefer," interview sequence with Keith Stroup, December 10, 1978.

38. Stephen Magagnini, "An Unlikely Pot Champion Drops Back In," *San Francisco Chronicle*, April 7, 1981.

39. The Drug Abuse Council, *The Facts About "Drug Abuse,"* p. 17, The Free Press, 1980.

40. Johnson, Bachman, and O'Malley, op. cit. Also *Highlights From Drugs and American High School Students, 1975–1983*, op. cit.

41. James Coates *(Chicago Tribune)*, "Harmful to lungs, reproductive system. A grim report on pot," *San Francisco Examiner*, March 28, 1980.

42. Secretary of Health, Education, and Welfare, *Marijuana and Health*, Eighth Annual Report to the U.S. Congress, NIDA, 1980; also *Marihuana and Health*, editions of 1971 through 1977.

43. Institute of Medicine, *Marijuana and Health*, National Academy Press, Washington, D.C., 1982.

44. Robert L. DuPont, "Marihuana: An Issue Comes of Age," in *Pharmacology of Marihuana*, p. 3, edited by Monique C. Braude and Stephen Szara, Raven Press, New York, 1976.

45. Federal strategy, op. cit., pp. 73–75.

46. N. B. Eddy, *The Question of Cannabis: Cannabis Bibliography*, United Nations Economic and Social Council, 1965, cited by Coy W. Waller in *Handbook of Natural Toxins*, v. 1, chapter 15, edited by R. F. Keeler and A. T. Tu, Marcel Dekker, Inc., New York, 1983. Also Coy W. Waller, Jacqueline J. Johnson, Judy Buelke, and Carlton E. Turner, *Marihuana: An Annotated Bibliography*, Macmillan Information, New York, 1976. Also Coy W. Waller, Rashmi S. Nair, Ann F. McAllister, Beverly Urbanek, and Carlton E. Turner, *Marihuana: An Annotated Bibliography, Volume II*, Macmillan Publishing Co., New York, 1982. Also Coy W. Waller, Kathleen

P. Baran, Beverly S. Urbanek, and Carlton E. Turner, *Marihuana: An Annotated Bibliography, 1980 Supplement*, University of Mississippi, 1983.

47. "Teenagers View Drug Abuse as Their Biggest Problem," *The Drug Educator*, v. 8, issue 4, pp. 1 and 6, 1983.

DRIVING

1. Joseph H. Davis, director, "Marijuana and Driving Performance," audiotape, transcribed in "A Drug is Guilty Until Proven Innocent," statement directed by the late J. Elmer Blanchard, attorney general, and Gordon Bennett, minister of education and justice, Prince Edward Island, presented to the Commission of Inquiry Into the Non-Medical Use of Drugs, Charlottetown, Prince Edward Island, Canada, November 6, 1970.

2. Arnold W. Klein, Joseph H. Davis, and Brian D. Blackbourne, "Marihuana and Automobile Crashes," *Journal of Drug Issues*, v. 1, n. 1, pp. 18–26, January, 1971.

3. J. E. Morley, P. Logie, and A. D. Bensusan, "The Subjective Effects of Dagga," *South African Medical Journal*, v. 47, pp. 1,145–49, 1973.

4. Andrew T. Weil and Norman E. Zinberg, "Acute Effects of Marihuana on Speech," *Nature* (England), v. 222, p. 437, May 3, 1969.

5. Reginald G. Smart, "Marihuana and Driving Risk Among College Students," *Journal of Safety Research*, v. 6, n. 4, pp. 155–58, December, 1974.

6. California Marijuana Initiative Committee, "California Marijuana Initiative-80," 1980.

7. Lloyd D. Johnston, Jerald G. Bachman, and Patrick M. O'Malley, *Drugs and the Class of '78: Behaviors, Attitudes, and Recent National Trends*, National Institute on Drug Abuse, Rockville, Maryland, 1979.

8. George E. Woody, "Visual Disturbances Experienced by Hallucinogenic Drug Abusers While Driving," *American Journal of Psychiatry*, v. 127, n. 5, pp. 143–46, November, 1970.

9. William Pollin, statements on "Health Consequences of Marijuana Use" before the Subcommittee on Criminal Justice, Committee on the Judiciary, U.S. Senate, January 16, 1980, and "Health and Educational Effects of Marijuana on Youth" before the Subcommittee on Alcoholism and Drug Abuse, Committee on Labor and Human Resources, U.S. Senate, October 21, 1981.

10. Smart, op. cit. Also Harry Klonoff, "Marijuana and Driving in Real-Life Situations," *Science*, v. 186, p. 323, October 25, 1974.

11. Patricia M. Fishbourne, Herbert I. Abelson, and Ira Cisin, *Highlights From the National Survey on Drug Abuse: 1979*, pp. 20–22, National Institute on Drug Abuse, Rockville, Maryland, 1980.

12. Bureau of Criminal Statistics, Department of Justice, State of California, "Statewide Arrest Statistics: Driving Under the Influence of Alcohol or Alcohol and Drugs, 1976," cited by Victor C. Reeve in *Incidence of Marijuana in a California Impaired Driver Population*, p. 13, Department of Justice, State of California, 1979.

13. Strategy Council on Drug Abuse, *Federal Strategy for Drug Abuse and Drug Traffic Prevention*, U.S. Government, 1979.

14. Alfred Crancer, Jr., James M. Dille, Jack C. Delay, Jean E. Wallace, and Martin D. Haykin, "Comparison of the Effects of Marihuana and Alcohol on Simulated Driving Performance," *Science*, v. 164, pp. 851–54, May 16, 1969.

15. Gerald Le Dain, chairman, *Cannabis: A Report of the Commission of Inquiry Into the Non-Medical Use of Drugs*, Ottawa, Canada, p. 62, 1972.

16. D. F. Caldwell. S. A. Myers, E. F. Domino, and P. E. Merriam, "Auditory and Visual Threshold Effects of Marihuana in Man: Addendum," *Perceptual and Motor Skills*, v. 29, p. 922, 1969. Also Ernst A. Rodin, Edward F. Domino, and James P. Porzak, "The Marihuana-Induced 'Social High': Neurological and Electroencephalographic Concomitants," *JAMA, The Journal of the American Medical Association*, v. 213, n. 8, p. 1,302, August 24, 1970.

17. Harold Kalant, "Marihuana and Simulated Driving," *Science*, v. 165, p. 640, August 22, 1969.

18. Alfred Crancer, Jr., and Dennis L. Quiring, "Driving Records of Persons Arrested for Illegal Drug Use," State of Washington, Department of Motor Vehicles, Report No. 011, May, 1968, cited in *Drugs and Driving: A Selected Bibliography* p. D-12, edited by Kent B. Joscelyn and Roger P. Maickel, National Highway Traffic Safety Administration, Washington, D.C., January, 1977, and in *Drug Users and Driving Behaviors* (Research Issues 20), pp. 33–34, edited by Gregory A. Austin, Robert S. Sterling-Smith, Mary A. Macari, and Dan J. Lettieri, National Institute on Drug Abuse, Rockville, Maryland, June, 1977.

19. O. J. Rafaelsen, P. Bech, and L. Rafaelsen, "Simulated Car Driving Influenced by Cannabis and Alcohol," *Pharmakopsychiatrie Neuro-Psychopharmacologie* (Stuttgart, Germany), v. 6, n. 2, pp. 71–83, 1973.

20. Herbert Moskowitz, Satanand Sharma, and William McGlothlin, "Effect of Marihuana Upon Peripheral Vision as a Function of the Information Processing Demands in Central Vision," *Perceptual and Motor Skills*, v. 35, pp. 875–82, 1972. Also Herbert Moskowitz and William McGlothlin, "Effects of Marihuana on Auditory Signal Detection," *Psychopharmacologia* (Berlin, Germany), v. 40, pp. 137–45, 1974. Also Herbert Moskowitz, Richard Shea, and Marcelline Burns, "Effect of Marihuana on the Psychological Refractory Period," *Perceptual and Motor Skills*, v. 38, pp. 959–62, 1974. Also Herbert Moskowitz, Slade Hulbert, and William H. McGlothlin, "Marihuana: Effects on Simulated Driving Performance," *Accident Analysis and Prevention*, v. 8, pp. 45–50, 1976. Also Herbert Moskowitz, "Marihuana General Hallucinogens," in *Drugs and Driving* (NIDA Research Monograph 11), pp. 77–90, edited by Robert E. Willette, National Institute on Drug Abuse, Rockville, Maryland, March, 1977. Also Margaret Blaskinsky and George K. Russell, editors, *Urine Testing for Marijuana Use: Implications for a Variety of Settings*, pp. 31–32, The American Council on Marijuana and Other Psychoactive Drugs, New York, 1981.

21. Joseph E. Manno, Glen F. Kiplinger, Norman Scholz, Robert B. Forney, and Susan E. Haine, "The Influence of Alcohol and Marihuana on Motor and Mental Performance," *Clinical Pharmacology and Therapeutics*, v. 12, n. 2, part 1, pp. 202–11, 1971.

22. Le Dain, op. cit., pp. 131–44.

23. Insurance Bureau of Canada, "Drinking, Drugs, and Driving," album including "The Combined Effects of Alcohol and Common Psychoactive Drugs," part 1, "Studies on Human Pursuit Tracking Capability," by R. Burford, Ian W. French, and A. E. LeBlanc, and part 2, "Field Studies With an Instrumented Automobile," by Alison Smiley, A. E. LeBlanc, Ian W. French, and R. Burford, 1975.

24. Klonoff, op. cit., pp. 317–24.

25. Klein, Davis, and Blackbourne, op. cit.

26. Robert S. Sterling-Smith and David D. Graham, *Marijuana and Driver Behaviors: Historic and Social Observations Among Fatal Accident Operators and a Control Sample* (Final Report), National Highway Traffic Safety Administration, U.S. Department of Transportation, 1976. Also Robert S. Sterling-Smith, "Alcohol, Marihuana and Other Drug Patterns Among Operators Involved in Fatal Motor Vehicle Accidents," cited in *Drug Users and Driving Behaviors*, pp. 54–56, op. cit.

27. U.S. Congress, *Marihuana-Hashish Epidemic and Its Impact on United States Security* (hearings before the Subcommittee to Investigate the Administration of the Internal Security Act and Other Internal Security Laws, Committee on the Judiciary, U.S. Senate, 93rd Congress, Second Session), pp. 299–300, 1974.

28. E. J. Woodhouse, "The Incidence of Drugs in Fatally Injured Drivers," cited in *Drugs and Driving: A Selected Bibliography*, p. D-15, op. cit.; and in *Drug Users and Driving Behaviors*, p. 59, op. cit.

29. Lawrence C. Kier, "A Simple Method for the Determination of the Smoking of Marijuana," presented at the Sixth International Conference on Alcohol, Drugs, and Traffic Safety, Toronto, September 8–13, 1974.

30. J. D. Teale, Elvyne J. Forman, L. J. King, and V. Marks, "Radioimmunoassay of Cannabinoids in Blood and Urine," *Lancet*, pp. 553–55, September 7, 1974. Also Derrick Teale and Vincent Marks, "A Fatal Motor-car Accident and Cannabis Use," *Lancet*, pp. 884–85, April 24,

1976. Also J. D. Teale, Jacqueline M. Clough, L. J. King, V. Marks, P. L. Williams, and A. C. Moffat, "The Incidence of Cannabinoids in Fatally Injured Drivers: An Investigation by Radioimmunoassay and High Pressure Liquid Chromatography," *Journal of the Forensic Science Society* (Great Britain), pp. 177–83, July, 1977.

31. National Transportation Safety Board, *Highway Accident Report—Ford Courier Pickup Truck, Fixed-Object Collision, Patuxent Road Near Crofton, Maryland, April 23, 1979*, September 6, 1979.

32. Arthur J. McBay, "Drug Analyses and Driving," Office of Chief Medical Examiner, Chapel Hill, North Carolina, March, 1981. Also personal communication.

33. George Cimbura, R. A. Warren, Ross C. Bennett, Douglas M. Lucas, and Herbert M. Simpson, *Drugs Detected in Fatally Injured Drivers and Pedestrians in the Province of Ontario*, Traffic Injury Research Foundation of Canada, Ottawa, March, 1980.

34. Peggy Mann, *Arrive Alive: How to Keep Drunk and Pot-High Drivers Off the Highway*, p. 302, Woodmere Press, New York, 1983.

35. Leonard G. Epstein, "Driving Under the Influence: Alcohol and Other Drugs," Division of Substance Abuse, Department of Health, State of California, September 14, 1977.

36. Victor C. Reeve, *Incidence of Marijuana in a California Impaired Driver Population*, Department of Justice, State of California, 1979.

37. V. W. Hanson, M. H. Buonarati, R. C. Baselt, N. A. Wade, C. Yep, A. A. Biasotti, V. C. Reeve, A. S. Wong, and M. W. Orbanowsky, "Comparison of [3]H- and ^{125}I-Radioimmunoassay and Gas Chromatography/Mass Spectrometry for the Determination of Delta-9-Tetrahydrocannabinol and Cannabinoids in Blood and Serum," *Journal of Analytical Toxicology*, v. 7, pp. 96–102, March/April, 1983. Also Victor C. Reeve, William B. Robertson, Jim Grant, James R. Soares, Emery G. Zimmermann, Hampshire [misspelling of Hampton] K. Gillespie, and Leo E. Hollister, "Hemolyzed Blood and Serum Levels of Delta-9-THC: Effects on the Performance of Roadside Sobriety Tests," *Journal of Forensic Sciences*, v. 28, n. 4, pp. 963–71, October, 1983. Also Victor C. Reeve, James D. Grant, William Robertson, Hampton K. Gillespie, and Leo E. Hollister, "Plasma Concentrations of Delta-9-Tetrahydrocannabinol and Impaired Motor Function," *Drug and Alcohol Dependence* (Ireland), v. 11, pp. 167–75, 1983.

38. James R. Soares and Stanley J. Gross, "Separate Radioimmune Measurements of Body Fluid Delta-9-THC and 11-nor-carboxy-delta-9-THC," *Life Sciences*, v. 19, pp. 1,711–18, 1976, and in *Cannabinoid Assays in Humans*, pp. 10–14, op. cit. Also Stanley J. Gross and James R. Soares, "Validated Direct Blood Delta-9-THC Radioimmune Quantitation," *Journal of Analytical Toxicology*, v. 2, pp. 98–100, May–June 1978.

39. Ljubisa Grlic, "Identification of Cannabis Users by Detecting Cannabinoids in Biological Media," *ACTA Pharmaceutica Jugoslavica*, v. 24, n. 2, pp. 63–72, 1974.

40. Stig Agurell, Bertil Gustafsson, Bo Holmstedt, Kurt Leander, Jan-Erik Lindgren, Inger Nilsson, Finn Sandberg, and Marie Asberg, "Quantitation of Delta-1-tetrahydrocannabinol in Plasma from Cannabis Smokers," *Journal of Pharmacy and Pharmacology* (Great Britain), v. 25, n. 7, pp. 554–58, July 19, 1973.

41. Mann, op. cit., pp. 144–45.

42. Robert E. Willette, editor, *Cannabinoid Assays in Humans* (NIDA Research Monograph 7), pp. vii–ix, National Institute on Drug Abuse, Rockville, Maryland, May, 1976.

43. Ibid., p. v.

44. Mary-Carol Kelly, untitled, news release for the U.S. Department of Health, Education, and Welfare, March 10, 1977.

45. Al Hicks, "Breatholizer for Marijuana Developed," UCLA news release, February 25, 1981.

46. Agneta Ohlsson, Jan-Erik Lindgren, Kurt Leander, and Stig Agurell, "Detection and Quantification of Tetrahydrocannabinol in Blood Plasma," in *Cannabinoid Assays in Humans*, op. cit., pp. 48–63. Also Marianne Nordqvist, Jan-Erik Lindgren, and Stig Agurell, "A Method for the Identification of Acid Metabolites of Tetrahydrocannabinol (THC) by Mass Fragmentography," ibid., pp. 64–69. Also Stig Agurell, Jan-Erik Lindgren, and A. Ohlsson, "Introduction to Quantification of Cannabinoids and Their Metabolites in Biological Fluids," in *Marihuana: Biological Effects*, pp. 3–13, edited by Gabriel G. Nahas and William D. M. Paton, Pergamon Press, Oxford and New York, 1979.

47. José Bonzani da Silva, "Identificação de Cannabinol Através da Analise Cromatográfica no Sangue, Urina e Saliva de Toxicômanos de Cannabis Sativa L.," *Revista da Faculdade de Farmácia e Bioquímica da Universidade de São Paulo*, v. 5, n. 1, pp. 205–14, January–June, 1967.

48. Leo E. Hollister, Saul L. Kanter, Frances Moore, and Donald E. Green, "Marihuana Metabolites in Urine of Man," *Clinical Pharmacology and Therapeutics*, v. 13, n. 6, pp. 849–55, 1972.

49. Kier, op. cit.

50. Kenneth E. Rubenstein, Richard S. Schneider, and Edwin F. Ullman, " 'Homogeneous' Enzyme Immunoassay. A New Immunochemical Technique," *Biochemical and Biophysical Research Communications*, v. 47, n. 4, pp. 846–51, 1972. Also "Enzyme 'Manipulation' Used in New Assay," *JAMA, The Journal of the American Medical Association*, v. 221, p. 1,343, September 18, 1972. Also G. L. Rowley, T. A. Armstrong, C. P. Crowl, W. M. Eimstad, W. M. Hu, J. K. Kam, R. Rogers, R. C. Ronald, K. E. Rubenstein, B. G. Sheldon, and E. F. Ullman, "Determination of THC and Its Metabolites by Emit(R) Homogeneous Enzyme Immunoassay: A Summary Report," in *Cannabinoid Assays in Humans*, op. cit., pp. 28–32. Also "New 'Breakthrough' Pot Detection Test," *Newsletter* (The American Council on Marijuana and Other Psychoactive Drugs), v. 3, issue 1, pp. 1 and 4, winter, 1981. Also Syva Company, various booklets and fliers on the Emit Cannabinoid Assay.

51. J. D. Grant, S. J. Gross, P. Lomax, and R. Wong, "Antibody Detection of Marihuana," *Nature New Biology* (Great Britain), v. 236, pp. 216–17, April 19, 1972. Also S. J. Gross, J. R. Soares, S-L. R. Wong, and R. E. Schuster, "Marijuana Metabolites Measured by a Radioimmune Technique," *Nature*, v. 252, pp. 581–82, December 13, 1974. Also Soares and Gross, 1976, op. cit. Also Gross and Soares, 1978, op. cit.

52. J. D. Teale et al., op. cit. (three).

53. Arleen R. Chase, Paul R. Kelley, Allison Taunton-Rigby, Reese T. Jones, and Theresa Harwood, "Quantitation of Cannabinoids in Biological Fluids by Radioimmunoassay," in *Cannabinoid Assays in Humans*, pp. 1–9, op. cit. Also Blasinsky and Russell, op. cit., p. 12.

54. Clarence E. Cook, Mary L. Hawes, Ellen W. Amerson, Colin G. Pitt, and David Williams, "Radioimmunoassay of Delta-9-Tetrahydrocannabinol," *Cannabinoid Assays in Humans*, op. cit., pp. 15–27. Also M. E. Wall, T. M. Harvey, J. T. Bursey, D. R. Brine, and D. Rosenthal, "Analytical Methods for the Determination of Cannabinoids in Biological Media," ibid., pp. 107–17. Also S. Michael Owens, Arthur J. McBay, Howard M. Reisner, and Mario Perez-Reyes, "125-I Radioimmunoassay of Delta-9-Tetrahydrocannabinol in Blood and Plasma with a Solid-Phase Second-Antibody Separation Method," *Clinical Chemistry*, v. 24(4), pp. 619–24, 1981.

55. Arthur J. McBay, "Marihuana/Other Drugs," in *Drugs and Driving* (NIDA Research Monograph 11), National Institute on Drug Abuse, edited by Robert E. Willette, pp. 91–99, March, 1977; idem, "Marihuana: A Forensic Problem," in *Legal Medicine*, W. B. Saunders Co., Philadelphia, 1980. Also Arthur J. McBay and S. M. Owens, "Marijuana and Driving," in *Problems of Drug Dependence, 1980* (Proceedings of the 42nd Annual Scientific Meeting, The Committee on Problems of Drug Dependence, Inc., NIDA Research Monograph 34), edited by Louis S. Harris, pp. 257–63, February, 1981. Also Arthur J. McBay, "Drug Analyses and Driving," Office of Chief Medical Examiner, Chapel Hill, North Carolina, March, 1981.

AVIATION AND OTHER TRANSPORTATION

1. News stories on the Molokai accident, *Honolulu Star-Bulletin*, March 16, 17, 18, and 19, 1981. Also National Medical Services, Inc., Willow Grove, Pennsylvania, toxicology report on four blood specimens from Hawaii. Also documents in the National Transportation Safety Board file on the aviation accident fifteen miles east of Molokai, Hawaii, Airport, March 14, 1981.

2. "Crash of Cessna kills young pilot," *Honolulu Star-Bulletin*, May 23, 1968; and "Student Flier Is Killed In Crash of Light Plane," *Honolulu Advertiser*, May 24, 1968.

3. David S. Janowsky, Martin P. Meacham, Jack D. Blaine, Michael Schoor, and Louis P.

Bozzetti, "Simulated Flying Performance After Marihuana Intoxication," *Aviation, Space, and Environmental Medicine*, v. 47, pp. 124–28, February, 1976; idem, "Marijuana Effects on Simulated Flying Ability," *American Journal of Psychiatry*, v. 133, n. 4, pp. 384–88, April, 1976.

4. "Marijuana in the Workplace. Issues Surface at ACM Symposium," *ACM News* (The American Council on Marijuana and Other Psychoactive Drugs), v. 4, issue 4, p. 1, 1982.

5. Albert R. Karr, "Sky High/Air-Traffic Controllers' Abuse of Drugs Alarms many in the Profession. They Believe Use off the Job—And Occasionally on—Is Worse Than FAA Says. A Heroin Dealer is Rehired," *Wall Street Journal*, p. 1, May 27, 1983.

6. Mark F. Lewis, Douglas Peter Ferraro, Henry W. Mertens, and Jo Ann Steen, "Interaction Between Marihuana and Altitude on a Complex Behavioral Task in Baboons," *Aviation, Space, and Environmental Medicine*, pp. 121–23, February, 1976.

7. Mark F. Lewis and Douglas P. Ferraro, "Flying High: The Aeromedical Aspects of Marihuana," U.S. Office of Aviation Medicine, December, 1973. Also Mark F. Lewis, editor, *Current Research in Marijuana*, Academic Press, New York, 1972.

8. U.S. Government, *Code of Federal Regulations*, Title 14, Government Printing Office, Washington, D.C., 1981.

9. National Transportation Safety Board, *Railroad Accident Report—Rear-End Collision of Consolidated Rail Corporation Freight Trains ALPG-2 and APJ-2 Near Royersford, Pennsylvania, October 1, 1979*, February 14, 1980.

10. John A. Miller, *Fares, Please! From Horse-Cars to Streamliners*, p. 78 et seq., Appleton-Century, New York, 1941.

11. David Young, " 'L' Driver had smoked pot, crash panel told," *Chicago Tribune*, March 18, 1977. Also (among sources) various news stories in the same newspaper and *The New York Times*, February and March, 1977.

12. National Transportation Safety Board, transcript of testimony at hearings of March 16 and 17, 1977.

13. Idem, *Railroad Accident Report—Rear End Collision of Two Chicago Transit Authority Trains, Chicago, Illinois, February 4, 1977*, November 29, 1977.

14. Young, op. cit. Also editorial. "A motorman's appalling record," ibid.

15. Railroad accident report, 1977, op. cit.

16. Stephen Engelberg, "Error by Signal Operator Is Called Likely Cause of Amtrak Collision," *New York Times*, July 27, 1984.

THE NONSMOKER

1. Takeshi Hirayama, "Non-smoking Wives of Heavy Smokers Have a Higher Risk of Lung Cancer: a Study from Japan," *British Medical Journal*, v. 282, pp. 183–85, January 17, 1981.

2. Dimitrios Trichopoulos, Anna Kalandidi, Loukas Sparros, and Brian MacMahon, "Lung Cancer and Passive Smoking," *International Journal of Cancer*, v. 27, pp. 1–4, 1981. Also Pelayo Correa, Linda Williams Pickle, Elizabeth Fontham, Youping Lin, and William Haenszel, "Passive Smoking and Lung Cancer," *Lancet*, pp. 595–97, September 10, 1983. Also Lawrence Garfinkel, "Time Trends in Lung Cancer Mortality Among Nonsmokers and a Note on Passive Smoking," *Journal of the National Cancer Institute*, v. 66, pp. 1,061–66, 1981.

3. Ira B. Tager, Scott T. Weiss, Alvaro Muñoz, Bernard Rosner, and Frank E. Speizer, "Longitudinal Study of the Effects of Maternal Smoking on Pulmonary Function in Children," *New England Journal of Medicine*, v. 309, n. 12, September 22, 1983.

4. Phillip Zeidenberg, Raymond Bourdon, and Gabriel G. Nahas, "Marijuana Intoxication by Passive Inhalation: Documentation by Detection of Urinary Metabolites," *American Journal of Psychiatry*, v. 134, n. 1, pp. 76–77, January, 1977.

5. Mark Gladstone and Lewis Leader, "Sex act sparked hotel fire," *San Francisco Examiner*, February 12, 1981. Also related stories in *San Francisco Chronicle*, January 16, February 18, and March 24, 1982.

6. Gilbert E. Stecher, *Fire Prevention and Protection Fundamentals*, The Spectator, Philadelphia and New York, 1953. Also Paul W. Kearney, *I Smell Smoke*, Simon and Schuster, New York, 1955.

7. Louis Derry, "Fatal Fires in America," *Fire Journal*, September, 1979.

8. Jon C. Jones, "1980 Multiple-Death Fires in the United States," ibid., September, 1981.

9. Associated Press, "Brownie party causes chaos at the Dade County courthouse," *The Tribune (Oakland)*, June 18, 1983.

10. United Press International, "Dance Teacher Puts Pot in Seniors' Brownies," *San Francisco Chronicle*, December 31, 1983.

DEPENDENCE

1. Robert P. Walton, *Marihuana: America's New Drug Problem*, pp. 128–39, J. B. Lippincott Company, Philadelphia, 1938.

2. J. D. Fraser, "Withdrawal Symptoms in Cannabis-Indica Addicts," pp. 747–48, *Lancet*, October 22, 1949.

3. A. D. Bensusan, "Marihuana Withdrawal Symptoms," *British Medical Journal*, p. 112, July 10, 1971.

4. Nathan B. Eddy, H. Halbach, Harris Isbell, and Maurice H. Seevers, "Drug Dependence: its Significance and Characteristics, *Bulletin of the World Health Organization* (Geneva), v. 32, pp. 721–33, 1965.

5. Council on Mental Health and Committee on Alcoholism and Drug Dependence, American Medical Association; and Committee on Problems of Drug Dependence, National Research Council, National Academy of Sciences, "Marihuana and Society," *JAMA, The Journal of the American Medical Association*, v. 204, n. 13, pp. 1,181–82.

6. *Cannabis: Report by the Advisory Committee on Drug Dependence* (Edward Wayne, chairman), pp. 8–53, passim, Her Majesty's Stationery Office, London, 1968.

7. Vera Rubin and Lambros Comitas, *Ganja in Jamaica: A Medical Anthropological Study of Chronic Marihuana Use*, chapter 10, Mouton & Co., The Hague and Paris, 1975.

8. Hardin B. Jones, "The Dangers of Cannabis Smoking," *AMA Gazette* (Australia), pp. 20–25, April 27, 1978; also "On the Problems Executives Must Anticipate With the Growth of Marijuana Smoking," *Executive Health*, October, 1977.

9. James Olds, "Pleasure Centers in the Brain," *Scientific American*, v. 195, pp. 105–16, 1956; and "Self-stimulation of the Brain: Its Use to Study Local Effects on Hunger, Sex, and Drugs, *Science*, v. 127, pp. 315–25, 1958.

10. Reese T. Jones, "Cannabis Tolerance and Dependence in Humans," presented to the symposium "Marijuana: Biomedical Effects and Social Implications" at New York University Post-Graduate Medical School, sponsored by the American Council on Marijuana and Other Psychoactive Drugs, June 28–29, 1979. Also Reese T. Jones, Neal L. Benowitz, and Ronald I. Herning, "Clinical Relevance of Cannabis Tolerance and Dependence," *The Journal of Clinical Pharmacology*, v. 21, pp. 143S–151S, August–September, 1981.

11. U.S. Congress, Health Consequences of Marihuana Use (hearings before the Subcommittee on Criminal Justice, Committee on the Judiciary, U.S. Senate, 96th Congress, Second Session), pp. 20–35, 1980.

12. Committee for the Investigation of Chronic Cannabism, M. I. Soueif, chairman; A. M. El-Sayed, Z. A. Darweesh, and M. A. Hannourah, members, *The Egyptian Study of Chronic Cannabis Consumption*, pp. 186–87, National Centre for Social and Criminological Research, Cairo, Egypt, 1980.

13. Julia Ross, "Addictive Marijuana" (letter), *San Francisco Chronicle*, July 7, 1981.

14. Joe Reilly, "Marijuana Intensive: A Treatment Modality," presented to the symposium "Treating the Marijuana-Dependent Person" at Bethesda, Maryland, sponsored by the American Council on Marijuana and Other Psychoactive Drugs, May 4, 1981.

15. J. M. Scher, "The Marihuana Habit," *JAMA, Journal of the American Medical Association*, v. 214, n. 6, p. 1,120, November 9, 1970.

16. Stanley R. Dean, "Marijuanics and Marijuanism," *Bulletin of the American Association for Social Psychiatry*, pp. 34–35, October 4, 1980.

17. Robert G. Niven, "Marijuana in the Schools: Clinical Observations and Needs," presented to "Work Group on Marijuana Abuse in Adolescence" at Rockville, Maryland, sponsored by the National Institute on Drug Abuse, June 3, 1981.

18. Peggy Mann, "The Parent War Against Pot," *Washington Post*, January 6, 1980.

19. Harold M. Voth, "How to Get Your Child Off Marijuana," Patient Care Publications, Inc., for Citizens for Informed Choices on Marijuana, Inc., Stamford, Connecticut, 1980.

20. Ingrid L. Lantner, "How I Get Users Off Pot," *Listen*, March, 1980.

21. Mitchell S. Rosenthal, "Marijuana and Effects on Adolescents," presented to the symposium "Marijuana: Biomedical Effects and Social Implications," cited above.

22. Harold M. Voth, "The Effects of Marijuana on the Young," presented to "Work Group on Marijuana Abuse in Adolescence," cited above.

23. Roul Tunley, "The School That Went Straight," *Ladies' Home Journal*, p. 114, May, 1982.

24. Donald Ian Macdonald, "Remarks on Relationship of Moderate Marijuana Use and Adolescent Behavior," presented to "Work Group on Marijuana Abuse in Adolescence," cited above.

25. David E. Smith and Richard B. Seymour, "Clinical Perspectives on the Toxicity of Marijuana: 1967–1981," presented to "Work Group on Marijuana Abuse in Adolescence," cited above.

26. David E. Smith, discussions, in *Final Report on the Work Group on Marijuana Abuse in Adolescence*, National Institute on Drug Abuse, 1981.

27. Ingrid L. Lantner, "Marihuana Abuse by Children and Teenagers: A Pediatrician's View," presented to "Work Group on Marijuana Abuse in Adolescence," cited above.

28. Marsha Manatt, *Parents, Peers, and Pot*, National Institute on Drug Abuse, 1979.

29. Hardin B. Jones, "What the Practicing Physician Should Know About Marijuana," *Private Practice*, January, 1976.

CRIME

1. Indian Hemp Drugs Commission, *Report of the Indian Hemp Drugs Commission, 1893–94*, first of seven volumes, Government Central Printing Office, Simla, India, 1894; reproduced in *Marijuana Report of the Indian Hemp Drugs Commission, 1893–1894*, Thos. Jefferson Publishing Co., Silver Spring, Maryland, 1969.

2. Walter Bromberg, "Marihuana Intoxication. A Clinical Study of Cannabis Sativa Intoxication," *American Journal of Psychiatry*, v. 91, pp. 305–9, 1934; idem, "Marihuana: A Psychiatric Study," *Journal of the American Medical Association*, v. 113, n. 1, pp. 4–12, July 1, 1939.

3. R. N. Chopra and Gurbakhsh S. Chopra, "The Present Position of Hemp-Drug Addiction in India," *Indian Medical Research Memoirs* (Supplementary Series to the *Indian Journal of Medical Research*), Memoir No. 31, pp. 27, 92–94, July, 1939.

4. Ram Nath Chopra, G. S. Chopra, and I. C. Chopra, "Cannabis Sativa in Relation to Mental Diseases and Crime in India," *Indian Journal of Medical Research*, v. 30, n. 1, pp. 168–71, January, 1942.

5. Mayor's Committee on Marihuana, *The Marihuana Problem in the City of New York—Sociological, Psychological, and Pharmacological Studies*, pp. 14–15, Catell, Lancaster, Pennsylvania, 1944.

6. C. G. Gardikas, "Hashish and Crime," *Enkephalos* (Greece), v. 2, n. 3, pp. 201–11, 1950.

7. James C. Munch, "Marihuana and Crime," *Bulletin on Narcotics*, v. 18, n. 2, pp. 15–22, April–June, 1966.

8. Bromberg, 1939, op. cit., p. 9.

9. John K. Imahara, "Marihuana, Narcotics and Dangerous Drugs—Medical and Psychiatric Observations of Drug Abuse in Vietnam," *The Prosecutor* (presented to the National District At-

torneys Association's Third National Institute on Narcotics and Dangerous Drugs), v. 7, n. 1, pp. 15–20, January–February, 1971.

10. C. J. Miras, "10 Studies on the Effects of Chronic Cannabis Administration to Man," in *Cannabis and Its Derivatives*, pp. 150–53, edited by W. D. M. Paton and June Crown, Oxford University Press, 1972.

11. U.S. Congress, *Marihuana-Hashish Epidemic and Its Impact on United States Security* (hearings before the Subcommittee to Investigate the Administration of the Internal Security Act and Other Internal Security Laws, Committee on the Judiciary, U.S. Senate, 93rd Congress, Second Session), pp. 297–99, 1974.

12. B. P. Sharma, "Cannabis and its Users in Nepal," *British Journal of Psychiatry*, v. 127, pp. 550–52, 1975.

13. John A. O'Donnell, Harwin L. Voss, Richard R. Clayton, Gerald T. Slatin, Robin G. W. Room, *Young Men and Drugs—A Nationwide Survey* (NIDA Research Monograph 5), pp. 81–97, National Institute on Drug Abuse, 1976.

14. Committee for the Investigation of Chronic Cannabism, M. I. Soueif, chairman; A. M. El-Sayed, Z. A. Darweesh, and M. A. Hannourah, members, "Drugs and Crime: The Case of Chronic Cannabis Taking," chapter 12 in *The Egyptian Study of Chronic Cannabis Consumption*, National Centre for Social and Criminological Research, Cairo, Egypt, 1980 (Presented at the Third International Symposium on Drugs and Criminality, São Paulo, Brazil, 1976.)

15. Marsha Manatt, *Parents, Peers and Pot*, chapter 1, National Institute on Drug Abuse, 1979.

16. Frederick W. Lundell, "Marijuana Alert. II. Enemy of Youth," *The Reader's Digest* (Canadian), pp. 55–58, November, 1980.

17. "What ethics scale do you play?" *Boston Globe*, August 4, 1980.

18. Maxwell Glen and Cody Shearer, "Ethics of the 'Me' generation," Field Newspaper Syndicate, *Oakland Tribune*, p. 11, September 3, 1980.

19. Editorial, "Legislative Proposals on Marijuana Problem," *Honolulu Star-Bulletin*, March 11, 1982. Also editorial, "Our pot problem," *Honolulu Advertiser*, September 10, 1981.

20. U.S. Congress, "Community Action to Combat Drug Abuse" (hearings, in Los Angeles, before the Select Committee on Narcotics Abuse and Control, House of Representatives, 97th Congress, First Session), p. 8, 1981.

OTHER DRUGS

1. Joseph Julian, *Social Problems*, p. 99, Appleton-Century Crofts, New York, 1973, cited by O'Donnell and Clayton below.

2. Lee N. Robins and George E. Murphy, "Drug Use in a Normal Population of Young Negro Men," *American Journal of Public Health*, v. 57, n. 9, pp. 1,580–96, September, 1967.

3. John C. Ball, Carl D. Chambers, and Marion J. Ball, "The Association of Marihuana Smoking With Opiate Addiction in the United States," *The Journal of Criminal Law, Criminology and Police Science*, v. 59, n. 2, pp. 171–82, 1968.

4. National Commission on Marihuana and Drug Abuse, *Marihuana: A Signal of Misunderstanding*, Appendix to the Technical Papers of the First Report, U.S. Government Printing Office, Washington, D.C., March, 1972.

5. Hardin B. Jones and Helen C. Jones, *Sensual Drugs*, pp. 246–47, Cambridge University Press, 1977.

6. Committee for the Investigation of Chronic Cannabism, M. I. Soueif, chairman; A. M. El-Sayed, Z. A. Darweesh, and M. A. Hannourah, members, *The Egyptian Study of Chronic Cannabis Consumption*, pp. 39 and 86, National Centre for Social and Criminological Research, Cairo, Egypt, 1980. (Originally published in *Bulletin on Narcotics*, v. 23/4, 1971, and delivered in testimony to U.S. Senate judiciary subcommittee, 1974.)

7. Albert S. Carlin and Robin D. Post, "Patterns of Drug Use Among Marihuana Smokers," *JAMA, The Journal of the American Medical Association*, v. 218, n. 6, pp. 867–68, November 8, 1971.

8. Lester Grinspoon, *Marihuana Reconsidered*, p. 246, Harvard University Press, Cambridge, Massachusetts, 1971.

9. David F. Duncan, "Marijuana and Heroin: A Study of Initiation of Drug Use by Heroin Addicts," *British Journal of Addiction*, v. 70, pp. 192–97, 1975.

10. Norman E. Zinberg, "The War Over Marijuana," *Psychology Today*, p. 51, December, 1976.

11. John A. O'Donnell, Harwin L. Voss, Richard R. Clayton, Gerald T. Slatin, and Robin G. W. Room, *Young Men and Drugs—A Nationwide Survey* (NIDA Research Monograph 5), pp. 98–104, National Institute on Drug Abuse, 1976.

12. John A. O'Donnell and Richard R. Clayton, "The Stepping-stone Hypothesis: A Reappraisal," *Chemical Dependencies*, in press.

13. William Pollin, statement on "Health and Educational Effects of Marijuana on Youth" before the Subcommittee on Alcoholism and Drug Abuse, Committee on Labor and Human Resources, U.S. Senate, October 21, 1981. Also Associated Press, "New Study Links Pot, Hard Drugs," *San Francisco Chronicle*, October 22, 1981; idem, "Marijuana, Then Harder Stuff. Study: 'Significant Relationship' To Crime Shown," *The Columbus* (Georgia) *Ledger*, October 22, 1981.

14. O'Donnell and Clayton, op. cit.

15. National Institute on Drug Abuse, "National Household Survey on Drug Abuse," press release, April, 1983.

16. O'Donnell et al., 1976, op. cit.

17. U.S. Congress, *Health Consequences of Marihuana Use* (hearings before the Subcommittee on Criminal Justice, Committee on the Judiciary, U.S. Senate, 96th Congress, Second Session), pp. 30 and 25, 1980.

18. Edwin G. Williams, C. K. Himmelsbach, Abraham Wikler, Dorothy C. Ruble, and Bolivar J. Lloyd, Jr., "Studies on Marihuana and Pyrahexyl Compound," *Public Health Reports*, v. 61, n. 29, pp. 1,059–83, July 19, 1946.

19. Jack H. Mendelson, *Final Report. Behavioral and Biological Concomitants of Chronic Marihuana Use*, Alcohol and Drug Abuse Research Center, McLean Hsopital, Belmont, Massachusetts, to the Department of the Army, September 23, 1974.

20. Robert Nowlan and Sidney Cohen, "Tolerance to Marijuana: Heart Rate and Subjective 'High,' " *Clinical Pharmacology and Therapeutics*, pp. 550–56, November, 1977.

21. Robert G. Heath, one of four participants in a telephone discussion, "Time to Change Attitudes on Marijuana?," *Patient Care*, p. 199, April 30, 1978.

22. *Cannabis: Report by the Advisory Committee on Drug Dependence* (Edward Wayne, chairman), p. 14, Her Majesty's Stationery Office, London, 1968.

23. Denise Kandel, "Evidence for Stages in Adolescent Drug Involvement," in *Marijuana: Biological Effects and Social Implications*, v. 2, pp. 60–79C, The American Council on Marijuana and Other Psychoactive Drugs, second annual conference on marijuana, New York University Post-Graduate Medical School, June 29, 1979.

24. United Press International, "Teen says he was hooked on drugs and booze, stole to feed his habit at age 11," *San Francisco Examiner*, September 2, 1983.

25. Congressional hearings, 1980, op. cit., pp. 208–13.

26. Albert J. Siemens, "Effects of Cannabis in Combination With Ethanol and Other Drugs," in *Marijuana Research Findings: 1980* (NIDA Research Monograph 31), pp. 167–98, edited by Robert C. Peterson, National Institute on Drug Abuse, Rockville, Maryland, June, 1980.

27. Advisory committee report, op. cit., p. 7.

THE MILITARY

1. David E. Kaplan, "Where the Bombs Are," *New West*, v. 6, pp. 77–83 and 144–47, April, 1981.

2. Ibid.

3. David Jackson, interview on "Eyewitness News," KPIX, San Francisco, December 28, 1981.

4. David Kaplan, interviewed on KCBS, San Francisco, April 24, 1981.

5. United Press International, "Sailor Tells of Dope on Navy Subs," *San Francisco Chronicle,* December 17, 1976.

6. "Army Disqualifies 33 MP's for Alleged Drug Use in Germany," *Narcotics Control Digest,* December 18, 1974, reprinted in *Marihuana and the Question of Personnel Security,* p. 43, cited below.

7. Felix Kessler, "Unrest in the Ranks: Overseas Military Unit Beset With Problems of Race, Drugs, Dissent," *Wall Street Journal,* September 1, 1970.

8. "Grass and LSD: SAC Officers Drug Arrests," *San Francisco Chronicle,* August 20, 1970.

9. U.S. Congress, *Department of Defense Appropriations for 1982* (hearings before the Subcommittee on the Department of Defense, Committee on Appropriations, House of Representatives, 97th Congress, First Session), pp. 505–7, 1981.

10. U.S. Congress, *Drug Abuse in the Armed Forces of the United States* (a report of the Select Committee on Narcotics Abuse and Control, House of Representatives, 95th Congress, Second Session), pp. 11–12 and 34–35, 1978.

11. Congressional hearings, 1981, op. cit., p. 508.

12. John H. Johns, prepared statement to the Subcommittee on the Department of Defense, Committee on Appropriations, House of Representatives, April 1, 1982.

13. Susanna McBee et al., "How Drugs Sap the Nation's Strength," *U.S. News & World Report,* p. 56, May 16, 1983.

14. Associated Press, "N-plant guards fail drug tests," *The Tribune* (Oakland), August 10, 1983.

15. Los Angeles Times, " 'Widespread' Drug Use at Nuclear Plant," *San Francisco Chronicle,* October 24, 1983.

16. Morris Duncan Stanton, "Drug Use in Vietnam. A Survey Among Army Personnel in the Two Northern Corps," *Archives of General Psychiatry,* v. 26, pp. 279–86, March, 1972. Also Treanor and Skripol, cited by Edward Colbach, "Marijuana Use by GIs in Viet Nam," *American Journal of Psychiatry,* v. 128, n. 2, p. 205, August, 1971.

17. Hardin B. Jones and Helen C. Jones, *Sensual Drugs,* chapter 7, Cambridge University Press, 1977.

18. John A. Talbott and James W. Teague, "Marihuana Psychosis," *JAMA, The Journal of the American Medical Association,* v. 210, n. 2, pp. 299–302, October 13, 1969. Also Gordon Chaplin, "Vietnam: Pot Is Everywhere," *San Francisco Examiner and Chronicle,* May 4, 1969. Also Gloria Emerson, "G.I.'s in Vietnam Get Heroin Easily," *The New York Times,* February 25, 1971.

19. "Fury Over Viet Pot—Try at Murder," *San Francisco Chronicle,* August 19, 1970.

20. U.S. Congress, *Marihuana and the Question of Personnel Security* (prepared by the Subcommittee to Investigate the Administration of the Internal Security Act and other Internal Security Laws, Committee on the Judiciary, U.S. Senate, 94th Congress, First Session), pp. 37–42, 1975.

21. Joel H. Kaplan, "Marijuana and Drug Abuse in Vietnam," *Annals of the New York Academy of Sciences,* pp. 261–66, 1971.

22. United Press International, "Amnesty Program for GI Drug Users," *San Francisco Chronicle,* August 21, 1970.

23. Edward Colbach, "Marijuana Use by GIs in Vietnam," *American Journal of Psychiatry,* v. 128, n. 2, August, 1971.

24. Associated Press, "Senate Told of Drug Use by Servicemen," *Los Angeles Times,* August 20, 1970.

25. NEA, "Pot Use by Yank Troops: Secret N. Viet Weapon?" *Berkeley Daily Gazette,* December 17, 1969.

26. John Steinbeck IV, *In Touch;* quoted in "Can Marijuana Save the U.S. Military?" *Los Angeles Free Press,* part one, p. 3, April 21, 1972.

27. Associated Press, "GI Hero of Viet Raid 'Was High on Marijuana,' " *Oakland Tribune,* June 21, 1971.

28. R. N. Chopra and Gurbakhsh S. Chopra, "The Present Position of Hemp-Drug Addiction in India," *Indian Medical Research Memoirs* (Supplementary Series to the *Indian Journal of Medical Research*), Memoir No. 31, pp. 3 and 25–26, July, 1939.

29. Michael T. Klare, "U.S.S. Nimitz. Cruising on the Edge of War," *Mother Jones*, v. 7, n. 111, p. 28, April, 1982.

30. Congressional hearings, 1981, op. cit., pp. 399–405.

31. Ibid., pp. 503–4.

32. Ibid., pp. 503–71, passim.

33. Ibid., pp. 500–501.

34. Ibid., pp. 519–20.

35. U.S. Congress, *Drug Abuse in the Military—1981* (hearing before the Select Committee on Narcotics Abuse and Control, House of Representatives, 97th Congress, First Session), p. 6, 1981.

36. Marvin R. Burt and Mark M. Biegel with the assistance of Yukiko Carnes and Edward C. Garley, "Highlights From the Worldwide Survey of Nonmedical Drug Use and Alcohol Use Among Military Personnel: 1980," in congressional hearings, 1981 (defense), op. cit., pp. 429–71.

37. Ibid., pp. 509 and 584–85.

38. Ibid., pp. 397–585, passim.

39. U.S. Army, "Human Readiness Report No. 5," ibid., p. 525.

40. United Press International, "Half of sailors in Navy test had smoked pot within week" (attributed to CBS News), *Oakland Tribune and Eastbay Today*, July 8, 1981.

41. Congressional hearings, 1981 (defense), op. cit., p. 406.

42. Congressional hearings, 1981 (narcotics), op. cit., p. 6.

43. Ibid., pp. 1–316, passim.

44. Ibid., pp. 200–201 and 204–5.

45. U.S. Congress, *Drug Abuse Among U.S. Armed Forces in the Federal Republic of Germany and West Berlin* (hearings before the Select Committee on Narcotics Abuse and Control, House of Representatives, 95th Congress, Second Session), pp. 98–143, passim, 1978.

46. Congressional hearings, 1981 (narcotics), op. cit., p. 6.

47. Johns, op. cit.

48. Ibid. Also *Federal Strategy for Prevention of Drug Abuse and Drug Trafficking*, 1982, pp. 66–67, Drug Abuse Policy Office, Office of Policy Development, The White House, 1982.

49. Irvin Molotsky *(The New York Times)*, "Navy's drug use lower," *Berkeley Gazette*, September 19, 1982.

50. Robert M. Bray, L. Lynn Guess, Robert E. Mason, Robert L. Hubbard, Donald G. Smith, Mary Ellen Marsden, and J. Valley Rachal, *Highlights of the 1982 Worldwide Survey of Alcohol and Nonmedical Drug Use Among Military Personnel* (report by Research Triangle Institute to the assistant secretary of defense, health affairs, Office of Drug and Alcohol Abuse Prevention), July, 1983.

MEDICINE

1. Richard Lance Christie, "Attention: Smoking Grass May Be Good for Your Health," *New Times*, cover and pp. 24–32, December 13, 1974.

2. Robert L. Du Pont, Jr., "Marijuana: A National Outlook," in *Marijuana: Biomedical Effects and Social Implications* (transcript of symposium at New York University Post-Graduate Medical School), The American Council on Marijuana and Other Psychoactive Drugs, June 29, 1979; idem, "Is U.S. Becoming a Drug-Ridden Society?" (written statement), April 19, 1980.

3. Emory Wheel Entertainment Staff, "NORML Chairman Keith Stroup talks on pot," *Emory* (University) *Wheel*, interview conducted January 26, 1979.

4. Supreme Court of Alaska, "Irwin RAVIN, Petitioner, v. STATE of Alaska, Respondent," *Pacific Reporter, 2d Series*, v. 537, pp. 494–516, May 28, 1975.

5. S. Julien, Paris, 1849, quoted by R. Mechoulam and E. A. Carlini, "Toward Drugs Derived from Cannabis," *Naturwissenchaften* (Heidelberg, West Germany), v. 65, p. 174, 1978.

6. Carlton E. Turner, *The Marijuana Controversy* (booklet), pp. 12–13, The American Coun-

cil on Marijuana and Other Psychoactive Drugs, New York, 1981.

7. Sidney Cohen, "A Progress Report: Marijuana as Medicine," *Psychology Today*, p. 62, April, 1978.

8. Robert P. Walton, *Marihuana: America's New Drug Problem*, p. 3, J. B. Lippincott Co., Philadelphia, 1938. Also Gabriel G. Nahas, *Marihuana—Deceptive Weed*, p. 1, Raven Press, New York, 1973. Also Ernest L. Abel, *Marihuana: The First Twelve Thousand Years*, pp. 11–12, Plenum Press, New York and London, 1980.

9. Turner, op. cit., p. 16.

10. J. D. P. Graham, "If Cannabis Were a New Drug," in *Cannabis and Health*, edited by Graham, Academic Press, London, 1976.

11. *The Pharmacopoeia of the United States of America*, eleventh decennial revision, p. 104, U.S. Pharmacopoeial Convention, 1936. Also *Epitome of the Pharmacopoeia of the United States and the National Formulary, With Comments*, p. 54, American Medical Association, 1936.

12. Horatio C. Wood, Jr., Charles H. LaWall, Heber W. Youngken, Arthur Osol, Ivor Griffith, and Louis Gershenfeld, *The Dispensatory of the United States of America*, centennial (22nd) edition, p. 278, J. B. Lippincott Co., Philadelphia, 1937.

13. Raphael Mechoulam, "Current Status of Therapeutic Opportunities Based on Cannabinoid Research. An Overview," *Journal of Clinical Pharmacology*, v. 21, pp. 2S–7S, August–September, 1981.

14. Shirley Y. Hill, Robert Schwin, Donald W. Goodwin, and Barbara J. Powell, "Marihuana and Pain," *Journal of Pharmacology and Experimental Therapeutics*, v. 188, pp. 415–18, 1974.

15. Russell Noyes, Jr., S. Fred Brunk, David A. Baram, and Arthur Canter, "Analgesic Effect of Delta-9-Tetrahydrocannabinol," *Journal of Clinical Pharmacology*, v. 15, pp. 139–43, 1975. Also Stephen L. Milstein, Keith MacCannell, Gerry Karr, and Stewart Clark, "Marijuana-Produced Changes in Pain Tolerance. Experienced and Non-Experienced Subjects," *International Pharmacopsychiatry* (Basel), v. 10, pp. 177–82, 1975. Also W. Crawford Clark, Malvin N. Janal, Phillip Zeidenberg, and Gabriel G. Nahas, "Effects of Moderate and High Doses of Marihuana on Thermal Pain: A Sensory Decision Theory Analysis," *Journal of Clinical Pharmacology*, v. 21, pp. 299S–307S, August–September, 1981.

16. John A. Scigliano, "THC Therapeutic Research by Independent and State-Sponsored Investigators: A Historical Review," *Journal of Clinical Pharmacology*, v. 21, pp. 113S–121S, August–September, 1981; idem, "Summary of Selected Provisions of State Laws Relating to Therapeutic Use of Marihuana" (chart), January 1, 1983.

17. Richard M. Cooper, "Therapeutic Use of Marijuana and Heroin: The Legal Framework," remarks prepared for delivery at the annual meeting of the American Bar Association, Dallas, Texas, August 14, 1979.

18. HHS, "Proposed Recommendation to the Drug Enforcement Administration Regarding the Scheduling Status of Tetrahydrocannabinol," *Federal Register*, v. 47, n. 46, p. 10,080 et seq., March 9, 1982; idem, "Proposed Recommendations to the Drug Enforcement Administration Regarding the Scheduling Status of Marihuana and Its Components and Notice of a Public Hearing," ibid., n. 125, p. 28,141 et seq., June 29, 1982.

19. Scigliano, op. cit.; data for 1983 (on states and INDs) compiled and furnished by Dr. Scigliano as FDA consultant.

20. Stuart L. Nightingale and Seymour Perry, "Marijuana and Heroin by Prescription? Recent Developments at the State and Federal Levels," *JAMA, The Journal of the American Medical Association*, v. 241, n. 4, pp. 373–75, January 26, 1979.

21. Charles G. Moertel, Thomas R. Fleming, Joseph Rubin, Larry K. Kvola, Gregory Sarna, Robert Koch, Violante E. Currie, Charles W. Young, Stephen E. Jones, and J. Paul Davignon, "A Clinical Trial of Amygdalin (Laetrile) in the Treatment of Human Cancer," *New England Journal of Medicine*, v. 306, pp. 201–6, January 28, 1982. Also Arnold S. Relman, "Closing the Books on Laetrile," ibid., p. 236.

22. Department of Health and Human Services, news releases of June 26, 1980, and September 10, 1980.

23. David Abraham, Kenneth R. Pina, and J. Paul Davignon, "Mechanism for National Distribution of Delta-9-Tetrahydrocannabinol (NSC-134454)," *The Journal of Clinical Pharmacology*, v. 21, pp. 122S–127S, August–September, 1981.

SOURCE NOTES 519

24. Cooper, op. cit.
25. Abraham, Pina, and Davignon, op. cit. Also NCI, "Group C Guidelines for the Use of Delta-9-Tetrahydrocannabinol . . . ," September, 1980.
26. Gordon J. Dow and Frederick H. Meyers, "The California Program for the Investigational Use of THC and Marihuana in Heterogeneous Populations Experiencing Nausea and Vomiting from Anticancer Therapy," ibid., pp. 128S–132S.
27. Research Advisory Panel, State of California, "Eleventh Annual Report of the Research Advisory Panel for 1980. Prepared for the Governor and Legislature," 1981.
28. U.S. Congress, Therapeutic Uses of Marihuana and Schedule I Drugs (hearing before the Select Committee on Narcotics Abuse and Control, House of Representatives, 96th Congress, Second Session), 1980.
29. Associated Press, "Legal marijuana capsules on way to 4 cancer victims," Albuquerque Tribune, January 17, 1979.
30. "Pot—a New Prescription For Cancer?" San Francisco Chronicle, July 24, 1979.
31. "Pot for cancer available," Berkeley Independent and Gazette, February 17, 1981.
32. Joseph H. Skom, Henry Brill, Sidney Cohen, David E. Smith, Jokichi Takamine, and Rogers J. Smith, "Marijuana in the '80s" (report of the Council on Scientific Affairs), House of Delegates, American Medical Association, 1980.
33. John Laszlo, "Tetrahydrocannabinol: From Pot to Prescription?" Annals of Internal Medicine, v. 91, n. 6, p. 916, December, 1979. Also John S. Penta, Don S. Poster, Salvador Bruno, and John S. MacDonald, "Clinical Trials with Antiemetic Agents in Cancer Patients Receiving Chemotherapy," Journal of Clinical Pharmacology, v. 21, p. 11S, August–September, 1981.
34. Department of Health and Human Services, news release of September 10, 1980.
35. "Marijuana," Medical World News, p. 43, July 19, 1971. Also Reginald W. Rhein, Jr., ibid., p. 40, April 28, 1980. Also Stephen E. Sallan, Norman E. Zinberg, and Emil Frei III, "Antiemetic Effect of Delta-9-Tetrahydrocannabinol in Patients Receiving Cancer Chemotherapy," New England Journal of Medicine, v. 293, pp. 795–97, October 16, 1975.
36. Ibid.
37. W. Regelson, J. R. Butler, J. Schultz, T. Kirk, L. Peek, M. L. Green, and M. O. Zalis, "Delta-9-Tetrahydrocannabinol as an Effective Antidepressant and Appetite-stimulating Agent in Advanced Cancer Patients," in Pharmacology of Marihuana, pp. 763–76, edited by Monique C. Braude and Stephen Szara, Raven Press, New York, 1976.
38. Alfred E. Chang, David J. Shiling, Richard C. Stillman, Nelson H. Goldberg, Claudia A. Seipp, Ivan Barofsky, Richard M. Simon, and Steven A. Rosenberg, "Delta-9-Tetrahydrocannabinol as an Antiemetic in Cancer Patients Receiving High-Dose Methotrexate. A Prospective, Randomized Evaluation," Annals of Internal Medicine, v. 91, pp. 819–24, 1979.
39. Stephen Frytak, Charles G. Moertel, Judith R. O'Fallon, Joseph Rubin, Edward T. Creagan, Michael J. O'Donnell, Allan J. Schutt, and Neal W. Schwartau, "Delta-9-Tetrahydrocannabinol as an Antiemetic for Patients Receiving Cancer Chemotherapy. A Comparison with Prochlorperazine and a Placebo," ibid., pp. 825–30.
40. John Laszlo, "Tetrahydrocannabinol: From Pot to Prescription?" ibid., pp. 916–18. Also Virgil S. Lucas, Jr., and John Laszlo, "Delta-9-Tetrahydrocannabinol for Refractory Vomiting Induced by Cancer Chemotherapy," JAMA, The Journal of the American Medical Association, v. 243, n. 12, pp. 1,241–43, March 28, 1980.
41. Penta et al., op. cit., pp. 11S–22S.
42. Terence S. Herman, Lawrence H. Einhorn, Stephen E. Jones, Catherine Nagy, Aurelia B. Chester, Judith C. Dean, Becky Furnas, Stephen D. Williams, Susan A. Leigh, Robert T. Dorr, and Thomas E. Moon, "Superiority of Nabilone Over Prochlorperazine as an Antiemetic in Patients Receiving Cancer Chemotherapy," New England Journal of Medicine, v. 300, pp. 1,295–97, June 7, 1979. Also Murray E. Jarvik, "Necessary Risks," ibid., p. 1,330.
43. J. Thomas Ungerleider, Therese Andrysiak, Lynn Fairbanks, James Goodnight, Gregory Sarna, and Kay Jamison, "Cannabis and Cancer Chemotherapy: A Comparison of Oral Delta-9-THC and Prochlorperazine, Cancer, v. 50, pages 636–45.
44. Don S. Poster, John S. Penta, Salvador Bruno, and John S. Macdonald, "Delta-9-Tetrahydrocannabinol in Clinical Oncology," JAMA, The Journal of the American Medical Association, v. 245, n. 20, pp. 2,047–51, May 22/29, 1981.

45. Alfred E. Chang et al., op. cit., p. 823.

46. Congressional hearings, op. cit.

47. L. E. Hollister, H. K. Gillespie, A. Ohlsson, J.-E. Lindgren, A. Wahlen, and S. Agurell, "Do Plasma Concentrations of Delta-9-Tetrahydrocannabinol Reflect the Degree of Intoxication?" *Journal of Clinical Pharmacology*, v. 21, n. 8–9, p. 177S, August–September, 1981.

48. James A. Neidhart, Mary M. Gagen, Henry E. Wilson, and Donn C. Young, "Comparative Trial of the Antiemetic Effects of THC and Haloperidol," ibid., pp. 38S–42S.

49. Solomon Garb, "Cannabinoids in the Management of Severe Nausea and Vomiting from Cancer Chemotherapy. Some Additional Considerations," ibid., pp. 57S–59S.

50. Donald L. Sweet, Nancy J. Miller, William Weddington, Edward Senay, and Lisa Sushelsky, "Delta-9-Tetrahydrocannabinol As An Antiemetic For Patients Receiving Cancer Chemotherapy. A Pilot Study," ibid., pp. 70S–75S.

51. Carol M. Cronin, Stephen E. Sallan, Richard Gelber, Virgil S. Lucas, and John Laszlo, "Antiemetic Effect of Intramuscular Levonantradol in Patients Receiving Anticancer Chemotherapy," ibid., pp. 43S–50S. Also John Laszlo, Virgil S. Lucas, Jr., Dean C. Hanson, Carol M. Cronin, and Stephen E. Sallan, "Levonantradol for Chemotherapy-Induced Emesis: Phase I-II Oral Administration," ibid., pp. 51S–56S.

52. Robert B. Diasio, David S. Ettinger, and Barbara E. Satterwhite, "Oral Levonantradol in the Treatment of Chemotherapy-Induced Emesis: Preliminary Observations," ibid., pp. 81S–85S.

53. Manfred E. Heim, Wolfgang Römer, and Wolfgang Queisser, "Clinical Experience with Levonantradol Hydrochloride in the Prevention of Cancer Chemotherapy-Induced Nausea and Vomiting," ibid., 86S–89S.

54. J. Thomas Ungerleider, Therese Andrysiak, Donald P. Tashkin, and Robert Peter Gale, "Contamination of Marihuana Cigarettes With Pathogenic Bacteria—Possible Source of Infection in Cancer Patients, *Cancer Treatment Reports*, v. 66, n. 3, pp. 589–91, March, 1982.

55. L. S. Harris, A. E. Munson, M. A. Friedman, and W. L. Dewey, "Retardation of Tumor Growth by Delta-9-Tetrahydrocannabinol (Delta-9-THC)," *Pharmacologist*, v. 16, n. 1, p. 259, 1974. Also A. E. Munson, L. S. Harris, M. A. Friedman, W. L. Dewey, and R. A. Carchman, "Antineoplastic Activity of Cannabinoids," *Journal of the National Cancer Institute*, v. 55, n. 3, pp. 597–602, September, 1975. Also R. A. Carchman, L. S. Harris, and A. E. Munson, "The Inhibition of DNA Synthesis by Cannabinoids," *Cancer Research*, v. 36, pp. 95–100, January, 1976. Also L. S. Harris, A. E. Munson, and R. A. Carchman, "Antitumor Properties of Cannabinoids," in *The Pharmacology of Marihuana*, op. cit., pages 749–62.

56. Government statistic cited by Keith Green, Keun Kim, and Karen Bowman, "Ocular Effects of Delta-9-Tetrahydrocannabinol," in *The Therapeutic Potential of Marihuana*, p. 49, edited by Sidney Cohen and Richard C. Stillman, Plenum Medical Book Company, New York and London, 1976.

57. Robert S. Hepler and Ira R. Frank, "Marihuana Smoking and Intraocular Pressure," *JAMA, The Journal of the American Medical Association*, v. 217, n. 10, p. 1,392, September 6, 1971.

58. Robert S. Hepler and Robert J. Petrus, "Experiences with Administration of Marihuana to Glaucoma Patients," in *The Therapeutic Potential of Marihuana*, op. cit., pp. 63–75.

59. A. B. Lockhart, M. E. West, and H. I. C. Lowe, "The Potential Use of Cannabis Sativa in Ophthalmology," *West Indian Medical Journal*, v. 26, pp. 66–70, 1977.

60. Paul Cooler and John M. Gregg, "The Effect of Delta-9-Tetrahydrocannabinol on Intraocular Pressure in Humans," in *The Therapeutic Potential of Marihuana*, op. cit., pp. 77–87.

61. Congressional hearings, op. cit. Also "For Glaucoma and a Host of Other Ills, It's Still Wait and See," *Medical World News*, p. 48, April 28, 1980. Also Patrick Anderson, *High in America*, The Viking Press, New York, 1981.

62. Congressional hearings, op. cit.

63. John C. Merritt. William J. Crawford, Paul C. Alexander, Alfred L. Anduze, and Solomon S. Gelbart, "Effect of Marihuana on Intraocular and Blood Pressure in Glaucoma," *Ophthalmology*, v. 87, n. 3, March, 1980.

64. Congressional hearings, op. cit.

65. Ibid. Also Merritt et al.

66. Ibid.

67. Ibid.

68. James S. Tiedeman, M. Bruce Shields, Paul A. Weber, James W. Crow, David M. Cocchetto, William A. Harris, and John F. Howes, "Effect of Synthetic Cannabinoids on Elevated Intraocular Pressure," *Ophthalmology*, v. 88, n. 3, March, 1981.

69. D. Shapiro, "The Ocular Manifestations of the Cannabinols," *Ophthalmologica* (Basel, Switzerland), v. 168, pp. 366–69, 1974.

70. William W. Dawson, Carlos F. Jiménez-Antillon, José M. Perez, and Jeffrey A. Zeskind, "Marijuana and Vision—After Ten Years' Use in Costa Rica," *Investigative Ophthalmology and Visual Science*, pp. 689–99, August, 1977.

71. Editorial, "Marijuana as Medicine," *The New York Times*, August 27, 1983.

72. Bruce E. Spivey, "Marijuana's Drawbacks in Treating Glaucoma" (letter), ibid., September 15, 1983.

INDEX